Trading in Santa Fe

Number Five: DeGolyer Library Series

Published in cooperation with the William P. Clements Center for Southwest Studies

Trading in Santa Fe

John M. Kingsbury's Correspondence with
James Josiah Webb, 1853–1861

Edited by Jane Lenz Elder and David J. Weber

Southern Methodist University Press
DeGolyer Library
Dallas 1996

First edition, 1996

Requests for permission to reproduce material from this work should be
sent to:

Permissions
Southern Methodist University Press
P.O. Box 750415
Dallas, Texas 75275-0415

Library of Congress Cataloging-in-Publication Data

Kingsbury, John M., 1829-1907.
    Trading in Santa Fe : John M. Kingsbury's correspondence with
James Josiah Webb, 1853-1861 / edited by Jane Lenz Elder and
David J. Weber. — 1st edition.
       p. cm. — (DeGolyer library series)
    Includes bibliographical references and index.
    ISBN 0-87074-389-9 (cloth). — ISBN 0-87074-390-2 (paper)
    1. Santa Fe Trail. 2. Frontier and pioneer life — Southwest, New.
3. Kingsbury, John M., 1829-1907 — Correspondence. 4. Webb, James
Josiah, 1818-1889 — Correspondence. 5. Santa Fe (N.M.) — Commerce. 6. Businessmen — New Mexico — Santa Fe — Correspondence. I. Elder, Jane Lenz. II. Weber, David J. III. Title IV. Series
F786.K575 1996
979'.02—dc20   95-43120

Designed by W. Thomas Taylor
Printed in the United States of America on acid-free paper
10 9 8 7 6 5 4 3 2 1

To our spouses

Tim Elder and Carol Weber,
who share our affection for Santa Fe.

To our parents

Nina and Bill Lenz and Frances and Ted Weber,
who first taught us about the world of business.

Contents

Illustrations, following page 152

William S. Messervy, c. 1849
Letter written by John Kingsbury to James Webb, Santa Fe, January 9, 1859
James Josiah Webb, late in life
Traders standing on the southeast corner of the Santa Fe plaza
Unfinished "state house" (Federal Building), Santa Fe, New Mexico, c. 1870s
Elsberg-Amberg wagon train in the plaza of Santa Fe, New Mexico, October 1861
Gravestone of Kate Kingsbury, Santa Fe, New Mexico
Map of the Santa Fe Trail

Acknowledgments

Trading in Santa Fe began in the DeGolyer Library at SMU in the late 1970s when David Weber came across a small cache of forty-four letters from John Kingsbury to James Webb in the library's manuscript holdings. No record remained of the letters' provenance except that Everette Lee DeGolyer, Sr., had purchased them from Edward Eberstadt in 1945. The letters had been transcribed, and both the originals and transcriptions handsomely boxed. Kingsbury had affixed a piece of calico to one letter, dated September 10, 1859, in which he chastised Webb for misjudging the tastes of their Santa Fe customers by sending cloth in dull colors: "I have only found one single piece [in a] bright color and send you the sample, all the balance are dead wood colors while at least ½ should have been <u>pink</u>, <u>blue</u> and <u>orange</u> or <u>yellow</u>." Kingsbury's letters from Santa Fe seemed as vivid as those colors and as tactile as the cloth he sought. Properly transcribed, introduced, and annotated, the letters would make a valuable source for historians who hardly knew of their existence and an interesting firsthand account for aficionados of the Southwest.

Other projects took precedence until we began our collaboration in the summer of 1987, thanks to the generosity of the Robert and Nancy Dedman Chair in history. We imagined a small book, to be published under the auspices of the DeGolyer Library and its enthusiastic director, David Farmer. Those modest plans fell apart when we learned that the Missouri Historical Society in St. Louis held an additional 150 letters from Kingsbury to Webb, as well as letters from Webb to Kingsbury, account books, and notebooks. When the Missouri Historical Society generously gave us permission to publish the Kingsbury letters in their holdings, our project quadrupled in length. David Farmer's interest in publishing the letters, however, did not diminish, and we are grateful to him for his unwavering support.

We have incurred a large number of other debts. The staff of the Missouri Historical Society has been unfailingly kind. We owe special thanks to Director Robert Archibald; to Peter Michel, the director of the library and archives who arranged for photocopying as well as airport retrieval; and to Archivist Martha Clevinger, whose appreciation for the richness of the Webb Papers rivals our own.

Ann V. Reddington at the Hamden Historical Society in Connecticut placed herself entirely at our disposal one long and busy afternoon. She fed us pie made from home-grown fruit when our energy flagged, stayed late to see that we obtained all the material we needed and, to our amazement, brought forth the most unusual item in their Webb Collection—James J. Webb's ponytail. We would never have known of this collection had it not been for the database networking skill of the DeGolyer Library's reference librarian, Kristin Jacobsen. Nor could we have made sense of much of Webb & Kingsbury's business records without the enthusiastic assistance of another member of the SMU community, Professor Michael Van Breda of the Cox School of Business.

In New Mexico and Colorado, our thanks go to a small army of people who have given their time, shared their knowledge and resources, extended their hospitality, and generously provided a wealth of information that greatly enriched our work: Glenn W. Bertrum, Secretary of Santa Fe's Montezuma Lodge #1; Santa Fe Trail historian Marian Meyer; Homer E. Milford of the New Mexico Abandoned Mine Land Bureau; Richard Rudisill, the curator of Photographic History at the Museum of New Mexico; and Richard Salazar of the New Mexico State Records Center and Archives. We are especially grateful to Mary Jean Cook, Mark L. Gardner, and Marc Simmons, who answered many questions in the course of this project, and then carved a considerable amount of time out of their schedules to read and correct the completed manuscript.

In the course of this project Jane has made several research trips, leaving her husband and two small children to their fates. She extends her heartfelt thanks to Pat and Alex Elder, whose practical support in domestic matters allowed her to abandon her family secure in the knowledge that all would be well. Jane thanks Bruce and Melissa Husel for providing lodging and company after long hours at the microfilm readers at the Boston Public Library; Mary Price and Brian Davidson arranged for her introduction to the splendors of the collections (as well as the dessert cart) at the Boston Museum of Fine Arts. Jane's two trips to Santa Fe were made possible in part by a grant from the Lenz Foundation, and greatly enlivened by the company of her mother and fellow survivor of Webb Young Tours, Nina Lenz. And to those who underestimate the power of positive familial influence, Jane would like to point out that if she had spent her childhood vacations at the beach like other people, instead of roaming the byways of northern New Mexico with assorted Lenzes and Callaways, she probably would never have taken a course with David Weber, set foot in the DeGolyer Library, or undertaken any of the endeavors that have made her working life such a pleasure.

We have been editing John Kingsbury's letters for seven years, nearly as long as he traded in Santa Fe. Both of our spouses have completed law school and embarked on careers, wondering when we were going to finish this single book. David's son, Scott, and his daughter, Amy, have both married. Jane's son, William, has grown from a newborn to a grade schooler and budding soccer star. In 1991 David became a grandfather for the first time, and in 1992 Jane's daughter, Margaret, was born. Other projects also derailed us from time to time; David worked on many of these chapters during a year in Spain where he was writing a different book; Jane has completed a master's degree. We have set no Francis X. Aubry–like speed records, but we have followed a "steady" course in the manner of Kingsbury and Webb, and in the end we have delivered the goods.

Foreword

The invitation to write a foreword to this collection of letters was based, I presume, on the desire to get the reaction of a twentieth-century retailer to the problems and accomplishments of two pioneer southwestern retailers, John M. Kingsbury and James Josiah Webb, who opened a general goods store in Santa Fe in the middle of the nineteenth century.

In these days of sophisticated retail operations, experience is important. If an individual desires to enter the field with a good college education, but no experience, he or she will be put through a rigorous training program to learn the key elements of the retail business before being assigned to a remotely located job requiring on-site decisions on stock content and basic operations. Kingsbury and Webb did not do it that way. When the two New Englanders forged an alliance in 1853, twenty-four-year-old Kinsgsbury, who had little experience, went to Santa Fe to manage sales and collections. James Webb, age thirty-five, with previous ownership of stores in New England, Savannah, St. Louis, and Santa Fe, supplied him with the kinds of goods that he presumed the residents of Santa Fe and army personnel posted there would want to buy.

The experienced Webb knew the problems of maintaining a consistent flow of goods. To meet the general scarcity of merchandise in Santa Fe, stores such as Webb & Kingsbury's needed to be kept supplied by seasonal overland shipments that often arrived late, or were delayed when hostile Indians assaulted the wagon trains. With the communication and transport systems of the 1850s, it was impossible to get the flow of goods that the neophyte merchant found to be of vital importance in meeting his customers' needs. Kingsbury's comment to Webb on July 26, 1853, that "since the new goods came in business has improved" reflects the obvious sales benefits from the receipt of new merchandise. Webb, however, was unable to ship more frequently than once a year, when the overland trains were organized and weather was friendly.

From long residence in New Mexico, Webb also knew the idiosyncracies of local customers, but tastes changed in New Mexico in the mid-1850s and Webb was far from the scene. Kingsbury's correspondence reveals his dissatisfaction with the character of the merchandise that Webb was shipping to Santa Fe. His complaint is no different than similar protestations from Dallas and Los Angeles today about the failure of eastern market representatives to select appropriate stocks.

In today's retail world, even with fax and telephone, it is difficult to anticipate customers' needs. Buyers are reluctant to let others pick merchandise for them, preferring to wait until the next market trip three weeks hence to place the order in person. It's an inherent quirk of buyers to believe that no one else can select as well as they can.

Webb's shipments were a mixed bag. In the spring of 1853 one shipment included "27 trunks, boots and shoes, 99 bales of domestics, 1 bale carpeting, 6 cases merchandise, 1 half barrel mackerel." Webb had to be an astute buyer to handle merchandise assortments like that, and Kingsbury had to display ingenuity to sell the mackerel to customers who were interested in printed cambrics.

Kingsbury offered good operating advice to Webb, his experienced partner. In October 1855 he wrote, "Where you buy goods on time, extend the payment as much as you can, so as to make payments early next year, particularly if you buy largely Indian goods, with the understanding that we are to wait for the payment until the appropriations are made by Congress." He concluded, "It will be a great advantage to us to get our goods out early. The first trains are bound to make money. Many things will be scarce in the spring. I think the market will be pretty well cleared before new goods can arrive." This is known in current retail practice as a "pre-selling pitch."

Kingsbury learned the vicissitudes of the retail trade quickly. In January 1856, he wrote Webb, "Debus and Bunker complained bitterly of the Cloak tassels, say they were badly moth eaten, and think they ought to be entitled to a discount." *(Welcome to the world of retailing, Mr. Kingsbury.)* Kingsbury counseled Webb on April 29, 1857, "I think the ox trains will be close on to the mule ones, and for ourselves I think our goods are safer with Oxen. Should the Indians be bad they will trouble the mule trains most." In addition to learning about moths and mules, Kingsbury had to cope with the financial crisis of 1857, to understand the intricacies of insurance coverage, and to haggle with the freight shippers who had quoted a different price to Webb than they tried to collect when the merchandise reached Santa Fe.

It is interesting to observe from the interchange of letters between the two how Kingsbury had to shoulder more responsibilities than just storekeeping. Dealing with tough fellow merchants and demanding customers, he grew to be a sagacious businessman. Kingsbury learned that taking care of individual requests for merchandise not ordinarily stocked was a good way to develop his business. In January 1858, he advised Webb, "Frank [Green] has received the <u>ring</u>. It fits exact and he is much pleased with it. The Bible has not yet come." In May 1858 he added, "Frank [Green] rec.d by this mail the Valise of clothes and is much pleased with them. There is no vest with the black suit, he expected one & thinks perhaps it was left out in packing. Did you get one or no? . . . Business is dull but we could hardly expect anything else at this season." This is exactly the kind of conversation that goes on today between buyers in small stores all over the country and the offices that represent them in the East and West Coast markets. They still talk shop and are concerned with the same trivia, for that *is* the essence of the retail business, now as then.

Kingsbury wasn't awed by his senior partner, for he complained on May 31, 1858, "Kitchens train got in yesterday with goods for Levi [Spiegelberg]. This gives him a decided advantage and then I am told he only pays 8 cents. It somehow happens that we always pay more freight than any one else, understand me right, I do not complain of your bargain. I have no doubt you done the best you could, but it is the principal. It gives our neighbors too great an advantage over us."

In contrast to today's merchants, Kingsbury had to be concerned with the unreliability of transport. Indians, weather, and trail conditions placed a heavy toll on merchants of the early West. On June 30, 1858 he wrote Webb, "The loss of cattle will weaken the teams so much that it will be difficult to calculate when they will arrive. They are loaded very heavy. <u>Three</u> have over 5500 pounds in them." He pleaded for deliveries of new goods in the same letter: "I think <u>Early</u> spring goods would help our business much, if I can have an <u>even show</u> with my neighbors. I am not afraid to stand side by side with anyone here. . . . All I ask is an <u>even show</u>."

This was a request from a seller to the buyer located 2,500 miles away to try to get him to understand his feeling of helplessness when his competitors received earlier deliveries than he was getting. It can be very easy for a seller to become frustrated by the apparent lack of understanding for urgency by his buyer. Many a present-day store manager, whether at Walmart, Saks, or Neiman Marcus, has voiced a similar message to a centralized buyer.

From our perspective, it is amazing that an enterprise like that of Webb & Kingsbury was able to survive and actually make money considering the inexperience of one of the partners and the absence of rapid communications and delivery systems. The partners succeeded because they learned from experience that retailing was a fairly simple business dealing basically with two elements—goods and customers. When retailers take good care of their goods, they stay sold—they *don't* come back. Conversely, when retailers take good care of their customers, they *do* come back. It is just that simple—and just that difficult.

Stanley Marcus

Introduction

The life of John M. Kingsbury is not the stuff from which western legends are made. Born in Boston, Massachusetts, in March 1829, Kingsbury chose to pursue the decidedly unromantic vocation of bookkeeper and probably hoped to rise through the ranks of accountancy until he achieved the kind of sober-sided success to which Bostonians of his day aspired. While this future did indeed await Kingsbury, his path toward that end did not lie along a predictable trajectory of modest promotions at regular intervals. Instead he achieved the "small, safe" prosperity he craved by means neither small nor especially safe.[1] For eight years, Kingsbury lived a high-stakes life replete with adventure, in which he took risks, battled the elements, found love, faced danger, and survived tragedy and hardship in an exotic land. And he hated it.

Between 1853 and 1861, as the junior member of the firm of Webb & Kingsbury, John Kingsbury belonged to that group of westerners known as Santa Fe traders, who have since come to seem larger-than-life. His quiet, conservative nature stood in contrast to the colorful characters with whom he lived and worked. Yet he was not an anomaly. He represented the future in an industry whose get-rich-quick days were over. The Santa Fe trade in the 1850s was no longer a venture that yielded a quick return on a small investment. While the decade saw greater and more dependable profits than ever before, the trade had evolved into a highly capitalized and complex business increasingly linked to financial interests in St. Louis, Boston, and New York. Freewheeling frontiersmen still maintained their place in the Santa Fe trade, but long-term, large-scale success fell to those who could wed western gumption to the sound business methods of the East.

Such was the case with the firm of Webb & Kingsbury. Characterized by one historian as "the largest and best-known firm trading in Santa Fe" in the mid-1850s, Webb & Kingsbury wielded an economic influence in Santa Fe that more closely resembled mercantile capitalism than storefront retailing or frontier barter.[2] Like other successful New Mexican trading associations, most notably the Spiegelberg Brothers of Santa Fe, the firm of Messervy & Webb, from which Webb & Kingsbury evolved, had maintained a full-time presence in the East to facilitate purchasing, shipping, and collections.[3] These activities required the support of a clerk and bookkeeper, and young Kingsbury apparently fit the bill. The skills that initially qualified John Kingsbury for his position as clerk, then later junior partner, of the firm included penmanship more

1. Kingsbury to Webb, Santa Fe, Dec. 30, 1855, MHS.

2. Barbour, *Reluctant Frontiersman*, 20, 128; Atherton, "Santa Fe Trader as Merchant Capitalist," 2.

3. Business historian Thomas C. Cochran estimates that by 1850, still about one-third of retailers in the interior of the United States, particularly the South, bought their goods in northeastern centers rather than rely on orders placed through catalogs and regional agents, or through traveling salesmen. *Business in American Life*, 71.

than horsemanship, proficiency with numbers as well as guns, and organizational ability more than courage or bravado.

As he exercised these skills, John Kingsbury produced a detailed chronicle of trading in Santa Fe in the 1850s—a time when commerce over the Santa Fe Trail reached new heights. Kingsbury's business activities resembled those of many Anglo-American merchants who traded in Santa Fe, both before and after him, but unlike nearly every other trader, Kingsbury has had his story preserved in his own correspondence—letters that provide a wealth of details about public and private spheres in recently conquered New Mexico. Writing regularly from Santa Fe to his seasoned, but mostly absent, senior partner, James J. Webb, Kingsbury reported on the day-to-day operations of their firm, the business climate in New Mexico, and what they might expect from their rivals. In the course of placing orders and charting cash flows, Kingsbury sent Webb gossip about New Mexico politics and politicians, some of whom were themselves involved in the Santa Fe trade and with whom Kingsbury and Webb enjoyed close relationships. Kingsbury's letters to Webb also offer intimate details about social and cultural life in Santa Fe and provide insight into the transformation of the territory's material culture. They reveal that the prominent John S. Watts was unable to meet his financial obligations, and that white paint had grown scarce in 1855. They also reveal the personality of Kingsbury himself, who entered the Santa Fe trade with high expectations, before personal tragedy befell him.

I.

The Santa Fe Trail had entered its fourth decade as a trade route when twenty-two-year-old John Kingsbury followed it westward to New Mexico in 1851.[4] To be sure, the Trail had a longer history. Beginning with Francisco Vázquez de Coronado in 1541, a stream of Spaniards from New Mexico had followed Indian trails eastward across the Great Plains. By 1792, Pedro Vial had linked Santa Fe to St. Louis. So long as Spain's empire embraced the western half of the continent, however, government restrictions made trade with foreigners illegal. Thus the Santa Fe Trail did not become viable as a commercial wagon route until newly independent Mexico opened its northern borders to merchants from the United States in 1821. Once American entrepreneurs realized the threat of incarceration in a Spanish prison had evaporated, a robust traffic sprang up between Mexican Santa Fe and the American frontier settlements in Missouri.

The Santa Fe Trail acted as an international commercial route supplying Mexicans, both in New Mexico and beyond, with inexpensive yet well-made manufactured goods. Starved for such staples as cloth and hardware, Mexicans bought American merchandise with alacrity and

4. Kingsbury began working for William Messervy and James J. Webb at least as early as 1849, but he only traveled as far west as St. Louis that year. He probably first went to Santa Fe with the spring trains in 1851. Messervy made a note in his purchase journal the following winter to buy a Spanish dictionary to ship out to him in the spring train in 1852. Had Kingsbury gone out in 1850, he would have needed the dictionary the year before. Additionally, he is listed in the Boston City Directory for 1849 and 1850, but is absent from it thereafter. Purchase Journal of William S. Messervy, Nov. 12, 1851-Apr. 1, 1852, Vol. 8, Webb Papers, MHS; and S. G. Bean to James Henry Webb, Las Cruces, NM, postcard, n.d., Misc. File, Box 8, Webb Papers, MHS.

paid for it with silver from the mines of northern Mexico. The lure of profits quickly attracted merchants from both countries. Beginning in 1822, Anglo Americans set out every spring in wagons from Franklin, Independence, Westport, and other Missouri towns to hawk their wares in New Mexico villages and points farther south—Chihuahua, Durango, and Zacatecas. Meanwhile, Mexican merchants began to ply the trail from Santa Fe to Missouri, some continuing on to Philadelphia and New York, buying American goods to bring to northern Mexico.[5]

Nearly eight hundred miles in length, the Santa Fe Trail took traders through the level Indian country of what is today Kansas, the Oklahoma panhandle, and northeastern New Mexico. Indians and the elements made the journey dangerous, but the "Commerce of the Prairies," as Josiah Gregg termed it in a popular book first published in 1844, also represented adventure and romance. Santa Fe itself, with its one-story adobe buildings clustered around a dusty plaza where the Mexican women wore revealing, loose-fitting clothes, epitomized the romantic allure of the exotic. As traders and teamsters approached New Mexico's foreign capital after a journey that usually took two months, Gregg noted, they "grew more and more merry and obstreperous as they descended towards the city. I doubt, in short, whether the first sight of the walls of Jerusalem were beheld by the crusaders with much more tumultuous and soul-enrapturing joy."[6]

By the time Kingsbury became acquainted with Santa Fe in the early 1850s, the city still retained much of its exotic air, but its trade with Missouri had changed from foreign to domestic. In the fall of 1846, the United States Army had marched westward over the Trail to occupy Santa Fe in the opening stages of the United States–Mexican War. In the victor's peace that officially ended the war at Guadalupe Hidalgo in 1848, the United States acquired all of southwestern America. Soon new routes to new destinations—California and Oregon—eclipsed the Santa Fe Trail in the American imagination.

Although the Santa Fe Trail lost some of its glamour as an international highway after 1848, the volume and value of its commerce reached new heights as the number of customers in New Mexico Territory grew. Some of those customers merely passed through Santa Fe. In the early years, supply-hungry gold-seekers bound for California took southern trails west by way of Albuquerque or El Paso. In 1859–60, a new wave of American gold-seekers heading for the new strikes in Colorado came west over the Santa Fe Trail and swelled demand temporarily. The United States Army, however, represented the largest and most stable group of new consumers in Santa Fe.

The army, as one historian has argued convincingly, "was the single most significant factor in the economic development of the Southwest."[7] American forces remained in New Mexico after the war, and a string of new military posts began to stretch westward from Fort Leavenworth,

5. The best introduction to the Santa Fe Trail and its literature is Rittenhouse, *Santa Fe Trail*; for the beginnings of the Santa Fe trade in its Mexican context see Weber, *Mexican Frontier*, 125-30. The activities of Mexican traders, long ignored by Anglo-American scholars, have been illuminated by David A. Sandoval in three articles: "Who Is Riding the Burro Now?," "Montezuma's Merchants," and "Gnats, Goods, and Greasers." Sandoval's essays end with the Mexican-American War, but Mexican traders remained active on the Trail, as Kingsbury's letters make clear.

6. Gregg, *Commerce*, 78. Rittenhouse, *Santa Fe Trail*, 112, reports that Gregg's work appeared in fourteen editions between 1844 and 1933.

7. Frazer, *Forts and Supplies*, ix.

Kansas, along the Santa Fe Trail to Fort Union, just east of Las Vegas, New Mexico. Using Fort Union as the hub, the army built posts throughout New Mexico Territory. In addition to defending lives and property against raids by hostile bands of Navajos, Comanches, Apaches, and Kiowas, the army introduced men and money into the territory. In 1849 New Mexico's military force consisted of 987 troops manning seven permanent posts. A decade later, those numbers more than doubled to 2,000 troops and sixteen posts.[8]

The soldiers, some of whom retired in New Mexico, not only swelled the local population, but their very presence probably contributed to Anglo-American emigration. The crude census count of 1850, which excluded so-called "wild" Indians, revealed 61,547 persons in New Mexico Territory. That figure included 1,600 Anglo Americans, of whom nearly 1,000 were military personnel. By 1860 the population of New Mexico Territory had increased by over 50 percent, to 93,516. At the same time the number of Anglo Americans had quadrupled to 6,300—3,100 of them in the military.[9]

The federal revenue the army drew into New Mexico was staggering by local standards. One historian estimated the cost of defense for one year in the early 1850s at more than $3,000,000; better than half of that figure probably represented the expense of shipping material from Missouri over the eight-hundred-mile Santa Fe trail.[10] Put another way, in 1849 when the cost of a day's ration for one soldier was 12 ½ cents on the Atlantic coast and 19 cents in Texas, in New Mexico the cost was 42 cents per man.[11]

The military became the biggest business in the territory. It transformed the markets of New Mexico, creating a permanent demand where only a few years before a seasonal one had existed.[12] The army's need for construction materials, food, hay, and grain represented a bonanza for the freighters and the merchants, who benefited most directly from this change. Prior to the United States–Mexican War, the year 1843 had probably been the high point of the Santa Fe trade, when 230 wagons imported goods valued at perhaps $1,500,000.[13] In 1858 over $3,500,000 worth of merchandise passed over the Trail to Santa Fe; in 1860 the figure may have reached $10,000,000—or roughly one-eighteenth of the total value of goods (60 percent of which was bulk cotton) shipped through the port of New Orleans that same year.[14]

Despite its significant size and expenditures, the military force in the Southwest proved unable to carry out its principal function as the civilians' defense against hostile Indians. To the contrary, one historian has argued that the increased hostility on the part of the Plains Indians in this period corresponded directly to the ever-expanding traffic on the Santa Fe trail: the greater number of supply trains, the operation of regular mail and stage routes, and the increased number of immigrants.[15] Throughout the 1850s, scarcely a year went by that Kingsbury did not

8. Connor and Skaggs, *Broadcloth and Britches*, 155-56.

9. We are using these figures only to suggest the rapid increase in population size. The 1850 and 1860 census figures do not lend themselves to easy comparison; New Mexico at that time included today's Arizona, and the 1850 census did not include El Paso. For details, see Frazer, *Forts and Supplies*, 185-86.

10. Lamar, *Far Southwest*, 95; Walker, *Wagonmasters*, 232.

11. Walker, *Wagonmasters*, 232.

12. Lamar, *Far Southwest*, 96, 107.

13. Josiah Gregg put the figure at $450,000, but Moorhead, *New Mexico's Royal Road*, 185-86, believed that figure was far too conservative and estimated $1,500,000.

14. Rittenhouse, *Santa Fe Trail*, 26. Simmons, "Santa Fe in the Days of the Trail," p. 126, gives different figures. In 1860, the Santa Fe trade engaged 5,948 men, 2,170 wagons, and 17,836 oxen. The total value of goods transported that year was $3,500,000. That is, his 1860 figure is Rittenhouse's 1858 figure. Johnson, et al., *Domestic and Foreign Commerce*, 1:243.

Business historian Elisha P. Douglass has characterized the Santa Fe Trade as small in dollar volume compared with the amount of trade conducted through the United States' eastern ports. Nevertheless, when one considers that the trade centered almost exclusively on manufactured goods transported by means of a slow and rudimentary system, these figures become more significant. *Coming of Age*, 313.

15. Oliva, *Soldiers*, 93.

mention hostilities of some sort. In 1856 he reported Indian raids in the Rio Abajo,[16] and in 1858 he noted the theft of cattle belonging to some Mexican trains on the Jornada del Muerto, a stretch of desert along the road from Santa Fe to Chihuahua. That same year Comanche attacks on outlying ranches increased and Kingsbury feared for the safety of their goods.[17] By 1859 several bands of Plains Indians had succeeded in disrupting all three mail lines to Santa Fe, to the extent that Kingsbury confessed, "I am timid about sending remittances untill some confidence is restored."[18]

Between 1859 and 1860 as many as 300 citizens of New Mexico lost their lives to Indian attacks, with the biggest threat coming from Navajos to the west of Santa Fe.[19] By then New Mexico–Navajo relations had deteriorated into full-scale war.[20] Kingsbury expressed what must have been a widely held view among Anglo Americans when he argued that the Navajos "must be exterminated or they will be worse than ever when this Compagne [campaign] closes."[21] Despite the public's outcry, however, Navajo raids posed a threat the army could not seem to control.[22]

Like all communities that depend on military budgets and payrolls, New Mexico lived with the threat that the army would pull out, leaving in its wake not only a shattered economy but a defenseless population. This was no idle fear, given the cost of defending the territory. Some officials, including one secretary of war, gave serious thought to buying up the territory's private property and leaving New Mexico to the "wild" Indians.[23] In 1852 the military department commander, Col. E. V. Sumner, put it this way:

> Would it not be better to abandon a country which hardly seems
> fit for the inhabitations of civilized man by remunerating them
> for their property in money or in lands situated in more favorable
> regions?[24]

Such was the region's dependence upon the army that a proposed military reorganization in 1860, intended as an efficiency measure, threw the population of the territory into a panic. While the reorganization involved greater government expenditure, it decreased the overall number of posts, causing anxiety among the merchants in New Mexico. The outbreak of the Civil War prevented the plan's full implementation, however. Instead it introduced a new crisis, as southern officers throughout the West resigned their commissions to join the Confederacy. Altogether 313 officers, 182 of them graduates of West Point, left western commands, reducing the officer corps of the entire United States Army by about a third.[25]

The threat of depredations at the hands of hostile tribes became much more immediate when four companies of soldiers stationed in New Mexico and Colorado were ordered East. The threat of a Confederate

16. Kingsbury to Webb, Santa Fe, Jan. 30, 1856, MHS.
17. Ibid., Apr. 30, 1858, MHS.
18. Ibid., Oct. 22, 1859, DeG. Kingsbury's misspelling of words such as "untill" is commonplace; we have chosen to keep the errors but not clutter his writing with "*sics*."
19. Horn, *New Mexico's Troubled Years*, 80.
20. Twitchell, *Leading Facts*, 2:316-17; McNitt, *Navajo Wars*, 382.
21. Kingsbury to Webb, Santa Fe, Sept. 20, 1860, MHS.
22. McNitt, *Navajo Wars*, 364-75.
23. Twitchell, *Leading Facts*, 2:288.
24. Lamar, *Far Southwest*, 96.
25. Josephy, *Civil War*, 34.

invasion from Texas compounded the problems posed by the Indians.[26] Many Anglo Americans in Santa Fe beat a hasty retreat to the East, as New Mexico made the transition from professional to volunteer defense.[27]

John Kingsbury joined the exodus, but because he had spent the preceding few years systematically concluding his business in Santa Fe, he left few loose ends. It seems likely, however, that he kept informed about the events that followed in New Mexico. After his return to New England, North successfully battled South for control of New Mexico's munitions supplies, mineral wealth, and strategic location along the only all-season route to the Pacific. From Boston, where he had settled, Kingsbury probably read with satisfaction how Kit Carson pursued the war with the Navajos that led to their "long walk" and their final subjugation in 1863.

II.

We know that John Kingsbury was born to George and Eliza McElroy Kingsbury in Boston in March 1829 and that he had at least two sisters,[28] but until he was drawn into the orbit of the two western adventurers, William S. Messervy and James J. Webb, the record remains silent as to his background and activities. Even after his initial employment with the Santa Fe trading firm of Messervy & Webb, he remained among the many clerks, bookkeepers, and agents who contributed to the smooth flow of operations, but whose lives cannot be easily reconstructed. In the mid–nineteenth century, white-collar workers such as these, living in hopes of a partnership or promotion, tended to identify themselves more with their employers' interests than with those of the independent tradesman or artisan classes into which they had been born. A bestselling book called *The Bible in the Counting House*, first published in 1853 and in its fifth edition before the end of 1854, advocated just such a course of action in a chapter devoted to "Principals and Clerks," which began by stating, "Every clerk should identify himself with the house he is engaged in."[29] Such was the case with John Kingsbury, who typified the businesslike attitudes that helped shape the emergent urban middle class: discipline, fidelity in discharge of all duties, and sound moral character.[30] On the eve of Kingsbury's promotion to junior partner, after he had made his first trip across the plains to New Mexico, he began to write letters that clearly reflect these attitudes. For whatever reason, his future partner, Webb, decided to preserve these letters.

By joining forces with James Webb, Kingsbury found himself in the company of a man of considerable experience, perspicacity, and wealth. One writer, in describing a prototype of the most successful of the Santa Fe traders, could have had Webb in mind when he wrote: "There were the old Santa Fe traders, who counted their gains by thousands, and whose signatures were good in St. Louis to almost any amount."[31] Born

26. Ibid., 36.
27. One of these Anglo Americans was Webb's and Kingsbury's friend Tom Bowler, who apparently wanted to join his wife, Refugia, then living with his mother in Jackson County, Missouri. In May she signed over a power of attorney to W. A. Street, authorizing him to dispose of her dower, the house and garden known as Bowler's Garden. By June they had sold not only Bowler's Garden but the Exchange Hotel as well. Santa Fe County Deeds, Book C, p. 297, NMSARC.
28. Kingsbury's death certificate, Aug. 21, 1907, Massachusetts Registry of Vital Records and Statistics; Kingsbury's own letters indicate that he had two sisters.
29. Bode, ed., *Midcentury America*, 42-43.
30. Cochran, *Business in American Life*, 72; Bode, ed., *Midcentury America*, 44-45.
31. Brewerton, *Overland with Kit Carson*, 183-84.

in Litchfield County, Connecticut, on February 5, 1818, Webb began working at the age of sixteen in the dry goods stores of uncles in New Jersey and then in Connecticut before trying his hand at his own stores— first in Savannah in 1841 and then in St. Louis in 1843. In 1844, at age twenty-six, Webb took a shipment of goods to Santa Fe and, thanks in part to generous credit from a well-capitalized partner, made a small fortune within a few years. Webb set up a permanent store in Santa Fe, boasting in 1849 that he had "the largest store and premises in town." That year, Webb's partner, George P. Doan, son of the senior partner of the St. Louis wholesaling firm Doan, King & Company mentioned so frequently in these letters, withdrew from the business.[32]

Webb found a fine replacement in William S. Messervy, another Santa Fe trader, older than Webb by five and a half years and with greater experience.[33] A native of Salem, Massachusetts, William Sluman Messervy came from a seafaring family. He was the oldest son of ten children born to William Messervy, a ship captain, and his wife, Eliza. Unlike his younger brother Thomas, who pursued an ocean-going life that included a stint as a whaler, Messervy chose to navigate a sea of grass on the western plains.[34] He moved to St. Louis in 1834, then in 1839 to Santa Fe, where his maturity and business acumen allowed him to amass more than enough capital to invest in Webb's business when the opportunity arose.[35]

Between them, Messervy and Webb had the intelligence, experience, and financial resources to build a business of formidable scope. In 1851, for example, their spring train, with which Kingsbury most likely first came to New Mexico, numbered between sixty and seventy wagons filled with goods bound for wholesale and retail trade; their customers ranged from the United States military and the territorial government of New Mexico to the smallest itinerant peddler.[36] Accounting records indicate that the firm continued to maintain this volume and breadth of trade until Webb and Kingsbury made the final decision to close it down.

In addition to their business interests, Messervy and Webb also became actively engaged in the affairs of their adopted community. Webb served one year in the New Mexico legislature, in 1856, but Messervy was the more politically minded of the two.[37] Following the American conquest, Messervy joined with other merchants who hoped to use New Mexico as a springboard for a political career. A small group of those merchants wrote a constitution for the new "state" of New Mexico and engineered its overwhelming ratification in June 1850. In the election that followed, representatives of that same clique of merchants won the highest offices—Henry Connelly as governor, Spanish-born Manuel Alvarez as lieutenant governor, and William Messervy as delegate to Congress. Messervy never filled the position since Congress refused to recognize the new state. Instead, New Mexico became a territory, as some of the opponents of statehood hoped it would.[38] Nevertheless, Messervy continued his involvement in politics and became secretary of the Territory

32. Webb to Doan, King & Co., Aug. 15, 1849, in Webb, *Adventures*, 32; Bieber's introduction to Webb's memoirs contains a biographical sketch.

33. Webb was born Feb. 5, 1818. Messervy was born Aug. 27, 1812. Webb and Messervy formed their partnership in Jan. 1850.

34. Salem City Directory, 1850; Messervy to Kingsbury, Salem, Oct. 13, 1856, MHS; and Messervy, Généalogie, n.p.

35. Webb, *Adventures*, 33.

36. Ibid., 33.

37. Ibid., 35.

38. Lamar, *Far Southwest*, 56-82.

of New Mexico on April 8, 1853. In early 1854 he served as acting governor in the absence of David Meriwether.[39] Soon after his retirement from the Santa Fe trade, Messervy continued to pursue his political interests by serving two terms as the mayor of Salem.[40]

Webb's approach to involvement in the community took a more spontaneous course, perhaps a reflection of what Messervy perceived as his inability to maintain an interest in anything for long. "Webb is very changeable," Messervy once told Kingsbury, "and there is no [telling] what his virus will be six months ahead."[41] Messervy may have been correct. Webb could be impulsive, marrying a woman in December 1853, for example, whom he had met only the previous October.[42]

Webb apparently did have a kind heart and a social conscience. Like many of his countrymen, he noticed the woeful state of education in New Mexico. Rather than merely deplore local ignorance, he claimed a "deep interest in the dissemination of the means of education among the poor of this country" and arranged with the Mission Society of the Methodist Episcopal Church to import first, second, and third grade readers in Spanish. "We are willing," he wrote to the Society,

> to act as your agents for the sale of all books in the Spanish language, not of a sectarian or religious character, without commission, provided you put the price so low as only to cover the cost. The want of school books in the Spanish language is lamentably felt in this country.[43]

On a more personal level, in 1856 Webb arranged with Bishop Lamy to have the daughter of one of his servants placed in the Convent of Our Lady of Light at his expense, $125 a year. As Webb explained to his wife, he had feared that otherwise she would have become a prostitute.[44]

This act of charity was not an isolated incident. Years before, sometime around 1849, Webb had taken under his wing a six-year-old Mexican boy named José Hernández.[45] Where José came from and how he drew Webb's attention are not known, but from that time until well into the 1860s Webb seems to have regarded José as his responsibility. During that time, José shuttled back and forth between Connecticut and New Mexico, first staying with Webb and then with Kingsbury and working at a variety of odd jobs. Reports on José's character and progress run through Kingsbury's correspondence, and Webb's letters reveal an anxious regard sometimes touching on disappointment or disgust when Kingsbury sent a negative assessment.

Whether Webb's care and concern were well placed is difficult to determine. He certainly exerted a great deal of effort on José's behalf. One of Webb's memo books, with which he kept track of purchases made and merchandise still to buy, contains the following entry:

39. Webb, *Adventures*, 34.

40. Kingsbury to Webb, Salem, Jan. 12, 1857, MHS.

41. Messervy to Kingsbury, Salem, Dec. 31, 1858, MHS.

42. Webb to Kingsbury, Cornwall Bridge, CT, Oct. 5, 1853, and Nov. 5, 1853, MHS.

43. Webb & Kingsbury (Webb's handwriting), Santa Fe, to Thomas Carlton, treasurer of the Mission Society of the Methodist Episcopal Church, Dec. 31, 1854, MHS.

44. Webb to Lillie Webb, Santa Fe, July 10, 1856, MHS.

45. S. G. Bean to Jimmie Webb, Las Cruces, NM, postcard, n.d., Misc. File, Box 8, Webb Papers, MHS.

Get for Jose M. Hernandez—
    blk cloth for coat
    vest pattern
    [cloth] for pants
    Spanish Dictionary, large ed.
    Webster's Do. [ditto], Large ed.
    Prescott's Hist. of Mexico
    "Buchers Letters to Young Men"
    "Specimens of American Eloquence"[46]

José occupied a position within Webb's family circle. He felt sufficiently comfortable, for example, to correspond with Webb's wife Lillie, addressing her as "Mother Webb," and he knew the members of Webb's extended family by name. José's letters to him express fulsome appreciation for all Webb's support, along with repeated promises to practice the kind of thrifty industriousness that Webb seemed to expect. By Webb's lights, however, stability eluded José.

In 1853, Messervy decided to withdraw from the business and return to Salem. Webb cast about again for a partner and offered the opportunity to his young clerk, John Kingsbury. Had Kingsbury refused, Messervy advised that Webb's second choice be Tom Bowler, who had worked in their store before becoming the co-proprietor of the Exchange Hotel.[47] Kingsbury had little capital to bring to the business, but he was about to marry Messervy's youngest sister, Kate,[48] and had probably impressed Webb with his hard work and integrity. Several years before when Webb looked for a partner he observed, "I would prefer an honest poor man to a legally honest one with capital. Poverty is a stimulant at least to industry and economy."[49]

Kingsbury accepted Webb's offer that fall, after returning to Massachusetts to prepare for his wedding to Kate Messervy. The youngest of the family, Kate was William Messervy's junior by fourteen years, and she suffered from tuberculosis, or consumption as it was called at the time.[50] Apparently she and her family felt that the move to Santa Fe might improve her precarious health. If she was "strong enough to stand the trip" there was, William Messervy opined, "no doubt it is the only thing which will prolong her life—if there is hope—it is well to attempt it."[51]

In tendering this advice, Messervy expressed a belief widespread among American physicians that lengthy journeys and changes of residence benefited many ailments. By midcentury, the dry Great Plains were well established as a favorable site for therapeutic travel, and the journey to Santa Fe was the most favored of western routes in Daniel Drake's influential study, *A Systematic Treatise . . . on the Principal Diseases of the Interior Valley* (1850).[52] Santa Fe trader Josiah Gregg, author of the

46. Webb Memo Book, n.d., Box 8, Webb Papers, MHS.
47. Messervy to Webb, Santa Fe, Oct. 27, 1853, MHS.
48. Messervy, *Généalogie*, n.p.
49. Webb to Doan, King & Co., Nov. 29, 1849, in Webb, *Adventures*, 32.
50. Messervy, *Généalogie*, n.p.
51. Messervy to Kingsbury, Santa Fe, Jan. 29, 1854, MHS.
52. Jones, *Health-Seekers*, 37-41.

widely read *Commerce of the Prairies*, had made his first journey across the plains as an invalid, but found travel so salubrious that within weeks he had taken on the duties of bookkeeper for one of the train's merchants. Experienced plainsmen such as Messervy, and Webb who complained of the colds he inevitably caught on his trips to the East, must have witnessed many instances where an individual's health improved in New Mexico's clear dry climate.

Kate Messervy and John Kingsbury married in December 1853, as did James J. Webb and his bride, Florilla Mansfield Slade, or "Lillie" as she was called. Earlier that fall, Webb had announced his intentions of marrying, although he had no one specific in mind at the time.[53] When he found Lillie shortly thereafter, he found a remarkable woman indeed. Not only did she commit her life to his on the basis of a short courtship, she willingly accompanied him, along with the Kingsburys, to Santa Fe. There she and Kate set up their first homes, assisted by a serving woman whom Webb described as "strong as a horse; a real Yankee high pressure steamboat."[54]

Beginning married life under these circumstances could not have been easy for Kate Kingsbury and Lillie Webb, but they had each other to rely upon. Although not unheard of in Santa Fe, Anglo-American women were still fairly rare. As one New Mexican frontiersman later remarked to Webb's son,

> I was thinking what a brave heart your mother must of [have] had to come to New Mexico in those days of peril. The number of American Ladies who did come are very few and I can count them on the fingers of one hand.[55]

These two women formed a close-knit circle with the wives of J. J. Davenport, New Mexico's chief justice; Frank Tolhurst, the Baptist minister; and perhaps others. Together they could provide one another with emotional support beyond that available from their husbands, who operated mainly in a masculine sphere, or from Hispanic women, whose alien customs and Catholic religion offended their Protestant Yankee sensibilities. Complicating Santa Fe's social life still further was a group of seemingly disreputable Hispanic women, with whom self-described decent ladies imagined they should not mix. These two social circles appear in a contemporary description of two Santa Fe gatherings, which included very different sets of guests. The first, a Mexican *baile* hosted by Col. John B. Grayson on December 4, 1856, was "a grand Fandango— Everyone was there almost (except the decent American ladies)— officers, gents, gamblers & all with their mistresses. Champagne &c. flowed in abundance & the party was a lively one." In contrast, the same visitor described a more sedate party given by Col. B. L. E. Bonneville ten days later as "a very handsome affair far surpassing what I expected

53. Webb to Kingsbury, Cornwall Bridge, CT, Oct. 5, 1853, MHS.
54. Ibid., Mar. 2, 1854, MHS.
55. S. G. Bean to Jimmie Webb, Las Cruces, NM, postcard, (ca. 1890), Box 8, Misc. File, Webb Papers, MHS.

to see here. The ladies were dressed beautifully, & the officers in full dress—epaulets & sashes presented a fine appearance."[56]

Fashion constituted another area in which the customs of the "American ladies" clashed with those of the New Mexican women, although the influx of trade goods from the East had begun effecting significant change throughout the territory. Even before the Mexican War upper-class Hispanic women began to adopt European-style gowns in place of their traditional short skirts and loose, revealing blouses.[57] After the American occupation, the pace of change accelerated. In 1856 W. W. H. Davis commented on the far-reaching influences of New York and Parisian styles, stating that "the national costume of the Mexicans is fast disappearing among the better classes, who are learning to adopt the American style of dress."[58] Kingsbury's merchandise orders reflect this shift. In September 1858, he asked Webb to ship some silk capes, which the Mexican women had begun to wear at dances and out on the street. In the same order he also requested more sunbonnets, whose introduction he credited to the Sisters of Loretto. Sunbonnets, he predicted, would replace *rebozas* as head coverings.[59]

Social life in Santa Fe separated itself into many parts. Anglo-American politicians, army officers, and traders formed their own enclave within which still further divisions existed. The non-Hispanic mercantile community, for example, consisted of large, established firms, such as Webb & Kingsbury, as well as individuals or partners who traded for a season or two and then moved on to other ventures, or who imported goods as a sideline. At one time or another, many of the merchants Kingsbury mentions held political office, owned and worked land, practiced a profession, mined, milled, freighted, or brewed, and one, Siegman Seligman, briefly operated a photographic studio on the east side of the plaza.[60]

A large proportion of these traders were Jewish. Kingsbury perceived them as a separate clique, referring to their enclave on one occasion as "our little Jerusalem of Santa Fe."[61] Although the number of Jews in New Mexico in the 1850s was very small—perhaps sixteen in the 1850 census and thirty-six to forty-three in the 1860 census—nearly all were merchants or merchants' clerks, and their names appear frequently in the letters among Kingsbury's competitors and buyers: Jacob Amberg, Louis Felsenthal, Louis Gold, Joseph Hersch, and Selig Weinheim of Santa Fe; Simon Rosenstein of Albuquerque; Moses Sachs of Los Lunas; Nathan Appel of Socorro and other points south and west. Most of these men had been born in Poland or Germany and were young, single, and related to one another by blood or friendship. Several were brothers: the Beuthners of Taos, the Seligmans, Spiegelbergs, and Staabs of Santa Fe, and the Zeckendorfs of Albuquerque. Although Kingsbury saw them as a faction, their competition with one another must have been no less fierce than it was amongst the trading community at large. Kingsbury's letters also reveal his deep anti-Semitism, but as minorities in Hispanic

56. Barbour, ed., *Reluctant Frontiersman*, 108-10.

57. Weber, *Mexican Frontier*, 218.

58. Davis, *El Gringo*, 61.

59. Kingsbury to Webb, Santa Fe, Sept. 18, 1858, MHS.

60. Richard Rudisill, Curator of Photographic History, Museum of New Mexico, to Jane Elder, personal correspondence, June 24, 1993.

61. Kingsbury to Webb, Santa Fe, Feb. 6, 1859, DeG.

New Mexico, Jewish and Anglo merchants, including Kingsbury, seemed to develop a sense of mutual dependence that transcended ethnic or religious differences to a larger extent than might have been the case elsewhere.[62]

III.

When John Kingsbury arrived in Santa Fe in 1851, he entered a society undergoing radical transformations, as New Mexico's Hispanic population came under the administrative control of the United States. The government of the United States had just granted New Mexico territorial status, introducing a new political structure with its attendant bureaucracy and monetary system. Pope Pius IX was about to elevate New Mexico to a bishopric, removing it from the authority of the diocese of Durango in Mexico, making it subject to the American church in St. Louis, Missouri, and appointing the reform-minded French priest Jean Baptiste Lamy as its first bishop.[63] Other elements contributed to this period of flux in Santa Fe: Protestant missionary activity, a mounting interest in exploiting New Mexico's agricultural and mineral resources, and a local economy increasingly linked to the fluctuations of a national one. In short, new political, economic, and religious forces had begun to reshape the destiny of the city and the territory. Kingsbury's letters reflect some of the turmoil and repercussions that these assaults on the status quo initiated for both Anglos and Hispanics as they adjusted to the first decade of territorial rule.

Kingsbury's descriptions of political campaigns and the day-to-day affairs of government indicate that the establishment of civil rule did not go smoothly. Hallmarks of the electoral process as first practiced in Santa Fe included intrigue, fraud, and violence. Kingsbury reported to Webb in 1859: "We got safely through Election day without any serious fights, only one man killed in Santa Fe over the election."[64] Kingsbury came to understand the nuances of New Mexico's complicated power structure well, perhaps from his early days as a clerk listening to conversations in the store between Messervy, Webb, and their customers. Political factions reflected the conflict of two cultures, each with its own deep divisions. The Americans, who mirrored disparate segments of the national political scene, compounded their lack of cohesion by tending to protect their own individual business interests. At the same time, the Hispanic community was plagued with what one historian characterized as "an elaborate and complicated politics of faction and disunity," based on whether to cooperate with the Americans. Family feuds, personal grievances of long standing, and church politics created additional rifts.[65] The extent to which these divisions hampered government operations was demonstrated in the territory's second legislative session when it took three ballots to elect the doorkeeper.[66]

In addition to the violence and factionalism of its politics, the fledgling civil government faced the problem of insufficient funding. Little

62. Tobias, *Jews in New Mexico*, 29, 39-40, 44-49.
63. Horgan, *Lamy*, 156.
64. Kingsbury to Webb, Santa Fe, Sept. 10, 1859, MHS.
65. Lamar, *Far Southwest*, 86-87.
66. Ibid., 88.

revenue found its way into the territorial coffers during this period because of the assembly's reluctance to impose taxes on anyone except the proprietors of saloons, gambling dens, and mercantile establishments. The merchants balked at the idea of bearing a disproportionate share of the tax burden and fought the decision in the courts.[67] Kingsbury hoped for a change, reporting to Webb in 1856: "They have made no new revinue law. Merchants license remains the same as always."[68]

Short of local revenue, officials paid the bills by issuing warrants, thereby creating a thriving speculative market in government drafts, in which Webb & Kingsbury participated.[69] By 1855 the "major local business" of issuing warrants nearly bankrupted the treasury, according to the acting governor, W. W. H. Davis.[70] When the newly appointed governor, Abraham Rencher, took office in 1857, the outstanding warrants drawn on the government that year equaled $10,973, while revenues totaled only $7,664. The resulting deficit, combined with those of previous years, came to $9,872.[71] Before his term of office ended in 1861, Gov. Rencher had reduced the debt to $3,673, but throughout the 1850s, government operations ran in the red.[72]

For the most part, the territorial government looked to Congress to provide for its financial needs. In addition to paying the salaries of territorial officials, the federal government subsidized both the prosecution of Indian wars and, briefly, the maintenance of peace with Indians through gifts.[73] It also reimbursed three New Mexican citizens for the $10,000 they loaned the first territorial assembly to meet its expenses,[74] and it opened a profitable pork barrel when it authorized construction of new public buildings, including a statehouse, for Santa Fe. Between 1853 and 1860, Congress made three appropriations for the statehouse totaling $150,000, yet by the outbreak of the Civil War, only one and a half stories of the statehouse had been erected.[75] In 1856 Webb & Kingsbury purchased the hardware for the building in the East, but the government had not paid the bill by 1861, when Kingsbury left Santa Fe, and may never have paid it.[76] Joab Houghton, the opportunistic superintendent of construction, drove costs up when he succeeded in convincing Washington that the federal buildings should be made with dressed stone. New Mexico, he solemnly assured them, had become increasingly humid, a change that might cause traditional adobe bricks to melt.[77]

Kingsbury's correspondence reflects the interdependency of civil government and private enterprise, and their overall dependence on federal money. The government's issuance of drafts and warrants made it possible for Kingsbury to send revenue to the East safely, while his inability to procure drafts and warrants from time to time hampered the operation of his business. Conversely, Webb & Kingsbury fronted the expense of purchasing and shipping the hardware for the new statehouse, or the "state house irons" as Kingsbury calls them, believing that an order based on the promise of a Congressional appropriation involved little risk. A myriad of smaller examples of this convoluted financial network exist in

67. Ibid.
68. Kingsbury to Webb, Santa Fe, Jan. 30, 1856, MHS.
69. Lamar, *Far Southwest*, 88.
70. Ibid., 88-89.
71. Horn, *New Mexico's Troubled Years*, 76-77.
72. Ibid., 88.
73. Twitchell, *Leading Facts*, 2:326, 284, 292, 295.
74. Lamar, *Far Southwest*, 90.
75. Davis, *El Gringo*, 42; Lamar, *Far Southwest*, 90-91.
76. Kingsbury to Webb, Salem, Oct. 13, 1856, MHS; Kingsbury to Webb, Santa Fe, Feb. 10, 1861, MHS.
77. Lamar, *Far Southwest*, 90-91; *Santa Fe Weekly Gazette*, Feb. 1853; Twitchell, *Leading Facts*, 2:326.

rich detail in these letters, as well as Kingsbury's own unexpurgated assessment of the personalities involved.

One individual about whom Kingsbury remained silent, however, was Jean Baptiste Lamy. His letters provide almost no insight into the activities of New Mexico's first and perhaps most influential bishop, who worked vigorously to establish order out of what he perceived as a moral chaos that plagued the territory. Devoting his immediate attention to establishing his authority and bringing recalcitrant priests to heel, Lamy also initiated several long-term projects for the good of the community.[78] In his first ten years in office, which corresponded almost exactly with Kingsbury's tenure in Santa Fe, Lamy imported groups of nuns and priests, who assisted in the establishment of the convent and girls' Academy of Our Lady of Light and the boys' school that later grew into St. Michael's College.[79] Yet the only written notice Kingsbury took of him was in relation to Lamy's construction projects, when they competed for the attention of local builder Calvin Scofield. Scofield apparently placed a higher priority on the bishop's work, thereby delaying completion of the floor in Kingsbury's store.[80]

Kingsbury's failure to describe Lamy's activities or any of the Catholic celebrations and ceremonies that occurred regularly on his very doorstep constitutes a curious omission. Perhaps he found uninteresting the religious drama that Lamy's arrival provoked. Or he saw no need to describe the everyday affairs of a religion whose practitioners represented the overwhelming majority of Santa Fe's small population and with which Webb was intimately familiar. Kingsbury's correspondence contains no anti-Catholic sentiments expressed in the virulent terms sometimes employed by his fellow Protestants, but on one occasion he indulged in a wry observation. After the roof and tower of the new Protestant church collapsed in a rainstorm, he reported to Webb with some satisfaction that "about the same time the end of the Bishops new Chapel fell out, showing that their faith & chapels are no stronger than ours."[81]

Kingsbury was more comfortable in the Protestant sphere. Only two denominations, the Methodists and the Baptists, had attempted to challenge Rome's New Mexico monopoly.[82] Charged with introducing an unadorned form of Christianity to Native Americans and Hispanic Catholics, they found their task daunting. In 1852, after two years of work, the Methodists gave up.[83] Whether they did so for financial reasons, or because of the notoriously licentious attitude adopted by many Americans in Santa Fe, is unclear. The Baptists, on the other hand, prevailed. They came to Santa Fe in 1849, hard on the heels of the invading army, and founded a mission school to teach English. They erected the first Protestant church in the city, which they dedicated on January 15, 1854.[84] The bell of the church cost over two hundred dollars, purchased by subscription by American merchants and mercantile firms, who probably financed most of the four-thousand-dollar edifice as well.[85] Fred K.

78. Horgan, *Lamy*, 285.

79. Horgan, *Lamy*, 181, 283-84; Russell, *Land of Enchantment*, 42.

80. Kingsbury to Messervy, Santa Fe, Oct. 31, 1854, Webb Papers, MHS.

81. Kingsbury to Webb, Santa Fe, July 26, 1853, MHS.

82. Although Twitchell mentions that a Presbyterian missionary came to New Mexico in 1851, he describes him as more of a politician and does not discuss his religious activities or whether he abandoned them. Twitchell later states that the Presbyterians and Episcopalians made no serious attempts to establish themselves in Santa Fe until after 1863. *Leading Facts*, 2:325-26, 352.

83. Ibid., 2:325-26.

84. Ibid., 2:350.

85. Misc. File, Box 8, Webb Papers, MHS.

Tolhurst, attached for a time to this congregation, and his wife numbered among the few close friends Kingsbury could count in the territory. Friends, too, although not as close, were the Rev. Samuel Gorman and his family, who lived and worked as Baptist missionaries among the Indians at Laguna Pueblo from 1852 until 1861.[86]

But whether Protestant or Catholic, church affairs apparently held little abiding interest for John Kingsbury. When not reporting to Webb about their own business prospects, Kingsbury kept him as fully informed as possible on the status of their competitors, as in 1858 when he warned Webb: "The Mexicans are now selling good sugar at 20 cents on 6 months. We cannot compete with them in groceries."[87] In addition, he passed on to Webb what he knew of developments in other areas of the economy, such as agriculture and mining. The needs of the large U.S. military presence had stimulated agricultural production, which rose throughout the 1850s. Corn, wheat, and bean yields more than doubled, while the number of cattle nearly tripled.[88] Sheep ranching in particular boomed between 1851 and 1861 with the appearance of a new, lucrative market in the gold fields of California.[89] In 1853, for example, a group of Hispanic New Mexicans drove a flock of over 25,000 sheep to California, selling them for $5.50 a head and returning home with a net profit of $70,000.[90] New Mexican wool found a market in the opposite direction. In 1854 merchants and freighters sent it east for the first time in an attempt to wrest some kind of profit from the empty wagons they sent back to Missouri every season. By 1857, they had sent at least 865,000 pounds of wool to Kansas City, and in 1859 agents from New York and Boston began traveling west to buy it.[91]

Kingsbury watched each new economic development closely, gauging the extent to which he and Webb should invest their own income, as well as ascertaining the moneymaking possibilities open to their debtors. Although Webb & Kingsbury exercised caution in the extension of credit, at times they could not avoid it. In fact, the collection of outstanding debts kept Kingsbury in Santa Fe far longer than he wished, once he and Webb decided to close their business.

What was good for business in general was good for the merchants who, throughout the antebellum West, tended to dominate local economies, performing their traditional roles as communities' financial agents and chief sources of working capital.[92] Thus, Kingsbury faithfully reported fluctuations in the expanding markets for livestock, produce, and raw materials in the Southwest. For example, a drought at the end of the decade imposed severe hardships on the land and its people. It increased the prices of grain, fodder, and livestock, but in general acted as a damper on the economy as crops failed and money grew scarce.[93] A slump in the prices New Mexican sheep could command in California in the second half of the 1850s put a cap on spectacular profits, although the market remained a good one for those willing to risk the dangers of

86. Twitchell, *Leading Facts*, 2:350; Webb & Kingsbury ledger, vol. 16, Webb Papers, MHS.

87. Kingsbury to Webb, Santa Fe, Sept. 18, 1858, MHS.

88. Frazer, *Forts and Supplies*, 186.

89. Lamar, *Far Southwest*, 106.

90. Baxter, *Las Carneradas*, 119-20.

91. Walker, *Wagonmasters*, 148-49.

92. White, *It's Your Misfortune*, 273; Porter and Livesay, *Merchants and Manufacturers*, 116.

93. Frazer, *Forts and Supplies*, 154; Kingsbury to Webb, Santa Fe, May 6, 1860, MHS.

the drive west.[94] Dealing in the coarse-fibered New Mexican wool remained a risky venture as well. Kingsbury advised a freighter in 1859:

> Unless you have a sure purchase for the wool, my advice to you would be to let it alone. I am told that New Mexican wool at best is a poor sale in the States and slow. It often has to lay there in storage one or two years before it can be sold. Dr. Conelly [Connelly] is my authority. He has tried it repeatedly and is well posted.[95]

The potential wealth of New Mexico's mineral deposits seemed to occupy far more attention than agriculture and stock raising, in some minds at least. A variety of speculative schemes focused on the operations located at the old colonial placers in the Ortiz Mountains, twenty-five miles from Santa Fe. Kingsbury kept Webb fully informed about one of these companies, the New Mexico Mining Company, which organized in 1854 when its investors acquired the Ortiz land grant upon which the mine was located. Part of the New Mexico Mining Company's prominence sprang from the presence among its shareholders of a great many territorial officials. Indeed, one of the company's directors—a fact concealed from Congress when the company applied for confirmation of its title to the old Mexican grant—was Governor Abraham Rencher. Rencher had turned down an appointment as secretary of the navy to become governor of New Mexico. His keen personal interest in developing New Mexico's mineral wealth, stemming no doubt from his heavy personal investment in it, manifested itself in many of his official pronouncements, including his inaugural address.[96]

Yet mining in the period before 1861 failed to develop, and even the Ortiz claim remained unprofitable until after the close of the Civil War. Kingsbury attributed Rencher's lack of success to poor management and inadequate funding.[97] Perhaps more importantly, despite its proximity to Santa Fe, the mine still lay open to Indian raids, which discouraged large-scale development.[98] For the most part, however, Santa Fe businessmen like Kingsbury, as well as their eastern counterparts like Webb, bided their time and waited for the kind of resolution to the Indian question that would safeguard their investments and their lives.[99] Until that time the New Mexico Mining Company and others like it remained undercapitalized and underdeveloped.[100]

The shortage of capital lay at the heart of New Mexico's overall failure to develop during this period. One of the forces contributing to this shortage was the national economy, which experienced slumps in both 1854 and 1857. The Panic of 1857, for example, and the ensuing two-year national depression created a climate of uncertainty as far away as New Mexico. Precipitated by the failure of an Ohio investment house and a sharp fall in agricultural exports to Europe at the close of the Crimean War, the panic threw thousands out of work and made money tight.[101]

94. Baxter, *Las Carneradas*, 141-43.

95. Kingsbury to J. B. Kitchen, Santa Fe, Feb. 6, 1859, MHS; Baxter, *Las Carneradas*, 149.

96. Horn, *New Mexico's Troubled Years*, 75-76; Townley, "New Mexico Mining Company," 57-59, 63-65; and Homer E. Milford, Environmental Coordinator, Abandoned Mine Land Bureau, Santa Fe, to Jane Elder, personal correspondence, July 21, 1993.

97. Kingsbury to Webb, Santa Fe, July 25, 1858, DeG.

98. Twitchell, *Leading Facts*, 2:324.

99. Connor and Skaggs, *Broadcloth and Britches*, 157.

100. See chapter 10.

101. Faragher et al., *Out of Many*, 459.

Webb's letters to Kingsbury reflect the nation's anxiety. Throughout the fall of 1857, he reported the failure of investment houses and banks, and even the suspension of operations of Webb & Kingsbury's chief supply house, Doan, King & Company in St. Louis.[102] "The Brokers are failing everywhere, and there is no telling how long the banks will maintain specie payments," Webb advised. He urged Kingsbury to take no drafts in payment except those written on the U.S. Treasury or on houses in Boston and New York.[103] "I presume the effect of the hard times will not reach you before next summer," Webb wrote hopefully.[104] Nevertheless, neither man doubted that this ripple in the nation's economic pool would eventually have a negative impact in the remote markets of New Mexico.

Merchants siphoning capital out of the local economy constituted another force directly affecting development in New Mexico. Most of the American traders, including Kingsbury, Messervy, and Webb, had little desire to make Santa Fe their permanent home, yet they acted as the entrepreneurs whose speculative activities drove the developing economy. Personal preference prompted their decisions on disposal of the profits these activities yielded, and neither Messervy, Kingsbury, nor Webb preferred Santa Fe. Many other Anglo Americans of the period felt the same way. Young men seeking their fortunes might perceive the city as exotic, foreign, and full of adventure. Older men, who had succeeded in accumulating some property and who wanted to begin a family and build a life, frequently regarded Santa Fe as dirty, corrupt, and alien. "When shall I get out of this hole of dissipation?" complained Kingsbury to Webb, who by that time had used the profits generated by his years in the Santa Fe trade to buy and improve an extensive estate in Connecticut.[105]

Like the merchants, freighters generated revenue that never made its way into territorial coffers. Operating out of the Missouri Valley on local capital,[106] these men received army or private contracts to haul goods to Santa Fe. Most of their profits probably did not circulate through New Mexico. In 1851, for example, 452 wagons of supplies left Fort Leavenworth for New Mexico, but the windfall from the more than one million dollars that the freighting contractors received most likely went to Kansas and Missouri where the freighters based their businesses.[107] So although Santa Fe was the center of trade in this period, it was not necessarily the main financial beneficiary.

A number of historians have characterized the western economy as extractive. Richard White sees three interrelated components as the foundation of western economic development: sufficient labor and capital to exploit existing resources, a market for the commodities derived from those resources, and a transportation system to move those commodities to market.[108] If White's model is correct, then New Mexico of the 1850s occupies an anomalous position within it. Its mining potential could

102. Webb to Kingsbury, Cornwall Bridge, CT, Oct. 5, 1857, MHS; ibid., New Haven, CT, Oct. 19, 1857, MHS.
103. Webb to Kingsbury, Cornwall Bridge, CT, Oct. 5, 1857, MHS.
104. Ibid., New Haven, CT, Oct. 19, 1857, MHS.
105. Kingsbury to Webb, Santa Fe, Dec. 24, 1859, MHS.
106. Walker, *Wagonmasters*, 75.
107. Ibid., 237.
108. White, *It's Your Misfortune*, 243-44.

not be realized with the same ease as that of California or Colorado during the same period. More geographically remote than Texas, New Mexico had a rudimentary transportation system that precluded an efficient method of capitalizing on its agricultural potential. Thus its appeal to eastern investors, the main source of capital in the West, fell short when compared to other western states. Arguably, New Mexico's most readily exploitable resource was the revenue generated by the market for goods that the military's presence had created. Ironically, however, one of the reasons the army occupied the territory in the first place was to protect the lucrative Santa Fe trade.

IV.

The collaboration of John M. Kingsbury and James J. Webb resulted in an organized, methodical, and businesslike approach to trading in Santa Fe in the mid–nineteenth century. Their financial success attests to their entrepreneurial acumen, but they also left a legacy of rich historical sources. Kingsbury's meticulous attention to his work made those sources invaluable, and the foresight and care of James J. Webb and his family prevented their loss or destruction. The Kingsbury-Webb correspondence, much of it published here, preserves in rich detail the day-to-day activities of antebellum merchants in Santa Fe. In addition, a complete and carefully organized set of the firm's business ledgers and a significant amount of related notebooks, shipping lists, invoices, and telegrams complement the correspondence. These can be consulted at the Missouri Historical Society in St. Louis.

In many cases, the firm's ledger books enabled us to provide a full name for individuals and business entities mentioned in the letters. The ledgers also allowed us to confirm various facts that the letters did not reveal clearly. And, when consulted in tandem, the correspondence and the ledgers have much to tell us about the nature of Kingsbury and Webb's business and the financial world in which they operated.

In the merchant's world of the mid-nineteenth century, promissory notes (any written promise to pay) and bills of exchange (directions in writing to another to pay a sum for the writer to yet another person at a specified date) played an important part. These paper instruments permitted the collection, purchase, shipment, and distribution of goods without the use of currency. For example, Kingsbury might sell $1,000 worth of goods to Tom Bowler, taking in payment a bill of exchange due in three months. Rather than wait three months to realize the cash, he could purchase $1,000 of goods from Doan, King & Co. and pay for it by giving them Bowler's note upon which they could collect at that note's date of maturity. Another option would be for Webb & Kingsbury to assign a collection of these bills of exchange to a banker, who would then extend them credit based upon the total amount, less interest. Webb &

Kingsbury could then use their bank credit to pay their own notes as they matured or to purchase more goods to continue business.[109] This kind of system streamlined financial transactions throughout the United States and allowed trade to flourish in a territory as cash-poor as New Mexico.

John Kingsbury used the standard double-entry method of book-keeping, consisting of a main ledger of accounts to which each of the cash and sales journals referred, with individual accounts cross-indexed.[110] His scrupulous attention to maintaining the firm's records according to the accepted procedure of his day suggests that he should have taken the next step and prepared a profit statement, a record that shows revenues and expenses in a zero-sum account form. Yet no Webb & Kingsbury profit statements seem to remain in archival collections. Furthermore, while Kingsbury mentions trial balances in his letters, no balance sheets showing all the debits, credits, assets, and liabilites have come to light.

The absence of profit statements and balance sheets can be account-ed for in several different ways. First, if Kingsbury or Webb drew up such profit-related statements, they may have since been lost. Webb would have been the most likely partner to create them, since he had to present at eastern banks many of the bills of exchange and government drafts the firm accepted as payment. Kingsbury had no way of knowing exact-ly how much some of those papers would yield, given the custom of dis-counting notes written on certain institutions, or the fluctuating value of such items as land warrants. Sometimes a draft would be protested and the partners received no money at all. Once Webb knew the actual amount realized from these kinds of paper, he could have prepared the statements and sent them to Kingsbury in Santa Fe, where they were lost—not unlikely since it was Webb, not Kingsbury, who preserved all of the correspondence and records that remain to us.

The second possibility is that the partners did not draw up balance sheets. Until the middle part of the twentieth century, the traditional method of teaching bookkeeping had been to divide the course into two parts: the first encompassed bookkeeping up to the point of making a trial balance, the second covered the preparation of financial statements. Kingsbury might not have taken the second course and therefore not have known how to prepare such a record. Moreover, Webb may not have needed one. No accounting ledgers survive from Webb's previous two partnerships, and perhaps he never kept them.[111] Webb might have kept the firm's bottom line in his head rather than on paper. In any event, the cash balance the partners maintained in their various bank accounts, pre-sumably in the East, would approximate their total profits.

Although Webb might have known the bottom line, we historians cannot calculate the profits of Webb & Kingsbury with any degree of accuracy. No record exists of Webb's initial investment in the business,

109. Colwell, *Ways and Means*, 205-6, 210.

110. The following analysis of the ledgers of Webb & Kingsbury is based on a series of conversations with Professor Michael Van Breda of SMU's Cox School of Business. Prof. Van Breda contributed his special expertise in the history and theory of account-ing to our project and made this discussion possible.

111. However, various memo books and purchase lists dating before 1853 are included in the Missouri Historical Society's collection.

or how much of that money carried over when he brought in Kingsbury as a junior partner. Kingsbury himself invested $10,000 when they created the firm in 1853, but he apparently borrowed a good portion of that money from either Webb or Messervy or both. The partners' investments in real estate present an added complication, since it is unclear whether that money came from personal or business funds. In the absence of such data, the evident prosperity of their later lives will have to suffice as an index to their business's profitability.

By the time they closed their store in Santa Fe in 1861, Webb & Kingsbury had accumulated 262 accounts on their books, 19 of which related to the running of their business: agent, personal, rental, and firm accounts, and one entitled "sundry." Of the remaining 243 accounts the majority, numbering 150, belonged to non-Hispanic individuals, of whom 16 were military personnel, 4 were clergymen, and 1 was a woman. Hispanic individuals, of whom 1 was a woman, numbered only 27. Similarly, there were far more non-Hispanic businesses and partnerships—42—than Hispanic or Anglo-Hispanic businesses and partnerships—4 and 2, respectively. Thirteen accounts dealt with government operations and funds, 2 with social organizations (the Masonic and I.O.O.F. lodges), and 3 with real estate parcels Kingsbury had accepted in payment in lieu of cash.[112] These accounts included retail as well as wholesale transactions. We are unable to determine if the books reflect small retail purchases made by people who might not have maintained formal accounts with Webb & Kingsbury.

V.

Kingsbury entered the Santa Fe trade at a time of unprecedented growth, but, paradoxically, those years between the end of the Mexican-American War and the onset of the Civil War also represent a low point in our knowledge of the trade. The opening decades of the Santa Fe trade, like any pioneering moment, have attracted writers. So, too, have the years before and during the war with Mexico. We have Gregg's *Commerce of the Prairies* (1844); the memoirs of Kingsbury's partner, Webb, *Adventures in the Santa Fe Trade, 1844-1847* (first published in 1931); and such colorful and authoritative secondary accounts as David Lavender's *Bent's Fort* (1954) and Bernard de Voto's *Year of Decision*. Writing on the 1850s, when no war raged and the American flag flew over Santa Fe, has paled in comparison.[113]

Glimpses of the story of the Santa Fe trade in the 1850s can be found in several firsthand accounts: the classic work of contemporary description and commentary by W. W. H. Davis, *El Gringo; or, New Mexico and Her People*, published in 1857; memoirs of residents, such as Marian Russell's lyrical recollections of her girlhood in Santa Fe between the summers of 1854 and 1856;[114] and memoirs or diaries of persons who simply

112. Index, Vol. 17, Webb Papers, MHS.

113. Bieber, "Aspects of the Santa Fe Trade," 158, made this point in 1924. Barbour, ed., *Reluctant Frontiersman*, 7, made the point again in 1990 and offers a good discussion of sources. For an example of the poverty of information and interest in the 1850s, see Connor and Skaggs, *Broadcloth and Britches*, 155-60.

114. Russell, *Land of Enchantment*. Russell came to New Mexico in 1852 at age seven, with her mother and brother, and settled first in Albuquerque. She did not stay settled for long, however. Between 1852 and 1862, she crossed the Santa Fe Trail five times. Rittenhouse, *Santa Fe Trail*, 186. Similarly, Franz Huning, who came to Santa Fe in 1849 at age twenty-two, wrote his memoirs in 1894 at sixty-seven; those memoirs were published as Huning, *Trader on the Santa Fe Trail*. The memoirs of David Meriwether, who served as territorial governor from 1853 to 1857, were dictated at age eighty-six and published as Meriwether, *My Life*.

traveled the trail to New Mexico but did not linger there.[115] Fine scholarly treatments of the political, economic, or military history of New Mexico in the 1850s also illuminate the trade,[116] but the full story of the Santa Fe trade in the 1850s, with its political and social implications, remains to be written.

The letters of John Kingsbury will constitute an indispensable source when the story of the 1850s is told, for they explain the inner workings of the Santa Fe trade as a long-time participant understood them. In contrast to accounts written from memory long after the event, these contemporaneous letters possess remarkable vividness and fidelity to detail. Since Kingsbury did not write for publication, his candor remained uncompromised and his meaning unclouded by literary pretensions, although he unnecessarily belittled his skills when he wrote to Webb, "I am a poor hand with private letters."[117] That Kingsbury wrote with just one reader in mind may weaken his letters as literature but gives them strength as historical sources. They become a private window through which we can catch tantalizing glimpses of the excitement and drudgery, the adventure and skulduggery, and the risks and rewards of trading in Santa Fe before the war economy and evolving patterns of industrialization changed the face of mercantile capitalism.[118]

115. The most recent publication of such a work is Barbour, ed., *Reluctant Frontiersman*. Other examples include: Napton, *Over the Santa Fe Trail*; Möllhausen, "Over the Santa Fe Trail through Kansas"; and Majors, *Seventy Years on the Frontier*, 102-106, 128-41.

116. Notable examples include: Keleher, *Turmoil in New Mexico*; Lamar, *Far Southwest*; Larson, *New Mexico's Quest*; Frazer, *Forts and Supplies*; Oliva, *Soldiers*.

117. Kingsbury to Webb, Santa Fe, Sept. 24, 1859, DeG. See, too, Kingsbury to Webb, Santa Fe, Apr. 3, 1859, and Nov. 27, 1859, DeG.

118. In *Nature's Metropolis*, 319-40, William Cronon presents a rich discussion of the ways in which the railroad alone transformed the world of the frontier merchant. It decreased the expense and eliminated the seasonality of shipping, diminished the chronic uncertainties of matching supply to demand, freed up capital, shifted national distribution patterns, and made possible such direct marketing techniques as advertising, traveling salesmen, and catalog sales.

Conventions

This book may be read in many ways. On one level, it tells Kingsbury's own sad story. On another level, it should serve as a reference work for those interested in economic, political, social, cultural, and material aspects of Santa Fe and its trade with the "States" in the tumultuous decade between the United States–Mexican War and the Civil War. Readers interested in business or the prices of commodities can skip over the sections treating politics, while those interested in material culture may not wish to read that A. Zechendorf lost a thousand dollars at a billiard table in a single night. We cannot anticipate the way in which readers, with their own questions and interests, will interrogate these letters. We have, then, resisted the temptation to cut seemingly extraneous passages and have reproduced Kingsbury's letters in full, with one exception. Each letter begins with "Mr. Webb, Dear Sir," and closes with "Yours truly J. M. Kingsbury"; we have not reproduced these formulaic salutations and closings.

Just as we have not attempted to anticipate readers' interests by deleting letters or portions of letters, we have not tampered with Kingsbury's text. His grammar occasionally suffers from problems of subject-verb agreement such as "there was three" or "I done." Kingsbury possessed a mind sufficiently ample to spell words inconsistently. In general, Kingsbury's spelling remains fairly predictable, although it deteriorates badly in those passages he wrote when angry or upset. In addition to the traditional problems with "to," "two," and "too," and "there" and "their," he could refer to his assets as "capital" or "capitol" and his business as "trade" or "traid" in the same letter if not the same paragraph. Other words he spelled consistently but incorrectly. He doubled consonants and vowels, spelling words like "lose" and "move" with two *o*'s, "wagons" and "widow" with an extra letter in the middle, or adding an additional *l* on words like "until" and "careful." From time to time he added an *e* to the end of words like "won," "whom," and "control." He used *s*'s and *c*'s interchangeably, as in "advise" for "advice" and "mashinery." When in doubt about a vowel he relied on *i*'s in words like "honisty," "corrispond," and "revinue," *ai*'s in words like "strainger" and "dainger," and he usually spelled "straight" "streight." Other problem words include "necessity," "attack," and "miracle."

Some of his spelling errors, such as the word "sayd," look jarring on the page, but the reader who remembers that Kingsbury spelled phonetically will have no difficulty translating "sayd" into "said." When his meaning seems murky, we have offered clarification in square brackets, and when his spelling seems particularly improbable we have added an occasional [*sic*] to make it clear that we made no transcription error.

Because we wished to have the book speak with one voice and because John Kingsbury did most of the trading in Santa Fe in the 1850s, we have chosen to reproduce only his letters. But where Webb's or Messervy's correspondence illuminates Kingsbury's, we have quoted or paraphrased it in a note. We have occasionally chosen to identify individuals in the notes at the point where Kingsbury actually discussed them rather than at the point where their first mention is made as part of a list. In some cases an individual, while prominent, may appear only once in these letters; we have not identified people Kingsbury mentioned only in passing, although we often supply first names of people Kingsbury identifies only by surname.

Kingsbury's Correspondence in Manuscript

Kingsbury's letters to Webb: Letters no. 1 to 92, July 26, 1853 to Dec. 26, 1858, and no. 137 to 194, Jan. 8, 1860 to May 12, 1861, are from the collections of the Missouri Historical Society, St. Louis, Missouri. Letters no. 83, Oct. 31, 1858, and no. 93 to 136, Jan. 2, 1859 to Jan. 1, 1860, are from the DeGolyer Library, Southern Methodist University, Dallas, Texas. We would like to thank each institution for giving us permission to publish these letters.

Abbreviations Used in the Notes

DeG	DeGolyer Library, Southern Methodist University
HHS	Hamden Historical Society, Hamden, CT
MHR	Missouri Historical Review
MHS	Missouri Historical Society, St. Louis, MO
NMHR	*New Mexico Historical Review*
NMSRCA	New Mexico State Records Center and Archives

I.

Business, Fandangos, and "poly sticks"

Summer in Santa Fe, 1853

Letters 1 & 2

John Kingsbury's letters to James Webb begin in July 1853 in Santa Fe, with Kingsbury then serving as a clerk for the mercantile company of Messervy & Webb. Webb had returned to the east that summer,[1] and Kingsbury kept him informed of local matters in two news-filled letters.

First, in regard to business, Kingsbury explained that sales were up thanks to the impending arrival of more United States troops.[2] The soldiers and their payrolls, merchants anticipated, would bring more buyers and capital into the territory. Messervy & Webb, in particular, Kingsbury believed, stood to profit more than its competitors. The firm had a stock of goods from the previous year for which they had paid cheaper freight than current charges for sending goods to Santa Fe with the annual spring caravans. Thus, the firm could undersell its competitors, whose goods had just arrived. However well-founded, Kingsbury's optimism proved short-lived—a pattern that repeated itself throughout his years in the Santa Fe trade. Although sales were brisk in July, he reported to Webb that they fell off in August.

In addition to his analysis of the firm's performance and prospects, Kingsbury sent Webb gossip about competitors, mutual friends, and local events, from the building of the territorial capitol to the collapse of part of the parish church. An influx of Anglo-American adventurers, lawyers, merchants, and soldiers—most of them young, male, and on the make—had given Santa Fe the rough edges of an American frontier town, yet the underlying foreignness of the city remained a reality for the Anglo Americans.[3] The unruly newcomers, possessed of political and economic power, still constituted a minority in Hispanic Santa Fe, heightening ethnic and class tensions. Kingsbury's letters, written clearly from an Anglo-American viewpoint, reflect those tensions. Nowhere are they clearer than in his description of a brawl and murder at a dance in Santa Fe's main hotel, the Exchange, the forerunner of today's La Fonda, then owned by William Messervy. Kingsbury also kept Webb informed of tensions in the southern part of the territory, where war with Mexico seemed imminent. The United States and Mexico seemed unable to agree

1. Webb traveled east by stage with the July mail from Santa Fe, arriving in Independence on July 20. Barry, *Beginning of the West*, 1172.

2. Gen. John Garland, the new commander of the Ninth Military Department, had assigned three hundred new troops to New Mexico. Connor and Skaggs, *Broadcloth and Britches*, 156.

3. Barbour, *Reluctant Frontiersman*, 38.

on ownership of a large tract of what is today southern New Mexico and southern Arizona—the so-called Mesilla strip.

Local politics held special fascination for Kingsbury that summer in Santa Fe. In July, if not before, he became private secretary to William Carr Lane, the interim territorial governor. That position probably amplified Kingsbury's knowledge of New Mexico politics—"poly sticks" as he called them—and explains his vivid characterizations of local politicians, would-be politicians, and political factions. On September 6, New Mexicans would elect their first delegate to Congress (a non-voting member), and various groups vied vigorously in August for the prestige, power, and patronage that would come from a direct link to the nation's capital. The Democrats split into two camps, one described as "pro-American" and the other as "pro-Mexican," but they did not divide along strict ethnic lines. William Carr Lane, the outgoing territorial governor, represented the "pro-American" faction but enjoyed the support of some Hispanics as well as of Anglo Americans such as Kingsbury. José Manuel Gallegos was nominated by the more populist "pro-Mexican" faction but received support from some Anglo Americans, including the incoming governor, David Meriwether.[4]

~

Letter no. 1, Kingsbury to Webb, Santa Fe, July 26, 1853

I received your letter written at Fort Union,[5] and made the entries.

We have rec.d nothing from Moore & Rees[6] yet. Moore is going to the Fort Union and says he will send some money soon as he returns.

The mail arrived on the 24th and brought some news about extry troops having been ordered here, which is general[l]y believed, if they come it will help thing[s] here wonderfully.

Since the new goods came in business has improved with [us], and if it continues we will have a fair show of closing out by Spring. The Sales this month are close on to $10,000 Ten Thousand Dollars and we expect to make it that sum before the month closes. The goods that came out this year cost so high in the State[s] that we can undersell them all, and have a fair profit left. People have found it out and are willing to buy. [William S.] Messervy[7] is determined to sell low and at the same time work off hard stock such as Clothing &c. He has succeeded very well so far. We are holding on to Manta, Lienzo, & Shoes.[8] Brogans bring $15 easy.[9] The assortment is still good. I hardly miss anything that has been sold since you left. The whiskey market is looking up a little, and I think ours will come in after a while. [Preston] Beck [Jr.][10] bought none common.[11] Yesterday he bought from [John] Flourney $2,500 worth, which must pretty near take his pile, so that all the whiskey is with [George] Wethered, Beck, & ourselves.[12]

4. Lamar characterized Hispanic politics of this period as "an elaborate and complicated politics of faction and disunity" based on "family feuds, personal dislikes, and general division" over cooperating or resisting the Americans, who themselves were almost equally fragmented along economic lines. *Far Southwest*, 86-87.

5. Fort Union, founded in 1851 near Las Vegas, New Mexico, served as an important supply depot throughout this era.

6. William F. Moore and Burton F. Rees of Tecolote were the major suppliers of corn and hay to the U.S. Army in New Mexico between 1851 and 1858. Frazer, *Forts and Supplies*, 102-3.

7. William S. Messervy was still Webb's partner at this time, while Kingsbury acted as bookeeper for the firm. See Introduction.

8. *Manta* generally meant unbleached muslin; *lienzo* was a type of linen. Manta was sometimes tacked up as an artificial ceiling in the homes of the wealthier classes of New Mexico. Twitchell, *Leading Facts*, 2:155.

9. Brogans are thick leather shoes.

10. Preston Beck, Jr., mentioned throughout these letters, was a native of Indiana and a Santa Fe merchant. He was disliked intensely by Messervy who, in his letter to Kingsbury of September 16, 1855, MHS, said that he would prefer to have his store remain empty rather than rent it to Beck.

11. Apparently a reference to the quality of the whiskey.

12. Kingsbury apparently means that the three firms had cornered the market in whiskey.

I think we have sold more goods this month than any of thoes with fresh stocks.[13] The fact being known that we sell cheaper than anybody else will give us the trade as long as our goods last and you may be sure we are doing all we can to Reap it before the freights,[14] letting some few things go cheap for <u>bait</u>.

The train brought out by the Jew, <u>Abriham</u> [A. M. Abraham] of Independence, reported for El Paso, will stop here, and open the assortment, (which from all accounts must be a pretty hard one) in [William Mitchell] Dalton's old store, and is to pay us $50 a month commencing 1st August, and make all repairs he wants himself.[15]

[Doctor Thomas E.] Massie has sold to [Solomon] Beuthner[16] & Levi Speigelberg [Spiegelberg][17] all his stock <u>except medicines</u>, at cost with 9 and 10 cents freight, and now holds his head above all <u>Grocery dealers</u>. I think he had enough of it and was glad of a chance to get out.

[T. H.] McKutchen [McCutchan] received 5 waggons containing a general assortment. He offered them at 12 ½ cents freight, and finally succeeded in selling the lot to Joseph Hersch[18] by lumping at <u>$9,000</u>. Mc. rather got the best of the bargain, he told me that it would turn out for him 13 ½ to 15 cents freight. I am sorry for this sale as <u>Joe</u> has probably enough for the present, and will prevent us from making a bill with him untill he sells off a little.[19]

We have had considerable excitement since you left. On the night of the 4th the Americans gave a Bila [*baile*, or dance] at the Exchange[20] which the Mexicans chose to brake up. They succeeded, and closed by shooting [S.] Finnigan the blacksmith who lived only 20 hours.[21] The circumstances are these, Candido Ortiz insulted Miss Conklin[22] who was at the time walking with the Governor [William Carr Lane]. Beck interfered and took him [to] one side, at which Mr. Ortiz very politely invited him out in the correl [corral] to settle the matter. Beck did not wait for a second invitation, but took him out by the callar [collar] and gave him a good hammering. In the meantime, little [Jesús Baca y] Sena[23] (the one who cut the Flag)[24] leaves the room and in a few moments all the windows on the street were smashed in with rocks, which did not leave a whole sash. This was done while Beck was at work with Candido. The women of course took a stampeed, most of the men went with them, particularly all who were armed to see them safe home, leaving only about Six men at the Exchange. At this time the mob returned headed by Candido. They fired some Twenty shots, the only one which took effect was on Finnigan, and we have positive proof that it was done by Tarpia [Tapia], the one who was convicted in San Miguel county for cutting a woman, sentenced for three years and broke jail first night. The shot was fired through the window, [Jules] Jean[n]eret[25] was out side and saw it all, but was not seen by them. Little Baca, Tapia, & Silver

13. Messervy was also optimistic about business that month. See Messervy to Webb, July 30, 1853, Santa Fe, in Bieber, *Papers of James J. Webb*, 292.

14. At this time the merchants' trains arrived in Santa Fe only once a year, between June and August, and would either return to the States that same summer or wait until early the following spring. Davis, *El Gringo*, 252.

15. Kingsbury's statement suggests that Messervy and Webb owned William Mitchell Dalton's old store, and that Abraham intended to rent it. We have been unable to determine where Dalton's store might have been located at this time.

16. Solomon Beuthner, along with his brothers Joseph and Samson, operated a mercantile house in Taos under the name of Beuthner Brothers. Parish, "The German Jew and the Commercial Revolution," 315-16.

17. Santa Fe had a large proportion of German Jewish merchants. The Spiegelbergs were prominent in the community, and are mentioned frequently by Kingsbury in his letters. Solomon Jacob Spiegelberg first established his mercantile house in 1846. One by one his brothers came to Santa Fe to join in the business: Levi in 1848, Elias by 1850, Emanuel in 1853, Lehman in 1857, and Willi in 1861. Fierman, *Guts and Ruts*, 8-9.

18. Joseph Hersch, whose name appears from time to time in these letters, was one of a group of individuals who regularly sold flour to the government throughout the 1850s. See chapter eight, Kingsbury to Webb, Santa Fe, March 14, 1858.

19. Kingsbury, in other words, doubted that Hersch would be buying goods from Messervy & Webb until his own stock is depleted further.

20. The Exchange Hotel, now La Fonda, was owned by William Messervy, and was operated by Tom Bowler and Frank Green. Messervy to Kingsbury, Salem, July 15, 1855, and Oct. 15, 1855, MHS. Hertzog, *La Fonda*, 6.

21. S. Finegan, blacksmith, appears in the 1850 census under the heading "men in Quartermaster Dept. U.S.A." Dates and places of birth are not shown for the members of this department. 1850 NM Census, 357.

22. Miss Conklin was probably Josefa Conklin, one of three daughters of James Conklin, who first settled in Santa Fe in the 1820s, and Juana Ortiz. Chávez, "New Names," 301.

23. The name Baca appears in Messervy's letter to Webb of July 30, 1853, which also provides a full account of this episode. Bieber, *Papers of James J. Webb*, 291. This seems to be Jesús Baca y Sena, who in 1850 was listed as sixteen years old and a laborer. 1850 NM Census, 331.

24. This phrase refers to an incident that was reported by the *Santa Fe Weekly Gazette* on Feb. 19, 1853: "A few days since one of our citizens gave a very fine and select ball; and for the purpose of adorning the dancing saloon the large flag, lately made by order of the Governor, was applied for and obtained. During the evening some malicious person cut and mutilated the flag to an extent as to render it, perhaps, unfit for further use."

25. Jules Jeanneret was a twenty-three-year-old matchmaker from Switzerland. 1850 NM Census, 348.

[Silva] came up together, Baca pointed through the window, Tapia then raised his pistol and fired. Silver afterwards fired 5 or 6 shots in the Bar Room, he & Candido walked in and took possession. Word was sent to Major [William T.] Brooks [at Ft. Marcy], and at the tap of the drum every mexican disappeared, did not show themselves again. The next morning the principal ones were arrested all except Silver who ran away and is still at liberty. They were brought up before Alcaie [alcalde] [J. W.] Reed, and committed for murder, Weightman, Tul[e]y & Baird for the prisoners, Ashurst & Smith prosecuting.[26] Weightman volunteered his services, a special court is called, the Grand jury have already found 10 bills and not done yet.

When they were first arrested Weightman was very busy in informing the mexicans, complained to the Governor and everybody else that the Americans would take them at night and hang them in presence of Judge Linch. He succeeded in getting a string [strong] military guard at the Jaol [jail] which has been keeped [kept] up ever since, so that Mr. Linch could not execute justice. They have been kept in very heavy irons, I think they cannot escape and hope they will get due justice under the law (pero quin sabi) [*pero quién sabe*—but who knows?].

A few days after, Joe Collins and Squire Mink meet on the street.[27] Joe gave him a good thrashing, then went before Reed pleaded guilty. There were 5 or 6 ready to pay his fine. Mink that night staid at Miguel Pino's house, under a guard of 20 mexicans.[28] He reported that the Americans wanted to kill him and he expected them that night. Next on the docket, Ex Lt. [Francis J.] Thomas[29] took occasion to call Weightman to account for something Weightman had written to [James S.] Calhoun sometime ago (you may have seen it in some of those papers of private correspondence which were floating about). High words ensued, upon which Mr. W. used his cane over Thomas's head as long as it lasted, then picked up the pieces and would have used them, had the Sheriff not interfered and demanded order.[30] Thomas made no resistance whatever, the enclosed papers made their appearance next morning which for the present is the end of that affair.

Poly sticks are as unsettled as usual, José Chavis[31] has not returned, and will not untill after election [for territorial delegate to Congress]. The Patent Democracy of Santa Fe have succeeded in appointing a committee to attend the convention, as follows [Charles L.] Spencer, [Caleb] Sherman, [Charles] Blumner, Mink, F. Pino, Manuel Chavis, &c., &c., &c. It is understood here that they will go for [Theodore D.] Wheaton.[32]

Thomas was offended by being left off the list and is now doing his best to get up another party of real, true & tryed Democrats.[33] I think he will not succeed. Weightman has withdrawn his name, and comes out in favor of [Spruce] Baird. Baird is working hard for the nomina-

26. Kingsbury is referring to two law partnerships: the firm of Richard H. Weightman and Murray F. Tuley, and Spruce M. Baird, and the firm of Merrill Ashurst and Hugh N. Smith.

27. John Henry Mink was then a clerk of the Probate Court for Santa Fe County. He was a native of Germany, and was thirty-six years old in 1853. Twitchell, *Leading Facts*, 2:371. 1850 NM Census, 346.

28. Miguel Pino was a twenty-seven-year-old farmer and native of New Mexico. 1850 NM Census, 353.

29. Formerly chief commissary officer, 1848-1851. Frazer, *Forts and Supplies*, 38, 54.

30. A flamboyant figure in New Mexico's history, Richard Weightman is described by Lamar as "an expansive temperamental Washingtonian who had come to Santa Fe with the army." *Far Southwest*, 74. Weightman did not stay away from a fight. In 1849 he provoked Joab Houghton into a duel (both survived). Poldervaart, *Black-Robed Justice*, 27-28. James Simpson described Weightman as "an ambitious little fellow, but his name is a misnomer with regard to his merits." Ibid. On August 18, 1854, he killed F. X. Aubry, a Canadian freighter known for setting cross-country speed records, in a duel in the store-cantina of Joseph and Henry Mercure, located on the south side of the plaza. In the course of an argument over the honesty of *Amigo del Pais*, a paper formerly edited by Weightman, Weightman threw his whiskey in Aubry's face. Aubry drew his gun, which misfired, whereupon Weightman drew his knife and stabbed Aubry, who died about ten minutes later. Chaput, *Francois X. Aubry*, 157-59.

31. Perhaps Kingsbury is referring to José Francisco Chávez, who was a member of the prominent Chávez family and had been educated in the United States. Chávez was a friend of Francis Aubry's and would invest in and accompany him on his second sheep-driving expedition to California, which left Santa Fe Oct. 10, 1853. He could have been away preparing for this trip. Chaput, *Francois X. Aubry*, 139-40, 190.

32. The convention was a local one to nominate a territorial delegate.

33. Many New Mexico politicians, seeing the advantage of joining the party which held national office, began their careers as Whigs. With the advent of the Pierce administration in 1853, however, local Whigs began calling themselves "National" Democrats, leaving true Democrats with such alternatives as "Buchanan," "Douglas" or "regular" Democrats. Lamar, *Far Southwest*, 100.

tion, and will get it if they don't through [throw] him off.[34] If they do they will take up Padre Galligos [José Manuel Gallegos]. So far as I can learn the padre has the best chance.[35]

Miguel Otero has returned from below, says they count him as an american and he has no chance.[36] There is but little said about [Governor William Carr] Lane[37]—no one can tell yet how the cat will jump.

The little boy who fell into the correll [corral] has suffered much, but is getting well fast, is now able to set [sit] up. Barry's bill was $35 money I think well spent. The other night a part of the back wall fell down, in the morning the dogs had full possession of the street, no one had currage [courage] to pass.

Since the rains commenced it has poured constantly. On Sunday last the 24th the tower of our new church fell bringing down exactly 1/3 the roof and all the front wall. [Joab] Houghton says the damage is not over $250, but I think it cannot be less than 4 or 5 hundred.[38] About the same time the end of the Bishops new Chapel fell out, showing that their faith & chapels are no stronger than ours.[39] Everybody is looking anxiously for the new Governor & commander, to know what will be done about the Messia [Mesilla] question.[40] Some think they will scare up a war, but generally they think it will be settled without any difficulty. Lane will leave soon as the new Governor arrives. Mr. Messervy will keep me here untill the first of October, and says he will certainly let me off then, so you can tell the folks pretty near when I will get home.

They have commenced the new State house. [Joseph] Nangle[41] has the contract for hauling and laying the stone. They are putting it in the open space in the rear of the military correll [corral], it is to face the street, leading to the plaza which runs by Brooks quarters.[42]

Paulina, Carina, & Squire[43] are well and wish to be remembered. Paulina is still keeping house alone. Mc would not take the things you left for him.

I send you by this mail a few copies of a pamphlet on the boundary question, it was written by Judge [John S.] Watts, and of course is all right, I have not had time to read it.[44]

Mr. Messervy will probably give you all the news.[45] I think of nothing more now.

P.S. I have rec.d the appointment of Governor Lane's private Secretary, to last as long as he remains.

Letter no. 2, Kingsbury to Webb, Santa Fe, August 30, 1853

I fear you will be disappointed with the tone of this letter after reading my last. We have had one of our old months again, all business has stop[p]ed just where it began. Sales this month make the gross Amount of ($2,000) Two Thousand dollars. We have however the

34. Spruce M. Baird, an unpopular lawyer from Texas, was known derisively as "Judge Baird." In 1848, when Texas brazenly claimed much of New Mexico as its "County of Santa Fe," Baird had the misfortune to represent Texas as the new county's district judge. Rejected by the New Mexicans, he returned home to Texas within a year. Binkley, ed., "Reports from a Texas Agent," 2:158-59. Baird ran unsuccessfully for the office of territorial delegate again in 1857.

35. Kingsbury was correct. Gallegos, an opponent of Americanizing influences within New Mexico, won the nomination. Handsome, vain, and ordained in 1840 at age twenty-five, Gallegos had served in the New Mexico legislature before 1846. In a controversial episode, he was publicly suspended from the priesthood on December 5, 1852 by Bishop Lamy. For Lamy's side, see Horgan, *Lamy*; for a pro-Gallegos account, see Angélico Chávez, *Trés Macho*. See, too, n. 46, below.

Although no longer a member of the priesthood, Gallegos maintained that he personally held title to the rectory of the church in Albuquerque and therefore refused to leave the house. His claim resulted in a legal action to eject him initiated by Bishop Lamy and his Vicar-General, Father Joseph P. Machebeuf, in October 1853. The matter eventually came to trial in 1855 and resulted in a hung jury. Gallegos retained possession of the house until February 1856, when Lamy paid Gallegos's attorney $1506, almost twice the appraised value, for the rectory. Steele, *Folk and Church*, 64-69.

36. Miguel Antonio Otero, who served as Governor Lane's private secretary (Lamar, *Far Southwest*, 104), was the son of a prominent New Mexico merchant, educated in the United States, and a member of the Missouri Bar. Little wonder that he believed that his compatriots "count him as an american." Nonetheless, he won the position of territorial delegate in 1855, 1857, and 1859. Weber, ed., "Samuel Ellison," 215-16. His son and namesake became New Mexico's first Hispanic territorial governor, 1897-1906.

37. William Carr Lane, second territorial governor of New Mexico, 1852-53, was from St. Louis, where he had been a surgeon and the city's first mayor. Horn, *New Mexico's Troubled Years*, 37. Later that year, Messervy wrote to Webb that "[Lane] is by far the best Governor we have ever had, or ever will have . . . he is possessed of great firmness & of indertermitable [*sic*] energy & industry & incorruptible <u>honesty</u> the only fault with him is that he is too particular about small matters." Messervy to Webb, Santa Fe, Oct. 27, 1853, MHS.

38. Kingsbury was closer to the mark in assessing the damage to the Baptist church, a pet project of Joab Houghton's, who was a circuit judge and native of Virginia. Davis, *El Gringo*, 130, noted that "the entire cost was about four thousand dollars, being increased about one third by the cupola falling down and damaging other parts of the building."

NOTES 39-45 ON PAGE FOLLOWING

satisfaction of knowing that we have sold as much as any of our neighbors.

I hardly know what to write that will be interesting. Gov. Lane is at last fairly in the field, running against Padre Gallegos, solo, the election comes off next Monday. It will be a hard race, no one can tell how it will turn out, it will depend principal[l]y upon San Miguel County. Lane will get all the counties below, at least 1,200 majority, he will probably lose Rio Ariba [Arriba] & Taos; Clark, Wheaton, & [James] Quinn go strong against him.[46] Weightman is lost sight of entirely. I am afraid we will lose Santa Fe county. The new Governor [David Meriwether][47] and chief Justice [J. J. Davenport][48] are messing with us, the Governor is a strong man & I think will keep every thing streight. He is very willing to hear & listen, then keeps his own ideas & opinions to himself. Some of the mexicans say he is "muy formal"— in short he is one of that sort, which will not be humbuged, and the génte are smart enough to see it.

The Chief Justice is full & boiling over with his democracy, & I think a little inclined to let himself be <u>taken in</u> by the [word illegible] Spencer Click [clique].[49] They are all after him. Sherman wants the clerkship, &c., &c.—by his conversation I see he nibbles at the bait of the <u>Patent</u> & uncompromising democrats—"Quien Sabe como salira [who knows how it will turn out]." I have got Lane's papers all written up; now nothing will do but I must go home by the way of Washington and if possible get them settled. I cannot get off untill the first of October. We will have the pleasure of crossing the plains together, and if he is elected will go in to Washington together. This will detain me a little longer on the road than I would like, but as he promises to pay for my time & trouble, I am compel[l]ed to submit.

On receipt of this, please write me and direct to Saint Louis, let me know where you are and what you are doing, have you been to Washington yet? Is there any chance of my meeting you there? Do not fail to write so that I may meet your letter in St. Louis. We have sent you by this mail First of Exchange for $1,000.00 which is charged to your Private account.

Mr. Messervy has probably written you all the news; The jail birds that I wrote you about in my last have made their escape by braking jail leaving their irons behind by way of compliment.

"Glutchalf" the dutch man who lived up the creek was struck (in his house) by lightning and killed.

Henry Cunniff [Henry J. Cuniff] has returned from California.[50] We are looking for [Francis X.] Aubry every day.[51]

There is no movement made yet, that I know of to move head Quarters.[52]

Do not get married untill I arrive. I want to be at the wedding.[53]

All the folks are well, Tom [Bowler] & [Lipman] Meyer wish to be remembered.

39. Kingsbury is most likely referring to the roof of the south chapel of the Parroquia. According to W. S. Stallings, who dated the roof beams by analyzing the tree rings, the roof of the chapel was completely rebuilt soon after 1851—a fact borne out by Kingsbury's statement. Based in part on Stallings's evidence, architectural historians George Kubler and S. G. Morley have hypothesized that at some point the original South Chapel was completely torn down and rebuilt. While the age of the roof beams neither confirms nor denies this idea, Kingsbury's reference to the chapel as "new" could give weight to their theory. Ellis, *Bishop Lamy's Santa Fe Cathedral*, 104-5.

40. La Mesilla, a rich agricultural valley in the eastern section of an area south of the Gila River and west of the Rio Grande, was claimed by both Mexico and the United States. The State of Chihuahua took possession and dispossessed Mesilla's residents, who considered themselves Americans, of their property, without compensation. They petitioned Lane's predecessor in office, J. S. Calhoun, for protection, but he did not taken action. Although the federal government had taken no steps to reclaim it, and Colonel Sumner refused him the support of federal troops, Lane considered the disputed territory New Mexico's. Lane and Chihuahua's Governor Angel Trias issued proclamations and counter-proclamations claiming the territory. Then, Trias, under orders of Santa Anna, marched to the border with a thousand troops. By this time, however, American troops were unnecessary as Lane had interested the federal government in the situation. In order to avoid conflict on the frontier and to gain a superior route to the Pacific, the administration entered into new negotiations with Mexico, leading to the Gadsden purchase. Garber, *Gadsden Treaty*, 70-74.

41. A Missouri merchant who came to Santa Fe in 1847, Nangle served as Commissioner of Public Buildings in the 1850s and was generally distrusted by many prominent members of the community. Chaput, *Francois X. Aubry*, 197-98. Messervy shared that distrust. At the beginning of David Meriwether's term as governor, Messervy wrote: "[I] rejoice that Beck and Nangle will have no further opportunity of handling the public money." Messervy to Webb, Santa Fe, Oct. 27, 1853, MHS.

42. In 1853 work had begun on a new Capitol building (now the Federal building) with $20,000 sent from Congress. An additional $70,000 was granted a year later. According to Davis, *El Gringo*, 42, it stood "on a vacant lot north of the palace, near the American cemetery." Despite repeated appropriations from Congress, however, the buildings were not completed for many years and were never used for their original purpose. Lamar, *Far Southwest*, 90-91.

43. Kingsbury could either be referring to "Squire" Mink, see above, or to James L. Collins, prominent merchant, editor, and part owner of the *Santa Fe Weekly Gazette* whose nickname was also "Squire." Weber, *Richard H. Kern*, 124.

NOTES 44-53 ON PAGE FOLLOWING

44. This was probably a pamphlet printed in Santa Fe in 1853 and entitled *A Review of the Boundary Question; and a Vindication of Governor Lane's Action in Asserting Jurisdiction Over the Mesilla Valley.* It was published under the pseudonym "Fernandez de Taos." McMurtrie, "History of Early Printing," 401.

45. Messervy, in Santa Fe with Kingsbury, also corresponded with Webb.

46. According to Gov. Lane's journal, in which he recorded the election returns as they came in in September, Kingsbury's predictions were fairly accurate (with the exception of Taos, which went to Lane by a margin of 104 votes). Lane wrote, "Dr. Howgle arrived with good Election News from Dona Ana, Socorro, Valenica, Bernalillo & Sta. Anna, my majority being 9399, which makes my election certain if the illegal votes in Rio Ariba & San Miguel can be set aside." The returns from Rio Arriba County were 826 for Gallegos, 128 for Lane, and in San Miguel County, Gallegos beat Lane by 1152 votes. Carson, ed., "Lane Diary," 293-98.

Messervy to Webb, Sept. 29, 1853, MHS: "Our election is over, thank God. Gallegos is elected by 445 Majority. Lane says he <u>will contest</u>, veramos." "The returns had so far used up 2 reams of foolscap paper," Messervy wrote Webb a month later, Oct. 27, 1853, MHS. Messervy expressed his sympathy for Lane in a letter to Kingsbury, Oct. 5, 1853, MHS: "I feel deeply interested in the success of Gov. Lane but very much fear he will be defeated. I really hope he may succeed but the prejudice against him on account of his being an American I fear will defeat him."

Lamar attributes Gallegos's defeat of Lane to two factors. The first was a curious alliance between Gallegos and the Missouri Democrats led by Thomas Hart Benton. The second was the newly enfranchised New Mexicans' discovery that a vote was a salable commodity. Lamar, *Far Southwest*, 103-05. Another problem was that, while many of the Taos ballots had been cast in Lane's favor, none had been reported. Larson blames Lane's defeat on Congress, which disallowed the ballots cast by the Pueblo Indians. Larson, *New Mexico's Quest*, 82.

In Congress, Gallegos was a disappointment to some constituents primarily because he spoke no English, but he was reelected for a second term in Sept. 1855. See chapter 4. In a letter dated October 27, 1853, MHS, Messervy wrote Webb that Gallegos took Santiago Abrea [Abreu] as interpreter to Washington. For some reason, however, Señor Abreu must have been unable to translate for Gallegos in the House, for Larson states that a friendly congressman undertook to find him an interpreter so that he could understand the Congressional proceedings. The efforts of both Abreu and the congressman were wasted, however, because the House refused to suspend its rules to allow for an interpreter. One scholar believes that New Mexico's choice of a delegate tarnished its image and probably further spoiled its chances for statehood. Larson, *New Mexico's Quest*, 82.

47. In 1852, David Meriwether, a Kentucky farmer and politician, was appointed to the U.S. Senate to fill the seat left vacant by the death of Henry Clay. In 1853, President Pierce appointed him governor of New Mexico, a position which he held until 1857. In his own account of his life, Meriwether claimed to have come to New Mexico in 1819 as a member of a trading party that was captured and imprisoned in the Palace of the Governors. Meriwether, *My Life*, 89.

Kingsbury's positive opinion of Meriwether matches Messervy's, who wrote to Webb on March 28, 1854, MHS, "You will probably meet Gov. Meriwether at Independence. John [Kingsbury] is acquainted with him and will introduce him to you. Cultivate his acquaintance, he is a trump."

48. J. J. Davenport, a lawyer from Mississippi, was appointed by President Pierce to replace Grafton Baker. Poldervaart, *Black-Robed Justice*, 45.

49. The Spencer clique could be the committee referred to earlier (note 32), which supported Theodore Wheaton for territorial delegate.

50. Cuniff returned to Santa Fe in August 1853 with $70,000 in coin and gold. In the wake of Francis X. Aubry's financial success in driving sheep overland to market in gold-rich California, many New Mexicans attempted drives of their own. Chaput, *Francois X. Aubry*, 140.

51. Francis X. Aubry was expected to return from his first sheep-selling venture in California. He remained in Santa Fe for only about a month before leaving with a second consignment of sheep assembled for him by his new partners, among whom was José Chavez. As mentioned in note 31, the party left for California October 10, 1853, with about fifty thousand sheep. Chaput, *Francois X. Aubry*, 138-40.

52. When Jefferson Davis became Secretary of War on March 7, 1853, he "declared that he was not in sympathy" with the frontier defense plan of his predecessor. Instead of stringing military posts in a long line among the Indians, he leaned more toward massing large bodies of troops at a few strategic positions. Perhaps this change in administration caused rumors about a change in Headquarters. Bender, "Frontier Defense," 345.

53. Webb married Florilla Mansfield Slade on December 1, 1853. Bieber, *Papers of James J. Webb*, 36. Although Kingsbury was in the East, he did not attend the ceremony.

2.

Facing the Parson and Becoming a Partner

Autumn in Salem, 1853

Letters 3–6

O n October 1, 1853, with summer sales behind him, John Kingsbury left Santa Fe. He followed James Webb to the states while William Messervy remained behind in Santa Fe to mind the store. For the time being, Kingsbury planned to go to Washington with William Carr Lane, whom he then served as private secretary. In Washington, Lane hoped to wind up his affairs as New Mexico's territorial governor and contest the election of José Manuel Gallegos as territorial delegate. Kingsbury's long-terms plans apparently included returning home to Massachusetts to marry and find a permanent position.[1]

Unlike the thirty-five-year-old bachelor Webb, who had returned to Connecticut to marry but had no particular woman in mind, Kingsbury planned to marry William Messervy's sister, Kate.[2] Kingsbury had carried Kate Messervy's picture with him to Santa Fe in 1853 and had spoken ardently of her to Webb.[3] Indeed, when Webb visited the Messervy home that same October, he, too, appears to have been smitten by Kate. As he told Kingsbury, he found her "a charming girl" and he tried to persuade her to join him and her future husband in Santa Fe. "How much I could and would do, to make her journey across the plains comfortable and agreeable, if we should ever cross them together." Then, apparently thinking that he had gone too far, Webb went on to explain to Kingsbury:

> You will perhaps say I am too enthusiastic, and perhaps have a little touch of jealousy—<u>John, I do love her</u>, but it is as a <u>sister</u>, and I have too much discernment not to know that I should be "fooling away my time" to aspire to anything more, even if my sentiments were of a deeper cast.[4]

As he rode eastward in October 1853, however, Kingsbury had come to no definite conclusions about his future. Webb had extended an offer to Kingsbury to join the firm. William Messervy had decided to pull out

1. Webb to Kingsbury, Cornwall Bridge, CT, Oct. 5, 1853; Messervy to Webb, Santa Fe, Oct. 27, 1853, MHS.

2. If Kate Messervy and John Kingsbury had not resolved to marry before Kingsbury set off for Santa Fe, they made their decision by correspondence while he was there.

3. Webb to Kingsbury, Cornwall Bridge, CT, Oct. 5, 1853, MHS.

4. Ibid.

of the business and had urged Webb to take on Kingsbury, his future brother-in-law, as a junior partner.[5] Webb, who seems to have been fond of Kingsbury, had accepted the suggestion, even though Kingsbury had little capital of his own to bring into the venture.[6]

Writing to Webb from St. Louis, Kingsbury explained that he could decide nothing until he returned home. He apparently needed to talk the matter over with his wife-to-be. His expected trip to Washington had not come about, so Kingsbury continued on to the Messervys' home in Salem, Massachusetts, where a week later he received good news. Kate and he would marry on December 21. Moreover, despite her precarious health, Kate would accompany him to Santa Fe the following spring. And so, on November 29, Kingsbury accepted Webb's offer to form Webb & Kingsbury—an acceptance contingent upon Kate remaining in good health.

⁓

Letter no. 3, Kingsbury to Webb, October 29, 1853, St. Louis, Missouri

I arrived here safe last night, had a very pleasant trip so far.[7] Shall not go to Washington as I had expected, but will go directly home.[8] I will leave here on Monday morning by the Rail Road line.

I have received your very kind letter of Oct. 5th and wish I could fill your wishes by giving you all the news but cannot begin to think of half you wish to hear, much less to write it. About the election [for territorial delegate] your fears were to[o] well founded. They have really swindled the Gov. out of his election. Gallegos on the returns gets 445 majority and on that he received the present Governor's certificate. Lane was elected fairly & on a true return would have a handsome majority. He intends to contest the seat, has got the papers and I hope he will succeed in obtaining the seat for himself or have the election returned to the people. Messervy gave no certificate, but gave copies of all the papers to Lane.[9] Mr. Messervy has probably written you some of the particulars about the election, and I will tell you all when we meet. I am very glad to know that you have been to Salem, and enjoyed your visit there so well.

With regard to business, for the present I can only thank you for your kind offers. I am unable to deside upon any future plans untill after I return home. I hope to meet you there & we will consult together. Soon as I arrive I will send you word.

I am sorry that you are not married yet, but hope you have everything fixed by this time.[10] I shall not want to wait, and it would not look well for a son to marry before the Father. You have no time to loose. However, if you are still in the market you can depend upon all my influence. I want to send you a long letter but I should omit so

5. Webb's letter (ibid.) makes this clear. The firm of Messervy & Webb stayed in business until February 1854, and Webb and Kingsbury did not formalize their partnership until June 1, 1855 (Webb, *Adventures*, p. 34), but the arrangement had begun in the fall of 1853.

6. Messervy's second choice as partner for Webb was another of the firm's clerks, Tom Bowler, whom Messervy described as "a very good salesman," and who probably had as little capital as Kingsbury. Bowler is mentioned frequently throughout Kingsbury's letters. Messervy to Webb, Santa Fe, Oct. 27, 1853, MHS.

7. If Kingsbury traveled with Lane, he likely returned home by the circuitous route outlined by Lane in a letter to William Carr Glasgow, September 7, 1853. Beginning in Santa Fe, Lane proposed they travel south through Albuquerque, along the Jornada del Muerto to El Paso, take a mail stage to San Antonio, then another to La Vaca, where they could catch a ship to New Orleans, and thence by steamboat up the Mississippi to St. Louis. Bieber, ed., "Letters of William Carr Lane," 199.

8. See chapter introduction.

9. Lane failed to gain the seat. He summed his situation up in a letter he wrote to his wife while in Washington that December: "There is an effort to enlist the aid of political bias, against me in the contest for the seat; and it may be, for aught I can say, entirely successful."

In this same letter, Lane goes on to remark of William Messervy: "Had it not been for a unexpected, inexplicable & indefensible move, of Mr. Secretary Messervy, I would have prevented the Padre, from taking his seat; & thus coerced an early decision of the question. But I will not trouble you with particulars." Bieber, ed., "Letters of William Carr Lane," 200-201. He is perhaps referring to the fact that ultimately Messervy did give Gallegos his certificate because, as Messervy explained in a later letter, "The returns that came to my office showed that he was elected. Had I refused to give it to him I would have been false to my duty and would have deservedly disgraced myself forever." Messervy to Webb, Santa Fe, Feb. 28, 1854, MHS.

10. Kingsbury's sympathetic remark is in response to Webb's letter to him: "Three months have passed John and I am no nearer getting married than when I left Santa Fé. I have seen one girl and shall visit her again a few times before I make up my mind whether I go a courting or not." Webb to Kingsbury, Cornwall Bridge, CT, Oct. 5, 1853, MHS. A month later, a triumphant Webb wrote: "Your favor from St. Louis came to hand yesterday, and I snatched a moment from my courting time to write a few words. To be brief—I am engaged—shall be married (providence permitting) about the first of next month. Shall go to Salem the last of next week—probably arrive on Saturday. Have not time to write more as I start in on hour to see my father-in-law—that is to be." Ibid., Nov. 5, 1853, MHS.

many things that I will leave it all untill I see you which I hope will be only a few days.

Letter no. 4, Kingsbury to Webb, November 4, 1853, Boston, Massachusetts

I arrived here last night, will leave for Salem today. Shall remain there untill you come down, shall expect to see you as soon as you can come.

Letter no. 5, Kingsbury to Webb, November 29, 1853, Salem, Massachusetts

I have not written before as this is the earliest moment that I could say anything definite in relation to returning to Santa Fe. I have now the pleasure to state that I have desided to accept of your proposition and have Kate's consent to accompany me, provided there is nothing received from Mr. Messervy contra to her going, which might induce her to remain, in such a case I shall expect to be let off.[11] Otherwise I hold myself & her in reddiness to accompany you in the Spring. Whatever arraingements you may make on the conditions you have stated to me will be right. This is the way I understand it. If Mr. Messervy will continue in the firm, right,[12] if not, you are to let all your capitol remain in the house untill such time as it can be withdrawn without injury to the business. That I am to receive one half profits, without paying interest. With regard to closing arraingements, purchasing Goods, &c. I leave entirely with you and expect you will be governed upon such advises as you may receive from Santa Fe.[13] I am sorry I cannot be with you when you get the next letters, but you can answer them with the understanding that I am to return with you and I will do the same in my letters.

I received your note of 21st inst. only last evening I regret that I shall not be able to be present on the 1st, but you have my best wishes and the satisfaction of knowing that you will have the start of me by three weeks.[14] We have set Wednesday the 21st Dec. as the eventful day [of their wedding], shall go directly to New York, intend to remain there a week or more, cannot tell exactly now. We will be very happy to see you and your wife here on the 21st 7 o'p.m., if you cannot make it convenient to be here then I hope to meet you in New York, or at any rate you must come to Salem and make us a visit after we return home. Before you start on your tour hope you will write me informing where you are going and what the chances are of our meeting, also send me all the particulars you may get from Santa Fe.[15] I shall be here untill the 21st address me at 65 Mill St., Salem.[16]

The letter you wish me to enquire for at the Post Office I had received & remailed to you, which I hope has come to hand before

11. Kingsbury was allowing for the contingency that Messervy, who was still in New Mexico, might not approve of Kate coming out to Santa Fe, due to the precarious state of her health. Messervy, however, was quite clear about where the duties of a wife lay, and strongly encouraged Kate to accompany him. Messervy to Kingsbury, Santa Fe, Jan. 29, 1854, MHS.

12. By this time Messervy had "positively determined to retire from business." Ibid., Dec. 15, 1853, MHS.

13. While the partnership was set up along the lines that Kingsbury describes here, he was only able to invest a small amount of capital toward the business and was, therefore, mistaken in assuming he would receive half the profits without paying interest back to the firm. Webb wasted no time in setting the matter straight. "The proposition I intended to make to you is understood by you, with one exception. I intended to make you a liberal offer, and said nothing, to my recollection, in regards to interest in any conversation I had with you. But do you think it would be an equal partnership on the terms you propose? In the partnership between myself and Mr. Messervy there was unequal capital, but the house paid interest on $5,000 to the credit of his sisters on our books, and I, by my own voluntary act paid interest on $5,000 which I had borrowed previous to our forming a copartnership, which individual note was taken up, and not of the firm given, but whenever the interest became due you know it was always paid and charged to my private account. I do not desire to charge you so large interest as to imperil your share of the profits, but think you ought to be willing to pay interest on a portion of the capital." Webb to Kingsbury, Cornwall Bridge, CT, Dec. 5, 1853, MHS.

14. Webb married Florilla Mansfield Slade on December 1, 1853. Kingsbury married Kate Messervy three weeks later on December 21.

15. The Webbs remained in Cornwall Bridge, Connecticut for a few days after their marriage, then traveled to Washington. They planned to remain in Washington for a few weeks, then proceed to New York around the 25th. Webb to Kingsbury, Cornwall Bridge, CT, Dec. 5, 1853, MHS.

16. This is the address of the Messervy home in Salem. Salem City Directory, 1855, 108.

this. Katy sends her very best respects to you & yours. All the folks wish to be remembered.

Letter no. 6, Kingsbury to Webb, December 20, 1853, Salem

I wrote to Mr. [Richard] Bigelow[17] to secure our quarters in N.Y. & he has sent me word that he will engage a room at the Metropolitan Hotel. I shall be there on the 23rd & will wait untill you meet me there.

Everything is going on well for tomorrow night, the house is turned up side down and everything in it.[18] I am mustering all the courage I can in order to face the parson. I look for a big crowd, expect the house will be full three or four times over. My best respects to your lady.

17. Richard Bigelow was the New York representative of the St. Louis firm of Doan, King & Co., mentioned frequently throughout these letters. Kingsbury to Messervy, Santa Fe, Oct. 31, 1854, MHS.

18. Kingsbury is referring, of course, to the preparations for his wedding. Messervy, still in Santa Fe, had urged Webb to take his place in "bestowing" his sister on "our faithful clerk," but Webb could not be in Salem either, perhaps because of his own marriage. Messervy to Webb, Santa Fe, Oct. 27, 1853, MHS.

3.

Shopping and Shipping in Boston

Late Winter 1854

Letters 7–15

As planned, John Kingsbury married Kate Messervy on December 21, 1853, at her family's home in Salem. The couple took a week-long honeymoon trip to New York, where they met Webb, who had succeeded in finding a woman who would become his wife. On December 1, 1853, Webb had married Florilla Mansfield Slade, known to friends and family as either "Flora" or "Lillie."[1]

After their reunion in New York, Kingsbury's correspondence with Webb lapsed for a month and a half, resuming with intensity in mid-February when Kingsbury began to acquire stock to ship to Santa Fe with the spring caravans. In Boston, Kingsbury purchased a variety of groceries, alcohol, hardware, clothing, cloth, shoes, and boots. By the time he finished, in less than a month, he had insured and shipped 375 containers of merchandise in barrels, packages, and bales.[2] At the same time, Kingsbury also investigated markets for New Mexico wool, beaver pelts, and minerals, samples of which Messervy had sent to him from Santa Fe.

While Kingsbury managed the details of shopping, insuring, and shipping from Boston, Webb engaged in similar activities in New York City. As the partner with the most capital in the firm of Webb & Kingsbury, Webb apparently gave the larger workload to his junior partner.

From Boston and New York, Webb and Kingsbury sent their merchandise by rail to Pittsburgh, then by boat to St. Louis and Westport. There, it would be stored until the wagons had assembled to cross the plains to Santa Fe. Beyond Westport, the cost of insurance coverage became prohibitive, so the owners themselves chose to exercise vigilance. Webb and Kingsbury would be on hand personally to count the packages and oversee the loading, and travel to New Mexico with their merchandise. Their new wives would accompany them.

1. Webb, *Adventures*, p. 36.
2. 101 packages on March 2; 74 on March 4; 56 on March 7; 144 on March 12.

Letter no. 7, Kingsbury to Webb, February 16, 1854, Boston

Inclosed I send you the letter of Introduction from Mr. Bennett to the Hat establishment.

I learned this morning from Mr. Conant that Edw.d Lambert & Co. (the firm you have a letter to from him) have moved from Broadway to the Street facing the Park, one or two doors from Stewart's large store, directly in the rear of Stewart's from Broadway. They have a large stock of rich fancy goods and would like to make a bill with you. I have seen the Packer about the baleing, am satisfied that the goods will go safe in the covering he has put on, the only objection to it is the looks. I have ordered three straps on all the balance which he has to put up and shall leave it so unless you write me that you would prefer Burlap for the outside. I do not know yet what the shoes brought, but will get returns tomorrow. Write to me care of Mr. Abbott.[3] Let me know from time to time where to address you.

Letter no. 8, Kingsbury to Webb, February 18, 1854, Boston

I wrote you a few lines on the 16th which I hope you have received.

Inclosed I send memorandum of the Brogans sold at Auction. I think they are well sold. The prices are rather small but it is full as much as I expected they would bring.

I forgot to tell you how many letters I had used for our private mark. In marking the New York purchases you can commence with letter (L) and use the balance of the alphabet.

I do not think of anything more now. Strong says he will want untill the 10th of next month to fill our order. Will get it in as soon as possible.

Letter no. 9, Kingsbury to Webb, February 22, 1854, Boston

I have not received any word from you since you left.

I got the sample of Nutral [neutral] Spirit this morning and have left it with Mr. Williams to try.[4] The young man at the Book Store succeeded in finding all the numbers of Harper's and has put them up complete. Your bill there amounts to $39.10.

The folks are all well and wish to be remembered.

Letter no. 10, Kingsbury to Webb, February 27, 1854, Salem

Your favor of 22nd, 23rd and 24th inst. from New York are received containing bills of purchases there, which I have placed on file with the other bills.

I am sorry that you could not make arrangements for freight on better terms than we had heard here. As you have left it with me I

3. J. C. Abbott was Messervy & Webb's agent in Boston.

4. In his study of bourbon in America, Gerald Carson defines neutral spirits as "a distillate run at or above 190 proof and obtained from molasses, grain or the redistillations of whiskey, brandy or rum. Used for blending with straight whiskey and making gin, vodka, cordials and liqueurs." *Social History of Bourbon,* 237.

shall do the best I can. I have been to all the different agents here and after hearing them, I consulted with Mr. Abbott and have about made up my mind to ship according to his recommendation, which is to send from here by Rail Road to Philadelphia care Leach &Co. and let them forward them to Pittsburgh care of the same agents which you have named at that place (Forsyth &Co.). This I think will be the best & quickest rout[e] and in all probability the cheapest at anyrate. It will be as low as any of the agents here will take it. I think I shall not wait to get all the goods together before I commence to ship. I shall send them along as I can get them ready. If they were all ship[p]ed on the same day there is no certainty that they will remain together all the way and the sooner they are on the road I think the better. I should prefer to send them on the same day and have them kept together, but some of the things cannot be ready untill the 10th and perhaps I may have to wait longer for the goods at Strong's, so that I am afraid it will make it late by waiting to send them all at the same time. I shall be particular to send them all by one rout[e]. Shall commence with the shoes, then the other goods soon as I can get them off.

I will have the New York purchases included in the policy of insurance.[5] I expect to be obliged to pay 2 ¾% in order to have the goods insured to Westport, which will be adding ¼% for the risk at Kansas. I have seen no notice yet of the arrival of the Santa Fe Mail.

I notice by the papers that Gallegos has succeeded in keeping his seat.[6] Kate has rec.d Lillie's[7] letter but has been so much engaged that she has not had time to answer it. She wishes to be remembered. We are going to Boston tomorrow and will stay the balance of the week.

I am glad to know that you have secured the woman to go with us.[8] My compliments to all the folks at Cornwall. Much love to Mother & Father Webb. Write soon, send as usual to care of Mr. Abbott, and let me know how I shall direct to you.

[P.S.] The 4 cases of Brogans which were to come at Du Boises have not arrived. I have settled the bill there today without including them and shall not take them now if they do come.

Letter no. 11, Kingsbury to Webb, March 2, 1854, Boston

I commenced yesterday to forward the goods by sending all the Boots & Shoes (except those at Strong's) One hundred and one (101) Cases marked "Webb & Kingsbury Santa Fe N. M. care Leach & Co. Phila. A #1 to 100." I sent them from here by the Boston & Providence R.R. and have sent letter of advise to Messrs. Harris & Leach at Phila. of the same with instructions to receive and forward them by Penn. Rail Road to Pittsburgh care of Messrs. Forsyth & Co. have also sent letter of advise to Messrs. Forsyth & Co. with instructions to receive

5. Apparently goods being shipped across the eastern half of the United States were insured. Beyond Westport, however, the cost of the insurance premiums was prohibitive, so merchants took their chances. See Davis, *El Gringo*, 252, and Walker, *Wagonmasters*, 147. Goods purchased at the eastern end of the Trail were insured for fire for the duration of their storage in warehouses. For example, Webb & Kingsbury set out the following instructions for the firm of Glasgow & Bro.: "Mr. Messervy informs us that he shall effect insurance on all our eastern purchases to Kansas. So you will not get insurance on our goods from the east unless instructed to do so by him. The memorandum sent to you, you will please get Insurance upon, including Fire Insurance in warehouse in Kansas." Webb & Kingsbury to Glasgow & Bro., Santa Fe, Feb. 27, 1855, MHS.

6. After over two months of investigation, the House of Representatives Committee on Elections announced February 24, 1854 that Gallegos was entitled to keep his seat as delegate from New Mexico. Bieber, ed., "Letters of William Carr Lane," 201 n. 54.

7. Webb's new wife, Florilla, was referred to as both "Lillie" and "Flora," although "Lillie" was used more frequently.

8. Kingsbury makes no further reference to this woman in his subsequent letters.

and forward the same on a good Boat to Saint Louis care of Glasgow
& Brothers[9] without delay. I have not yet written to G[lasgow] & Bro
but will wait to hear from you in order to know what to tell them
about forwarding, whether to forward them to Kansas in lots as they
receive them or to hold them in St. Louis untill all the goods arrive
there so as to make one shipment up the Missouri,—or if you prefer
you can write to Glasgow & Bro. and give them such instruction as
you think best. I could not get the policy of insurance to cover risk to
Westport without paying extry for it, but have taken insurance to cover
all risk from here to Kansas and at Kansas untill the goods are tran-
shiped into the waggons. I have got insurance for $24,000 which cov-
ers original cost of invoices with 10% added, the policies are made to
cover the goods which will be sent from New York. Mr. Abbott got it
taken for us at the Warren and Boston offices $12,000 each. They are
made in good form and payable to Mr. Abbott as our agent in case of
accident. I shall leave the policies with him for safe keeping. The premium is 2 ¾% 4 mos. $660.00 less 2% for cash. I shall start the goods
along as fast as I can get them ready. I have bought from Mr. Heard 3
Barrils of that high 95% proof n[e]utral spirits. I took it on Mr.
Williams recommendation. He thinks it is exactly what we want. I
shall advise you as I ship the goods and give you all the marks and
numbers with date of shipment. Please write me by return Mail. I
wrote you last on the 27th ult. and have not heard from you since. I see
that the Santa Fe Mail reached Independence on the 23rd ult. I am
afraid it will be late when we get our letters. Most of the goods are all
packed and will be ready to ship down as I settle for them. I do not
know yet where I shall use the cash which we have on hand. Let me
know how much you wish me to retain.

My love to all.

Letter no. 12, Kingsbury to Webb, March 4, 1854, Boston

I wrote you on the 2nd inst. and have received your letter of same
date.

I have today forwarded (74) Seventy four packages by the same
route as the Boots & Shoes, and have sent letters of advice to Harris &
Leach Phila. and Forsyth &Co. Pittsburgh, with instructions to forward them on a good Boat to St. Louis care of G[lasgow] & Bro.,

3	Barrels Mdse [merchandise]	I	#1. 2. & 3.
14	Casks do.	J	#1. to 14.
25	Baskets Champagne	"	#15 to 39.
16	Packages Mdse	K	#1 to 16.
16	Bales Mdse	do	#1 to 16.

74 (Seventy four) Packages.

9. Glasgow & Bro. was a prominent mercantile
house in St. Louis. They are mentioned frequently
throughout the Kingsbury letters. For a history of
the business see Gardner, ed., *Brothers*.

Will it be necessary to inform Messrs. Forsyth & Co. and Glasgow & B. that the goods are insured?

I notice what you say about holding on to our funds. I will keep enough to cover all the expenses that you mention, and if Necessary will send from here enough to Glasgow & B. say ($1,500.) to cover the freight. I do not send it now as I want to hear from Santa Fe first and know if there is any funds in this mail which we can use. It is very possible should there be any that it will be payable in St. L. If so we will save the exchange.[10] Should there be funds you will please give directions to place it at Glasgow's to our credit, or that is as much as you think we will want there, say $4,000 for freight outfit &c. Should there be more than this sum I suppose it would be well to have it sent here, unless you think of purchasing Groceries at St. L.[11] Soon as you get you letters write me what advices you receive about money and how you dispose of it. Should we get none I can fix all our settlements on what I have got so that I think we will be easy, that is provided Mills & Co. will make their Bill 10 & 12 months. You wanted me to settle this bill first as it is the largest, but it will be the last received and must be the last settled. I shall do the best I can. Inclosed I send an <u>estimate</u> of the settlements as I intend to make them provided I have no more funds and shall come as near it as possible.

I think I shall not be able to stop in Cornwall Bridge as the folks are very anxious to keep us here untill the very last moment. You will give me the latest day to meet you in New York. Also state where I shall find you.

I shall leave it with you to take receipts and send letters of advice for the goods which start from New York. I hope to have all the goods started from here by next Saturday week 11th.

Please send me the Santa Fe Papers after you have read them. Kate has a dressmaker Monday, Tuesday & Wednesday. We shall be occupied all the time untill we start. Please remember us kindly to all the friends at Cornwall. I would like very much to stop on our way through, but I think the folks at home have the best claim upon us. Our best respects to Mother and Father Webb. Also to Lillie.

Letter no. 13, Kingsbury to Webb, March 7, 1854, Boston

I sent yesterday 56 Packages, care Leach & Co. Phila. with instruction to forward all our goods by <u>Rail road</u> to care of Mssrs. Forsyth & Co. Pittsburgh,

The above packages are

9 boxes Hardware[12]
3 Packages do [ditto] (6 boxes)   }   E #1 to 13
1 Cask   do

10. Throughout his letters Kingsbury mentions a currency exchange, apparently a reference to the thriving market in bank notes current in the United States in this period. In 1850 there were 824 state banks issuing on an average six different denominations of notes. By 1860 the number of state banks had grown to over 1,500. Thus, a huge number of different types of notes were in circulation. Generally speaking, most notes submitted for payment at a bank a great distance from the issuing bank were paid at a discount of anywhere from 1 to 30 percent, because of the well-based fear that they were either counterfeits or issued from a bank that was no longer solvent. Only notes from the strongest banks, such as those in New York or Boston, circulated at par. The cross-country nature of Webb & Kingsbury's business made the problem of currency exchange particularly important. Walton and Rockoff, *American Economy*, 254; Douglass, *Coming of Age*, 131.

11. For Webb and Kingsbury groceries included "figs, sardines, pepper, cloves, chocolate, tobacco, cigars, candy, raisins, ketchup, pepper sauce, mustard, yeast powders, starch, sassafras bark, vinegar, saleratus [bicarbonate of soda], pickles, French olives, quinces, canned tomatoes, canned peaches, canned pears, and castile soap." See the analysis of the Webb & Kingsbury account books in Bieber, *Papers of James J. Webb*, 302-3.

12. "Hardware included such articles as iron pumps, skillets, frying pans, ovens, ploughs, coffee mills, corn mills, nails, bars of lead, hay forks, scythes, sad irons, locks, sheep shears, chisels, files, hand saws, bolts, knives and forks, pocket knives, Indian bells, Indian beads, axes, faucets, gun locks, bullet moulds, castors, scissors, zinc mirrors, and mouse traps." Ibid., 302.

8 Trunks Clothing[13]
10 Bales do   } F #1 to 10

19 do   Dry Goods[14]
2 Cases   do   } H #1 to 25
4 Trunks   do
_____
56 (fifty Six) Packages

I have now got all started except Mills Strong and Cerrant's. I hope to get everything off by next Saturday. I have not yet received my letters from Santa Fe and do not want to use anymore cash untill I here from there. You will advise me soon as you get your letters. I have not written to G[lasgow] & B. am waiting to hear from you first.

Letter no. 14, Kingsbury to Webb, March 8, 1854, Boston

I have rec.d your letter of the 7th inst, also a letter from Mr. Messervy. He does not say anything to me about Tom [Bowler] but must have been rather out of sorts at the time he wrote about our vacelating and changing our minds so often.[15] He does not seem to know whether we will come or not. I have been to enquire about wool, and find it is of no use to send little samples such as could be forwarded by mail. I will, however, get samples big enough to judge from and take them along with me. I am convinced the best way to find out about our wools is to get up a lot of it, say 1 or 2 Bales, bring it in here then you can find out what it is worth as it is. You can never get any satisfactory information on small samples, which would do to rely upon. As regards Beaver you know as much as I can find out here. In my letter to Mr. M. I sent him word for word the information I rec.d from the man I sold the samples to.[16] You at the time was satisfied that you could do better in St. Louis and I expect the best way is to get all the information we can as we pass through there. You remember Lacerne sent a large lot of Beaver to the States the funds was to go into Mr. Messervy's hands through Mr. Alverez[17] and I should think by the result of this lot (of which I have no doubt he can get all the particulars) he could obtain more reliable information on New Mexican Beaver than what we can find out here.

About the minerals. Mr. Abbott went to find Mr. Jackson the head man here about such things, but find he is gone on a visit to South Carolina. I will look up somebody else and have them assayed, but it cannot be done in time for this mail.

I have this day sent to Messrs. Glasgow & Brother Draft on James S. Watson Esq. St. Louis Mo. drawn by Mr. Abbott, for Three Thousand Dollars ($3,000) dated March 8th payable at Twelve days after date, this will place them in funds in season to meet the freight as soon as will arrive there. I have sent them advise of the goods which are already on the way. Told them we would like to get the goods together

13. Clothing included "cord pants, blue blanket coats, overcoats, coats, frock coats, dress coats, cotton vests, silk vests, fancy neckties, string collars, white shirts, fancy shirts, red flannel shirts, and hickory shirts." Ibid.

14. Dry goods (as opposed to fancy goods, which was a different category) included "pink cambric, check cambric, blue cambric, lienzo, manta, fancy cashmere, blue satinett, blue drill, Swiss muslin, victoria lawn, white wool flannel, black serge, blue blankets, red blankets, table linen, blue yarn, furniture print, blue cloth, alpaca, oil cloth, oil table covers, oil carpeting, and silk handkerchiefs." Ibid., 301-2.

15. A peevish Messervy, anxious to know what decisions and plans Webb and Kingsbury had made and impatient to retire from business, leave Santa Fe, and return to his family, had reproached Kingsbury: "You both remind me of two boys who have found bird's nests and think the whole world is in them. Would it not be well to give a thought as to where you are to live when you get out here—or do you intend to tumble in here with the whole crowd who come in at the same time with you." Messervy to Kingsbury, Santa Fe, Feb. 28, 1854, MHS.

16. Messervy had asked Kingsbury and Webb to make some inquiries about eastern prices for New Mexican wool and beaver pelts and also to have some minerals assayed. Webb to Kingsbury, Cornwall Bridge, CT, March 10, 1854, MHS.

17. Manuel Alvarez, a Spaniard who had come to New Mexico in the 1820s, where he traded, trapped, and served as U.S. consul. Sixty years old in 1854, Alvarez served as a business agent for a number of merchants. Chávez, *Manuel Alvarez*, 180.

and make on shipment up the Missouri, but that we are very anxious to get them up to Kansas as early as possible and must depend upon them to act for our interest. If the river is at a good stage & freight low I told them they could send them as they received them, but that I left it entirely to their judgment.

I have written them to acknowledge receipt of the draft by return of mail and address to care of Doan King &Co. 37 Pine St., N.Y.[18]

All the funds that I have left after setting up here, I will take along with me. I shall not want to leave here untill I get all the goods off, and settlements closed up, then I will leave soon as I can. I am sorry that I can not be with you in writing to Mr. Messervy this time but shall depend upon you to write him fully and if possible satisfy all his inquiries. He writes me that he has sent a memorandum to St. Louis of some things which will be well to purchase there. He urges us by all means to be in Santa Fe with our goods (if we bring any) early, and in regard to making money he says it must be done by saving and economising. I have instructed Glasgow & Bro. in case they send the goods up to [Westport] Kansas to send them to the firm which have the Brick Warehouse there J. Riddlesbarger & Co. I think it is. This is the name I find in Messervy's last Bills. In my next letter I will tell you more particular about which day and where I will meet you. I want to see Kate first. It is storming today. I have no goods ready and could not ship them if I had.

I wrote G[lasgow] & B. that we would both be in St. Louis about the 1st April.

Estimate

Due September			
6 mos: 10/13 Dana Farrar & Hyde		337.37	
10/13 J. D. & M. Williams		984.69	1322.06
Due November			
8 mos: 10 E. Lambert &Co.		997.02	
10 G. Bird &Co.		681.28	
10 J. H. Prentice & Co.		1039.44	
10 Tucker Neuten & Mills		1221.75	3939.49
Due January			
10 mos: C. H. Mills &Co.		2500	
Whitney F[illegible] Shaw &Co	950		
Horners & Ladd		1050	4500
Due March			
12 mos: C. H. Mills &Co.	cash	2500	
Lyman Tucker &Co.	650	1300	
Burbank & Rose	450	1000	

18. Doan, King & Co. was the wholesale dry goods establishment in St. Louis with which Webb & Kingsbury did much of their business. George P. Doan, son of the senior partner of the firm, had been Webb's first partner in the Santa Fe trade in 1845. Webb, *Adventures*, 28.

A. String &Co. <u>400</u>　　　1000　　　<u>5800</u>
　　　　　Cash　　$1500　　　　　　　　15561.55

Now on Hand $5600	Amt. Expended 5400
deduct　　　　1500	"to be paid
will leave　　$4100 Cash	as per this a/c　1500　<u>6900</u>
	Total Purchases　　$<u>22500</u>

Letter no. 15, Kingsbury to Webb, March 12, 1854, Boston

I have at last got all the goods started from here. I sent yesterday 144 packages which closes up all we have here.

Marked Webb & Kingsbury, Santa Fe, N. M. care Leach & Co. Phila.

| 27 Trunks Boots & Shoes | C #1 to 27 |
| 99 Bales Domestics | D #1 to 99 |

4 Trunks Dry Goods
4 Bales　do　　　　} I #1 to 9
1 Bale Carpeting

6 Cases Mdse
2 Trunks　do　　　} B #1 to 9
1 half Bbl. Mackerel

144 One hundred and forty four packages

Which makes in all 375 packages sent from this place. I have settled all the bills and closed them up according to the statement which I sent you. I shall start from here with $1,000 cash. You have $400 and with the $3,000 sent to Glasgow & Bro. will make $4,400 which I think will be sufficient to put us all through. At anyrate this is all the cash we have left and must make it go as far as it will. In settling the bills I have extended the time as much as possible and used as little cash as I could get along with. I have done the best I could and think the payments are so arranged that we will be perfectly easy. I have closed my letter to Mr. Messervy and sent it yesterday. I sent him all the information I could. I enclosed him a copy of our payments and sent him the amt of purchases up to the present.

I have left with a chemist 4 of the largest samples of minerals to have assayed. He cannot give me the result untill next Saturday. I have requested him to save a part of each sample and give me a full written statement of what they contain. His charge is $5 each.

I want to know exactly the number of packages which start from New York, from the bills I find,

Edward Lambert &Co.	1 Case	I
J. H. Prentice &Co.	15　"	M #1 to 15
George Bird &Co.	8 Bales	O #1 to 8
W. D. Cuthbertson	20 Baskets Champ.	N.
	44 packages in all, is this right?	

Was Lambert's goods all put in one case & numbered, was there any numbers put on the Champagne? Have you got the pistols with you or are they packed by themselves and sent with the other goods? We are making every preparation to leave here on the 21st Tuesday morning. If it should be pleasant we will go by the Stonington route & take the Boat to N. York so as to get a little sleep & be with you bright and early Wednesday morning. If it should be unpleasant we will come through on the Rail Road. We shall stop so short a time in N. York that it will make no difference to me where we are, let me know at what Hotel you engage rooms and I will go to the same place. I have had so much trouble getting the goods started that I have had very little time to myself. I have got all off now and feel a goodeal better. What have you done with your extra baggage? I have sent Kate's on with the Goods. I put it all in 2 Trucks & 1 box. The folks are expecting to have a good time with me this week, but the faces are beginning to look long and I shall be glad to get off.

Send your next letter to Salem. Kate wrote yesterday to Lillie.

4.

"Everything is quiet except the Indians"

Autumn and Winter in Santa Fe, 1855–56

Letters 16–24

After shipping much of their own baggage ahead with the merchandise, John and Kate Kingsbury and James and Florilla Webb started the long journey to Santa Fe in mid-March of 1854. Kate and Florilla may have gone West reluctantly. Florilla ("Lillie") Webb added a wistful postscript to one of her husband's letters to Kingsbury: "Kate—How do you feel now? Keep up good courage and send me a word of sympathy."[1] But notwithstanding the stereotype of male pioneers dragging reluctant women into the new country, many women expressed enthusiasm at the prospect of a move west—and that may also have been true of Kate Kingsbury and Florilla Webb.[2] Clearly, John Kingsbury had consulted with Kate and intended to respect her wishes. By the mid-nineteenth century, patriarchal marriages in which husbands demanded obedience from wives had given way to marriages that stressed mutuality and collaboration.[3] Kate and John seem to have enjoyed such a companionate marriage. Kate's brother, on the other hand, seems to have held a more traditional, authoritarian view and looked askance at the idea that a husband should respect his wife's wishes. As William Messervy later explained to John Kingsbury, "Kate is your wife—& it is her duty to consult your interests, wellfare—& desires, more than that of any other person living."[4]

In addition to "duty," Kate Kingsbury had a practical reason to accompany her husband to Santa Fe. She suffered from tuberculosis, or consumption as it was then known, and her illness was apparently well advanced. Indeed, Messervy had written to Kingsbury assuring him of his belief that the trip, however strenuous, was worth the effort. There seemed little reason to expect her health to improve in Salem, but perhaps New Mexico's clear, dry climate could offer her some hope.[5]

Kate received encouragement from several quarters to make the attempt, including the firsthand reports of Santa Fe traders—her husband's employer and partner-to-be among them. In early October 1853,

1. Webb to Kingsbury, Cornwall Bridge, CT, Mar. 7, 1854, MHS.

2. Myres, *Westering Women*, 99-102.

3. For a summary of the literature on the shift from patriarchal to companionate marriages, see Griswold, *Family and Divorce*, 4-17.

4. Messervy to Kingsbury, Santa Fe, Jan. 29, 1854, MHS.

5. Although Messervy does not identify consumption by name in this letter, it seems almost certain that the nature of Kate's illness was clear to her family for the disease was common and its symptoms well understood. Messervy to Kingsbury, Santa Fe, Jan. 29, 1854, MHS.

while John Kingsbury was still making his way home from Santa Fe to Salem, James Webb had stopped in Salem to meet Kate Messervy. As Webb told Kingsbury, "I talked much of New Mexico, and much of her going out there, provided you desired her to do so. I think she would go."[6] Fond of New Mexico's salubrious climate and plagued by "violent colds" in the East, Webb told Kingsbury he had pressed the point with Kate that "a residence of a few years in that country would establish her health upon a strong foundation."[7]

Webb's perscription for Kate was a common one, and her doctor and family would probably have concurred with his opinion.[8] From about this period until well into the twentieth century, the West's clear, dry climate lured countless health-seekers across the plains. Webb, whose firm fulfilled many banking functions, must have known some of these individuals, who carried letters of introduction to vouch for their good credit. For example, James Ross Larkin, a native of St. Louis with connections in the trading community, arrived in Santa Fe in 1856 armed with such a letter to Webb & Kingsbury introducing Larkin as "visit[ing] New Mexico for the purpose of improving his health."[9] Clearly those close to Kate had reason to believe that the journey to Santa Fe would be worth the try.

The Kingsburys and the Webbs arrived in Santa Fe in June 1854.[10] We know nothing of their journey, but it seems certain that neither Kate nor Florilla performed the routine chores that absorbed the energies of the wives of most emigrants on the overland trails of their day. Both women probably traveled with servants and enjoyed many of the comforts that Susan Shelby Magoffin, the wife of another Santa Fe trader, described so vividly in the well-known diary she kept in 1846, published as *Down the Santa Fe Trail and into Mexico*.[11]

In Santa Fe, John took up his new responsibilities as junior partner, and Kate's physical condition apparently remained stable.[12] In January of 1855, however, Kate gave birth to a son, George, who suffered a birth defect so serious that she and John attempted to conceal the nature of the infant's condition from the rest of the family. The only record of the trouble remains in a cryptic letter from Kate's brother, William, to John Kingsbury:

News of the 1st Febry. informing me of the birth of your child, I received with the other letters. You may rely upon my discretion, with regard to the contents of your letter. As soon as I received it— I consigned it to the flames—& have not communicated one word of it to any one not even to my wife—none of the family suspect that Kate has yet been delivered.

Should the child live there is no other way but to give it that place in your affections to which it would be entitled if it had been born perfect. We soon become to loose sight of the imperfections

6. Webb to Kingsbury, Cornwall Bridge, CT, Oct. 5, 1853, MHS.

7. Ibid.

8. Jones, *Health-Seekers*, 37-41.

9. Barbour, ed, *Reluctant Frontiersman*, 127.

10. Kate Kingsbury's obituary, *Santa Fe Weekly Gazette*, June 20, 1857.

11. Drumm, ed., *Down the Santa Fe Trail*, 1-29. For more normal work routines for women, see Faragher, *Men and Women*, 66-87.

12. Messervy to Kingsbury, Washington, DC, Feb. 16, 1855, MHS; ibid., Salem, Feb. 10, 1856, MHS.

of our children—in our strong natural love for them—such will be the case with you & Kate should your child live. Should it not live, then it would be well to say nothing respecting its misfortune, but should it live you must take what God entrusts to your care—& if helpless—then extend to it the more kindness & love.[13]

We know little of the Kingsburys' private or business life in the predominantly Mexican town of Santa Fe from their arrival in June 1854 until October 1855. During that time, both partners remained in the territorial capital, so there was no need to correspond with one another. One might suppose, however, that accommodation to local customs and to dark-skinned, Spanish-speaking peoples was difficult for the Kingsburys, both of them Protestant Yankees whose tradition included deep anti-Hispanic and anti-Catholic sentiments.[14]

For Kate Kingsbury, living in New Mexico for the first time, and in "delicate" health as her husband put it, the adjustment would have been especially difficult. Unlike her husband, she had no network of Anglo-American business acquaintances to help her reconstruct a familiar world in an alien land.[15] Moreover, the number of Anglo-American women in New Mexico was small and that would have imposed further hardship on her, for she lived in an era of rigidly distinctive male and female spheres, when women depended heavily on one another for emotional support.[16] New Mexican women probably provided little comfort for a Kate Kingsbury. To the contrary, they tended to scandalize Americans with their revealing clothes, cigarette smoking, gambling, and behavior that seemed improperly bold by Yankee standards, at least female Yankee standards.[17] Isolated by their sex and morality, the wives of other Anglo-American residents of Santa Fe formed a small circle, in which they tried to create a reassuringly familiar environment by keeping canaries, hosting genteel celebrations, and observing the niceties of middle class American social behavior.[18]

Kate was probably closest to Lillie Webb, with whom she shared a house.[19] Florilla Webb had given birth to a son the month before Kate delivered George.[20] The experiences already shared by these two wives of Santa Fe traders, together with the births of their first babies within a month of each other, probably strengthened their friendship.[21] Secretary of the Territory W. W. H. Davis described a gathering at Webb and Kingsbury's house, which the presence of these two ladies made more pleasant. Davis had invited a few friends to share a glass of wine at the house where he was boarding: "Mrs. Webb and Mrs. Kingsbury baked some nice cakes, and one in the shaped of a heart was handed to me. It had on it `Long live the Secretary' in large letters."[22]

Kingsbury's correspondence with Webb resumed again in October 1855, after Webb returned to the states.[23] Kingsbury's letters during the autumn of 1855 suggest that his interest in local politics had diminished

13. Ibid., Salem, Mar. 13, 1855, MHS. The number of disadvantages Kate must have experienced during her pregnancy make it difficult to speculate on the exact nature of George's "problem," although a later reference from Webb indicates that it involved a major deformity below the waist. Webb to Lillie, Santa Fe, July 5, 1857, HHS. In addition to Kate's illness and the quality of medical care she would have received in Santa Fe (which was probably primitive even by nineteenth-century standards), her age increased the odds against her. While her tombstone indicates that she was thirty years of age at the time of her death in 1857, the 1850 Massachusetts census lists her age as twenty-seven, making her about thirty-one at George's birth and about thirty-three at the time of her death. The tombstone's inaccuracy may have been a polite fiction. If the 1850 census data is correct and she was born in 1823, John Kingsbury was seven years younger than she.

14. Weber, "'Scarce More Than Apes',"295-307.

15. See Myres, *Westering Women*, 167-71.

16. Smith-Rosenberg, "Female World," 411-35.

17. Lecompte, "Independent Women," 17-35. If Kate came to know New Mexicans, as she might have known the family servant Facunda, whatever stereotypes she carried with her might have diminished. As Susan Magoffin noted, "What a polite people these Mexicans are, altho' they are looked upon as half barbarous by the generality of people." Drumm, ed., *Down the Santa Fe Trail*, 130. See, too, Russell, *Land of Enchantment*, 33.

18. Kingsbury to Webb, Santa Fe, Oct. 29, 1855, MHS; W. W. H Davis to his sister, Santa Fe, Aug. 26, 1854, Papers of W. W. H. Davis, WA MSS, S-1323, Beinecke Library, Yale University; Webb to Lillie Webb, Clasped Memo Book, Box 8, Webb Papers, MHS.

19. We have assumed that Webb and Kingsbury built a traditionally New Mexico style of house on the property that they purchased from Messervy. While it may have been one structure, it could have been a series of rooms around a placita (an open courtyard in the center of a building), which they divided into two homes, their store, and storage rooms.

20. "Mr. Webb was presented with a fine son on the 22nd inst. weighing 8 1/2 lbs. Mother and Boy are doing remarkably well." Kingsbury to Abbott, Santa Fe, Dec. 30, 1854, MHS.

21. Webb, *Adventures*, 22.

22. W. W. H Davis to his sister, Santa Fe, Aug. 26, 1854. Papers of W. W. H. Davis, WA MSS, S-1323, Beinecke Library, Yale University.

23. The Webbs left in September. Webb to Kingsbury, Fort Union, Sept. 3, 1855, and Westport, Sept. 22, 1855, MHS.

since the summer of 1853 and that business matters consumed him. The wholesale trade had declined, he thought, but retail business, including trade with individual Indians, still returned good profits. He and Webb had invested in a crumbling brewery, but the partners needed more capital. Characteristic of many Santa Fe merchants, Kingsbury devised a way to gain temporary use of $5,000 of public monies, a scheme that never came to fruition. The intense competition led Webb and Kingsbury to entertain the idea of buying teams and wagons to freight their own goods rather than hire the work out. And it may have been the keen competition that prompted Webb to entertain temporarily the idea of dissolving the partnership that autumn, to Kingsbury's dismay.

In addition to news of their business, Kingsbury's letters in the autumn and winter of 1855-56 provided Webb with gossip about mutual friends and acquaintances, local events, and homey details—the keeping of canaries, the fatal danger of sleeping under roofs covered with tons of dirt, the price of real estate in Santa Fe, the scarcity of white paint, and the uncertainty of the mails. Other than a few references to the health of his wife and son, and to their contentment with their household staff and the security of their home, Kingsbury's letters reveal nothing about Kate's deep unhappiness and declining health—concerns reflected in Messervy's letters of advice to Kingsbury but not in Kingsbury's letters to Webb. Not until the spring of 1856 would Kingsbury discuss his family life with his business partner.

❧

Letter no. 16, Kingsbury to Webb, Santa Fe, October 29, 1855

I have received your letter from West Port, and feel quite releaved to know of your safe arrival there. I got no letter from you at St. Louis and suppose you did not arrive there in time to write by this mail. We have at last got into the new house, and are very comfortably situated, although there is not a single room furnished.[24] We have had delightful weather since the first, not a drop of rain. If I can only get the portals up before storms commence I shall be satisfied.[25] I like my man very much.[26] He takes good care of the animals, is punctual and always on hand. He is very handy about the house and I have considerable confidence in his honisty. I found I had to give him his board and pay him $10 a month. Our little boy [George] had a long sick time of it. It appeared to be more like a slow fever than anything else, but I am thankful to be able to say that he is better and beginning to pick up again. The care and anxiety has been a hard task for Kate. Her health is delicate and it has been trying upon her. She likes the house very much but the delicate state of her health is always a drawback upon

24. Webb & Kingsbury purchased a large piece of property from William Messervy for $5,000 in August 1854 where, we assume, they built a house. The land included forty-two feet of frontage along the Plaza, at its southeast corner just across the street from the Exchange Hotel, and extended back as far as the Rio Chiquita, or present-day Water St. Santa Fe County deeds, Book B, p. 16, NMSRCA; and Mary Jean Cook to Jane Elder, personal correspondence, Santa Fe, July 24, 1994.

25. Kingsbury had written the year before that the store was completed except for a little adobe work and the portals—porticos or covered porches: "[Scofield] would soon have it ready for us if he would work steady, but he has so much to do for the Bishop [Lamy] that it is uncertain when he will get it done." Kingsbury to Messervy, Santa Fe, Oct. 31, 1854, MHS.

26. In a later letter Kingsbury mentions their servants by name: Talisfer, Facunda, and Blasa. Kingsbury to Webb, Santa Fe, Jan. 30, 1856, MHS. Perhaps the man to whom he refers here is Talisfer.

her happiness. She cannot enjoy the comforts around her like a well
person. We still have Blasa serving for us. She is very happy and wants
to remain with us.[27]

 . I hear from José [Hernandez] through Maj. [Cary H.] Fry's
Clerk.[28] He met him at El Paso. He was well and getting along well.
We are unfortunate with our Canarys. The one you gave us before you
left was well and singing sweetly in the morning and in the evening I
found him at the bottom of the cage dead. I could not account for it in
any [way]. Mrs. Fry lost hers in the same way. It fell from the perch
and died without a struggle.

Mrs. [Fred K.] Tolhurst has yours.[29] I rec.d the Box of seed and
turned it over to her. I think I have secured our money on the
Brewery.[30] I permitted Meyer to sell the Kettle with all the fixtures for
$150. payable 1st March. He sold to [Herrmann] Kessler with Dr.
[Edward] Guba's [Guba-Leidel] endorsement. I hold the note. The
[brewery?] house was about to fall down, and I made a conditional sale
to [James H.] Clift of the same for $250. payable June 1st 1856.[31] He
goes into it and puts it in good repair. When the note against Meyer
and [Henry] Ott comes due, I will forclose. If we buy it in, I give Clift
a deed on his paying the $250. If it should bring more at auction than
the mortgage, and Clift has to leave (of which there is very little
prospect) we are responsible to him for the improvements he makes to
the amt. of $50. I am very well satisfied with the traid and think it is
the only way we can get our money out of it, and think ourselves lucky
to loose nothing but the interest on money. I will get an additional
mortgage from Clift on all his Tools and shop fixtures for $250, draw-
ing interest from Oct. 15 at 10% per an. This will make our money safe
because I relinquish nothing on the Brewery.[32]

Ott has gone to the States. Meyer is here and cooking for Levi
S[piegelberg] at $30. a month. He is satisfied if we can save ourselves
out of the Brewery and clear him from the note. He expects nothing
beyond this.

I have sold this month $5,500. making in all since we took a/c stock
1st June last $42,800. Enclosed you will find Trial Bal. to Oct. 1st, also
an extract from same. You will see by this that I am short $5,000 to
meet the deposit a/c's

by this mail I remit to Boston	4,875
	9,875
deduct amt. of collection this month	4,000
	5,875
by next mail I have to send	4,500
to St. Louis to meet the freight note,	
making	$10,375

to be raised immediately. I shall not be able to remit you any more
at present, except I should collect some missionary's drafts,[33] say 4 or

27. "I am very glad you have got Blasa, hope she will stay with you. Tell her to be a good girl and all good people will love and respect her." Webb to Kingsbury, Boston, Dec. 10, 1855, MHS.

28. José Hernández is mentioned frequently throughout these letters. See Introduction. For Kingsbury's candid assessment of his character and prospects, see his letter to Webb, Santa Fe, July 25, 1858, DeG.

29. Rev. Fred K. Tolhurst was a Baptist minister in Santa Fe, apparently operating under the auspices of the American Baptist Home Mission Society. Webb to Abbott, Santa Fe, Sept. 30, 1856, MHS. He and his wife became close friends of the Kingsburys.

30. Henry Ott and Lipman Meyer, who had once been Webb & Kingsbury's cook, had formed a partnership in the brewing business. Webb & Kingsbury seem to have had some kind of financial interest in the business, in addition to facilitating Ott and Meyer's acquisition of essential materials such as hops. Webb & Kingsbury to Dr. J. Byrne (of Ft. Union), Santa Fe, n.d.; and Webb & Kingsbury to Glasgow Bros., Santa Fe, May 29, 1855, MHS. Frazer indicates that while no breweries existed in New Mexico before the Mexican War, by 1861 they were scattered throughout the territory. *Forts and Supplies*, 188.

31. James H. Clift was a carpenter from Virginia. 1860 NM Census, 470.

32. "I think you have done well, to secure the draft on the Brewery as well as you have. I considered it all lost, and all you get is so much made. What did they do with the hops?" Webb to Kingsbury, Boston, Dec. 10, 1855, MHS.

33. The drafts to which Kingsbury refers here and throughout his correspondence were bills of exchange drawn by an official or merchant on funds deposited elsewhere, and paid by the person or institution holding the funds, or as one contemporary book on finance defined them, "any direction in writing to another to pay a sum for the writer," at a specified date in the future (see Introduction). Colwell, *Ways and Means*, 205-6. An observer in Santa Fe noted, "The merchants generally make their remittances to the States in drafts obtained from disbursing officers of the general governments, which is a great convenience, and attended with less risk." Davis, *El Gringo*, 252. Drafts represented a convenience for firms such as Webb & Kingsbury, which would have been reluctant to risk sending cash across the country. The drawback of drafts, as later letters demonstrate, was that they were sometimes difficult to obtain and thus prevented a smooth transfer of funds from Kingsbury, who was selling the goods, to Webb, who needed the cash from Kingsbury's sales in order to purchase more goods to send out.

600 Dollars, which is possible I may get to send by next mail.

You have probably on hand	$500
I sent last mail	3,971
I send now	4,875
making in all	$9,346

for Cash purchases, if you need more you must make arrangement to get a loan there for 3 or 4 months as in addition to what I have to raise as per statement on the other side I must send 3 or $4,000 to meet you in St. Louis for Expenses and Cash purchases there. I have a little financial arrangement on foot, which if it succeeds will give you all the Cash you want without borrowing. It is this. Houghton wants to continue public work this winter, dressing stone &c.[34] He will send by this mail a requisition endorsed by [territorial Secretary W. W. H.] Davis with a request to Governor M[eriwether] to place $5,000 of the Building fund with Mr. Abbott to our Credit. If the Gov. consents to do it, it will give you the money at once and will be all that you can possible need. I hope he will do it as by so doing it will place you in funds and at the same time, be very easy for me to meet here. I shall not advance one cent untill I hear from Mr. Abbott that the deposit is made. This cannot come untill the end of January. You will have the money a month and a half, and I will only have a few hundred Dollars to pay weekly as the work advances. Where you buy goods on time, extend the payment as much as you can, so as to make payments easy next year, particularly if you buy largely of Indian goods, with the understanding that we are to wait for the payment untill appropriations are made by Congress.[35]

Sales and collections so far this year are very fair. I think the a/cs in the books look well, and I anticipate no trouble in collecting what is necessary to meet my obligations here. I am doing my best to reduce the stock, when I can place it in safe hands. I refuse no reasonable offers. I do not expect to make large sales but by working off small lots it will amt. up in the end. I made a barter trade with [Henry] Connelly[36] and took 14 sacks of Coopers Coffee at 20 cents. It retails easy at 25. If I had sugar to sell with it I could sell it all before spring. (Brown) sugar is retailing at 31 ¼.

Enclosed you will find a small book with a few memo. which I want you to examine before making purchases. It is not very full, because I have too much confidence in your judgment to dictate to you about purchasing. I would advise you to select a good stock for retailing. Wholesale profits are getting so small that counting the <u>risk</u> there is but a small margin for gain.

In the back part of the Book you will find an order from Tom [Bowler].

I have been so busy this month moving, taking off Trial Balance &c. that I have not been able to make a plan of the property as I

34. Joab Houghton drew the original plans for the territorial capitol, for which Congress made its first appropriation in 1850. He supervised its construction, as well as the building of a new penitentiary. Twitchell, *Leading Facts*, 2:326; *Santa Fe Weekly Gazette*, Feb. 19, 1853.

35. This is a good example of the kind of cooperation that existed between the merchants and the government at this time. See Introduction.

36. Henry Connelly was a prominent New Mexican whom Kingsbury mentions frequently. Connelly was a medical doctor and became a merchant in Chihuahua and later in New Mexico. He served as governor of New Mexico during the Civil War and died shortly after his term of office ended in 1866. Horn, *New Mexico's Troubled Years*, 93-111.

intended to. However if you deside to insure, I think you can easily give them an idea of the size, shape, situation &c. which will be all sufficient. If it can be done at a reasonable rate, I think you had better do it. Consult with Mr. Messervy and see what he says about it.[37] I think the danger is small. Still if we are insured it will guard against all contingencies. Be carefull in having the policies made, so that it will give us permission to keep in the store all foods that are in our line, Alcohol, Turpentine, Liquors and all other combustibles.

I have sent by this Mail to Mr. Messervy a Draft for $450.+ being for amt. of rents collected for him up to the present time.[38]

If you should need the money for the drafts which I send to Mr. Abbott before they can be collected, you can easily dispose of them to a Broker.

I have done my best to place you in funds and hope you will have no trouble for want of money.

Let me know where I shall address your letters from time to time, so that they may find you without delay. I expect you will see high times this winter at Washington. Brooks, Collins, Beck &c. will be there to work against the Gov.[39] Otero will go on to contest Gallegos seat.[40] Collins wants to be made Supt. of Ind. Affrs. and have it divided from the Office of Governor.[41] They feel confident of getting Gov. M. removed, and expect to put [Perry E.] Brockus [Brocchus] in his place.[42] Gene [William] Pelham also goes on with the view of getting his office divided making the Surveyors Office and the Court of Land Claims district Offices.[43] I do not know who they intend for this new Office, but I fear Pelham is a little tinctured with the Beck clique. We expect to have lively times here this winter. We have already had two bilaes [*bailes*—dances] for the genta fina [*gente fina*—the elegant folks]. [W. W. H.] Davis gave one at the Palase, which certainly gave him credit. Col. Grayson gave a very fine one at his quarters. Tonight there will be a subscription party at Manuel Chavis's house in honor of the departure of Gallegos. Each American family is expected to give a party during the winter.

Mr. [Thomas A.] Weirick is willing to remain with us, and I think it would be better for us to keep him than to bring a strainger from the state.[44] He is very attentive to business, and I doubt very much whether you would be able to find a better man. He has the advantage of knowing the language, and has lived here long enough to prove his character. Besides he is getting more acquainted with our business every day, and appears to be interested for us. I feel quite fortunate in having secured his services this winter. He is very quiet, attends to his own business and in time I think he will make a pretty fair salesman.

It will be a great advantage to us to get our goods out early. The first trains are bound to make money. Many things will be scarce in the spring. I think the market will be pretty well cleared out before new

37. Messervy had been elected as a director of a Boston insurance office in August. Messervy to Kingsbury, Salem, Aug. 15, 1855, MHS. Webb spoke with him, then wrote to Kingsbury: "We have no insurance, and if we had we had almost as well insure our own goods as guarantee the insurance offices. There is a great deal of insecurity in the offices, as a great many bogus offices [are] in operation now a days. I have talked with Mr. Messervy & Mr. Abbott about insuring, and they say we can get insured very easily, but no good, responsible office would take the risk without a higher premium than we would be willing to pay, so I have given it up." Webb to Kingsbury, Boston, Dec. 10, 1855, MHS.

38. The rents to which Kingsbury refers were probably derived from a storehouse and rooms along the plaza, which Messervy had leased to Preston Beck for $70 a month, as well as the Exchange Hotel, which stood on the site of today's La Fonda, and of which he was sole owner. Santa Fe County Records, Deed Book A, 351, 396, NMSRCA; Messervy to Kingsbury, Salem, Oct. 15, 1855, MHS.

39. Governor Meriwether's administration was a rocky one, and he encountered opposition from a number of people on a number of issues. Motives of the clique of Brooks, Collins, and Beck for working against Meriwether while in Washington are unclear in this instance. The governor remained unperturbed, however. Webb wrote to Kingsbury, "I rec.d a letter from Gov. M. . . . He says the clique cannot effect him." Webb to Kingsbury, Cornwall Bridge, CT, Jan. 15, 1856, MHS.

40. José Manuel Gallegos was reelected to his seat as territorial delegate by a majority of 99. Miguel A. Otero, whom Bishop Lamy and his friends supported, contested the vote, chiefly on the grounds that 1,400 of Gallegos's votes were cast by citizens of Mexico. Congress recognized Otero's claim. Otero held the office for three successive terms (1855-1861). Twitchell, *Leading Facts*, 2:309-10; Angélico Chávez, *Trés Macho*, 89-91.

41. At this time the offices of governor and superintendent of Indian affairs were combined.

42. The "clique" failed in this effort.

43. William Pelham was New Mexico's first surveyor-general, holding the office from 1854-1860. Westphall, "Fraud and Implications of Fraud," 190. The Confederacy later named Pelham governor of the New Mexico Territory. Waldrip, "New Mexico During the Civil War," 252.

44. Hired that winter, Thomas A. Weirick, who had lived in New Mexico at least since 1850, remained Webb and Kingsbury's clerk throughout the firm's tenure in New Mexico. He was a native of Kentucky, with the unlikely occupation of sailor. 1850 NM Census, 348.

goods can arrive. Perhaps it would pay to stock an early train. I can tell better by Jany. or Feby.

Remember us kindly to your family, and all the friends.

Letter no. 17, Kingsbury to Webb, Santa Fe, November 30, 1855

I have received your letter of Oct. 5th containing account of settlements made by you. I have not had time to examine them but suppose they are all right. The mail was detained at Independence untill the 5th and did not reach here untill the 28th. It brought news of the Santa Fe Mail robbery.[45] [George] Estes rec.d a telegraph dispatch[46] from [Reuben P.] Campbell, stating that he had rec.d letters that were in that mail cont.g Drafts, from [Maj. T. H.] Brooks, [Lt. Col. John B.] Grayson, Armijas [Armijos], [Henry] Mercure, & Beck, from this I hope ours got through safe, but fearing they might be lost or destroyed, I done my best to get duplicates, from [Albert J.] Smith, the pay M.[paymaster] & Col. Grayson, but they refused stating that they could not give duplicates untill we assertained certainly that the originals were lost. I send by this mail to Mr. Abbott a full discription of the drafts which I sent from here Oct. 1st in all $3,971.82. You are probably with him, and can see it there. If not, you can get a copy from him. I can do nothing about them untill next mail arrives.

I send by this mail Drafts to Doan King & Co. sufficient to take up our freight note. The Cloak Tassels came but were not what they wanted. They sent short ones, and they wanted long ones. [Wendell] Debus & B[unker] took them however.

By last mail I sent you a long letter, with Trial Balance and full statement of Cash affairs. I hope Gov. M.[eriwether] has turned over the $5,000 to you.[47] I also sent a small Book cont.g a few memo. about goods, and an order from Mr. Bowler for things for him. He has desided to send for a billiard Table, and wants us to fill the enclosed order on the best terms that you can get.

Business has been very dull this month. Our sales only amt. to $3,500.+ still I feel satisfied, as the most of it is retail. I have had only 1 large sale and that was today to old Chat.[48] He is not through yet, will buy 800 to $1,000.

Collections amt. to $4,500 which is very fair. Santa Fe never appeared so dull to me as it has the last month. I feel confident that no one has sold more than ourselves this month.

I send no money to Mr. Abbott by this mail, I rec.d a small Box, without any letter or advise cont.g 2 setts of Billiard Balls and one sett bagatell ball.[49] I do not know who they are from, what expenses there is on them, or w[h]ether there is anymore to come or no. Scofield[50] is still mooving on very slowly with the house no important addition since you left. His excuse now is that he cannot get lumber.

45. Robbery was common along the Trail. That summer Indian Agent John W. Whitfield wrote: "All the tribes from Council Grove to the headwaters of the Arkansas . . . have regular stands on the road, where they exact and enforce the payment of toll in the way of sugar, coffee &c. No train has been permitted to cross without having to submit to this imposition, whilst a large number of horses, mules and oxen have been stolen during the present season." Quoted in Taylor, *First Mail West*, 41.

Among the items lost in the robbery to which Kingsbury refers was a letter he had written to Messervy Sept. 30, 1855, and some daguerrotypes. All were recovered eventually. Messervy to Kingsbury, Salem, Dec. 11, 1855, and Feb. 10, 1856, MHS.

46. There was no telegraph line to New Mexico at this time. "Here our only telegraphs are Indian runners," one resident of Santa Fe noted in 1855. Whilden, "Letters from a Santa Fe Army Clerk," 156. The most plausible explanation for Kingsbury's term "telegraph dispatch" is that a message was telegraphed to the westernmost point, probably St. Louis or St. Joseph in Missouri, then dispatched overland to New Mexico. Ault describes this "slow, uncertain, and expensive" process in *Wires West*, 32-34. Diane DeBlois to Jane Elder, personal correspondence, Wynantskill, NY, Mar. 4, 1994.

47. This is a reference to Kingsbury's scheme of having Governor Meriwether place $5,000 in public money in the hands of Webb and Kingsbury's agent in Boston. See Kingsbury to Webb, Santa Fe, Oct. 29, 1855, above.

48. We have been unable to determine "old Chat's" real name.

49. Bagatelle is a game, similar to pool or billiards, played by striking balls with a cue.

50. Calvin Scofield was the contractor building the house (or houses) in Santa Fe for Webb and Kingsbury. "I hope you will get Scofield to finish up the house as soon as you can; he will be long enough about it anyhow, and would not finish it at all unless you crowd him. Don't advance him another cent. When the house is finished pay him, and not untill then." Webb to Kingsbury, Boston, Dec. 10, 1855, MHS.

I hardly know what to say more. I notice what you say in regard to retail sales, and of course will do all that I can. I find it impossible to trade for Corn long side of the Jews.[51] They have got strikers out in every direction, and every sack of grain is bargained for 5 miles before it reaches here.

I hope you will receive my last letter. You can judge very well of our present stock by knowing the amt. of sales since you left. I will sell all the Catawba,[52] without any trouble.

George is quite well again, he has no <u>tooth</u> yet. My love & a happy new year to all.

[P.S.] <u>Old Gordo</u> has gone to his long home.[53] He went to his house in usual health <u>and</u> was found dead in his bed next morning.

Letter no. 18, Kingsbury to Webb, Santa Fe, December 29, 1855

I have received your letter of Nov. 13th from Norfolk, also the Telegraph communication announcing the Safe arrival of all the remittances, which you may believe releaved me of a great load of anxiety. (I am sorry my letter to you was lost, it was the first after you left, and contained very little of importance about business, and I failed to keep a copy of it.[)]] I sent in it your Odd Fellows Certificate & card,[54] also a letter which you will find herewith. It appears that my letter must have been opened and this letter has found it[s] way back here. I wrote you at that time all the particulars of the death of Elias Spiegelberg. The roof of the room in which he was sleeping with his companion (Ries the youngest of the Goa[s] family) in the rear of his store fell in burying them both.[55] It happened in the middle of the night and was not discovered untill next morning, when they were both found lying side by side dead, having been smothered by the ruins. Our account against him will be paid when it comes due.

In the following Mail that is the one which left here, Nov. 1st, I sent you trial Balance of our Books, also a full statement of our business up to that time, with a small book containing a few memo. about goods, and an order from Mr. Bowler. In case you received this mail you will be fully posted in every particular relating to our affairs. I feel quite anxious to hear whether you got it or not. In the memo. Book I wrote you my expectations about reducing the stock so as to be able to close out the balance before new goods arrive. But sales have fallen off so that I fear I shall not be able to reduce it sufficiently. But I shall continue to do my best to sell all that I possibly can to safe men.

Sales this month amount to $2,500. I have collected this month $4,500.

By last mail I sent funds to Doan King & Co. at St. Louis to take up our freight note. I send by this mail to Mr. Messervy remittances to

51. We have been unable to determine why Kingsbury was trying to trade in corn.

52. A wine made from a reddish variety of grape, first raised on the Catawba River in South Carolina.

53. We have been unable to determine "Old Gordo's" real name.

54. The Independent Order of Odd Fellows is a benevolent, secret society that began sometime during the late eighteenth century in England. The American branch was founded in 1819 and "lodges" spread rapidly throughout the United States. Santa Fe's Montezuma Lodge no. 1 was founded in 1851. Webb apparently belonged to it, as did many prominent Anglo Americans in Santa Fe at that time. Weber, *Richard H. Kern*, 310 n. 16.

55. Elias Spiegelberg was one of the numerous merchandising Spiegelberg brothers. W. H. H. Davis described the way in which roofs were constructed in Santa Fe: "The only wood used about the roof is the sleepers, and the boards are laid across them to hold the earth, because of the high price of timber. They cover the sleepers with a foot or eighteen inches of dirt, which they pack down, and then besmear it with a top coating of mud to make it waterproof.... Sometimes a single roof will weigh several tons, the load of dirt accumulating from year to year." *El Gringo*, 40–41.

the amt of $875.+ which is all I send by this mail, $500 of it is on a/c of rents collected & $375 on a/c of money collected for Messervy & Webb. I have placed from the same funds to your credit on our books $550.+ which makes your accounts on the Books of M & W [Messervy & Webb] about equal.

I shall take off a trial Balance of our Books to January 1st and will send you a copy by next mail. I will also make up a grocery memo. to meet you in St. Louis.

By last mail I sent you an order from Bowler for a billiard table and all the fixtures complete.

I hope Gov. Meriwether has turned over to Abbott the $5,000. I shall be able to meet it here without any trouble.

Mr. Tolhurst has rec.d nothing from his board since June last. I will get his draft when it comes. I am advancing him a little money, just enough to live on.

Scofield has at last commenced to work on your rooms, he has laid the floors of the Kitchen and in the upper sleeping room in the placita. He appears to be going a head in good earnest and I have strong hopes of getting it finished in the Spring.

I shall not be able to repaint the store this winter as I had intended because it is impossible to get a keg of White Lead in the Territory. I have written to the Quarter master at Albuquerque requesting him to loan us enough to paint your rooms with. If he does not do it, Scofield will be obliged to send by mail and get 3 or 4 kegs.

Spiegelberg has just made a trade with [Alexander] Valle, for his property which a[d]joins Mr. Messervy's & ours, he paid $4,700 or $4,800 for it as it stands.[56] Will take it all down and make 2 stores, two stories high.[57] When Beuthner returns to the country he will be in that firm, and will remain here. They say Beck's house cost between 12,000 & 14 Thousand. Spiegelberg expects his will cost in the neighborhood of 15 Thousand or more. I have not heard from José [Hernandez] since he pas[s]ed through El Paso on his way down. Mr. Boyd who was here for his health, I learn died on the 13th Dec. at Caleb Sherman's house, of chronic diarrhoea [sic].

Remember us kindly to al the folks. Little George is quite well. Tom & Refuja[58] also wish to be remembered to you & wife.

Letter no. 19, Kingsbury to Webb, Santa Fe, December 30, 1855

I am in receipt of your favor dated Litchfield Nov. 13th 1855.

Your proposition is intirely unexpected and meets me with surprise, it is true I anticipated something of the kind in the future, but not for several years.[59]

I am at a loss to comprehend what should have influenced you to wish to make so sudden a change. Is it that you are loosing confidence

56. Spiegelberg purchased a piece of property on the south side of the plaza, next to the store Messervy was leasing to Preston Beck. In March 1854 Messervy bought eighty-three feet of land fronting the plaza at its southeast corner from Alexander Valle for $6,000. In August he divided the property and sold the easternmost forty-two feet of the frontage closest to the Exchange to Webb & Kingsbury for $5,000. We assume that the remaining, western half is the parcel he leased to Preston Beck. In 1859, when Messervy was able to sell that store to Gaspar Ortiz, the deed indicates that Levi Spiegelberg owned the land on the west side of it, while Webb & Kingsbury owned the land to the east. Misc. File, Box 8, Webb Papers, MHS; Santa Fe County Records, Deed Book A, 351, 396, and Book C, 152, NMSRCA.

57. A two-story home in Santa Fe would have been a novelty. Charles Whilden wrote in September 1855, "The only house with two Stories in Santa Fe is where the Catholic Bishop lives." "Letters from a Santa Fe Army Clerk," 149. See, too, Weber, *Mexican Frontier*, 222.

58. Tom Bowler's wife was named Refugia.

59. We have not been able to locate Webb's letter outlining the "proposition," but apparently he wanted to close the business. On Dec. 10, 1855, Webb wrote to Kingsbury (MHS), and referred to a conversation he had had with Messervy about buying Kingsbury out. Webb indicated that he and Kingsbury would talk about it when Webb arrived in Santa Fe. If, as Kingsbury supposed, Webb's desire to close up was due to the fact he did not want to come west, it represented a drastic change in Webb's attitude from two years before. Then he had written Kingsbury, on October 5, 1853 (MHS): "I cannot be contented in this country [the East] and my health would not allow me to live here long if I desired. I have taken three violent colds since my arrival, and each settles on my lungs. I <u>fear</u> to remain here even if I desire, which I do not by any measure." Perhaps his subsequent marriage and the birth of his son explains his reluctance to return to Santa Fe.

Messervy offered Kingsbury a psychological explanation: "The difficulty with Mr. Webb is he is too prone to change his mind. The only way to manage him is to hold him to his contract. I think after he wrote to you on the subject he was ashamed of it. Webb is honorable, honest, just, and generous, but very changeable. Give him time to <u>reflect</u> and he will allways come out right. He does some foolish things, sometimes in the spur of the moment, but will allways make amends when he has reasoned on the subject." Messervy to Kingsbury, Salem, Feb. 10, 1856, MHS.

in my integrity or are you dissatisfied with my ability as partner? The only reason you give for wishing to make a change is that you wish to settle in the states. If this is the <u>only</u> reason you have, I think we can arrainge it much more satisfactorily than by admitting a third person. The man you propose I have seen but once or twise. He is a perfect strainger to me, and I know nothing of his business qualifications. He is still in California. Connelly tells me he thinks he is inclined to that place, and may engage in some permanent business there before he returns. By our books since we have been together they show you at least 20% per annum on your capital. Let me ask can you invest it in the States where it will pay you the same interest with any less risk? You must at any rate come out with the goods you are now purchasing and remain here one year. At the experation of that time, I think we can arrainge it for you to return and remain there.

We have in our business,	Webb	36,000
	Kingsbury	1,000
	Stock Note	7,000
	Real Estate do [ditto]	5,000
	Profits to Oct 1st, 1855	<u>17,000</u>
		66,000
	Probable Profit on the Stock	
	you are now purchasing	<u>10,000</u>
		76,000

Now I have no ambition to do a big business, and when the goods which you are now purchasing, are paid for we can safely pay our Real Estate Note of

	5,000
and let you draw out $10,000 or say	15,000
add to this the cost of real estate	13,000
which is dead capitol, although paying	
a good interest while we occupy it	33,000

deduct this from 76,000 would leave $43,000 active capitol which I should think would be ample to carry on a small <u>safe</u> business. If this statement will meet your approbation and give you funds enough to settle in the States, you can remain in the States, buy the goods and send them out each year, and I will stay here and attend to selling & collecting. You will have it in your power to stop the supply of goods and close the business whenever it suits your convenience. Under this arrangement you would not be compel[l]ed to return to the country except in the event of my death. You can draw out each year your share of the profits and as much more as the business will admit, which will be reducing my interest account.[60]

If you have any ground for dissatisfaction with me, I beg of you as a man and a friend to tell me frankly, and I will not urge a continuance

60. Webb and Kingsbury remained in business, operating along the lines suggested by Kingsbury. Webb returned to Santa Fe only on business trips, except for a protracted stay in New Mexico in 1856-57 when Kingsbury had to be in Salem with Kate, who was ill. See Introduction.

of our partnership one moment longer than is actually necessary to close it up. If agreeable to you I would like to continue our business a few years longer, so that I might retire with sufficient means to insure me a support. I have no desire to remain here for years with the hope of accumilating a fortune. My only ambition is to make enough to support myself & family.

If you are determined to sell out and realize your capital as soon as possible then I would suggest that you sell my mite with it. It is so small that it cannot injure the sale of yours, and I will leave the Country with you. I shall do nothing in refference to a change of partners untill you return. Our firm is now established both here and in the States, and I do not think with my limited amount of means that it would be to my advantage to make a change.

In case you are willing to continue and want to draw out money to use in the States before the Stock you are now buying becomes due, then you must curtail the amt. of present purchases sufficient to meet that end.

I can think of nothing more to add on this subject. Think the above sufficiently explicit, and will leave it with you to act according to your own inclinations.

Letter no. 20, Kingsbury to Webb, Santa Fe, January 29, 1856

I am in receipt of your letters of Dec. 10th & 12th am pleased to hear that you are getting along so well with your purchasing. If you are pleased with them I know I shall be. I notice what you say about the a/c standing in the Trial Balance but I assure you I use every exertion to get in the hard accounts. I am afraid we will be obliged to loose something by [Peter] Saxel. The papers he sent us before you left Maj. Fry [paymaster] lost & I have been unable so far to get duplicates of them. The only show we have to get this debt is through his honisty. I have dun[n]ed him every chance & always get fair promises, but up to the present have not rec'd a cent of money. His property has been taken by a mexican for debt, & Levi [Spiegelberg] has secured himself by taking goods. I have today rec'd the balance from Old Sanchez.[61] In this we are lucky, he paid up with the hope of getting more. After I got the money I told him he could have anything he wanted cheap for cash, that his time was altogether too long for us. I am told he owes everybody in the Rio Baja [Abajo],[62] at least $10,000.+. We are out of this and I intend to keep so. [Rev. Samuel] Gorman[63] will be able to pay soon with interest. [Moses] Sachs has paid, and bought another bill for cash.[64] He is good, he tells me he is worth 15 or $16,000. Next year if we sell him cheap he will be a good customer with the money in hand. He bought from Connelly this year, about $10,000 at cost,

61. We have been unable to determine "Old Sanchez's" full name.

62. The region along the Rio Grande downstream from Santa Fe; the region upstream was referred to as Rio Arriba.

63. Rev. Samuel Gorman came to New Mexico in 1852 as a Baptist missionary to the Pueblo Indians at Laguna. He taught and preached there until 1860. Twitchell, *Leading Facts*, 2:350. His wife, Catharine, who died in 1862, is buried in Fairview Cemetery in Santa Fe, close to Kate Kingsbury's grave.

64. Moses Sachs was a trader in Los Lunas.

freight & 25%, and he thinks he done better than he would by coming to Santa Fe. He got what he wanted & saved the freight down.

Herewith you will find Trial Balance to Jany. 1st. I suppose you know before this that Gov M.[eriwether] has desided not to draw on the Building fund untill he returns here, so you will not have the $5,000 that I mentioned before.[65] I have collected this month $4,000, sales amount to $3,200. I remit to Mr. Abbott by this Mail Drafts amt.g to $3,101 97/100. Also to Messrs. Doan King & Co. at St. Louis $5,000 to meet you there. It is placed to our credit subject to your order, for Freight, Expenses, Groceries, &c. I also send by this mail a letter to their care for Jan. cont.g memorandum for Groceries &c. I may be able to send more money by next mail, it will depend upon collections.

I expect to get a Check for $5,000 from [W. W. H.] Davis to send in by the Mail which leaves here April 1st, on which we will get a credit of 6 mos. or more, which I want you to use for freight on the plains. Should [Amazon] Hays[66] back out, or from any cause be unable to bring our freight it will help you to make a good bargain, and perhaps get freight a little less. Mexicans are freighting to Rio Baja for 8 cents. The Otero's[67] would like to get ours [business] at that price, with mule teams & would start as early as you wish, for they intend to make 2 trips.[68] In case you think we would save money by having our own teams, this would help you to buy them, & if you could get 6 or 7 months on the balance I think we could stand it. I presume we could buy 20 Ox Teams for what our freight will amt. to this year, and whatever freight we got out of them afterwards would be profit. Do not think of buying unless you can find some capable man, such as Tom Akerman or some one in whome you have confidence and can make an agre[e]ment with him to take the entire charge of them for several years & give him some sort of an interest in them which would make it to his interest to take good care of the train & save expenses. I am told that many of [Joseph] Murphy's Waggons turned out mean last year. Connelly had 6 out of 7 new ones entirely used up.[69] I do not recommend the purchasing of Teams because I know nothing about them, but leave it for your judgment and experience. I hear every day that thoes who have their own teams count their freight at 4 or 5 cents, and of course give to the world to understand that they can undersell us.[70] If by having our own teams we could reduce freight one half, I should say it would be worth trying, but your experience on this subject is a better guide than anything I can suggest.[71] Perhaps Hays by getting $5,000 in advance would be willing to make some discount, or extend our note for the other half. My next letter will be directed to St. Louis.

65. Kingsbury is referring to an idea he had outlined to Webb on Oct. 29, 1855.

66. Kingsbury is referring to freighter Amazon Hays, not to Martin B. Hayes, another freighter involved in the Santa Fe trade at this time. Amazon Hays transported goods for Webb & Kingsbury until 1858, when they negotiated a new contract with freighter Charles Kitchen. Walker, *Wagonmasters*, 101, 135.

67. The Oteros were one of New Mexico's "old, aristocratic families" who had seen the profits made by Americans in the early days of the Santa Fe trade and decided to join in. Simmons, *Murder on the Santa Fe Trail*, xvi–xvii. See, too, Kingsbury to Webb, Jan. 29, 1856, below.

68. While it has been generally supposed that merchants did not begin to make two freighting trips per year until 1857, one trader, Norris Colburn, made two trips in 1846. Gardner, ed., *Brothers*, 152 n. 86.

69. Joseph Murphy was a well-known and reputable St. Louis wagon builder. In times of peak demand, however, wagonmakers sometimes used unseasoned wood, which began to shrink once out on the dry plains. The problems Connelly experienced with Murphy's wagons could have been due to that. Walker, *Wagonmasters*, 96, 99.

70. Freighters charged a certain price per pound, roughly eight cents at this time, for the goods that they shipped. Given the size of their shipments, a savings of a few cents a pound could amount to a good-sized sum of money. For example, in 1857, Kingsbury had a dispute with Amazon Hays, who said that they had agreed to a price of twelve cents, while Webb insisted that the agreed-upon figure was ten cents. Because the shipment consisted of 26,909 pounds of goods, the difference in the two prices amounted to $538.18. Kingsbury to Webb, Santa Fe, Oct. 27, 1857, MHS.

71. Webb and Kingsbury continued to hire freighters such as Amazon Hays and Charles Kitchen.

72. Easily overlooked in the flood of information about Anglo merchants on the Santa Fe Trail is the fact that the trail ran two ways. In his discussion of Hispanic merchants in the Santa Fe trade, David Sandoval credits New Mexican and Mexican merchants with achieving "economic dominance of the trade by the early 1840s." They were involved in every aspect of the trade "from the sending out of troops (to defend the caravans as well as the tax coffers) to civilian travel [children were frequently sent east to be educated in American schools] and retail and wholesale mercantile operations, including merchants who lobbied in Washington and traded in New York, Pittsburgh, and Europe." Sandoval, "Gnats, Goods, and Greasers," 22-31.

A more recent and expanded study by Susan Calafate Boyle challenges the previously held notion that New Mexico traders lost prominence after the Mexican War. Boyle develops the idea that wealthy New Mexican merchants played a significant role in the expansion of the trade through refining existing practices, and diversifying their activities and investments, placing them well to the fore in the growth of mercantile capitalism in territorial New Mexico. Boyle, *Comerciantes, Arrieros, y Peones*, 2-5, 96-123.

73. Horace L. Dickinson was about thirty years old when he died. A merchant from New York who had lived in Santa Fe at least since 1850, he was appointed auditor of public accounts in Dec. 1854 and served as territorial auditor through 1855. Weber, *Richard H. Kern*, 124, 310 n. 16.

74. Elias Spiegelberg was the victim of the roof cave-in Kingsbury mentioned in his correspondence the previous year. Both men were buried in the Independent Order of Odd Fellows Cemetery, which occupied the site of the present Masonic Temple just north of the Federal building in Santa Fe. Around the turn of the century, part of the cemetery was moved to Fairview Cemetery on Cerrillos Road and part to the National Cemetery.

75. A Santa Fe trader from Ireland who is mentioned from time to time throughout these letters, and should not be confused with the mountain man of the same name who died in the late 1840s. 1850 NM Census, 347.

76. W. W. H. Davis commented, as did other visitors to Santa Fe, on the "alarming extent" to which gambling prevailed there. *El Gringo*, 56-57.

77. Davis acted as Governor Meriwether's secretary at the time. Horn, *New Mexico's Troubled Years*, 65.

78. Residents of Rio Arriba need not have worried. Public education was defeated by popular referendum by a vote of 5,016 to 37. According to historian Howard Lamar, New Mexicans "saw in the American pressure for public schools a threat to religion, the likelihood of taxation, and an unwelcome process of Americanization." *Far Southwest*, 89.

79. Lamar notes: "Never having paid taxes, the Assembly showed a healthy reluctance to tax anyone but grog shops, gambling places, and American merchants—who in turn refused to pay up until the tax laws had been tested in the courts." Ibid.

80. Tom Bowler's mother lived in Missouri. The house, or hotel, to which Kingsbury refers is probably the Exchange, which Bowler was running. Hertzog, *La Fonda*, 6.

NOTES 81 AND 82 ON PAGE FOLLOWING

Letter no. 21, Kingsbury to Webb, Santa Fe, January 29, 1856

Herewith you will find a memo. for Groceries & also an order from T. F. Bowler. I have sent Messrs. Doan King & Co. by this mail Three Checks amt.g in all to $5,000.+, which they are to collect and place to our credit subject to your order.

Debus & Bunker complain bitterly of the Cloak Tassels, say they were badly moth eaten, and think they ought to be entitled to a discount. See if you can get anything off for them.

I have sent letters for you by this mail to Kent [CT], cont.g Trial Balance, &c. which I hope you received in due time.

My next will be sent to St. Louis.

[P.S.] The cry is that a great many goods will come out next year. I do not think there will be more than usual, however you can see what the mexicans are buying.[72]

Letter no. 22, Kingsbury to Webb, Santa Fe, January 30, 1856

I refer you to my other letters for business items, &c.

I hardly know what to write in the way of news. Your brother Mason & Odd Fellow H. L. Dickinson has gone to his long home. He was taken sick with a fever, lingered through it about 3 weeks, failing gradual[l]y.[73] He was buried with services of both orders, and a larg[e] crowd of Citizens. He was laid in the next grave to [Elias] Spiegelberg.[74]

Dick Owens[75] is very sick. It is doubtfull if he ever leaves his bed again.

Our town is full of Gamblers at present.[76] A large crowd has just ret'd from California, John Abell and others, all straingers to me. [W. W. H.] Davis has got along very cozy with the Legislature this winter.[77] They have passed more laws than at any previous session, among the rest a school tax for public schools, which is creating considerable excitement. Rio Ar[r]iba is opposed to it and say they will fight before they will pay it.[78] They have made no new revinue law. Merchants license remains the same as always.[79]

Tom has got his house full & must be making money. He will send his wife & child in by Connelly's train to spend the summer with his mother.[80] She is well & the baby is a cunning little thing.

Everything is quiet here except the Indians. They are stealing every day in the Rio Baja. Very little money in sirculation, and very little business doing. [James L.] Collins will go in in the next Mail, all the quarling [quarreling] spirits are at Washington.[81] We moove on very harmoniously at present. Thieves are hard pushed & make an occasion raise by br[e]aking in, they have not troubled us yet. Tip[82] & Beney's reputation is too well known, still I keep a sharp look out. I think we have the safest house in the place. Our house is a great protection as well as a great comfort. We still have Talisfer, Facunda and Blaza.[83] Mr. Weirick is a reliable man for the Store. We moove on very nicely together. Kate is well for her. I fear she never can be strong. Little George is in first rate health, never was better than at present. He is fat and looks well. He has cut no teeth yet. I think they will all come at once. He begins to eat quite well, and is certainly one of the best babies as far as trouble is conserned. I fear the Janduce [jaundice] which your wife had will cause little Jimmie's nose to be put out of joint one of these days.[84] Mrs. [Charles L.] Spencer has a fine little <u>Girl</u>! Mrs. [L. D.] Sturgis I am told has a bouncing boy.

Mr. Tolhurst has the Canaries. They are doing well, you must bring more seed for them when you come.

[Henry] Winslow[85] would like you to send him by mail 1 doz. of thoes letter balances such as you sent to Dr. [John] Byrne.

Geo. Estes says tell Webb <u>How</u>![86]

Letter no. 23, Kingsbury to Webb, Santa Fe, February 27, 1856

By last Mail I sent to Messrs. Doan King & Co. remittances amt.g to <u>$5,000.+</u> with request to collect the same and place to our credit subject to your order. I now send them $2,000+ now with the same instructions, if you should not need all of this money in St. Louis, you can instruct them to send whatever amt. you have over to Mr. Abbott to meet the Boston notes. I sent Mr. Abbott by last mail Drafts to the amt. of <u>$3101.97</u> to be used in canceling our first payments there. I shall send him nothing by this mail. Sales this month are $2,500.+ collections amt. to $4,000.+. I have rec'd the amt. of our claim against the [e]state of Elias Spiegelberg. We are also secured in the Saxel debt with interest, by taking back goods. It is the best I could do, and I think we are lucky to get it settled in this way. The balance of his creditors will have to wait his motion. I believe he is honest & would pay if he had the means but that I fear will be a long day off, as he is entirely broke up now. The goods we got are a pretty hard lot but I think it is better to have them than nothing. They are not here yet, will be here in a few days. I got [Henry] Winslow to receive them for us for which he had the politeness as a particular favor to charge 10% which I have paid. Upon the whole I think we are fortunate to get his note off of our books. It was a bad egg, and yet we will get something out of it.

By last mail I sent you a memo. about Groceries &c., and here with send duplicate <u>with a small</u> addition, fearing that the other may not have come to hand.

José [Hernández] has returned, and is heartily sick of Chihuahua. He comes with the determination to do whatever you may suggest for

81. James L. Collins was a Santa Fe merchant and editor of the *Santa Fe Weekly Gazette.* He was appointed superintendent of Indian affairs in 1857, when that office was separated from the office of territorial governor. Lamar, *Far Southwest*, 71, 88, 98.

82. Perhaps either William or Thomas Tipton of Las Vegas. Windham, ed., *New Mexico 1850 Territorial Census*, 3:122.

83. Kingsbury is referring to their servants.

84. Jimmie was Webb's son, James Henry Webb, born in Santa Fe on Dec. 22, 1854 (just a few weeks before George Kingsbury's birth). Webb, *Adventures*, 22.

85. An Albuquerque merchant and army agent throughout the 1850s. He was also, briefly, alcalde for Bernalillo County. Frazer, *Forts and Supplies*, 204.

86. George Estes was a merchant and a native of Virginia. 1850 NM Census, 347. He is mentioned regularly in the Kingsbury letters.

him. I have given him $50.00 on your a/c & started him for the States with Connelly's Train. He will meet you at West Port. Tom is sending his wife & child home. José will drive the Carriage, so that it will cost him nothing to go in.

March 3rd, 7 O' P.M. The Feby. Mail has not arrived up to the present moment, and of course I have no advises from you since my last letters. We have no news of the mail & the supposition is that it is lost. We learn from buffalo hunters who have come in that the snow is very heavy on the plains. That they suffered much from cold & storms, 6 of their party were frozen to death, lost about 260 head of animals & had to burn their wagons for fuel. This may account for the delay, others again think that the Indians have taken the party, but it is all supposition. We know nothing here. A relief party of Dragoons left Ft. Union on the 24th ult. to hunt for them.[87] We are in hopes to hear something from them soon. Nothing new here. We are all well, and hope you & family are the same.

Letter no. 24, Kingsbury to Webb, Santa Fe, March 28, 1856

I am in receipt of your letters of Jany. 15th and Feby. 10th. These are the only letters I got by this Mail. I am without advises from Mr. Messervy or from home. Katy got a letter so that we know they are all well there. I suppose the roads were so bad that the letters did not reach Ind. in time for our mail.

By last Mail I sent Messrs. Doan King & Co. $2,000, as follows, which I hope got there in time for you to use.

L. C. Eastin's draft no. 74 on Maj. D. H. Vinton		$700.00
ditto	82 ditto	1300.00
		$2,000.00

I now send them $5,500 viz
W. W. H. Davis Secty. check no. 20

	on Asst. Treasurer St. Louis	$4,000.00
War Warrant No. 10 part 7262 ditto		1,500.00
		$5,500.00

with request to collect the same & hold it subject to our order. I want you to use $5,000 of it for freight, make the most out of it you can, if you need any money you can take the other $500, if not use that also on a/c of freight.

I also send by this mail to Mr. Abbott remittances amt.g to $1887.50.

Business has been dull this month. I have sold only $2,300, Collections amount to $5,500. I hope you will be able to get the goods loaded & started in good season. I cannot say now that there will be a great demand for goods, but it is always best to get here as early as possible. The first trains always have an advantage over the later ones. I shall

87. The mail delay was most likely caused by the weather. Oliva states that at this time mail escorts were provided whenever the Post Office Department, the mail contractors, or the commander of Fort Union considered it a necessary precaution. In Feb. 1856, however, Lt. W. T. Magruder, Fort Union's commanding officer, recommended that they discontinue military escorts since the Indians were quiet. His recommendation was rejected. Oliva, *Soldiers*, 108.

look for you with the May Mail,[88] hope you will be able to come with it, at anyrate get here in advance of the train as early as you can. I think I shall have the house ready for you. Scofield is still at work, but it moves very slowly. The portals are not up but he says that the stuff is all got out ready to put up. I have succeeded in getting sufficient white lead to paint all the rooms & portals.

Prue [the Kingsbury cow] has not got a calf yet, & I am afraid she will not have one. If you are bringing your family, you had better buy a good Cow and send it with the train, if we should not want it we can always sell it without loss.[89]

I hope you have been very careful to keep your agent account correct so that I will have no trouble to put it in the books after you arrive. I hope the next Mail will bring me a copy of the Invoices so that I can enter them in the Invoice Books before I commence taking a/c stock. I send by the Mail conductor a small package of <u>Chile</u> for you to use on the road. You will find it at Boon's store.[90]

I am surprised that you did not write me what to do with José [Hernandez]. I did not need him here before the new goods arrived & sent him with Connelly to meet you at West Port. Should you have arrainged nothing for him in the States & want him with you untill you go in again, I think you could make him usefull here. If you have anything profitable for him there do not let him sacrifice it by bringing him back. If you deside to bring him he will be of great service to you on the road, should you come with the mail you can arrainge it for him to come with the Train at a small expense. I think his trip home was a good lesson. I feel more interested in him since he returned and would like to see him in a place where he would be contented & at the same time be doing well.

The Governor is expected by next Mail. I shall do my best to sell him every thing that we have got that he may want. Levi has received advises from Jake & Solomon which will prevent him from building.[91] He intends now to put up some warehouses in the rear and rent the stores. Geo. Estes rec'd your letter and wishes to be remembered to you. If you have time try and see Refuja [Refugia].[92] I think it would be gratifying to Tom. He is doing very well with his house, his table is constantly full. Several messes [boarding houses] have broken up and he gets all the bo[a]rders. Provisions & groceries are scarce & high. He laid in a large stock in the fall and is making money by it.

Kate rec'd your wife's letter, would answer it by this mail, but is very much pushed for time having many back letters she feels compel[l]ed to answer. We are very sorry to hear that little Jimmie has been sick.[93] Hope he has entirely recovered. Our little boy has no teeth yet. He has been very sick with them, but they have not made their appearance yet.

88. The Independence-to-Santa Fe mails were still monthly in 1856, although the four-year mail contract awarded to Jacob Hall in 1854 provided for additional compensation should he desire to increase the frequency to semi-monthly. Taylor, *First Mail West*, 39.

89. Webb brought neither his family nor a cow.

90. Albert Gallatin Boone and James Gillespie Hamilton were Indian traders in Westport. They owned a trading post in Council Grove that was run for a time by Seth M. Hays. Perhaps it is this store to which Kingsbury refers. Hays went on to own and operate his own store in Council Grove. Kathryn Gardner, "Conn and Hays," 34.

91. Kingsbury refers to the Spiegelbergs building plans, which he mentioned in a previous letter in 1855.

92. Tom Bowler's wife, who had gone to Missouri with their child to live with Tom's mother.

93. Webb wrote to Kingsbury, "Jimmie has been very sick. We considered him in a dangerous condition for some days. He is now well, begins to walk a few steps and try to talk a few words. Has four teeth." Cornwall Bridge, CT, Jan. 15, 1856, MHS.

5.

"The most trying time of my life"

Santa Fe to Salem, Spring 1856 to Autumn 1856

Letters 25–30

In late April 1856, Kingsbury dispatched surprising news to Webb. He had sent Kate and little George back to Salem while he remained in Santa Fe. Kingsbury addressed his letter to Webb at St. Louis for, as he knew, Webb himself was en route to New Mexico, traveling there without his family. Webb had decided in February, after considerable thought, to leave his wife and child in Connecticut. "It is a great task to take them across the plains," he told Kingsbury, "and Jimmie is getting his teeth and [is] subject to sick turns every few days."[1]

Teething had also made the Kingsbury's son ill, but Kingsbury had more serious reasons to send Kate and George across the plains. Kate was deeply depressed. Lillie Webb's departure in September 1855 may have added to her sense of isolation from family and friends, and the responsibility of raising a child suffering from a disability probably weighed heavily upon her. Although her health remained stable, New Mexico had not proven to be the tonic that Webb and others thought it would. "Kate is well for her," Kingsbury told Webb in January 1856. "I fear she can never be strong."[2]

Unwilling to suffer in silence, Kate expressed her unhappiness openly. Even the death of her canary seems to have caused her greater grief than might have been the case had she been home.[3] Her complaints brought her little sympathy from her brother William, who evinced no doubt about a woman's proper role or sentiments. In a letter to John Kingsbury, William explained that Kate should behave cheerfully, "without a murmur" of discontent:

> I am pained to hear that Kate complains so much of her <u>lot</u> & <u>misfortune</u>. She is the last person who ought to complain of her lot or afflictions & if she would contrast her condition with that of oth-

1. Webb to Kingsbury, Cornwall Bridge, CT, Jan. 15, 1856, MHS.
2. Kingsbury to Webb, Santa Fe, Jan. 30, 1856, MHS.
3. Webb to Kingsbury, Boston, Dec. 10, 1855, MHS.

ers, she would find cause for congratulation & thankfulness rather than from depression of spirits. With regard to the condition of your little boy—she has no right to complain or make herself unhappy. God has given him into your & her charge for a <u>good</u> & <u>wise</u> purpose & it is her duty—as a woman—as a mother—& as a Christian—to cheerfully, affectionately & pleasantly—& without a murmur—to cherish & <u>be proud</u> of <u>it</u>. Had it been my child—it would never have given me an hours unhappiness. My rule in life is "What we can't cure—we should cheerfully endure." Tell Kate that as hard as she thinks her lot is—that there are but few who have been as highly blessed as herself.[4]

The next month William Messervy sent another homily:

I am pleased to hear that Kate does so well in housekeeping and think that she is fortunate in having <u>pleasant work</u> enough to do to keep her constantly employed—most ladies are made unhappy from <u>idleness</u>—those who have constant pleasant employment are rarely unhappy and discontented not even when they have reason to be so.[5]

Notwithstanding her brother's admonitions and prescriptions, Kate Kingsbury's unhappiness in Santa Fe remained sufficiently acute that she and her husband agreed that she should return home to visit her family for the summer of 1856. John's business responsibilities, though, required him to remain in Santa Fe through the summer.

Kate left Santa Fe in the spring of 1856, apparently traveling as planned with W. W. H. Davis, one of New Mexico's key political figures. Davis, who was secretary to Gov. David Meriwether and would become acting governor of New Mexico in 1857, had written a manuscript on New Mexico that he would publish the following year and that would become a classic—*El Gringo: or, New Mexico and Her People*.[6] The party reached Westport, Missouri on May 22 and New York by mid-June, where Kate's brother William met her and accompanied her home to Salem.

Kate and George seem to have weathered the trip well, but on July 29, George died at her brother's home of what was described as an infection of the bowels.[7] Whatever the nature of his birth defect, he had been in "first-rate health" that spring, before he and Kate left Santa Fe, and his death must have come as a shock to the Kingsburys, although it apparently surprised few of their acquaintances.[8] Kate's illness, which may have become more severe before George's death, became accute.

John Kingsbury learned nothing of these tragedies until the fall, after he left Santa Fe for home. At the Arkansas River crossing of the Santa Fe Trail he met W. W. H. Davis, who was returning to Santa Fe and who told Kingsbury of his son's death and his wife's deteriorating health. At

4. Messervy to Kingsbury, Salem, Dec. 11, 1855, MHS.

5. Ibid., Jan. 8, 1856, MHS.

6 Horn, *New Mexico's Troubled Years*, 75.

7. A. G. Boone to J. J. Webb, Westport, May 22, 1856, MHS; and Messervy to Kingsbury, Salem, June 15, 1856, MHS. Messervy reported their "safe" return and mentioned no ill effects of travel, but if Kate and George were ill he may not have wanted to alarm Kingsbury with such news. George Kingsbury, record of death, 1856, vol. 102, p. 167, no. 247, Commonwealth of Massachusetts Archives Division.

8. Messervy to Webb, Salem, Aug. 16, 1856, MHS, mentions the date of George's death. Kingsbury to Webb, Santa Fe, Apr. 29, 1856, MHS, mentions George's good health. The cause of George's death is not clear to us. The day-to-day business correspondence of Webb and Kingsbury reveals the fact that his death did not come as a surprise to some people. Fred Tolhurst to Webb, Oct. 8, 1856, MHS: "I can scarcely say that I am surprised at the death of George Kingsbury but I deeply sympathize with them." D. D. Lore to Webb, Dec. 17, 1856, MHS: "I have heard that Mrs. Kingsbury's babe is dead. A blessing undoubtedly tho' the bereavement may be keenly felt by the parents."

St. Louis letters awaited Kingsbury including alarming news from Kate's brother, William. Kate's consumption, he reported, was so far advanced that "she will never be strong enough to return to New Mexico."[9] Neglecting some of his business at St. Louis, Kingsbury hurried home to find Kate "very sick." Only a return to Santa Fe, he believed, would prolong her life, but she seemed too weak to make the journey.

Through the remainder of the autumn Kingsbury busied himself with business. He made purchases to send to Webb in Santa Fe, collected or tried to collect debts, grieved over the death of his son, and kept watch over his dying wife, hoping perhaps for a miracle.

≈

Letter no. 25, Kingsbury to Webb, Santa Fe, April 29, 1856

I am in receipt of your letters of Feby. 20th & March 13th. I am very sorry to hear that little Jimmie is in so feeble health. I hope for your sake you have not been obliged to leave them behind. I have desided to send my wife and boy in under the care of Mr. [W. W. H.] Davis who will accompany them as far as New York. You will meet them with this mail. My object is that she may enjoy the summer at home & I am a little afraid to take her there at the commencement of one of those severe winters. By going in now she can make all her visits during warm weather & in the winter go south. They are both well now, the baby is very well for him. He has two teeth through at last. Scofield says you can depend on seeing the house finished when you get here. Mr. Tolhurst has been offered the chaplaincy at Ft. Fillmore & will probably accept. I shall do nothing about renting the house untill you arrive.[10]

We have had a very hard winter, it has been snowing & hailing fast today.

Our old friend Jerry Folger has gone to his long home.[11] He died at Ft. Union. His body was brought here and deposited in the Odd Fellows cemetery. The funeral started from Hugh Smith's[12] house, all the principal Citizens were present. Col. [John B.] Grayson[13] read the service at the grave, liquor wore him out finally.

I suppose you saw by the paper that Barkley is dead. He had the pluricy [pleurisy] & kil[l]ed himself by taking too strong medicine.[14] The Gov. has just returned. Pub[lic] Buildings will go on rapidly this season. The Military are making extensive improvements in the shape of a new warehouse & soldiers quarters. They also intend to build a new lot of Officers Quarters. Tom is doing first rate with his house, he has no opposition, his table is crowded with bo[a]rders. Nearly all the private messes are braking up for it is almost impossible to get any-

9. Messervy to Webb, Salem, Aug. 16, 1856, MHS.

10. In his letter of February 20, 1856 (MHS), Webb suggested that Kingsbury try to rent or sell Webb's portion of the house to Fred Tolhurst. Fort Fillmore was located six miles south of Mesilla, on the east bank of the Rio Grande. Frazer, *Forts and Supplies*, 64.

11. Jared W. Folger was the sutler at Fort Union. Emmett, *Fort Union*, 18.

12. Hugh N. Smith, an attorney from Kentucky, was mentioned in passing in Kingsbury's first letter.

13. Brevet Lieutenant Colonel John B. Grayson had been chief commissary officer for the department of New Mexico since 1855. Frazer, *Forts and Supplies*, 107. He was not popular with W. W. H. Davis who, in 1859, wrote Kingsbury asking, "Is Lt. Grayson as full of gas as ever? Whenever we have a western wind I wonder if he is not blowing on the Fonda corner." Davis to Kingsbury, Feb. 23, 1859, MHS. Nevertheless, he was certainly a colorful figure, as borne out by a careful notation Webb made in one of his notebooks: "Col. Grayson on the 9th day of April 1857 had for dinner a piece of bear meat which had been hanging in his larder since Oct. 19, 1856." Webb Memo Book, Box 8, Webb Papers, MHS.

14. Kingsbury is very likely referring to Alexander Barclay, the Englishman, who died in December 1855. Kingsbury's statement, if true, augments what little is known about the cause of death of this famous mountain man. Historian George Hammond, in his work on Barclay, had to rely on a letter written in November 1856 by Herbert George Yatman to Barclay's brother George, in which Yatman gives the cause of death as merely an "inflammation of bowels." Yatman himself pointed out, however, that this information was little better than hearsay, since it was a year old and had come to him indirectly. Hammond, *Alexander Barclay*, 233-34.

thing to eat. Onions are selling at 2 bitts a piece. Beck keeps his Billiard Table in the second story for the benefit of his friends. I do not think it pays. Prue has a fine calf. I shall let Tom have her untill you come; did you get the Chile which I sent you?

How does it go with fresh Buffalo meat?

By last mail I sent Messrs. Doan King & Co. $5,500.+ which I hope arrived in time for you to use. I also sent at the same time $1,887.50 to Mr. Abbott which I hope went through safe. I now send him Checks on the Asst. Treasurer of U.S. at New York for ($3,000) Three Thousand doll. Enclosed you will find copy of Trial Balance to April 1st. I have sold this month $1,800.+ collections are $3,500. They still continue to come in well, I think we can consider ourselves lucky in getting in our money so well this year. The Trial Balance certainly looks well. You will see there is only about $8,000 in it and of that I have rec'd this month $3,500. I am not satisfied with my sales but I really cannot do better. I never let a chance go by, customers are not to be found. The Merchants now are inclined to wait for new goods. Next month is the last of our fiscal year & I shall certainly do my best to get off what I can in order to leave as little stock on hand June 1st as possible.

I hope the goods started in good season & that no Ox train will arrive in advance of ours. I shall expect to see you with May mail. I am told grass is good & trains will come in early. It does not make so much difference about our goods getting here at an early period. The only thing is to be the first in. This goes a great ways in getting customers. I do not expect we can keep ahead of Mule trains, but I do hope ours will be the first Ox Train.

I can think of nothing more of importance try to get here yourself as soon as you can.

Letter no. 26, Kingsbury [in Kansas] to Webb [in Santa Fe], September 22, 1856

I reached Westport on Saturday the 20th at noon, safe & well, arrived here a little to[o] late to take the boat and will have to wait untill tomorrow Tuesday 23rd for the next one. The river is quite low. I suppose you have heard by Mr. [W. W. H.] Davis the sad news which he gave me at the Arkansas, the death of little George. Kate was quite sick & confined to her room. You can imagine my anxiety to get later word from her. I expect to find letters at Saint Louis. I met Sabine who is just from the East, says that he called upon your Father in company with Orin Spruce. Found the old gentleman & his wife well and said they passed a very pleasant day there.

You will see by the papers that the Army bill has passed.[15] There is still considerable excitement here about the Kansas difficulties. The

15. Kingsbury could be referring to a Congressional Act which was finally passed on March 3, 1857, appropriating $213,090.60 for militia service in 1854. *Legislative Blue Book*, "Resources of New Mexico," 25. Messervy, acting as governor in 1854, called out the Rio Arriba and San Miguel county militias to help protect the settlements from particularly troublesome Indians. Twitchell, *Leading Facts*, 2:299.

new Governor is at his post, it is hoped that he will succeed in quieting things there and be able to car[r]y out the law.[16]

Tell Gov. Meriwether that Mr. Majors[17] was not at home and I could not get the Pistol. I left word with their agent at Westport, who promises to send it to Santa Fe by the next Mail. If Gov. M. should not be at home when this mail gets there, inquire of the conductor for a package & receive it for him. Mr. [W. W. H.] Davis told me that he would be reap[p]ointed Mail agent.[18] This will suit us better than to have it ourselves, so I shall do nothing about getting it, and shall not go to Independence. I didn't meet Gilchrist[19] and do not know whether he has bought the mortice mashine or no, inquire of <u>Mr. McGlabe</u> and if Gilchrist does not bring one, there will be plenty of time for you to send me the order in time to come with the other State House goods.

I have settled with Riddlesbarger & Co. You will make the following entries on the Journal

J. Riddlesbarger & Co. Dr.
　　To Glasgow & Bros.
For amt. of our draft at sight
in their favor dated Kansas Sept. 22, 1856 <u>$99.27</u>
　　<u>(Ninety nine & 27/100)</u> dollars.
Merchandise Dr.
　　To J. Riddlesbarger & Co.
For Freight & charges on Sunday $7.50
Mdse. forwarded,　　　　　Seven & 50/100 dollars.
When the above entries are posted there will be a balance on our books to their credit of <u>$32.70</u>. They forwarded Aug. 31st by Yager & Briant's train the missing box of Siter Van Culen & Glass <u>No. 6</u>. and collected from them the above amt. of <u>$32.70</u> which you will find on the bill of Lading our charges, when you receive the box you will pay this amt. and charge it to Messrs. J. Riddlesbarger & Co., which will close their account.

Tell Mr. Davis that Riddlesbarger sent his box at the same time, <u>that is</u> by Yager & Briant's train Aug. 31st, 1856.

When I reach St. Louis I will close Glasgow & Bros. a/c and send you statement of same from there.

Tell [John S.] Watts[20] that [Alexander] Reynolds principal business in Santa Fe is to recover the property he formerly owned, and that he must watch him, see that he does not disturb the Exchange.[21]

Letter no. 27, Kingsbury to Webb, Salem, October 13, 1856

I wrote you last, dated at Kansas, containing a/c of settlement with J. Riddlesbarger & Co, which letter I hope you received. The letters which met me at St. Louis from my family were such that I felt

16. Kingsbury touches on a key issue in American history, "Bleeding Kansas." Organized as a state in 1854, Kansas entered the most tumultuous period of its history as a result of the slavery question. While most of Kansas's legal residents were anti slavery, thousands of pro slavery Missouri residents had crossed the border to vote in the elections of 1856, thereby setting up a government that condoned slavery and made speech or actions against it illegal. Violence and guerrilla warfare ensued until that fall, when the new territorial governor, to whom Kingsbury refers, negotiated peace.

17. Perhaps Alexander Majors, a prominent figure on the Santa Fe Trail at this time.

18. W. W. H. Davis was listed as agent for Hockaday & Hall. Taylor, *First Mail West*, 40, 195 n. 6.

19. We have been unable to determine whether Kingsbury refers to Duncan or James Gilchrist.

20. Judge John S. Watts, whom Kingsbury mentions regularly, was a native of Indiana involved in New Mexico government and politics for a number of years. He held the offices of associate justice of the Supreme Court of New Mexico, territorial delegate to Congress, and chief justice. Twitchell, *Leading Facts*, 2:392. Between appointments, he practiced law, and represented Messervy in various aspects of Messervy's New Mexico business. As Kingsbury's later letters reveal, however, he could be undependable and somewhat shady when it came to financial matters.

21. Watts had been called on by Messervy to defend his right to the Exchange Hotel against a claim made by Reynolds, Pino & Baca ("a piece of Mexican Rascality"). Messervy had instructed Kingsbury, in his letter of Oct. 15, 1855, to "let Judge Watts hold himself in readiness to defend my right & title in it." Messervy to Kingsbury, Salem, Oct. 15, 1855, MHS.

The history of ownership of the Exchange Hotel in the early territorial period is confusing and treated poorly in the one work on the subject (Hertzog, *La Fonda*). According to Messervy, who outlined it in the same letter to Kingsbury as well as a previous one written in July 1855, it was as follows: the hotel was purchased at a marshal's sale by Alexander Reynolds, who sold half to Runley & Ardinger's. Reynolds' other half was sold at marshal's sale to Beck, who in turn sold it to Messervy in March 1854 for $2,200. Beck's sale to Messervy is supported by the Santa Fe County Records, Deed Book A, 351, NMSRCA. Runley & Ardinger's half was purchased at marshal's sale by Messervy, giving him sole ownership. Messervy to Kingsbury, Salem, July 15, 1855, and Oct. 15, 1855, MHS. Messervy rented the Exchange to Tom Bowler for $100 a month. Rent Accounts Ledger, Box 8, Webb Papers, MHS.

Messervy did not trust Reynolds, and wrote of him, "When Smith was the agent of Beck and got hold of the property [the Exchange] on a suit brought by Beck against Reynolds, Reynolds knowing that he was behindhand with the government and others—or in other words insolvent, made a fraudulent conveyance to his infant children for the purpose of fraudulent concealment." Messervy to Webb, Salem, May 16, 1857, MHS.

compel[l]ed to come here as soon as possible, for this reason I did not spend quite as much time and attention to things in St. Louis as I had intended to, however I think I done all that was really necessary there. Gov. Meriwether requested me to get a written Statement from the man that you had previously refer[r]ed Mr. Davis to,—(the one that was to be [Lipman] Meyers partner in the Ind. trade). I wish you would excuse me to the Gov. and tell him I really had not time to attend to it. On my way home I stop[p]ed at Cornwall Bridge left there the $200 and the small package which you sent for your wife. I was very sorry not to meet her. Mr. Frink & family treated me with every attention. I stayed with them one night and arrived at Salem on the 3rd inst.—found Kate as my letters had indicated very sick. She is on her feet & able to move about the house but that is all. Her cough is very troublesome and has got a strong hold upon her. I have had a long consultation with her physician but could get no encouragement from him. He thinks her lungs are past cure. All that remains for me to do is to get her back again to Santa Fe if possible. You know I have intended to take her south to spend the winter, but in her present condition it is out of the question to think of starting with her. If she gets stronger I may travel with her but I fear she will not be able to stand the fatigue of a journey this winter. Since I have been with her I think she has brightened up some and if I can keep her spirits up, I have strong hope that she may be able to start with me in the spring. At present I can make no calculation on her.

Mr. Messervy has got into his new house. It is finished and furnished in the very best manner, it is a perfect little palace.[22]

Mr. Thomas M[esservy?] will start in a few days on a whaleing voiage [voyage]. I have desided to keep up the old homestead this winter and have Eliza Ann with us.[23] Facunda is in the kitchen and we will get along nicely. Kate will have more comforts here than I could supply her in any other place. I have sent a line to your wife requesting her to make us a visit, whenever it will suit her best, we are expecting her sometime this month. We are anticipating a pleasant time with her and little Jimmie.

You will probably get by this Mail stage Two boxes, which I sent from St. Louis by express to care of Hockaday & Hall marked with our address for them to forward. One is for [Vincente] St. Vrain, the other for J. M. Hunt. Tell Hunt that I hope the things I selected will suit him. I did not quite fill his order. The things that I sent over run the money he furnished as you will see by the inclosed bill $15.97, this sum with whatever expense is advanced for forwarding he must pay without delay as we charge him nothing for our trouble. Tell Vincente [*sic*] that I hope the seals will suit. I was compel[l]ed to get a separate one for each county, and the price of the whole is within his limit. Tell him by rolling the paper up under the arm of the press he can place

22. After returning to the East, Messervy had searched for a house in which he and his wife, who was expecting a child, could set up their home. He had purchased one in Boston before discovering that his wife preferred to live in Salem. Messervy to Kingsbury, Salem, Jan. 13, 1855, MHS. He apparently decided to build a new house in Salem.

23. Eliza Ann was Kate's sister. By "old homestead" Kingsbury might have meant the Messervy home in Salem, at 65 Mill Street. The year before William Messervy had outlined his domestic arrangements in a letter to Kingsbury: "Eliza Ann will keep house where she is. She will occupy one half of the house, and the other half will be let to some good family . . ., the rent of which will be given to Eliza Ann. I shall probably purchase Thomas and John's [Messervy's brothers] part of the house so as to keep the estate in such a way as to secure a home for Eliza Ann as long as she lives." Messervy to Kingsbury, Salem, Jan. 13, 1855, MHS. Messervy himself had moved his own family into a new residence at 91 Lafayette. Salem City Directories, 1855 and 1857.

the seal upon any part of a sheet of paper.[24] I could not find a copy of the Book he wanted. You will collect from him the bill of $29. and whatever charges you pay for forwarding. I sent by mail to our house the patterns for Debus & Bunker. I paid for them in St. Louis $150 also for Postage on same

 42     $1.92

I could learn of no fall train for Santa Fe—everything had started before I got in, so I did not purchase the things for Mr. Gruber. Enquire of him if he would like for me to fill the order and bring the thing out with our goods in the Spring. Or if he would prefer to make a new and more complete order for me to fill in the Spring.

Mr. Abbott has received & collected the Treasury warrant $750. sent him Aug. 25th—everything in the shape of goods that I have looked at up to the present is high. Belchers Clarified Sugar is selling in St. Louis at 11 cents. Mr. Abbott says that he thinks we will not be able to get Brogans for less than 80 cents.

Should James Gray ask about the notes he gave me to collect, tell him I have had no time to do anything with them yet.

I hope the detention in passing the army bill did not injure things in New Mexico.[25]

I met Otero in St. Louis.[26] He says he will be able to get almost anything that he will ask at Washington. He only asks now for the people of the Territory to make their wants known to him. He will not overlook the necessary appropriations. He intends to get the Office of Gov. & Supt. of Ind. Affs. separated.[27] If it is done I suggested to him Steck for Supt. of Ind.[28] He wants to get Messervy's Volunteers paid off, but says in the present form they will not pass.[29] I do not understand what he wants done. I mentioned the probability of your being in the legislature & he said he would write you on the subject.[30] I think the Gov. could put him on the right track to get these claims allowed.

I will get William [Messervy] to interest himself with it soon as he gets stronger. While inspecting a public building in Salem (he was one of the committe[e]) he fell through a staging a distance of about 10 feet and hurt his head pretty bad—so as to make him insensible & partly deranged. He has been confined to the house about two weeks but is now better & just getting about again. We were all very anxious about him, but now he is so much better that we think it will not be a permanent injury to him, it will be, however, a long time before he fully recovers.

Politics are running high everything is excitement. Fremont is much stronger in the east than I expected. It is very uncertain yet who will be the next President.[31]

I gave the order for the State House Irons to a good house in St. Louis.[32] They will be right and ready when we want them. Mr. King

24. The oldest son of famed fur trader and New Mexico entreprenuer Ceran St. Vrain, Vincente St. Vrain worked as a clerk according to the Santa Fe census of 1850; in 1862 he was named an assessor for the internal revenue for New Mexico. Hafen, ed., *Mountain Men*, 5:300 n. 11; *Legislative Blue Book*, 124.

25. Congress finally passed the appropriation bill in the spring of 1857. See note 15.

26. Miguel A. Otero, New Mexico's territorial delegate to Congress, 1855-1861.

27. The offices of governor and superintendent of Indian affairs were combined until 1857. Lamar, *Far Southwest*, 98.

28. Kingsbury's suggestion to Otero of making Dr. Michael Steck superintendent of Indian affairs was a good one since Steck had had experience serving as Indian agent to the Utahs and Jicarillas. He was commended in a newspaper editorial in 1853, which stated: "We believe that Doctor Steck has done more since he has been in the service than all the other agents that have been appointed for the Territory." *Santa Fe Weekly Gazette*, Feb. 19, 1853. In 1863 Steck followed James L. Collins in the office of superintendent of Indian affairs. *Legislative Blue Book*, 122.

29. Kingsbury is referring to the militia of Rio Arriba and San Miguel counties that Messervy called out against the Indians while he acted as governor in 1854. Twitchell, *Leading Facts*, 299.

30. In 1856, Webb was elected to the lower house of the New Mexico Assembly as one of the four representatives of Santa Fe County. He served for one year. Webb, *Adventures*, 35.

31. In the north Democrat James Buchanan's chief opponent was Republican John C. Frémont; in the south Buchanan faced the strongest competition from the Whigs' choice, Millard Fillmore.

32. We have construed Kingsbury's phrase "state house irons" to mean some kind of ornamental ironwork or hardware intended for use in the statehouse then under construction. The story of these goods constitutes an ongoing saga in his letters.

introduced me to the house. It is <u>Gaty McCune & Co</u>. I am not certain that I have put the firm down right as I did not take their card, but you know the house. We were there several times together when we were looking for a wheel for the church bell. They could not fix the price exactly but said it would not be far from 12 or 12 ½ cents per pound. I hope you will or have already sent me full orders about goods to purchase.

P.S. I shall ship our goods to care of Kirkman & Luke at St. Louis, and try them this season. They are a regular forwarding house, and spoken very highly of by Mr. King.

Enclosed is entries that will close Glasgow & Bros. a/c. The Knives I think will suit Davis for the Legislature, if not we can sell them. He will pay $24 for them if they suit without saying a word.

Letter no. 28, Kingsbury to Webb, Salem, November 12, 1856

I return many thanks for your very kind sympathies in my behalf, words cannot express what I felt on reading you kind letter for I know it is all sincere, & right from your heart. I can only hope you may never be placed under like circumstances.[33] It is indeed trying to me, I do not know what to do or how to act, I want to do my duty and what is right, but the thing is to know what that is. At presant I cannot look far enough ahead to take a single step. This is certainly the most trying time of my life. I have lost many kind friends, my mother was at last taken which I felt was hard to bear, & now my little boy. I have been reconsiled to all and was willing to feel & say it was for the best, but now to think for a moment that I must give up my wife, the dearest and nearest tye on earth, I cannot and will not admit it to myself. She is certainly far from well, but I must hope that she will yet be able to return in the spring with me. I cannot say she is any better than when I last wrote, but I think she is a little stronger. She is still up and about the house, walks out a short distance pleasant days, her cough is very troublesome, and she has some night sweats but they are not regular, upon the whole she appears to me to be mending. The disease every one knows is flattering and I may be deseived.[34] I do not think it would be advisable to go south with her now, if she does not have a set back I may start with her, but I would like to have her stronger first.[35] Our Physician think her in the consumption and past cure. Still if she is able to return to Santa Fe she may last a long time yet. He recommends her to go there, and of course all my energies will be exerted to take her. The thing is will she be able to stand to journey.

Your wife and boy are now in Salem. We have had the pleasure of their company since last Friday. They will remain several days yet. Today they went up to Williams house to stay a day or two.[36] We have

33. Unfortunately, Kingsbury's hope for Webb did not come true. Lillie Webb died in 1861 after a prolonged illness involving a tumor. See chapter 15.

34. The characteristic appearance of those afflicted with tuberculosis included large, bright eyes, a pale, thin face with hollow, flushed cheeks, and full lips. The "look" became fashionable in the nineteenth century, perhaps because so many people suffered from the disease (in 1880 it was the cause of twelve out of every hundred deaths in the United States alone), or perhaps because of the number of its famous "creative" victims, such as Keats, Shelley, Elizabeth Barrett Browning, and the Bronte sisters. René Dubois and Jean Dubois, *The White Plague: Tuberculosis, Man, and Society* (New Brunswick: Rutgers University, 1987), 44-46.

35. Webb had written Messervy that Dr. De León in Santa Fe suggested that Kate take a trip south: "He recommended her to go up to St. Johns River to Palatka or further in the interior of Fla. Says she should by no means go to St. Augustine but to the middle [of] Florida." Sept. 22, 1856, MHS.

36. Kingsbury is probably referring to William Messervy's house.

had a delightfull visit with them. Oh! what a boy, you may well be proud of him. Yes, you have every thing to live for & I hope you may long live and that they may be spaired to you. You may rest assured I will do all in my power to have you once more united to them. I have told your wife to make no change or calculation for the present about going out. I still hope it will be so ordered that it will be unnecessary. It is yet to[o] early to make any change or deside upon what we are to do, a month or two may make a desided change, and the way may be made more clear. I am compel[l]ed to look upon every thing here as uncertain, and I hesitate to make a single step for the future, for the present I can only thank you for your willingness to sacrifice every wish & inclination for me at this trying time. While I live it will never be forgotten.

P.S. Mr. Messervy is much better & says that he has entirely recovered from his fall, but he still looks feeble, and is troubled with severe head aches. His family are well, he rec'd your letter and will probably answer it by this mail.

Please remember me to all enquiring friends. Tell Clift that Facunda is well, but very lonesome. She feels the loss of George very much. She has been very happy since your wife came and is perfectly delighted with Jimmie. She is a good faithfull girl.

Letter no. 29, Kingsbury to Webb, Salem, November 12, 1856

I am in receipt of yours of Sept. 20th, with deed to Genl. [John] Garland[37] for the Brewery property which I have completed, and herewith return the same.

All the drafts which I brought in with me have been paid except the draft for $162.50 from Dodge. This has been sent on for collection but I have no return from it yet. Your last remittances (those which left Santa Fe Oct. 1st) I am holding to purchase shoes with. Meyer's draft was protested, and Mr. Abbott returns it to you by this mail. The proceeds of Davis check for $2,000 has been rec'd here. On a/c of the high price of leather all kinds of Boots & Shoes are scarce and high. Sole leather is now worth 30 cents a lb. and will probably go up. I have bought about $600 in Childrens Shoes, which is all that I could find in the way of Shoes up to the present that would do for us. I have attended several auctions. Prices range very high. I think I shall Order most of our shoes through Mr. Abbott. I have not seen a Brogan sell at auction under 85 cents. Mr. A. thinks he can get them for us at 80 cents which is as low as they can be bought this season. I have done nothing yet except look about, everything looks high. Cottons have advanced 1 cent since you purchased. I cannot now duplicate your bills of domestics, blue prints, and staple goods less than ¾ to ½ cents advance. It is not confined to cottons & leathers alone, but everything, woolens, silks

37. Gen. John Garland was in command of the Department of New Mexico from 1853 to 1858. Frazer compared him favorably to his predecessor, General Sumner: "He was less impressed by his own position, less concerned with minutia, and more inclined to delegate authority to subordinates. In his relations with representatives of the civil government he was generally cooperative, and in his dealings with civilians he was more often conciliatory than peremptory. As a result his period of commands was less fraught with the minor crises that had marked Sumner's tenure." *Forts and Supplies,* 87-88.

&c and of course fancy goods[38] go up with all staples. I shall be in no hurry about buying. I do not think goods can be any higher. Still they may go up. Those who have them for sale, say they are bound to go up. I write this so that you may not be afraid to hold our staple goods. Of course get off all the trash and old stock, but do not push staple goods. If they will not pay a fair or good profit, we will make money by keeping them over. They cannot be duplicated this year at same prices and we ought to get the advantage of the rise. The prices that is asked for goods here makes me quite timid. I begin to think money is not worth what it formerly was. It certainly will not buy as much. I shall keep our bills within reasonable amounts and be very careful not to "overcrop" ourselves with goods at the present prices. I intend to get a good stock of Boots & Shoes. Prices are high, still I think there will be room for a profit on them, and I think they will be scarce & in demand next spring. No one can take them out at less prices than we will.

I am pleased to see sales & collections keep up. I feel confident that you will make good sales. I want you to remit all the money you can for new purchases and get it here early, but do not cramp yourself. You will of course be limited by collections.

Don't pay cash for drafts on the departments at Washington if you can get any other. They are the most expensive for us. It costs ½ % for collection & it takes from 3 to 6 weeks to get returns. They take their own time & there is no way to hurry them through. New York are best, and St. Louis next. I am pleased to hear that you found a <u>cash</u> customer for the brewery; we got out of that affair <u>well</u>.

What was done with Peter Saxel's suit against us? Your letter does not mention it. I shall expect the memo. you speak of sending for odd goods. I hope you will think to mention the number of Bales left on hand of Manta & Lienzo, Blue Prints &c &c so that I can have some guide to purchase by. We have had very little profit on Manta & Lienzo the last year or two. I would like to see them scarce once. I really do not feel like buying at present prices. You will find in the papers all the news. Buchanan is elected without doubt, the returns are not all here yet in correct form and the Republicans are not willing to give up yet.[39] This mail will bring you much later news from the States than I can write.

Letter no. 30, Kingsbury to Webb, Salem, December 11, 1856

I am in receipt of yours [illegible] 31st, with Trial Balance Sheet, which I am delighted to see. It was unexpected and a pleasant surprise. It looks very well. I think from present appearances you will be satisfied with the year's business. <u>Small and safe</u> sales pay best in the end.

Your letters to Mr. Abbott with the draft amt.g to $5125.+ have been duly received. Our notes are all discounted in Bank and I cannot get

38. Fancy goods included "shaving soap, wash balls, hooks and eyes, face powders, vermillion, hair pins, bead bracelets, necklaces, finger rings, ear bobs, satin beads, buck gloves, white gloves, men's gloves, metal vest buttons, pearl buttons, coat buttons, military buttons, women's cotton hose, women's open-work hose, ladies' silk hose, worsted cord, piping cord, needles, black silk thread, white thread, crayon, India ink, ribbons, wax, matches, ivory combs, side combs, gold stars, silver stars, shoe laces, lamp wicks, wide lace, muslin dresses, silk dresses, fancy dresses, blue crepe shawl, feathers, cotton handkerchiefs, turkey red handkerchiefs, pink saucers, wool comforts, cologne, hair oil, case bonnets, and silk suspenders." Bieber, *Papers of James J. Webb*, 301.

39. James Buchanan, the democratic nominee, won the election of 1856, defeating Millard Fillmore, the Whig nominee, and John C. Frémont, the choice of the newly formed Republican party.

them to discount. Mr. Abbott will allow us 6% interest on the amt. in his hands untill our paper matures.

I have bought nothing yet, except shoes, most of which I have ordered through Mr. Abbott. They will cost more than we ever paid before, but I am satisfied that no one can get them at less prices, and owing to the high prices, the probability is that few will be taken out. Brogans we get at 78 cents cash net. They are now worth 85 cents. This is for as poor a shoe as will do to take to Santa Fe. There is so few Boots & Shoes in the market that they are all bought up clean at private sale. Nothing left for Auction. There has not been more than 3 or 4 Auction Sales in Pearl St. up to the present. I think there may be some along in January, which I shall watch closely. At anyrate I shall get a good & well assorted stock. I have seen no Prints yet that I could buy. I shall get our Hardware, Liquors[40] & heavy goods ready to start by the way of New Orleans, about the middle of January. The balance that I purchase here, I shall send by Rail road and want to start them by the end of Feby. I shall try to keep the purchases inside of the amt. you mention in your letter.

Miguel Cordova still owes the balance of $33.75, which he will not deny. When I settled with him I gave him up one note which was paid in full. He left knowing there was still a balance due of the above amt. which he agreed to send us by the first chance after he got home. Up to the time I left, we heard nothing from him, & of course he still owes it. You will find the note in the safe and the credits on the Ledger are full and correct. I see on the Balance Sheet a/c against James Gray, don't let him get anything on the strength of the papers which he gave me to collect. They are not worth one cent.

Tell [James] Gray after considerable trouble and expense of about five dollars, I found his man Thompson and am satisfied that he has got nothing. He is a thread bare gentleman, living on a small income which has been left to his children, but in such a way that he has no control whatever over the principal. The income is barely enough to keep the family above want. Mr. Gray can set his drafts down as worthless. I have done all that is possible with them, & have collected nothing.

Try to collect Labadi[e]'s a/c.[41] Push him pretty hard. Don't allow him to increase it. He will probably be one of the first removals.

You must be in good luck, and ought not complain when you can close up such a/cs as Ashurst, Eaton &c. I am pleased that B. has pledged himself to you, against all play. I hope it is in such a way as not to be broken. I hope for his sake & family that he will feel the importance of keeping it faithfully.

I have rec.d one letter from your wife since she was here. They arrived home safe & well. You will probably get later dates from them

40. Liquors consisted of "champagne, whiskey, fine whiskey, peach brandy, cherry brandy, wild cherry brandy, dark brandy, New York brandy, common cordial, madeira wine, port wine, schnapps, punch essence, and gin." Bieber, *Papers of James J. Webb*, 302.

41. Lorenzo Labadie was the Indian agent at Ft. Sumner in 1865. Lamar, *Far Southwest*, 125.

than I have. I never saw your wife looking better than when she was here. She appeared to be quite happy.

With regard to Kate's health I am sorry to say that I am as much in the dark as when I last wrote. She is certainly no better. Her cough is still very troublesome and in addition she is now confined to her chamber & most of the time to her bed with Rheumatism. This however we hope is nothing permanent & may soon be releaved. But it is very unfortunate as it deprives her the privilege of taking fresh air, which is quite important in keeping up her appetite. In losing her appetite she will of course lose what little strength she had gained. I felt at times quite encouraged but now, I do not know what to hope for. I fear every change & look with dread for the next. It is now two weeks since she was out. She is in as good spirits as can be expected. The weather is pleasant & cold for this season of the year. The cold does not appear to effect her unpleasantly. Mr. Messervy rec.d your letter. He is well. His little girl has frequent ill turns.[42] The rest are well.

42. In the letter Messervy wrote to Kingsbury, in which he offered Kingsbury consolation on the birth of George, Messervy said of his own daughter, apparently named Maria: "I feel that I love my little Girl much more than if she had been perfect in her physical development. The extra claim her helplessness has upon me causes me the more to love and protect her—such will be the case with you and yours." Messervy to Kingsbury, Salem, Mar. 13, 1855, MHS.

6.

"She may improve on the road"

Salem to Santa Fe, Winter and Spring 1857

Letters 31–35

The new year in Salem began as the old one had ended for John Kingsbury. He immersed himself in details of business and suffered such "anxiety for Kate that I am almost beside myself."[1] Kingsbury planned to return to Santa Fe that spring with or without Kate, for he had a strong sense of his "duty" to Webb, who probably wanted Kingsbury to relieve him so he could return home to his family. If Kate remained at Salem, Kingsbury believed she would die in the warm, humid summer months ahead. Dry Santa Fe seemed her only chance to prolong her life, but she might be too weak to make the trip. As her brother, William, predicted gloomily: "Mr. Kingsbury will, so he informs me, leave for Santa Fe about the first of March. My own opinion is he will be obliged to leave Kate behind him and probably forever."[2]

But John Kingsbury was not obliged to leave his wife behind. Gamely, she set out on the long journey accompanied by her sister, Eliza Ann Messervy. The two were apparently very close. There had been talk of Eliza Ann joining Kate on her first trip to Santa Fe, three years before, but she had decided to stay in Salem. As Webb put it, Eliza Ann and Mrs. Messervy[3] had "the greatest horror of that country, and the strongest attachment to home of any two persons I ever met."[4]

Traveling by train and boat, the Kingsburys' party made it to St. Louis, where Kingsbury bought a carriage to take Kate across the plains. Then, they continued to Westport where their merchandise would be loaded onto wagons and they would join one of the season's first caravans to Santa Fe. They reached Westport in late April, but little rain had fallen and winter had lingered. Until the prairie grasses greened up enough to support the animals, they would be delayed. Kate remained "very weak & feeble, but anxious to be on the plains," Kingsbury told Webb. "It is almost a mirical that she has kept up so well this far."[5]

After a wait of a few weeks, they set out across Kansas, riding slowly in a mule-drawn carriage across the plains. Kate's health did

1. Kingsbury to Webb, Salem, Feb. 15, 1857, MHS.
2. Messervy to Webb, Salem, Dec. 10, 1856, MHS.
3. The Mrs. Messervy referred to here is probably the wife of William S. Messervy, since the 1850 census shows no wife for William Messervy, Sr., aged seventy, living in that same household. 1850 Essex County, MA Census, 141.
4. Webb to Kingsbury, Cornwall Bridge, CT, Oct. 5, 1853, MHS. See, too, Messervy to Kingsbury, Santa Fe, Jan. 29, 1854, MHS.
5. Kingsbury to Webb, West Port, Apr. 29, 1857, MHS.

not improve as her husband hoped it would, but she remained stable. Suddenly, on the evening of June 4, she began to suffer severe shortness of breath, and she died at dawn the following day at the Lower Arkansas River Crossing of the Santa Fe Trail, near present-day Dodge City, Kansas. (Crossing that same river, less than a year before, John Kingsbury had first received the news of his son's death).[6]

Eleven days after her death, late in the evening of June 16, John Kingsbury, Eliza Ann Messervy, and two companions rode into Santa Fe with Kate Kingsbury's body in a metal coffin that Kingsbury had packed secretly in one of the trade wagons. The small party had traveled fast. From the Arkansas Crossing, they had covered some 375 miles, averaging thirty-four miles a day.[7] James Webb met them in Santa Fe and heard the heart-wrenching story of Kate's last hours, a story that he reported in moving detail to his wife, Lillie. In this chapter, we have reproduced Webb's description of Kate's death, much of which must have come from the lips of her bereaved widower.

The remains of most of those westering Americans who died on overland trails lie in modest graves near the site of their deaths,[8] but John Kingsbury took his wife's body home to the community where they had shared their first years of married life. On June 18, 1857, she was laid to rest in the cemetery of the Independent Order of Odd Fellows, to which Kingsbury belonged (the cemetery stood at the site of the present Scottish Rite Cathedral in downtown Santa Fe).[9] A group of friends and acquaintances attended the burial service and the *Santa Fe Weekly Gazette* published a lengthy, highly sentimental obituary two days later, which we have reprinted in this chapter.

Eight months after Kate's funeral, John Kingsbury dispatched an order to merchants in the East for "a neat white marble grave stone, with a base stone to set it in, & [a] small foot stone." He asked that the stone be inscribed "in distinct letters" with a simple message that stressed salvation (this in contrast to the lugubrious warnings of eternal damnation such as characterized gravestones of an earlier era):[10]

Mrs. Kate L. Kingsbury
Died June 5th, 1857
at the crossing of Arkansas River
Aged 30 years.
Blessed are the Dead which die in the Lord.

To enclose the gravesite, Kingsbury also ordered an iron fence, eight by five feet.[11] The gravestone and the fence were shipped to New Mexico over the Santa Fe Trail with Webb's and Kingsbury's other merchandise and placed on Kate Kingsbury's grave. A half century later, the gravestone, along with the rest of the Odd Fellows Cemetery, was moved to a new location on Cerrillos Road. There, in a grove of small trees, the

6. Kingsbury probably did not cross at the identical place when he journeyed to Salem in 1856. It seems likely that he used the more common Middle Crossing at present-day Cimarron, Kansas. According to her obituary in the *Santa Fe Weekly Gazette*, Kate died downriver at the Lower Crossing. That spot is about fourteen miles east of Dodge City, at present-day Ford, Kansas. Simmons, *Following the Santa Fe Trail*, 115-16.

7. Gregg, *Commerce*, 217. See, too, the map on the endpapers of Brown, *The Santa Fe Trail*.

8. Jones, *Health-Seekers*, 85; Unruh, *Plains Across*, 408-9.

9. Meyer, "100 Years of Area History," 6.

10. Karen Halttunen, *Confidence Men and Painted Women: A Study of Middle-class Culture in America, 1830-1870* (New Haven: Yale University Press, 1982), 125-26; James J. Farrell, *Inventing the American Way of Death, 1830-1920* (Philadelphia: Temple University Press, 1980), 103.

11. Kingsbury to Webb, Santa Fe, Feb. 28, 1858, MHS.

inscription on Kate's neglected and badly worn grave marker can still be read today.[12]

~

Letter no. 31, Kingsbury to Webb, Salem, January 12, 1857

(Direct the letters you send March 1st to St. Louis care of Doan King &C. I will get them there.)

I am in receipt of yours of Nov. 24th with small book of memorandum and shall be governed by it as near as possible. It came to[o] late for me to make any change in shoes, having given all my orders before. The only thing I would wish to change is Brogans. I have ordered 40 cases same as you had last year which is perhaps more than is nessesary, but upon the whole I think it is best to bring them all our for I feel quite sure owing to the high price they will be very scarce in our market, and we may make a good run with them.

I am pleased with your purchase of Groceries. I am sure they will pay. Sugar will not be had at St. Louis less than 12 cents in the Spring. It may be more. I wish you to send me complete memo. about Groceries to buy in St. Louis, Articles and quantity. I do not fear being cramped by your Santa Fe purchases. We have ample means, only keep a sharp eye on collections. It will be profitable whether we need the money or not. I shall be very careful in purchases and try to keep the amt. within your limit. I have bought all our heavy goods and shall ship them this week by way of N.O. [New Orleans]. Have not got the bills yet & do not know the amt. You will place many with Doan King & Co. to meet freights & expenses. I shall send all our goods to Kirkman & Luke at St. Louis, a commission house recommended by Mr. King. I have bought 100 Gross best Boston matches at 80 cents New York style round wood boxes. I have found it difficult to get good cigars, but have finally got such as I think will suit Tom. Our Liquors will be first rate, at a little higher cost than last year. I have ordered 10 bales of Manta same article as last year. It now costs 8 cents, for fine Lienzo I have ordered the same we had two years since at 10 ¾, now costs 11 cents. This is the best goods for the money that I have seen. I have bought no prints yet. If I can only get these right, I have no fear about other goods.

Your sales & collections keep up very fair so far, and remittances have been all that I could expect. I can use all you send but I do not need much.

I sent by this mail to Mr. [David V.] Whiting a ring which I have made to his orders. It cost $17.+ (Seventeen). He will probably pay you the amt. and you can place it to the Cr. of my agt. a/c.

I have not met with any one that I would risk to take out with me. If I should find one that I think will do I will bring him, but I think it

12. The gravestone is in the Independent Order of Odd Fellows Cemetery on Cerrillos Road, adjacent to Fairview Cemetery. Meyer, "100 Years of Area History," 6.

rather uncertain. Keep Mr. Weirick if he is willing to remain. It will be hard to find one to fill his place. He understands the Language & our business, and is more valuable to us than any strainger.

Mr. Messervy has not heard from Judge [John S.] Watts yet. He [Messervy] has been reelected Mayor. Rec.d about ⅔ of all the vote polled. Is now very busy with matters of his office, and will not be able to write you this mail.

They had a fine little boy arrive on the 2nd inst. Mother and son getting along nicely. Maria has frequent ill turns, caused by water overflowing the brain. They have but little to encourage them about her remaining long here.[13]

You cannot tell what a great loss it is to us that little George is taken away. Even imperfect as he was, we feel it deeply. It makes a void which nothing can fill. I think it has much weight upon Kate. She is now about the house again. I think she is as well as when your wife was here. If the weather would permit I think it would be safe for her to go out as she did then. I cannot complain of the weather, so far it has been a favorable for her as we can expect at this season of the year.

I thank you for your kind wishes in her behalf. You have certainly been very kind. I cannot however give up the idea but that she will be able to start with me, and that we will reach Santa Fe together. I am so fully of this opinion that I do not think it advisable for you to make any preparation for your wife to come. It is true Kate is very feeble & it is uncertain what change may occur, but if possible I wish to take her back & am making all calculations <u>now</u> to that effect. Should it prove impossible for her to go, then I feel that it will be my duty to go without her. I shall not give up untill the last moment. If she has nothing to put her back I think there is a chance for her yet.

Letter no. 32, Kingsbury to Webb, Boston, January 17, 1856

I have sent you a letter at the usual time this month. I send this that you may know that the Drafts of Davis $500 and Deavenport $625, payable Jany. 1st are collected. I shall get our heavy goods off probably on the 19th

Spiegelberg was here this week. They bought nothing in Boston but shoes. Their Brogans I understand cost them 82 ½ cents <u>net cash</u>. Seligman & Cleaver have also ordered some shoes from here about <u>$2,000</u>. Since my last I have found some prints that I have ventured to buy 20 bales at 8 and 8 ½ cents. I think I shall be able to get a very pretty stock. Nothing new. Kate is about the same. The rest are all well.

[P.S.] I have subscribed for the Boston Weekly Post, called the <u>Statesman</u> which you will receive.

13. Maria, William Messervy's daughter, suffered from some kind of defect and did not live to adulthood. Messervy, *Généalogie*, n.p. See note in chapter 5.

Letter no. 33, Kingsbury to Webb, Salem, February 15, 1857

Dear Sir, Your letter of Dec. 29th did not reach me untill the 12th inst. Your letter at same time to Mr. Abbott cont.g drafts amt.g to $9,943.85 has been rec.d and acknowledged by him, also the letter with 6 Land Warrants, which were sold at 98 cents per acre (say $940.80). This is the highest price in Boston market for them now. They are continually raising & falling. I hope [John] Dold will be satisfied. The funds you have sent will be ample for all immediate purposes, and will make me quite easy. Estimate for Notes Payable 1857

June	320.00
July	2500.00
Sept.	3000.00
Oct.	6000.00
Nov.	2000.00
	13820.00

If I have any funds left after starting all the goods from here, I shall take up some of the first notes. I notice all your instructions about goods, and will do my best to have things come out right. I have waited untill the last moment hoping to give you advice of payment of some of the drafts; it being Feby. short month, I do not dare to wait longer. We have no returns yet.

I see that a bill has passed the <u>house</u> for completing the Capitol Building in N.M.[14] This is I suppose sufficient for me to fill the order. I do not know what amt. is appropriated and it has yet to pass the Senate. I do not think Mr. M[esservy] will interest himself in New Mexican appointments. He is very much occupied with his [mayoral] cares here & I think he is fast being weaned of everything connected with N.M. It has been a very severe winter throughout the state. Boston harbor was froze up about three weeks. Our goods laid at the wharf all of that time, started finally on the 6th inst., which I think will give them time to go through in season. Rail Roads are all blocked up now with goods. A week or so will releave them much. I shall try to get the balance of our goods started by the end of the month.

Since my last letter the weather has been very changeable, extreme cold and then warm, which has been very trying for Katy. The last week she was again compeled to take to her bed, suffering severe pain in the chest and side—something like <u>pleurisy</u>. She is now just sitting up again. It has reduced her strength much. I have no encouragement from her Doctor of any one else. She has already lived beyond their expectations. I am satisfied there is little hope for her here. I may be deseived but I cannot give up the hope but that she may be able to start with me. The time is fast approaching and still it looks very dark. My mind is so harassed with anxiety for her that I am almost beside myself. I hope I shall have strength to do my duty. The disease is very

14. In 1850 Congress appropriated $20,000 for the construction of a capitol building in Santa Fe, approving an additional $50,000 in 1854 and $60,000 in 1860. Twitchell, *Leading Facts*, 2:326. The bill to which Kingsbury refers may have been defeated in the Senate.

flattering, and so far has been slow, and I think in spite of all opposition it will be a case of long & protracted termination. Her friends think different. They say if we start she will never reach St. Louis. If she remain there is but little hope of her getting though the spring months, and no chance of her getting through the summer. What am I to do? She is willing to start & wants to leave here, is very unwilling for me to leave her only for a single night. It is a very hard and trying case for me. I feel very anxious to go out with the goods and relieve you and still intend too, but it may prove otherwise, a week's time may prostrate here so as to put it beyond a doubt and show me plainly what course to pursue. You may rest assured I will not encroach upon your indulgence more than the necessities of the case will warrant.

P.S. Our Mr. Abbott is to be married tomorrow to a widdow Lady who has three children. She is the Lady who has been his housekeeper for some time. Facunda is well.

Letter no. 34, Kingsbury to Webb, West Port, April 29, 1857

I am in receipt of yours of Feby. 27th & March 31st—Moore did not instruct Mr. Reese or Mitchell about paying over the $2,200, untill this mail. They have used all their funds and cannot pay it now untill Moore sends further remittances. I have seen Mr. Reese, he says that next mail will certainly bring him funds and he will then turn it over to Doan King & Co for us. Of the money you sent on I forwarded to J. C. Abbott $1,000. to be used on our notes, the balance I used in St. Louis, and left one bill unpaid Tellman Rozier & Co. with the understanding that D.K. & Co. would pay them on receipt of money for our a/c from Moore & Rees. I did not buy anything but the Irons for the State House, these were [on] order, and I had to take them. Whole amt. of purchases including this bill is about $35,000, add for Insurance Freight & forwarding say 3,000, which will make the gross amt. of bills that I have contracted.

[There appears to be a page missing at this point.]

On my arrival here, I found Mr. A[mazon] Hays sick in bed, he is still quite sick but out. He has made arrangement with James Davis (our Jim) to load the waggons and take them out, before I came he had given up the idea of mule teams. Mules are so high that it could not be done. He still thinks he can make 2 trips, and is counting on a full Train for us. The Spring is very backward, no grass is the cry from everybody. Corn is selling at $5. a Bbl. and hard to find at that. There are several trains loaded & on the plains, but I can only hear of two that have started. That is [Charles] Kitchen[15] for Auberg, and Moore & Rees. mule Trains, and these are actually starved out. Beck has taken his mules on the other side of the river to keep untill there is some show for grass. There has been no rain for a month. There has been snow & hard freezing within the last 12 days. We are loading and getting the waggons out on the prary [prairie] before the roads get wet. Today we finished the 12th waggon. There will be about 21 or 22. Hays say that they shall start just as soon as they can live on grass. He has about 70 Bbls. of Corn, when this is gone he will not buy more. All his new Cattle he is to receive on the 1st. He has now nearly enough to make up his teams engaged. I do not think there is any chance for our train to start before the 10th, perhaps not until the 15th. Kate keeps up remarkably well. She is very weak & feeble, but anxious to be on the plains. We all think it will benefit her. Her spirits are very good, at time[s] she is pretty nervous owing to her being so low & feeble. It is almost a mirical that she has kept up so well this far. It has been a very cold bad spring and very trying on her. I have bought a Carriage and Mules (cost $700 out of money sent to St. Louis) shall come out with Tom. I see no chance now but to start with Davis and urge him along. I shall strain every nerve to be with you at the earliest moment. I cannot possibly reach Santa Fe before the June Mail. You can look for me with it. I hope to come in as we did 3 years ago. All trains are bound to be late this year. I think the Ox Trains will be close on to the mule ones, and for ourselves I think our goods are safer with Oxen. Should the Indians be bad they will trouble the mule trains most.[16] Our loading is very bad. I counted on the heavy goods for the State house and have too many light goods. I don't know how we will get through with it. Your order for groceries I have filled, and they are so high that I did not dare to buy more. Belchers clarified sugar 12 ½ cents, crushed 15 cents, soap 8 cents, Candles 26 cents, Lard 14 ½, Coffee 12, these are the prices that I paid cash net, and money could not buy them less. Sugar advanced ¼ cents only 2 days after I bought. Some of the Santa Fe folks got it at 12 but they were a little ahead of me in time.

Notwithstanding the high prices of everything there will be a large amt. of goods taken out. We have less waggons than anyone for our place. Besides all the waggons that are loaded & on the plains Riddlesbarger and Walker & Chicks wharehouses are now piled and cram[m]ed with goods for N.M. Mexicans have hardly got here yet. I think there will be at least 800 waggons, and this is probably too low an estimate.[17]

I would like much to come with this mail & could have got ready in time, but it is not safe for me to think of starting with my wife to travel with it. She is entirely too feeble. I shall be content if she can go through by ox speed. It is the only chance for her. She may improve on

15. Freighter Charles Kitchen, who later transported goods for Webb & Kingsbury and is mentioned frequently in these letters, also acted as a corn contractor to the army during the 1850s, holding four contracts at one time or another throughout the decade. Kitchen was a native of Virginia, where the 1850 census lists him and his brother as merchants and farmers. Frazer, *Forts and Supplies*, 78, 102, 212.

16. Used as early as 1829, when Major Bennett Riley of the U.S. Army escorted the annual caravan to Santa Fe, oxen had several advantages over horses and mules. Oxen and their harness cost less, their cloven hooves provided better traction in mud and sand, they subsisted more easily on range grass, and Indians found them less attractive to steal. Oxen had drawbacks, however, which included tender hooves that sometimes required shoeing, an intolerance of the extreme heat and cold that could be encountered on the plains, and a tendency toward disease. Walker, *Wagonmasters*, 106-9.

17. We have been unable to determine the exact number of wagons that left Kansas in the spring of 1857.

the road. If so & any opportunity offers we will be prepaired to travel faster.

Tom has turned over to me Six Land Warrants of 160 each, which will go to his credit when sold.

Letter no. 35, Kingsbury to Webb, Santa Fe, May 30, 1857

I have sent you under another Envelope 16 Small drafts & checks, amounting in all to $3,019.50, which I hope you will receive safely in due time. I also send by this mail $5,000 to Mr. Messervy for his Exchange Property.

P.S. Kind regards to all, many Kisses for Master Jimmie. Weirick wishes to be remembered, is congratulating himself on having another chance at this coming Legislature.

[James J. Webb described the circumstances of Kate's death to his wife, Lillie, in this letter of June 18, 1857, which first appeared in Ralph Bieber's *The Papers of James J. Webb*.]

To-day we have performed the last sad offices of duty and respect from the living to the dead. John, and E[liza] A[nn] Messervy and Tom Bowler and wife arrived here on the 16th, about 9 P. M. and brought the remains of Mrs. Kingsbury who died on the 5th of this month at the crossing of the Arkansas. Mrs. Kingsbury was at no time improved in health on the whole route; but while on the plains her appetite had much improved, and she had enjoyed her food, was as comfortable as usual until they stopped for the night on the river bottom just below the lower crossing. Soon after they arrived in camp she was taken with shortness of breath, which had troubled her at spells for some week or ten days before, but this time with greater violence and she could get no relief until her death at 6 o'clock the next morning. She could not feel convinced that she was about to die until 12 or 1 o'clock at night, when E. A. and J. assured her that they had done everything in their power to relieve her but without effecting relief, and they thought she must die. She urged them to continue their efforts and not give up. Said she, "if I was in your place I would not give up, but would persevere in trying to do something to give relief until the last, and never give up." They assured her they had done everything in their power, and wished her to realize that her end was approaching, but they should continue to do everything to alleviate her distress as long as she breathed. She said "is it possible that I have come this far on my way and must now take leave of you all?" She then commenced with perfect composure, and took leave of her sister and John. She wished to assure them that the course they had pursued was in every respect to her satisfaction, asked forgiveness for every hasty expression, or unkind word that had passed her lips during her illness, her every wish had been complied with, and everything in the power of man had been done to promote her comfort. "And now," said she, "if my Heavenly Father has sent for me, I am ready to go. I leave myself in His hands, having the fullest confidence in His justice and mercy. Don't regret, or grieve over the step you have taken. I have taken leave of everything behind; I have got everything with me. Oh" (said she) "I am very tired and now let me go to sleep." Knowing it was her last sleep, in her struggles she aroused and articulated a few words faintly, but these were nearly her last words . . . Eliza Ann says that the whole scene of that night was the most overwhelmingly sublime that she had ever witnessed or imagined, transcending the power of man to describe. Not a cloud in the sky—not a breath of air swept over the plain—not a sound of man, beast or fowl to break the stillness of the night—all nature seemed hushed and subdued to silence by the sublimity of the scene. The moon shone in her most dazzling splendor, and the majesty and power of God seemed to pervade all nature. At 6 o'clock, all was over, and as the train had made every possible preparation to cross the river, John and E. A. left the carriage to the charge of Tom Bowler who took it over the river, and Mrs. Bowler and Facunda laid out the corpse, and about 9 o'clock at night it was put into a metalic coffin and sealed up, and they brought the corpse into Santa Fe. John had been very prudent and discreet,—had prepared for any emergency which might occur unknown to any but himself and Tom. And all were struck with surprise when he went to a waggon and took out a box marked "private stores" and opened it and disclosed a coffin. She (Mrs. K.) a short time before her death asked John in regard to her burial. Said she, "John what are you going to do with this body?" He replied, that she could rest assured he should take good care of it, and she said no more about it—seemed to have confidence that he had prepared himself for any emergency; but he said he could not tell the arrangement he had made, but she was satisfied.

[This obituary first appeared in the *Santa Fe Weekly Gazette* of June 20, 1857, a difucult issue to obtain, even on microfilm. We are grateful to Marian Meyer for furnishing us with a copy.]

"Died, at the lower crossing of the Arkansas, on the Santa Fe trail, on the 5th of June, instant, of consumption, Mrs. Kate C., wife of Mr. John M. Kingsbury, junior partner of the house of Webb and Kingsbury, merchants, of this city, aged thirty years.

The circumstances attending the decease of this estimable woman are of a more melancholy nature than usually fall under our notice. She arrived in Santa Fe in June, 1854, a bride, with the intention of making it her permanent home and resided here until May, 1856, when she made a visit to her friends, at Salem, Massachusetts. Her husband followed her to the States in September of the same year, with the intention of returning to this place with his wife the present summer. Soon after her arrival at her family home, she was called to mourn the death of her darling little son, a bright and intelligent child about eighteen months old. Before the summer closed, consumption, that deadly enemy of the human race and with which she had been afflicted for years, seized upon her system [words illegible] she gradually grew weaker [words illegible] away, and when spring arrived hope for her recovery had almost departed.

Imperative business engagements compelled her husband to return to this country this summer, and she [words illegible] by the strength of womanly [word illegible] determined to be his companion while life should last. They left Salem in March last, and, traveling by easy stages, arrived at West Port, Missouri, the starting point for Santa Fe the latter end of April. By this [words illegible] much reduced [words illegible] the carriage [words illegible] her departure for this place, but her friends hoped that the pure and bracing air of the Plains would restore her failing strength. Herself and husband in a comfortable traveling carriage left West Port on the thirteenth of May in company with the merchant caravans enroute for New Mexico. She accomplished the first part of the long and tedious journey with comparative ease; but as they approached the Arkansas she began to sink rapidly. They encamped on the eastern bank of that river on the fourth instant, and remained there until the following morning. That night was one of the most beautiful and bright that ever smiled upon the earth; and as in preparation for the solemn scene about to take place, all the elements were hushed in awful stillness. All night the Angel of Death hovered over the little encampment, and as the morning dawned in the east, the pure spirit of our dear friend took its flight from earth to Heaven.

The deceased died as the Christian dieth. She had long put her trust in things not of this earth. A short time before she breathed her last, when asked if she was willing to bid adieu to this world, she replied "If my Father calls I ask not to stay." Through all her sufferings she exhibited a wonderful degree of patience and fortitude; and, although she died hundreds of miles out upon the great Plains, her last moments were soothed by every attention the hand of love could bestow. She was accompanied by an elder sister, who left home and friends on this mission of holy affection, and whose devoted attention blessed her dying hour. After proper care had been bestowed upon her mortal remains, the mournful cortege resumed its journey across the Plains, and arrived in this city on the evening of the sixteenth inst.

The body was interred in the cemetery at this place on the eighteenth, and was followed to the grave by a large concourse of friends. ·

The deceased was a woman of many virtues. She was a pure Christian, a devoted and affectionate wife and sister, a firm friend, and possessed all those beautiful traits of character that endeared her to all who knew her. To the husband, whose heart is left desolate, and who finds his home robbed of all he cherished and to her who has been deprived of a sister's love by this dispensation, and to the family and friends generally, we tender our heartfelt sympathy, and pray that our Heavenly Father, "who tempers the wind to the shorn lamb," may sustain them in this their hour of trial.

"Leaves have their time to fall,
And flowers to wither at the north wind's breath,
And stars to set—but all,
Thou hast all seasons for thine own, O death!"

7.

"Business continues very dull"

Summer and Autumn 1857

Letters 36–45

Having lost his child and buried his wife, John Kingsbury turned his attention to overseeing his firm's interests in Santa Fe. He was alone. Webb had returned home to his family, reaching Connecticut in September after escorting Eliza Anne Messervy safely as far as New York.[1]

Kingsbury faced bleak economic prospects. The Panic of 1857 had restricted the money supply throughout the country and slowed business to a crawl. That autumn William Messervy described the symptoms to Kingsbury: "We are now going through one of the severest money pan-ics the country ever knew & the strongest & richest mercantile houses are filing [for bankruptcy] or suspending . . . and all the Banks have suspended."[2]

Long before he heard from Messervy, Kingsbury had already felt the effects of that "Panic" in far off New Mexico. Business was "dull," he reported repeatedly to Webb, and he began to accept land warrants instead of cash from his customers. Between 1846 and 1856, Congress had passed four bills that gradually extended the number of veterans who could receive grants of a quarter section of the surveyed public domain as a reward for military service. Applicants who served as far back as the Revolutionary War received bounty warrants, which Congress ruled could be assignable to other parties.[3] In the belief that his cash-hungry customers were selling land warrants at deep discounts, Kingsbury began to pay cash for them. By the end of the year Webb had difficulty unloading those warrants at a profit, and Kingsbury stopped buying them.[4]

That same autumn, Webb and Kingsbury decided to close down their business, but not solely for financial reasons. The idea originated with Webb, who probably made the suggestion before he returned to the East.[5] Closing the store, he explained, would benefit his bereaved partner. "I am yet of opinion that it would be as much to your interest and proba-bly much more for your pleasure and comfort to wind up our business and return permanently to the States."[6] Kingsbury agreed, but believed that he would need to stay into the next spring and that Webb would have to send him a partial shipment of goods to give him sufficient stock

1. Webb to Kingsbury, Norfolk, CT, Sept. 17, 1857, MHS.

2 Messervy to Kingsbury, Salem, Oct. 16 1857, MHS. Throughout the latter half of 1857, both Webb and Messervy filled their letters to Kingsbury with news of the hard times.

3. Oberly, *Sixty Million Acres*, 8-16.

4. Between February and November of 1857, aver-age land warrant prices fell from around one dollar an acre to something less than eighty cents. Ibid., 108.

5. Webb to Kingsbury, Norfolk, CT, Sept. 17, 1857, MHS, makes it clear that he had come to that opin-ion earlier, and discussed it with Kingsbury.

6. Webb to Kingsbury, New Haven, CT, Oct. 19, 1857, MHS.

to lure customers into the store to buy goods he would still have on hand. On the other hand, if Webb wanted to terminate business immediately, Kingsbury would raise no objection.[7] Unloading their real estate in Santa Fe, however, would take considerable time.

Notwithstanding his litany of "dull" business, Kingsbury ended the year with sales of over $53,000, down by only $2,000 from the year before. The firm still had $30,000 to $35,000 worth of goods, which Kingsbury would have to sell in order to liquidate the business.

In his letters to Webb in the summer and autumn of 1857, following Kate's death, Kingbury generally kept his feelings about his personal life subordinate to matters of business. There were exceptions. In late September he lamented the death of the family dog, Barney. In October he revealed that he was "anxious to get away & am at times very uneasy."[8] One of his two sisters in Boston, whose name we do not know, caused him concern. Her husband, who had a reputation for heavy drinking, was unemployed, the family lived in poverty, and she was in poor health. Kingsbury asked Webb to check on his sister, and Webb later confirmed Kingsbury's worst fears. His sister, too, appeared to be dying of consumption. In none of these letters to Webb, however, did he mention his late wife or how his life went on without her.

∾

Letter no. 36, Kingsbury to Webb, Santa Fe, August 31, 1857

I send by this mail under another Envelope Thirteen Land Warrants

9	160 Acres Each	
1	80	"
3	40	"

to you to be sold for our accounts.

Also to Mr. Abbott Remittances amt.[g] to $1,100 to be used on our notes.

Also to St. Louis Doan King & Co. $737.56 to our credit.

Letter no. 37, Kingsbury to Webb, Santa Fe, August 31, 1857

Business has been very quiet and dull this month. I think we have had our share of what is doing. Sales amt. to $9,000.+ collections $5,000.+ I have rec.[d] nothing from below, Smith, Hoppin & Appel, Sachs &c &c

I shall try to take off a Trial Balance of our books to send you by next mail. I will then send you some items which will be usefull in commencing the books which you intend to open. I hope you closed

7. Kingsbury to Webb, Santa Fe, Oct. 27, 1857, and Nov. 14, 1857, MHS. Webb remained firm in his conviction; see Webb to Kingsbury, New Haven, CT, Nov. 20, 1857, MHS.

8. Kingsbury to Webb, Santa Fe, Oct. 31, 1857, MHS.

all business in St. Louis to your satisfaction. I have sold the 30 boxes soap for Tillman Rozier & Co. & send them a/c of the same by this mail showing a loss of $88.47 which amt. I have charged to their account.

Simon Delgado[9] has bought Geo. Estes stock and takes our store. Geo. gave him a good bargain, States cost, without freight 6 months. George will bring a fresh stock in the spring and will then want the store again.

I have found a customer for Messervy's Store.[10] Elsberg & Amberg[11] take it as it is for one year at $35.+ per month. I had to clean the store and repair the roof. Expense about $20.00.

Enclosed you will find Thirteen Land Warrants, which I have bought for Cash as per the following bill.

9	160 acres	Warrants Ea.	1440 @	75 cents		1080.00
1	80	"	80	"	75	60.00
3	40	"	120	"	85	102.00
						$1242.00

You will dispose of these to the best advantage, 160's are worth at least 90 cents. Don't sell them less, in the Spring say Jany. or Feby. they will bring 95 cents to 100. I will however leave it to you to hold them or not, whatever profit is made on them is to the advantage of the firm. The amt. of cost $1,242.+ is charged to your Agent account. Soon as they are realized advise me. I send this as an outside remittance, I will remit <u>Checks</u> from here to meet all our payments so that you will not be compel[l]ed to sell these warrants unless you want the money for your private a/c.

Money is very <u>tight here</u>, that is why I have got these papers at the prices named, I shall buy all I can get at these prices unless you advise me to the contrary.[12] Have them examined and if there is anything [w]rong in them, send them back at once.

I send by this mail to Mr. Abbott, remittances amt. to <u>$1,100.</u> on a/c of our Notes.

Also Doan King & Co. at St. Louis Drafts amt.^g to $737.56 with instructions to collect the same and place amt. to our credit.

Letter no. 37, Kingsbury to Webb, Santa Fe, Sept. 14, 1857

By last mail I sent you Thirteen Land Warrants to be sold for our a/c, cost to us $1242.+ <u>Cash</u> which amt. is charged on your agent a/c.

I also sent to Doan King & Co. St. Louis $737.56 and to John C. Abbott $1,100.+ Herewith you will find Trial Balance of our Books to the 1st inst.

Business has been very dull so far this month I have not sold one wholesale bill. Everybody is full of excitement & liquor over the

9. A merchant and native of New Mexico, 1860 NM Census, 484.

10. Located next door to Webb & Kingsbury's store on the south side of the plaza. Much of Messervy's correspondence with Kingsbury during 1855-56 was devoted to berating Kingsbury for not renting his store, and advising him on the right people to whom to rent it and at what price. Messervy approved of Elsberg and Amberg. Messervy to Kingsbury, Salem, Oct. 16, 1857, MHS.

11. In 1855, Jacob Amberg, formerly partners with Henry Connelly, formed a mercantile operation in Westport, Kansas with Gustav Elsberg. In 1856, they moved their firm to Santa Fe. Parish, "The German Jew and the Commercial Revolution," 315.

12. Money was becoming tight nationally and the value of land warrants was decreasing. In October, Webb wrote that land warrants had been quoted as low as 80 cents an acre, and advised Kingsbury not to take any over 60 cents, except in collections. In December, Webb wrote that their value had fallen to 76 cents per acre. Webb to Kingsbury, Cornwall Bridge, CT, Oct. 15, 1857; New Haven, CT, Oct. 19, 1857; and New Haven, CT, Dec. 7, 1857, MHS.

election & its returns, so far as heard from Otero is a long way in advance and is probably elected by a heavy majority.[13]

I have rec.^d from Mr. [Moses] Sachs $502.+ on account. He is broke. Levi forced a settlement with him, his a/c was $5,000. He took 50% cash, $2,500. Sachs was afraid of Levi and had put everything out of his hands. He writes us that he will pay every cent all he wants is time to realize what he has outstanding. Capt. Ewell is in town after talking with him, I feel more easy about our account.[14] He says Sachs was smart to settle with Levi, and that he certainly has a large lot of Wheat & Corn, also that he sent a large lot of goods not less than ($2,000) to Tucson by the Luners [Lunas].[15] This he will realize & have in his opinion enough to pay all his debts and something more.

Herewith you will find Land Warrant No. 38.627, for 160 acres, which came in the way of collection at 90 cents—say $144.00, which amt. is charged to your agt. a/c. Dispose of it same as the others.

I send by this Mail to Messrs Doan King & Co. St. Louis Drafts amt.^g to $1,317.87.

I hope next mail will bring me full a/c of your money matters in St. Louis so that I can make my calculations according.

Should you go to Washington do not fail to go to Fant and take up Wingfield's note which you left with them for collection, in case it is not paid. It has my endorsement on it and it may some day if left in their hands make its appearance against me.

[P.S.] I also send by this mail $502.+ to Mr. Messervy in a/c of Rents.

Letter no. 38, Kingsbury to Webb, Santa Fe, Sept. 30, 1857

I received your note from Kansas, did not get anything from St. Louis. By last mail I sent you one Land Warrant 160 acres #38.627.

I have nothing very encouraging to write, in the first place business is very dull. I never saw anything like it before. Money is so scarce it is almost impossible to do anything. I have made no large wholesale bill this month. Sales are only $3,000.+ Collections $4,700.00+. The Saxel suit was desided in this court and went against us.[16] I settled it by paying back the money rather than to take an appeal and run the risk of further costs. It gives me pain to write that our faithfull dog B[ar]ney is dead. He was sick about a week. I done all I could for him but I could not save him. Dolores Moya gained her suit with Mink, has got him out of her house & has rec.^d the rent due from him. She has meet [met] with quite a bad accident, in closing a window the sash fell upon her right arm, a piece of Glass came in her wrist in such a manner as to cut the main art[e]ry. She came near bleeding to death before it could be taken up. Frank Green[17] was wounded by an accidental shot

13. Incumbent delegate Miguel A. Otero was running for reelection against Spruce M. Baird. As he had been in the election in 1855, Otero was backed by Bishop Lamy and his friends, while Baird received the support of such prominent New Mexicans as former delegate José Manuel Gallegos and Territorial Secretary Samuel Ellison. Weber, ed., "Samuel Ellison," 216.

In a letter to Kingsbury, Webb commented on the current state of New Mexico politics and advised Kingsbury to stay out of them, an opinion echoed by Messervy who said, "I see by the papers that Otero is re-elected. That being so settles the Matters of New Mexico. You can rest assured that Collins, Beck & Co. will have it all their own way & it will be of no use to oppose them. This I tell you in confidence that you may govern yourself accordingly—I would advise you therefore to attend strictly to your own business & keep on good terms with all men of all parties and have nothing to do with politics, but let the politicians manage the affairs of the Territory & you look to making money honestly." Messervy to Kingsbury, Salem, Oct. 16, 1857, MHS.

14. We have been unable to determine Capt. Ewell's full name.

15. A prominent New Mexican family strongly identified with the sheep trade. Baxter, *Las Carneradas*, 142.

16. Webb refers to this suit in passing, but provided no details: "I am glad that the Saxel suit is decided and settled. Close it up the best you can and balance it." Webb to Kingsbury, New Haven, CT, Nov. 6, 1857, MHS. Existing records indicate that judgment against them amounted to $285.30, but the nature of the suit remains unknown. Secretary of the Treasury, Santa Fe, vol. 1853-1858, NMSRCA.

17. Reuben Frank Green, a native of Missouri, was co-owner of the Exchange Hotel with Tom Bowler and is mentioned with increasing frequency throughout these letters. The shooting was described in detail by Samuel Ellison: "Frank Green was shot through his two thighs, I mean he was wounded in his two thighs by a pistol ball on the 27. inst. by José Sacon. Some Soldiers met at the Exchange and called for liquor, and Frank refused to let them have it, when a difficulty ensued. Frank in attempting to put them out, one of the Soldiers drew a Slungshot, and Sacon supposing that Green was in danger, drew his pistol and fired, as he supposed at the soldier, but unfortunately hit Frank. Whereupon Frank, wounded as he was gave Sacon a devil of a thrashing, to the great amusement of the bystanders—Frank is suffering a good deal at present, by [but] he will soon recover, as the ball did not touch the bone." Weber, ed., "Samuel Ellison," 220.

of a pistol in the hands of Joe Seacon [José Sacon]. The ball passed through the upper part of both thighs. They are ugly painful wounds but not daingerous. José [Hernández] has just got the interpreters berth through Collins, with the new agent for the Nabijoes [Navajos].[18]

I send by this mail to Doan King & Co. St. Louis Five Thousand five hundred and fifty dollars, with request to remit to J. C. Abbott Thirteen hundred dollars. I also send direct to Mr. Abbott, Nine hundred and Eighty dollars which with the $1300. from St. Louis will place him in ample funds to take up all our notes.

P.S. Mrs. Tolhurst, Maj. Thornton, Henry Mercure and Otero & wife, are passingers in with this mail. Deavenport is talking of taking his family in but did not get off. We have no new Gov. yet. Davis will probably stay untill he arrives.[19] J.M.K.

Kind regards to Mrs. W.

Letter no. 39, Kingsbury to Webb, Santa Fe, October 14, 1857

I am in receipt of yours from St. Louis with copy of Invoices also of Sept. 7th from New York, stating that the drafts on Watts were protested.[20] Watts was at Westport on the 15th and writes to Hovey from there that he had found & paid the $1,000. (which we got from F. Green and used in paying freight)—also that he had arrainged to pay all the drafts which Pelham drew on him. I have rec.d Bills Lading for the goods. The mail passed the wagons at Little Arkansas. Hays said he should try to get here so as to go back on the 1st Nov. I send no remittances by this mail. Business continues very dull. Davis & Deavenport go in with their families this mail. I have been very busy with their accounts but have got everything settled up to suit myself. I have managed to keep all the cash I could. I shall probably have funds enough to meet the freight bill on arrival. Tom agrees to Mr. Messervy's conditions and takes the Exchange Jany. 1st at $5,000.+.[21] He will have the money ready in time. Frank [Green] has just got out. He got along very well in on [sic] crutches. Frank wishes you to do him the favor to purchase for him & send by express to Care of Hockaday & Hall Ind., Mo.—One large copy Family Bible, superior bound the finest you can find and large size cost $20 to $30.+ have his name R. Frank Green, printed in fine gilt letters in the cover.

The package by express to Debus & Bunker arrived safe.

I rec.d this mail a letter from Jacob Forsyth Jr. of Pittsburgh (formerly Forsyth & Ballard our com. agents there) stating that he had just effected a settlement with Leach & Co. for the two cases Brogans shoes closed the matter by receiving of them One hundred dollars, which amt. he holds subject to our order. You will please draw for it,

18. José wrote to Webb describing his new position: "I am now getting ready to start for Navajo as an interpreter for the Agent of the Navajos Wm. R. Harly. My wages are $500 Dollars a year and therefore I think that I will not be able to see you this winter, although I give you my word that I shall never live in this Country. My intention is and has been to seddle [sic] down in the States when ever I am able to do so." Hernández to Webb, Santa Fe, Sept. 29, 1857, J. J. Webb Collection, NMSRCA.

19. Abraham Rencher, of North Carolina, succeeded David Meriwether as Governor of New Mexico in 1857. W. W. H. Davis, territorial secretary, was acting as governor for Meriwether who had left the territory in May. Contrary to what Kingsbury supposed, Davis did not wait for Rencher's arrival, but left New Mexico in mid-October. Rencher arrived in Santa Fe on November 11 to find Samuel Ellison, Davis's private secretary, holding down both the office of secretary and governor. Horn, *New Mexico's Troubled Years*, 75.

20. Webb had written that Watts's draft had been protested and that Watts had gone west to move funds to meet them. Webb to Kingsbury, New York, Sept. 7, 1857, MHS.

21. The terms of Messervy's sale of the Exchange Hotel to Tom Bowler, who had been renting and managing it up to this point, were dictated by Messervy in a letter he sent to Kingsbury, who acted as his agent. "Your Mr. Webb has informed me that Mr. Bowler desires to purchase my Exchange property. Therefore, out of regard to Mr. Bowler for his kindness to my sisters and his faithfulness to me, I have determined to accept his offer & give him a quit claim deed to the Exchange property for Five thousand dollars, the property to be delivered to him on the first day of January next . . . & in the mean time he is to pay the Rent up to that date." Messervy to Kingsbury, Salem, Sept. 5, 1857, MHS.

and let me know when you receive the amt. so that I can charge it to you.

The Gov. has not yet arrived. We have now very few Officials at their posts. Collins is intending to go in with the next mail. We know of no appointment yet to fill the Secretary's Office. I hope I shall be able to write soon something more incouraging about business.

I have today delivered the State House Irons, on the Supt.[s] receipt and given the account to Davis as disbursing agt. to fwrd. to Washington which he has done with his recommendation that it should be paid out of the first appropriation for State House here.

I see no prospect at present to sell our Real Estate.[22] I have written to day to Messervy requesting him to put the lowest price on his Stores, so if I get an offer for the whole I can be fully posted about his position. In haste.

Letter 40, Kingsbury to Webb, October 27, 1857

I am in receipt of yours under date of 17th ult. I am sorry to hear that [General William] Pelham's drafts had not been paid. Watt's arrangements had not had time to reach Washington when you wrote. I have every assurance from the partners here that they have been paid, other drafts of the same class given at the same time to other parties here have been realized, and I feel quite sure you have rec.[d] the money on these before this.[23]

The delay on these drafts has probably detained you in making your a/c current. I do not yet know whether the Carandolet [mining] notes and Smiths drafts of $1,500 is paid or not.[24] There are several parties here interested in Smiths Drafts and they are getting quite impacient for the money. In my last letter I wrote you that Jacob Forsyth Jr. at Pittsburgh had rec.[d] $100 from Leach & Co. for the two cases missing Brogans and for you to draw for the same.

Business has been exceedingly dull this month. Collections $2,500.+ Sales amt. only to $3,000.+ and $900 of this amt. is for the bill of State House Irons. From present prospects it will be ut[t]erly impossible to reduce our stock to anything near the usual items by June 1[st]. Still if the money which is reported to be on the road is once distributed, I may be able to reduce the present stock considerable.

I think it will be advisable and to our advantage to have a small stock in the Spring to assort up with and assist in disposing of what may be left over. I imagine that there will be a pretty fair business next year, yet I can state no certain grounds for such an opinion. I have at last sold the old Pack Saddles by this I conclude that our good luck has not entirely left us. I will send you some memo. for Goods by Jany. or Feby., to fill up with, and you can do as you think best about buying. I still hold to your opinion that it is best for us to close up here,

22. Kingsbury concurred with Webb's decision to close the business and leave Santa Fe. Messervy offered the following advice on their real estate there: "I desire also to sell my stores & from what Mr. Webb says, I am in hopes you will be able to sell them together with your Real Estate. It is well enough to own Real Estate in Santa Fe so long as you can be on the spot to watch it but it is not worth much unless you can attend to it in person. Therefore if you should think of leaving the Territory I would advise you to sell out everything before you leave." Messervy to Kingsbury, Salem, Sept. 5, 1857, MHS.

23. Webb had still not received payment on Watts's drafts, but was still attributing the delay to hard financial times: "I . . . should not be much surprised if he [Watts] failed to meet them. Times are very tight and it is hard to raise money anywhere in the country." Webb to Kingsbury, Norfolk, CT, Sept. 17, 1857, MHS.

24. Kingsbury often refers to Carondelet notes, apparently issued by a mining company represented, and possibly owned and operated, by Eugene Leitensdorfer and his brother, Thomas, who lived in Carondelet, Missouri. Webb & Kingsbury Ledger, vol. 16, and Webb & Kingsbury to Mr. C. McCauley, Mar. 13, 1858, Webb Papers, MHS.

and shall do everything in view of this end.[25] This year so far has proved so unfavorable that I am at times almost discouraged. I see no prospect at present of getting the property off our hands at any price. I have rec.[d] nothing since you left on Wm. T. Smith's note. I fear that this is a bad egg and that we shall loose the balance. From the best information I can get I learn that he is largely in debt and but little chance of working out.

Enclosed please find 3 One hundred and Sixty Acre Land Warrants, to be disposed of same as those previously sent. 480 Acres at 75 cents say $360.+ which amt. is charged to your agent a/c. I hope there is margin enough on these warrants to make a good profit. If not I would prefer not to buy more. I have to get them through Hovey with considerable trouble; I have no confidence in him and I do not wish to take any risk on Warrants through him. Should any prove bad there is little hope of recovering anything of him. He continues to spend money fast & foolishly if anything more extravagantly than when you was here. Somebody is bound to be left in the rear by that outfit.[26]

29th The wagons got in today. The goods came out very well. The 4 Cans Lard Oil and 1 Box fine cut Tumblers (cost 10.50) are missing. Hays did not receive them. They are not on his B/L [bill of lading]. I have written to McCauley & Miller to hunt them up. The Prints open well and I hope they will help me. I have been unable to settle the Freight with Hays. In your letter to me Aug. 28th you say "I made an arrangement with Mr. [Amazon] Hays to take out our freight at 10 cents per pound." This he positively denies, says that not a word passed between you in regard to the price of freight or terms. The only question was whether he would take it or not, there not being 10 Loads. He claims that it comes under our old contract and that the price is 12 cents. I have paid him 10 cents as per your letter, and left the other 2 cents for him to settle with you. There is 26,909 pounds making a difference of $538.18 in dispute. The B/L is dated Kansas Sept. 4th, 1857 and the price of freight left blank.[27]

I enclose an extract from our letter to him Feby. 24th 1855, which is the only article in writing that I know of in regard to our contract with him.

I hope you have some evidence of your arrangement made with him in regard to this freight, that you will be able to convince him & make him acknowledge it. He is very positive, says he is willing to forf[e]it the whole freight, if he made any such arrangement as you state.

I send no remittances by this mail. When Davis left I had to draw on some of the money which I had remitted to St. Louis. By this mail I have requested Doan King & Co. to take up our Freight Note $4,750.+ which will ex[h]aust all the funds which I have sent them. I have anticipated about $3,000 after I collect this; I shall commence to

25. Webb had written, "I have had but little time to look about and decide what it may be best to do next year, in regard to buying goods, but am still of the opinion that we had best close up our business as soon as we can do so." Webb to Kingsbury, Norfolk, CT, Sept. 17, 1857, MHS.

26. Kingsbury refers to Oliver P. Hovey, a printer and native of Vermont. 1850 NM Census, 343. Webb agreed with Kingsbury's assessment and advised him to collect their account against Hovey as soon as possible. Webb to Kingsbury, New Haven, Oct. 19, 1857, MHS. W. W. H. Davis once referred to him as "the great `Lord Hovey'." Davis to Kingsbury, Doylestown, PA, Aug. 21, 1859, MHS.

Historian Mark L. Gardner confirmed that Kingsbury's fear that the warrants might "prove bad" was justified, finding "evidence in two bounty land application files that Hovey as attorney representing an applicant was a party to fraudulent claims. These were both instances where an individual in Santa Fe falsely claiming to be a particular veteran applied for that veteran's bounty land." Gardner said he suspected that Hovey got a list or muster roll of members of the Traders Battalion and went about finding people to make applications. Mark L. Gardner to Jane Elder, personal correspondence, Dec. 13, 1994.

27. Webb responded to this disagreement over the blank bill of lading: "I am surprised that Mr. Hays should dispute the bargain I made with him. I made a fair bargain at 10 cts. freight and so instructed McCauley & Miller to fill our B/L. I will look into the matter and write him." Webb to Kingsbury, New Haven, CT, Dec. 7, 1857, MHS.

28. The firm of Messervy & Webb held a note against Robert Cary of Taos. He had arranged with Webb to pay twenty-five cents on the dollar over the course of two years, and had written to Kingsbury, as Messervy and Webb's agent, that he was now in a position to comply with the terms of the note. Cary to Kingsbury, Taos, Oct. 29, 1859, MHS.

29. Webb's response to this proposition was, "I will write Mr. M. in a day or two about a power of attorney, but can see no necessity of it. You have the notes there and can effect any compromise which may be offered without power of attorney, but if Mr. M. thinks it best we will forward one." Webb to Kingsbury, New Haven, CT, Dec. 7, 1857, MHS.

30. Captain Antonio Sena, a prominent citizen of Santa Fe during the era of Mexican rule, retired from public affairs after the American Occupation. Bloom, ed., "Historical Society Minutes, (Concl.)" 421.

31. José Hernández to Webb, Santa Fe, Feb. 13, 1858, NMSRCA: "I am now at Santa Fe very sick and without imployment know body to look after me not to give me advise but all alone in this wide World; now I can appreciat the advices that you use to give me. The Agent Mr. Wm. R. Harley has resigned and have gone to the States. I have saved very little money this year."

32. The addition to Gorman's family must have been Eugene, his third son. 1860 NM Census, 490. Apparently the idea of appointing Rev. Samuel Gorman Indian Agent to the Navajos came to nothing. Gorman remained at Laguna until 1859, although, as Kingsbury suggests, his efforts at Protestant evangelization met with mixed success. In her biographical sketch of her husband, Gorman's second wife described the situation at Laguna as one in which "the Roman Catholic priests and the leaders of sun-worship were very hostile to them and their work. They told the people not to sell them anything but to starve them out, which they came very near doing." The timely intervention of an army captain, Henry L. Dodge, saved their evangelical enterprise from becoming a complete failure. Dodge convinced the Indians to accept the presence of the Gormans, and suggested that Gorman set up a store as a way of gaining a foothold in the community. Gorman, "Samuel Gorman," 318-20, 321.

33. We have been unable to determine Miss Duty's name.

34. Charles Blumner, who is mentioned frequently throughout these letters, was a native of Germany and held a variety of posts in the early territorial government, including an appointment as the first territorial treasurer in 1846. Twitchell, *Leading Facts*, 214. At one time or another he also served as U.S. Marshal, U.S. Collector of Internal Revenue and, according to later Kingsbury correspondence, U.S. census taker in 1860. Description, Hiltrud von Brandt Collection, Museum of New Mexico Manuscript Collection, Santa Fe.

Clever's expectations were fulfilled. He acted as U.S. Marshal while continuing his mercantile enterprise with partner Siegmund Seligman. 1860 NM Census, 486; Richard Rudisill to Jane Elder, personal correspondence, June 24, 1993.

NOTE 35 ON PAGE FOLLOWING

lay by money for you. I shall endeavor to start $10,000 to you by Jany. 1st for you to use in buying goods, or if you deside not to buy, it will be that much to reduce your stock account. Inclosed is a copy of a letter which I have just rec'd from R. Cary. In the absence of any information from you on the subject I think I shall accept his proposition as stated, and hope it will be satisfactory to you. I would like to know from you what your proposition was to him, all the particulars, Interest, mill &c &c.[28]

If you think it is best and worth while I wish you would send me a Power of Atty. with the authority to settle any of the old claims of Messervy & Webb. Write to Messervy and see if he also is willing to give me this authority. It might assist me in settling some claim like the present where it would be inexpedient to wait to receive special instructions.[29]

Kind regards to Mrs. W. Hope you will have a pleasant time this winter.

[P.S.] I have just found the missing Tumblers. They were packed inside the crate.

P.S. 30th Things are getting much more quiet in the political strife since Deavenport & Davis left. Sam [Ellison] holds possession of the office, and everything appears to move on quickly again. Collins will leave on the 15th for the States in his own outfit and travel with the mail. Our Tom is dubd. Gov. for the present, the lobeys [lobbyists?] make him stand treat once a day on the strength of his title.

Wm. Drew was married last night to Francisca one of old Capt. Sena's daughters.[30] Tom [Bowler] furnished the supper & they had a fine layout. Nearly the whole town & all Jeresulam [*sic*] are tight today in Ale. It came out fine, only on Bbl. worked a little. We have opened the Glasses they came out safe. The new Ind. agt. for the Navajoes is much dissatisfied will not remain.[31] Collins says he will use every exertion to get parson Gorman appointed for them. Says he thinks he is just the man for them. The Laguna's are tired of him and under the influence of the Bishop [Lamy] & are putting every obstacle in his way. There is little hope of his ever doing anything there more than he always has, just keep the Pueblo in constant strife. He has lately had an addition to his family.[32] [Julius C.?] Shaw with his family have gone to Socorro. He is appointed Post Master there. Miss Duty is coming up here to open School.[33] She is a humbug as far as teaching is concerned. [Charles] Blumner has resigned. [Charles Peter] Cleaver expects to be appointed Marshal[l] in his place.[34] A Court Marshal [*sic*] will commence here on Monday. Maj. [William H.] Gordon to be tried.[35]

Crops are fine this season. Moore & Rees have 10 to 12 thousand Fanegas Corn. Potatoes have succeeded in nearly every place they were planted. They are very plenty here now. We have had no rain this season to speak of. Not enough to try the roofs. Grass in consequence has entirely failed. Fodder is leasing extremely high.

Tom's Jardain [*jardín* or garden]—turned out fine.[36] He has sold all his mules—will clear about $1500 on taking in the mail.[37]

J.M.K.

Letter no. 41, Kingsbury to Webb, Santa Fe, October 31, 1857

We have just tapped one of those Bbls fine Whiskey. Tom is much dissatisfied with it, and grumbles not a little that the Tillman should send such Whiskey for that price. There must be some mistake or else Tillman won't do. We compaired it with some of the old and there is as much difference as night and day. Tom says this is not as good as the second quality which he sent in the Spring at $1. We ought to have a discount of at least $1.25 a Gall on these two Bbls. I have not written to them. I am tired making complaints & reclamations. I don't beleive Tillman's house is a bit more reliable than Glasgow's. If we buy goods in the Spring, we had better try some other house.

P.S. You will get another letter from me by this mail with 3 Land Warrants 160 Acres ea.

Letter no. 42, Kingsbury to Webb, Santa Fe, November 14, 1857

I am in receipt of yours of 5ᵗʰ inst. I hope you will realize those Land Warrants whenever you think best. We certainly cannnot loose anything on them. The news by this mail has made me very uneasy about money matters. Tillman Rozier & Co. have failed, and there is a report here that Doan King & Co. also have failed. This last I can find no foundation for and can only hope it is not so.[38] If it should be true I fear we are bound to suffer by them. I will inclose a statement of our a/c with the. Owing to the tightness of the money market <u>I suppose</u> Ganuche[39] did not pay his notes to Tillman and we will escape there. It is too late now & I am too far off, to make any moove in regard to these two a/cs. I trust you are fully posted in regard to them, and have taken all necessary steps, in case my fears are realized. If we are in for it, I cannot blame myself. I have only followed the regular routine of our business. Your letter contains good instructions but it is come too late for me to alter what is already done. It was impossible for me here to anticipate anything like what the papers bring of money matters. I do hope that our agents are sound and that we will escape. If not I must depend upon you to do the best you can under the circumstances. I do hope the drafts on Watts have been paid. There is little

35. Gordon must have been acquitted at his court-martial, since Frazer mentions that in 1859 he was in charge of selecting a site near the Gila River on which to build a replacement for the recently abandoned Fort Thorn. *Forts and Supplies*, 143.

36. Tom Bowler's Garden was apparently the name by which a property of Bowler's, which included a house and plot of land, was known. Lying somewhere along the north side of the Santa Fe River, it apparently included a garden of some sort, for which Webb sent slips of willow quince and instructions on how to plant and care for them, promising that they would yield fruit within three years. Webb to Tom Bowler and Frank Green, St. Louis, April 8, 1858, v. 20, MHS; Santa Fe County Records, Deed Book C, p. 297, NMSRCA.

37. Because of a disruption in mail service due to weather in early 1857, the Santa Fe postmaster made a special contract with Tom Bowler to carry the mail to Independence for $1,200. He made the trip between Feb. 3 and 27, taking twelve days to get from Santa Fe to the Arkansas River crossing, under what were claimed to be the worst road conditions ever known. Taylor, *First Mail West*, 41-42.

38. Doan King & Co. had indeed failed. "Doan King &Co. have suspended but what funds we have in their house is [*sic*] safe. They are getting an extension, show a very large surplus, but no one can tell what he is worth or form any idea what he will be worth at the end of the next year." Webb to Kingsbury, New Haven, CT, Oct. 19, 1857, MHS. They apparently weathered the storm, though, as Webb wrote to Kingsbury the next month: "I consider Doan King &Co. as safe as ever. They show a surplus of ($10,000) dollars." Ibid., Nov. 6, 1857, MHS. The following month Webb confirmed the news: "All our business with Doan King & Co. is <u>safe</u>, and you need apprehend nothing on that score." Ibid., Dec. 21, 1857, MHS.

39. We have been unable to determine Ganuche's full name.

hope of recovering the amt. from the parties here. All business men make mistakes, as the present times prove and we with the rest.

Business continues very dull. I have sold very little outside of what Tom has take[n] of his order. We certainly will not want a full stock next Spring. Our intention is to close and we only want such things & quantity as will help to realize what we already have on hand. I think $12,000 or 15,000 will cover the first cost bills of all we shall require including groceries.

I send you herewith an order for Shoes so as to give you time to have them made if necessary. In my last I gave you my views in regard to business. I have no reason now to change them. Tom will want to order a few goods. If you do not agree with me and think it is best to cut off at once, then do not buy one cents worth and I will try to do the best I can with what is here.

The real estate troubles me more than the goods. I see no prospect of a purchaser. Since I have desided to close up here, I am anxious to get away & am at times very uneasy, but I hope to be contented to remain as long as our interests require it. Feeling as I do, I do not wish to entangle myself here with the hope or view of making more money. I am only willing to go in so far as it may be necessary to realized & recover what has already been made.

We have no Secty. yet. The Gov. arrived on the 11th. He was rec.d with due form of ceremony. His family are in our house. I have made no bargain with him yet about rent &c. He has been so busy I have had no time to talk with him about it.[40]

I sent the papers to R. Cary at Taos but have no return yet. I am told that he has gone to Ft. Union, which accounts for the delay.

Collins, Levi, Smith & [Henry F.] Brittingham go in with this mail. I understand B. has quit Connelly, goes in to buy a stock on his own hook. Connelly has packed up the balance of their stock here and will take it down home with him.

By last Mail I sent you <u>Three</u> 160 Acre Land Warrants. I send no remittances by this mail.

Letter no. 43, Kingsbury to Webb, Santa Fe, November 30, 1857

I am in receipt of yours of the 19th & 22nd ult. Watts did not come out with this mail. He is expected with the next. I do hope you have realized the money on those drafts. Business continues dull and everything quiet here. I cannot answer your questions about the future. There is nothing new developed here to base any future calculations upon. I still think it is best for us to import but a few goods in the Spring and try and wind up soon as possible and make the most we can out of what we have got. I do not fancy the Gov. much. He is rather on the <u>old fogy</u> order.[41] He has brought a young man to super-

40. The new governor was Abraham Rencher of North Carolina, a former Congressman and minister to Portugal, who turned down President-elect Buchanan's offer of the post of secretary of the Navy to become governor of the territory. Horn, *New Mexico's Troubled Years*, 73. Rencher rented Webb's and Kingsbury's house.

41. Whether or not Rencher was an old fogy, he was a poet and essayist. Ibid., 74. Webb wrote a curious passage regarding Rencher, the mines and New Mexico politics: "The new Gov. will try and ride both horses in which effort he will essentially fail and will finally find himself on the side of the 'Nationals.' There has been all sorts of means used to get him on that side of the question. Connelly and Beck have both, through Judge Watts, bought stock in the mining Co., which will create an identity of interest and of course of political sympathies. So you can see how to steer." Webb to Kingsbury, New Haven, Oct. 19, 1857, MHS. Rencher was closely involved with the New Mexico Mining Company. See note 42.

intend the mines. [William] <u>Idler</u> goes in with this mail. I do not thing [*sic*] we can calculate on anything from the mines for a year or two.[42] The Lectensdorfer [Eugene Leitsendorfer's Carondelet Mining company] outfit will be a complete failure.[43] The Gov. has rented our house at $500. a year. He talks of building in the Spring.

I have sold my furniture, after reserving my chamber outfit. I have realized out of the balance $1,000.+. The Gov. took about half. I sold what I could at private sale, and put the balance up at Auction, so that I have realized the above amt. out of what was sold.

Sales this month amt. to <u>$8,500.+</u> Considering the times this will do very well. Collections have been first rate. We have rec.[d] <u>$9,000+</u>. Joseph Hersch has paid his account. I think he was a little afraid of Connelly, and has taken from him in good[s] nearly all that was coming to him, so that I have been unable to sell him anything more. I sent Tom down to see Sachs. We can get nothing from him at present. He says he owes none now but us. He has paid all his debts below in grain & by shifting round has settled with everyone but us. He has put everything out of his hands long ago, so that we would gain nothing by pushing him, except by intreaty. He says we shall not loose a cent by him & will pay us just as soon as he can make collection. He has sold his little Store at Belin [Belen] on credit, is trying to settle up his business, is taking annuals or anything he can get for his old accounts. He has sent also some sheep to Cal. by the Luners [Lunas]. I think he will pay us in full in the Spring.

Bob Cary, has signed the note which I sent him, but failed to get the necessary security sent them down by Mostin (Carson's clerk)[44] who says he will get securities here or raise the money before he leaves town. He Mostin has been on a big spree ever since he arrived, and I can get no satisfaction out of him. I think he is in some way expecting money from Watts &Co. and intends to raise the money to settle these notes through them. Hovey has stop[p]ed all transactions and waiting Watts arrival. Mostin will probably stay untill Watts comes.[45] I have said nothing about the Cary matter to Messervy and shall not untill I get it all settled. I send him M. by this mail a Check for Five Thousand dollars, which is from Tom for the Exchange property.

I send you enclosed Drafts amounting to <u>$3,019.50</u>, which is charged to your agents account. I send nothing to Tillman. They have failed & I do not know who are the proper receivers for them. I must leave it for you to settle out of this money. We are honestly entitled to all the discount you can get on those two Bbls Whiskey 81 Gall at 2.25 $184.98. The balance of their a/c as per your bill Aug. 27th 1857 is (<u>$402.17</u>) Four hundred and two 17/100 dollars. This Whiskey has turned out worse than Glasgows Peach Brandy. Tom could not use it at all at the bar. He had to stop it up and there it lays. People would not drink it, even the soldiers grumbled at it. If they had sent us

42. William Idler had been the superintendent of the New Mexico Mining Company. Webb & Kingsbury Ledger, vol. 16, Webb Papers, MHS. Apparently Rencher was unhappy with his management and had decided to replace him.

The evidence suggests that the mines to which Kingsbury refers could be the Ortiz Mining Grant. In 1854 a group of investors, headed by Abraham Rencher, purchased the Ortiz Mine from John Greiner. Rencher, who owned 28 percent, acted as president and signed stock certificates from 1854 to 1864. This fact probably accounts for a segment of his first speech as governor, in which he extolled the potential of New Mexico's mineral resources. Horn, *New Mexico's Troubled Years*, 75-76. The company was incorporated as the New Mexico Mining Company on February 1, 1858 and, according to its prospectus, formally organized on January 15, 1859. Rencher remained a major stockholder, with certificates being issued to him as late as 1878.

The Ortiz grant consisted of land four leagues square, or about 92,160 acres, located at Dolores in the Ortiz Mountains. Records indicate that by 1860 a steam-driven quartz mill, used to crush ore and extract gold, had been placed on the property. Homer E. Milford, Environmental Coordinator, Abandoned Mine Land Bureau, Santa Fe, to Jane Elder, personal correspondence, July 21, 1993.

43. Kingsbury is apparently referring to the large amount of equipment Leitensdorfer had imported for use at the mines, and part of which he instead sold to Joseph Hersch to power his gristmill. See chapter 8.

44. John Mostin worked as Kit Carson's interpreter and clerk from January 1854 until his death in October 1859. Carter, *'Dear Old Kit'*, 136, 153.

45. Watts seems to have put a kink in Santa Fe's commercial life.

common rectified Whiskey it would have been better. Settle this the best way you can.

This money I send you now is for new purchases, and is probably all I shall send for that purpose to be used East. By mail from here Jany. 1ˢᵗ I shall try to send you $10,000.+ on your stock account.

By last account from Mr. Abbott, he had not received the $425.+ amt. of T. H. Hopkins Salary. This will be paid & probably is before now, by some cause or other it has been delayed. If it is not paid Mr. Abbott will be that much short in paying our old notes. Then if Doan King & Co. have failed to send him the $1,300.+ which I directed them to do under date of Sept. 30ᵗʰ, he will be that much more short. Write to him immediately about these two amts, and if he has not rec.ᵈ them, you must make it good to him out of the amt. which I send herewith, so that our old notes can be taken up. I notice what you say about private drafts. I hope all that I send now are good & will be met promptly. The two on the Miss[ionary] Society I was compel[l]ed to take. [George] Smith's draft on his farther [*sic*] at St. Louis is good and will be paid. It is for a part of the letter of credit which he brought with him when he came out and can be no question about it.[46] You can use it in settling with Tillman. The balance are all on the Gover.ᵗ and must be good. They make a big pile for so small amt. but they all come in in collections and I send them as I get them. That one of Davis I passed here but it still comes back and you will notice I have endorsed it to you individually, so as not to send it through the mail in blank. I am working of[f] the goods to the best of my ability, and shall try every safe method of reducing the stock. I have not a piece of Manta in the house, and no Lienzo, except a little of the fine which is always good. I believe prints won't sell any more in this country or else the market is over stocked with them. I have not sold a single peice of those you sent at wholesale, and at retail they go very slow. We will not want more than 3 or 4 bales choice patterns to assort up with in the Spring. I will try to send you memo of all the goods we will want by next mail, which will give you ample time. We will want very little beside Manta & Lienzo.

Groceries go slow but I think I will get all the sugar off. The Lard Bacon & hams are all sold to Tom. Don't send any German rebosoes here if they are given to you. They are not worth freight.

I don't know what to say further about Doan King & Co. I sent you their a/c by last mail. I hope we will not suffer by them. Should there be any stoppage of our funds in their hands, perhaps it would be best for you to go on and try to arrainge it with them. Get it secured the best you can.

Hovey & Co. owe us here about $1700+ which I have the promise of soon as Watts arrives. I may have to take it in warrants.

Our new Secretary has not yet arrived. I have advanced some money and goods in preparing the Halls for the Legislature, if he

46. On the contrary, there was a question about Smith's draft. As Webb wrote to Kingsbury, "Those are unhealthy drafts to take. He [George Smith] is only an adopted son of Mr. James Smith, and from what I can learn he is not expected back, that is Mr. James Smith does not desire his return, unless he mends his ways." Webb to Kingsbury, St. Louis, Aug. 28, 1857, MHS.

should not come I shall supply them with stationary.

I can think of nothing more now.

P.S. When you are in Boston, if you have time I would like to have you call at my sister's house & see them. They have moved from the old house. Now live at South Boston <u>Point</u>. Omnibusses will take you from Boston to the Point. <u>Enquire for Sam Spirmey's house</u>. They live not far from him.[47]

J.M.K.

Letter no. 44, Kingsbury to Webb, Santa Fe, December 14, 1857

The mail from St. Louis did not get up in season to connect with our mail of the 15th and I am consequently without advices from you or anyone else since my last. In my last under date of Nov. 30th I sent you drafts & Checks amt.ᵍ to $3,019.50 which I hope you received in due time and that they were all met promptly. Watts did not come with this mail. The parties here got no letters from him. Business is quite dull again. Still I hope to bring the sales up to a respectable amt. before the month closes. Collections are nothing so far. What few goods are selling go at very low prices, good manta is quite scarce and the price has not raised over 14 cents. I have brought everything out of the Warehouse except Liquors, and got them nicely piled up in the Bale room. They are very handy and I am in hopes to work off all the odds and ends. Ellison is acting Secretary under the direction of the Gov. I have furnished the Legislature with most of their Stationary. I have not been able to complete the memo. to send you by this mail.

I have finally succeeded in closing that matter with R. Cary. Enclosed you will find a statement of the settlement. I hope it will be satisfactory to you. Frank Green is secured in his endorsement of these notes by certain papers turned over to him out of which he is to make the money & soon as he realizes the amt. he is to take up the notes, I deducting interest for prepayment. I consider these 4 notes perfectly secure should the parties live, and I am in hopes to get them discounted. I think there is a fair prospect to make the money on them in the course of six months. I send by this mail to Mr. M. a full statement of above settlement. I have nothing particular to add.

[P.S.] The house have just passed a bill carried 4 to 10 that the Clerk be required to furnish 2 candles each night to each member wether they sit or not, also that he is[s]ue to them Stamp Envelopes. Ashurst is Speaker of the house. He made a speach against it but nothing could stop it. They must and would have the candles and it is now a matter on record.

Don't you wish you was a member. It is the hardest lot we have had yet.

47. This could be the mother of the nephew with whom Kingsbury made his home in Boston in his later life. Webb eventually complied with Kingsbury's request to check on his sister, visiting her that winter, but not describing his visit to Kingsbury until the following June. The picture he painted of her situation provides an explanation for Kingsbury's concern: "I have intended every time I have written you since my visit to your sister last winter, to have told you how they were getting along. I found your sister in very feeble health, much more feeble in my opinion than she could realise. I think she evidently has consumption. She appeared rather destitute, but told me that she had been able with your assistance to get along very comfortably and had kept free of debt. From what I could judge they were getting along tolerably comfortably except that she was entirely unable to do her work as well as she wished to and could not afford to pay a girl. I told her I thought she was entirely unable to do her own work, and that she ought at least to hire by the day to do her heavy work. She said she thought she would as soon as her husband could get work. I saw him and he appeared to have as little energy as ever but I was rejoiced to learn from your sister that he had quit drinking entirely. I had a private conversation with her and asked such questions as would elicit such information as you would desire and she answered them freely. I do not know how her health is since spring has opened, but think she has not long to live. She will disguise her situation from you as much as she well can, and I think it would be well for you to have some confidential friend in Boston to keep an oversight of them and supply their wants in case an emergency should arise. Eliza Ann will call on her as often as she can, but she cannot go about much and it would be better to have Mr. Abbott or Mr. Steel call and see them occasionally and write you about them." Ibid., Hamden, CT, June 18, 1858, MHS.

Letter no. 45, Kingsbury to Webb, Santa Fe, December 31, 1857

By this mail I am in receipt of your favor of the 6[th] Nov. with the drafts on Watts returned.[48] This is the latest date I have from you. The Secty with his family[49] and Judge Watts came passingers. Watts assures me on his honnor that he sent you the money for these drafts on the 5[th] Nov. I am compel[l]ed to take his word and wait untill next mail for further advices from you in regard to it. Watts has with him some $50,000.+ in Land Warrants but no available means except through these warrants. These are yet to be transfered, then sold, which will take several months. I have got from them $500.+ on their a/c here which is every cent I could squease out of them. I hope the money he sent you was in such form as you could have got it safe. I shall buy no more Land Warrants and shall have no more unless I am compel[l]ed to receive them in settlements. I hope you have rec.[d] before this from J. Forsyth Jr. Pitts[burgh] the $100 amt. recovered by him for the two cases lost Brogans.

I have by this mail from Mr. Abbott all our <u>Eastern</u> notes cancel[l]ed with his a/c current showing a balance in his favor of $158.86. This is occasioned by the failure of T. H. Hopkins remittance of $425 which he had not rec.[d] up to <u>Nov. 18[th]</u> date of his a/c current. I still hope this $425 will be sent to him from Wash. Should it still be behind, I depend upon you to reimburse Mr. A. the above amt. of $158.86 and charge the same in your agent a/c. The $1,300.+ from St. Louis reached him safe without delay. I feel that D. K. & Co. are all right. McCauley & Miller Kansas City write that the 4 cans Lard Oil are not on their B/L and that they were never shipped to them by Tillman Rozier & Co. They McC & M. would write to them on the subject and let me know the result. It takes so long to get returns and answers here, that I think you had better write T. R. & Co. on this subject and try to settle it with them.

Sales this month a little over $4,000+ making in all up to this time $53,000+ which is within $2,000+ of the amt. sold last year at this time. Considering the times this will do very well and we should be satisfied. I have sold a large portion at retail bringing good prices which will bring our profits up to a fair average. We have now on hand at a fair estimate from $30,000 to 35,000+ cost and freight. This amt. I hope to reduce ⅓ or ½ before the end of our fiscal year. Collections this month 3,500.+ They have held up very well so far, and I shall use every exertion to keep them up. We may have a few losses but upon the whole I think we have done a safe business this year. Money continues scarce. Hovey has absorbed every dime his credit would raise on high interest. They owe in town between $40 & 50,000. Every merchant is more or less effected by their delay. It will all be good in the end. All they ask is time & they are bound to get it by paying for it. I

48. Having made a trip to Washington in October to see Watts, who was unable to pay the drafts, an exasperated Webb had returned the drafts to Kingsbury in hopes he could collect on them in Santa Fe. As Webb said, "I have had more anxiety on account of these confounded drafts than on account of all our other business." Ibid., New Haven, CT, Nov. 6, 1857, MHS.

49. The new territorial secretary was Alexander M. Jackson, of Mississippi.

send you herewith enclosed remittances amt. to $8,000+ which you will please receive as a portion of your capitol. I could easily make the amt. up to $10,000 by anticipating bus. at the presant state of money matters. I don't choose to run any risk of being cramped, and I think it will be more satisfactory to you to know that what I send is of our own realized means. I have no deposit accounts and still have a little left in the safe to operate with. I shall continue to remit you as collections come in. I intend to send you soon as our business will admit <u>$28,000</u> of your capitol so that next year I will have no Int. to pay you. The drafts I send now are all good. It is possible the Dept. may send the Gov. a Warrent for the amt. he has drawn if so he will turn it over to me, so in case his draft is not paid do not have it protested, but send it immediately back to me and you will get from me the Warrant in place of it. He has written instruction to draw for his salary & he thinks this will be paid, but when in Wash.[n] he was told they would send him the first Quarter, at any rate you will get this amt. the only question is about the time.

You will also find herewith a small book of memo. of things which I think will be necessary and help to work off what may be left over. If I have ordered too much I leave it for you to curtail as you think best. Do not increase anything except it be Manta and it must be very <u>cheap</u> to make it an object to increase that.

I send these memo. with the understanding that it is to be our last importation. Next year goods are bound to be sold cheap in this place and we must look to our retail for our principal profit. I hope by good luck and fair management to have a perfectly clear & clean house one year from this date, that the balance of time I stay here may be entirely devoted to collecting and closing up.

Soon as I get your a/c current I shall take off a Trial Balance. I can think of nothing more at present.

8.

"It is by no small sacrifice
that I stay here"

Winter and Spring 1858

Letters 46–64

Kingsbury & Webb planned to shut down their business, but they could not close the doors and walk away. They held real estate, inventory, and a number of uncollected debts. At Kingsbury's suggestion, Webb planned to ship more goods to Santa Fe in the spring of 1858 so that Kingsbury could fill his shelves and attract customers who would buy the old stock along with the new. Sales remained "dull" in early winter, then quickened in March, becoming so brisk that Kingsbury lamented not ordering additional goods.

By the time that Kingsbury sent this news of healthy March sales, Webb was on his way to St. Louis to buy goods for a spring shipment. Webb's enthusiasm for staying in business had revived and he anticipated making still another shipment to Santa Fe in the autumnm of 1858. Instead of closing the store, then, Webb seemed intent on stocking the shelves twice a year instead of only once in the spring.

Kingsbury balked. In a letter to Webb of April 30, he indicated his inclination "to stick to my wish to quit"—provided he could sell the firm's Santa Fe real estate. He remained in Santa Fe, he said, only out of duty. "I have no society, and very little pleasure except only the pleasure of making money," he explained, and that pleasure had lost its allure. "I have not the same objects to work for, and my whole calculations of life are changed."

Kingsbury continued to liquidate stock, but he could not find a buyer for the real estate. "I cannot make up my mind to order goods for a fall train," he wrote to Webb on May 31. That same day he complained to Webb that "prospects of business are not very encouraging here," and then, in the same letter, reported that he had closed the books for the fiscal year with record sales at $76,500.

For his part, Webb tried to persuade Kingsbury to remain in Santa Fe and keep the profitable business going, even as he assured Kingsbury that he would respect his wishes. Responding to Kingsbury's letter of

May 30, Webb pointed out the uncertainties of doing business in the East and argued that the business in Santa Fe was "worth too much to abandon."

> I presume you intend to do business sometime yet somewhere. You have a considerable portion of your capital in real Estate and our business will require some time to settle up. My impression was that it was not worth while to leave a certainty for an uncertainty. It is true that it will take as long at any other time to close up our business as at present, but should we do as well as we can with good reason anticipate, you will be better able to loose a year or two in closing up and commencing anew two or three years hence than now. I shall leave the matter with you to decide. Should we continue, I think we could do well with a full train, but perhaps it would be better in the long run to close out as close as possible this year and commence with a new stock.[1]

Webb expressed these sentiments in a letter of July 5, but Kingsbury had reconciled himself to Santa Fe long before receiving that message. He could not sell the real estate and he would have to stay. As June of 1858 ended, so did some of Kingsbury's gloom; his letters that month suggest a renewal of his entrepreneurial spirit. In mid-June he berated Webb for failing to assess the kinds of goods that other merchants were sending to New Mexico, noting that he could not make those judgments because "a small portion of the goods for the territory come to Santa Fe." And he chided Webb for not staying in Westport long enough to oversee the loading of the goods onto wagons. In late June, Kingsbury lamented the late arrival of his spring shipment, planned the next fall and winter sales, and negotiated a three-year freighting contract with Charles Kitchen (Webb, Kingsbury had complained, paid too much for freight, putting them at a competitive disadvantage). Webb & Kingsbury seemed ready to continue trading in Santa Fe.

❧

Letter no. 46, Kingsbury to Webb, Santa Fe, January 1, 1858

The mail does not leave until tomorrow. I have sent you under another Envelope, memo. for Goods, also remmittances amt.g to $8,000.+ on account of your capital, which I hope you will receive safely in due time. Enclosed you will find a full memo. of the same. Should they not come punctual you can stop the payment of them. New Years day we have a lovely quiet day. Southern Mail got in last night. I have nothing from below. Kind regards to all.

1. Webb to Kingsbury, Hamden, CT, July 5, 1858, MHS.

Letter no. 47, Kingsbury to Webb, Santa Fe, January 14, 1858

I am in receipt of yours of 20th ult with a/c current, and have made the entries on our books accordingly. I shall not be able now to take off a trial Bal. untill the first of the month, will send you a copy soon as corrected. By last Mail I sent you remittances amt.g to $8,000 on your capital also memo. for goods to purchase, which I hope you rec.d in due time. I am sorry to be disap[p]ointed again about those Watts drafts. Their hands are completely tied here. I cannot get a dime out of them. Enclosed you will find copy of a letter from Watts to his agents on the subject, which if complied with will be the quickest & surest way of our realizing this amt. I have lost all confidence in the whole outfit do not believe any of their statements. Still, as there is no chance of getting anything here for the present I hope this amt. will be forthcoming according to the enclosed instructions. Watts has also written to you on the subject.

You will probably receive in a few days from W. W. H. Davis who is now at Davisville Penn.a a check for $52.10 which I have paid here for him.[2] Please receive it in your agent a/c, and let it appear in your next a/c current. Business continues dull, no wholesale, and but little retail. Our collections continue pretty fair, by the next mail I will send you all of this month's collections on you stock account.

Enclosed you will find a small order from [Jim] Hunt, which I have take[n] to be filled subject to your option. He has no means of paying it except out of the goods. You can send them or not as you think best. He is trying to work along here and is quite certaine he can make money on these things and sell them re[a]dily. I do not know how much it will amt. to but I would not (if you deside to send them) let the bill be over $500 to 800. Have them packed by themselves separate and marked so I will know them. If you deside not to send them let me know by return mail.[3]

Letter no. 48, Kingsbury to Webb, Santa Fe, January 31 1858

Since making up my letters I have rec.d a draft for 1,000 which is also inclosed with the other remittances. This I send to be used on new purchases.

I send you by this Mail under another envelope remittances amt.g to $7,000. Seven Thousand dolls. which I hope you will receive in due time, Memo. & discreiption [*sic*] of the same herewith enclosed. I also return the Drafts on Watts. He goes in with this Mail & will be in funds before any of the parties here. Agent Harly also goes in with this mail. José is here. I believe it is understood that he is to be retained in the Office here at his present Salary untill Harly returns.[4] José will probably write to you, and state more fully. He has just deposited with

2. After serving as secretary of the Territory, and acting governor for eleven months, W. W. H. Davis had returned to Pennsylvania, where he settled at Doylestown to run a newspaper, *The Democrat*. During the Civil War he served with the 10th Pennsylvania, then returned to Doylestown where he remained until his death in 1910. Twitchell, *Leading Facts*, 314-15, n. 241.

3. Webb declined to fill the order, a wise decision since Hunt drank himself to death a few months later.

4. The new Indian agent to the Navajos. As Kingsbury mentioned in his letter of Oct. 27, 1857, the previous agent, who hired José, had resigned.

me ($90.00) which he says he has saved since he went to the Navajo Country.

John Ward was married in Church yesterday morning. It is a good thing for the children and I hope it may help him.[5]

Mrs. [Joab] Houghton has a fine little daughter, both are getting along nicely.[6] Isabel our washwoman, also has a little daughter.

The Old Vicario was taken with Apoplexy & died in about 15 minutes. He was buried after considerable manovering [*sic*] with the Bishop, in the Church with full honors & in full Dress as a Vicar.[7]

Judge Beard [Baird] is here occupied with some Land Claims before the Surveyor Genl. Full harmony appe[a]rs to exist. Since Deavenport & Davis left, we have had no troubles. [C. B.] Magruder is clerking for Joe Hersch.[8]

I have kept entirely clear of all politics. The Gov. has his a/c at Beck's. I did not fish for it. I saw it was no use. They have also got the Secty. deposit which they are welcome too. Let them make all out of it they can. I have enough to do in attending to our own business. Deposits alone are not worth a cent at present while money is so scarce. I should not dare to anticipate a cent with the view of paying for it in cash as the only circulation now is drafts.

I have sold this month across the counter for <u>Cash</u> $1,000.+, which I believe is more than any other house has done, excepting only Joe Hersch. Our Show case is worth to us One hundred dollars a month.

The Gov. is a very quiet man and exceedingly reserve[d]. The Legislature will soon adjourn, without having accomplished any important measures. They are now trying hard to repeal the Gambling law, and permit it again by licence.[9] It will not pass the Gov. They have made a new license law for the Merchants increasing the sum to be taxed on up to $50,000, where formerly the largest amt. was only $6,000.+ I have not seen it and do not know the provisions.[10]

Kind regards to Mrs. W. I am pleased to know that little Jimmie talks of me. Do not let him forget me.

P. S. Smoking has this season been prohibited in the Assembly while in session [words illegible].

Letter no. 49, Kingsbury to Webb, Santa Fe, January 31, 1858

Since closing my letter I have rec.d on collection from Seligman & Cleaver the enclosed draft. viz. dated Santa Fe New Mexico, Jany. 30th 1858, on messrs. Sweeny Rittenhouse Fant &Co. Perm.a Aux Wash. City D.C. payable on or before the 10th day of March next for One Thousand dollars ($1,000.+) drawn by John S. Watts, payable to the order of Messrs. Seligman & Cleaver, by them endorsed to our order,

5. John Ward acted as New Mexico's first Territorial librarian between 1852 and 1854 and as the chief clerk for the superintendent of Indian affairs between 1852 and 1857. He later served as an Indian agent to the Navajos and then to the Pueblos. Bloom, ed., "Historical Society Minutes," 274-75.

6. Houghton's wife, Ann, had given birth to Clara. 1860 NM Census, 42.

7. Juan Felipe Ortiz, appointed *vicario foraneo* in 1832 and still vicar at the end of the Mexican era. Salpointe, *Soldiers of the Cross*, 165, 193. As Kingsbury indicates, the relationship between Bishop Lamy and Father Ortiz was a stormy one, which began with Ortiz questioning Lamy's appointment as bishop to New Mexico and culminated with Lamy suspending Ortiz, along with Padres Martínez and Gallegos. Even then, Lamy continued to be troubled by "the few native clergy that are out of their office that keep a bad spirit against us." Ortiz died of apoplexy on January 20, 1858, after receiving last rites. After lying in state at his home for three days, he was buried with great ceremony in the Cathedral. Horgan, *Lamy*, 107-14, 241, 256.

8. C. B. Magruder, a merchant with a penchant for gambling, is mentioned consistently throughout Kingsbury's later correspondence because of the debt he owed the firm. Kingsbury's indication that a onetime merchant had taken a position as a clerk would alert Webb to the possiblity that collecting their money might be a problem.

9. Gambling, remarked upon frequently be Anglo visitors to New Mexico, had been abolished by law, if not in practice, under the administration of David Meriwether. Horn, *New Mexico's Troubled Years*, 68.

10. The territorial legislature's unwillingness to tax anyone but American merchants during this period is noted in Lamar, *Far Southwest*, 88. Kingsbury is probably referring to another of their attempts to do so.

which amt. is charged to your agent a/c. Please collect the same and apply proceeds on our present purchases.

Letter no. 50, Kingsbury to Webb, Santa Fe, January 31, 1858

I am in receipt of yours of 7th and 21st ult. I thank you for the encouraging tone of these letters. They have helped me much.[11] One of the principal objects which I am constantly laboring for is to please you, that you may continue to be satisfied with the trust & confidence which you have always placed in me.

I am sorry to hear that you have been cramped for money. I was under the impression that there would be a larger balance in your hands untill I rec.d your account current. I had intended that the proceeds of Watts drafts Land Warants & Corandolet Notes when realized should be rec.d by you on your private a/c in order to make that account equal with mine. The fatality which has followed these three claims (though good) is the cause of your being out of funds. Business has turned out more favorable this month than I could possibly anticipate. Sales amt. to $4,500.+, collections $8,000.+. Herewith you will please find remittances amt.g $7,000.+ which you will receive as a portion of your Capital, making with the $8,000 sent Jany. 1st $15,000.+ on this account. This is all I shall be able to send you for the present on this a/c. It is in advance and exceeds your requests. My next month's collections I must remit to met you at St. Louis for expenses & the purchase of Groceries, after that all the collections must be applied to the purchases you are now making untill they are all paid up. Then I intend to send you $13,000+ more on your capital, soon as practible [*sic*].

In case you adhere to the determination as stated in your letter to buy this stock only for <u>Cash</u>, of course you will be compel[l]ed to invest a portion of your capitol again, in which event you can reimburse yourself out of the first monies which I send to pay for these Goods. I shall continue to keep a sharp eye to collections & shall remit as fast as possible. I have succeeded in getting our a/c here with Hovey settled. In the remittances of today are two drafts of John S. Watts on Sweeny Rittenhouse Fant & Co., one I rec.d on collection from Bowler the other in settlement with Hovey. These drafts are good but it may be necessary for Watts to reach Washington before they are paid. He goes in with this mail, and to avoid any trouble with them I would advise you to hold them a few days in order to give him time to get them before these drafts are presented. He takes with him a large amt. of Warrants and other papers not less than $80,000 or 90,000. Beck and Spiegelberg together have advances for him here about $50,000.+ so that they have been able to settle all their indebtedness here. I also enclose the three protested drafts on Watts, so that in case

11. "I am sorry to find you are in so low spirits. Trade with us is dull, and we have not done as well this year as we could have wished, yet when we compare our situation with hundreds of others, who have been considered <u>rich</u>, we have great reason to be thankfull. You have no idea of the reverses which many have met. Don't be discouraged. Do the best you can, excercise [*sic*] your best judgment and if we sometimes miss it, we should not indulge in self-reproach." Webb to Kingsbury, New Haven, CT, Dec. 21, 1857, MHS.

they are still unpaid that you may have them to follow Watts up with and get the money from him. I seen [see] no chance for the present of getting them paid by the parties here and think it best for them to be in your hands as Watts is bound to have funds before any of the parties here.

I am not satisfied with the appearance of the Mining Co. operations, don't you be induced or persuaded into an investment there untill it is proved beyond a doubt to your satisfaction that all is right and that it is paying.

I notice what you say about our Real Estate and will be governed accordingly.[12]

Frank [Green] has rec.d the <u>ring</u>. It fits exact and he is much pleased with it. The Bible has not yet come. Frank has just returned from the Pass [El Paso]. There was a failure of the Southern Mail & Tom got the contract to take it down for which they are to get $1,300.+[13] Frank says O'Bannon, (who still holds Smiths note) told him that it was good and in time we would get the amt. in full.

I shall send my next letter to New Haven after that to St. Louis care of Doan King & Co.

We will want from Goodwin Murray & Co. 25 Gross or 50 (fifty) Boxes of Scafalate Tobacco and about 10 Boxes La Clade. We shall have plenty of the common left over. I could get no Scafalate last spring and perhaps you had better send them our order immediately for the above to have it ready when you want it. The Pure Havana Tobacco is too expensive. It was a profitable mistake in sending double quantity of Scafalate. I have not a box left. Have retailed it all.

Letter no. 51, Kingsbury to Webb, Santa Fe, February 14, 1858

I am in receipt of yours of the 4th ult. I hope you have been able to get a satisfactory settlement of those Carondolet Notes. In case you have not, I still beleive they are good and will be paid in time. Leitensdorfer has sold the whole outfit. The Engine to Hersch for $2,000.+ six months, and the balance of the machinery here & at West Port to the Gov. at cost of 15 cents freight, half on delivery & the balance 3 & six months.[14] He Leitensdorfer says he shall remit to his brother Tom, funds as fast as he collects it. He is now turning over the works and is in hopes to get through so as to receive a portion of the payment to send in by next mail. It has turned out as I said a failure. They loose their time, improvements, and expenses if nothing more, which is a pretty heavy sum, and the sooner we get our amt. secured the better. I am glad to hear that the Land Warrants are sold. I hope the remaining three proved good and that they also are disposed of. I am sorry they turned out so unfavorable & that you had so much trouble with them. I hope this is to be our last Warrants. I got the very best settlement

12. "You had better not try and <u>force</u> the real Estate, watch out and if an opportunity offers, sell; if not, we must keep it, and after our business is closed up, and if it is unsold at that time, we must settle between ourselves for one or the other to take it, at a price at which it will pay as an investment." Ibid.

13. Taylor, *First Mail West*, does not mention this.

14. Eugene and Thomas Leitensdorfer, proprietors of the Carondelet Mining Company, had imported some mining machinery, which included a steam engine and four stamps, to New Mexico. When their enterprise failed they sold the engine to Joseph Hersch, who used it to power his grist mill on the Rio Chiquita. The remaining equipment was sold to Abraham Rencher and the New Mexico Mining Company. Kingsbury & Webb to C. McCauley, Mar. 13, 1858, MHS; Frazer, *Forts and Supplies*, 106-7.

possible with Watts & Co. without taking Warrants, and hope the papers which I have sent will prove good, and that you will get all the money from Watts without delay.

I am pleased to learn that you have found & purchased a farm to suit.[15] Hope it may prove a pleasant home for you & that you may not be disapointed in your calculations. The sum you require $20,000+ shall be forthcoming in the time specified. The amt. I have already sent if realized will make you perfectly easy for the present. By last mail I sent you $7,000+ on your capital & 1,000 more for new purchases, all of which I hope you rec.d in due time, and that all the amts. were collectible without delay. By the last mail I learn from Mr. Abbott that the $425. from T. H. Hopkins is still unpaid. I now send to Mr. A. Hopkins' draft on the department for the sum and trust it will be paid without further delay. I have instructed him to use the amt. when realized according to your instructions and in absence of any instructions from you to apply it on our first payment. I send no other remittances by this mail. By next mail I shall send all I can to St. Louis. I shall enclose the remittances that I send to you care of Messrs Doan King & Co. with my orders for Groceries &c. I expect you will follow the goods and see them loaded at Kansas.

Sales continue dull but upon the whole we have sufficient reason to be satisfied with our business this year. Retail continues pretty fair. I hope to collect enough to send you at least $5,000 to use in St. Louis. Herewith you will find Trial Balance from our books to Feby. 1st by which you can see the condition of all the accounts. Those marked X a[re] doubtfull the balance I beleive to be good. You will notice that the Cr. of our Int: a/c has increased considerably. I have made this off of Hovey & by financing with specie. In making your calculations from the Trial Balance, I think it would be safe to Estimate the Stock on hand at $27,000+ counting it at cost & freight. Louis Falsenthal [Felsenthal] is a bad egg. He has squandered every thing, what he owes us will be a dead loss. He owes Joe $700, Levi $1200.+ & Amberg $1300.+ and nothing left to pay with except a few outstanding a/c about $800 against Mexicans & soldiers, which will probably never be collected. The Bible for Frank has not yet come to hand. Enclosed is a small private order from him which please fill according to directions.

I can think of nothing more at present. Kind regards to Mrs. W. Take good care of that little man & don't let the cows kick him over. He will be a fine fellow to break in those fine colts. I would appreciate a small cheese from the first dairy in the new farm.

Letter no. 52, Kingsbury to Webb, Santa Fe, February 28, 1858

I wish you to get for me a neat White Marble grave stone with a base stone suitable to set it in, & small foot stone. Have the following cut on the slab in distinct letters

15. Webb had purchased an estate in Hamden, Connecticut, near New Haven, which he named "Spring Glen." He eventually became a proficient farmer, turning Spring Glen into a model stock and dairy farm. Webb, *Adventures*, 37. In the twentieth century, the property was developed as a residential area through which "Santa Fe" street runs.

Mrs. Kate L. Kingsbury
Died June 5th 1857
at the crossing of Arkansas River
Aged 30 years.
"Blessed are the Dead which die in the Lord."

have it put on in such form and shape as the cutter may think best. I also Want, a light iron fence to enclose the grave, it must be 8 foot long & 5 foot wide (this measure is for the outside), with 4 corner posts, select something neat which you think will be appropriate.[16]

At the same time I wish you would get for Mr. Tolhurst, a small head stone with this inscription {Our first born}. Have them all packed with care, and try to send them with our goods, when I know the cost it will be placed to your credit.

Letter no. 53, Kingsbury to Webb, Santa Fe, February 28, 1858

I am in receipt of your favor of Jan 20th 1858. I think the papers which I sent Mr. A. by last mail will secure the payment of the $425 from Hopkins.

By last mail I sent you trial balance from our books which I hope you rec.d in due time.

Business continues dull but I have arranged to keep collections up pretty well. Sales amt. to $2,500.+ Collections $5,000.+ Here with you will find orders for the goods we will require from St. Louis, also remittances amt.g to $5,511.75 and in addition to this I have made arrangements for ($1250.+) Twelve hundred and fifty dollars, to be placed with Doan King &Co. to our credit for your use. This amt. is coming from Moore & Rees, through the house of Robert Campbell and is to be paid immediately on the arrival of Bill Mitchell at St. Louis. He is now on the road with their train. I hope there will be no delay in this payment as there was by them last year. If this is paid it will give you in all $6,761.75 which I think will be ample for all the St. Louis bills and other expenses. If possible I think it would be best to pay for everything in St. Louis, reserving enough for river and Warehouse charges, also to settle the balance which is in dispute with Hays on our last freight, provided we have to pay it in the end. After providing for all of the above should there be any balance on hand, remit it to be used on the eastern purchases. The New York checks which I send now if used in St. Louis ought to bring a premium as they are the best class of exchange.

Our outstanding a/c's are fast maturing and I am in hopes to keep up our collections. My next remittances I shall send to Mr. Abbott with instructions to use in [illegible] the notes you have made this spring unless otherwise instructed by you. I expect you will advise me at the earliest moment the amt. of cash which you have applied to them so that I may know the exact amt. and time which it is necessary

16. While somewhat worn, and missing the last line quoted here, Kate's tombstone today is as Kingsbury described it. It lies in the Odd Fellows cemetery adjacent to Fairview cemetery on Cerrillos Road in Santa Fe. The fence and posts are gone, perhaps lost when the cemetery was moved from its former location where the Masonic Temple now stands.

for me to remit to meet them. I make no account of these $1,250 from Moore & Rees in my calculations untill I hear from you that it is paid, which I wish you to do as early as possible. In my last I wrote that [Eugene] Leitensdorfer had sold his mashinery to the Gov. at cost & 15 cents freight. In this I was misinformed. He sold here at 15 cents a pound, without including cost. I think our notes against his Co. are now secure. In case you have already rec.d the money for them or got them secured beyond a doubt, let me know in your first letter and if not let me know so that I can stop the money here. Leitensdorfer leaves in a day or two for the Picket Wire,[17] he says to trade with Indians, and has left me full power to receive and receipt for the company for all sums coming to them, and all the papers are turned over to me with the understanding that our notes are to be paid out of the proceeds in case they are not previously paid in the States by the parties there, and in case they are I am to send the money as collected to Mr. Thomas Leitensdorfer to be used for the benefit of the company. There is a small portion of the works left behind at Kansas or on the road, for which I have agreed to become responsible for all expenses which may have accrued on them, storage &c. and am to pay it out of Co. funds in my hands on receipt of the same here. I have nothing to do with forwarding of what is left, only to receive the pay for it on arrival here and pay whatever charges are due on it. I shall depend upon advises from you whether to stop an amt. here, or send it all to Thomas Leitensdorfer as I receive it.

I hope you will be able to get a fair discount on the 2 bbls. sup. Whiskey also repay & damages for the 4 cans Lard Oil which were charged in our last bill and not sent.

The present prospect for traid is so limited that I have sent very light orders. The principle portion of these orders are for Tom [Bowler] and I want you to do the best you can for him. Don't have any mistake in the Whiskey this time. He does not limit you in price, but wants a reliable article.

Letter no. 54, Kingsbury to Webb, Santa Fe, February 28, 1858

I send you under another envelope Memo. for goods to be purchased in St. Louis also remittances amt.g to $5,511.75 as per enclosed memo. You will also find herewith No. 4870 Treasury Warrant No. 5573 dated Washington Jany 8th, 1858, at sight on the Asst. Treas. of the U. S. at New York, for Four Hundred Twenty One 19/100 dollars ($421.19) Quarterly Salaries, signed Sam. Casey Treas. of the U. S. registered Jany. 8th, 1858, F. Bigger reg: of the Treas. payable to the order of Abraham Rencher, Gov. of the Ter. of N.M. and by him endorsed to your order. As I anticipated, this Warrant has been sent to him for his first Salary, and you will please receive this in the place of his draft sent you

17. A common Anglo-American rendering of the Purgatoire (Purgatory) River in southeastern Colorado.

In addition to trading with the Indians, Eugene Leitensdorfer may have had other business on the Purgatoire. He owned a one-sixth interest in the Vigil and St. Vrain Grant, which he transferred in trust to Spruce M. Baird in January 1858. Taylor, *Trinidad*, 33–34.

Jany. 1st for $416.65, which in concequence of this warrant being sent, in all probability has not been paid, and according to advise it is I expect on its way back to me. The difference ($4.54) Four 54/100 dollars, I have paid the Gov. here, and charged the same to your private account.

[P.S.] The Bible for Frank has not come to hand yet. I shall direct my next letter for you to Kansas City.

Letter no. 55, Kingsbury to Webb, Santa Fe, February 28, 1858

I have closed two letters to you today. Each enclosing remittances. I then stated that I expected to get another check in season to send by this mail, but I did not succeed in getting it.

Soon as you get through with our transactions with Watts & Co. let me know the final results as early as convenient. How did the 3 warrants turn out which you sent to Washington for approval? I hope it has turned out well with those drafts on his agent. I have stop[p]ed all transactions with Hovey, and do not intend to have anything more to do with him untill I heare that all is paid and settled up. I frequent[ly] have opportunity to make big profit through him but I prefer to take no further risk in that quarter.

I intend to start in the morning for Los Lunes [Lunas], with the intention of stir[r]ing [Moses] Sachs up a little and if possible get something on account.[18]

Letter no. 56, Kingsbury to Webb, Santa Fe, March 14, 1858

I am in receipt of yours of Feby. 25 acknowledging receipt of remittance of $8,000.+—also containing Land Warrant #60558 Ernest Falk. I have recovered from Hovey the cost of this Warrant $120.+ One hundred & twenty dollars and placed the same to cr. of you agt. a/c. I am informed by Mr. Abbott, that he has at last rec.d the $425.+ Hopkin's salary and it is placed to our Cr. In my last sent care of Doan King &Co. I enclosed remittances amt.g to $5,511.75 also notice that they would receive for us $1,250.+ of Bill Mitchell, all of which was intended for your use in St. Louis. I also sent as above under another envelope Treas. War. for $421.19 for you to receive in place of the Gov's draft sent Dec. 31st. I send by this mail to Mr. Abbott remittances amt.g to $2,058.44, also to Mr. Messervy a check of $540.+. I have succeeded in obtaining the cash on those 4 notes against R. Cary by allowing discount for prepayment, have received net for this old account $715.+.

Louis Gold, Joe's nefhew [*sic*] has returned and commenced business here again.[19] We got him to take the few remnents left in the

18. Kingsbury's attempts to secure Sachs's debt against their firm are a prominent feature of his correspondence throughout 1858.

19. Louis Gold was a merchant and a native of Poland. The Joe referred to here as his uncle is probably Joseph Hersch, who is mentioned frequently throughout Kingsbury's correspondence and was also a native of Poland. 1860 NM Census, 480.

hands of Louis Felsenthal on one years cr., and in the sale I have secured $116.+ of our a/c against Felsenthal. Should Felsenthal ever make a raise I believe we will get the balance from him.

I found Sachs, but could get nothing from him. He made a very poor mouth. Said he had lost everything in sacrifices closing up. He now intends to go to California with sheep, in company with a nefhew of Judge Otero.[20] He says Otero will furnish the outfit and he can make something handsome by going and offers Judge Otero as security to us for what he owes. On my way back at Burnillo [Bernalillo] I met Judge Otero, and had a long conversation with him about the matter in which he coroborated Sach's story and said he had agreed to go his security to us provided he (Sachs) would start on the trip but would not go his security now as he did not wish to insure his life from now to the time of starting which is to be about the 1st of October. He (Otero) says he thinks we can count what Sachs saves as Safe. Should he get ready to start Otero will be his security and should he not go Otero sayd he will have plenty to pay us & we will get it sooner than we would should he go.

Sales continue slow, but collections are fair as you may judge by my remittances.

In closed you will find a small order of things for Tom, which I hope will reach you in time to send them with our goods. If it should be to[o] late he wants you to fill it and forward them to Kansas, with such instructions as will insure their coming with one of the first trains starting from there. Louis Gold has written for his son to come out about 13 or 14 years and has requested as a favor that you will make arrangments with our train or some other to bring him & his baggage. He requests this of you as a special favor not knowing anyone in Kansas to do this for him. The boy will be directed to look for you at Kansas. Hersch has got the Flour contract for here & Albuquerque and has repurchased his mill from Connelly at $9,000.+. Says he can clear the price of the mill the first year.[21]

[Henry F.] Brittingham has returned, and appears like a dog with his tail cut off. I don't know what the trouble is but am certain something is wrong. He is too fond of cards for a young man. A. Zechendorf lost $1,000.+ in one night playing at Billiards. We have just got word from Taos that Samson B. lost in one night $3,000.+ at Billiards playing with Hicklin [Hickler],[22] and settled it next day by paying $1,500.+. Hicklin, [P.] Stephens and a number of gamblers are going to Salt Lake with Capt. Marcy's Company.[23]

I have no knowledge yet of our last freight note being paid, but presume it is, when you close you business with Doan King &Co. send me a copy of their a/c current.

20. Antonio José Otero was a prominent New Mexican, who at one time studied with Antonio Martínez of Taos. Appointed to the New Mexico Superior Court by General Kearny, he presided over the Third District Court, which at that time consisted of everything south of Santa Fe and all of Arizona. According to Twitchell, he was greatly respected both personally and as a judge. Twitchell, *Leading Facts*, 2:273-74.

21. Joseph Hersch installed the first steam-powered grist mill in New Mexico in 1858, capable of turning out large quantities of flour every day. In 1858 and 1859 he received contracts for 266,500 and 320,000 pounds of flour, respectively. In 1860, however, his flour was deemed unacceptable by the Secretary of War, and his flour contract was not renewed. Frazer, *Forts and Supplies*, 106-7.

22. We have been unable to determine if Kingsbury refers to M. Hickler or Samuel Hickler.

23. Albert Sidney Johnston, on his way to Utah to wage the "Mormon War," sent Captain Randolph B. Marcy to New Mexico to seek additional support when he learned of rumors indicating that the Mormons were trying to unite various Indian tribes against the United States. Marcy arrived in Taos on January 21; he left for Utah on March 9, having assembled a company consisting of an officer with a command of twenty-five riflemen, thirty wagons, and sixteen hundred animals. Emmett, *Fort Union*, 209-13.

Letter no. 57, Kingsbury to Webb, Santa Fe, March 14, 1858

I send by this mail to St. Louis a letter for you which I hope you may receive before leaving there. I fear you will be obliged to pay a high price for freight this year, however, make the best bargain you can. If it will help this matter much by paying all cash on delivery I think it would be safe to do so, as I feel confident I can raise the money in case you should think it to our advantage to make a bargain for <u>cash</u>. And will hold my collection from this on for this purpose untill advised by you. For fear you have not got the letter mentioned above, I will state in this that I now send to Mr. Abbott remittances amt.g to <u>$2,058.44</u>. Also that Louis Gold has written for his son to come out and requests of you as a special favor that you will make arrangements for him to come with our train or some other one. He is a boy 13 or 14 years old, and is directed to look for you at Kansas. His Father relies upon you to do this favor not knowing anyone at Kansas in whom he can rely for such a favor.

Letter no. 58, Kingsbury to Webb, Santa Fe, March 30, 1858

I am in receipt of your letters of 16th & 20th ult, also the Telegraph Dispatch. I am much pleased to know that those drafts are at last paid.[24] I have no doubt but that you will receive the interest for delay on these drafts. I am also pleased to know that the two warrants proved good & are disposed of. You say that the Gov's draft was not paid but would be from the next quarter, and having no other instructions from me, you have kept this draft. Now you could not have read my letter accompanying this draft or else you had forgotten what I then wrote, which was this. Should the draft not be paid do not have it protested but send it <u>immediately</u> back to me and you will get a warrant in place of it. Now as I anticipated the draft was not paid, the Warrant came, I received it & have forwarded the same to you. Now I trust this first draft is on its way back to me. As I do not intend or wish to advance anything on it, I know the Gov. has drawn for the full amt. of the following quarter, and the draft you hold cannot be paid without conflicting. The Gov. has queer notions about business, and I am sorry you retained the draft.

I am glad that you desided not to fill Hunt's Memo. He is drinking pretty hard and the chances are that it would have been a bad arraingement for us.

Business is more incouraging. This month sales amt. to $6,000.+ collections a little over $3,000. I am in hopes to have a good trade next month. The prospect now is fair to bring this years sales close up to last years.

Could I have anticipated our sales to have come up so well, I believe I would not have ordered anything, but I hope it will all prove

24. While it would be interesting to know how Watts at last managed to pay the disputed drafts, the letters Kingsbury refers to here are not present in the collection at MHS.

for the best. I am satisfied I shall be able to sell all you send and at the same time be reducing the old stock. It is quite clean now & in good order.

I am sorry to have to tell you that Tom [Weirick] is about to leave us. He will start for Utah in a few days, on a salary of $125 per month and all expenses paid. He would remain if I demanded it, but he thinks it is best for him to go. He is not saving anything of his salary here, and by leaving this place, he thinks he can save the whole of his salary. His intention is to go home next Winter & he wants a little money to do it with.[25] He goes in the employ of Dr. [F. E.] Kavanaugh, Nick Pino & [Oliver P.] Hovey.[26] They are sending 10 Wagon loads of goods and he has the full control of the goods. I have engaged old Uncle Tom Rowland[27] to stop with me for the present. I could get along with Talisfer untill new goods arrive, but would be very closely confined & be compel[l]ed to trust him more than I wish to.[28] Old Uncle Tom is reliable and I consider it safer to have some one with me.

I hope you will be able to make a good and reasonable bargain for freight. Endeavor to get the goods here as early as possible.

I sent by last mail to Mr. Abbott remittances amt.g to $2,058.44 to be used on new purchases. I send nothing by this mail. I shall make no more remittances untill I hear what arrangements you make about freight. My next letter I will direct to St. Louis care of Doan King & Co. Should you finish your business there and leave for home before it arrives you can leave word for them to forward it to you. You will get all the news in a letter from Tom, which I have just directed to you. José has not received a letter from you for a long time & appears quite down-hearted that you do not write to him. He is here doing nothing at present.

I can think of nothing more now.

Letter no. 59, Kingsbury to Webb, Santa Fe, April 14, 1858

The letters from the East did not reach Indep. in season to connect with our Stage, and I am without advices from you since my last. I have very little to write at this time, nothing of importance. Mr. Weirick went with the Hovey expidition. I miss him much. I am however well pleased with Uncle Tom. Think he is the best person I can get at present. Talesfor [Talisfer] has also left me. He took it into his head that he must go home & plant his ranch. He probably will be glad to return in a month or two. If he should not I will get another boy & break him in before new goods come. Business continues slow and quiet, very little sold so far this month yet I hope to bring the sale up to a desent amt. by the end. The store looks thinner now than it ever did. It is perfectly impossible for me to make the shelves full. I have

25. Webb wrote that he believed it was in Weirick's best interests to go to Utah, and that he was sending out a replacement for him—Weirick's brother: "I think he will do a great deal better by leaving Santa Fe and altho' he was faithful to our interests, and it may be a sacrifice to your feelings to part with him, hope his interests will be promoted thereby, and more than [that], that his relations with that woman will be forever broken off and that he will again feel and act like a free man. I respect him. I like him, and from my heart hope he will succeed. His brother is here on his way out to see him. He has had five years experience in selling goods and I like his looks. I have told him that Tom has left for Salt Lake and he says he starts for Santa Fe and will still go on. I have given him encouragement that you would give him employment on his arrival, and thought you would give him trial at thirty dollars a month." Webb to Kingsbury, New Haven, CT, Apr. 27, 1858, MHS.

26. Dr. F. E. Kavanaugh, at one time the sutler for Ft. Fauntleroy, served in the territorial legislature during the term convened in December 1859. In 1864 he was indicted, but not tried, for treason, and had had property confiscated by the U.S. Army. *Legislative Blue Book*, 106; Tittman, "Exploitation of Treason," 130, 142.

27. Thomas Rowland was a one-time merchant about whom little is known. His more prominent half-brother, John Rowland, trapped and traded in New Mexico in the 1820s and 1830s, then moved to California in 1841 where he prospered at La Puente, near present Riverside. Tom Rowland, who stayed behind in New Mexico, was robbed in his store at San Miguel that year by a "mob" of New Mexicans who associated the Rowlands with Texas expansionists. Gregg, *Commerce*, 162. Tom Rowland married Tomasa Trujillo of Santa Fe in 1843 in Taos, and had a daughter, María Luz, who later married one of Donaciano Vigil's sons (see chapter 10). Weber, "John Rowland," 275-81. Our apreciation to Max A. van Balgooy at the Workman and Temple Family Homestead Museum in the City of Industry, California, for providing us with a genealogy.

Webb apparently did not care too much for Rowland. He advised Kingsbury: "You will soon get sick of old [Uncle] Tom. He is lazy and has no energy or judgment about business. He is clever & honest and a good fellow but unfit to sell goods." Webb to Kingsbury, New Haven, CT, Apr. 27, 1858, MHS.

28. Talisfer was one of Kingsbury's servants.

spread the things untill now when anything is taken down it leaves a gap. I have sold all the Groceries, have got no bad stock now but the prints. I have been quite successfull in working off old trash, which makes the shelves empty.

Mr. [Preston] Beck finally died from his wound after a painfull illness of 13 days.[29] It has casted a deep shaddow of [*sic*] the whole community. Henry Oneil and Briwort have charge of the business untill Johnson arrives. Mr. Tolhurst goes in with this mail. He is in hopes to meet you, if he should not he will try very hard to make you a visit at your new home.

Tom [Bowler] is about building a new dining room.[30] The foundation of the old one gave way and the walls are badly cracked so that it is not safe to enter. I think Messervy done well to get that property off his hands.

We have quite an important event to come off at 8 o'clock P.M. Frank Green is to be married to Mary. Tolhurst will perform the cerimonies.[31]

Tom is very sanguine about getting the mail contract and has sent Maj. Wells down into old Mexico to purchase Mules. They are very high here now, and if the Major has good luck in getting the animals here safe it will at any rate be a profitable speculation. Houghton says "tell Webb it is time for him to write to me"

I can think of nothing more at present. Kind regards to all.

P.S. I send by this mail to Mr. Messervy his a/c current with us, also a Trial Balance from the old book of Messervy & Webb.

Letter no. 60, Kingsbury to Webb, Santa Fe, April 30, 1858

Yours of the 6th with account current and 17th ult are at hand. The entries are made on our books accordingly.

You state that probably you will use some $4,000. of the Capital which I have sent you in these new purchases. I think it hardly nessesary but should you find it so I will soon be able to reimburse you. At present collections are a little cramped on account of the Q. M. Dept. not being able to draw. Soon as I hear what arrangements you make for freight I will commence my calculations about remittances, and will send as fast as you can possibly require funds. You speak about a fall train. I have no doubt but we might have one and that to our profit but, my last orders were made only to assort our old goods and not with a view of continuing and as it stands I think it is best to go on with these and try to sell out, and for once have a clean house even at a little sacrifice. Should I succeed in this, and after sending you your surplus Capital, then we will see what is best for future arraingements. My actions will be governed a goodeal by our real Estate. If I can

29. Webb's reponse to the news of Beck's passing was probably a common one, considering the violent nature of life in Santa Fe in the 1850s. "I am very sorry to hear of Mr. Beck's death. He will be a great loss to New Mexico. I hope it will be a lesson to the living to be more cautious in attempting to settle difficulties with deadly weapons." Webb to Kingsbury, New Haven, May 19, 1858, MHS.

30. In the Exchange Hotel, which he purchased from Messervy in 1857.

31. Two years after the wedding, the Green household consisted of Frank and María Green, as well as Virginia, age sixteen, Laura, age nine, John, age seven, Grayson, age four, and William, age one. 1860 NM Census, 10. Upon learning of the marriage, Webb remarked: "I am glad to hear that Frank is going to marry Molly [a nickname for Mary/María?]. I think it his duty to his children to do so. Hope they will both be good and happy." Webb to Kingsbury, New Haven, CT, May 19, 1858. Green was a widower with children, whose first wife is said to have been one of the early Anglo-American women in Santa Fe. Mary Jean Cook to Jane Elder, personal note, n.d.

dispose of this to a fair advantage I shall be inclined to stick to my wish to quit, if not why then we will see what we can agree upon for the future. It is by no small sacrifice to my private feelings that I stay here. Still I hope to be contented to remain so long as our interest makes it my duty. I have no society, and very little pleasure except only the pleasure of making money. This of course is a strong inducement, but with me it has not the weight now that it once had. I have not the same objects to work for, and my whole calculations of life are changed.

Our Sales continue encouraging. This month they amt. to $3,800.+—Collections $2,400.+. I find now that we were a little to[o] fast in pushing off Groceries. They are more in demand now and would bring a good profit over the prices I sold at. I have just sold the last Keg of Nails. Shoes this year have been rather slow & stick a little. I have done my best to work them off, but in spite of all I shall have a good lot left. Hats still drag and prints are worse. I have just sold ½ of the prints on retail shelves the bad end as they are remnents and all at 10 cents—1,800 yds. I have retailed all the dark prints you sent from St. Louis, but the white ground large figures lay over. The reason of so many prints being on the shelves is I have nothing else to fill up with.

Since Talisfer left I have found no boy that I dare trust. I miss him more than I do Weirick. I shall take a/c stock at the usual time, will send you a copy with trial Balance soon as I can. It will be rather a hard job as there are many broken packages. You have probably seen by the papers that our Tom has the Mail contract from here to El Paso. He still expects to get it also from here to Independence.[32] They are going on in their house well as usual. It has turned out well that you did not buy those things for Hunt, though I believe I could have sold them myself to a good profit. Poor Jim [Hunt] has been called to his long home, and leaves his little family perfectly destitute. The [Masonic] Lodge will assist them some. The poor woman will have a hard time to raise the little children.

I will send you a file of back [Santa Fe Weekly] Gazettes. We have a report here and I believe it is true that the Indians have taken all the cattle from several Mexican Trains on the Jurnada [Jornada del Muerto] and they are left with their waggons on foot. The Comanches are on our borders and are very bad. They have wiped out Water's ranch & threaten Giddings and others. I fear our goods will be in much danger this year.[33]

Poor Old Juno is at last dead. She had a hard fight with Nelly in the night I got up & seperated them, but Juno was bit through the Jaw so that she could not eat. I could do nothing for her. She died about three days after.[34]

Kind regards to all.

32. Tom Bowler worked hard for his success. Of the fifty-one proposals submitted to the postmaster general in 1858, twenty-seven were Bowler's. Taylor, *First Mail West*, 47-48.

33. Various Indian groups were particularly troublesome to plains travelers during 1858.

34. Kingsbury is apparently talking about his dogs. His private account book indicates that Dog "feede" counted as one of his principal expenses. Kingsbury's Private Account Book, Box 8, Webb Papers, MHS.

Letter no. 61, Kingsbury to Webb, Santa Fe, May 14, 1858

I am in receipt of yours of 2nd ult. from New Haven and 8th from St. Louis. If I have rec.d the first without the last I should have felt very bad. In regard to the Gov. Warrant I done what I thought was the Safest. Not knowing when you would leave the East, I was afraid that by sending it there it might pass you on the road and by sending it to St. Louis it would be sure to meet you and would be only a few days difference in time. In your last you say you would write again on the 10th. This letter did not come. I look for it by next mail. I am sorry about those Marcy drafts, when here he stated that $140,000. had been placed to his cr., and these could be no question against them or delay. I hope you have been able to use them in the purchases. They are certainly good and will at any rate be paid soon as the deficiency bill passes. In reply to my letters with remittances I wish you would be particular and inform me when the money is realized. I have no knowledge from you whether the remittances sent Feby. 1st were all paid or not but presume they are as you say nothing about it.

The drafts I sent Mr. Abbott March 15th when paid will be more than enough to meet the notes you gave there.

If you use the remittances I send as directed there can be no danger of our a/c's conflicting or getting mixed up. I now enclose the following checks for your private use thinking perhaps you may be out of funds. These are charged to your <u>private a/c</u>. If you have invested again a portion of $4,000 as you stated of your Capitol in these purchases, do not take these drafts in the amt. because soon as I learn the sum you may have reinvested I will make other arrangements by which you will be placed in possession of it again.

In settlement with Col. Grayson yesterday he claims by his memo. book to have paid to Webb & Kingsbury on or about the 1st of Jany. 1857 <u>One hundred dollars on a/c</u>. He says that it was paid during his illness for that reason he has not got the precise date. Our book does not show any credit to corrispond to this amt. and he thinks he should have cr. for it now. Perhaps you can remember something about this amt. which you can explain so that I can satisfy him about it. I mistrust [*sic*] it occurred perhaps in some private account between you and him, try and recollect what you can about it & inform me by your first letter.[35]

Frank [Green] rec.d by this mail the Valise of clothes, and is much pleased with them. There is no vest with the black suit, he expected one & thinks perhaps it was left out in packing did you buy one or no? The box of slips came safe. They are very glad to get them & return many thanks. Business is dull we could hardly expect anything else at this season. Still I am pushing along quietly and manage to sell whenever I can find a customer. Collections come in slow, but I will have

35. He is referring to a transaction that may have occurred while Kingsbury was in Massachusetts looking after Kate and Webb was seeing to business in Santa Fe.

enough to pay the freight in case you have made a cash bargain. Sachs has not kept his word with me and I have determined to commence suit on his note in the next court in order to compel him to give the security which he promised or to make him pay the money.[36] He has not treated us right and I am not disposed to let it stand long without security.

I have rec.d nothing yet on [George] Smith's note. I have got Sherman to take it again and have authorized him to take 50% on the balance if by so doing he can effect an immediate settlement with him. I was in hopes to hear something from it today but the Southern Mail has failed.[37]

I have had very good luck this month in closing out little odd remnents. I have finally closed out all the old lot of Ribbons, and have not a piece of clothing in the house.

Letter no. 62, Kingsbury to Webb, Santa Fe, May 31, 1858

I am in receipt of all your letters to first inst. We'll make the entries to corrispond with Tillman Rozier & Co. a/c current. I am much pleased with your letters bringing evidence of your esteme and confidence. I am completely at a loss to know how to deside about future arrangements. In my letter of Apl. 30th you have my views in advance. It will require a great effort on my part to change them. I want to do what is just to myself and others and the trouble is to know what my duty is. Prospects of business are not very encouraging here, still judging from our last year's sales we have sufficient insurance that we can continue a limited and safe business. However at present I cannot make up my mind to order goods for a fall train.

With this month closes our fiscal year. Collections are $3,000.+ Sales amt. to $4,500.+ making our sales $76,500.+ for the year which is more than they ever have been before. I notice what you say about trusting out goods. In this matter I can only say that I act to the best of my judgment, sometimes being compel[l]ed to take up your motto "trust your bread on the Waters." Simon's [Delgado's] bill is not due yet, he will be able to pay it if he chooses, but should he wish to play the rascal he has us in his power. Our Sales this year did not commence untill late and of course collections will be late coming in. I have pushed all I could in getting off goods to fair men and in making collections.

By last mail I sent you on your private a/c $1,841.81, which I hope was duly rec.d and drafts honored. I must again urge upon you to inform me of the payment of each & every remittance sent you. That little draft on [James Ross] Larkin has occasioned me much trouble on this a/c.[38] There are 8 or 10 persons here interested, and they cannot get their portion untill I hear that you received the <u>cash</u>. That $1,250.+

36. Extant Santa Fe Court records do not reveal the details of this suit.

37. The Southern Mail ran along a route from Memphis or St. Louis through Fort Smith, El Paso, and Tucson, then on to Los Angeles. Taylor, *First Mail West*, 18.

38. James Ross Larkin crossed the plains as a health-seeker, arriving in Santa Fe with a letter of introduction to Kingsbury from the firm of Glasgow & Brother, St. Louis. Barbour, ed., *Reluctant Frontiersman*, 10.

of Moore & Rees was a transaction beyond my controle, and in which we had no interest untill the money was paid to us. It was simply a little finance on my part to give you the use of all the funds I could in St. Louis.

I hope to receive your a/c current by next mail so that I may know what you have advanced. However, you may expect to receive by next mail a remittance of $3, or 4,000. I shall fix matters so as to send you this and also have ample funds to meet our freight. Your invoices came safe and look well. Have no doubt but that everything will turn out right and well.

Kitchens train got in yesterday with goods for Levi [Spiegelberg]. This gives him a desided advantage and then I am told he only pays 8 cents. It somehow happens that we always pay more freight than anyone else, understand me right, I do not complain of your bargain. I have no doubt you done the best you could, but it is the principal. It gives our neighbors too great an advantage over us. We have always paid our freight punctually and we ought to get it as low as any one. It has been used as a handle against us with some of our customers. Should we continue we must look well to this item in freight. Kitchen did not come with these wagons. He is on the road with his other train. I have commenced taking stock. It is a pretty hard job this time. I now miss Weirick badly. I hope his brother is the right kind of man.[39] I shall be compel[l]ed to do all the work this season, Uncle Tom nor no stranger to our business can help me much

I have been quite sick the last two weeks with influenza. It is an epidemic here, scarce anyone has escaped. It is accompanied with high fever. Uncle Tom and myself were both down at the same time. I have lost about six pounds. I am much better now and in a few days hope to be all right.[40]

Frank Green starts to day with his family for the States, in his own outfit will travel with the mail. I will try to send you by next mail Trial Balance and copy of a/c stock.

Letter no. 63, Kingsbury to Webb, Santa Fe, June 14, 1858

I am again without advices from you since my last. I rec.d a letter with B/L from Miller & Co. The[y] state that the Waggons started on the 13th. The latest word I have of them is from Johnson. He got in last Saturday and says he passed our train on the 30th of May at Turkey Creek.[41] They will probably be late in getting here. I am sorry you did not stay to see them loaded and hurry them off. You could then have examined the goods and being on the spot could have traced up immediately any package or packages which might be missing. I have examined carefully the B/L but it is ut[t]erly impossible for me to tell by it whether the goods are all in the wagons or not. Hope however

39. Tom Weirick's brother had become Webb & Kingsbury's clerk when his brother left for Utah with the Kavanaugh, Pino, and Hovey outfit (see note 25). "I think you will be pleased with young Weirick and find him a better clerk than Tom." Webb to Kingsbury, Kansas City, Sept. 2, 1858, MHS.

40. "For a week past an epidemic similar in its symptoms to what was known in the States as `Tyler Gripe,' has prevailed in this city to a considerable extent, and also in the vicinity of Taos. It is nothing more than severe cold, accompanied by light fever, which is readily broken. The disease is not considered dangerous." *Santa Fe Weekly Gazette*, May 22, 1858.

41. Turkey Creek, in the vicinity of the Rabbit Ears, along the Cimarron Cutoff, was a site known for good water, wood, and grass. Brown, *The Santa Fe Trail*, 126.

they will come out right. Miller & Co. state that a small stove was left behind having been broken, and that they will arrange it with you.

Business is exceedingly dull this month. We could hardly expect anything else in June. Beck & J[ohnson] Mule Train will be in tomorrow. There is very little incouragement for business this season. The prospect now certainly is slim, yet it may turn out well in the fall and spring as you say. We will have rather a small stock. You will notice since I sent you my memo. I have sold over $20,000.+ which has materially changed the stock which I expected to have left over. With regard to finding out the stocks that are coming, the amt. and what foods will be scarce is quite impossible for me to do in season to send for you to purchase for a fall train. For that purpose my orders should go in by the next mail. In the first place few goods will have arrived here, and then you know but a small portion of goods for the Territory come to Santa Fe at any rate, so that I have not half so good an opportunity of judging or making a calculation about it as you who were at Kansas when nearly all the goods for the Ter. meet and you had the opportunity to see them all and judge correctly. I believe I could sell more goods, and perhaps a fall Train would be profitable for us, provided we do not pay to[o] high freight. We cannot well afford to pay over 10 cents even for fall goods. I do not expect Kitchen or Hays to get here before the next mail leaves and I shall be unable to learn anything about the price of freight. Herewith I send you a correct copy of the a/c of stock by which you can see what I have to work with. I see no prospect to dispose of our real Estate and I am more than half inclined to accept your offer to continue our business.[42] Still I do not think it advisable to send a heavy stock this fall. I will make out orders to the best of my ability to send by next mail, and leave it to your judgment to buy or not. You will also find on the last sheet of the a/c stock a full abstract of our affairs, showing just what we have got to work with, and by examining the Trial Balance you will see the condition it is in. Unless we are very carefull in purchasing for a full train it will cramp operations for the following Spring importation which is always the most important. I have written to Messervy to see if he is willing to let the $7,000.+ still remaining, in case we continue our business.

You will herewith find check dated Albuquerque N. M. May 31st 1858, at sight on Asst. Treas. of the U. S. at New York for <u>One Thousand dollars</u>, drawn by J. C. Ives 1st Lieut. Top. Engrs. payable to Simon Rosenstein on order and by him endorsed to our order.[43]

Also Check No. 2 dated Santa Fe New Mexico June 1st 1858, at sight on the Asst. Treas. of the U. S. at New York, for <u>Three Thousand dollars</u> ($3,000.+) drawn by Alex. M. Jackson, Secretary of the Territory of New Mexico, Payable to our order, making in all <u>$4,000.+</u>, which I send to reimburse what you may have advanced of your own funds in spring purchases. If this sum is not sufficient to cover the amt. when I receive your account current I will forward whatever is

42. See note 12.

43. Lt. J. C. Ives had headed an expedition of Topographical Engineers that set out to navigate the Colorado River in the winter of 1857-58. They made their way to the Gulf of California, where they assembled a steamboat and made it up the Colorado to the Virgin River. Returning to the Mojave villages, Ives divided the party and led half overland to the east. In April, he became the first white man to walk onto the floor of the Grand Canyon. He and his group reached "civilization" on May 23, when they trudged into Fort Defiance in western New Mexico. Goetzmann, *Army Exploration*, 378-93.

deficient, and in case it is more than enough, receive whatever balance there may be on your <u>private</u> account. I also send by this mail to Mr. Messervy check for <u>$420.00</u> to cover interest on note in his favor, for one Year July 1st 1857 to July 1st 1858.

There is no question but that the Gov. [Abraham Rencher] is having the Palace repaired in such a manner that he can move his family there, and it is evidently his intention.[44] He has said nothing to me yet about vacating our house, but will probably leave soon as he gets the other fixed. I hope to find a good tennant again.

P.S. You must have forgotten to subscribe for the New York papers, which you promised when you left. I have not rec.d a copy yet. I would like one <u>good</u> New York paper, also the Boston Weekly Statesman, published at the office of the Morning Post. J.M.K.

Letter no. 64, Kingsbury to Webb, Santa Fe, June 30, 1858

By last mail I sent you two Checks, amt.g to $4,000.+ which I hope you have received safely.

I am now in receipt of your little note of May 19th written in the "Suds." This is the first I have rec.d since those written at West Port. I have no bill of the chairs and I see no invoice of Hats. I can hardly think you left St. Louis without writing to me, and I fear the letter must be lost. I expect your next letter with a/c current and hope by it to learn how you closed up matters in St. Louis &c.

Estes & Mercure's Goods got here on the 22nd. This makes almost 70 wagons up to the present. Levi's ox team will be here in a few days. Since the new goods commenced arriving my sales have stopped short. I have only sold <u>$750.00</u> this month—Collections amount to $5,000.00.

The last a/c of our wagons they were at Pawnee Fork[45] on the 11th had lost <u>26</u> yoke of cattle run off with Buffalo. They sent me word that they expect to be here by the 8th of July.

The loss of cattle will weaken the teams so much that it will be difficult to calculate when they will arrive. They are loaded very heavy. <u>Three</u> have over 5,500 in them.[46] Our wagons being so far behind will make a big difference to us. I have already lost the sale of from 12,000.+ to 15,000 which I cannot recover. Country Merchants were here and were bound to buy when they could get goods. They were all anxious to go home with a little asst. of <u>new</u> goods. Levi must have sold over $30,000 this month. It may prove all the better for us in the end. We will have a full fall and winter asst. and perhaps prices may go up a little, but our sales being behind will bring our collections in late, and may push us a little in money matters.

Kitchen came in with Levi's last wagons. I had a long consultation with him about future freight &c., and made a partial bargain with

44. The governor was renovating the palace in the face of considerable criticism. He had scavenged materials from the old post office building, a move that led Colonel Fauntleroy to forbid him to continue under threat of martial law. Horn, *New Mexico's Troubled Years*, 83-84. In an article in the *Santa Fe Weekly Gazette* of May 22, 1858, the editors questioned Rencher's use of congressionally appropriated capitol building funds to pay for the repairs, there being some question as to whether the palace was owned by the federal or territorial government. They also questioned his decision to move the Indian Department's office out of the palace, implying that "the space to be vacated by the Indian Department will have to be occupied for other than public purpose." Perhaps, as Kingsbury states here, he intended to move his family to the palace and needed the space. Rencher's household consisted of his wife, Louisa, two daughters, Sarah and Charlotte, and four black servants (possibly slaves): Margaret, age twenty, Susan, age one, Samuel, age eighteen, and Mary Ann, age seven. 1860 NM Census, 41.

45. South of present Larned, Kansas, where the Pawnee Fork joins the Arkansas River. Simmons, *Following the Santa Fe Trail*, 103.

46. The usual payload of the wagons of Santa Fe traders was two to three tons, or four to six thousand pounds, so Webb and Kingsbury's wagons were on the heavy side. Rittenhouse, *Santa Fe Trail*, 18-19.

him for 3 years, as you suggested.[47] 15 Early Spring wagons, and 15 fall each year. He wants (9) <u>nine cents</u> for spring goods and (10) ten cents for fall goods. He will be back this fall when I can close the bargain. What do you think of these prices? Will it answer? He agrees to start the Spring wagons <u>mules</u> on the 15th of April or as soon as you can get the goods up after the river opens. And for fall freight he will start as late as the 15th of September. I think <u>Early</u> Spring goods would help our business much, if I can have an <u>even show</u> with my neighbors. I am not afraid to stand side by side with anyone here. I believe we can sell as many goods as we want too and select our customers, but it will not do for the competition now here for them to have all the advantages on their side. All I ask is an <u>even show</u>.

Kitchen has also agreed to bring our fall freight this year, provided Hays does not want it. Will bring as many wagons as we want and be glad to get it, at (9 ½) nine and a half cents, and will give us our own time to pay it in. Should Hays not want it on these terms I have agreed to give it to Kitchen. He will start as late as Sept. 15th but of course would like the goods and will start as early as you can possibly give him the goods. Herewith you will find a small book with memo. for the East which I think will do to buy. I have made them to the best of my judgment as full and as explicit as possible. In buying you can make such changes as you think best. I also enclose herewith, Three checks on New York amt.g in all to <u>$3,216.50/100</u> which is all that I can send for this purchase. This with whatever balance may be in Mr. Abbott's hands, you must make the best of, and make it go as far as possible. What you get on Credit, extend it as far as you can. By the Mail of the 15th I will send all I can raise to St. Louis for purchase of groceries with my orders. I will use my best cards then at financing and try to send enough to but all these for <u>cash</u>. I will also make arrangements from here to meet the two Boston Notes due in Sept. and have it there in season. I am now retaining enough to see my way clear to settle with Hays for the goods on the road. It will be in Drafts & Checks, unquestionable so that I will have no necesity of drawing on you as you proposed in yours of Apl. You then said you would have a written contract with Hays & Fogelson, covering this spring bargain. I am sorry I have not got a copy of this contract or at least all the points in it, so that I might be fully posted before settling with them.

This <u>$3,216.50</u> is charged to your agent a/c, and you will take it up in your papers as such.

We are much pleased with the prospect of a weekly mail.[48] If one starts from here on the 7th I will send you a few lines and direct them to care of Mr. Abbott. By the following Mail that is the 14th or 15th I will send my letter cont.g memo of checks to you as I did last spring to care of Doan King & Co. I do not think I have omitted anything. Kind regards to all.

47. A good indication that Kingsbury had agreed to continue business.

48. Jacob Hall contracted to carry the mail weekly from Independence to Santa Fe with a running time of twenty days for $39,999. The mail left from each terminus on Monday morning at 8 a.m. The contract was awarded in April and the weekly mail began on July 1. Taylor, *First Mail West*, 48.

9.

"There is no merchant here more popular than myself"

Summer and Autumn 1858

Letters 65–84

In the summer and autumn of 1858, Kingsbury's letters continued to reflect the optimism and engagement that characterized his correspondence with Webb in late spring and early summer. His letters also became more expansive, reflecting perhaps a renewed interest in affairs beyond business. He had become a "senior deacon" in the Santa Fe lodge of the Masonic order, and he had plastered the outside of their house in Santa Fe.

Kingsbury's new ability to communicate more frequently with Webb may also have inspired him to write more fully. Beginning in July 1858, mail service between Santa Fe and Independence, Missouri, became more frequent, moving from semimonthly to weekly deliveries. The coaches that hauled the mail out of Santa Fe on Monday mornings usually carried a letter to Webb from his partner in New Mexico, who kept him more fully informed about business and local gossip than ever before. Samuel Ellison, the territorial secretary, "loves gambling as well as ever," Webb learned. "It will always keep him poor."[1] Dick Owens, who once rode with Kit Carson and John Charles Frémont, "continues to drink all he can . . . . He totters . . . at a gait of an old man of 90. It is astonishing to all that he is still with the living."[2] William Pelham, the surveyor general, scandalously eloped with a young girl who had been in the convent.[3]

Wagons carrying the spring shipment from Webb arrived late, in July, but came in safely with nothing missing except a box of "Italian macaroni." Kingsbury sold the new mechandise quickly, and urged Webb to fill his orders for the fall and winter. Sales slowed as summer wore on, but would increase at harvest time, Kingsbury reckoned. "The fact is," he told Webb on August 29, "the people are poor." And competition had become keener. In the autumn he reported to Webb that "Santa Fe is full of goods, and more stores open here now than I have seen since I have been in the country." But, Kingsbury assured Webb, "I am getting my share of the trade."[4]

Webb & Kingsbury got their share by anticipating local demand and locating the right supply. "You know how it works here," Kingsbury wrote

1. Kingsbury to Webb, Santa Fe, Aug. 14, 1858, MHS.
2. Ibid.
3. Ibid., Oct. 17, 1858, MHS.
4. Ibid., Oct. 31, 1858, MHS.

to Webb on September 18. "If an article . . . is scarce the price goes up for the season, and the next year every one brings a lot and the market is overstocked." Kingsbury suggested that he could sell more if only Webb would send him the right goods. He chided Webb for failing to send him scarlet yarn, in demand by Pueblos as trim for their cloaks, or *tilmas*. When the fall shipment arrived Kingsbury deplored the "dead colors" of the "Boston fancy Prints," explaining to Webb that he needed colors like pink, blue, orange, and yellow.[5] Fashions had changed.

In previous years, Kingsbury had been able to depend on Webb to know local tastes, but as Webb's absence from New Mexico lengthened Kingsbury had to describe the newest fashion. Young girls had begun to wear shawls and capes instead of *rebozos*, he told Webb, and sunbonnets had become "very common."[6] The more that women wore sunbonnets to cover their heads, Kingsbury predicted, the less they would wear *rebozos* and the more they would wear shawls and capes. Ironically, the unlikely source of the sunbonnet craze, according to Kingsbury, were Sisters of Loretto—nuns from Kentucky who had established a school for young women in Santa Fe in 1852.

∾

Letter no. 65, Kingsbury to Webb, Santa Fe, July 11, 1858

I am in receipt of yours of June 2nd with a/c current, also a/c current of Mr. Abbott. I have not had time to examine them thoroughly but presume they are all right. You paid C. Marlow $36.+ this bill I have not got, neither have I Miller & Co. Bill at Kansas. These must have been in the letter you sent from St. Louis which I never got. By last mail I sent you some memo. for fall goods, also check amt. to $3,216.50 as per enclosed a/c. which I hope you get. By the mail which leaves here on the 19th, I will send to St. Louis orders for Groceries with all the money I can raise. In case you should have determined to send <u>no</u> goods this fall, write immediately to C. W. Kitchen care of W. R. Bernard at Westport and inform him of the fact. You had better write to him anyhow, and if you are buying tell him what time you will probably get the goods up, and also to hold himself and Wagons in re[a]diness to receive the freight <u>provided Mr. Hays does not want it.</u> He will know whether Mr. Hays wants it or not, and can on your letter make his arrangements.

Our Spring Wagons have got here at last, are on the hill and will unload tomorrow.[7] Soon as I get a little time I will make all the entries to agree with your a/c current. I cannot however untill I get the two missing bills. According to this a/c we owe you $3,961.51. and to offset

5. Ibid.

6. Ibid., Sept. 18, 1858, MHS.

7. Prairie travelers rarely failed to mention their first glimpse of Santa Fe spied from a hill above the city. After weeks on the dusty plains, members of the caravans frequently stopped to spruce up a bit before making the final descent into the town.

it I sent you June 14th $4,000.+ Now you had better take the difference $38.49 on your private a/c as I suggested and settle this a/c up.

Mr. Abbott's a/c I think is all right. I believe I understand it although it begins in the middle, and will balance his a/c accordingly. Balance in our favor $726.41 this I calculate you will use for fall goods, and I will send other funds from here to meet our notes. Business is dull now but if I have the right sort of goods I believe I can bring up a years business which will be satisfactory to you.

I have desided to have the out side of our house plastered in Lime. Geo. Walls has returned from California and I have got him to do it.

I can think of nothing more now.

Letter no. 66, Kingsbury to Webb, Santa Fe, July 18, 1858

By this mail I send to you care of Doan King & Co. St. Louis, letter cont.g memo. of goods to purchase in St. Louis also check on the Asst. Treas. there amt.g to $6.500.+ expecting it will meet you there. I also send at this time to Mr. Abbott Check on New York amt.g to $2,025.+ to meet our Boston notes due in Sept. This makes my remittances for the last month as per enclosed memo. $24,299.47. To do this I have anticipated some, still I can see my way clear, and feel perfectly easy in money matters.

Letter no. 67, Kingsbury to Webb, Santa Fe, July 18, 1858

My last to you was addressed to Boston. Our wagons were unloaded last Monday to 12th. I rec.d the written agreement for freight by Mr. Weirick and I have settled it accordingly. The goods came out in good order, so little damage that I made no claim on them. Mr. Hays did not come and I could make no settlement of that old matter of $50.+ which he claims as I do not know what it can be. He certainly has no just claim of a cent against us. I miss nothing yet of these spring goods except one box Italian Macaroni which could not have been put in the Wagons. Must have been lost at the warehouse or the other side.

I have had only five days to work on the new goods and I assure you I have been hard at it every moment, trying to make up for lost time. I have sold $12,240.+ besides what goods are delivered to Tom. His I haven't had time to enter yet. If you will be carefull in selecting goods & send me the right sort, you need have no fear but that I will sell them. I flatter myself that there is no merchant here at present more popular than myself. I hope this will meet you at St. Louis and that you have been able to fill the order which I sent east to a good advantage. Herewith you will find a book of orders for St. Louis. Do the best you can. Some of the items may look large to you but if all goes well I believe I can dispose of them all to good men. You are to remember always that my orders are subject to your approval and you can make such alterations as sircumstances may suggest to you. I have made these orders up carefully and believe the goods will be needed here before spring goods can arrive. You will also find herewith checks on the Asst. Treasury at St. Louis, amt.g to Six Thousand Five hundred dollars, which is charged to your agent a/c. This I think will be enough with the balance which may be left of M[oore] & Rees $1250. and the first note of Carandolet Co. to enable you to make the most if not all these purchases for <u>Cash</u>. However save enough of it to pay all expenses as I shall not be able to remit any more funds just at present. By this mail I also send to Mr. Abbott, check on New York for $2,025.+ which will enable him to take up our two notes due in Sept. at Boston. Don't draw on this again as I may not be able to replace it in time to meet them. With the amt. which goes this mail it will make my remittances and payments for the last month come up to $24,300.+, It has taken no small financing on my part to do this. Tom [Bowler] on a/c of his mail contracts has been unable to assist me, and still owes a good sum on his last years a/c, before these new goods arrived. He is doing well and soon as he gets his 1st quarter payment for Mail Service, he will be easy in money matters. In these remittances I have anticipated some but I do not think there is the least fear of being cramped. I have made my calculations carefully and can see through, only I will not be able to send more just at present.

Weirick takes hold well.[8] I think I shall be pleased with him. He wishes to be remembered to you. I shall keep Uncle Tom [Rowland] for the present, untill Weirick gets learnt and picks up a little Spanish.

The old goods are moving off with the new ones. I have sold nearly all the old prints, and I will work off all our shoes this year. I have not got shelf goods enough to fill up the store and it looks heavy. If you fill my orders, I will have a good fall & winter stock and will be ready for any traid that may offer. I see no reason now why we should not make a good years business of it before it closes. Try to get the goods started as soon as you can. I hope Hays will not want our fall freight and that they will be brought out by Kitchen.

I can think of nothing more now

P.S. We have a judgment against [Moses] Sachs and Judge Otero has obligated himself to sign a joint note with him payable June 1st, 1859 with interest from date of Judgment, so we can consider that claim secured. J.M.K.

Letter no. 68, Kingsbury to Webb, Santa Fe, July 25, 1858

I am in receipt of yours under date of June 18th acknowledging receipt of remittances amt. to $1841.81, you say on your "stock a/c." This

8. This Weirick, to whom Kingsbury usually referred as young Weirick, was the brother of Kingsbury's long-time clerk, Tom Weirick, but we have been unable to discover his first name.

I sent on your private a/c and not on your stock a/c. You will see by my letter accompanying it that I intended it for your private use and that I charged it to your private a/c. I hope the drafts were all paid promptly.

We have no word here to coroborate the reports about Gold & silver discoveries at Tucson.[9] I hear of many parties on the road and others coming, bound for the new Territory of Arizona. I believe the gold & silver stories are humbug got up to induce emigration, for the end of creating the proposed Territory [of Arizona] and making Offices for Office Seakers. Beard [Baird?] is one of the prime moovers and principal letter writer. I believe he expects to be Governor.

The Gov. is still prosecuting this work at placers, but is going on very slow. I hear nothing encouraging from them. I think it is deterred much by bad management and the fear of expanding money. He is too much of an old fogy to open the mine and work it successfully. It may be that he is cramped for means which would account for the delays there. I believe he is trying to make it pay without further investment while every body can see that to make it profitable they must push the mashinery, work it night & day and spare no expense to feed it and keep it going.[10]

By the mail of the 19th last Monday I sent you to St. Louis orders for purchases there also Drafts amt.g to $6,500.+ which I hope you have received. Since then I have sold in addition to what I then reported $5,000.+. Do not be afraid to fill my orders, or to increase them. If you buy carefully I believe I can sell all the goods you send. My sales, now counting in Tom's orders, will make nearly if not quite the whole sum of your spring purchases and freight. I have worked off many of the goods which were left over, and our stock at present as far as it goes is in as good a condition as we could wish. The house in spite of me looks thin and I cannot fill it up even with the help of what is left of new goods. I have sold so much of the old trash off the shelves that I cannot fill them again.

If our goods had come 2 or 3 weeks earlier I believe I could have sold nearly out. I have sold nothing to Joe [Hersch?] yet. I have had all I could attend to, and have not had time to work with him and get him up to look at our goods. He has bought heavy this spring of Levi [Spiegelberg] and I expect since my assortment is now so broken that I had better let him go untill the fall train arrives.

Be sure and send the Billiard Table & fixtures for [E.] Branford. I have already received from him a portion of the money on it.

I do not think of anything now to add to my orders, but leave it with you to send whatever you may see that you think is desirable and a profit can be made on it.

I sold yesterday the pair of Paintings for $40.+. My sales have commenced so fair that we cannot expect for them to keep up. You must look for limited sales now untill the fall train arrives. I shall now turn my attention to retail and try to get in all the cash I can. I have hardly

9. Webb had written on June 18 that he had read a report in the papers of large gold and silver discoveries in Tucson. He may have read about the strike that year at Gila City, north of present Yuma, or of earlier strikes near Tubac. Wagoner, *Early Arizona*, 383-92, 406-8.

10. Kingsbury is referring to Gov. Abraham Rencher and the operations of the New Mexico Mining Company, mentioned briefly in chapter 8.

The New Mexico Mining Company was set up to exploit the mineral riches of the Ortiz grant at Dolores in the Ortiz mountains, twenty-eight miles south of Santa Fe. The gold deposits there had been discovered in 1828, and in 1833 Lt. José Francisco Ortiz was granted surface rights to an area of about 1,500 linear feet along the Santa Rosalía outcrop, one of the largest producers of bullion in the district before the American occupation. In addition to those mineral rights, Ortiz was granted the use of natural resources, such as water and pasturage, on the four square leagues of land surrounding the opening of the mine.

In 1854 a group of investors headed by Abraham Rencher purchased the Ortiz grant from John Greiner, who had acquired it from Ortiz's widow, Maraquita Montoya, in 1853. Rencher, who owned 28 percent, acted as president and signed stock certificates from 1854 to 1864. The company was incorporated as the New Mexico Mining Company on February 1, 1858 and, according to its prospectus, formally organized on January 15, 1859. Rencher remained a major stockholder, with certificates being issued to him as late as 1878.

In 1860 the company, whose prominent shareholders included a number of territorial officials, moved to confirm their claim to the Ortiz grant. They sought, and were awarded, rights to the four-league-square area rather than just the mineral rights to the Santa Rosalía vein, plus water and pasturage on the larger plot of land. In their application to the territorial legislature to pass an act of incorporation, Rencher's name was prominently listed, yet his name was removed completely, as were the names of other territorial office holders, in the bill before Congress to confirm the company's claim to the grant. Townley, "New Mexico Mining Company," 57-59; 63-65; Homer E. Milford, Environmental Coordinator, Abandoned Mine Land Bureau, Bureau of Land Management, Santa Fe, to Jane Elder, personal correspondence, July 21, 1993.

been behind the counter yet. I have to leave it so far entirely to Uncle Tom. He has taken in since the goods arrived about $800.+. These items will give you a pretty good idea of what we are doing.

The grave stone came out safe also the fence. I like them much. Many thanks for your attention in this matter.

Letter no. 69, Kingsbury to Webb, Santa Fe, July 25, 1858

José has gone with Mr. Brevourt [Elias Brevoort] to Ft. Buchanan.[11]

How far astray José has gone I cannot say. I think he is desiring of some sympathy & considerable leniancy. He was too young and of to[o] little experience in the world to be thrown on his own resources at the time you set him free. He needs an adviser in whom he has confidence and some one to direct him. I do not think he is bad at heart, but evidently has done many things wrong. I have kept an eye to him the past year and have advised him when I thought he would listen. I have seen him several times when I thought he was under the influence of Liquor. I never heard of his gambeling. He certainly has been carefull with his money and now has on deposit with me about $400.

His greatist misfortune has been in his associates. He is of a lively disposition, natur[al]ly fond of fun and having nothing to do he had got very thick with a crowd here which by associating with them was very much against his character. Had it not been for this I would have given him a trial in the store again, but was afraid to trust him while he kept such company, and so long as he stayed here it was impossible for him to get clear of them. I talked with him freely about it and advised him to leave, and be more carefull in future about forming associates, to profit by his experience. I finally got him this chance to go with Brevourt [Brevoort], recommended him highly that he would not play cards or drink and am personally responsible for his honisty. He knows this, and I told him plainly that should he <u>drink gamble or prove dishonist</u>, he could expect no further assistance or favors from me, that I would have nothing more to do with him.

Brevourt [Brevoort] did not promise him steady employment, the understanding was for him to go out for which he would pay him and after they got there if he had a place for him in his store or suitable employment for him he would then hire him to stay with him. I advised him to go and do the best he could to please Mr. B.—not so much for the prospect of a salary but to get away from this place and the associates he had here.

Before he left I charged him over & over about things which I thought would be to his benefit, had he been my own brother I could not have been more faithfull in my advises to him.

11. Elias Brevoort was then sutler at Fort Buchanan, established in southern Arizona, thirty-two miles east of Tubac, to protect ranches and mines.

I have written to him today & enclosed your letter, have advised him to stay with Mr. B. should he want him. If not & he is again out of employ to return here by the first safe chance that would not be expensive to him and I would consult with him about further plans.

Should he come and I learn nothing more against him than I now know, I shall certainly advise him to go to you.

Letter no. 70, Kingsbury to Webb, Santa Fe, July 25, 1858

I send my letter to you by this mail to St. Louis care Doan King & Co thinking it may find you there. Otero is politically dead here. His party even those who were his warmest friends are not sparing in their remarks against him. They say he has done nothing for the Territory and I fear there is too much truth in it. Appropriations do not come up to anyone's expectations.[12]

The next deligate is talked of they say no one but a Mexican can hope to be elected. Joachin Perear [Perea] is spoken of as a fit subject.[13]

Letter no. 71, Kingsbury to Webb, Santa Fe, August 1, 1858

The month closed rather dull. I have had but one wholesale customer in the last week. That was La Carne[14] and he had bought some $4,000 of Capt. St. Vrain before he came down. My whole sales for the month of July foot up $28,000+ Collections amt. to $5,000+ Tom Weirick returned yesterday with the mail. He could not agree with Pino, and left them at Fort Larina,[15] went to Independence and came immediately back. What he intends to do now, I have not learned yet.[16] Should he deside to open on his own a/c, I think I shall let him have goods. He tells me that all the Trains now loading and on the road are loaded with groceries. I fear I have made a mistake in ordering so many groceries for this fall, however, they will allways be good and will sell in time. I hope you have filled my orders, and especially the prints and fancy goods that I may have a good assortment for fall and winter trade. In keeping up our business it will be very important that we continue to keep up a good assortment. In ordering goods it is impossible to order every little item and keep up with the times. One in buying often sees little things which will sell at a good profit, while one ordering would never think of them. These I must leave to you to fill up according to you[r] own notion. I still believe I shall have a good trade this fall. I see that all the troops which were taken from here for Utah have been ordered back.[17] The prospect for crops in all parts of the Territory were never more promising than at present. We have had an unusual quantity of rain so far this season and everything looks well. There has been no appropriation this Congress for our state house and I see no prospect at present of getting our money for those

12. Despite being politically dead, Miguel Otero was reelected for a third term as delegate in 1859. Twitchell, *Leading Facts*, 2:310. Twitchell assesses Otero favorably.

13. A Francisco Perea was elected territorial delegate in 1863, and perhaps that is who Kingsbury has in mind.

"I notice what you say about politics. Perea is not the man. He will disappoint the people worse than Otero has done. Let the people hold on to Otero untill they can do better. They ought to send an American." Webb to Kingsbury, Kansas City, Sept. 2, 1858, MHS.

14. Perhaps Augustin or John La Come of Taos County. Windham, ed., *New Mexico 1850 Territorial Census*, 3:54.

15. We have been unable to determine what Kingsbury means by Fort Larina.

16. "I am sorry to hear that Tom has returned. My opinion is that he ought to have continued on, and acted with firmness in protecting the interest of parties he went out to represent. . . . If Tom wants to go into business for himself you can rely on him. He will not do a large business but I think would be very safe. Try and get him to quit that woman." Webb to Kingsbury, Kansas City, Sept. 2, 1858, MHS.

17. From Utah, Albert Sidney Johnston had requested reinforcements from Fort Union to help fight the Mormons. See chapter 8.

Irons. It is good and will be paid some day but I am getting impatient for the use of the money. Can you suggest any way by which the payment can be hurried?[18] The papers are all at Washington in proper order and we ought not to be kept out of our money longer. Otero must have been asleep not to have got that appropriation through. Some here say he is in favor of moving the Capitol South. His party of friends appear to be very much dissatisfied with his operation this winter or rather at his doing nothing. This is their private talk. The Gazette this week has a long article about what he has done, but this is all moon shine and only put in for party sake. He could not be reelected.

[Tom] Weirick says that the Gold discoveries north are no humbug. That it is on the north fork of the Platt [Platte River], some two hundred and fifty mile from Taos. That he saw some parties coming in from there and a large party some 300 Cherikees going out.[19] If this turns out true it may help New Mexico some.

Hays has declined to receive our freight on the terms Kitchen offered, stating that Kitchen was a Mexican freighter and he declined coming down to a level with them.[20] So you will give the freight to Kitchen who you will find in re[a]diness for it soon as the goods get to Kansas. I think this is a poor excuse of Hays'es [sic]. He probably did not like the price. He no doubt expected to get a big price out of us 12 or 14 cents or some w[h]ere in that neighborhood, and is no doubt disapointed. I gave him the refusal at the same price Kitchen offered and by his declining I consider he forf[e]ited all claim in this freight and have so written to him. I hope you will take advantage of the weekly mail and write me as often as anything important offers.[21]

P.S. I wish you would send me a copy book for letter press for my private letters. Send a small one 300 to 500 pages. Get good white paper that is paged.[22] By leaving one end open you can send it through the mail for 1 cent the ounce. J.M.K.

Letter no. 72, Kingsbury to Webb, Santa Fe, August 14, 1858

I am now in receipt of yours of July 5th and 17th. Business so far this month has been rather limited. The fact is I have very few goods left for wholesale. I have sold all the Liquor & Manta except the 5 bales best manta, and nearly all our staple goods are gone. I have about 10 Bales old prints left. Your brogans this year did not turn out as well as usual. The regular article is not as smooth and neat as formerly. The fine ones that is the waxed are a good shoe but not desirable. They are not bound, heavy and large sizes. The balance of the shoes disapeared like hot cakes. Those Wms. sewd boots 2/5 are a fine article to see here

18. Webb was correct in replying, "We shall have to wait for our money for those Irons. I doubt if any appropriation for the capital [capitol] is made for years." Webb to Kingsbury, Kansas City, Sept. 2, 1858, MHS. Although another congressional appropriation for $60,000 was secured in 1860, it was "off-set by the direct war-tax of 1862." Twitchell, *Leading Facts*, 2:326.

19. The Cherokees to whom Wierick referred were veterans of gold mining operations in both north Georgia and in California, although their number was perhaps closer to sixty. In June of 1858 this party and various groups of whites began gold-hunting operations in the vicinity of Ralston Creek. After a few weeks with poor results, the Cherokees gave up. The whites, whose numbers were swelling, spread out across the Pike's Peak region or moved up to the South Platte River. By the end of the summer, news of potential gold discoveries spread quickly to an American public hit hard by the financial panic of 1857. Great anticipation marked the winter of 1858-59, as eager "fifty-niners" prepared for the coming spring. Hafen and Hafen, eds., *Reports from Colorado*, 14-17.

20. Amazon Hays's insult apparently refers to Charles Kitchen's low charges rather than his ethnicity. According to a contemporary article, "Native Mexicans are employed as teamsters mostly by traders of the same nationality. Some American freighters, however, hire them likewise on account of the low wages they are paid. While they receive only about $15 per month, their Anglo-American colleagues receive from $25 to $30." Gardner, "Trade with New Mexico," 21.

21. The Santa Fe-Independence mail began to run weekly on July 1, 1858.

22. This type of letterpress book was the sort that Webb used as well. They contained thin, tisuue-like paper, upon which copies of letters could be preserved. While Kingsbury's private correspondence books were not preserved, some of Webb's were. These can be consulted at the Missouri Historical Society.

& profitable. Retail at present is slim but I hope it will improve. [Tom] Weirick is again with me. He was afraid of the responsibility of starting on his own account, and is much pleased to get back with me. He says he intends to stay with me as long as I remain in the country and will be perfectly satisfied. I have also got Talisfer back. He got poor and is very willing to return on the old terms and says I may now depend on his services as long as I want him. Young Weirick I have turned over to Tom Bowler. He has put him at keeping his books and so far is much pleased with him. Old Uncle Tom is still with me and will remain untill our fall Train arrives. He intends to open a small store for himself. Will go to San Miguel and open there if no better place offers before then. He has some money and I expect to furnish him his first goods. [Charles] Blumner will open this fall in Santa Fe, take one of his stores down at the corner. He has agreed to buy of me if I have the right kind of a Stock. Wholesale goods are not plenty here, and if you send me a well assorted stock, you may expect to hear of prompt sales. Tom [Bowler] has engaged all the Liquors we have on hand, will take them as he wants them. They are doing well with their house. It is crowded all the time. The gardain [*sic*] is a neat profit and advantage in supplying the Table.[23] Their new dining room seats about 75 persons, and they have so many boarders that many have to wait for the second table. Tom has another fine daughter just one week old. They call it "Ellen Grayson." Mother and baby getting along nicely. Poor Dick [Owens] is still on his feet. He continues to drink all he can. He has failed much the last 3 months. He totters up as far as the Exchange & back to his store, at a gait of an old man of 90. It is astonishing to all that he is still with the living. He cannot last much longer.[24]

[Henry] Brittingham has completely ruined himself with Liquor. He has had 3 Whisky fits, and looks like an idiot, perfectly simple. He has no goods yet, and I think he has no prospect of getting any. Still he claims to have some coming. I fear I shall have trouble with him about Messervy's store. He leased it for one year and is unwilling to give it up. If he does not pay the rent punctually I shall compel him to give up the Keys. I have a chance now to rent it to Frank Abriu [Abreu?] and will take it from the first of next month. Elison [Samuel Ellison] is still employed in the Gov's Office. He loves gambling as well as ever. It will always keep him poor. As I predicted the Gov's mine with his management has turned out a failure. He has now suspended all operations there, and discharged his men. He talks now of getting Mr. Idler back again. All he has expended has been sunk. Up to the present he has realized nothing from the outfit. He is hard pushed for funds, is unable to pay for the mashinery which he bought of Leitensdorfer, and Leitensdorfer has commenced suit for it. It will come up in the next court.[25] The overseer he had, evidently did not

23. See chapter 7.
24. See chapter 4.
25. Prior to 1858, the management of the New Mexico Mining Company had extracted gold without machinery, deriving about three ounces of gold per ton of ore, bringing in $60 at the mint or $100 in greenbacks. With machinery, the partners of the company had hoped that the mine would begin paying for itself, since their investment alone was financing its operations. According to Webb, for example, Rencher had everything he owned invested in the mines. But clearly, their scheme failed; the mine alone could not generate sufficient funds to purchase equipment and develop new deposits simultaneously. Townley, "New Mexico Mining Company," 62; Webb to Kingsbury, Hamden, CT, Oct. 25, 1858, MHS.

understand his business. Our new secretary is a very good man. Is becoming popular and will get along well.[26]

I have heard nothing yet from José [Hernández]. I wish you would send me by mail <u>Two</u> copies of a good Masonic Manuel or text book. Get the best work you can find. Our Lodge is getting along well & harmoniously. I am much interested there. Hold the office of Senior Deacon & flatter myself that I fill it well.[27]

I have nothing from Mr. Tolhurst by this mail. Kind regards to all.

P. S. On account of the weather and other inconveniences, I have been much delaid in plastering the house, which will increase the expense, but when it is finished it will be well worth all the outlay & increase the looks & value of the property. If you could see what is finished I think you would be pleased with it. The roof has stood well so far. The pretil[e]s are some worn, if I can get adobies I shall have them all raised one adobie.[28]

Letter no. 73, Kingsbury to Webb, Santa Fe, August 29, 1858

I am without advices from you since my last. I have nothing Special to write but send these few lines to let you know how the month's business foots up. Sales amt. to $4,500.+ Collections are $2,200.+ Business is rather quiet but we have our share of what is going. I shall be unable to make any large sales untill the fall train arrives. I hope then to do well. Retail is limited this season. Money is very scarce and the fact is the people are poor. After the crops are gathered which now promises to be very fair we can expect to find more money is the hands of the people. [Joseph] Hersch has got his steam [grist]mill started. It works well and he is delighted with it. Mr. Easterday is to have the management of it.[29] [T. H.] McKutchen is trying to buy Joe [Hersch] out, has offered him $60,000.+ for the property and all his interests in the Territory including his last flour contract. H. Oneil has gone to the States for goods, will bring a fall train this season. I think he and Mc are together in trying to buy Joe out, however, there is little prospect that Joe will make the trade. Elic Duvall is very anxious to buy Tom's [Bowler's] interest in the Exchange. Tom is willing to sell but will do nothing about it untill Frank returns. If Frank consents, Tom will probably sell, and then give his whole attention to his mail contract.

Their house is doing well, but it takes every dime they can raise to start these Mail outfits. They have paid us nothing on this Spring goods and still owe a small balance on old a/c, however we will get it in time for next purchases.

The Southern Mail is just in by it I rec.[d] a letter from A. B. O'Bannon containing a check of $500.+ to cover the balance due us from W. T. Smith with interest. He, O'Bannon, claims 10% for collecting which

26. Alexander M. Jackson of Mississippi.

27. Kingsbury was initiated into Masonry on September 5, 1857, elected Senior Deacon in December 1857, and served as such in 1858, 1859, and 1860. He missed only two meetings out of forty-eight during his tenure as Senior Deacon. Webb and Messervy were also members but rarely attended meetings. The Masonic Lodge in Santa Fe, Montezuma Lodge No. 109, was chartered on May 8, 1851, making it the oldest lodge west of the Rocky Mountains. It was the successor to two military lodges from the 1848 war with Mexico. Glen W. Burttram, Secretary, Montezuma Lodge No. 1, Santa Fe, New Mexico to Jane Elder, personal correspondence, May 21, 1993.

28. Pretiles are low walls or parapets formed by extending the walls of an adobe structure above the flat roof line.

"How are you gettin along fixing the house and what is the expense? Since you have commenced I would do the thing thoroughly, but when you have done that, <u>stop</u>, don't go to any larger outlay. Patch up if any repairs are necessary and get along with that for the present. What I refer to is don't go into any new ideas about roofs, or inside plastering. (Your idea to plaster the outside with lime is an economical one.)" Webb to Kingsbury, Kansas City, Sept. 2, 1858, MHS.

I am to send him. This I shall do with pleasure and count ourselves very lucky to get out of this debt so well. I didn't exactly understand how this money could come from O'Bannon.[30] Last April I requested him to send the note to Sherman, and expected it was in Sherman's hands since that time. At that time Sherman wrote me that he would do all he could to collect it (although he did not acknowledge its receipt) and mentioned from what source he thought it could be made. However, we have got the money from O'Bannon and he claims the commission, and I conclude that he must have kept the note and never sent it to Sherman. This is one hard case less on our books. The only bill that troubles me now is the one I sold to Kavanaugh Pino & Hovey. It is not due yet, Still I fear I shall have trouble to get it. I am confident it will eventually be paid but not promptly. Hovey is the only one here, and it is impossible for him to pay untill some returns come from the outfit sent off. The last a/c of them they had opened the goods for return on the river Jordan, near Salt Lake. Hovey says he expects Kavanaugh back with Col. Loring's command. We must wait till then to know the result. I hope all will turn out right.[31]

Letter no. 74, Kingsbury to Webb, Santa Fe, September 4, 1858

Your letter of Aug. 3rd with a/c current is before me, also noting the safe arrival of the Drafts amt.g to $3,216.50 with my memo. for goods. I hope you are sending me a good lot of Prints. Our stock needs them badly. I have not a desirable piece left. When you will have rec.d all my letters you will be fully posted as to what I done about this fall freight. I hope it will be all right and be no conflicting. The way it stands I expect Kitchen to bring it and hope you have given it to him. When he returns if I hear nothing from you to the contrary I shall do the best I can to make some arraingement for future freights with him, at any rate make a bargain for next spring. Tom [Bowler] was well pleased with his whiskey, he did not order more of the same, as what you sent was enough of that quality to last him this year. I hope that will be a fair article you are sending this fall. It is for him. I think Chick & Co. have desieved you about Miller & Co. having quit the commission business. I have heard nothing of it here. Your question about how the goods opened I believe I have answered in a previous letter. They arrived in good order, the damage was so little that I claimed nothing of the freighters, and on opening I have found nothing injured. The goods looked well and the best proof is they have sold well. There was much competition this year which prevented me getting big prices but I have done the best I could and if I have made no bad debts I shall be perfectly satisfied. There was hardly enough of the New York goods for me to judge well about them. I have sold but few silks. The reason is the late arrival. They will, I think, sell this fall, the price Black Silk is

30. This must have been a tough debt to collect. Webb's reaction to the convoluted way in which it was collected was similar to Kingsbury's: "I am glad to get the money, enough so to pay O'Bannon his ten per cent whether he is entitled to it or not." Webb to Kingsbury, Hamden, CT, Sept. 28, 1858, MHS.

31. Webb echoed Kingsbury's concern: "You must look sharp for our account. Don't place too much confidence in Hovey. He is sure to slip up some day and I would only credit him to a limited extent, and on very short terms. Kavanaugh is honorable, but his ability to do as he would depends on a good many contingencies. Pino is uncertain always. So I consider that debt a little dubious." Ibid., Kansas City, Sept. 2, 1858, MHS.

good and nearly all sold. Those childs clothing you sent are not desirable. It is to[o] fashonable & expensive. Childs Pants & Jackets <u>with Sleaves</u> will sell well that odd lot I bought all sold at retail for good profit. The Silk Hdkfs were just what I wanted. I have some left, but they have sold well. I enclose you the statement you wish. I think it is correct enough to base any calculation upon. Soon as I get the total of the fall goods I will send it to you to be added to this.

I wish you would send me a copy of the bill of chairs you bought for Tom last Spring, so that I can enter it in our books to your Cr. and know how to charge them to him. Also explain what that $300 is for, paid to Miller & Co. July 24th for R. F. Green, so that I may collect it from Frank [Green]. I believe your a/c is all correct with the exception of 10 cents in amt. for Doan King & Co. However, I will make our books to show a balance same as you render <u>$3,569.41</u>. That is when the chair bill is entered.

I do not remember now whether I replied to your explination about the $100 Cr. claimed by Grayson. It was all right and he is satisfied that our a/c is correct. I hope you sent all the Coffee that I ordered. They are asking now 26 & 28 cents. Ours has been gone some time. Levi bought a bill last week of a Mexican on fair terms, Sugar 19, Coffee 21, Candles $12 a box, good <u>heavy wide</u> Manta 11 cents all on 6 months. He bought in Albuquerque and paid the freight up.

You will remember I made my orders before the Spring goods arrived. If I had it to do over I could make important and valuable change in them. I shall want Manta & Lienzo badly, but I could not forsee it then. However, if you send me a good stock I feel sure I can do well with it. I have now so poor an assortment that I cannot sell any big bills. Our retail stock with the exception of shoes is pretty fair yet. I have but a few bot. fine Pomade left. That St. Louis bill of Cologne is a poor outfit.

Letter no. 75, Kingsbury to Webb, Santa Fe, September 18, 1858

Your long letter of Aug. 23rd is before me. I have rec.[d] no books or copy of invoices yet, hope it will come by next mail. I will try to answer all your inquiries in full before I make any more orders. I will commence now on a few. In the first place you have made a desided mistake in not sending the Scarlet Yarn. I had the 100 lbs all sold at $2.50 a pound, and am sorry to disapoint those who want it, besides loosing our profit. In regard to that yarn in the a/c stock, it is unsaleable, for three reasons. First it is not yarn but worsted,[32] then it is in ½ lb bundles, then there is no color but blue, orange and green which is unsaleable. This is worsted we bought of Siter, Price & Co. when we first commenced and I do not remember having an enquiry

32. Worsted is a smooth, compact wool spun from long wool fibers and used especially for firm, napless fabrics, carpeting, or knitting. Yarn is a continuous, often plied, strand composed of either natural or man-made fibers or filaments, and used in weaving and knitting to form cloth.

for it since Dodge closed his business at Cibolete [Cebolleta].[33] I have repeatedly offered it at 50 cents a pound and cannot get clear of it. It stands now a portion of our dead stock and likely to remain so. The Scarlet Yarn is used by all the Pueblos in working borders on the black Tilmas which they make.[34] They use no other color but red or scarlet for this purpose 1 oz skeins sell at 25 cents which gives the retailer $4 a pound. The 30 lbs you sent this Spring did not last me five minutes after it was opened.[35] I conclude from your letter that you have not bought the Barcelona Hdkf. 100 ps. is a good many but I believe I could sell them all, as none were bought this year. They would have been good to us for $8 a piece. The last you bought you paid $6 a piece. Next spring 100 pieces would be too much as they are in demand now and of course everybody will bring them next year. You know how it works here, if an article say sugar is scarce the price goes up for the season, and the next year every one brings a big lot and the market is overstocked. So it is with every particular article which is used here.

Blue Denims I know are good and I will do my best to make them take. Blue Drills[36] for several years have not paid the consequence is no one brings them, and they are now scarce. Johnson brought 3 or 4 Bales, inferior which he has sold here in town at 16 and 17 cents. You have done right in filling my order for Drills. In case the prints you are sending prove desirbale [sic] patterns you may be sure I will get my own price for them. I wholesale[d] about half you sent this spring at 14 ½ & 15 cents. The French Prints sold well. I retailed a portion at 50 cents and wholesaled the balance at 40 cents. A few prices might answer from time to time but not many. I have no fa[u]lt to find with the shawls sent, but I must confess that I cannot sell shawls, and don't care ever to have another cotton or wool shawl while in business, except perhaps black. A few will always sell for mourning. The Jews sell a great many fancy cheap silk or silk & cotton shawls.[37] If we could hit the right kind I might sell them but as we have never had any I cannot say how they would turn out. Fancy capes silk and other material are being worn here at Biles [*bailes*, or dances] and on the street by Mexicans. I am willing to try a few next season. Since the Sisters at the convent introduced the sun bonnet they have now become very common and they are eventually to take the place of the rebozo.[38] Then shawls, capes &c will be used. They are now confined principally to children and misses. You speak of having made a pretty little bill of clothing as being cheap and less cost & money. I don't know whether you refer to the bill of Past spring or one which you are now sending. Clothing is a good article for this country if we could only get the right kind at fair prices. I shall want you next spring to go to Jakes house in New York and try a bill from them. Levi for several years has had the whole controle here in clothing and I see no reason why we cannot get a share of it. [James] Johnson bought this year at their

33. Siter, Price & Co was a firm in Philadelphia. Cebolleta, near Mt. Taylor, was where agent Henry Dodge ran a trading post for Navajos before he was killed in 1856.

34. A watercolor done in 1849 by the artist Richard Kern and reproduced as a chromolithograph shows "Whar-te (The Industrious Woman)," wife of the governor of Jémez Pueblo, wearing a black cloak, or tilma, with a scarlet border as noted by Kingsbury. Weber, *Richard H. Kern*, 78.

35. Webb did not send any scarlet yarn because he could not find any in St. Louis. Webb to Kingsbury, Hamden, CT, Oct. 21, 1858, MHS.

36. Drill is a durable cotton fabric in a twill weave.

37. Webb took a philosophical view of Kingsbury's inability to compete with Santa Fe's Jewish merchants when it came to selling shawls, and advised him to "let them slide" if he could not sell them at a profit. Webb went on to advise that "the Jews sell fancy goods that it would be impossible for us to dispose of. They sell by per cent, and have their customers, who will go nowhere else. Jake [Spiegelberg] gave me a little insight into his manner of doing business and he skins to the quick. Even Levi does not know the cost of his goods until they are sold. This is private, but goes to show that to attempt to do business as they do, you must have your customers under your thumb and do business in a way which neither you nor me [sic] care to." Webb to Kingsbury, Hamden, CT, Oct. 21, 1858, MHS.

38. Kingsbury is referring to the nuns from the convent of Loretto, who first came to Santa Fe in 1852. Horgan, *Lamy*, 160. Rebozos were described by W. W. H. Davis as long scarves, made of silk or cotton, which were worn over the head, with one end thrown across the left shoulder. *El Gringo*, 61.

house and since Levi has got through with his, Johnson is doing a good business in clothing.[39]

The Bills from Jeffray & Son and Davis & Co. have turned out so far very well. Gloves are slow sale. I shall not want any more for a long time, unless it is a heavy buck for Teamsters or Gentlemens riding gloves. Fancy muslin dresses I cannot retail. If you send any more they must be cheap for wholesale. Those 4 dz Hdkf in fancy boxes I sold at my own price. Those that cost 4.50 sold for $12. The others I sold at $15. The 36 ps silk hdkf are all good and will sell. I will in time sell the printed Linen and shirt bosoms, but do not want any more. Plain white Linen is the best sale, that from Becke this year was good, the 80 cents goods I sold at $2.50 Now in regard to De Lains [sic], you copied my bills too closely. Tissues, Bar[r]age & challe does not sell well.[40] I bought all kinds as an experiment, and find that cheap De Laines are the best, 16, 18 or 20 cents not over 20, but they must be plain distinct figures, something in the order of those all wool which you sent, clear figures on solid ground. J. C. Howe & Co. in Boston is the best house in these goods, but my impression is that they only sell by the package. The next time you are in Boston you had better see their goods & if they do not break packages, they will give you the names of houses who job thier goods. The all wool De Lains were beautifull and sold [word illegible—crazy?] at $1 a yd. all except one price and I send a sample of that. This would also sell easy were it not for the purple & green stripes. As it is, it is too much mixed up for Mexicans. The narrow ground with one or 2 distinct figures is sufficient, however in regard to this goods it is too costly to send any great quantity. It is something like silk dress patterns, a few is enough say 10 or 20 in a stock.

I have cleared the house of challes, Barage & cheap De Lains, after selling all the desirable patterns at a good profit. I got an offer for the balance old stock, remnants and all, a little over cost & freight and thought it best to let them slide. I have not a yard left. I found there was a prospect of many of them sticking as mules if I held them for a profit. Now for the future don't send any unless you think you understand what I want, even of the right sort 20 or 30 pr are enough for any one stock. I am satisfied you could have done better in the East with many of the things which I ordered from St. Louis, but the goods coming so late I had no fair chance of making out my fall orders. The most of it had to be done by g[u]ess work, under the circumstances I think I done very well. I have not made many mistakes. If I had it to do over with the knowledge I now have I should change some few things and add a good many more which are left off.

I think I wrote you planely about the Whiskey. That 10 Bbl which you sent this Spring is all right and gave entire satisfaction to Tom [Bowler] and his customers. He does not object to the quality nor the

39. James Johnson, a native of Maryland, came to Santa Fe in 1852 and became a prominent citizen and merchant. The two-story Catron Block/Blatt Building located on the northeast corner of the plaza was originally named for him. Sherman, *Santa Fe: A Pictorial History*, 40.

40. Delaine is a light muslin, usually woolen, used chiefly for women's dresses. Barrage is a worked linen, interwoven with worsted flowers, used for inexpensive dresses and furnishing. Montgomery, *Textiles in America*, 157. Perhaps by challe Kingsbury means challis, a lightweight soft clothing fabric.

price, but he ordered a cheaper article this fall thinking he could make it go on the cr[edit] of the other and at the same time give him a margin for a better profit.

You speak of filling another order for [David V.] Whiting.[41] I was not aware that he had ordered anything untill this. Neither did I know anything about the spring order untill I got the bill. He would order all the goods in St. Louis if he thought you would send them. Now do not trouble yourself any further about orders from him or in fact any one else unless they send them through me. I am here for this purpose and if they do not wish to send through me let them get somebody else to bring them. It is all right so far, but I write this to avoide trouble in the future. Whiting at present is good and can pay, but he is very slow. If you were to make a practice of filling everybodies order, we would in the end slip up, besides causing you much trouble they are not willing to allow any profit, and then we run the risk of getting our money back or keeping the goods which perhaps no one else would want. The watch for Frank [Green] is a very different thing, or any little thing which might be ordered by a good man. I mean asst.g [assisting] orders when there is risk.

I am very anxious to get your Invoices to know what is coming. I hope you have sent the Billiard Table, also the Two casks big Hoes. All the Hoes sent out by Gov.t to [James L.] Collins are little garden hoes which are no use in this country. When I ordered the second cask from St. L. I had just sold all you sent this spring.[42]

The Mexicans are now selling good sugar at 20 cents on 6 months. We cannot compete with them in groceries. The only way for us is to wait and keep back till they get through and along through the winter if any article gets scarce then we can make a fair profit. Our great profit and the best of our business now lies in fancy and asst.[d] goods both for retail and wholesale. This is why I have urged upon you to send me anything that was desirable and that would help the looks of our assortment.

The Looking Glasses for Tom came all safe and were satisfactory. I will write you about cigars and the shoe bills after they arrive. The New York & Boston papers have commenced coming. Sperm Candles are poor for this market.[43] They run worse than the [word illegible]. I can perhaps sell a few but I would not send any more. The bill of Looking Glasses which you bought at Kimball Whittemore & Co were the best packed we have ever had. There was only one glass broken in the whole bill and that only one little corner. I had it cut off and the frame cut down to fit and it is as good as new. The Glasses were what I wanted and reasonable. Don't send any more Oval glasses, nor 2 Glasses in one frame. They are not desireable. I don't know what is the matter with Brogans this year. I can't sell any. Business generally has been very dull so far this month.

41. David V. Whiting was interpreter and secretary to Gov. James L. Calhoun. He later moved to Kansas City, Missouri, where he and Miguel Otero ran a forwarding and commission business under that name of Whiting and Otero, New York and Kansas City. Mary Jean Cook to Jane Elder, personal correspondence, n.d., n.p.

42. James L. Collins was the superintendant of Indian affairs, who had been making purchases for the Indians through Webb & Kingsbury in 1858 and 1859.

43. Kingsbury is referring to fine wax candles made from whale oil.

P.S. In case you will want any private funds you must let me know when it will be required and in what sums so that I may send it to you. I prefer to send you what you may want for private purposes outside of my business remittances.

Letter no. 76, Kingsbury to Webb, Santa Fe, September 18, 1858

"Private"

Dear Sir, I succeeded in getting José [Hernández] a good chance to work his way to the States on good pay. After having a long conversation with him he finally desided not to go. He has some little delicacy and a goodeal of feeling about returning to you.[44] He says you have no confidence in him, have believed all the reports that are to his discredit many of which are false. He feels & acknowledges now that he is under many obligations to you for what you have already done for him and he does not wish to increase them. He says he had rather starve than go back and be a berden [burden] to you. If he was sure that there was an opening where he could make himself usefull perhaps he might go but as it is, he did not know what he would do when he got there. He would like to see you and the rest of the family, but he could not see that he would be justified to go there just for a visit. He does not wish you to forget him or loose track of him, will always be glad to get your letters and receive your advise. He says he has no claim upon you. He does not expect any assistance from you. You have set him free to shift for himself and he hopes yet to live, and prove to you that he was worthy of your confidence. He acknowledged to me that he has indulged in strong drink. This he said he had done in times, when he felt perfectly desparate, and done it to forget himself. He feels his situation is anything but a pleasant one. He finds himself in the world with no one to encourage him in well doing and only to find fault with what he does wrong. He says he has been very unfortunate in not being able to keep steady employment. He declairs it is no fa[u]lt of his and he don't know how he could have prevented it by any act of his, that it has been purely by cercumstances beyond his controle, that he has been so much out of employ.

He is now living at the [word illegible] waiting for the first opportunity which may offer for him to do something. I urged upon him to accept this chance to go in only for the trip and get the pay for it, told him the probability was such he could see as well as myself that he would be here all winter on expenses, and if he went in and wintered in Missouri it would not cost as much and he would be there in the early Spring & perhaps get a good situation on the road. He replied that he had rather be here out of employ than to be there, that he thought there were more chances for him here. He did not know of anything there that he was capible of doing. He had no trade and he

44. Webb had asked Kingsbury to send José to him in Connecticut. "He [José] seems to want to come to the states. I am afraid he has learned bad habits, but am willing to do anything I can for his good and think he would do better here and with me. He will be out of the way of temptation and I can restrain him more or less and perhaps save him yet. I have written him to come on if you advise him to come. Now unless he has become too abandoned you may advise him to come." Webb to Kingsbury, Hamden, CT, June 18, 1858, MHS.

was not willing to take the risk there of other employment, that here he felt more secure, the little money he had made he wanted to save, and would do so to the last moment. So he finally desided to take the chances here.

He says he never felt free in your presence, was always down whenever you were in conversation with him, and for this reason he expects you thought he acknowledged to the many charges which you have told him of when it was only through fear of diffidence in replying to you. He knows that you can be very hasty and has been afraid of making you angry with him. He is now afraid that if he was with you he could not satisfy you and it would only make him more unhappy to see you displeased.

I have told him very planely how he stands in this community and how it is that he is so, also the opinions of others about him that he is lazy and cannot be trusted, and that he can only over come this by regular and correct deportment, that if he was determined to do right it would take time, but in the end he could reistablish his character, but it depended entirely upon himself. He appeared greatfull to me and said it was always his intention and that he would do the best he could and was willing to stay right here, and abide the consequences of his future conduct.

I do not know that I can say anything further in regard to him. With this and previous letters you will know all that I know of him. I shall continue to keep an eye on him & if he is disposed to do what is right I will assist him all I can & be very willing to do it.

Letter no. 77, Kingsbury to Webb, Santa Fe, September 25, 1858

Yours of the 2nd, 3rd & 6th inst. are before me. I have written you fully my opinions about Watts. I hope you will not let him have any more money unless you obtain undoubted security.[45] Hovey has full power to use Watts name and it is flying round here at any amt. of interest just to raise money. I am watching Hovey closely, have stop[p]ed all transactions with the whole outfit. You need not fear that they will take us in. I have had already full enough trouble and anxiety in the transactions we have had with them and have no idea of opening any fresh negotiations. With regard to those goods I sold for Salt Lake.[46] I knew at the time there was an extry risk, but after considering well I concluded to take the risk and wait the result. In the first place I was very anxious to sell what they took and then I put my own prices on the things. I could have sold them three times the amt. I did if I had have had full confidence in them. We have reliable information here that Kavanaugh has disposed of everything (except the Teams which are with Pino) at a good profit & I have every reason to believe that we will get our money from them. At present I am more

45. Webb had written that he had given Watts $2,500 out of his private account to give to Tom [Bowler] to pay for his carriage and harness at Concord. "Watts promised the money in a few days, but Frank [Green] informs me that Tom will have to send me the money from Santa Fe. I am glad it was in my power to do Tom a favor." Webb's letter continues, "Watts is a man of but little judgment in a business way, and if Tom follows all his recommendations, the first he will know he will mire down." Ibid., Kansas City, Sept. 2, 1858, MHS.

46. Kingsbury refers to the Kavanaugh, Pino and Hovey expedition with which Tom Weirick was briefly involved. The Mormon settlement of Utah, which began in 1847, had given birth to a prosperous trade. Prices were relatively stable until 1858, the year of the Mormon War, when prices spiraled upward. Where sugar and coffee had sold for forty cents a pound year after year (the early traders had set a price policy), in 1858 they sold for sixty-five cents a pound. Walker, *Wagonmasters*, 161.

anxious about the little bill I sold to [George M.] Alexander than the other. Alexander was sutler for the troops, and has come out at the little end of the horn. Report says he has lost on the expedition not less than $8,000 or 9,000+. His first bad luck was to loose his cattle by the weather, then had to cash [cache] a large portion of his goods on the prairie, and then heavy losses by the soldiers stealing. They helped themselves from his goods when they pleased and he could not prevent it. Absolutely robbed him from day to day.[47] You may rest assured that I am not getting wild or over ambitious. Every business transaction is protected with all the caution at my command, in fact I am at present more cautious and timid than when I had you present to consult with. I know [E.] Branford well and am not going too far with him. I watch all our accounts carefully and our collections will prove that I work faithfully in them, with many I have succeeded far beyond my expectations. I have even collected those little bills of Jesus Baca and N. Quintana. I have not yet given up that debt of Louis Felsenthal. He is still here and if he remains I will catch him some day. If I only had a judgement on his note I could now secure $150 on it. I got clear of Uncle Tom on the first of the month.[48] He went with Collins to assist in distributing presents to the Indians. He still intends to open a small business at San Miguel, soon as our goods arrive, will buy from us and it will be safe as I have now on deposit from him some $1,400.+ for that purpose & by the time the goods get here he will have some $500 more which I know is sure. He will not want over $2,000 or 2,500 stock to start with. As you had left the Neutral Spirits to buy in St. Louis I am glad you have sent none. It was ordered for Tom [Bowler] and nothing but the best (Atwoods) will answer for him. He wants nothing common, and I have no use for it whatever except for him. I could have found sale for all the Coffee. I am only afraid of the sugar. I am not sorry you that you did not fill Whitings order. I have always kept copies of my orders, you will learn before this that I did not duplicate the Hoes without knowing it. You will find enclosed a list of my principal sales this season, with the amt. to each. Hoppin & Apel is the largest out side.[49] I did not let this bill go untill I was convinced that they were good for it. It is 4 & 6 mos. They are both honest men and unless some great misfortune happens to them, we can count the debt sure and rely upon the money coming when it is due. I took note of what you said in the Spring about [Henry] Connelly and have kept clear of him, have refused to sell him except for cash, offered him good bargains for <u>cash</u> but could not trade.[50]

[Moses] Sachs starts for California in miserable health. I doubt very much if he will ever reach there. I am done with him, hope for his own sake and family that he may come out well and ahead.[51]

The improvements I have put on the property will cost between $500 & 600. It is all out side and was necessary, by doing it with lime

47. "He [Alexander] is not a business man and is too much dependent upon others, and his selection of agents I don't think any too well of." Webb to Kingsbury, Hamden, CT, Oct. 25, 1858, MHS.

48. Webb had warned Kingsbury earlier to get rid of Thomas Rowland (see chapter 8), and now elaborated: "You had better dispense with the services of Old Tom as soon as you can. I think perhaps he is strictly honest, but he is an old fool about women and I never knew him to do any good for himself or anybody else. These facts did not strike me so forcibly untill I had a talk with Mr. Messervy." Ibid., Kansas City, Sept. 2, 1858, MHS. "I wrote from Westport about Uncle Tom. I have but little confidence in him as a clerk, no confidence as a salesman, and if he succeeds in doing good for himself now it will be a new streak. I would not credit him much at the start. Probably you cannot get along without letting him have a few goods, but the less the better, and you will have a good time collecting it. Look out sharp for him." Ibid., Hamden, CT, Sept. 28, 1858, MHS.

49. Mercantile partners who had stores in Tubac, in today's Arizona, and in Mesilla.

50. "You had better be a little carefull of Connelly & Co. Connelly is [a] hard man. I am told there are several thousand dollars indebtedness about here two years old. He owes a good deal in St. Louis and I presume in the East also." Webb to Kingsbury, Kansas City, Sept. 2, 1858, MHS.

51. Sachs's debt to Webb & Kingsbury was secured by Judge Otero.

it cost about double, but I am convinced it will be the cheapest in the end. This winter I intend to repaint the store and if the house should be empty will paint that. I fear that next spring I shall be compeled to put a thin coat of dirt on the whole roof. I am carefull about increasing expense and will ex[h]aust nothing in experiments or in unnecessary outlays.

We have nothing here except favorable reports about the new Gold discoveries. Some few have gone but we have not much excitement about it. Louis Simons formerly of this place you probably know him, is just from there & now on his way back with a small party & provisions. He says that when he left there were about 60 men at work with pans, that they averaged about $8 a day to the man. There are no rich pockets discovered yet. The Gold is fine and so far is even & regular. No one doubts that there is gold there. It only remains to prove whether it will turn our profitable or not to work it.[52]

I am very anxious to learn more about those lost goods. I hope your papers are so that you will know exactly what was on the boat and the value. Are they insured in St. Louis or East? is the office sound? how long will it take to recover from the office what is coming to us? I hope you have already written me all the particulars.[53] I am sorry to loose the Boots and Shoes and chewing Tobacco from our Asst. [assortment]. I can do very well without the other articles you mention and hope that the balance was unimportant in our Asst. did you not have time to replace the chewing Tobacco? I do hope you will have no trouble with the office and that they will settle everything fair.

Watts agreement with Tom [Bowler] was to furnish half the money in these mail contracts, but he has fooled him and up to the present has not put in a cent. This cramps Tom in money matters. He says however that your $2,500 is all right and will be paid in full with interest, but he can do nothing about sending it untill Frank [Green] arrives. He is expected about the 10th next month. The El Paso mail has been increased to weekly service and Tom has all he can do to get up the Teams. He would not have been cramped attal [at all] had Watts come up to his bargain. In case you do not want your money immediately, and would like to let it stand on interest, it would suit Tom to let it stand as he has now no confidence of getting any assistance from Watts. Tom says he will be able to carry it all through without him and declairs that Watts shall have no share of the profits.[54] Should you however require your money immediately, send word to Tom and he will make arraingement to send it to you at once.

José [Hernández] has gone out with [R. E.] Clemin's surveying party. He has a contract for some work south which will take 3 or 4 mos. and Jose will get good pay for that time.[55]

My letter book has arrived. It got pretty well greased in the Mail coach but it will answer. It was just what I wanted. I will give you the

52. Kingsbury is commenting on the new discoveries in Colorado. Webb wrote in answer to this letter: "We have conflicting reports about the Pike's Peak Gold diggings, but the reports are rather favorable than otherwise. There have [been] large number gone out this fall and should the reports from them be favorable there will be a rush out in the spring. If there are mines there which will pay, there will be new discoveries made all along that range of mountains and all over the Territory." Webb to Kingsbury, Hamden, CT, Oct. 25, 1858, MHS.

53. Kingsbury need not have worried about the soundness of the insurance office. Webb had insured their goods through Shoe and Leather Dealers Fire and Marine Inc. whose president was their Boston agent, J. C. Abbott, and one of whose board members was his former partner, William S. Messervy. Ibid.

54. "I have written you about Tom's transactions with Watts, and am glad to find that Tom has thus early found out that he will not be a very profitable partner. He [Watts] will try and assume to Tom that he cannot get along without him, and that his influence is necessary to his success, but I would rather not have his influence at so great a sacrifice. Watts is clever enough and I beleive [sic] honest, but he is a reckless business man, and will always be in hot water." Ibid.

55. Webb was happy to hear that José was working again, and asked that Kingsbury send him to Connecticut once he was through with Clemin, since he had need of a teamster for his farm. Webb to Kingsbury, Hamden, CT, Oct. 25, 1858, MHS.

footings of this months business in my next letter. It is rather slight so far. Soon as I get your list of Bills payable, I will begin to send funds to meet them. By a little arraingement I will have plenty of funds there ahead of the time.

Letter no. 78, Kingsbury to Webb, Santa Fe, October 3, 1858

I hope you have rec.ᵈ all my letters up to the present. I rec.ᵈ this morning your letter of Sept. 9ᵗʰ also Book of Invoices and Bill of Lading. I have just had time to glance at the invoices and nothing more. When [Charles] Kitchen arrives I will make the best bargain I can with him for what freight we may have next year. When you ascertain the exact amt. of goods lost send me the figures and when you recover the same from the Ins. Office give me the amt. and how you dispose of it as early as you can. Sales for Sept. amt. to $2,600.+ Collections $2,500.+ You will find herewith Trial Balance from our books made up to Oct. 1ˢᵗ by which you can see the exact state of all the a/c's on our books. You will discover a Cr. of $3,000.+ to J. Mercure. This amt. I borrowed that you might have it to use in St. Louis. Tom Bowler is to pay the Int. on it and also the amt. whenever Mercure may want it.

Tom has certainly broken the pledge he made to you. Still I see nothing in his conduct as yet, for us to be especially alarmed at. When I have more time I will write you more fully on this subject.[56]

How is it about that Insurance note, is it to go on our books? If so send me the date, amt. and time.

I understand from your letter that you will pay the bills of Doan King & Co. and Berthald Rozier & Co. This will leave me only the notes payable to meet. Are the Notes given in St. Louis payable at any particular house and where? By this mail I have made arraingements for Mr. Abbott to receive in our account $525.+ direct from Washington. It is for One quarter Salary due D. V. Whiting for Services in Gen.l Pelham's Office.[57] Have requested Mr. Abbott, when rec.d to pay it out as you may direct. There are more fall trains this year for Santa Fe than ever was known in one season before.

Letter no. 79, Kingsbury to Webb, Santa Fe, October 10, 1858

I am in receipt of yours of Sept. 14th from St. Louis. [Henry] Oneil & [James E.?] Sabine have arrived and report that Kitchen's trains were getting along well. I look for the mule waggons here about the 20th. When the goods arrive I will examine everything as closely as possible, and try to assist you in your memorandums. I hope you have got sufficient information to enable you to settle for the insurance justly for all parties. Business is exceedingly dull so far this month. I hope however it will take a start soon as the good arrive. José has returned

56. Bowler, who ran a gaming table, must have been gambling himself, and had pledged to Webb that he would stop. This brief comment by Kingsbury elicited the following from Webb: "What you say about Tom alarms me. They are owing us too much money. I should feel perfectly safe and there is scarcely anything which would give me more pleasure than to do all in my power either individually or as a member of our firm to assist him, provided he was true to himself, to his own interests, to his former character, to his solemn pledges, but when he violates them all, I must confess I felt some alarm. I feel a particular interest in Tom's success. I like him. He was a faithful clerk and I do believe a true friend. I always felt that Tom loved and respected me. I know that these sentiments were entertained by me towards him in a very great degree. But when he violates his most solemn pledges to me I cannot but feel that his respect for me is gone. I know of no individual who has had a better chance to make money than Tom Bowler. If he will sacrifice himself, his family and his friends by gambling, I cannot help it, but I want him to quit it. I want him to be Tom. I want him to [be] attuned to his business, be prudent, persevering, industrious, and he can soon make enough to do him. But I cannot write on this subject any longer. It makes me too nervous. I leave it for the present, by exhorting you to talk with him, council him, if you have any influence with him do make use of it. Tell him if he has any respect for me or my feelings to quit it. I don't want the mortification of hearing that he has again been gambling." Ibid., Nov. 1, 1858, MHS.

57. David Whiting, a native of Vermont, had acted as secretary to New Mexico's first territorial governor, James S. Calhoun. Windham, ed., *New Mexico 1850 Territorial Census*, 4:146; Horn, *New Mexico's Troubled Years*, 26. Whiting is mentioned often in Kingsbury's letters from 1858-59.

again. I am beginning to loose the little confidence I had in him. I notice what you say about sending him to you, but shall do nothing for the present in regard to it. I wait your reply to my last letter in regard to him before I say anything more to him on the subject.[58]

I hope you will succeed in getting the $100 from Forsythe.[59] Frank Green has not arrived yet. Tom [Bowler] is getting anxious about his delay, as he counts on the outfit with Frank to start back. The 15th is the date he has to start a mail in from Albuquerque.

Mr. [David] Whiting requests that you will purchase for him and forward by express to Ind. & come out by mail coach about $20.+ in toys and little tricks suitable for his children. He wants them to get here before Christmas. For the little girl send a large Wax doll with eyes to open & shut. Select what you please for the boys.[60] If his draft has been sent to Mr. Abbott, then it is all right and you can fill the above little order. What he wants is little present for the children to give them at christmass [*sic*] time.

I learned yesterday that Mr. [George M.] Alexander had left for the States with his family. I have written out to his clerk to know if he had made any arrangements before leaving to meet our bill which is now due, and urging him to send us the amt. at once. Send me another copy of Dana Farrar & Hyde's bill, also a copy of the bill of chairs you bought last Spring for Bowler if you have not already done so. I have nothing special to add now, will write as often as anything important occurs.

P.S. Old man Bailey is very low with dropsy will probably never recover.[61]

Poor Dick is still able to take his allowance of Whiskey. His case is a perfect miracle. The Gov's family will probably moove next week.[62]

Letter no. 80, Kingsbury to Webb, Santa Fe, October 17, 1858

We have no mail today. This is the first failure of the weekly mail. We have word from it by Judge Watts. He started with it as passinger, found they were several days behind the time, and left them on the cimorone [Cimarron] with teams giving out, came in with [Miguel] Pino in his carriage to Red River and from there came on foot to Fort Union, got in here last night. He reports that he passed Kitchens Ox waggon at Las Vegas, his Mule Waggons at red river, and Yagers Train at Whitstone [Whetstone Creek] so I expect we will have all our goods here some time next week.

I have nothing important to write, business is exceedingly dull. [Dr.] Kavanaugh got here from Salt Lake last evening. He brought no funds, every dime they have got is in the teams and goods which Pino is bringing. When they get here I may save our debt by taking goods. I

58. If Webb wrote a response to the letter Kingsbury mentions we have been unable to find it.

59. We have been unable to identify Forsythe.

60. One of the Whiting boys later died, in April 1863 at the age of fifteen, while attending school in St. Louis. *Santa Fe Weekly Gazette*, May 2, 1863.

61. Dropsy is a synonym for edema, which is an abnormal accumulation of fluid in connective tissue or in a serous cavity.

62. Rencher had been renting Webb & Kingsbury's house while he had been renovating the old Palace of the Governors in order to live there.

can do nothing untill they arrive, will then do the best I can. Kavanaugh brings encouraging accounts from the new gold region, passed right through the diggins say they are all doing well there. Brought in a small lot of gold about $50. which he bought from the miners. Says they get from each pan 2 ½ cents to $3.00 not a pan of dirt but what yields gold.

Mercure wants his $3,000 and I expect I will have to pay it to him as Tom will be unable to raise it just now unless Watts comes forward and puts in his money according to agreement.

I can think of nothing more now.

Letter no. 81, Kingsbury to Webb, Santa Fe, October 17, 1858

Private

The Town has been full of gossip the last week on a/c of a novel case of Gen.l Pelham.[63] Something new for New Mex. No more nor less than an elopement. The Genl. last Sunday morning eloped with Miss Papia [Tapia?] (the girl that Henry Oneil had some time in the Convent.) He took her in his buggy and started with all possible speed on the road to Vegas, was meet and both of the parties recognizing [*sic*] at Aroya [Arroyo] Hondo[64] by McKutchen and at the canon [canyon] by Maj. Smith paymaster. It has turned out that they went to Valies (Pigeons)[65] and spent the honey moon, have since returned, and he keeps the bird closely confined in his office.

I understand the family will present the whole affair to the President and request his removal. Many whom he counted as his friends are opposed to his conduct in this affair and it will probably appear in many of the papers in the States. He has rather overshot the mark and I think it will go bad with him.

From appearance of things now, should an American run for next Congress, it will be [Oliver P.] Hovey. He is working hard for the nomination and if any American is put up, I think it will be him.

José [Hernández] is running with the El Paso Mail. Last accounts Frank [Green] had not started from Neosheo, was still waiting for his carriages. Tom [Bowler] started an outfit from Albuquerque on the 15th under charge of Maj. Wells for Neosho.

The Gov's wife has been quite sick the last week. They have done nothing yet toward moving. They will now probably keep the house a full year, which ends Nov. 11. Soon as it is vacated Tom or Frank will probably take it. Tom has already requested me to hold it at any rate untill Frank arrives. Their house is so crowded that they must have more room. Tom's idea is to take our house, one of them moove here and use the surplus room for Sleeping rooms when the Hotel is crowded.

63. A native of Kentucky, William Pelham held the federally appointed office of surveyor General of New Mexico Territory from 1854 until he resigned in 1860, disillusioned with his superiors in Washington. Westphall, *Mercedes Reales*, 88–93.

64. Six miles from Santa Fe. Brown, *The Santa Fe Trail*, 31. Not to be confused with present-day Arroyo Hondo, twelve miles northeast of Taos.

65. Pigeon's Ranch was a twenty-three-room complex at Glorieta Pass, fifteen miles east of Santa Fe, near the site of a pivotal Union victory in 1862. It was owned by Alexander Valle, whose nickname was Pigeon—purportedly for his penchant for "cutting the pigeon's wing" at dances. Portions of Valle's old hostelry remain standing today. Simmons, *Following the Santa Fe Trail*, 185.

Letter no. 82, Kingsbury to Webb, Santa Fe, October 24, 1858

The mail is just in but brought nothing from you. I am now without advises from you by two mails. Kitchen has just come in and says the waggons will come on the big hill tonight and be ready to unload first thing in the morning. His ox and mule waggons are together. Yager's Train is close behind and perhaps will be in tomorrow if now will be here Tuesday morning.

I have rec.d B/L of one case merchandise ship[p]ed by Parker #8587 230 lbs. this is all the goods that I have notice of being shipped since you left West Port. Pino has nothing in his train for us, if any other goods have been forwarded I have no notice of it. Business continues dull. I have nothing to communicate of interest for the last week.

Letter no. 83, Kingsbury to Webb, Santa Fe, October 31, 1858

I am in receipt of Yours of Sept 28th & Oct. 4th I rec'd the Goods by Kitchen on Monday & by Yager on Tuesday. I have been drove the whole Week without a minute to spare, and today have closed the doors for a little rest. I have a great deal to write you, but my head is too full of the week's excitement and fatigue to put down ¼ what I wish to.

Collections this month amt. to $2,000. I sold before the Trains arrived $3,000. Since then I have sold & billed $5,000.+ making our sales for the month $8,000.+. This is without including anything for Bowler, besides the above I have sold to Blumner about $3,000 which is not entered yet it will appear in next month's sales.

I have examined all the bales carefully, and find I have rec.d E #13 & #17. also F #4. but E #31 and #46 are still short. I have rec.d the case Vermillion, but on opening it I find only 3 Glaziers Diamond and in the Bill we are charged with 4. 1 plain Diamond charged at $3.50 was never put in the case. We are also short 6 Bbls Kennett's Ale charged in Berthold Rozier & Co's Bill. I leave these two items for you to settle and adjust with them.

I have rec.d nothing of J. R. Jeffray & Son's bill, presume however that the case Parker is bringing will contain the whole of their bill.

The case hardware CR #3 did not come. The Cask Pale Sherry C #4. is here. The Balance of the goods have come out all right with the exception of such as you have marked on the invoices with the X as short.

Out of the 10 dz common Buckets sent I will not have more than 3 or 4 doz, they all shook to pieces, if ever you send Buckets again be sure to have them covered with Baleing it protects them from rubbing and holds them together. I am not much pleased with the clothing, the worst feature in it is the quantity of moths, particularly in the coats

#510, 531 & 588.—the whole Lot #531 is nearly eat up, if I get N.Y. cost on these three lots coats I will do well. The coats are not desirable here anyhow and much less since they are moth eaten.

The Satt. Pants are good but a little too high cost for wholesale. I must say I am disapointed in your Boston fancy Prints. They are a little better qua[l]ity than those I bought but the colors & patterns not a bit more desirable. They are all dead colors and altogether to[o] modist for this market, as yet I have only found one single piece bright color, and send you the sample, all the balance are dead wood colors while at least ½ should have been pink, blue, and orange or yellow. As the prints stand on the table they look like one & the same thing both old & new, nothing bright and lively in them. The little figured prints from Doan King & Co. are at present the most desireable prints that we could have both for wholesale and retail. The mourning Prints from Tucker Newton & Co cant be bettered, the only trouble with these the cost is a little to[o] high for quick sales. Next to these are the blue Merimack's from Crow McCarey & Co. these are first rate.[66]

We have retailed all the Fancy Shawls at a good profit. The Chinese Shawls just suit the Mexicans, if you had sent 1 or 2 dz I beleive they would all have sold the first day. Santa Fe is full of goods, and more stores open here now than I have seen since I have been in the country. You may be sure I am getting my share of the trade. Groceries are slow with me simply because there are so many in the market. If I had 50 sacks less sugar, Our groceries would not hurt, however it is a prime article and should it lay over it will not spoil.

I told [Tom] what you say about the $2,500. He will write you by this mail.[67]

I cannot write more now.

Letter no. 84, Kingsbury to Webb, Santa Fe, November 14, 1858

I am without advises from you since my last. I am confident you have written. There must be a failure of the mail between St. Louis & Ind[ependence].

Business has been pretty fair so far this month. Dry & fancy goods moove off well, but Groceries are a little heavy. I am still in hopes they will take a start before Spring. I have today rec.ᵈ a B/L of 4 packages sent by Broadwell. He only brings them to Vegas, and I am to get them in the best way I can.

Viz.	1 Box Chocolate	220
	1 Box Whips	102
	1 Bale E #31	160
	1 Bale E #46	275
		757

The Box Whips I presume to be Box Cr. #3. Hope it may prove so as the Secty. is quite anxious to get his seal. I have sent no remittances

66. Kingsbury is referring to the St. Louis firm of Crow, McCreery & Co.

67. Webb had said that if Tom could pay him $500 of the $2,500 Webb had given Watts to give to him, Tom could wait until april 1, 1859 to pay him the remaining $2,000 plus 10 percent. Webb to Kingsbury, Hamden, Ct, Oct. 25, 1858, MHS.

for some time, as I was compeled to keep all my collections to meet
what I had anticipated in forwarding funds on our last purchases.
There is no dependence now to be placed on deposits and I have to
work pretty close. I have paid up everything and will soon commence
making remittances. I think I will be able to collect as fast as you will
need funds and get it to you in season.

When that Carandolet M[ining] Co. debt is finally settled I wish
you would send me a full statement of it. The interest and different
amt.s so that I can enter it correctly on our books. It stands now in the
original amts. as you will see by reference to the last Trial Balance. I
could not change it as I never rec.^d a statement of the settlement and
extention given them, when it is finally closed send me all the figures
so that I may enter it up right.

I am very anxious to know how you came out with your insurance
settlement. Hope however you had no difficulty. Soon as I get your a/c
current I will send you more figures to base calculations upon.

The Gov. [Rencher] has finally mooved. Tom [Bowler] has taken
the house at $500.+ a year, has moved his family over, and uses the
extry rooms for sleeping rooms for his bo[a]rders. His house is full all
the time he has done better there this season than anytime since they
commenced.

Frank [Green] left Neosho on the 16th Oct. and was due at Albuquerque on the 10th. It is now 4 days over the time and not a word
from him. We are all getting anxious at the delay.

I don't want to complain too much about your Fancy Prints, but I
tell you honestly they are hard and slow sales. The balance of the
goods I believe I can get along with very well except those moth eaten
Coats. I think we are justly entitled to a discount on the three Lots
that is if you bought them for perfect. They certainly must have been
[two words illegible] on you in that condition. If it was only one or
two damaged I would think it was a natural consequence and say
nothing about it, but it runs through the 3 lots every one is more or
less eaten and especially in Lot #531. There are many round holes that
a quarter or half dollar would go through easy.

Nothing more now,

10.

"I have sold the property"

Autumn and Winter 1858–59

Letters 85–103

On November 20, 1858, Kingsbury sent surprising news to Webb. Kingsbury had found a buyer for the property in Santa Fe, but the buyer was John S. Watts, whose failure to pay previous obligations to Webb and Kingsbury had caused the partners considerable anxiety. Watts had given Kingsbury a draft for $5,000 as the initial payment, and promised to complete the transaction on June 1, 1859, with an additional payment of $5,000. Kingsbury assured Webb that he would not surrender the property until he had "every dime of the money in our possession." Meanwhile, Kingsbury would stay on and sell a final shipment that Webb would send to him on the earliest wagon train in the spring of 1859.

Kingsbury recognized that his decision to pull out of the trade would surprise Webb, who might think him "fickle." Business had been good, and Kingsbury had not recently mentioned his unhappiness in Santa Fe. But, he explained to Webb, he was "far from being happy here." Only the real estate had kept him in New Mexico. Moreover, the future of the business looked gloomy. He faced increasing numbers of competitors, including some of his former customers who had gone into the wholesale business, and the potential for more defaults from his customers, to whom he had advanced goods on credit. He had good reason for concern. Debts due Webb & Kingsbury totalled $25,300 by late winter.[1]

Kingsbury blamed stiffer competition on his "thieving" Jewish competitors. Since Webb was familiar with the trading practices to which he objected, Kingsbury did not bother to explain them. Kingsbury's anti-Semitism is apparent from several of his remarks, and he became more shrill as competition increased. Webb's anti-Semitism can be inferred from his tacit agreement with Kingsbury's statements. Yet, while both partners privately condemned the "sharp paractices" of the merchants of "Little Jerusalem" as a group, they nevertheless maintained cordial relations with some of them as individuals.[2]

Kingsbury's assessment of business conditions once again proved unduly pessimistic. Although Kingsbury had told Webb on November 20 that Santa Fe was full of merchandise, two weeks later he reported

1 Kingsbury to Webb, Santa Fe, Mar. 13, 1859, MHS.

2. Kingsbury's letters, for example, frequently mention the various Spiegelbergs in such a way as to indicate they were on good terms.

some short supplies among the merchants. "Dry goods are not plenty," he wrote on December 5, and he had succeeded in selling some manta and lienzo that ordinarily did not sell in the local market. "Cheap or rather common clothing for Mexicans is scarce," he told Webb, and prints and shoes were also selling well.

Kingsbury's plan to wind the business down depended on Watts honoring his commitment to buy the property, but as winter advanced and Watts's bank draft failed to clear, prospects looked dim. Kingsbury, then, continued to send orders to Webb, on January 30, March 5, and March 13, for everything from bacon to petticoats. He also continued to keep Webb apprised of what would and would not sell. He urged him to send satin wallpaper—"select light & flashy patterns . . . plenty of border paper to match," and he complained about a whiskey with a "smell, taste and flavor which is obnoctious [*sic*] to the Whiskey drinkers here."[3]

Beyond business concerns that winter, Kingsbury called a number of events to Webb's attention: Tom Rowland was murdered at his store in San Miguel and Kingsbury made funeral arrangements in Santa Fe for his fellow Mason; travelers and the mail came and went from Santa Fe at the sufferance of Indians through whose lands they passed; Tom Bowler and Frank Green sold the Exchange Hotel, the predecessor of today's La Fonda, to Leonard Rose, a wealthy Iowan whose emigrant train had been attacked by Indians; Lt. Beale arrived in late December from Fort Smith, Arkansas, to do further work on the 35th parallel route; reports of gold at Pike's Peak drew men into what Kingsbury called the "upper country"—a craze fueled by "too much humbug," he feared, but from which a merchant could profit "from the emigration."[4]

~

Letter no. 85, Kingsbury to Webb, Santa Fe, November 20, 1858

Yours of Oct. 21st with a/c current of Oct. 25th are before me. I have only had time to glance at the a/c current. I see no Cr. of the $100 of Forsythe, how is it with that claim do we loose it?

Parker is just arrived and I have rec.d the case of goods from Jeffries & Sons but have not opened it. I just got it at dark.

That Kavanaugh Pino & Hovey outfit has turned out a poor thing. I found it was to be a grab game and I had to grab with the rest. I have taken goods for our bill, on their terms done the best I could and think we will in the end come out even. I took the goods today. They are in the wharehouse, will get the bill tomorrow or next day. I had to give them 10 cents freight and 25% on original cost, in selecting the goods I had little or no choise. I had to take what I could get & no grumbling.

3. Kingsbury to Webb, Santa Fe, Mar. 8, and Mar. 5, 1859, DeG.
4 Ibid., Feb. 6, 1859, DeG.

It is principally in Whiskey, sugar, coffee, soap candles, and Lard. I think I have got enough to cover our claim, and you can consider the debt closed. Hovey has about run through with his interest in the Watts consern. I found there was little show of getting any money from them and I thought it best to get what I could while it was going. I consider what I have taken today far better than the debt.

Now I have something more important to communicate, about the last words you said to me before leaving, were these "John I want it distinctly understood that this Property is for Sale, and at the first reasonable offer let it go. Should we require a house longer why then hire." Well the offer has come and I have sold the property to John S. Watts—stop now don't be alarmed.[5] I have no confidence in him, and do not intend to relinquish one inch of our title untill we have every dime of the money in our possession. The sale and conditions are these. He pays us $10,000+ Ten Thousand dollars—one half cash by his sight draft on his Banking house in Washington, the other half by his note payable at New York or Boston on or before the 1st day of June next, with interest from date at the rate of 10% per annum. We are to collect the rents from and after 1st Jany. next for his a/c and hold them untill his note is paid. Then we have rent free for what we occupy untill July 1st 1859—after that time We are to have possession to our store as long as we want it at seventy-five doll. per month. I am to give him a bond under penalty of Fifteen Thousand dollars that We will make him a quit claim deed of the property on the prompt payment of said note due June 1st 1859. The papers are not made yet, soon as I get them I will send you copies of all. Now I hope this sale will meet with your approbation. I am pleased with it myself and if he comes up prompt I real[l]y believe it will be a good thing for us. If he should not we loose nothing by the transaction. The draft and note are now in my possession. I shall send the draft by this mail, with another check for $2000.+ to Mr. Messervy to lift the note he holds against us of $7,000.+. Wait a few days to give Messervy time to collect Watts draft and then write to him to know if he has got the money.

Now in regard to selling the property I have many reasons for having done it. I am very far from being happy here, and it is my wish and intention to leave the country as soon as I can with justice to ourselves. I know I have sold it cheap, but if we had been forced in to market for a purchaser, it would not bring ⅔ of what I sold at. The fact is it is no easy matter to find a man in the country with $10,000.+ loos[e] money who is willing to put it into real Estate. I have tried every possible chance and I know well what I say when I state the above. I have also given him the refusal of Messervy's two store[s], and he will take them soon as he can raise the funds. This I know will please Messervy.

I had completed a bargain with [Charles] Kitchen to run two years, 16 mule Waggons spring and fall, at 9 ¼ cents, and what other Spring

5. Despite previous trouble with Watts, Webb approved of the terms of the sale: "The information you give me about the sale of our Real Estate is unexpected but I am pleased with the sale. It has brought all I ever expected to get for it. I consider it a good sale, and a good purchase for Watts. He expects to remain there, and it will pay him good interest. The terms are liberal and just on both sides, and I think Watts will comply with them. You must send me a deed for myself and wife to execute so I can return it to you in time, but, of course, if he makes his note payable in New York or Boston, you will want to be advised of its payment before delivering the deed, which will take till the 15th of July at least." Webb to Kingsbury, Hamden, CT, Dec. 27, 1858, MHS.

freight we might want to come in Ox Teams at 9 cents. All payable 6 months from the arrival at Santa Fe. The conditions however were these. If either of the parties die, he loose his stock or we sell our real Estate, then the contract to be void. So by my sale that contract is void, and he is not bound to bring us any freight.

Now it is my intention for you to send me a good stock of goods next spring and try to wind up on that, and with this view have made another proposition to Kitchen to pay him 10 cents for his early Mule Teams (16) and 9 cents for 12 Ox Wagons more or less as we may have. Should he not accept I am disposed to stop where we are, but I think there is no question about his accepting as I believe he is more anxious for the freight than we are to give it to him. You may look with confidence for my shoe order by next mail. Let me say a little more about this continuation of our business. You may think I am getting fickle and changeable in my ideas, but it is not so. I was absolutely compeled to continue in spite of my own wishes. I never have had but one idea about it and that was to quit at the time you set, but found it impossible on account of our real Estate. Now if Watts comes up prompt to the stipulations why this difficulty is removed, and we can wind up when it pleases us. To take up the statement I sent you at the close of our last fiscal year, our business certainly looks incouraging and up to the present time we have no reason to be dissatisfied. You will remember up to that time we had made few or in fact you may say no bad debts. In fact I tell you truly that the track of the country at present is so cut up, and the profits are getting so limited that there is really no margin left for bad debts, one or two losses in a season would consume all our profits. You remember when I arrived last year you asked me where I expected to find purchasers for my stock. I really could not reply and you who had had the whole run of the business the year previous could not surmize or point them out. It is true the year wound up and I sold more than we had in any previous year, and I believe the most of it has been realized in cash. Now to look ahead it is darker than ever, in the first place Santa Fe is crowded with goods, every little hole is a store with a fair asst. [assortment]. How they all live I do not know. Goods being so plenty Credits are getting every day more loose. The result will be in a year or two New Mexico is bound to see another turnover. This I wish to escape.

Now where and who are our customers. The best men are dropping off one by one. Sach's is done, Cummings at Manzana [Manzano][6] brings his own goods from the states so we have lost him. Peter Joseph is now in the States, will bring his own stock next year. Beuthner did last season and will next. Col. [Ceran] St. Vrain supplies the balance of the upper country,[7] the little merchants find the goods right at their doors and are under no necessity of coming to Santa Fe for them. Now in the place of our old and tried customers, who are coming up? Why

6. The town of Manzano, in the Manzano Mountains southeast of Albuquerque.

7. One of the nineteenth-century Southwest's most prominent figures, Ceran St. Vrain, along with various members of his family, is mentioned fairly regularly in Kingsbury's letters. St. Vrain was born in St. Louis County, Missouri, in 1802 and pursued various trapping and trading enterprises on the frontier throughout the 1820s. In 1830 he formed a partnership with Charles and Willian Bent, resulting in one of the West's most successful and well-known trading operations. He was an important figure in Taos both before and after the American conquest of New Mexico. By the 1850s he had withdrawn from his association with the surviving Bent brother, William, and had settled in Mora where he managed his diverse and numerous business operations. He died in 1870. Thrapp, *Encyclopedia*, 3:1260.

a sett of unprincipaled, thieving Jewes [*sic*]. They have nearly got possession of the country and if they increase as they have done they will get it all sure. Yes, take Tom's [Bowler's] business from us and I see little to encourage us to continue—and his business you know what it is. It is as uncertain as anything can be. You can form no possible idea of the little, low, mean act that these Jews are constantly at. It is true I fight and work along with them, and I will say it I have just as good a show as any one in the country, but their influence is tending to ruin the whole trade of the country.

Now if we can carry through the mill, one good stock, come out safely with ordinary luck and wind up on that, I think we ought to be satisfied. If all goes well, you certainly will have enough to make yourself and family independent, and as for myself I will to[o] be satisfied.

If you are displeased with what I have done do not hesitate to tell me so. I am most sure that on due reflection you must come to the same conclusions I have. It was well to sell the property and that it is best for us to close up soon as we can. I have full confidence that by having an <u>early</u> train in the Spring, I can manage one more stock, and that with advantage to us both. Tom will want a full stock and that with what I can pick up out side will carry us through, but it all depends upon that <u>early train</u>. If I cannot have this advantage next spring, then I would not give a fig for our chances. Kitchen's agreement is to load those 16 Wagons and start as early as 1st day of April. My calculation is to get the goods here and sell them before any others can possible arrive. My sales this month keep up well. Profits are small but I am bound to sell. To the present I have sold about $12,000.+ add this to what I have already reported and you have the sum of $57,000.+ for our sales sine June 1st. I deliver nothing to Tom only as he requires. I think there is at least $10,000 + for him not delivered or charged up. Add this in and it only leaves me 8,000 to sell between now & spring to make our sale up to the usual amt. <u>$75,000.+</u>

I have spoken to Tom about what you say of that <u>$2,500.+</u>, and he says you may expect by next mail to get the $500 with interest as you request.[8]

The last word we have from Frank Green he had waited at Fort Smith for Lt. Beal's [Edward Fitzgerald Beale's] party and did not leave there untill the 1st of this month.[9] We have news to day from Antonchice [Anton Chico] that Tom's mail which left Albuquerque on the 15th last month has been wiped out by the Comanche, not one of the party saved.[10]

[Henry or Joseph] Mercure has consented to let that $3,000+ stand 6 months longer. I have now on hand plenty of funds and by a little management could send you at once funds enough to take up all our eastern notes, but no one of the Offices are drawing at present. I must wait untill they get funds to there [their] Cr. to draw on. [James L.]

8. As mentioned in chapter 9, Webb had given Watts $2,500 to give to Tom.

9. Although Congress had authorized a mail route between Neosho, in the Southwest corner of Missouri, and Albuquerque in 1854, service did not actually begin until October 1858. In charge of the new service was Frank Green, who apparently intended to travel with Lt. Beale's surveying party, consisting of 130 men and two pieces of artillery, but instead went on ahead to Albuquerque. Rumors flew back and forth as to the party's whereabouts and safety, as Kingsbury's letters reflect. Kingsbury reported their safe arrival at Anton Chico on the Pecos River southeast of Santa Fe in his letter to Webb of Jan. 2, 1859. Taylor, *First Mail West*, 54-56.

Webb wrote, "I see that Frank has not yet arrived. I don't think you need be under much apprehension for his safety, but he may not arrive untill this month or next. I see there is some prospect of Lt. Beall's [*sic*] going into winter quarters. It may be collusion between Beall and the other company, in order to embarrass Frank and get new lettings on the grounds of failure to fulfill the contract. There is no telling what may be in the wind. I mention this to you in confidence everything <u>may</u> be right and in good faith, but I have none too much confidence in Beall." Webb to Kingsbury, Hamden, CT, Jan. 5, 1859, MHS.

10. A later letter of Kingsbury's revealed this rumor to be false. Kingsbury to Webb, Santa Fe, Dec. 26, 1858, MHS.

Collins expects every mail to get authority to draw.[11] I intend to send you funds to take up all our notes before you commence making fresh purchases.

The Warns Boots I had refference [*sic*] to came from Johnson & Co. cost 50 cents. I cannot give you the Nos. as there were others at the same cost. When I make my orders I will describe them so that you will know them. The Shoe bill from New Haven is a pretty clean bill. I am much pleased with it. It is just what I wanted but it is only suitable for retail, and of course they will last some time. I think now I shall not require any more from that house for Spring. What I have got will be enough to carry us through. All the shawls you sent this fall sold well. I have retailed the whole at good profit except 4 or 5 of the black ones, and these will soon be gone. In regard to Cigars, those sent in the Spring gave general satisfaction. You know the cigars are all for Tom's house. He wants a good reliable Havana Cigar, that he can sell at a bit each, one at less price he would not have. Anyone here who uses them will pay a bit and not complain, and they want a fair cigar. The Manilla cigars will not do, don't send any more of them. The highest price cigars sent this fall are wrapped so tight that there is complaint about them. The balance are fair. What Tom wants is a good havana Cigar to cost in the State[s] from $30 to 60 or 65 a thousand.

We have favorable reports from Pikes Peak. There is no question about there being plenty of gold there. From the best information I can get it is from 3 or to 350 miles from here.[12] However, it has created no excitement here, and I think very few will go from here unless it attracts a few of the Gamblers which we shall be glad to get shed of. Col. [Ceran] St. Vrain is about starting a train loaded principally with Flour under charge of St. James.[13] This is about the first benefit I can see that New Mexico has got from the discovery. In the Spring no doubt the place will be over run with everything direct from the State[s]. I cannot see that this discovery is to help N. M. any more than the discoveries at Fraziers diggin[g]s.[14] It is too far off and the States will get the whole benefit. I have written you fully all I know about the Gov. mining operations at Placers. I was there myself. You done well to let it alone. I believe there is gold there. They have plenty of water and the mashinery works well[15] but they have had no one who could separate the gold after the ore was ground up. This together with bad management has ex[h]austed all their funds in salaries and in getting ready to work and now they find they do not know how to get the gold out. I believe the Gov. has some hope of getting Mr. Idler back and if he succeeds will try it again. He [Rencher] has got his all invested there and it is his only show. It has nearly cost the old man his life. He has been sick nearly all the time since the mines stop[p]ed and Doc Hoan says it is nothing but nerves [nervous] excitement

11. The extent to which Santa Fe's commercial life was wrapped up with government agencies as a source of currency and revenue is revealed in Kingsbury's explanation of his temporary shortage of ready cash. See Introduction.

12. Webb had inquired about the rumors of gold at Pike's Peak in his correspondence during the fall of 1858. See chapter 9.

13. We have been unable to identify St. James.

In addition to his other business interests, Ceran St. Vrain was involved in the production of flour. Around 1849 he set up a gristmill in the Taos Valley, near Cantonment Burgwin, later expanding his milling operations until he became one of the territory's principal suppliers of flour to the Army. Frazer, "Purveyors of Flour," 217-21.

14. In the spring and summer of 1858, reports of gold drew 25,000 to 30,000 people to the Fraser River in British Columbia. Paul, *Mining Frontiers*, 38. Kingsbury has made his point emphatically.

15. Historian Barton Barbour cites the use of the quartz-crushing machinery at the mines at the placers in the Ortiz Mountains at Dolores as "arguably the first tangible application of the Industrial Revolution to New Mexico." *Reluctant Frontiersman*, 39.

caused by over excitement. The fear of loosing his all is too much for the old man.

Your fall clothing bill may be reasonable enough that portion for retail goes very well. I am well satisfied with it. But the balance is all to[o] good for Mexican trade. There is nothing low cost enough to reach their limit. I have finally got clear of the moth eaten coats. I sold them at New York cost. I am convinced it is no use for us to try to wholesale clothing long side of the Jews. I have sold all the muslin dresses from Beche & Co. I wholesaled the most of them at $2.50 each and closed out the balance at $2. The others I sold to Hoppin & Appel at a profit.

The Hoes from St. Louis will sell, but they are not quite so desirable as those we got from Boston. Those from Boston are polished & that makes them go. The whole bill of Howe Pierce & Co. has turned out well except Bale $4 Trenton Cass: these are too high or too good for me to make a profit on. The few prints in this bill are the only thing that has saved us on prints with the help of these few I have worked off about half the balance. The Sattines are all gone and I could sell 5 bales more of the same if I had them now. The Champlain Jeans sold fast at 20 cents. Those 12 ½ cottonades from Beche are a little slow on a/c of the collar. They are black & White check, look to[o] much like the Gerger[16] of the country to take with Mexicans.

This will do now. Kind regards to all.

P. S. Jose is still running with Toms El Paso Mail. We have just rec.d word that Jeanerett is dead. He sold himself a long time ago to old King Alcohol and he has finally taken him.[17]

Letter no. 86, Kingsbury to Webb, Santa Fe, November 27, 1858

I sent you a long letter by last Mail, stating that I had sold our property &c. The mail arrived this evening but brought me nothing from you.

Kitchen has accepted my last proposition for freight. That is 10 cents for the early mule Teams and 9 cents for the Ox Train

Herewith you will find my order for shoes, fill it as near as you can and on the best terms the market will allow.

Business has been very fair this week and my whole sales for the month will close very encouraging. I will send you the figures by next mail. The bill of Groceries it took of Kavanaugh, Pino & Hovey came to a little over $2,100.+ leaving them still in our debt about $300.+ for which amt. I think they are good, and hope to get it of them soon. I succeeded in disposing of the whole bill at the same prices I paid them, to Chas. Blumner on 6 mos.[18] He took the whole bill with the exception of one small cask of fine Brandy which he concluded was

16. Jerga is a coarse woolen cloth, locally made and often in a check pattern with natural light and dark brown yarns. See Boyd, *Popular Arts*, 181-86.

17. Jules Jeanerett, the matchmaker from Switzerland, was mentioned in Kingsbury's first letter in 1853 as one of the witnesses to the riot at the Exchange Hotel.

18. "I am also advised of your disposition of the goods taken from Kavenaugh, Pino & Hovey. I am glad to get rid of the goods in a lump and lose the outfit, but are you sure that you have not got too many goods in that nest? Blumner is honest, and I presume will not gamble, but he is a slow business man, that is, he has but little energy, and will be apt to do business upon the old fashioned mexican plan—have his goods scattered about in little stores, which will not do at the present day. I do not speak of this from want of confidence, but you have never seen anything of his way of doing business, and you might from his popularity, personally, be induced to credit him farther than you would do knowing his business qualifications." Webb to Kingsbury, Hamden, CT, Jan. 5, 1859, MHS.

too high cost for him. I consider this a good sale. It is true I made nothing by the transfer, and we are kept 6 months longer out of our money, but I consider Blumner safe, and in the end we will come out all right. At the prices I paid them I saw at once I could make no profit on the goods, and in fact when I took them, I considered it that or nothing and was glad to get all I could. And now to get them off our hands at cost I consider that we are lucky.

No one of the Officers are drawing at present, for this reason I send no remittances. I have now in the Safe $7,000.+ above my deposits and collections coming in every day. Soon as I can get drafts you may expect funds enough to take up all our Eastern Notes and some for Cash purchases.[19]

Herewith you will find copy of my agreement with Watts, also his note for Five Thousand dollars, payable on or before the 1st day of June next with int. from Nov. 19th, 1858. He expects to take this up before it is due, so as to stop the interest from the time he may be ready to meet it. For this reason I send it to you to hold untill such time as he may offer you the money. The conditions of the note are imbodied in it and will explain itself.

I also send you the deed signed by myself which we are to give him when he has complied with our agreement, which is the prompt payment of the full sum of Ten Thousand from Nov. 19th 1858 untill paid at 10% per annum. Look carefully at this deed and if it is right when you have all the money in your possession, then perfect it by your signature and Mrs. Webbs and give it to him, or if he has returned to Santa Fe then send it out to me. But do not under any circumstances let this deed out of your hands, untill you have got all the money cash in hand. We are not to guarintee the deed or title. We give only such as we rec.d I have looked this over carefully and believe we can sign it with safety.

We have not a word yet from Frank Green. Tom does not send you now the $500.+ promised in my last letter for the same reason I have given before, which is that is is impossible to get Drafts or Checks. Tom has got a proposition to sell out his two mail contracts. Butterfield & Co. the mail contractors for the overland rout to California offer him $80,000.+ Eighty thousand dollars for the two contracts cash down.[20] He has only to go to Washington sign the papers and get the money. They will probably take his stock and outfit on the lines at cost. The above they offer just for his contracts. Tom has made up his mind to sell, and is only waiting for Frank to get here so that he can leave. If nothing has happened to Frank and he gets here safe, you may expect to hear soon that Tom is starting for Washington.[21] Should he go on he will come directly to see you. In going to Washington he expects to get the contracts transferred by consent of the Post Master General to the other parties so as to entirely release him and his securities from all responsibility from and after the date of transfer.

19. As mentioned in chapter 4, Kingsbury's inability to obtain drafts in order to send money to Webb safely tended to slow down their business operations.

20. The Butterfield Overland Mail, one of the West's most famous lines, began operation in this same year, running from Memphis and St. Louis to Los Angeles and San Francisco by way of an oxbow route through Fort Smith, El Paso, and Tucson. Taylor, *First Mail West*, 18. Bowler would have been better off accepting this offer, as later letters reveal. See chapter 12.

21. Both Messervy and Webb had expressed concern that Tom Bowler was overextending himself with the mail contracts. In December Messervy had written, "I am afraid Mr. Bowler has made a mistake in that Mail Contract. He will I think lose money at it. He had better confine himself to his Tavern." Messervy to Kingsbury, Salem, Dec. 31, 1858, MHS. Webb was delighted with the Butterfield offer. "I am rejoiced to hear that Tom has an offer to sell out his contracts so well. Advise him by all means to take the offer. It is more than he can under any circumstances make out of them, and it relieves him from all embarrassment and anxiety and he can shape his business as he chooses." Webb to Kingsbury, Hamden, CT, Jan. 5, 1859, MHS.

P.S. Maj. [John R.] Wells was married last night to James Hunt's widdow. The Maj. appears as happy as a King with his little family.[22]

Letter no. 87, Kingsbury to Webb, Santa Fe, December 5, 1858

We have no mail today, we had two snow storms last week and it is probably detained by heavy roads.

By last mail I sent you my order for shoes, and all the papers pertaining to the sale of Property to Watts, that you could see the whole transaction on paper. I also enclosed his note payable June 1st, 1859 for the last $5,000.+ all of which I hope you received safely.

Our business for the last month closed very favorable, as you will see by the following figures, whole amt. of sales are $20,000.+ Of this amt. 2,000.+ is for goods delivered to Tom, and two thousand sold to Blumner (the goods taken from Kavanaugh Pino & Hovey) without profit. The balance $16,000+ is in our side sales. Collections amt. to $6,000.+ The moment I can get Drafts I intend to send to Boston $12,000.+—6 of it to meet our Notes there and the other six for you to use in new purchases. Kitchen has written me that he would start his mule train as early as 10th March if you can get the goods there, and if we can do it promises to make us an F. X. Aubry Trip.[23] Now I will try to make up my orders so to send by next mail or certainly by the one following so that you may have all the time possible, and get the goods up on the first opening of the river.

My sales last month has nearly closed out all my wholesale goods. I have not Dry Goods enough left to secure a wholesale customer should one come along. The Truth is dry goods are not plenty and it is lucky for us that it is. So far it has enabled me to push off many hard lots. My retail stock is pretty good yet, and I have plenty of Groceries to last untill Spring. I think now they will all go. The Manta and Lienzo you sent from St. Louis was all hard. In the first place it was too narrow, and then the manta from Doan King & Co. was too light & fine for this market. Still I have sold it all at a fair price, have not a piece left, but could not have done it only that Manta and Lienzo is scarce. All my old Prints are gone except about 30 or 40 pieces. My boots & shoes are nearly all gone. I have only 2 cases Brogans & 5 or 6 cases those fine boots from Strong's left. Warm high shoes are very scarce. I have not a piece of blue or black prints except what is on the retail shelves. In fact all my staple goods are gone. I believe now if I had 40 bales Manta & Lienzo, a few blue & Blk Prints and about 10 cases Warm high shoes that I could clean our whole house and sweep it out. Now if we only succeed in getting that early train here in advance of anyone else I feel quite certain that I will be able to close out clean. I shall want the whole train loaded with Staple & fancy Dry goods. My Groceries and Liquors will be mostly for Tom and can

22. As Kingsbury mentioned in his correspondence in the spring of 1858, Jim Hunt had drunk himself to death and the Masonic lodge had been helping his widow, Ana María Sandoval, get along. Major Wells lived in Albuquerque and became a secessionist. He was a friend of Spruce McCoy Baird, retreating in 1862 with the Confederate soldiers and the Baird family to San Antonio, where he died in the Baird home in 1863. Emmett, *Fort Union*, 254; Archives of the Archdiocese of Santa Fe, microfilm POS #7B, Marriages, 1858-1889, Santa Fe; Cook, ed. "Reminiscences of Andrew Bowdry Baird," 6.

23. A reference to the transcontinental speed demon Francis X. Aubry.

come in the Ox Train. They will be a sure sale on arrival. Cheap or rather common clothing for Mexicans is scarce. Levi and Beck's establishment are sold out clean. I could sell now $10,000.+ of clothing if I had the right sort.

Henry Oneil has a small but good stock of Goods and is now the only man who can fill a wholesale customers wants. I have finally sold the last of that striped shirting manta, my Marlboro Plaid and the bale Denims but do not want any more of these articles. Those fancy goods in Jeffries bill would have been sold had they come with our other goods. I have not been able to get those package from Vegas yet which Broadwell brought out.[24]

Herewith you will find my estimate of stock on hand to Dec. 1st amt.g to $25,450.+. Its bearly possible that the goods in the house may not hold up to these figures, from the fact that I have sold many things at cost and some hard lots mules & shopkeepers at less just to get them out of the house. Still on the whole my profits have been fair and if sales continue good untill spring, I will certainly bring up the profits to the regular average that is divide the sale by 5, same as the estimate is made. I am certain this paper is near enough to make any calculation upon that you may wish.

I will close this now. 10 P.M. and no word from the mail.

Letter no. 88, Kingsbury to Webb, Santa Fe, December 12, 1858

Dear Sir, Under another envelope I send you by this mail Check no. 42 on the Asst. Treas. of the U.S. at New York for Twelve Thousand dollars $12,000.+ drawn by J. L. Collins Supt. of Ind. Aff. N.M.—which I hope you will get without delay.[25]

Herewith you will find enclosed No 6404 War Warrant part 5467 dated Washington Oct. 25th 1858, at sight on the Asst. Treas. of the U.S. at New York for Six hundred Thirty Three & 79/100 dollars ($633.79/100) drawn by Sam Casey Treas. of the U.S. registered Oct. 25th, 1858 F. Bigger reg: of the Treasury, payable to the order of Capt. A. W. Bowman 3rd Infy. by him endorsed to John R. Wells or order and by him to your order. The above Warrant you will received on a/c of money advanced to John S. Watts for T. F. Bowler Aug. 9th 1858 as per a/c rendered on the opposite page leaving a balance still of $1,956.54 in your favor, for which I have taken his note according to your request.

Mr. T. F. Bowler
1858   To James J. Webb
Aug. 9th For amt. turned over to
John S. Watts for his a/c $2,500.00

24. We have been unable to determine the full names of Jeffries and Broadwell.

25. Apparently by this time Collins had received permission to draw and Kingsbury had the cash to send east, but needed to convert it to a draft for safety.

For Int. on above from Aug 9th
to Dec. 9th 4 mos. @ 10%   83. 33
For amt. paid J. S. Watts for Expenses   7.00
                                                       $2,590. 33
Or By Treasury Warrant   633.79
                                                       $1,956.54

Balance for which I have taken his note payable on demand with interest at the rate of 10% per annum from Dec 9th, 1858.

Letter no. 89, Kingsbury to Webb, Santa Fe, December 12, 1858

Dear Sir, I am in receipt of yours of Nov. 1st. I will do my best with those old notes, but I think the c[h]ances of their being collected very slim.

I have found your a/c current all right and made the entries in our books showing a balance to Cr. of your Agent a/c of $27.48. I have found it impossible to get my orders ready to send by this mail & then Tom [Bowler] does not want to give me his order untill Frank [Green] arrives or we get some reliable information in regard to him. We have not a word yet, and cannot surmise what is the cause of his detention. We fear now that it will turn out bad.

I consider our claim against [Moses] Sachs perfectly secure. I have in my possession a joint note signed by him and Judge [Antonio José] Otero for $1687.40. payable June 1st 1859 drawing Int. from June 25th, 1858 at 6% per annum. This will certainly be paid at maturity w[h]ether Sachs return from Cal. in time or not.

I am watching Tom closely and doing all in my power to keep him straight. I think he will be more carefull in future and not suffer himself to be led into anything that is not right. He never has been guilty of playing heavy. It is only little petty game, a few dollars now and then. It is not the amt. but the principal of the thing and the danger he exposes himself to by tampering with that he should not touch. I am in hopes he will now quit it entirely.

Under another envelope I send you War Warrant no. 6404 on Asst. Treas. of the U.S. at N.Y. for $633. 79/100, which amt. I have rec.d from T. F. Bowler on a/c of the $2,500.+ you advanced to Watts for him.

Herewith you will find Check no 42, dated Santa Fe N. Mex Dec 13th 1858 at sight on the Asst. Treas. of the U.S. at New York for Twelve Thousand dollars. ($12,000.+) drawn by J. L. Collins Supt. of Ind. Aff. N. Mexico and payable to our order.

I have taken this check from Collins knowing that he has no advises of money being to his Cr. at the Treas. in New York. He has estimated for it and it should be there long before this reaches you. Now that you may have no trouble with it, he has written again by this mail to the dept. at Wash. that in case he has no cr. there to place this sum there immediately so as to meet this check. I think there can be no question about the payment of it. There are $7,000.+ of Ind. appropriations not drawn for. Don't protest this check but hold it a few days in order for his letter of advice to reach Washington and the funds to arrive in N.Y. to meet it.

You will also find enclosed two 160 Acre Land Warrants, No. 81.852 Francisco Armijo, and No. 81.851 Marcus Lucero.

The above Land Warrants I have rec.d in collections at 87 ½ cents the acre or $140 each making $280.+. You will take this figures up on your agent a/c, this making $12,280.+ The land warrants you are to turn into cash on the best terms you can, and the parties here are responsible for any discount you may have to make on them. Sell them the first chance and let me know what you get for them, so that I can collect the difference here and give you credit for it. When you have realized the amt. of within remittances, you can take up all our Eastern Notes, due at New Haven and Boston, getting what discount you can and use the balance on new purchases.

I have also made arrangement for Mr. Abbott, to receive direct from Washington $525.+ [David V.] Whitings Salary from Oct. 1st to Dec 31st, 1858. This sum may be a week or two getting to Boston but I think you can count that it will come then. When the notes are taken up (if you receive all the above moneys) it will leave you some $4,000.+ to use on new purchases East. I want to send you some $5,000 or 6,000 more for this purpose and feel confident I can do so by the close of this month. The only difficulty will be the scarcity of remittances. I should not have taken this check of Collins if I could have got Army drafts but none of the Officers are drawing, and to place you in funds had to take what I could get, however I think you will have no trouble with it except the delay of a few days.

10 p.m. 13th. The mail due today has not arrived. Whiting says should it not get here tonight he will not start the mail back untill Tuesday. Should anything offer in the meantime I will send you another letter.

Letter no. 90, Kingsbury to Webb, Santa Fe, December 14, 1858

The mail came in late last night. By it Collins rec.d notice that he had his Estimate of money placed at the Treasury in New York to his Credit, so you can send his check at once for collection and it will be paid on presentation.

Letter no. 91, Kingsbury to Webb, Santa Fe, December 18, 1858

Dear Sir, I am in receipt of yours of 18th ult stating that you had rec.d the insurance money and how disposed of. I will make the entries as you request. We have not a word yet from Frank Green. Tom is doing the best he can, and has managed very well so far. Frank's delay comes very hard on Tom. Their house is full the whole time and that with the mail outfits keeps Tom pushed all the time. Herewith you will find Tom's draft on John Marron, 3rd Asst. P.M. General, at Washington D.C. for ($1,872.50) One Thousand Eight hundred and Seventy two 50/100 dollars for the 1st quarters service on the El Paso Mail route, payable to our order and endorsed to your order. This amt. you will receive on a/c of the money advanced to Watts for him. His contract reads that the Dept. are to send him drafts or Warrants for each quarters service, that is why he has not drawn before. He expected that each mail would bring his Warrant, but now as it has not come he thinks it is safe to draw without danger of its passing the warrant on the road. Soon as we can get checks here he will send you the balance due you on private a/c with interest. By last mail I sent you for him War Warrant for $633.79 on this same a/c which I hope you got all safe.

I will get Tom's draft for the next quarter which will be double the amt. of this one, so as to send it to you by next mail. (This he will turn over to us on a/c.) He cannot drawer [*sic*] before the full expiration of each quarter as before his draft will be paid the dept. requires the Post Master here to certify that the service has been performed and this Whiting cannot do untill the full time is up. But in this case I will get him to do it a few days before so that I can start the draft to you by next mail.

Herewith you will find my orders. I have made them out the best I could. The prospect is now that I shall have very few goods left over. All I can say is send me a good stock of Goods, and get them started as soon as you can. Kitchen will be ready with his mule Teams to receive them the moment you get them up the river. I shall want all the Dry Goods, Fancy Goods, and Asst.d goods to come in the first train, leaving the Liquors and Groceries to come in the Ox waggons. The most of these will be for Tom and it will do just as well for him if they are a little later. My idea is to get the principal part of my stock there early and sell it out if possible before other trains get here.

I sent you by last mail remittances amt.g to $12,280.—also arrainged for Mr. Abbott to receive $525.+. This will enable you to pay all our Eastern Notes and leave a good sum for purchases new. Then you can count on Tom's draft of $3,745.+ to come by next mail. Should my collections allow me to send more I will do so if not you must use our credit and get along without any more. If that Carandolet Note is paid you can use that, any way you please, I will not count upon it but make my calculation from here to meet all the notes at St. Louis. Also when it comes time to b[u]y groceries I will see that you have funds enough or at anyrate I will remit every dime I can, if collections come in prompt I will have plenty for you, if not why I will anticipate all I dare to so as to give you all the cash there that you will want. We have plenty of means and should be perfectly easy, but the whole trouble is as I anticipated & wrote you sometime ago, that our last spring train getting here so late would make our collections late coming in. Then being obliged to extend that K[avanaugh] P[ino] & Hovey debit 6 months. Then add to this the large amt. which we are wanting on Tom, and you can readily see why it is that we are a little cramped for ready funds. Now don't you get uneasy about funds, leave it all to me and if there is no failure in the mails I will arrainge it all so that you shall have enough and in time.

I am glad you sent me the copy of D. F. & Hyde's bill. I wanted it to make my books straight. Whenever you make a settlement with Mr. Abbott, send me a full copy of his account current.

Look at my orders carefully, but in buying be governed by your own judgement. If you send me a good clean stock of goods, you may rest assured that I will sell them readily. Business continues encouraging. I have every assurance that I will get my share of what is going.

I hope you have sent me full & long letters in reply to mine since the Sale of the property.[26]

Letter no. 92, Kingsbury to Webb, Santa Fe, December 26, 1858

By last mail I sent you Tom's draft on your private a/c for money loaned him, amt.g to $1,872.50. I also sent my orders for eastern goods, all of which I hope you rec.d in due time. You may think perhaps that the orders are not explicit or full enough, but I done the best I could and do not see now how I can alter them to make them any better or plainer. The probability is before they can get here I shall have sold out pretty clean. I want you to send me a good clean stock that you think will sell readily, try to avoid mules. I want to sell everything you send before next January, so that the balance of the time I remain here may be entirely devoted to collecting and closing up. I must again urge upon you the great necesity and importance of starting these goods early, everything depends upon this, first prices will be better and then it will assist me greatly in winding up if the goods get here a few weeks before other trains arrive. Goods are not pleanty at wholesale, and are now in fair demand. I calculate by this that in the spring I will be able to find ready sale for what you send on arrival, provided they get here early.

I wrote you that your a/c current was correct, and my entries made to agree with it, which is true as far as it went. On looking carefully over the book of Invoices I find that you have omitted to take Credit for amt. pd. S. R. Niles for subscriptions $4.00 and $1.66 for T.

26. Webb had the following to say about the sale of the real estate to Watts: "I am satisfied with the sale, and hope he will comply with his contract. The papers are rather one sided. You give bonds to the amt. of fifteen thousand dollars for the faithful fulfillment of our part of the contract, but there is no forfeiture on his part. Had he given you cash in hand, for the five thousand dollars, a failure on his part to pay the note at maturity would have been equivalent to a forfeiture of his contract, and we could have held the amt as forfeit, but as the matter now stands, he has everything in his own hands with the deed to the property partly executed. You must try and have the five thousand dollars paid in some way. . . . The chickens are to be hatched, raised, and sold, before the cash is realized." Webb to Kingsbury, Hamden, CT, Jan. 17, 1859, MHS.

Gr[illegible] & Co. for stationary, making $5.66, which amt. you will enter on your agent a/c to your credit.

You also omitted to reply to my enquiry in regard to that $100.+ of Forsyth at Pittsburgh. How will that turn out? will we loose it or is there a chance of getting it yet?

I have rec.d this week the 4 packages all safe which Broadwell brought out. The enclosed letter from W. H. Chick & Co. will explain to you, what detained the 6 Bbls. Ale also 1 Case Ginger. You had better write them to sell or dispose of the Ale, as it would not do to send it out in the spring and especially after being kept there a year.

I have sent them no money I leave their account for you to settled with them when you reach Kansas. Keep this letter so that you can claim the value of the Ale and Ginger. Also remember to claim of Bacur Hyde & Co. $3.50 for one Glaziers Diamond short.

By this mail we have newspaper reports from the State that Tom's mail which left Albuquerque Oct. 15th had reach Niezo [Neosho] all hands safe.[27] Also that Frank Green had remained with Lt. Beals [Beale's] party[28] waiting for an escort which was then 3 or 4 days behind them. If this is true, we can look with confidence for Frank to arrive in the next 10 days.

Enclosed you will find draft dated Santa Fe Dec. 20th, 1858 at sight on Sweeny Rittenhouse Fant & Co. for $500.+ drawn by John L. Watts payable to the order of O. P. Hovey and by him endorsed to our order. This draft should be paid on presentation and probably will be. If however, it should not be met promptly do not have it protested but hold it a short time and the funds will be there to meet it. The case is this. Genl. Pelham started for the states by last mail. Takes with him papers to meet this draft & a number more of the same sort. He must have time to reach Washington & arrange matters there before it can be paid. Also draft dated Santa Fe Dec. 31st, 1858 at sight on John Marron 3rd Asst. Post Master Genl. for $4,062,50 Four thousand Sixty two & 50/100 dollars drawn by T. F. Bowler payable to our order, making in all $4,562.50 which amt. is charged to your agent account. Now this draft of Tom's you must not send on till February, as it will not be paid untill then. This is the best I can do for you in the way of remittances, and you must do the best you can with it. I shall not send anymore for cash purchases east. Now in case you require this money before these drafts can be collected, then you must get Mr. Abbott or someone else to discount them or advance you the money untill they can be collected. They are both good and will be paid. It is only a question of a little time and if you need the money before they are paid I think you can easily raise what you want on them.

I shall make up my Trial Balance to Jany 1st will send you a copy soon as corrected.

Enclosed is a small order for D. V. Whiting do the best you can to fill it.

27. This is the mail that was rumored to have been wiped out by the Comanches.

28. During the Mexican-American War, Edward Fitzgerald Beale served in California, where he met and accompanied Kit Carson on his transcontinental dispatch assignment. Beale was also involved in the government's attempt to introduce camels as pack animals, using the beasts in his 1857 survey along the 35th parallel. Beale found the results of this experiment successful enough to purchase many of the camels for use on his own ranch near Bakersfield, California, when the War Department decided to sell them. Thrapp, *Encyclopedia*, 1:76.

P.S. Levi Spiegelberg and Seligmann go in with this mail both to buy goods.

Letter no. 93, Kingsbury to Webb, Santa Fe, January 2, 1859

I have now yours of Dec 1st. I got my Trial Balance off yesterday but there is a small error in it of $2. which I have not had time to correct. Our sales this month amt. to $5,900.+ Collections amt. to $9,000+. By last mail I sent you Tom Bowler's Draft on Washington $4,062.50 and a small draft of Watt's on Sweeny Rittenhouse Fant & Co. for $500.+ which I hope you have rec'd safely.

Frank Green has at last got here all safe, we are all much relieved, he came through all the way under protection of Lt. Beals [Beale's] party. His whole outfit came through well, lost no mules, he had two horses die with distemper.[29]

You will see by the amt. of my sales last month that business has kept up pretty fair. The house looks rather thin, my wholesale goods are getting low, in Groceries I am well assorted yet, and have now no fear but that they will go and it is possible that I may sell all the sugar. My retail Stock is good yet, it is clean and well asst'd. We retailed last month about $2,000+. In my sales I am confident we will come out all right. Now if collections come in fair, all will be well, and I see no reason why they should not. In looking at the a/c's I am a little anxious to get them in. I don't like to see so large amt. standing out. They will soon be coming due and I shall push hard to collect. This comes partly by having the Two Trains come so near together, I was obliged to let some of the customers have second bills before the Spring ones became due.[30] Then Tom's amt. is large but there is no help for it at present, I am confident he will come out all right, and we are compeled to keep him going. Soon as he can get to handle 1 or 2 Quarte[r]s more pay he will be out of the woods. He owes nothing except to us worth mentioning. His whole outfit on both lines are paid for, and he pays the men and all contingenc[i]es cash up. The El Paso line is now well provided with corn fodder &c., all of which is paid for. He may owe out side of our house perhaps $4,000.+ but he says it will not pass that. The House [Exchange Hotel] is doing well. They are making money there just as fast as it is good for them. They are crowded all the time, with good paying men. If they have no misfortune, in one year they will be out of debt with plenty of cash ahead.

P.S. <u>Poor Dick</u> [Owens?] has gone to his long home. King Alcohol took him off at last, he fought him a long time but finally went under. He was buried in the Church [the Parroquia] on the Plaza.

Geo. Estes will administer the estate.

29. Frank Green's mail party, believed by many to have been wiped out by the Comanches, finally arrived at Anton Chico southeast of Santa Fe on the Pecos River around the New Year. Kingsbury's report that they traveled the whole way with Lt. Beale's surveying party contradicts Taylor, who said they had gone ahead of Beale and his men through the most dangerous country before arriving at Anton Chico and continuing on to Albuquerque. Taylor, *First Mail West*, 56 (Taylor bases this on *Kansas City Daily Western Journal of Commerce*, Jan. 11, 1859, p. 2,; Feb. 1, 1859, p. 2). Beale's party stopped at Hatch's Ranch for two months to rest. Beale had gone on ahead to Santa Fe, then on to visit Kit Carson during January, so there is no reference to when or where Green left the group. Since Beale makes no mention of Green going ahead earlier in the journey, we are inclined to believe Kingsbury's version, which Beale's journal supports by default.

30. Due to various mishaps Kingsbury mentioned previously, Webb & Kingsbury's 1858 spring train did not arrive in Santa Fe until early July.

Letter no. 94, Kingsbury to Webb, Santa Fe, January 9, 1859

I got nothing by the mail today from you. Herewith you will find a correct Trial Balance from our books showing the balance of each a/c up to Jany 1st.

Kitchen started his mule Teams in on the 4th—he will be ready soon as you can give him the goods.

I am suffering today with one of my ugly head aches. I have nothing of importance to write so I will stop.

P. S. Collections are coming in well so far this month.

Letter no. 95, Kingsbury to Webb, Santa Fe, January 16, 1859

Dear Sir, I am now in receipt of yours of Dec 14th. I hope the shoe order reached you in time. I delaid it longer than I intended on a/c of being about to effect the sale of our property and then to make fresh bargain for freight. You understand all long before this. You also have an answer about the Shoe bill from Bristall & Hall, it was all right just what we wanted for retail. Our groceries will all sell before Spring, I have no fear about them now. All the Lard was for Tom. I have finally sold all the head dresses, at fair profit, for two of them I got 100%. The flowers go slow but will all sell in time. They are most to[o] high cost to wholesale but they have so far retailed well. The goods from Jeffries & Son would all have sold readily had they come with the other goods. As it is they are left over but will sell. I have not sold one of the mantillas yet but they will all sell in the Spring. The new style dress goods from Doan King & Co are still on hand they do not take here. The Bayetta [bayeta] is all sold, it brought $1. a vara,[31] $12 a piece over cost. In regard to Flannela,[32] I cannot tell how it would go or the price never having sold a yard in my life.

You will see that I have ordered a few more hoop skirts. I have sold about half of the red Petticoats but don't want any more. The comb bill was all right and the goods all sold long ago. I have not heard a word from Branford since he got the [billiard] Table, presume however it gave satisfaction. I have heard others speak of it in high Terms. They say it is better than either of Tom's. The Butterfield Co. have rather backed out in their proposition to Tom. They still want to buy but object to giving what was first offered.[33] Tom has decided not to go in at present, but gave Watts a full power of atty. to act for him in that matter, if they come up to fair terms the sale will be made.[34] Watts left here last Monday, for the States will see the parties at El Paso and go on in their line. The fact is it is allmost an impossibility for Tom to leave here, their house requires all of his and Frank's attention to keep thing[s] streight and going. So they finally desided to trust this mail

31. Bayeta is a type of cloth. A vara was about 33 inches.

32. Flannela is one of several kinds of soft-spun cotton flannel fabrics, many of which have generic names like 'flannela' or 'flannelette.'

33. Kingsbury had mentioned previously that Butterfield had offered Tom $80,000 for his two mail contracts. Kingsbury to Webb, Santa Fe, Nov. 27, 1858.

34. Apparently Watts acted as Tom's partner in the mail contract business. In a September 1858 letter, Kingsbury mentioned that Watts had agreed to furnish Tom with half the money to start his mail deliveries, but then never gave him the money. This cramped Tom's finances, delaying payment of his debt to Webb and Kingsbury. Ibid., Sept. 25, 1858, MHS.

matter to Watts. You tell me that you have rec'd the $2,500. by Watts, well this is all right hold on to it, and place the other money which Tom sent, on your Agent a/c and I will pass it to Tom's Credit here. Take it up according to the following figures.

Warrant sent Dec 12th		$633.79
Draft " " 18 "		1872.50
from this deduct what is yours Private		$2506.29

Cash to Watts	$7.00	
Interest on Amt. Loaned	83.33	90.33
	leaving	$2415.96

which amt. I will charge on your agent a/c and place the same to Tom's Credit on our books. By this mail I send to Messrs Doan King & Co. at St. Louis a Check No 49. drawn by J. L. Collins, Supt. Ind. Affs. N.M. on the Asst. Treas. of the U.S. at New York for $2,500.+ with request to them to take up our several notes due there in February. The notes amt. to $2368.44, and I have instructed them to hold the small balance subject to your order. This check is the last cent of exchange on the States that can be bought today in Santa Fe. It would have pleased me better to have sent them a remittance direct on St. Louis, but it is impossible. I hope this will answer just as well, and perhaps it may be worth a premium there. Soon as I can get exchange, I shall continue to remit to them funds to take up the two freight notes and for you to buy groceries with. Collections continue to come in fair, sales are small but I am satisfied. I have not been able to make a wholesale bill this month, but retail keeps up well, and by the end of the month I hope to make the sales foot up well.

If I have omitted anything now, I don't know it, I always try to give you every item of importance in regard to our business so that you may be fully posted, in everything connected with it, not only for your benifit but mine also, so that should anything happen to me, I shall feel easy to know that you are in possession of every matter pertaining to it. You say that my letter of Nov. 14th "is short" and "nothing about business."[35] Had you been in the same situation I was when that was written I doubt whether you would have written atall. It was just at a time when I was pushed and hurried almost beyond my abilities, you must remember that I have no easy task to perform, managing customers, fishing for them, then to sell the goods. Keeping the books. And coupled to this the care and anxiety to have everything come out right, is pretty heavy on little John. If there is anything now in our business that you do not understand or that you want any information about, mention it to me, and it will be my first pleasure to explain every particular to you, and I promise to do it to the best of my ability.

Since I have been writing this I have made some enquiries about

35. "Yours of Nov. 14th is just to hand. It is short, and not much news. You say nothing about business sales collections, &c, except that you hope to place me in funds to make spring purchases. I had expected your shoe memorandum, but it has not come. . . . You have not said a word." Webb to Kingsbury, Hamden, CT, Dec. 14, 1858, MHS.

Flannela it is selling here now by the pieces at 87 ½ cents, Blue, Green & red are the collers wanted but it sells in proportion of about 6 pieces red to <u>one</u> of the other colors. I think I might sell some, this and Bayetta is always more or less used.

I shall continue to send your letters to New Haven when you leave there, leave orders to have them forwarded to you so that you may get them.

Letter no. 96, Kingsbury to Webb, Santa Fe, January 23, 1859

I am without advices from you since my last. By the last mail I sent to Messrs Doan King & Co. check for Twenty five hundred dollars ($2,500.+) with request to take up our notes due in St. Louis. Business continues very dull that is sales are small, but collections are coming very fair. I think now that I shall get in plenty of funds to meet all that you will want and have it in good season. Tom Bowler has sold his and Frank's interest in the Exchange to a man by the name of Rose.[36] He is one of the party of Californians that was defeated by the Indians, he had there heavy loss in Stock &c. but has still means, and is said to be a man of property. The conditions are these. They give him possession on the 1st day of March next, he paying $5,000. cash down the balance in Equal payments of 6, 12, 18 & 24 months. He takes all their fixtures and stock at cost which is not injured and things which are worn and partially used up, at a fair valuation. Tom still keeps the property and rents it to him for three years at $100 per month payable monthly, and give[s] him the privilege of a 5 years lease after that time if he should want it. The gardain [*sic*] they keep for their mail outfit. They are both tired of the house, and glad to have the chance to quit. They are pretty well broke down and want a little rest. If this man does not come up all right, they will have the papers fixed so that they can get possession again & go on as before. But the probability is that it is a sure sale and that the man's means are all that they are represented to be. He is also to take all the goods which we have for Tom on the same terms that we have been giving them to him, and also to take all that is now ordered and the balance which Tom will order from St. Louis which the house will want. In fact he takes Tom's place and we have his business just as we have had Tom's.[37]

I have just got a letter from San Migu[e]l bringing the sad news that Old Uncle Tom Rowland is murdered.[38] It appears that whoever done it, entered his store between 7 & 8 in the evening, he had just finished shaving, and while he was behind the counter they made an atact [*sic*] upon him, with Knives. There are 24 cuts upon his head, hands and body, he must have given them a hard fight he succeeded in getting out of the store and clear from them (there was evidently several against him) went about 120 feet and fel[l] dead in which condi-

36. Leonard J. Rose, a well-to-do resident of Iowa, had led a group of emigrants and a large herd of cattle toward California in 1858. From Albuquerque, they followed the 35th-parallel wagon road explored by Lt. Beale in 1857. Mojave Indians, friendly to Beale the year before, attacked Rose's party on the Colorado River. The survivors, who included Rose, his wife, and his mother, retreated to Albuquerque, going much of the way on foot. Rose later filed a claim against the United States government for losses totaling nearly $28,000. Dodge, *The Road West*, 133-54, 207-14.

37. Kingsbury was probably relieved. As these letters reveal, supplying Bowler's needs as manager of the hotel constituted a significant part of their business.

38. Webb reacted to this news with regret, but not surprise. He had warned Kingsbury against employing Rowland for any longer than he had to, expressing both his own and Messervy's opinion of the old man's character (see chapter 9). Hearing of Rowland's murder, Webb wrote, "I am very sorry to hear of the fate of poor old Thom. You may rest assured that a woman was in that scrape. You do not say as suspicion rests on any one, but certainly every means ought to be made use of in order if possible to furnish the perpetrators." Webb to Kingsbury, Hamden, CT, Feb. 21, 1859, MHS. Gov. Abraham Rencher responded by offering an $800 reward for the capture of his murderer. *Santa Fe Weekly Gazette*, Feb. 5, 1859.

tion he was found, the murderers made their escape and no clue left to discover them, as he spoke to no one after he was cut. The suposition is that they were thieves and killed him just to rob the store but his getting out and hollering alarmed them so that they made good their escape and probably took nothing as his watch was found just as he laid it off and some little money in the draw[er] about fifty dollars. The people here wish me to administer on his estate. I shall go out tomorrow with preparations to bring in the body for interment here, and if I cannot find a suitable person there to take charge of it, I may do it myself.

It is only yesterday that I sent him out a few goods which he ordered and if I get these back, he will owe us nothing. I know that he owes very little and must have left plenty to pay all if it is properly managed.

I am expecting by every mail to get a remittance from Hoppin & Appel, have got nothing from them yet. I hear that they have been doing a good business, and we ought to hear from them soon.

Letter no. 97, Kingsbury to Webb, Santa Fe, January 30, 1859

Yours of the 27th ult. is to hand. I have received $400. on a/c from Geo. M. Alexander[39] also $100. from Kavanaugh Pino & Hovey. So you see we will come out all right with the Utah outfit. Collections are coming in fair and as soon as I make up funds for our freight notes and purchases in St. Louis I will then settle the amt. with Mercure in case Tom cannot by that time.[40]

I have no advises from Messervy for a long time, not even an acknowledgement of the $7,000. which I sent him. I am surprised he does not write to me. In regard to the Three thousand which you will want for private use next summer, I have not the least doubt but that I can arrange it for you & not miss it, particularly if Watts should pay that note of $5,000. promptly. However it is impossible for me now to make a certain calculation about funds, nor will I be able to untill I know the whole amt. of the purchases you are making this Spring. There is always more or less uncertainty about collections, and at the time you will want this amt. is about the time our notes will be maturing. Still you will be safe to start your improvements and go on with it. Soon as our notes are provided for, I will then send what you need, and in all probability a goodeal more, the only risk is that it may not reach you quite as early as the time you state, but it will be sure to follow soon after.

The prospects now are that Tom will not keep us long out of our money since he has sold out, I know his first object is to pay us, and that to[o] as soon as possible. He has today made arraingements for $2,500. to be placed in the hands of Doan King & Co. at St. Louis to

39. Alexander is the man who had had all the bad luck the previous fall. See chapter 9.

40. Kingsbury had borrowed $3,000 from Joseph Mercure on Tom Bowler's behalf.

our Credit, it is a part of the $5,000 Cash he gets on his sale. This sum of $2,500. you will probably find there all safe when you reach St. Louis. I shall not count on it to meet our notes, but leave it extra for you to use in purchases.

I received today a letter from Messrs Hoppin & Appel, which I will enclose to you that you may know just how it stands. I am disapointed in not getting a remittances from them, and have written them the best pushing letter in reply that I could. I believe firmly that they are good for it but fear now that they will be slow, and I shall be uneasy untill we get our money from them.

I have one more day to go on in this month but will now give you the figures for the month's business which will be near enough for your calculations. Sales amt. to $6,500., Collections Amt. to $10,000.

I started for San Miguel on Monday last, & in the Canion [*sic*] met the body coming in, I then turned and came back, it was burried with due Masonic honors. There is no clue yet as to who the murderers were. I have got <u>Vigil</u> who is married to a daughter of Uncle Tom's to administer on the estate. He is a son of Donaciano Vigil.[41] I have started Weirick out to take possession of the last bill I sent out and to make arraingements to have them brought back. There will be no trouble about it. The goods have been deposited at the Sheriff's house subject to my order.

I have your memo. of amt. paid Bula & Co. and for Butter, will enter it a[t] once be sure to get the butter along to come with the first train. It will come then as safe as in a fall train. I have not the most remote idea what the weight of the goods I have ordered will make nor can I make any satisfactory estimate. Thinking perhaps you may require some heavy goods to fill up the train, I will send by this mail a small order for groceries to meet you in St. Louis. They are for things which will be wanted here on arrival and will sell imediately. I shall afterwards duplicate nearly all the Articles to come in the Ox waggons but can't give the quantity of each now.

Enclosed you will find a small order for Whiting fill it if you can. I think of nothing more now. <u>Kind regards to all.</u>

P.S. José has been discharged from his situation with the [El Paso] mail. He is now idle and getting more trifling every day.

Letter no. 98, Kingsbuy to Webb, Santa Fe, January 30, 1859

I have sent you a full letter under this date to New Haven, which I hope you have received.

Memo for a few groceries to come <u>in the first train.</u>

3 Bbls best Whiskey, to cost about $1

500 " best powdered bar sugar

41. Donaciano Vigil, who served as acting civil governor of New Mexico following the death of Charles Bent in January 1847, was one of the territory's most influential residents.

1,000 " crushed sugar

50 cans lard

2,500 " canvassed hams

1,500 " side meat

10 sacks coffee

30 boxes candles

20 "   white soap 1 " bars

20 doz. cans fresh oysters

6 Bbl. Kennet ale

at all events send the oysters and ale and if possible the balance.
I do not send you any money now to make payments for above, as I
depend upon the $2,500.+ coming from Tom's successes being in Doan
King &Co's hands waiting for you.

Attached you will find a memo for some stove plates. They are
wanted to repair Tom's hotel stoves and will be needed soon as we can
get them here. I send the order just as they give it to me in order to
avoid any mistake. They have since added some more things and I
must copy it.

Letter no. 99, Kingsbury to Webb, Santa Fe, February 6, 1859

I am now in recpt. of yours of Jany 5th, am glad to know that you
have got my papers all safe so far. Mr Messervy writes me that Watts'
draft of $5,000 is not yet paid.[42] I am a goodeal an[n]oyed and per-
plexed that it should turn out so, but still trust it will all be made right
and satisfactory on his arrival in the States. Should he finally back out
we must look for another purchaser, and I shall be uneasy untill I hear
more about it. I do not know where a letter would find him in the
States he will probably be on the move all the time he is there. You
had better corrispond with him direct your letters to care of his banking house in Washington, that will be the surest way of his getting
them, if he does not pay the first draft, of course he will not pay the
note. Try your best to hold him to the contract and get the money out
of him soon as you can.

I believe Blumner is perfectly good for all I have sold him, but from
this on I will be governed by your suggestions in his case.

Watts never told Tom that he had made arrangement for you to get
the $2,500. and I doubt if Watts knew it himself when he left here. Of
course you will keep it, and appropriate the amt. Tom sent from here
on our new purchases. In case you have collected Tom's mail drafts or
sold them, you will certainly have all the ready funds that you will
want east. Before Kitchen started in I paid him $2500 on a/c of our
freight note to him which was $5,000.+ leaving still a balance in his
favor of $2,500.+ to be paid in St. Louis then for freight we owe to
Yager & Kerr $2,150.+ Making $4,650.+ which is all we owe on last

42. Apparently Watts's draft for $5,000, consti-
tuting the first payment for the real estate of Webb
& Kingsbury, had been protested. Webb to Kingsbury, Hamden, CT, Jan. 17, 1859, MHS.

years business. I have now $3,000.+ on hand above all deposits and will soon have enough to remit all you will want to use in St. Louis. I think my collections keep up as well as we could expect, when you take into consideration the dates of the sales. At any rate I am doing my best to get them in as fast as possible.

I think that Lt. Beale is acting in good faith with Tom & Frank.[43] Tom has now gone out to Hatche's [Hatch's] ranch in Company with Lt. Beale and some others to have a talk with the Comanche Chiefs, about a right of way for the mail coaches to pass through their country.[44] They are in hopes to make a compromise with the Indians and buy their good will, I hope they will succeed, if they do not it will be impossible for Tom to run his Mail. The Indians have the power and are not willing that a road should be made through their country. The emigrants that returned from Rio Colorado, were a large party on the way to California with Cattle, from what I can learn they got into a fuss with the Indians which could have been avoided, the Indians being strong, succeeded in running off their stock and they were compeled to return, on foot and in a miserable destitute condition having lost several of their party in the different encounters, but the whites are themselves to blaim having made the first attacts on the Indians without cause. Simply because they thought they were strong enough to defend themselves but it proved othewise. The Yuma rout[e] is not opened yet, soon as the weather will permit Lt. Beale with his party will proceed from Albuquerque through and work the road in places, where it is most needed.[45]

The whole upper Country (Missouri and the borders I mean) are perfectly crazy on the subject of Pike's Peak gold mines, we have accounts here that the excitement is equal to that for California in 1849. Men are starting out on foot with their Kit on their backs. I hope they will not be disapointed but I fear there is too much humbug in it. The gold is there but no one up to present can tell how profitable it will be. Much money will at any rate be made off of the emigration.[46]

We have had considerable excitement the past weeks in our little Jerusalem of Santa Fe. The case is this [Selig] Weinhem has been gambeling and ruined himself at it. He made an as[s]ignment and turned all his effects over to Cleaver, it carried on its face a Jew swindle, I did not like the looks of things and immediately in company with [J. J.] Beck & Johnson took out an attachment and shut him up.[47] Some of the goods had been removed and conseald, we then got out a Sirch Warrant and I believe the most of them are now in the hands of the Sherriff. He owes us about $760. His whole debts are between 5. & 6,000. If our attachments hold good Beck & ourselves will be paid in full as we are first. My lawyer's [Merrill] Ashurst & [Hugh N.] Smith say that we are perfectly safe, and to rest easy that we will get every cent. For my part I do not like law suits and would

43. This was probably written in response to Webb's suspicions that Beale might be acting for the good of a rival mail carrier. See Webb to Kingsbury, Hamden, CT, Jan. 5, 1859, MHS.

44. Hatch's Ranch was on the Gallinas River, a tributary of the Pecos, some eighty miles from Santa Fe by Beale's reckoning. Traveling from Fort Smith, Arkansas, Beale arrived at the ranch on December 26 and left most of his survey party there until March while he attended to business and social calls in Taos, Santa Fe, and Albuquerque. Jackson, *Wagon Roads West*, 251-53, 369 n. 51.

Although Kingsbury does not mention the episode, apparently mail contractor Jacob Hall, whom historian Charles L. Kenner credits with obtaining the contract for the Neosho to Santa Fe to California mail route, had been attacked by the Comanches the previous November on his initial trip over the route. The Indians burned his wagon and the mail, while Hall succeeded in escaping. Apparently this incident brought home the necessity of treating with the Comanches. Kenner, *A History of New Mexico-Plains Indian Relations*, p. 127-28.

45. Kingsbury here confuses Beale's 35th-parallel route, which crossed the Colorado River at the Mojave villages, with the 32nd-parallel route, which crossed the river at Yuma.

46. Of the estimated 100,000 gold hunters who set out from the Missouri River that spring, most found the rumors of gold "Pike's Peak Humbug" and returned home disheartened. One exception was John H. Gregory of Georgia, who struck it rich near Central City on May 6, 1859. The stampede to Colorado resumed, bringing prosperity to many of the Missouri River merchants who supplied the trains heading west. Hafen and Hafen, eds., *Reports from Colorado*, 16-19.

47. Kingsbury is probably referring to Dr. J. J. Beck. Kingsbury to Webb, Santa Fe, March 3, 1860, MHS. Preston Beck, who was mentioned frequently in the early correspondence of Kingsbury, Webb, and Messervy, died in the spring of 1858 (see chapter 8).

not have done this if I had not thought they were bound to swindle us. As it is I have made fair propositions for a compromise to withdraw my attachment and let him go on. If those who are more interested than we are do not accept my terms, I shall carry it through & sell out what is left and wait the disision of the Court. My offer is this to take 50% Cash for our debt, or extend it 6 & 12 month with 6% interest, with good security.

The whole Jew outfit are more or less interested in this nest, and the excitement is really laughfable [*sic*]. Beck & Johnson and myself have got the start of them and they know it, and are badly plagued about it.

This is only another case of the uncertainty of our Customers, he was doing a good and profitable business, had good credit, but suffered himself to play off all his profits and much more, deceived his best friends and country men. We are lucky to have no more at stake there.

Pigeon's luck has come back to him again, in the last two or 3 weeks he has wone between $12,000.+ & $14,000. The most of it from Old Falez [Félix?] Garcia. The probability is he will not keep it long.[48]

Letter no. 100, Kingsbury to Webb, Santa Fe, February 20, 1859

I am now in receipt of both your favors of Jany 17th. I think my previous letters will explain to you fully that matter of the $2500.+[49] There can be no difficulty about it whatever, you have only to hold on to all the money & apply it according to your letter. There is no mis-understanding with the parties here. Tom & Frank are willing to keep in with Watts if he will only do what is right. The two drafts I sent you on this account were both started from here before I got yours stating that it had been paid from S[weeny] R[ittenhouse] Fant & Co. It is true Watts said the amt. had been paid to you, but he had nothing to show for it and we did not believe it, and I insisted that it should be sent to you forthwith. This is the reason why you got it from both par-ties. As it has turned out it is all the better for us it gives you that much more to use in cash purchases East. You request me to send you $500. on private a/c. I regret that I cannot get exchange if I could I would send it by this mail.

However I feel easy about it as I know you are not going to suffer for money while you have so much of the firms money in your hands. If my calculations are right, after paying all the Eastern Notes, you must have at your disposal between 11 & 12,000. That is provided all the remittances are realized which I sent.

I hope you found ready sale for the two Land Warrants.

In my last I wrote you all about the case of Weinheim, well I have now got that affair settled for the present. The other creditors paid me the 50% cash and I have released the attachment. They pay all the costs

48. Kingsbury is referring to Alexander Valle, nicknamed Pigeon. See chapter 9.

49. Webb's continued confusion regarding the matter of the $2,500 apparently stems from the fact that both Watts and Tom Bowler paid him back. Webb to Kingsbury, Hamden, CT, Jan. 17, 1859, MHS.

except my lawyers' fees. I have rec'd this amt. as settlement in full and given a receipt to that effect and we have no further claim on Weinheim for our debt. But he assures me on his honor (what little he has left,) that as soon as he gets out of debt that he will pay the whole amt. That he does not intend that we shall loose a cent by him. I believe he is sinsere, should he live & be lucky enough to get out of the woods and ahead he may pay us as he says. Under all the circumstances I am well plased with the settlement as it is, and think we have got of[f] cheap.

I shall try to get the balance of my orders started to you in a week or two by that time I hope also to be able to get remittances to send with them. Mr. Rose with his family is now here, will probably take possession of the Exchange according to their agreement. I shall send my orders just as soon as I can learn what he will want us to bring for him. I like his appearance pretty well, he appears like a smart business man. I believe it will all be right with him. Col. [William A.] Street and Mr. [W. A.] Davidson, the officers of the Land office, have bought the McKutchen house will moove their office there. Soon as they vacate our house Frank will moove in. So I shall have Tom & Franks families for neighbors for the present. I hope your next letters will tell me your calculations about traveling, if not I shall be at a loss to know how to direct my letters to you that you may get them without delay.

Business continues pretty fair for this time of year, and my sales are very good considering my assortment. Collections are coming in gradually. After I get the amt. together nessesary for cash purchases in St. Louis & the freight notes, it will be almost impossible for us to be pushed any more for money. I hope Watts has arrived safe, and by this time had ample time to arrange his matters so as to comply with our bargain. I shall be uneasy untill I hear more from you about it.

P.S. Brittingham started for Pike's Peak in company with M. Pollock of Las Vegas & others. Pollock writes back that Brittingham died at Platte river on the 12th of January, no particulars. Little Tom Smith the Pay Masters brother is also dead. He died of consumption and was laid in our Cemet[e]ry.

You will see by the [Santa Fe Weekly] Gazette that a party have been arrested on suspision of being the murderers of Uncle Tom. The evidence against them is all circumstancial and there is enough to commit them for trial, but no positive evidence. I believe the whole party are guilty, but think it will be impossible to convict them unless some further evidence comes out or one of the party turns States evidence.

I will not forget your <u>chile</u>.

Letter no. 101, Kingsbury to Webb, Santa Fe, March 5, 1859

Dear Sir, I am now in receipt of yours of Jany 31st containing a/c current of Mr. Abbott, which I am glad to see, also yours of Feby 7th. I trust the drafts of Watts for $5,000 and $500. are both paid long before this. I must again request you to let me know, when you receive the Cash, on each and every remittance I send you. You always acknowledge receipt of the remittances but I want to know when each is paid. Was Tom's first mail draft paid? and how about the other? Have you sold those two Land Warrants yet?—and what amt. did you realize for them. It is important I should know so as to colle[c]t here what ever discount was made on them less than the price they were charged to you. I had no date to give you for Tom's draft his advise from the dept. was that it would be paid any time after the 1st of February. I trust it is all right, and that you have realized the money on both of them. Tom's first Neosho Mail got through safe a little behind the time, and returned. They have lost no mail. The next return mail will be due in a few days. If it gets through safe, they anticipate no more trouble from the Indians. They are expecting to get full pay from the commencement of the contract.[50]

[James H.?] Clift closed out his shop, and in Company with old man [James?] Conklin started with a carriage through Country peddling. I furnished them with goods and they had paid nearly all up. They could not agree and seperated, and left with me the carriage or ambulance with harness, to sell to cover the balance of their a/c. It is not sold yet but if I can find a purchaser it is good for the amt. Clift afterwards opened a house, for the accomidation of travelers, with a little store, at the foot of the Mesa.[51] I assisted him to start, he is doing well and will be able to pay us. he bought a goodeal of corn of the people of Pinablanca [Peña Blanca]. Soon as he sells this he will have the cash. Corn is in demand. It is worth $4.50 a Fanega[52] at Albuquerque, and is selling here at $4.

Bob Cary has already paid his account. He is doing well, has got the sutlership at Taos. Is making money fast. If he will let cards alone, he will soon be able to pay the old a/c of Messervy & Webb, that is the discount which I allowed him. You have no claim on him for it as the settlement was in full, but he has told me that he intends to pay every cent of that old debt, soon as he can do so without injury to his present business.[53] I believe Bob is perfectly honest and means what he says. The only danger with him now is that he will drink & while on his sprees will gamble. Speaking of gambeling, I do not know what has got into the people. Since the law has prohibited it, I beleive that there is more gambling than formerly and that of the most dangerous kind as it is done in secret, men have got infacinate [sic] that never to[u]ched a card when it was public.[54] Such men as Sampson

50. According to Taylor, the short-lived Neosho to Albuquerque mail route was so underutilized that in February the postal officials ordered that half the mail sent through St. Louis be directed west via that route. With the advent of a new postmaster in March, however, came cost-cutting measures that spelled an end to several western mail lines. Service on the Neosho route was discontinued on July 1, 1859. *First Mail West*, 56-57.

51. Probably at Bajada, at the foot of La Bajada Mesa, a stopping point on the road from Albuquerque to Santa Fe. Peña Blanca, where he bought corn, is nearby.

52. A fanega was a unit of measurement equal to about two and a half bushels, although in early territorial New Mexico its exact size varied greatly. In 1852 Capt. E. S. Sibley fixed the unit at a weight of 140 pounds for the purposes of army contracts. This ultimately became the fanega's accepted size. Frazer, *Forts and Supplies*, 80.

53. Webb had written that Bob Cary still owed them over $500 and that he wanted Kingsbury to collect it as quickly as possible. Webb to Kingsbury, Hamden, CT, Feb. 7, 1859, MHS.

54. Gambling had been abolished during the administration of David Meriwether. Horn, *New Mexico's Troubled Years*, 68.

Beuthener and Henry Mercure play as heavy as any one. This is private. I would not have it come from me to their injury. I could mention others but we are not interested and I will not put their names down. From the nature of circumstances down below Hoppin & Appel are bound to be slow, but it is caused by things beyond their controle. I rely upon their being honest men & not card players. They have property and means, and I feel confident they will pay us but we must wait on them. To be sure I shall be uneasy about that a/c untill the money comes, but I see nothing at present to be especially alarmed about. Vincente St. Vrain is just from there. He tells me that they have a large amt. of corn on hand, and are expecting to sell it to the Butterfield Mail Co. It is worth there now $3.25 a Fanega and on the rise.

Collins has full confidence in our house I can do almost anything with him in Money Matters. He has bought no goods here in Santa Fe the last year, except Mexican Blankets, he received direct from the States all the goods which was required for the Indians. He has bought nothing in the Territory except Blankets, Corn & Provisions.[55] With the Secretary I stand all right. I furnished the last Legislature as far as our stock would go all the things they wanted. When I sold the property [to Watts] I considered it a legitamate sale beyond a question, and still think Watts will pay all damages and stick to the bargain. I rec'd from him that draft as cash, and his note for the balance, and made the entrees on the books immediately, which I thought at the time was the only correct way.[56] The real estate got Cr. for $10,000, Cash a/c charged with $5,000. & Notes receivable charged with $5,000. I then sent the Draft of 5,000 in company with a check of $2,210. as a cash remittance to Messervy to lift our note to him of $7,000. and the interest in full to Jany 1st 1859. The $7,000. was charge against his note and the interest $210. to my private a/c as usual. That you may understand fully our Notes Payable a/c as it stood at the time of the last Trial Balance, I will send herewith a statement of the names and amts. I will try to profit by your suggestions in regard to extending credits next year. I know it will be impossible to sell those goods without letting them go on Credit, and wherever credit is given there is more or less risk. We are liable to be desieved with the best men.

You may rely that I am doing my best to collect as fast as possible and getting in all the money I can. My collections during the month of February amt. to $5,500.+. Sales for the same amt. to $3,400.+ You may judge by this what I am doing.

Herewith you will find my orders for Groceries. I want what is ordered here in addition to my order of Jany 30th. I have no possible idea of what amt. of freight you will have left over after filling the mule Waggons. I would like to give Kitchen freight for the 15 Ox Waggons, but our understanding is for 15 more or less to be governed by our wish, so I think you will have no trouble about the quantity of

55. Webb had asked Kingsbury if Superintendent of Indian Affairs Collins had confidence in their house and if he was buying goods from them. Webb to Kingsbury, Hamden, CT, Feb. 7, 1859, MHS.

56. Webb had criticized Kingsbury for entering Watts draft for $5,000 as cash on their books, as if the real estate deal had gone through. Ibid.

Freight. In making my orders I have been very carefull not to order anything except what is already engaged or staple articles, nearly all the heavy goods are engaged, such as Lard, Bacon, side meat, whiskey, and about half of the Sugar, Coffee, Soap & Candles. If you wish to increase my orders, to enable you to fill up the Wagons you may do so, but I leave that with you, what I have ordered I feel sure I can sell.

Now let me explain to you about the Whiskey, the 8 Bbls. you sent last have got that same smell, taste and flavor which is obnoctious to the Whiskey drinkers here. It may be the best kind of Whiskey but they won't drink it. I have now 6 Bbls left, and do not know how I shall ever get it off. The two BBls belonging to Tillman Rozier & Co. I put onto Hovey in that Utah outfit last Spring. Have not rendered them a/c of it yet, I am waiting to get a full settlement with Hovey first. I consider that I sold it on their risk, & they must wait untill I get the pay for it, before I send it to them. Now to avoid any mistake about the 15 Bbls. which I have sent for in the Exchange order. I send you by mail a small box containing two of the Samples which you sent out last fall, one is of the 8 Bbls. sent, be careful to avoid getting any more like this. The other is marked "Bourbon". This Tom selected of all the samples you sent and says this will do, send the 15 Bbls like this!! if you cannot get the same lot of Whiskey this was sampled from do your best to find something as near it as you can, that is the same flavor and <u>about</u> the same price.

Herewith you will find No 8439 Treasury Warrant pt. 7999. <u>Interior</u>, dated Washington Nov 3rd 1858, at sight on the Asst. Treas. of the U.S. at St Louis, for Eighty five ($85.+) dollars, signed Sam Casey Treas of the U.S. F. Bigger regist. of the Treas. Payable to the order of R. H. Tompkins U.S. Atty., and by him endor[s]ed to our order. <u>Also</u> Check No 67, dated Santa Fe New Mexico Jany 17, 1859 at sight of the Asst. Treas. of the U.S. at New York for One Thousand Dollars ($1,000.+) drawn by J. L. Donaldson A.Q.M. payable to our order.

<u>Also</u> Check No. 10 dated Santa Fe N. Mexico, March 4, 1859, at sight on the Asst. Treas. of the U.S. at Saint Louis for Six Thousand dollars ($6,000+) drawn by J. L. Donaldson A.Q.M. payable to our order. Making in all Seven Thousand and Eighty five dollars (<u>$7,085+</u>) which amt. is charged to your agent account. I send this to meet expenses and for cash purchases, also count that you will find the $2,500+ from Mr. [Leonard] Rose deposited at Doan King & Co for your use,—and possibly you may have rec'd the balance due from the Carondolet Mining Co. Now I cannot send any more funds at present, dispose of this to the best advantage. Should you require any funds immediately for your private use you must take it out of these funds. My next remittances will have to go to meet those two Freight Notes. Soon as you get your bills fixed up send me a full a/c of all the settlement so that I may know how to make remittances to meet what will be left unpaid. It will probably take all my collections this month to

meet those freight notes, after that I can begin to remit on unpaid a/c's of the new purchases.

Tom gave possession of the Exchange to his successor [Leonard Rose] according to agreement. They have not got through yet taking a/c of the fixtures, that is they have not fixed on all the prices yet. Tom thinks it will amt. to $15,000 or 20,000. Mr. Rose appears to be a very fine man and will probably make a popular Land Lord. I had 5 strings of Chile ground for you, packed it nicely and sent it in by the last mail, you will find it at "Bernards."[57] I would send the Buckskins now, but the mail charge 50 cents per pound on packages and are very unwilling to take them at that. Make Kitchen let you have what you want he took in a large lot, & can certainly spare the little you want.

I cannot think of anything more now.

Letter no. 102, Kingsbury to Webb, Santa Fe, March 13, 1859

By last mail I sent you to care of Doan King & Co St. Louis my orders for Groceries, with remittances amt.g to $7,085.+ which I hope you have rec'd all safe before this. If there is still time I wish you would send One Case or about 200 rolls paper hangings not less than 25 rolls of any one pattern, get good <u>Satin</u> Wall paper to cost from 30 cents to 50 cents. Select light & flashy patterns, also send plenty of border paper to match. I do not think of anything more to order now. I have no letter from you by this mail. Business so far this month has been very dull, sales very small & collections coming in slow. I hope however to be able by next mail to send in sufficient funds to meet the Freight notes. I hope the funds I have sent you together with what you will find at St. Louis on your arrival, will be enough to enable you to arrange all matters there to your satisfaction.

I have no letter from Mr Messervy. I am getting very impatient to hear more about that draft of Watts, to know whether it is paid or not.

I have no advises direct from Hoppin & Appel since that letter which I sent to you.

Simon Rosenstein came up yesterday and paid me $800. on account.

When you leave St. Louis give directions there for them to forward to you any letters which may come. I do not know when you will get through there & do not know exactly where to send your letters.

I think of nothing more now.

[P.S.]

Chas. LaRouge	1,500.00
Seligman & Cleaver	2,800.00
S[elig] Weinheim	1,600.00
Hoppin & Appel	5,500.00

57. Bernard & Co., Westport. See chapter 15.

Miguel Cordova	2,500.00	
cash down	1,100.00	1,400.00
Simon Rosenstein		700.00
J. Hersch		1,200.00
Louis Gold		600.00
T. F. Bowler		10,000.00

The balance is in <u>Cash Sales</u> and <u>in small bills</u>. If we confine our business to Cash Transactions it would be very limited, and wherever we let goods go on credit, there is certain to be some risk, so far, we have been very fortunate in collecting, our losses have been so small that they are hardly worth mentioning. In the above list I see nothing to be especially alarmed about. I believe myself that they are all good, yet there is risk on each one of them untill they are paid, and the money in our possession again. J. M. Kingsbury

Letter no. 103, Kingsbury to Webb, Santa Fe, March 20, 1859

Dear Sir, The Mail came in yesterday but I am without advises from you or Mr. Messervy.

By this mail, I send to Doan King & Co Five checks on the Asst. Treas. of the U.S. at St. Louis in all amt.g to <u>$4,684.83</u> with request to collect the same & with proceeds to cancel out two notes for Freight.

I have also advised them that they would receive from Mr. Thos. Allen of Batesville, Independence Co. Arkansas, a sum somewhere between $4,000.+ & 6,000.+ to our Credit, which when received to dispose of according to your instructions. It is coming to us in this way, C. B. Magruder has sent Power of Atty. to the above man to sell his place at Batesville, for the most he could get for it, and to forward the proceeds to them to our credit.[58] He Magruder thinks it will not under any circumstances bring less than $4,000.+. He has given instructions to have it sold immediately without reserve. It may take some little time to realize this money, but as soon as it is made it will be sent as directed, now you had better not count to[o] strong on this sum for immediate use as the Amt. and time of its being realized is uncertain but leave instructions with them that whenever it may be received to advise you of the Amt. & then you can dispose of it as circumstances may require—do not fail to let me know at the earliest moment of the receipt Amt. &c. that I may settle with Magruder here. He owes us now <u>$3,000.</u> and I can sell him goods for the balance whatever may be over that sum. He has gone into business here & I have rented him Messervy's store which Owens formerly occupied.

I now enclose to you three small drafts which I hope will reach you in time to be of service in closing up a/cs in St. Louis. viz.

Check No 157. dated Galesteo [Galisteo] N.M. October 11th 1858, at sight on the Asst. Treas. of the U.S. at New York, for One hundred &

58. Magruder's debt and his farm in Arkansas become an issue in these letters second only to the payment for the statehouse irons.

Eighty ($180.+) dollars, drawn by Jno. Pope Capt Tp. Eng. payable to the order of G. B. Cosby and by him endorsed to our order.

Also Check No 163. dated Galesteo N.M. Oct. 16th 1858. at sight on the Asst. Treas. of the U.S. at New York for One hundred & Eighty ($180.+) dollars, drawn by Jno Pope Capt. Top. Eng. payable to the order of Robert McAfee & endorsed by him. (It is endorsed so high up that I must let it go in blank).

Also draft No 24. dated Santa Fe December 9th 1857, at sight on Maj. Genl. T. S. Jesup, Qr. Mr. Genl. U.S.A. Washington D.C. for Six hundred and Seventy five 15/100 ($675.15/100) dollars, drawn by L.C. Easton on Capt. A.Q.M. payable to the order of Maj. D. H. Rucker, Asst. Qr. Master, by him endorsed to order of H. Connelly & Co. by them endorsed to order of James Cumming by him endorsed to our order.[59]

Making in all $1,035.15 which is charged to your Agent a/c—have these papers collected as soon as you can & let me know when they are paid.

Tom's bill of fixture which he sold to Mr. Rose, amt'd to $16,800.+. Soon as Tom can get his papers fixed with him, I shall try to get a settlement with Tom & shall probably take these notes for our a/c, They will draw 10% interest.

59. Kingsbury's previous remittances don't seem to involve checks with such complex endorsements.

William S. Messervy, c. 1849. Courtesy of the Museum of New Mexico, neg. no. 88121

Santa Fe Jany 9th 1859.

Mr Webb
    Dear Sir,
                    I got nothing by the
mail to day from you. — Herewith
you will find a correct Trial Balance
from our books, showing the balance of
each a/c up to Jany 1st. —
        Kitchen started his mule teams in
on the 4th — he will be ready soon as
you can give him the goods. —
        I am suffering to day with one
of my ugly head aches, — I have nothing
of importance to write so I will stop,
                            Yours truly
                            J. M. Kingsbury

P.S.
Collections are coming in well
so far this Month. —

Letter written by John Kingsbury to James Webb, Santa Fe, January 9, 1859. Courtesy of the
De Golyer Library, Southern Methodist University, Dallas, Texas

James Josiah Webb, late in life. Courtesy of the Hamden Historical Society, Hamden, Connecticut

Traders standing on the southeast corner of the Santa Fe plaza. The Exchange Hotel is in the center and at the right is the storefront of Seligman & Clever, formerly Webb & Kingsbury, c. 1860. Courtesy of the Museum of New Mexico, neg. no. 10685

Unfinished "state house" (Federal Building), Santa Fe, New Mexico, c. 1870s. Courtesy of the Museum of New Mexico, neg. no. 10242

Elsberg-Amberg wagon train in the plaza of Santa Fe, New Mexico, October 1861. Courtesy of the Museum of New Mexico, neg. no. 11254

Gravestone of Kate Kingsbury, Independent Order of Odd Fellows Cemetery, Cerrillos Road, Santa Fe, New Mexico. Courtesy of Neil Jacobs, Santa Fe, New Mexico

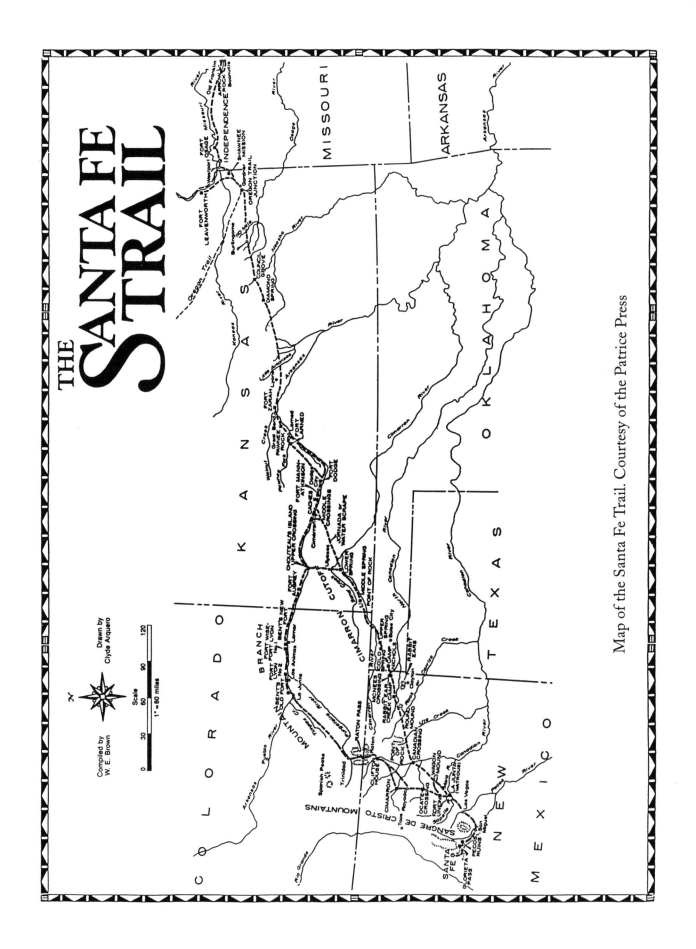

Map of the Santa Fe Trail. Courtesy of the Patrice Press

II.

"I am . . . disgusted with the whole country"

Spring and Summer 1859

Letters 104–122

Spring began with a stormy correspondence, laden with metaphors. With Congress cutting army appropriations, Webb predicted that business in New Mexico would suffer. "You may be sure a squall is arising," he advised Kingsbury, "and if you take in sail . . . the ship will ride through the storm."[1] Kingsbury, Webb charged, had "become excited and too ambitious to do a large business," and had spread too much sail by advancing too many goods on credit. A note from Leonard Rose for $2,500, which Kingsbury had sent to Webb, had not been honored. Nor could Webb collect John Watts's note for $5,000, which represented down payment on the purchase of the Kingsbury-Webb-Messervy property in Santa Fe. Kingsbury, Webb complained, had entered that payment on the books as though it had been received. "Let me ask you plainly and frankly if <u>you</u> consider these indications of a prudent healthy managed business," Webb asked Kingsbury.[2]

Aggrieved, Kingsbury turned the accusation around. Webb, he said, was captain of the ship and it was he who took unnecessary risks by spreading too much sail. Kingsbury had always urged "a small safe business," but under Webb's direction the business had "enlarged beyond the natural increase."[3] The mutual recriminations included Webb's charge that Kingsbury should not have trusted John Watts, and Kingsbury's retort that Webb had failed to force Watts to pay on his note.

Kingsbury seemed more determined than ever to quit the business, and wished that Webb had shipped him no more merchandise. But on May 19, Charles Kitchen's freight train arrived, the first of the season, full of goods for Webb & Kingsbury. Able to get a jump on his competitors, Kingsbury tallied $22,860 in sales before the month ended.

Then Webb himself arrived in Santa Fe. As was his custom, he had traveled from Connecticut to St. Louis and Westport to complete purchases and oversee their shipment. This time, instead of returning

1 Webb to Kingsbury, Hamden, CT, Feb. 21, 1859, MHS.

2 Ibid., St. Louis, Mar. 8, 1859, MHS.

3 The quote is from Kingsbury to Webb, Santa Fe, Apr. 3, 1859; the paraphrase is from Mar. 27, 1859, DeG.

home he had continued on to New Mexico for reasons he made plain to Kingsbury:

> I have thought much of our business, and about closing up, and have come to the conclusion that I had better go out in May and stay untill Sept. or so long as I can be of any service. Some question might arise in which you would prefer my opnion and advice.[4]

In face-to-face discussions in Santa Fe, Kingsbury and Webb apparently resolved their differences amicably. Webb stayed only from early June to mid-July, not until September as he had planned. The partners' correspondence ended, of course, during their time together.[5] One of the subjects they must have discussed, however, was the ever-promising John Watts, who had showed up in Santa Fe in May, telling Kingsbury that he had paid Webb the initial $5000 and that he would have the remainder ready in a few weeks. "I do not credit his story," Kingsbury wrote, "but am willing to let the matter rest untill you arrive."[6] Webb arrived and Watts was discredited once again. However much he wanted to close up shop, Kingsbury still lacked a buyer for the property and he had an inventory of newly arrived goods that he still needed to sell.

While Webb returned home, Kingsbury remained in Santa Fe. There, with the coming of summer, business slowed as usual. Kingsbury began to complain of surpluses of goods and of competitors underselling him. This summer he did not blame Jews for his slow sales, but rather a Hispanic New Mexican, Felipe Delgado.[7] To make matters worse, several parties of Colorado-bound gold seekers, whom Kingsbury counted on as potential customers, passed through Santa Fe without buying provisions. They had brought their own.

If business was dull again, life was not. Kingsbury and Tom Weirick fought off a drunk with a large knife who invaded their store, Miguel Otero won a hard-fought contest for territorial delegate, to Kingsbury's delight, and politicians dueled.

～

Letter no. 104, Kingsbury to Webb, Santa Fe, March 27, 1859

Dear Sir, By last mail I sent you remittances amt.g to $1035.15 also to Messrs. Doan King & Co checks amt.g to $4,684.83 all of which I hope have safely come to hand. I am now in receipt of your three letters of Feby 21st together with the book of Invoices. From what I can see they look well and I shall have a good stock of Goods, and in all probability shall be able to sell them well. Your figure about the ship & its sails is very clear, but you must have forgotten that you are Capt. of this craft and when you saw the squall so near at hand you certainly ran a great risk in ordering the sail spread. Now it remains for me to

4. Webb to Kingsbury, Westport, Mar. 25, 1859, MHS.

5. There is a gap from June 4 to July 16.

6.. Kingsbury to Webb, Santa Fe, May 28, 1859, DeG.

7. Felipe Delgado was a successful New Mexican merchant who owned a general store in Santa Fe and operated ox and mule trains along the trails that linked Santa Fe with both the United States and Mexico. Like many sons of prominent New Mexican families, Delgado had been educated in St. Louis. His home on West Palace Avenue, built in 1890, still stands today. Loomis, ed., *Old Santa Fe Today*, 13; Kingsbury to Webb, Santa Fe, July 30, 1859, DeG.

pull them in if I can. The goods are bought and of course must be sold. I shall however do my best with them & try to avoid all extry risks. How it will turn out time only will tell.[8]

Tom Bowler has gone down to El Paso and I have got him to look after our interest with Hoppin & Appel.[9] He will be back in a week or two, I will then be better advised and know how to proceed with them.

Business has been very dull this month. I will give you the figures in my next letter.

P.S. - Blaza died a few days ago. She had what I call quick consumption. I with the assistance of a few others had her body decently buried at the Guadalupe Church.[10] From all I can learn she died an honest virtuous girl.

Letter no. 105, Kingsbury to Webb, Santa Fe, April 3, 1859

I am now in receipt of yours from St. Louis of Mar 5th also two of the 8th. If I did not know you so well I would not attempt to answer these letters. You must have been in one of your wild tanterums [*sic*], and all because you did not find that $2,500.+ at Doan King & Co's.[11] Now I am in no way to blame for this. Mr. Rose was in Albuquerque (he lived there with his family) I got my information from Tom, and acted upon that. It appears now that Tom was mistaken about it or there was a misunderstanding between him and Mr. Rose. It is only since I got your letters (last night) that I learn that Mr. Rose did not send the order to have that money placed to our Cr. untill he arrived here to take possession of the house, which was the last week in February. This being the case it was impossible for the money to be there untill the last of March. By letters and papers here in the hands of Mr. Rose I am fully convinced that the money was paid over according to agreement without a moment's delay.

You assert that I am excited and over ambitious to do a big business. I must deny this. You have been the one to urge an extension & expansion on all occasions. I leave it to yourself if I have not always urged the principal of keeping things within our own controle being fully satisfied to do a small safe business. And I cannot see now that it is enlarged beyond the natural increase of such a business.

You seem to think that you have much cause of complaint, while I am convinced that the whole trouble arrizes [*sic*] from the fact that we live too far seperatid [*sic*] to do business with a full understanding. You know that I am no letter writer and cannot half explain myself. I would this moment willingly give $500.+ to have a personal interview with you for one half hour. I did think we fully understood each other in regard to Watts. I would not trust him for $50.+. If there is anything wrong in that matter it is since that papers left my hands and you have allowed Watts to ring in on you. The whole basis of my contract with

8. Webb had written: "I see Congress has cut down the Army apppropriation bill two million dollars, items transportation and forage. A good captain takes in sail before the squall strikes his ship. You may be sure a squall is arising and if you take in sail, and stand firm at the helm, the ship will ride through the storm without accident. I must say again, collect close, attend closely to your own business, and keep it under your own eye, and all will come out right." Apparently, Webb was adding this in reference to a passage he had written in an earlier letter, also dated the 21st: "You must keep your eye skinned for a smash up. Congress has determined to retrench army expenses, and when retrenchment commences, little folks must stand from under. Retrenchment is sure to commence when there is the least necessity for it, where it will create the greatest amount of distress, and produce the greatest amt. of outcry. So New Mexico is sure to be victimized. Collect all doubtfull or slow accounts, and be carefull about extending credit except to responsible parties. I can think of nothing more except to say look well to collections." Webb to Kingsbury, Hamden, CT, Feb. 21, 1859, MHS.

9. Kingsbury's statement here is somewhat misleading. From his reference to Tom's trip to El Paso in the same sentence with Hoppin & Appel's debt, one could assume that Hoppin and Appel were located in El Paso. The firm, however, had locations in Mesilla and Tubac. Both Webb and Kingsbury were concerned about money owed them by Hoppin & Appel, and Webb had recommended that Kingsbury send somebody at once to collect it. Ibid., Feb. 21, 1859, MHS.

10. Blaza had been one of Kingsbury's servants. Guadalupe Church on the corner of Agua Fría and Guadalupe Streets (where it still stands) was probably Blaza's parish church.

11. Annoyed, Webb had written at length to Kingsbury, in a tone suggested by these excerpts: "Doan King & Co. have rec.d no money on our acct. and you must not rely upon such remittance, and if Tom relies on such payments, he will make a bad business of it. Now, a draft of a private individual on another is not cash and is not negociable [*sic*] for cash untill accepted and should never be recd in payment for any property, particularly in that country." Webb to Kingsbury, St. Louis, Mar. 5, 1859, MHS. "Now look at this transaction. Was it prudent in Tom to deliver his property to `Mr. Rose,' and receive such payments as cash. Was it prudent in you to consider Mr. Rose's promise to pay $2,500 to our credit at D K & Co. as cash, for me to buy goods with. I admit, John, that I have scolded a good deal lately, but what can I do?" Ibid., Mar. 8, 1859, MHS.

him was made (and so expressed in the papers) upon the <u>prompt payment</u> of those two obligations according to their <u>tenor & date</u>, now when he failed in this, there was nothing binding upon us, his failure to comply made the contract null & void. The Simple entry on our books had nothing to do with binding either party to the trade.[12]

I am willing to acknowledge that I was very anxious to convert the property into <u>cash</u>—and perhaps over anxious to do so, thereby suffering myself to accept a proposition which was liable to fail, but I was very care full to relinquish nothing. It was an experiment on my part to get the money without any risk, trusting you to see it carried out. Now when you found that he was vacelating [*sic*] and putting the payments off beyond a reasonable period, you should have taken the draft from Messervy, canseld [*sic*] the papers and ordered me to look for another purchaser. I wrote you afterward urging you if possible to make him comply to the sale, and am still very willing to let him or anyone else have the property for that money but never consented or entertained the idea of taking any risk. The property is far better than anybodies promises.

You say he is about to get an extension of 6 or 12 months from Messervy on that $5,000.+ by paying interest—have you nothing to say in the matter? If you are satisfied or have any security that Watts will pay the note June 1st without vacilation or defalcation,[13] and then Messervy is willing to give him an extension on the other $5,000. for a consideration of the interest, <u>by releasing us</u> and taking Watts alone for it, then it would be right. But if Messervy does not release us, give up our note, and look to Watts alone for his money, then I am desidedly opposed to any such extension, and rely upon you to bring the whole matter to a close at once. Let Mr. Watts slide and we keep our property.

I will continue to pay the Interest to Messervy, untill the principal can be paid without injury to our business.

If that little draft of $500. is not [paid] send it to me immediately and I will get the money from Hovey.

I think your surmises of my calculations about forwarding your letters a little harsh. You left me in the dark about your moovements and that was the only place I could send them to that was safe.[14] By sending them there I knew if you was not there they would be forward[ed] to you so that you would surely get them. They contained no money and a few days could make no important difference. I never suspected that you would neglect any part of your duty, you have too much at stake to admit of such a suspision. But I did not know but that matters might require your presence in the <u>East</u>, and that you would be kept behind by things beyond your controle and that the first train would have to be started without your presence. I considered every contingency and followed the only safe course. I have sent all the funds to St.

12. "You should never have entered Watts draft on our books as rec.d in payment on our property, untill you had been advised of its payment. . . . Now don't sell property to Tom, Dick, and Harry, on their drafts on Tom Nokes or Bill Stokes, and endeavor to impress yourself with the idea that you have rec.d a <u>cash</u> payment. . . . I hope, and presume, that after much tribulation we shall get these slow, and irregular exchanges straightened up, and now let us return to our old system of doing buisness, <u>carefull</u>, <u>systematic</u>, and <u>cautious</u>. Not trusting too much in the smooth protestations and promises of `clever fellows.' Judge W. has given us a deal of trouble, and it is hard to resist implicit confidence in all he promises, but we know he does business loosely, draws drafts at random, and our experience is that they <u>invariably</u> go to protest." Ibid., Mar. 5, 1859, MHS.

"Now let us look at your transaction with Watts. You sell our property to him for $10,000 half cash, half 1st June. Now our experience with Watts has been that his drafts are bad, and we take no more of them in business negociations, but in the face of this you take his draft for $5,000 as cash, enter it on our books as cash, close our real estate account, on our books by Cash, none receivable & leaving a balance to be closed by profit and loss, then send me another draft for $500 as cash. Now let us look at the <u>trifling</u>! [*sic*] amount involved in these transactions— No I will leave you to foot them up yourself, but let me ask you plainly and frankly if <u>you</u> consider these indication of a prudent healthy managed business. You <u>may</u>, and <u>perhaps</u> will bring them all out right, but have taken large risks." Ibid., Mar. 8, 1859, MHS.

13. A legal term meaning failure to meet an obligation.

14. "Then again, look at your system in planning, and arranging our spring buisness. All your letters sent to New Haven when you know I ought to be in Saint Louis. When have I so far failed in my duty as to lead you to suppose I would not perform it at this time? You arranged for Mr. Kitchen to start 15th March. You wish me to prepare to start him at that time. You know I ought to be in St. Louis (or ready to leave) to accomplish that end. But still direct your letters to New Haven. All this is not in accordance with your usual system. Now, John, I do not want to harrow your feelings, or be unkind to you, but I want to show you where I think you have been imprudent." Ibid., Mar. 8, 1859, MHS.

Louis that I could command, for the purchase of Groceries if you exceed that amt. of course they will have to come on <u>Cr</u>. I have no funds now to reimburse Mr. Abbott, for the amt. you drew on him for but expect <u>you</u> must have done so out of the funds which I have sent for <u>cash</u> purchases of groceries.

Now I come to a much more difficult matter, the goods which you are now sending. I do wish they were not purchased. I would be very glad to take cost, freight & expenses, <u>Cash down</u>, for the whole outfit the moment it arrives. If you mean what you say in your letters and expect me to go by that strictly, my hands are completely tied, what am I to do? I do not know one man in the country that will want goods of us on credit where there is no risk.[15]

Shall I shut the doors and say no goods leave here except for <u>Cash on delivery</u> or undoubted security? If I am only to sell them this way, it would take 10 or 15 years to realize the money. I am not willing to give that much time to it. I would sooner blow my head off at once, & let my body be put in the mother earth. If this is what you want you must come and sell them yourself. I cannot think you mean what you wrote, you was in a <u>fret</u> at that time, & probably have forgotten all about it before this time. You say don't credit Rose over $500.+ at any one time, now just think how the matter stands, you are sending me $15 or 18,000+ worth of goods that I have no prospect of ever selling except to that house & you say the house must realize the money on them before they get the goods.

Now I think that any honest man who has that house is good for all the house requires to keep it going provided he gets value received whenever he buys anything, & obligates himself to pay for it. This Mr. Rose is a good Business Man, less extravigant and far more prudent than ever Tom or Frank were and I have unlimited confidence in him.

Soon as Tom Bowler gets back I will get some sort of a settlement with him by which we will be secured. The only thing in his case which I can see that looks bad is the appropriation bill for Mail service not passing.[16]

I hope to give you a full statement of the settlement by next mail. You close your letter, saying "I hope that I may be mistaken in my surmises, and that you will write me a letter which will explain the condition of things satisfactorily." Now I do think you are mistaken, and trust I have explained my position so that you will be satisfied. I will continue to explain matters as they develope themselves.

I am confident I have got a hard season before me. I will try to prepair myself for all immergencies [*sic*], and am willing to work night and day and do all I know how.

My Sales the last month amt. to $1,800.+. Collections $3,500.+. I shall take a/c of stock this year before the usual time, make my calculations to have it done before the first train can get here. You will then

15. Kingsbury was responding to Webb's urging that he extend as little credit as possible.

16. "I would also advise you that the Post Office appropriation bill failed to pass Congress. So there will be no funds for mail service after July 1st unless the President calls an extra session of Congress which is doubtfull." Webb to Kingsbury, St. Louis, Mar. 5, 1859, MHS.

get all the papers as usual and know exactly how everything stands. I have paid Mercure the $3,000. borrowed money.

If I can get remittances I shall try to send by next mail, about $2,000. to Kitchen on a/c of freight. I partialy promised him to send him some money that he might use in the states before starting. If I can do it it will be a great help to him and in the end we will make more than the interest on it by accomodating him. I have rec'd the duplicate bill from Beebe & Co.

I think of nothing more now.

Letter no. 106, Kingsbury to Webb, Santa Fe, April 10, 1859

My last letter was written under the sting of your scolding letters from St. Louis. I could not avoid being grieved on receiving letters of such a tenor from you. I am liable to make errors like all other men, but I do know that I have tried hard to do my duty and I have a clear conscience to sustain me in all our business matters, and that pure motives have dictated all my moovements. Knowing this it was hard to receive complaints when I had a right to expect your approval and support. I have always had a watchfull eye to your interests, and it is my firm determination to continue every honest effort in my humble ability to that end knowing that as I protect your interest so will my own be advansed. From the first you have placed me under many obligations to you, I trust I have not been ungreatfull, I have no means of proving it except by my action, guarding your interest and carrying out your wishes faithfully as far as my powers extend.

I am now in receipt of yours of Mar 10th from St. Louis and 19th from Kansas these letters are dictated with reason and I see plainly the force of your suggestions. I can only repeat that every exertion on my part shall be enlisted to carry them out. By this time I think you must be perfectly easy in money matters. You know I am never backward in making remittances when I can do so in safety. The remittances which I have already started to you place me at this moment about $4,000+ ahead or in advance of my collections. In my last I stated to you that I intended to send something by this mail on account to Kitchen, I could easily send him at this time $2,000.—if it were possible to procure drafts. But it is out of the question to get any sort of exchange at this moment, and now since I cannot send it by this mail, any following mail will be too late to meet him there and consequently I shall not send him any, but will gather all I can to pay him on arrival here. So you will advise him of the circumstances, and tell him not to expect anything there from us.

Now in regard to Mr. Abbott. You say I must remit him at the earliest moment say $6,000.+ to cover the $2,500+ which you drew on him for the note to Beebe & Co. which he would have to pay for us

provided Tom's mail draft should not be realized. Now I rely upon you
to refund to him the $2,500+ (which you by draft on him anticipated)
that you will or have already received from Mr. Rose. The note to
Beebe & Co is now due, no remittance from me could reach there in
season to meet it. If they have failed to pay Tom's draft, we must rely
upon Abbott under your request to protect our note. And of course it
will fall upon me to reimburse him with money from here for so
doing, which I will be prepaired to do, soon as I am informed that
Tom's draft is not paid. However, should my collections admit of my
making remittances and I be able to get drafts, I will without delay
begin to send him funds. But of course I want to know how this draft
of Tom's turns out, whether I can count it in my calculations as cash or
have to leave it out for another year. You still ask for $500. private
funds. You may be expecting a special check for this and therefore disapointed in not getting it, but I have already told you to take whatever
you might want for private use out the amt. I sent to St. Louis, and I
certainly think there was enough for you to do so, without cramping
your purchases. This request I know you are making in conformity
with my wish expressed some time ago, let me explain what I me[a]nt
by that. It was this. I did not wish you to apply for private use what I
was then sending to meet special payments, for fear I might be behind
in getting funds there in season to meet our liabilities falling due. Now
when I sent money this Spring for new purchases, some $12,000.+
East and about $10,000+ to St. Louis all of which I charged to your
agent a/c, I did not imagine that you would hesitate to take out of this
whatever you might want for Expenses or for any private necesities. I
also knew that you had on hand $2,500+ private funds which you
loaned & I knew had been returned. My calculations were well founded to furnish you with all the private funds you could possibly wish,
for building or any other purpose. My intention was and still is for you
to take the proceeds of that note of Watts $5,0000+ on your private
a/c, and I had relied upon it being realized in ample season to meet
your wants. This amt. was never used as active capital in our business
and consequently the business could not suffer by your drawing this
out whenever it might be realized. I had never counted upon this amt.
in any of my business calculations.

    I have now got through with sending open remittances, and from
this on I must send special remittances untill all our liabilities on the
spring goods are covered. Now then should Watts fail in his bargain
for the property so as not to give you that $5,000+, & you require
funds for private use beyond what you have taken let me know and I
will send you a special remittance.

    You speak of a probability of your coming out this summer. I would
be greatly releaved by your presence, many things you might assist me
in. However the heft of my sales will probably be over before you can

get here, and for my part I do not see the actual necesity for you to take the risk of such a trip. I would be very glad to have you here, principally to satisfy you on all pending business, not that I think you could change matters much. I firmly believe that God sparing my health I will be able to carry everything through safely, and in the end I am confident you will be satisfied. Should you finally deside to come the sooner you get here after the goods are started, the better it will be. I will send my remittances as you direct, untill further advised. You must give Mr. Abbott a full list of our payments, names, dates, amts. &c.

You may not approve of my course taken with Magruder. It is true I have nothing in my hands, but I count upon nothing in that matter untill I hear from St. Louis that the money is duly deposited. Under any circumstances I feel confident we are safe with him.

Tom has not yet returned, another week must pass before he can get here. You would not have done less for him than I have. If the dept. had funds so as to honor his drafts when they are due we would not be kept long out of our money by him. But the failure of that [postal] bill is something that could not have been foreseen & in which the whole country must suffer more or less. Should he be compeled to continue running these mails without any funds for so doing, it is easy to see the danger & difficulty he will soon find himself in.

Mr. Rose has started off to be a <u>cash</u> man—and if his business continues as it now is, I see no danger of his wanting credit beyond what we would be safe & willing to let him have.

I will send my next letter same as this to care of Chick & Co. Should you leave Kansas before it arrives, leave word with them how to forward it.

P. S. Jose, has been laying here idle all winter, and very sick part of the time with Billious Fever. I yesterday got him started to go in with Pigeon's Train, as far as Counsil Grove. He goes with the full assurance of a situation as interpreter for the house of Conn Hill & Co[17] at that place, I hope he may do well. J.M.K.

Letter no. 107, Kingsbury to Webb, Santa Fe, April 16, 1859

My letter for you by this mail, is sent as you requested to St. Louis. I hope you may get it there. It contains <u>no drafts</u> remittances can not be had. I hope you have had funds enough to arrange everything to your satisfaction. I have nothing further to add only get that ox train started as soon as you can.

I will send the balance of my letters in this month to West Port, after that in the way mail to meet you on the road.

17. A firm in Council Grove consisting of Malcolm Conn, Thomas C. Hill, and James C. Munkres. Gardner, "Conn and Hays," 36, 38.

Letter no. 108, Kingsbury to Webb, Santa Fe, April 16, 1859

Dear Sir, I am now in receipt of yours from West Port of March 25th in which you request me to send this reply to St. Louis but fear it will be too late to meet you there.

I am sorry to learn that Kitchen has been delayed in getting his waggons. I did not anticipate any such delay on his part. I am very impatient to get the goods here at the earliest moment possible.

Mr. Messervy writes that he has declined to accept Watts proposition for an extension, and I sincerely hope you have done the same, that you have either held Watts to the original bargain, or closed the whole matter by letting him slide and we hold on to our property. My only fear now is that you may have consented to some extension and allowed him to deseive you with fresh promises. I have no confidence whatever in him or any arraingement he might propose and I do hope you have not allowed him to get your confidence. His repeated failures with us does not entitle him to any and I shall be sorry to hear that you have allowed him any further credit in the matter.

I am much relieved by the prospect of your coming out this summer. I did not venture to propose it although I have wished it very much. If you can arrainge to leave your home matters safely I think it will be to your interest to come and I am confident it will give you great satisfaction to be here and see for yourself just how all our business stands. I hope nothing may intervene to change your present calculations about coming.

Tom has returned. He has not yet got his settlement & papers fixed up with Mr. Rose. The settlement has been retarded by various causes which could not be avoided. Rose's Notes are to be secured by Real Estate in the States. I think they will be perfectly good and safe for us to take if we can wait for the money untill they mature. Tom's a/c with us is now about $16,000+ with a Cr of $2,500.+ to come off provided Mr. Rose pays that sum as agreed upon to Messrs Doan King & Co.

Tom could bring me no reliable information about Hoppin & Appel, except that they were bound to be slow. Every one below appears to have confidence in the expedition which Appel is on and thinks he will by his trip be able to bring all out streight. Now that I may leave nothing untried to secure that debt I have desided to send a man out to meet Appel with full power to act for us, and have instructed him to secure it in every possible way, by taking whatever he can get hold of from them that can be turned into money. He will start down in the mail on Monday next, and must leave it so for the present. I will get returns by the time you arrive here, and will then explain everything to you.

Contrary to your instructions and advise, I have consented to take Tom's mail drafts for service on the Neosho Mail rout[e] for the first two quarters of his Contract and send them on by this mail for Collection to Mr. Abbott. Tom is confident that they will be paid and is anxious to have them presented. I make no calculation upon them and give him no credit on them untill I hear that they have been paid. I do this to favor Tom and at the same time if they should be paid to have the money in our hands.

Business is pretty dull so far this month. Mr. Rose intends to be a cash customer with us. I have sold him this month about $2,000.+ which he expects to pay on the arrival of our first train. I could send by this mail a pretty fair remittance to Mr. Abbott If I could get drafts but it is impossible. I got by this mail duplicate bill of 10 dz Hoes from Mooney Cohn & Co. You must keep a correct a/c of all your money matters, and of all amts. unpaid. The way the accounts are coming to me it is impossible for me to do so correctly. I rely upon you to give Mr. Abbott a correct list of everything unpaid, dates &c.

Nothing more now.

Letter no. 109, Kingsbury to Webb, Santa Fe, April 24, 1859

I am now in receipt of yours of Mar 31st also B/L of 15 mule waggons and the letter book.

My last letter for you was sent to St. Louis, I have endeavored to write you fully on all business matters and hope you may have rec'd all my letters.

Sales are small this month. We could not expect much considering my stock. Collections are not heavy but coming in gradually. I could send in by this mail a very handsome remittance if I could only get drafts, but it is quite out of the question. Not one of the departments have a cent to draw on.

I shall take a/c of stock and close up my books to the 1st of next month and have everything fixed up ready for the new goods by the time they can arrive. I am told the road is in fine condition, hope he will make a quick trip. I have engaged little Bob Riddlesbarger to assist in the store untill the rush is over.

Your letter indicates that you are not fully desided whether you will come out or not.[18] I would like much to see you and have you here for a short time that you might satisfy yourself as to the condition of all our unsettled business—at the same time I would be very sorry to urge your coming and expose you to the risk of such a trip unnecesaraly. I will try to give you my ideas about matters with a view to assist you in your determination about coming. In the first place I am determined to close up our business on the goods now under way. I do not want any more goods. I want to get our Capital in and it can only be done by stopping our purchases at once. It cannot be done by curtailing. I have no ambition to do a big business and in fact no desire to continue our present amt. My great desire now is to realize what has already

18. Kingsbury had an unexpected ally in his difficulties with Webb over business that year. In his letter of March 31, Webb announced, "I shall fill your next order and attend to it personally, but have not yet fully determined whether I go out or not. I shall unless my wife raises too strong objections. She says you are doing better than if I was there, and there is no sense in it."

Webb went on, however, to express his interest in coming out to make a final decision about the firm's future: "I think I ought to go out and arrange definitely about our future business. Some of our friends say you ought not to leave, but I am of your opinion that you can make as much money in a ten years business here as you can there, and can moreover live at home all the time, and prepare a house for old age." Webb to Kingsbury, Westport, Mar. 31, 1859, MHS.

been made. Of course my wish is to do it to the best advantage consulting the interests of both parties.

Now the greatest difficulty in the way is this Property. If Watts has made you satisfied, and takes the property off our hands, then I can see no real necesity of your coming, unless you are unwilling for me to sell the goods now under way & credit them out on my judgement. If this is so then of course you must come, and see these goods disposed of. However if you will be satisfied and content to let me go on trusting it all to me as formily [formerly], I can only say I will do the best I can to realize these goods and all present out standing a/c's and you shall have your share just as soon as it is in my power to consumate it. Now on the other hand if Watts has failed (which is to me from all accounts much the most probable) and the property is still ours, then I think you had better come. You no doubt want to quit as much as I do, and by being present here you can assist me much and suggest perhaps the most practable [*sic*] method for me to carry out. I will be prepaired to accept any reasonable proposition you may make with a view to close our business and realize what we have got at stake here. I will be willing to buy or sell at once, or go on together untill we can wind up, but am determined and desided not to continue this business beyond what is already contracted for.

From this you can I think fully understand my ideas, and know whether it is best for you to come now or no.

Should it be your wish to close our partnership at once you must certainly come out, because I will not do so by letter. I want you present in order for us to understand fully all the conditions and contingencies, which may arrise. Do not for a moment think that the above is dictated by any fealings of discontent with you. It is only this. I am very unhappy here and am determined to quit. At the same time I know & feel my indebtedness to you, and am willing to make any sacrifice on my part to satisfy you and secure your interest, in all that we have undertaken, but am not disposed to continue our business here with a view of making money.

I have a letter by this mail from Beebe & Co. stating that they had rec'd from you our note for $9960.06 and of the following allowances that is passed to our credit to be deducted from that amt.—viz.

—#141 27 yds Flannel Short	@24	$6.48
on 50 dz Cot. Hose #15	2 ½ cents	1.25
" 30 " " " #50	6 cents	1.80
" 39 " Coats Spools	2 ½ cents	.98
" Prints #8, 9, & 10.		12.15
	Making	22.66

In my last I wrote you that I had taken Tom's drafts for two quarters on the Neicho [Neosho] route,—by information that he has got from the Dept. now, he thinks that there is no question but that they will both be paid in time and in all probability the first one will be paid at once. I hope it may be so and that the money will be paid to Mr. Abbott without delay.

P.S. My letters following this will be directed to you and sent by the mail conductors outside of the mail.

Letter no. 110, Kingsbury to Webb, Santa Fe, May 1, 1859

I am now in receipt of yours from St. Louis of April 4th noticing receipt of Drafts amt.g to $7,085.+ together with orders for Groceries. I am not a little disapointed that you do not inform me of the receipt of monies on the remittances which I send you from time to time. Since last November I have sent you a large amt. of checks and drafts, and up to this moment I do not know from you that a single one has been paid or realized. You say when in Washington you will see about the P.O. draft, now I have certainly sent you two on the P. O. Dept. I supposed one must have been paid, but I do not know which. I am sorry to know that there is so much delay with that $2,500+ from Mr. Rose, but it is a transaction from being [illegible] beyond my controle. I trust however that you have such assurances in regard to it that you can count with cirtinity [*sic*] upon it and be able to use it in your settlements. I expect you have arrainged it when paid to go to Mr. Abbott to reimburse him for the Amt. you drew on him for.

The department[s] here are still without funds and it is impossible for me to make any remittance.

I write this letter hoping it may meet you on the road out. However if circumstances have convinced you that it is unnecessary for you to come, you can rest assured that I shall go on with the business giving it my whole attention and I will leave no point untried to further and secure your interests here. I may make errors, but my whole energies are enlisted to do what is right & if possible to satisfy you in every particular. I have felt hurt by some of your previous letters sensuring [*sic*] me when I know that I have been doing all in my power to protect your interest and to please you. I am determined to close up the business with the stock now on the road, and consequently will want no more goods bought. The mail which came in yesterday passed the Mule Wagons on the Cimmaron [Cimarron]. I count by this that they will get here in about one week from this time. If so they will be far in advance of other goods, and I hope to make a big hole in them before the others can arrive. I trust that the Ox wagons were started in good season and that they will make a reasonable trip. My collections for April Amt. to $3,700.+—Sales for the same time amt. to $3,726.+ making the gross sales for the past eleven months $86,963.+. I am now taking a/c of stock—and on a/c of those mule Teams coming so early must close my fiscal year and make up my papers one month earlier than the usual time.

I will try to have the whole statement ready so as to give you the figures by next mail, with Trial balance &c.

I am pleased to see by your letter that you know to some extent the liabilities of Watts and by this I feel comparitively easy, judging that when you found that he had failed to satisfy Messervy for the $5,000.+ that you have not consented to any new bargain about the property baised upon fresh promises which he might make, only to be broken again.[19] Our property is far better in our own hands than anybodies promises.

I have not been able to yet make a settlement with Tom. He starts tomorrow for El Paso again. It will have to lay over untill he returns. I hear nothing more from Hoppin & Appel.

I can think of nothing more now.

Letter no. 111, Kingsbury to Webb, Santa Fe, May 7, 1859

Dear Sir, I have no letter from you today. Herewith you will find a letter from Messervy which he must have enclosed to me by mistake.

Kitchen left his Wagons and came on ahead, I have a note from him in which he says I may expect the wagons about the 15th and can count certain on there [their] being here by the 18th. This would make 48 days rather a <u>long</u> trip to brag on. I had expected them much earlier. However they will be the first to arrive and I hope to do well with the goods. You will find enclosed Trial Balance also Statement of our business made correct up to the 1st of this month. I look for you here so soon that I will omit comment on the outstanding accounts, trusting that I will be able to explain everything to you satisfactorily on your arrival. I am urging & pushing collections as fast as possible. I have rec'd from Berthane Rozier, a full statement of settlement with The Carondolet M[ining] Co. showing balance in there hands of $260.+ to our credit. They report that they have furnished you with a copy of the same. I suppose you got this in time to use in St. Louis.

I am still unable to procure exchange and can remit nothing by this mail.

I have nothing further from Hoppin & Appel.

Everything is dull here. Santa Fe is at a perfect standstill just now. I hope the arrival of fresh goods will start things up a little. I hope you will have a pleasant trip, get in as soon as you can.

Letter no. 112, Kingsbury to Webb, Santa Fe, May 11, 1859

Yours of May 23rd from West Port is now before me. I shall look for you here next Saturday. I can now get drafts but as you will be here

19. Webb was obviously fed up with Watts and had written, "There is no use in fooling with him any longer. . . . He is embarrassed and is not likely to be any other way soon, at least, I do not want anything more to do with him." Ibid., Hamden, CT, Apr. 14, 1859, MHS.

so soon I have thought it best to let it be one week longer & then remit as you may think best. Up to the present I am without advices from Mr. Abbott, have not rec'd his a/c current, and do not know yet the result of the $2,000.+ balance on the P.O. Draft. In the mean time I may hear and know better how to make my remittances.

The $2,500.+ from Mr. Rose has all been paid in full. Doan King & Co's receipts are here in his hands to show for it. Weirick returned today. He succeeded in getting the Money on that [Moses] Sachs debt. It is now secure in our own Safe.

My mind is now at rest about Watts. I have closed that matter with him by annulling the contract on terms of mutual consent. He has given up the bond and I have given him a receipt to return his Draft & note when they shall arrive here.

Tom Bowler has just got back he has had no time to do anything yet. I hope he will get his matters arrainged with Mr. Rose before you arrive. I shall not urge Tom to a settlement untill you arrive. My sales this month so far have been small but what I have sold has been principally for _cash_ in hand. For the past week during Weirick's absences I have averaged $100.+ a day cash sales from the retail shelves. I think collections will sum up well at the close of the month.

Letter no. 113, Kingsbury to Webb, Santa Fe, May 14, 1859

Yours of Apl. 14th from home is received. I feel quite easy about the property, being satisfied now that you have not licen[s]ed or consented to any new proposition from him.

I learn by the mail that Kitchen's wagons would be at Las Vegas last night. I look for them here by Wednesday which will make it the 18th. The trip is a long one but they will get here early enough to give me a good start in advance of any other house. I have full confidence and assurance that I will be able to manage the stock well. I now count for certain that you must be on the road coming out. This is a great source of relief to me.

By last Mail I sent you Trial Balance accompanied by a full statement of our business up to May 1st, which I hope you have received. Since then I have collected about $2,500.+. I am still unable to get drafts and consequently can make no remittances.

The man I sent to Tucson has just returned. He brought from Hoppin & Appel only $500. in cash, but I am fully satisfied that we will get that debt by allowing them time to realize their means. Before you get here I hope to have papers from them which will fully secure us. I have every assurance that they have enough to pay everything, provided it is properly managed. I have every confidence in Appel and believe he is capable of bringing all out streight, and I am more than ever convinced of his honisty.

Tom Bowler has not returned yet.

Letter no. 114, Kingsbury to Webb, Santa Fe, May 28, 1859

I did not write you by last mail. Our goods got here on Thursday the 19th and I had all I could attend to. Since they arrived I have sold about $20,000. I am now in receipt of yours of Apl 26th from Hamden with a/c current, also a/c current of Kirkman & Luke & Chick & Co. I have not had time to examine them.

It is impossible for me to get drafts and consequently can not make a remittance to Mr. Abbott. I hope to be able to send him a check by next mail. Judge Watts is here. He came out with the last mail. I do not know what to think of the man. He now assures me most positively that he has sent you the first $5,000.+ and that he will have the other $5,000.+ ready to pay me in about three Weeks. I do not credit his story but am willing to let the matter rest untill you arrive, as I feel confident you will get here before he leaves again. He talks of going back in a month from this time. Had you sent me back his note and draft I should have given them to him at once and got the bond canceld. Then if he wanted to buy and had the money to do it with, we could make a new bargain. As I have not these papers I have desided to wait for them or wait untill you came. He appears perfectly willing to give up the bond at any moment on receipt of his obligations—or if we wish to hold him to the traid will make everything satisfactory.

I will get the balance $300. on that little draft in a few days.

I hope you will soon be here when I can explain everything.

P. S. Tom & Frank occupy the house and you need have no fear of Watts getting possession of any part of the premises untill he pays the cash.

Letter no. 115, Kingsbury to Webb, Santa Fe, June 4, 1859

I am now in receipt of your note from St. Louis May 13th—I am at a loss to know why that $2500 from Mr. Rose was not paid in full. I still believe him to be perfectly honest in the matter and that the balance will cirtainly come.

The Officers here are still without funds to draw on, but I have had the good luck to obtain second hand Three checks of $500 each making $1500.+ which I send in by this mail to Mr. Abbott. It certainly will not be long now when some one will get authority to draw, and I shall be able to get checks to send him for the balance due also for a good sum to be applied on our Notes Payable list.

My whole sales last month fut [foot] up $22,860.+ Collections Amt to $7,000.+ So far sales this month commenced slow. I have not had a wholesale customer in yet. Cash retail is pretty fair—about $125.+ a day. I hope yet to have a good trade this month & bring my sales up to a good amt.

By what I learn from the Mail Conductor the Trains on the road will be slow getting here, which still leaves me a good margin to go on.

I have rec'd from Watts the $300.+ balance on the draft you returned. I am disapointed not to get his draft & note back, but am trying to get possesion of my bond by giving him a receipt for his Draft & Note to be turned over on your arrival. I am fully convinced that the only safe way for us to do, is to anull this thing and have nothing to do with him.

I have rec'd from Hoppin & Appel $480. more on a/c. It is in drafts of the Overland Mail Co. at 30 days after sight. I send them by this mail to Mr Messervy on a/c of rents collected for him.

Sachs has returned from California. I shall start Mr. Weirick of[f] in the Stage on Monday next for los Lunes [Los Lunas][20] and try to get that amt. from him.

Mr. Rose has paid up very well all he has bought of me so far. His house is crowded all the time and there is no doubt that he must be making money there.

[Here, the correspondence breaks for six weeks, while Webb was in Santa Fe]

Letter no. 116, Kingsbury to Webb, Santa Fe, July 16, 1859

I am in receipt of your note from Fort Union. I have nothing new to note since you left. Everything is moving on slow. In fact I do not expect to do much in the way of business untill the Train arrives.

Yesterday I had a pretty big scare. A lot of old dry goods boxes in Levi's Corral took fire, and for a few moments untill I learned how and what it was, I was not a little frightened. It happened in the middle of the forenoon and was soon put out with no serious damage to any one. Had it occured at night it might have been a serious affair.

Herewith I enclose draft No. 1971. dated Agency at Milledge Geo. Apl. 19th 1859 Planters Bank of the State of Georgia at Sight on Bank Republic New York for Four hundred dollars ($400.+) drawn by A. M. Niebet Agt. payable to the order of Reuben H. Johnson and by him endorsed to our order.

This check I rec'd for collection and am to pay over the amt. here when I know that it is realized. We have no interest in it whatever further than this. I think there is no question but what it will be paid on presentation, however should it not be paid have it protested and send it immediately back to me. If it is paid take up the amt. on your agent

20. Los Lunas, a farming community on the west side of the Rio Grande some twenty miles south of Albuquerque, where Moses Sachs apparently had a store.

a/c.—and notify me of its payment as early as you can that I may settle with the owner here.

The enclosed letter is all that came by this mail for you.

Did you take José on with you?

Letter no. 117, Kingsbury to Webb, Santa Fe, July 30, 1859

The wagons got here last Saturday late and took till dark to unload them. Then on Sunday I was busy making the Settlement with Kitchen so that I did not write to you by last mail.

In my last letter July 16th I sent you a check on New York for Four hundred dollars which I hope you have received.

Business remains very dull. I was in hopes that when the train got here that it would take a start and give me something to do, but the last week has made no chainge. It is just as dull and quiet as when you left.

The whole sales for the month foot up $6,650.+ collections for the same time amount to $7,000.+

I have rec'd nothing yet from Vicente St. Vrain. Today the mail brought a mortgage deed from Hoppin & Appel to us for certain lands and property 8 pieces. They sent it to H. N. Smith for him to deliver it to us, provided we would accept it and be satisfied if not to send it. It would have been right had there been no errors in it, and I should have accepted it, that is if the paper covered what they intended that it should. But on examining it with [Merrill] Ashurst [an attorney] we found so many errors that he desided that it was no paper attall, and consequently I am obliged to send it back and urge them to fix it [with] St. Vrain, he having the right papers and authority from us. I believe in time this whole thing will be adjusted & that we will get out of it all right but it will require patience.

Goods are being forced on the market just now and it looks rather squally for Business. I am in hopes there will be a turn by & by and I am keeping quiet. Groceries are being hawked about for cost and freight, and yet I have heard of no big Sales. There are three new outfits here with goods (principally Groceries) which started from the States for Pikes Peak. I hope there will be no more of this sort of outfits come here.[21]

Filipe [Felipe] Delgado is at present the hardest one to contend with. He has plenty of goods now, and more coming. He is offering Groceries & Staple Dry goods, Manta, Lienzo &c at prices less than I can let ours go at and keep even. Fancy and Assorted goods are not plenty. Of these goods you know that I have not a large quantity, but I shall try to make what I have got tell. For the next month I do not anticipate much. The surplus goods on the market must be worked off and prices come down to something steady before the people will have

21. Kingsbury apparently hoped that parties bound for Colorado would arrive in Santa Fe without provisions and make purchases from him.

any confidence to buy. This will take at least a month or six weeks, after that I have some hopes that business will begin to look up again, and things that are really wanted bring their fair value. I am trying to make myself as easy as I can under the circumstances. I cannot help fretting a little but I am very cautious not to let any one outside see it or know it. I do not relish this season of the year passing off without seeing my sales sum up better.

Letter no. 118, Kingsbury to Webb, Santa Fe, August 6, 1859

I learn by the Mail Boys that they met you at Charvis [Jarvis] Creek[22] getting along all well. I hope you got home safe. I have finally got a settlement with the Governor by taking his draft on Washington which I now send you viz draft dated Executive department Santa Fe Aug 4th 1859, on Hon. Howell Cobb Sec'y of Treasury, for One Thousand dollars ($1,000.+) to be paid out of Appropriation for the Contingent Expenses of the Executive Dept. of the Terr. of N. M.—Signed A. Rencher Gov. N. Mexico payable to our order. You will also find herewith Check #1068. dated June 18th 1859, at sight on the Asst. Treas. of the U.S. at New York, for One hundred and thirty nine 43/100 dollars, drawn by Albert J. Smith Paymaster U.S.A. payable to the order of Fredk. Bartram and by him endorsed to our order. Making in all $1,139.43 which Amt. I have charged to your agent account. If you get the money for these papers and the draft for $400. which I sent before you can begin to take up some of the Notes due in October. In case you want any more funds immediately you can draw on Mr. Abbott for whatever balance he may have in his hands. Perhaps you had better find out from him how much he will have left after paying & closing up all we owe there, and draw for it to use on the Oct. payments, as I shall have not use for it in Boston. I have not had time to get returns from him & consequently do not know the exact amt. there, but will leave it for you to take up and dispose of as you please, let it appear in your agency a/c.

I paid to Kitchen nearly $3,000.+ on the freight, leaving just $6,000.+ for which I gave our notes due Jany. 23/26 1860 payable at the office of D.K & Co in St. Louis. This with the previous note due Dec. 20/23 for $3,000.+, will make $9,000.+ we owe for freight. Add to this the list of Notes due at New Haven and you can see at once all our liabilities. I think now I shall be able to meet all of this without much trouble. Outside of this we owe nothing except the balance of $5,000+ to Mr M. on that Stock Note.

I have had a Settlement with <u>Old Chat</u>.[23] Closed up the old a/c all square, by taking an obligation on J. Hersch due in the month of Oct. next, for $1,000.+, and sold him a fresh bill yesterday of $2,669.43. This gives me a good start on sales for this month. Don't fail to post me on

22. A creek in eastern Kansas named for the wealthy Mexican trader José Antonio Chávez, who was robbed and murdered in its vicinity by a gang of American hooligans. Franzwa, *Santa Fe Trail Revisited*, 93. The story is the subject of a book by Marc Simmons, *Murder on the Santa Fe Trail*.

23. Old Chat is mentioned from time to time throughout Kingsbury's correspondence, but we have been unable to identify him.

Tom's mail papers, soon as you get them in proper shape. He has already used up all the $10,000.+ which he got from [James?] Hunt.

Letter no. 119, Kingsbury to Webb, Santa Fe, August 28, 1859

I am in receipt of yours of July 29 & Aug. 2nd, and releaved to know that you got in safe. Jim Kitchen has settled his note and it is not probable that he will want credit with us again. I have collected the exchanges from Gaspar Ortiz.

In my last I sent you two drafts amt.g to $1139.43 on which I hope you have rec'd the money before this. I have now made arraingements with A. M. Jackson Secty. by which you will receive direct from Washington a Treasury Warrant on the Asst. Treas. at New York for Five Hundred dollars ($500.+) being for his salary for quarter ending September 30th 1859. When you get this amt. take it up on your agt. a/c and notify me so that I can settle with him here. I see now that there will not be time for me to hear from you in regard to Tom's papers and I must therefore place you in funds from here to meet our payments falling due at New Haven.

You may expect to get from me by next mail a Check for $4,000.+ or $5,000,+ and more if I can make my collections sustain it. At all events I will start funds to you in season to meet all our notes there, provided I do not hear from you in the mean time that you have turned Tom's papers into cash. Magruder has come to the conclusion that his power of Atty. &c never reached his Agent as he has not rec'd a silable [*sic*] from him yet on the subject. Mack did not keep his promis[e] to you, and I have every day less confidence in him.[24] Tom & Frank I think are manageing badly. We are safe with them, but it will be a scratch if they do not loose all they have made before they get through with their mail outfit.

Mr. Rose up to the present is doing very well. He fills my notion of an honest business man. I believe he will not desieve us. He has sold his Texas Land and some other property to Dr. Cumming for Cattle and Salt, which he will soon be able to turn into money, which is so much more Capitol he will have to go on, and of course will make it all the better for us. I have nothing satisfactory yet from Hoppin & Appel. Vicente [St. Vrain] has returned the papers we gave him stating that they had already sent the Mortgage &c to us, which is true but in such a form that I could not receive them.[25] Now I would go myself and attend to this business, but I cannot see how I can leave just now without neglecting more important matters. It is absolutely necessary that I should be present here all the time, then if I should not find Appel below my trip would be useless. So I shall not go now, but will try again to get the security in proper form by having all the papers made out here right and then get their names to it. This debt is

24. Both Kingsbury and Webb frequently referred to Magruder as Mack.

25. See above, Kingsbury to Webb, Santa Fe, July 30, 1859, DeG.

causing me much anxiety but at the same time I have a good deal of hope, and believe in time I will get it. I have other slow ones to manage, and will follow them as close as I can, I have still plenty of courage and full confidence that in the end I will be able to bring up everything to your entire satisfaction. It requires time, patience and close attention. If my life is spared you may rest assured that I will neglect nothing.

They cry on every side dull times, still I am having my share of business. Not much it is true but what I am doing is with the best men of the country & I am trying to have all my new bills safe. I am not urging sales but rather picking for customers which [are] safe and sound. Soon as I can get my Trial Balance off, you shall see how all the accounts stand.

Don't get the blues but trust that I will have brighter accounts to report when a little more time shall develope them. The darkest of the night is just before day.

Letter no. 120, Kingsbury to Webb, Santa Fe, September 3, 1859

I have sold my poney for $125.+ cash.

Dear Sir, I am still without advices from you. In my last I notified you that you would receive from Washington a check for $500.+ A.M. Jacksons salary for one quarter, which I hope you have got all safe by this time.

My sales for the Month of Aug. Amount to $8,000.+ Collections $4,700+.

Herewith you will find Check No. 80, dated Santa Fe N.M. Sept. 3rd 1859 at Sight on the Asst. Treas. of the U.S. for ($5,000.+) Five thousand dollars, drawn by J. L. Collins Supt. Ind. Aff. N. Mexico, payable to our order. The Amt. I have charged to your Agent a/c and send it to be used in taking up our October Notes due at New Haven. I have received from Mr. Abbott, his a/c current in full to August 5th showing a balance in our favor of $165.87. Deduct from this the draft in favor of Messervy $12.44, which will leave $153.43 for you to receive from him. You have probably drawn it in conformity to my previous letter. I had counted on a larger balance there but in his a/c he has charged Commisson and Int. on Cash advanced which I had not allowed in my calculation and this makes the difference. I also enclose Trial Balance of our books up to Sept. 1st by which you can see how all matters stand up to that time. Mr. Abbott's a/c did not reach me in time to enter before taking off this Balance Sheet. I have put in a little Memo. taken from the Trial Balance which will assist you in making any calculations you may desire.

I have received from Doan King & Co. the Mortgage of L. J. Rose all safe & recorded. They state that they have to our Cr. $1.33 left out of the amt. which you left with them for recording the same. How is it about those Old St. Louis Notes? Amounting to $2,368.44 did you get them as you went through? I have never had notice from them or you of the payment of these notes and consequently the notes remain open on our books & their a/c is still charged with the amt. I sent them to cancel the notes with, which was under date of Jany 16th. They must have been paid and there is a discrepancy of $2.65 in this matter which I cannot account for, except it was for exchange or some such item. Before you left here I put in your book a full memo. of this so that you should not forget it. Write to me about it so that I can enter & settle this in our books.

What did you do with the Billiard Ball you took in for Mr. Rose? Did you make arraingements for his Grass Seed &c? Don't forget to notify me about these little things, it places me in an unpleasant situation. Whiting annoys me no little about his orders, have you sent anything for him?

If we owe the enclosed bill pay it and charge the same in your account.

Henry Oneil has closed out his Stock to J. Hersch at cost & 10 cents freight on time. Henry Mercure has also sold his stock on the same terms to old man Beaubien so we have just at present two less stores. I believe now I will have a pretty fair fall and winter trade. Veramos,

P.S. Please send me Mr. Tolhurst's address if you have it, from some cause I do not know what, he does not receive my letters. I am forced to believe that I direct them wrong. If you have time I wish you would drop him a line for me, say that I have sent him several letters which he has not acknowledged, that I am well &c.

Letter no. 121, Kingsbury to Webb, Santa Fe, September 10, 1859

I am still without advices from you. I am at a loss to understand how it can be. If you [wrote] from St. Louis or on your arrival home about St. Louis matters the letter must have been lost. I rec'd by this Mail Stage a box from St. Louis containing Castor Bottles and the Billiard Balls for Mr. Rose but no bill of them. The Bottles suit and he is very much pleased with the Balls. By last mail I sent you Check on Asst. T. U.S. at New York signed J. L. Collins Supt. I. Aff. N. Mexico for ($5,000.+) Five thousand dollars, also Trial Balance and other papers showing our business in full up to Sept 1st all of which I hope you have rec'd safely.

I now enclose Check No. 83. dated Santa Fe N. Mex Sept. 10th 1859. at sight on The Asst. Treas. of the U.S. at New York for ($1,200.+) Twelve hundred dollars, drawn by J. L. Collins Supt. Ind Affs. N.

Mex. payable to the order of O. P. Hovey and by him endorsed to our order.

Also, Check No 84 dated Santa Fe N. Mex Sept 10th 1859. at sight on the Asst. Treas. of the U.S. at New York for five hundred dollars (\$500.+) drawn by J. L. Collins Supt. Ind. Aff. N. Mexico, payable to the order of O. P. Hovey and by him endorsed to our order. Making the sum of \$1,700.+ which is charged to your agent a/c. With these two checks you will be in ample funds to take up all our obligations due at New Haven. Soon as you get them all cancelled send me your a/c of the Settlement so that I may cansel the same on our books. In sending the money to meet these Notes I have been obliged to antici-pate my collections about \$4,000. Now my next push will be to make up this sum and get in enough to meet those freight notes at St Louis. If I have ordinary luck I shall be able to do it without any assistance from those papers of Bowler's which you hold for collection. I do not count on them and shall make my figures to meet those notes from here. I have a letter from Mr. Messervy noticing receipt of the \$4,000.+ for his Stores also deed for the same signed by himself & wife. He expresses himself well pleased with the sale and returns his thanks to both of us for executing it. Business is very dull so far. This month has been the dullest we have had this season. I am a juror in this Court and have been kept out of the store all the week. Then everything is in a state of excitement about the election. The returns are not all in yet but the probability is that Otero is elected, and as a matter of course the Territory is saved.[26]

It has been raining the past five weeks constantly. Our house has leaked none to speak of. One of the rooms in the Exchange fell in last night, fortunately no one was hurt.

P.S. We got safely through Election day without any serious fights, only one man killed in Santa Fe over the election. Several weeks ago Jim Houston stab[b]ed Chasteure (who was formerly with Mahan at Algodonez [Algodones]) during a political argument, from which wound he died, Houston is now on trial for his murder. This probably kept the parties cool on election day. We have now by the mail today that Watts & Otero got into a fuss at Doñ[a] Aña and that a chalage [challenge] had passed between them the fight to come off on the 8th. Frank Green is there and is Watt's second. It may have been settled but everybody here thinks that they have had the fight.[27]

Santa Fe is getting worse and more unsafe every day, during the sit-ting of this Grand Jury they have brought in no other enditements [indictments] except those for murder. There are now 6 or 8 cases before the court. These wild sporting characters are increasing every week, and it is really unsafe here for a quiet man. If I escape with my life I shall consider myself lucky. It may prove necessary for you to

26. In 1859, Miguel A. Otero was elected to his third successive term as territorial delegate, defeat-ing José M. Gallegos. Twitchell, *Leading Facts*, 2:310.

27. In a speech he delivered at Mesilla, Watts made some disparaging remarks about the Otero family, precipitating a duel between Otero and him-self. Neither one was injured. Twitchell, *Leading Facts*, 2:310.

come out yet to close up things here. It is only this afternoon that I had a narrow escape, fortunately Weirick was present and took the fight off my hands. It was this. A drunken fellow came in the store, a strainger from California been here only about 2 weeks. (I have since learned that he was a daingerous man and of desperate character there.) He insisted upon riding over Weirick and myself. We put him out twise without hurting him and ordered him to stay out, threatened him if he did not I would call the Sheriff. At this he made a rush in, Weirick caught an axe handle out of a box full which happened to stand exposed for sale close to the door, and with it struck him a blow on top of the head. This did not stop him. I went for the Sheriff, and the fellow followed me out of the door and went into the Exchange. In the mean time while I was out hunting the sheriff, he returned again in the presence of a big crowd which had congregated and said he wished to make friends. Weirick called lowed [loud] to those outside, his friends or whoever might be there to stop him & not let him in, but he got past them all and close up on Tom & grab[b]ed him. Tom threw him and beat him pretty severely with his fist, before the crowd could seperate them. By this time I returned with a constable and had him arrested. I hope this is the end of it. Tom was not hurt except a slight sprain of his nuckles [*sic*] of the right hand while hitting the fellow. Neither Tom or myself were armed. The fellow had a big dirk Knife which he had been throwing in all directions by a slight of hand with great force, point first, sticking it into the portal posts &c before he came into the store. I did not see the Knife after he came in. If he had it, he had no chance to use it as Tom was too quick for him. This is only our first encounter what will come next I cannot imagine but can expect almost anything. I am perfectly disgusted with the whole country and want to get clear of it. The sooner the better. I am certain we have made no mistake in desiding to close, I only wish we had commenced sooner.

Letter no. 122, Kingsbury to Webb, September 17, 1859

Dear Sir, Yours of the 17th ult. is to hand. I am much relieved to know that you got home safe. Not having any letter for so long a time I began to fear something was wrong. I am sorry to hear that you had been sick, I hope however it is nothing serious.

By last mail I sent you two Checks #83 & 84, drawn by J. L. Collins Supt. Ind. Aff. on New York amtg. to $1,700.+ which I hope you have received. When you get this amt. according to my figures you will have funds enough to meet all our payments at New Haven. In order to send this money to you so early I have been obliged to anticipate my collections pretty strong and as money is getting very tight and scarce here I am afraid to increase it just now.

You ask for some private funds to reach you by 1st Feby. next. By that time or soon after in all probability I shall be able to send you pleanty, but how is it that you make no allowance whatever for those papers of Bowler's being realized? It certainly does appear to me reasonable to suppose that the Dept. will have funds and pay something on Mail Service before that time. If from my collections I am able to meet those freight notes at St. Louis I shall think I am doing well. This I shall certainly try hard to do, and I go so far as to count, that you will certainly get money on Tom's papers, and that to[o] from the Dept. without being compeled to raise it through private bankers, directly after Congress meets, so that by the first of January next you will have funds enough to take up our Note of $5,000.+ in the hands of Messervy. This will be the last debt we owe and I would like if all things go right to have it taken up at that time, and whatever amt. over this sum you get on Tom's papers you will be at liberty to appropriate for your own private purposes, and I will make the amt. good to him here. I only place this before you now, in the view of a financeing movement, subject of course to all contingencies which may arrise. By this mail, I have received from Doan King & Co. their a/c current also those old St. Louis notes canceld. I can now close their a/c on our books. By their a/c I learn that the difference of $2.65 which I mentioned to you in a previous letter, was for a telegraph Com. to you March 15th 1859. This item makes our a/c's agree and I presume it is all right.

On reflection I have determined to risk our Cr. a little further with the Squire [Mink?] and will send the amt. you request thinking perhaps that you may require it at once. Herewith you will find Check No. 85 dated Santa Fe N.M. Sept. 17th 1859 at sight on the Asst. Treas. of the U.S. at New York for Five hundred dollars ($500.+) drawn by J. L. Collins Supt of Ind. Aff. N. Mexico, payable to your order. This amt. I have charged to your private account, and you will receive it as such. Business continues very dull, I think of nothing more just now.

P.S. The fellow we had the fracas with last week is about again, rather the worse for ware. He is sober now and perfectly docile. I hope he will remain so. The famo[u]s duel has passed the[y] [Otero and Watts] fought with Pistols a[t] 15 paces. Each shot 3 times and neither hit. The Seconds then interfered and the matter was postponed, but I understand that it is not fully settled yet. It is generally admitted that Otero is elected though the returns are not all in yet. There are still some on the other side not willing to give it up yet. At all events it will be a very close election. There can only be a small majority on either side. Judge Watt's son How is to be married on next Thursday to the youngest Mis[s] Edgar.[28] We have had the unpleasant duty this week of laying the remains of Hugh N. Smith in their last resting place. He

28. Joshua Howe Watts married Henrietta Susana Edgar in September 1859. Archives of the Archdiocese of Santa Fe, microfilm POS #7B, Marriages, 1858-1889, Santa Fe.

was taken sick last Sunday and died very suddenly. It was supposed he had a fit during the night, on Monday morning he was found in a lif[e]less stupor and remained in it unconscious for 24 hours and then died. Every possible remedy was used to bring him to life but without effect.[29]

29. Webb was not surprised to hear of Smith's death, and offered an unexpected explanation as to its possible cause. "I regret much to hear of the death of Mr. H. N. smith, altho it was not unexpected to me to hear of it. He has drunk hard for a long time. Did he not take morphine? From your description I should think that was the case." Webb to Kingsbury, Hamden, CT, [Sept. or Oct.] 19, 1859, MHS.

12.

"This hole of dis[s]ipation"

Summer and Autumn 1859

Letters 123–135

On through the autumn, business remained "dull"—one of Kingsbury's favorite characterizations—even though sales as of October 1 were $8,000 ahead of the previous year. Kingsbury did not, however, place more orders with Webb. At last he was selling out the inventory.

By fall Kingsbury had finally found a dependable buyer for the firm's real estate holdings. On November 19, he reported to Webb that he had sold the Santa Fe property to Col. Thomas T. Fauntleroy, who had assumed command of the Ninth Military Department replacing Gen. John Garland's temporary appointment, Col. Benjamin L. E. Bonneville.[1] For $1,000 down, with the $9,000 balance payable on July 1, 1860, Fauntleroy would take immediate possession of the house and rent the store to Kingsbury for $75 a month. When Kingsbury vacated the house, he made the store his home, moving his bedroom furniture into the corner of the "bale room."[2]

Kingsbury needed the store. As of late November he had an inventory worth $22,000 to $23,000, and competition remained stiff. Moreover, numerous customers still owed money to Webb & Kingsbury. Kingsbury hoped to collect the outstanding debts, pay off the company's last bills including recent freight charges, and sell most of the merchandise before his commercial rivals imported new goods in the spring. At best he hoped to reduce his inventory to a point where he could sell it as a lot to a single buyer. Should that fail, he told Webb, he would move to smaller quarters in the spring and keep selling. The cutback in military expenditures and a slowdown of business at the Exchange Hotel, which had been his principal customer for liquors and some other goods, left him in one of his characteristically pessimistic moods.[3]

As Kingsbury wound down the business that autumn, Comanches stepped up raids on the plains to the east of New Mexico. Throughout his years in Santa Fe, Comanches, Kiowas, and other Plains peoples had disrupted the flow of goods and mail from Missouri. A number of Kingsbury's acquaintances in New Mexico, represented by John S. Watts, had filed claims for damages against the United States government for its

1. Frazer, *Forts and Supplies*, 147.
2 Kingsbury to Webb, Santa Fe, Feb. 19, 1860, MHS, describes his new living arrangements.
3 Ibid., Nov. 27, 1859, DeG.

failure to provide protection.[4] But in the autumn of 1859 Comanches on the eastern borders of New Mexico became more troublesome than ever. Squeezed between Texans who pushed them north and west, and New Mexicans moving eastward onto the high Plains, Comanches intensified their resistance. They stole horses, killed cattle and sheep, and destroyed ranch property.[5] "The present Indian trouble is another cause for us to be satisfied with our determination to quit," Kingsbury wrote. "We can count on no security for years to come."[6]

Mail service, in Kingsbury's opinion, became especially insecure that autumn. Three mail lines then served New Mexico: the Independence route, authorized in 1855, between Independence, Missouri, and Stockton California, by way of Albuquerque; and the Butterfield Overland Mail, authorized in 1858 to connect St. Louis and San Francisco by way of El Paso (from which point Tom Bowler had a contract to operate a subsidiary line to Santa Fe).[7] The third route, the Neosho route, which began operating less than a year before, had been ordered discontinued by Postmaster General Joseph Holt on July 1, 1859, although Tom Bowler and others hoped it might be reinstated.[8] "All three of the lines," Kingsbury told Webb, "are looked upon as unsafe," but he urged Webb to use the Overland Mail route as the least risky of the three.[9]

While Indians posed a threat outside of Santa Fe, within the city the residents themselves supplied an element of danger. Kingsbury continued to send Webb reports of drinking, gambling, and fighting among Mexicans and Anglo Americans alike. Judge Kirby Benedict, Chief Justice of the Supreme Court of New Mexico, "continues to soak it up like a fish," Kingsbury told Webb, and Lt. Julian May, who had slapped Benedict in the face and kicked him in the seat of the pants in a drunken fight, died a few days later of "appaplexy" following his "big spree."[10]

The interesting foibles of his neighbors notwithstanding, Kingsbury did not regard his time in Santa Fe "as living, it is only staying."[11] Like a prisoner anticipating release, Kingsbury poignantly pondered his future in the larger world. "I often wonder what I will do when I get through here. I shall be lost for a while at least."[12]

~

Letter no. 123, Kingsbury to Webb, Santa Fe, September 24, 1859

Yours of the 24th ult. is now at hand. I have very little in the way of business items to impart since my last. In that I sent you a Check #85, drawn by J. L. Collins Supt. Ind Aff. on N. Y. for Five hundred dollars ($500.+) for your private use, which I hope you have received all safe. Don't omit to advise me of the payment and actual receipt of the money on all the remittances which I have sent you. I am not particular to get your a/c current untill you have paid all those Eastern Notes.

4. Watts, *Indian Depredations.*

5. Kenner, *New Mexican-Plains Indian Relations,* 128-29; Wallace and Hoebel, *The Comanches,* 302-3.

6. Kingsbury to Webb, Santa Fe, Oct. 22, 1859, DeG.

7 Conkling and Conkling, *The Butterfield Overland Mail,* 1:90-92.

8. Taylor, *First Mail West,* 54-56; Kingsbury to Webb, Santa Fe, Sept. 24, 1859, DeG.

9 Kingsbury to Webb, Santa Fe, Oct. 22 and Oct. 31, 1859, DeG.

10. Ibid., Nov. 6 and Dec. 11, 1859, DeG.

11. Ibid., Nov. 6, 1859, DeG.

12. Ibid., Dec. 11, 1859, DeG.

I would like to have them all taken up and included in your a/c when you make it out, so that I can close our Notes Payable Account.

Every manner of Business remains exceedingly dull. Money is getting very scarce which has a tendency to cramp my collections. I hope Government will import some specie this fall, it is needed badly here now. Col. Fontelroy [Fauntleroy] is to superseid [sic] Col [B. L. E.] Bonneville and take charge of this dept. I understand that he is now on his way out.[13] We have a report here which appears well founded that the Overland Mail has been inter[r]upted by the Comanches on the Yano [Llano] Estacado,[14] two coaches were due at El Paso, and no word of them. I delivered your message to Ellison.[15] He promised to write by this mail. Tom Bowler is thinking some of going to Washington late this fall or winter. He thinks his presens [presence] there may secure him additional Mail Service either on the El Paso route or in the re-establishing the Neosho.[16] What do you think of it? Judge Watts will go in next week. Dr. [David C.] De Leon goes at the same time and has promised me that he would certainly give you a visit.

P.S. You well know that I am a poor hand with private letters, but will continue to do my best in giving you some of the leading news. I send a paper this week with a full a/c of the proceedings had at Hugh's [Smith's] death.[17] Wm. Cantwell who was sentenced at San Miguel, is the young man who came out with us, when we came ahead we left him in charge of the Cows.[18] Tom Smith the gambler has been tried at El Paso for the murder of [George H.] Giddings the Mail Contractor and a[c]quitted.[19]

Wm. Drew has been drowned, he was out with Garitson on a surveying trip and in crossing the Rio del Norte near Santo Domingo while the river was very high. He got in a hole and being unable to swim, was carried down. His body has not been recovered. There are letters here stating that by the death of his mother he is heir to property in England Amt'g to some $300,000.+.[20]

Pigeon is coming here with his goods. He will take the store which Henry Mercure occupied. He was here, stayed a little over a week, but I did not hear of his playing any. Henry O'Neal and H. Mercure are still fighting the tiger. This week they each got bit for a $1,000.+.[21] Frank Green is still below, I expect he is having a big spree, I cannot imagine what else is keeping him. As far as I can learn Tom is behaving himself very well, if he is doing otherwise he is very cautious to keep it from me. They had a grand wedding at the Squires. How[e] [Watts] appears delighted with his young bride.[22] She is Catholic and was married by the Bishop [Lamy]. Several of my friends have made a strong set on me to take the other [sister], I decline the honor. They do not know me.

Mrs. [D. V.] Whiting had a fine little son arrive a few days since, all

13. Fauntleroy took command on October 25, 1859, in camp at Cottonwood Springs on the Santa Fe Trail. Frazer, Forts and Supplies, 147.

14. On its loop from Fort Smith, Arkansas, to El Paso, the Butterfield Overland Mail Company passed through the Llano Estacado (Staked Plains), where a stone station was built about 1859. Conkling and Conkling, The Butterfield Overland Mail, 1:372.

15. Webb had asked Kingsbury to apologize on his behalf to Samuel Ellison, whom Webb apparently regarded as a highly esteemed friend, because he had not had a chance to see much of him the morning he left Santa Fe. Webb to Kingsbury, Hamden, CT, Aug. 2, 1859, MHS.

16. The postmaster general had eliminated the Neosho route in July 1859. See introduction to this chapter.

17. Hugh N. Smith, the attorney general of New Mexico, "departed for the eternal mansions," as the newspaper put it, after a brief illness described as a consequence of an apoplectic seizure, at the age of thirty-seven or thirty-eight. Santa Fe Weekly Gazette, Sept. 24, 1859.

18. Cantwell's case, involving the accidental death of George Wingate, received three columns on the front page of the Santa Fe Weekly Gazette, which printed Judge Kirby Benedict's remarks in passing sentence on the young man. Apparently Cantwell, like many other young men throughout the west, adopted the habit of attending fandangos "loaded down with knives and pistols," which he would use after becoming intoxicated, thus endangering those around him. In April 1859 Cantwell shot and killed George Wingate, a popular and upstanding member of the community, in what Benedict characterized as "the wanton, reckless, and bragadocio [sic] use of a pistol." Benedict's remarks, and the interest they generated, suggest that he and the community at large had lost patience with this kind of spontaneous, violent outburst. He sentenced Cantwell to three years in the San Miguel County jail. Ibid.

19. George H. Giddings, who operated the mail connection between Santa Fe and San Antonio. Taylor, First Mail West, 40.

20. The extant issues of the Santa Fe Weekly Gazette did not report this story.

21. Apparently a reference to gambling.

22. See chapter 11.

getting on well. Mrs [Joab] Houghton is expecting an addition soon, the Judge has gone to Pikes Peak.

Mr. [Leonard] Rose has got a contract to furnish this Post with Beef at a bit a pound, and he has a fair prospect of selling his salt soon to Col. Grayson.[23]

This is all now, I will leave the balance for Saml. [Ellison].

Letter no. 124, Kingsbury to Webb, Santa Fe, October 1, 1859

I have no letter from you since my last. Everything remains quiet here. My sales for the past month are $2,860.+. Collections amt. to $3,800.+. I now feel perfectly easy in money matters. The sales appear small but on looking over my figures I see that I am still $8,000.+ ahead of what they were last year at this date.

I will probably get Tom's mail draft for the quarter just ended to send to you by next mail. I have just sold a bill on 6 mos. to John Dole [Dold], perhaps it will come to something over $1,500.+—prices low, but I could not let a safe man go past.

I have nothing of importance to add.

Letter no. 125, Kingsbury to Webb, Santa Fe, October 16, 1859

All communication on the Independence rout[e] is stop[p]ed. On Tuesday three mails will be due and none through from either end of the route. Maj. [J. L.] Donaldson came in this week and reports that the Indians, (Camanches [*sic*], Ki[o]was & Kaws) had consentrated at Walnut Creek,[24] and had become desperate at receiving no present this year, say the white man has lied to them long enough and had threatened to attact the settlement at Walnut Creek the next day. We have no further news.[25] The Mails from this end, that is the two last, not meeting any from the States got timid and turned back. There were two mails ahead of these and this side of Walnut Creek going in. What luck they had we do not know. With the first, Otero and his family were pasingers, also Judge Porter & Mr Crenshaw mail contra(c)tors were with it. With the one following was Mr. E. Branford of Albuquerque & some others as pasingers, straingers to me.

With the Otero Mail, that is the one that left here Sept. 19th, I sent you to be used on your private a/c Check No. 85 dated Santa Fe N. M. Sept. 17th 1859, at sight on the Asst. Treas. of the U.S. at New York for Five hundred dollars ($500.+) drawn by J. L. Collins, Supt. of Ind. Aff N. Mexico, made payable to your order. I trust that this check will get through to you safe. In case you have not got it and you learn that the mail that it was in is lost, you will take steps to prevent it being collected by anyone but yourself and notify me so that I may procure a duplicate here for you. This is the last money I have sent through the

23. A "bit" represented 12 ½ cents, which was a relatively high price for a pound of beef. Comparable figures are 7.92 cents in 1860, for a Fort Buchanan order—the only contract purchase for that year—and 6.74 to 11 cents a pound in 1861. The price may have been higher in the fall of 1859 because a drought affected the availability of forage and the price of hay. Frazer, *Forts and Supplies*, 52, 154, 167, 179.

24. Walnut Creek is located about two miles east of Great Bend, Kansas, the point at which the Santa Fe Trail joined the Arkansas River. Maj. Donaldson had come through with a small train, which included the paymaster carrying $50,000. Simmons, *Following the Santa Fe Trail*, 96-98; Oliva, *Soldiers*, 116.

25. Indian Agent William Bent reported seeing roughly 2,500 belligerent Kiowa and Comanche warriers at the mouth of Walnut Creek on September 16, 1859. The Indians had become increasingly hostile and bold in their attacks on plains travelers. On September 24, a party of 15 Kiowas murdered two members of a mail party, Lawrence and Michael Smith, whose military escort had orders not to proceed farther west than Pawnee Fork. The third member of the party, William H. Cole, escaped by abandoning the wagon and hiding in the tall grass. Oliva, *Soldiers*, 113-19. Interruptions in the mails are borne out by Webb's letters throughout the fall, which provide a detailed record of which of Kingsbury's letters he eventually received and which he did not.

mail except a small Treasury Warrant of $30.15 which I mailed as a present to Mr. Tolhurst. Drop him a line and see if he has rec'd it. My last month's business closed with very slim figures. viz. Sales $2,860.+ Collections amt'g to $3,800.+

So far this month Business has been a little more lively & encouraging. Sale & Collections sum up pretty well and if I can make it hold out at the same rate to the end of the month I shall have respectable figures to report to you. In the morning they will start another mail on our road with an escort of thirty-five men. I shall start no more remittanc[e]s untill the road is opened again, and I have assurances that all is safe. The first freight note is not due untill Dec 20/23, so I have yet a full month before I shall be compeled to start funds to meet it. I am confident now that my collections will give me plenty to meet these freight notes and I count on a good sum over. In reply to this send me a letter by the Overland mail, let me know what success you had at Washington & Co.

Letter no. 126, Kingsbury to Webb, Santa Fe, October 22, 1859

Yours of Sept 8th is just to hand, written after your visit to Washington on the subject of Tom's business. Watts is still here, has been getting up papers for Tom, and has already covered most of the points which you suggest. I have read to them both all of your letter applying to Tom's business, that they might profit by any remarks there that they had not already provided for, and I suppose they will do so. At least I have given them all the information you sent and leave it for them to act on.[26] Watts will (so he says) leave on Monday next for the States will go by the Overland route. Tom wants very much to go, and will if it is possible for him to arrainge matters here so that he can leave them, his aim is now to start some time in December. I have posted him privately about Watts, also written to Vincente [St. Vrain] about the fate of his draft. I am pleased to hear that you have one quarter pay secure $4,062.50. This will nearly put us eaven with Tom. Now all I can say is hold on to this and not let it out of your hands to go back to him on any conditions. Now then, if you can get out of him or his papers about $2,000.+ more, I want you to do so and retain it, so as to cover Frank's a/c, the rent, and other little items. Tom has not given me his draft for the next quarter now already due on the El Paso route. He appears a little o[a]fish about it and I have not pushed it. Can you not get a certificate covering this quarter (from June 30th to Sept. 30th) 1859, on the authority now in your hands without a draft from him?

My collections this month so far have come in very well, and I am beginning to make new calculations about remittances. My aim now is to meet from here the $9,000+ freight and $5,000. to Messervy, so as

26. Webb had written that Tom could not be paid for providing mail service on the now suspended Neosho to Albuquerque route until he gave the mail department sufficient excuse for nonperformance of his contract. Webb provided an interesting outline of specific objections raised by the government, stating that the service had not been performed according to contract: "The mail was recd. and delivered at Neosho, sometimes in two horse waggons, sometimes in two horse spring coaches, and sometimes on horseback, and at other times there was entire failure. Again, when the service was performed according to contract, mail was left at Neosho in every instance, and on the annulling of the contract there was three thousand pounds of mail matter left at Neosho." The leftover mail apparently consisted of books franked by Miguel Otero, which Webb suspected might have been part of some ploy to keep Tom from fulfilling his contract, since it would be difficult to carry such a heavy load over the unbroken road between the two points.

Webb went on to say that he believed that mail contractor Jacob Hall had unduly influenced one of the clerks in Washington in order to embarrass Tom, who had taken some mails when Hall had failed to arrive and who had bid against Hall for the Independence mail route. He concluded by advising Kingsbury not to count on Tom being able to pay his debt using revenue from this mail contract and suggesting that "if Tom has any friends who can help him by their influence, he wants them now. . . . Manage your affairs with him so as to help him if you can, but always be safe, and very safe." Webb to Kingsbury, Hamden, CT, Sept. 8, 1859, MHS.

to leave in your hands for your own private use all that you may get from Tom. The certificate you have already got must certainly be paid in time to meet your wants already expressed to me, that is Feby 1st. Now if I have any luck with my collections, I shall be able to meet all that I have laid out to[o] and also have enough to send you in time to meet your farm note. What was the date you told me? I have forgotten as I did not set it down. Was it March 1st or Apl 1st? With regard to this I shall write you with more certanty some time in January after I have provided for the $14.000.+ mentioned above. Nothing but bad luck will prevent me from taking it all through swim[m]ing and never once touch bottom. One little drawback against me is the present trouble with the Indians and the insecurity of our mails.[27] I am timid about sending remittances untill some confidence is restored. All three of the lines are looked upon as unsafe. The Indians are hostile and range on all the routes, The last mail from Independence came through with a big train. The mail party before that were all killed.[28] The mail bags were recovered and brought through. No passingers with the coach. Geo. Beall[29] had taken passage in it but they made some objection to the weight of his trunk and he desided to come with Moore & Reese's train and there by saved his life. They found 12 dead bodies on the road 11 men & 1 woman, mostly small parties returning from Pike's Peak. These were all found between the Arkansas and Walnut Creek, and right on our road, it is supposed that other parties have been wiped out, and not yet discovered.[30] The over land [Overland Mail] have lost a goodeal of stock but no men yet. It is a good thing for Tom that his Neitsho [Neosho] route has been stop[p]ed. The Texas line is also in dainger, so I shall hold up with my remittances untill the last minute. I am truly thankfull that you was ahead of all this difficulty and also that we have no goods on the road. I believe however that the trains will get through safe, still they are in dainger of loosing their animals at anytime. It appears so far that the Indians have only attacted small parties.

Mr. Rose is about selling out the Exchange. He is satisfied that it is profitable but the business does not suit him, and I think he will make the traid, but will not give possesion untill 1st March next. The men who want to buy him out are two men from Arkansas with means.[31] They came out with a large drove of cattle, and sold a part of them to Gov. for Beef on good tirms. The balance Rose will take in part payment if he makes the sale. I am not willing to bring any more goods for that house on any condition, so you need not anticipate any orders. If I get the cash out of what we have already on hand I shall be perfectly satisfied. You can trust to me for this, but I don't want any more to put through the mill.

The present Indian trouble is another cause for us to be satisfied with our determination to quit. I think it is a matter that will not be

27. See previous letter, Kingsbury to Webb, Santa Fe, Oct. 16, 1859, DeG.

28. Perhaps a reference to the murder of the two Smith brothers, mentioned in note 25.

29. This is the only mention of George Beall in Kingsbury's letters.

30. Oliva refers to an eastbound mail party discovering three dead Pike's Peak emigrants in September, as well as to a report by the commanding officer at the military camp at Pawnee Creek estimating that at least nine gold-seekers had been killed that season. *Soldiers*, 118-20.

31. We have been unable to ascertain who these two men might have been.

soon settled and we can count on no security for years to come, that is such as we have had for 8 years past. I am very willing to be clear of this extra risk.

In your letters be particular to state the receipt of each of mine so that I may know that you get them all, and I will do the same.

P.S. The Otero mail, with check of $500.+ for you got through safe.

Letter no. 127, Kingsbury to Webb, Santa Fe, October 31, 1859

I sent you a long letter last Monday. The mail from Ind. has just got here it came through with Col. Fontelroy's [Fauntleroy's] Escort, by it I got yours of Sept 21st & 24. I had nothing to write yesterday and have no letter for you ready now. Tom's mail is now before the door and I just scratch this to let you know that I am all right, and will give you good news from H. & A. [Hoppin and Appel] by next mail. Apple [Appel] is here & I will get a settlement today. There is no hope of a regular mail by the Ind[ependence] route for the present.[32] One of the men of this party was killed at Red River.[33] Send all your letters for me from this out by St Louis and the Overland Mail!! My sales and collections are good this month. I will give you the figures in my next.

Keep all that money of Tom's Certificate. This is $4,000.+ & we want about $2,000. more from him to put us even.

Letter no. 128, Kingsbury to Webb, Santa Fe, November 6, 1859

I scratched you a few lines last Monday stating that I had received yours of Sept 21 & 23rd. Since then I have rec'd nothing more from you. I know by your letters that you must have written and owing to the trouble with our mail it is still on the road. Yesterday a mail got through from Ind[ependence] all safe but it brought nothing but Newspapers. The supposition is that the letter mail is all sent by the Overland route. If you have got all my letters you will find that I have written you very regular and long letters, posting you fully on business and also other matters.

Tom is doing all he can to get the required papers to sustain his claims, and now talks of getting off in about two weeks, will take his family on, wants to go on the Ind[ependence] route. At that time an escort will be started to accompany the mail, so that it will be safe and he will probably get ready to go with it. It is his intention to come direct to you and get you to go with him to Washington to assist him.

I have had a Settlement with Hoppin & Appel and now believe that we will not loose a cent by them. On the contrary we will get the whole debt in time with interest. This is the way it now stands and you can judge for yourself. They have sold their house at Messilla [Mesilla] to Alex'r Duvall for Three Thousand Dollars, on third cash, ⅓ at 4

32. For the Independence route, see the introduction to this chapter.
33. We have been unable to identify the victim.

Summer and Autumn 1859 185

mos. note & ⅓ 8 mos. note—all of which they have turned over to me together with a note of Sylvester Mowry[34] for $500.+ which has 5 months to run, payable at Washington City—leaving a balance still due of $1,300.+ on which I have given them 6 months extention by taking a mortgage on all the balance of their property. I have made out all the papers in proper form and Apple [Appel] will take them down to be completed & recorded. He states to me on honor that they only owe besides our $1,300.+ a balance of $500.+ to Juaquin Pea[r]se. This is every cent they owe in the Territory. That there property is clear, and that they have wagons, mules and merchandise at Tubeck [Tubac] amt'g to at least $5,000.+.

Now the only case that I am an[n]oyed about is Magruder—and this I should not consider desperate attall if the rascal would only quit gambeling and attend to his business. He plays constantly, a few dollars every night, and in the end I fear it will eat him up. If I can do no better I think I shall buy his Farm in Arkansas, and take the chances for the balance of his a/c. He cannot increas[e] it one cent, all I want is to get even with him once and let him look for favors in some other quarter.

By having patience with Cha. La Rouge I believe he will work out.[35] He is getting in a good lot of corn and corn this season is money. We had early frosts and all the crops are cut short, and this will make all grain high. New corn is now selling at $4.50 per fanegue [fanega], & it is certain to go up & be very high in the Spring.

Mr. Rose has made the trade I wrote you about he has sold and gives possession on the 1st of March next. He sells same as he bought that is takes the Cattle for cash the balance 6, 12, 18 & 24 mos. He will take no goods of me except what is wanted to keep the house going, and this he is to pay cash for. What I have left the other parties are to take & they understand that it is cash when they get it. Now the only trouble to me is having these goods in the way of my closing out. I want to close off all our goods before Spring trains get here and believe I can sell all but these goods for the Hotel. These I can sell to no one else and I can only sell them there as they are wanted. If these things were off my hands I feel sure I could sell the balance so you see how it stands.

Col. Fontleroy [Fauntleroy] has arrived. I second your motion, that is that the citizens attend to their own business & let him manage military matters under his instructions. But you know what Santa Fe is, we have so many big men here they must show themselves. One thing certain I will not meddle in what does not concern me, let the balance do as they please.[36] They have already jumped Col. Bonnevill[e] & the military about the Indians on our route, had public meetings in the court House &c &c. I have attended none and shall not mix in anything of the kind. I look upon it as a political spite because they [the military] opposed Otero in the election. That side have jumped on the

34. A former army officer and owner of the Mowry mine in the Patagonia Mountains near Tubac, Mowry was involved in the effort to have Arizona made into a separate territory from New Mexico. In 1859 he became the owner and publisher of the *Weekly Arizonian*. Twitchell, *Leading Facts*, 2:408.

35. Beyond his name, we have been unable to identify Charles La Rouge, but he is mentioned fairly often in Kingsbury's later letters. See chapter 13.

36. Santa Fe was divided over the best way to handle the current Indian troubles. One faction, led by Gov. Rencher, supported independent action by the citizens under the direction of the governor. This method was supported by territorial law and had been the practice up to this time. Col. Fauntleroy, as departmental commander, objected to the intervention of civilians and threatened to withdraw regular troops if Rencher authorized a volunteer campaign. Matters came to a head when two companies of volunteers were raised and Fauntleroy refused to issue them either arms or ammunition. Keleher, *Turmoil in New Mexico*, 102-3; Horn, *New Mexico's Trouble Years*, 81.

first thing that offered and tried to make it appear that it was a public thing—and by their great demonstrations streingthen there [their] party. They were all great men at the meetings, big indian fighters, each one would kill & eat his 100 indians and swallow them in a glass of Whiskey. The misfortune is that it takes transportation to move the whiskey and our great fighters could not think of starting without a sufficient amt. in the front ranks. This fail[e]d and so the matter ended, and Mr. Indian is left free. We may expect hot times in the Legislature this winter.

Col. Fontelroy [Fauntleroy] in looking for quarters has got his eye on our house and wants to get it. I have half got him in the notion of buying the whole property, the only trouble is that he has got no ready money. He does not object to the price and if he had the funds I could make the sale. I have proposed to sell to him for ½ cash and ½ on time. He replies that he can only raise $1,000.+ just now, having invested all his sirplus funds in the States just before leaving.[37] Johnson goes in now for a new stock to bring here. He wants to rent our Store and is anxious for Fontelroy to buy so that he can get it. He aims to get here early say in May and wants to be sure of getting our Store. I may be able to make the sale yet. Qui[e]n Sabe.

My sales for the month of October amt. to $7,500. Collections for the same time sum up $7,300.+. Since Nov. came in I have not sold a bill, so far nothing but a little retai[l]ing, but my collections have started off well. If they continue good through the month I will have plenty of money. I can now see my way clear to pay the Freight and Messervy, and in all probability I will have something soon for you. I shall try to send you the $1,000.+ in time to reach you by Feby 1st. We cannot count on selling off our old remnant to Joe [Hersch?]. He has got his teams and says that he will go in the winter and bring his own stock in the Spring. He wants to sell all his goods now on hand for grain and leave his house shut up, this is the way he talks. However he may change his notion. If he does & I can get our stock down a little more say sell about $10,000.+ I shall try hard to sell him the balance.

This is all now.

P.S. I hope you have sent me a bill for those Castor Bottles and charges on the billiard Balls so that I may know what to recover here of Mr. Rose. He has not heard a word about the Grass seed.

If you cannot collect that draft against Watts, I wish you would return it to Vincinte [Vincente] direct, and write him just how it is. address him V. St. Vrain & Co. El Paso, Texas.

P. S.

I have already given you the principal news. I do not remember any one being killed except Chasteure he was stabbed by Houston, & Houston is still in jail waiting trial. We have had any number of fights

37. Fauntleroy, who had fought in both the War of 1812 and the Mexican War and who was by this time past sixty years old, was an excellent prospect to purchase Kingsbury and Webb's real estate. Although he was temporarily short of ready funds, Fauntleroy's net worth was roughly $50,000 in real estate and personal property. Keleher, *Turmoil in New Mexico*, 138; 1860 NM Census, 40.

but nothing fatal.[38] Our town is full of <u>Sports</u> I could not begin to give you all the gambeling items, the changes are so constant & rapid that I on the spot can hardly keep pase with them much less give you accurate account. For the last 2 or 3 weeks the mania has run at a high pace. H. Mercure, Oneil, Col. St. Vrain, Pigeon, Wilbar Hovey, Kavanaugh &c &c all in the ring fighting the tiger. Pigeon brought his goods here, and has sold the whole lot to Simon Delgado at <u>first</u> that is invoice cost and 10 cents freight without any other charges, on 3, 6, 9 & 12, months, it came to about <u>$8,000.</u>+. Simon has got his house finished so as to open his store there. He occupied one & his brother Pablo the other. Col. Collins fell from his horse and hirt his leg badly. It is mashed just above the ankle, not broken but a serious injury. It confines him to bed.

[William] Drew's widdow (you remember he married one of Anto. Sena's daughters[39]) since the news of his death, has denied herself every comfor[t], such as sleep &c. untill she has finally died of grief, she was buried today. They leave one little boy about one year old. I just learned that John Mostin of Taos is dead. You remember him red hair, drank hard was clerk for Beuthner a long time. He has had the jaunders [jaundice] very bad for 6 month.

I am told that the new commander is loaded down with instructions as to economy and retrenchments in the expenses of the army.

Watts has got possession of the Alverez [Alvarez] Estate on Power of Atty. from the heirs, this may keep him up for a while.[40] Hovey still keeps up his extravigance but is pushed to the utermost [*sic*] to get money is in hot water all the time. He appears to owe everybody, cannot appear on the plaza without being dunned on all sides, for my part I cannot see how he can keep going much longer.

You caution me to take care of myself, life, &c. This is the first instinct of nature. All I can say is I shall do my best to avoid all dainger or extra hazzard. I do not know what I am to do. I am now as it were in a complete Prison. I will not hunt up any difficulties but if they are crowded on to me, I must do the best I can to defend myself. I have no recreations. The balance of the time I remain here I do not count as living, it is only <u>staying</u>. This much I have to be thankfull for, I am in <u>excelent health</u>; getting fat & Lazy every day.

Letter no. 129, Kingsbury to Webb, Santa Fe, November 13, 1859

I am still without letters from you, I am at a loss to understand it, three letters are now due from you. I am sure you have written, I begin to fear that they have been carried through to California.

In my last I gave you several items of business and a full account of my settlement with Hoppin & Appel. You may be sure that this will all come right in the end. I have now to report settlement with

38. Webb had inquired, "Tell me who was killed in Santa Fe since I left?" Webb to Kingsbury, Hamden, CT, Sept. 23, 1859, MHS.

39. William Drew had married Francisca Sena in October 1857.

40. This was the estate of Manuel Alvarez, who died July 5, 1856. The heirs, to whom Kingsbury refers, were Eufracio, María, Bernadino, Matias, Pelago, Antonio, Atanacio, and Josefina. Santa Fe County Records, Direct Index to Deeds A–D, 1848-1934.

Magruder. I got very uneasy about that debt and the way he was
manovering [*sic*], and finally bought his farm for what he owed us. I
took it with the hope of saving ourselves there. He assures me that the
title is clear and perfect, and gives a Warantee deed. The deed is in my
name (to save signatures) I enclose it to you, also a full power of Atty.
to you, to dispose of it as circumstances m[a]y seem best. If your home
affairs are such as to permit you to leave, I would like to have you go
there and see what can be done with it. It cost us just the sum stated in
the deed. There is over 300 Acres in land besides the improvements.
Now I am satisfied that the place is worth all that it cost us & perhaps
more, but the trouble is to find a purchaser with the ready cash to buy
such a place. If you cannot go send the deed there at once that it may
be recorded. But if possible it is better for you to go there and see to it
yourself. Inclosed is a letter of introduction to Dr John F. Allen, who
has been Magruder's agent since he left there and knows all about the
place. This Mr Allen has had a Power of Atty and instructions from
Magruder for some time to sell the place and the proceeds to be
deposited with Doan King & Co. to our credit,—but up to last advices
from him it was still unsold and his advise to Mack was to hold on as
it was bound to increase in value. Now if it should be sold before you
get there then you will take the proceeds and pay ourselves and if there
be any surplus it goes to Mack.

In order to get this settlement with Mack, I was obliged to give
him a written obligation that I would resell to him the place any time
between now and the 1st of Jany 1862 for the same price. He paying
12% Interest on the amt. also Taxes, improvement & all repairs—and I
to allow him the rents that may be received from it. This obligation to
expire on the date above stated, and is only binding on me for the time
being provided the place is un-sold. The Amt. is this, it is sold to me
and I have full power to dispose of it at any moment as I please and
that moment it goes from my possession he has no further claim upon
me or any one else. It is his home place and he parts with it reluctantly,
and this reserve is made that in case he can in that time make the
money and I am unable to sell it, then he wants the privalidge [*sic*] of
buying it back & this is what I have granted him.

Now I have taken it to make our money and for no other object. I
want you to go there and see it. Sell it if possible. If I have paid to[o]
much for it, and by making a discount you can find a cash purchaser
make the loss at once and get clear of it. If it cannot be sold at present
leave it in the hands of some good man if this Mr Allen does not
please you give it in charge of some other person who will attend to it.
Have the taxes paid regular, and whatever rents we get over and above
the taxes let it go to keep the place in repair. These are only suggestions as they occur to me here, you on the spot would know much better what is best than I could imagine, you may find it a profitable

investment for the money just to let it lay, (whatever you do will be right and I shall be satisfied. The farm adjoines the town of Batesville Independence Co.—on White river a stream which I am told is navigable all the year,—and regular packets run there once or twice a week to Memphis. There is also Stage communication to St. Louis, Don't scold, it is the best I could do with Magruder, at all events we will not loose much on it, and by letting him go on we might loose the whole debt, so just make the best of it.

You will also find herewith Tom's Mail draft for quarter ending Sept. 30th 1859 on the El Paso route, for Four Thousand Sixty two 50/100 dollars ($4,062.50) On this draft I have advanced him $2,000.+ in cash to enable him to arrange matters here so that he could go to the States, so now the whole draft is ours. The balance we are to retain to cover what he owes us—if you have already got a certificate to cover this quarter all right if not you certainly can get it now on this draft. The Amt. of this draft, and the other certificate of $4,062.50 say $8,125.+ you are to hold on to as our money,—and when you get it use it as you please on your own private account. What other monies he gets from Mail Services he has a right to dispose of as he chooses, he wants to leave tomorrow by the Independence route, and will if there should be an escort allowed, which Col. Fontelroy [Fauntleroy] has promised. He will come direct to you and get you to assist him in his matters. They will Travel slow, and if you can go at once to Arkansas you will have time to return before he can get to you. Now about Tom's Money he is owing a goodeal here and will want to pay just as soon as he can. He says he will deposit what he gets with you and for me to pay it out here to save time before he gets back to Santa Fe. If he does this be carefull and instruct me how much I shall pay here, always reserving the $8,125.+ before mentioned in this letter as ours.

By this Mail I send to Doan King & Co. checks sufficient to meet our first freight note of $3,000.+ business is very dull this month, collections keep along pretty steady. By giving this $2,000+ to Tom, I may not be able to pay Messervy quite as soon as I intended, but, with ordinary luck I will soon have enough to pay him, and soon as the appropriation passes you will have a good sum in your hands, so as to be perfectly easy in your private matters. You remember the little bill I sold to Nat Macrae when you was here, well he has paid it promptly and I have sold him another small bill. Blumner is paying up very well.

I hope you are receiving all my letters regular. I will continue to write you each mail. Nothing more now.

P.S. Old Dr. Guba, had been sick with Asthma about two weeks, he was about attending to his business, and one evening last week while in his little store fell over on the floor and expired immediately.

Letter no. 130, Kingsbury to Webb, Santa Fe, November 19, 1859

I am now in receipt of yours of Oct 6th. I have rec'd all your letters except the last one mentioned that is the one of Sept 30th. Your little note of Aug 2nd from St Louis came duly to hand but there were other matters from St. Louis which I was anxious to hear from and as you did not mention one of them after you got to your home, I thought certainly that there must have been a full letter from St. Louis missing.—but I see now I have got all except that of Sept 30th. Mr Rose has rec'd the Grass Seed but not a word from you on the Subject. I still have no bill of those thing[s] you sent from St Louis for him. From the letter now before me I presume that the check for $5,000.+ was rec'd all safe and promptly paid. In a previous letter I wrote you all about my settlement with Hoppin & Apple [Appel] which I trust you have rec'd. In my last I wrote you about my settlement with Magruder having taken his farm for our debt, also sent you the deed and a Power of Atty. At the same time I also sent you T. F. Bowlers draft for the quarter ending Sept 30th 1859 on the El Paso route $4,062.50. This whole amt. now belongs to us and when you get the certificate or money you are to retain it as ours. Tom with his family got of[f] last Tuesday, goes by the Ind. route with the mail party under a military escort. They will get through safe but will not be able to travel fast. The Indians are still lurking about the road and troublesome, so that it is unsafe for a small party to attempt to cross.

I have again sold our property on Credit, this time I trust with a little better success than before. I have sold to Col. Fauntleroy for $10,000.+ on thousand cash in hand and the balance 9,000.+ payable on the first day of July next, with interest from date of sale at 6% per an. He taking immediate possession, and we paying $75.+ per month for our store so long as we want it. I have signed the deed to him, and have given him my bond that I would get the deed completed by you & Mrs Webb's signatures to deliver to him here on or before the 1st day of July next. I now enclose it in order to give you ample time to complete it before the commis[s]ioner of deeds for your State so that it may get back to me in time. His note for $9,000.+ is secured by a deed of trust to us on the same property, with power of Sale by giving 30 days notice, provided he does not meet and pay the same promptly with interest &c. From all that I can learn the Col. is a Man of Ample means and responsible, so that I aprehend not the least possiblity of a failure on his part. I have made this bargain believing that it will insure us the quickest mode of realizing our money on the property. I have tried every possible chance to sell it for Cash since you left, and am fully convinced that it will always be a difficult matter to find any one with that much cash in hand willing to pay it out for property. If I were so fortunate as to find one willing to pay our price, the money would look so big that he would at once back out. I have seen no chance favorable for a sale or anything approaching it except the hope of a trade with Gaspar Ortiz, he is a grand scamp & I put but little reliance in him. I could not consent to let him have it on credit and in order to trade with him we would have to wait untill he returns and then wait untill he could realize his means and after that be subject to all his notion and deli[n]quencies. I have no idea that he would come up with the cash and pay our price. If when he returns he finds that I could not sell it, and I go to him to buy, he would play off and want a discount of 1. or 2 Thousand.

In the sale I have now made if all goes right I am confident that we will get the money much sooner and surer than waiting and taking the chances with Ortiz, —and then if Ortiz should in the mean time change his notion, then I would be perfectly at a loss to find anyone to take it. It is no easy matter here to sell property of this value, and considering all things I have let it go again on the first fair offer I have had.

My sales so far this month have been very small. Parker's train got in a few days since. He brought freight for a new Jew house. They are straingers, have got the house Henry Mercure occupied. They have a large lot of goods and a good assortment. This outfit dampens my prospects considerable.

Rose keeps his a/c about the same that is pays just about as much as he takes. He has slip[p]ed up on his Salt outfit, that is fail[e]d to get the contract as others under-bid him. The Salt is still on hand and he may sell it to the one who got the contract. It is a great disapointment to him and us as it stands as he had intended to turn the money he got for it immediately over to us. There is about 12 or 15 hundred dollars worth, so we are kept out of this amt. untill he can sell it. He had intended to pay it on the March note. His house is full and doing a good business, at all events I think he will be able out of his house to pay us what he owes and also the Note in March, before he gives possession to his successors. He Takes nothing now except what the house actually requires. He understands that I am not to let him have our goods to sell to them on Credit—and if I have anything left for them they are to pay for it as they take the goods.

J. Hersch's a/c will be due on the 21st of this Month soon as I get a settlement with him I shall try to send you some funds for private use. This is all now.

[P.S.] How did that bar of Silver turn out that you took in? Do we loose on it or not? They are getting plenty here & I want to know if it is safe to take them at marked value.

I have had no further trouble with our Californian, he has kept sober since & appears to behave like a gentleman.[41] I do not know that

41. Webb was understandably concerned by Kingsbury's report of his encounter with the violent man from California, and advised him on the dangerous climate in Santa Fe and the best way to guard himself and their property: "You know my impressions in regard to the insecurity of human life when I was in Santa Fe. I did not know but these things appeared to me in an exaggerated form, as I had been so long absent, but I think not to any great extent. Those who were formerly in Santa Fe, have become by continued association more hardened and desperate, and the influx is from every part of the world, of the most desperate characters. New Mexico is now the place of resort of the worst characters. My advice is to have nothing to do with them. Don't cultivate their acquaintance, even for purposes of trade. We can get along without it. Of course I would not advise you to refuse to trade with any one who visits the store, but I would close all business arrangements which will bring them about. Take no deposits or orders which will place you in the position of friend or confidant. This was my reason for my advice in regard to deposits when I was in Santa Fe. I hope nothing serious will result from your encounter, and hereafter my advice is to cut all acquaintance of that class. Play no billiards, keep away from the fonda [Exchange Hotel] as much as possible and pursue such a reserved course as will be rather a barrier to the cultivating of your acquaintance." Webb to Kingsbury, Hamden, CT, Oct. 6, 1859, MHS.

he entertains any animosity toward either of us. His friends convinsed him that he was entirely to blame,—and so it rests. I have never spoken to him. I intended to say in that letter that the Grand Jury brought in <u>no</u> other inditements, that is that their whole time was occupied in investigating murder & asolt [assault] cases so that they had no time to take up gambeling or other crimes.

The little Judge B. is running a fast race, he continues to soak it like a fish, just as he started when you was here.[42] He has had several little fusses, and is loosing the little favorable impression that he started with. One night this week he had some high words with Lt. Julian May,[43] both under a high steam of Liquor. They finally got to blows no <u>weapons</u>, Lt May cuffed his face or in other words slapped his face—and as the little judge turned applied his boot to his posterior in a most violent man[n]er. He has not appeared on the Plaza since. I have heard some talk of a challenge but think it will all blow over though I am not certain. Fighting and quarreling is the order of the day. There is scarcely a fandango that does not break up in a row. This morning in open day light two Mexicans, Talisfer Salizar & Anto. Abati took a notion to shoot at one another right in the street near Hirsche's [Hersch's] Store. Three shots were fired, but I am told no one was injured or at least not serious. So it goes I do not know what to expect next.

Letter no. 131, Kingsbury to Webb, Santa Fe, November 27, 1859

Your little note of Nov 3rd is now received by it I see that you got mine of Sept 17th which contained a check for $500.+ for your private use, so I know that you got it safe. This is the last money I sent you up to the present except Toms mail draft for <u>$4,062.50</u> on El Paso route quarter ending Sept 30th 1859. The next three mails following that of Sept 17th were intercepted by the Indian troubles and all returned to this place and were afterwards sent forward by the "Overland route," which will account to you for the delay, since then I have sent all my letters that way. I have written you under the following dates, Sept 24th, Oct 1st, 22nd, Nov 6, 13 & 19. if you have all these you are fully acquainted with all the important items of our business. The last three were important Nov 6th with full a/c of settlement with Hoppin & Appel, Nov 13th purchase of Magruder's farm in Arkansas with deed, power of Atty and Toms mail draft, Nov 19th sale of our own property to Col Fauntleroy with deed for you to sign, I want you to acknowledge each and all the letters you get from me. Yours of Sept 30th is still missing & I fear it is lost would like for you to send me a duplicate, that of Oct 19th may yet come.

You can do nothing more about Tom's mail business untill he gets there, except perhaps to get a certificate to cover that last draft

42. Kirby Benedict, serving a four-year term as chief justice of the Supreme Court of the Territory of New Mexico since his appointment in May 1858, was a notorious drunk for much of his life and a man with an uncontrollable temper. Hunt, *Kirby Benedict*, 41-42, 184-85, 196, 199-200, 219-20, 223.

43. Lt. Julian May, a decorated veteran of the Mexican-American War, died on November 22, 1859. Heitman, *Historical Register*, 1:699.

mentioned in this letter. I have sent to Doan King & Co. $3,000.+ to take up our first freight note, and have taken up one here for $1,500.+ favor Dick Kitchen leaving still one for $4,500.+ payable at St. Louis Jany 23.26. I have not been able to collect our a/c from J. Hirsch [Hersch] yet, he has sold 1,000 Fanagers [fanegas] corn at $4.50 to Govt. with which he expects to pay us and as soon as it is delivered will turn the money over to us.

Business this month has been dull, dull, dull, and I am getting the blues. I am anxious to sell out but my stock is alltogether too heavy at present, and sales are so limited that it appears like an imposibillity [*sic*] to reduce it. The town is full of goods & judging from my present sales, I fear I cannot close out this winter, one thing looks well that is grain of all kinds is high, but on the other hand the crops are short and the high price is caused by its scarcity and not by any extra demand.

I can count safely on my collections to meet our last freight note, and in a short time will have enough to pay the $5,000.+ to Messervy. Thinking some ready money may assist you in your private operations, I now enclose to you for your own private use, Check No 90, dated Oct 1st 1859 at sight on the Asst. Treas. of the U.S. at New York for One Thousand ($1,000+) dollars drawn by J. L. Collins Supt. Ind. Affs. N. Mexico, payable to our order. which amt. I have charged to your private account—by observing the date of this Check, you may be surprised at my having it on hand so long. —let me explain, I received it in a settlement I made for Dr Steck, it is his money, I have held it for him as a deposit, and now send it to you knowing that I will be able to collect the amt. before he will want it. About the first of Jany I will get from Mr Rose drafts for Salaries of the different clerks in the Surveyors Genl. Office, amt'g to about $1,000.+ which I shall also send to you. They will be due and cash soon as you get them, so you see I am calculating to give you plenty of private funds. Of my collections I cannot complain, so far they are good and the prospect ahead is fair, but my sales are truly discouraging, especially as I had counted on fall sales to reduce the stock so that the Amt. would be in the reach of one man to take the balance in a lump. True Oct. footted up well and possibly Dec. may turn out better than I know anticipate, but this month has been so small I am ashamed to give you the figures, will wait till the next week so as to put in every cent I can, and if possible make it appear respectable. I am in hopes to get your account current with settlement of all the New Haven notes before I take off another trial balance, so that these items may appear closed on the books.

I trust you have rec'd all my previous letters, I do not remember anything of importance that I have omitted to communicate to you. For your satisfaction I shall continue to write each week if it is only a few lines, and try to post you in every matter. Kind regards to Mrs W. also the Father W. & his lady. Do you hear anything from José.

Letter no. 132, Kingsbury to Webb, Santa Fe, December 3, 1859

Dear Sir, I have still to report that I have no letter from you. I have a letter from Sisters at home as late as Nov 12th and it really seems to[o] bad that I do not get your letters. It breaks into my calculations very much in not getting regular replies from you.

By last mail I sent you check #90. on the Asst. Treas. at U.S. drawn by J. L. Collins Supt. of Ind. Affs. for One Thousand dollars, for your private use which I hope you have received. My Sales the last month Amt. to $3,600. —making gross sales since May 1st $56,000.+. I estimate my stock on hand now at $22 to $23,000.+ and think it will hold out fully. I shall do my best to reduce this amt. and if possible close it all out before Spring Trains arrive. If I cannot I see no way but to take it patiently and sell as I can, one thing certain I do not intend to crowd Sales unless I see a fair prospect to collect the money when it comes due. If I find I cannot close out, my intention now is to take a smaller house in the Spring, and moove, where the goods will be more compact and manage[a]ble. My assorted goods do not trouble me, it is only the Liq[u]ors and other goods bought for the Exchange. This is bound to be slow stock, and it will only go as I feel authorized to trust them with it, money being so very scarce here, reduces very materially their receipts, and consequently they are not requiring so much of our goods as last year. My Collections for November amt. to $5,300.+ and $1,000.+ on Real Estate, making $6,300.+ I have now on hand over and above all deposits just enough to meet our last freight note. Soon as Joe Hirsch [Hersch], pays his a/c it will give me the means to pay Messervy in full, and I can confidently expect to get this settlement some time during this month and shall apply it to that end. We will then be entirely out of debt, and all my collections from that time, I shall forward without delay to you. I aim now to be able to send you between this and the time Col. Fauntleroy's note will be realized the whole of your surplus capitol, so you may begin to look for a profitable and safe place to invest it.

I read this morning several letters of introduction written by Judge Benedict to Douglas and other members of Congress for Tom B.[44] They will be sent by Frank to Tom at Washington. They read well and if Tom will take advantage of them they cannot fail to assist him. Stir him up and try to make him fill what those letters represent him to be. Tell Tom he must have courage and confidence in his cause and not be bashfull with those big men, to be open and frank will help him, warn him not to trust too much in Watts and his fine promises.

My sales the last day or two have started off fair and I am in hopes to make a good month of it. Spring bills are coming due, and I shall push collections all I can. Do write me full and long letters.

44. Kirby Benedict, originally from Illinois, knew Stephen Douglas. Hunt, *Kirby Benedict*, 11, 24. Bowler's contract for mail service over the El Paso and Santa Fe route was annulled about this time and he wanted to travel to Washington to reinstate it. In April 1860 he "appealed for damages. The committee reported in his favor, but in January, 1873, the decision was reversed." Conkling and Conkling, *The Butterfield Overland Mail*, 1:91-92.

P.S. I am no hand at writing private matters, and shall not attempt it now, I think of nothing really important. [E]very thing appears to be mooving on at the old Santa Fe speed. Weirick is getting in the notion of making a visit home this winter. Mrs Houghton presented the Judge with a fine son one night this week, 9 ½ lbs.—all doing well, the Judge is delighted at its being a boy.

Did you get Ellison's letter?

The Legislature will meet on Monday. There is all sorts of man-overing for the petty offices, the town is full of straingers, and may help retail sales a little. I can furnish the Secretary [A. M. Jackson] with everything we may have that he will want. It is not much but all helps.

Letter no. 133, Kingsbury to Webb, Santa Fe, December 11, 1859

Yours of Nov 15th with duplicates of Sept. 8 & Oct. 8th is now received. These two I had already red'c. and acknowledge but yours of <u>Sept 30th Oct 19th & 25th are still behind.</u>

I am much relieved to get this late date from you and know that my letters are getting to you although a long time on the road. When you get them all you will find that I have posted you in all matters as fast as they develope themselves. In my last of the 3rd inst. I gave you the result of transactions for Nov. I am well pleased with the footing, and I think you cannot fail to be satisfied. It is unnessary for me to repeat that I have not lost sight of those hard cases you mention. No I never allow an opportunity to pass where I can spur them up without doing it, and if I do not mention to you particular cases it is because I have nothing favorable to report, when I accomplish anything in the way of a settlement or partial payment it is my first object to notify you that you may be relieved of any anxiety you may have entertained. By my silence you must not think that I am overlooking these nest eggs. My whole energies are constantly at work not only on these old cases but in trying to avoid new ones. Look at the following figures and I know you must be pleased with the result of my labors. On the first day of May last our outstanding accounts amt'd to $44,000.

To Dec 1st I have sold to the Amt of   <u>$56,000.</u>

                                                                    100,000.

Amt of outstanding a/c's Dec 1st   <u>$40,500.</u>
                         Showing $59,500.

which is $3,500 collection over and above the amt of sales for that period. In this calculation I count the two drafts of Bowler $8,125,—& the debt of Magruder $4,250. as collected. Much of the $40,500. now outstanding are bills of late date and not yet due. Hirsches' [Hersch's] a/c will be paid soon which will reduce this sum $5,000.+ and then it will leave very pretty figures.

I do not write this for you to think for a moment that my dander is raised by your letter, it is only with a view to post you more fully as to the real state of our business matters. You have the figures in your own hands with which you can easily prove the above statement.

For my every day guide I have our whole business before my eyes. the gross figures corrected every month and consequently have them always at my fingers ends, in this way nothing can escape my attention.

For the last 18 years my whole study has been centered on business. In fact I don't know anything else. I often wonder what I will do when I get through here, I shall be lost for a while at least.

You state that Jo[s]é had come on. I do hope that he has sown all his wild otes, turned over a new leaf, and determined to be a <u>man</u>. When he left here on adjusting his a/c he had to his credit in our hands a balance of <u>$350.+</u> since then I have paid for him to Dr Kavanaugh $25.+ and for forwarding his Trunks $4., leaving still to his credit <u>$321.00</u> Three hundred and twenty one dollars. Now it strikes me that it would be more to his advantage to have this money where it would be bringing him something in the way of interest, and I would suggest that if he has no immediate use for it, that you place it for him in some safe place where it would be earning something for him. I enclose herewith the following checks to give you the means to pay him. viz. Check No 1236, dated Santa Fe N.M. Oct 31st 1859. at sight on the Asst. Treas of the U.S. at New York, for Two hundred and twenty two 50/100 dollars (<u>$222.50</u>) drawn by John B. Grayson Bvt. Lt. Col. & C.S. payable to the order of Lt. M.S. Davis USA. and by him endorsed to our order. <u>Also</u> Check No. 8, dated Santa Fe N.M. Dec 2nd 1859. at sight on Messrs Clark Dodge & Co. at New York for One hundred dollars, <u>$100.</u> drawn by David Hood payable to the order of L. J. Rose and by him endorsed to our order. Making <u>$322.50</u> which amt. I have charged to your agent a/c, and you will please take it up and account for it there. Send this check of <u>Hood</u>, on for collection immediately and let me know if it is paid promptly. He is a new banker who has established himself here and is putting his check on the community pretty heavy, and I wish to know, whether it will answer to take them in my collections or not.

You will also find a bill against José in favor of Geo. Carter. This is Geo. the Barber, and he claims that it is a just a/c which José left unpaid. Now if José acknowledges this a/c and wishes to pay it deduct the amt. from the balance due him and instruct me to pay the same here for him. I sent José['s] Trunks to him a long time ago, and have felt quite uneasy about them. If he has received them he ought to let me know it.

4 ½ P.M. We have just got a coach through from Independence bringing 4 back Mails, —by it I have got yours of Oct 19th & 25th—

leaving that of Sept 30th still behind. I now count this as lost and if you have not already sent me a copy of it, I wish you would do so now. I will attend to your requests. Piñeones [piñon nuts] are not to be had this year. Vigil says he has got the Wheat but it is at his house yet. Tom is on the look out for your Onion Seed. I will see Geo. about the other matter and try to get him to write to go next week. I hope you will continue to write every week and if I omitt anything that you want to know about just jog my memory with it.

[P.S.] I forgot to tell you that the fuss between the little Judge & Lt May all blowed over, the Judge keept out of sigh[t] a few days and while May remained here, he keeped up a big spree. He finally left for Union and died at Moores house in Tecolote, that is I mean <u>Lt. May died,</u> he went off very much the same as poor Hugh did, they call it appaplexy [*sic*]. The little J. Has keeped himself very scarce since not showed himself up town more than once or twise, I understand now that he has gone to Taos.

This mail party report that they had a fight with the Indians at Cold Spring they had an escort, killed <u>6 Ind</u>. We can expect no security on this route for the present. I shall continue to send everything by the "Overland."

Letter no. 134, Kingsbury to Webb, Santa Fe, December 17, 1859

I sent you last week a letter as usual and in it inclosed two checks amt'g to <u>$322.50</u> for the express purpose of giving you the means to pay José the amt. he had deposited here. —which letter I hope you have rec'd before this. I have again to say that I am without advises from you since my last. I have nothing in particular to communicate for the week just closed. Business so far this month mooves on slowly Sales pretty fair, but collections moderate, I shall send by next mail, $4,500.+ to St Louis to take up our last freight note there. It will then give it 1 month to get there and it should reach there in ample time to meet the note at maturity, —after this we have nothing more to pay in St. Louis, and I want your advise about remittances. Suppose in my collections I get drafts on St. Louis, what shall I do with them. Shall I send them direct to you and let you send them back for collection, can you do this without paying premium, or would you prefer for me to send them to St Louis there to be collected and afterward the amts. sent forward to you—perhaps Doan King & Co would like to receive the money in St Louis and let their house in N. York pay it to you, write me on this subject and let me know how I shall manage it to best please you. Soon as I can collect José's a/c I intend to send it to Messervy to close up with him, and after that all my collections will be for your exclusive benefit, and I shall loose no time, in sending forward. You can safely count on soon having plenty of funds. When you are in Washington, I wish you would call on Mr Faunt and enquire about that note of mine against Maj. E. H. Wingfield the old indian agt. which you left with him a long time ago for collection, if it has been paid receive the money, if it has not, get the note and send it to me, don't forget this I want it taken up and out of the way as it has my endorsement on it.

I mentioned your request to Geo. and tried to get him to write you on the subject, he replies that had you come to him according to agreement he would have told you all he knew about it, but that he <u>could not want</u> to put it on paper. So I sup[p]ose you must learn from some other source how to cure your horse.

[P.S.] The Gazette is not published regular, I have sent you copies as they come out & will continue to. I send you today a copy of the Gov's. message. The Legislature has got fully under way. O. P. Hovey has been elected <u>public Printer</u> he represents that he will have a new press and all the nessisery materials here in the Spring.

We are just in the midst of our gay season & the usual compliment of Fandangoes and rows are in full force.

Letter no. 135, Kingsbury to Webb, Santa Fe, December 24, 1859

Yours of Nov 30th is now before me. I do not send you duplicate of my letters for the reason that I firmly believe that you have got them all by this time, and if so you know already the reason those missing were so long on the road. I wrote you last week that I should by this mail send <u>$4,500.+</u> to Doan King & Co to meet our last freight. I have just now closed the letter to them covering remittances for $4,511.55. Also closed one to Messervy covering remittances for $5,266.25 which with the balance of $58.75 which he owes us on open a/c will make <u>$5,325.+</u> which I send him to cancel the balance on our note together with the interest on same in full to Feby 1st 1860. Write him and enquire if he gets this letter in due time.

I have had a settlement with Hersch and collected all he owed except a balance of $425.+. I have also collected from Old Chat, the full amt. of the bill he bought last summer after you left. I was a little disa-pointed in not getting your account current, I shall now wait another month before I take off my Trial Balance.

Next week I shall try to fix up a remittance for you. If I do not then, I shall certainly the week following so you may be sure of getting plenty of money soon. Under date of Nov 27th I sent you a check for <u>$1,000+</u> for your private use which I hope you have already received. All my collections from this on shall be for you im[m]ediate benefit. I wrote you some time ago that at the first of Jany, I would get from Mr

Rose the Salaries for clerks in the Surveyor Generals Office, well I am informed that two of them (that is their a/c's) will go on by this mail. One of T. H. Means and one of Philip Smith each for $333. and some cents. These you will or should receive immediately direct from the Dept at Washington. The other is D. J. Miller's of the same amt. and I am told he cannot get his papers off untill next week now as you receive these three sums I wish you to acknowledge them <u>seperately</u> so that I may give Mr Rose Credit and he be able to settle with the parties here.

Mr Rose has had to good luck to get the Contract to furnish Govt. with 200 head of Beef Cattle. They will amt. to something near $5,000.+ he has three weeks time to deliver them in, so we may expect to get some money there at the end of that time. He also has a good prospect of getting his Salt in though at a very low price, so low that he makes nothing on it, but is willing to let it go, only to get it into money. <u>I think</u> the parties will take it at his offer if so we will get this money also. I have a disagreable job on hand for Monday. I am about to get out an attachment against our old friend [G. A. J.] Noel he owes us about ($400.00) Four hundred. He went into partnership last summer with a man by the name of Maxwell at San Miguel now this fellow Maxwell is about to play the rascal and by at[t]aching them I can secure our debt. I should do it today but Ashurst and the whole town is on a Christmas spree and I must wait for him to get sober.

I have received from Hoppin & Appel the Mortgage securing the balance of $1300.+ all properly signed and recorded. Rosenstein came up in the stage this evening and I am in hopes to get something from him. My collections will foot up well this month, I will give you the figures next week.

This is all now.

[P.S.] Two men were froze to death this week while on the road from Taos to Neos[h]o, when I tell you who they are I think you will remember them. One was old man Barry Clerk of the Rio Ar[r]iba Court for several years. The other was Printer Davis, a little Red headed fellow who was formerly partner with Hovey in the printing business, he afterwards went to California with that party which left here in '52 to hunt gold on the Gila river. They both left Taos drunk and it is suposed they got stuped [stupid] and got off their Animals, layed down & then froze. They were found together the Animals that they were riding came back to town. Whiskey will get them all after a while. Kavanaugh is drinking very hard if he does not hold up he will go off as poor Hugh did. Geo Estes takes all that he can chaimber, there are lots more in the same fix.

When shall I get out of this hole of disipation.

13.

"Clear of our goods just in time"

Winter and Spring 1860

Letters 136–160

With their real estate sold to Col. Thomas Fauntleroy in November 1859, Kingsbury focused his attention on collecting bills and disposing of the remainder of the inventory. Both tasks seemed especially difficult because New Mexico suffered from a shortage of hard currency. Thus, he complained to Webb, "the most trying and vexatious part of our whole business is now before me."[1] "True money," as Kingsbury put it, had become "very scarce."[2]

The proposed military reorganization probably contributed to New Mexico's constricting cash flow. Col. Fauntleroy had submitted a comprehensive plan incorporating many of the suggestions of his predecessors as well as his own ideas on how to meet the demands of an increasingly less isolated territory with efficiency and economy. Although reorganization involved greater government expenditure, the uncertainty it caused most likely produced sufficient economic anxiety to make money tight.[3] As Webb pointed out, "All these things will create confusion, and have a tendency to embarrass trade, but if all parties will keep cool, and wait until affairs get settle down, I am still of opinion that a large and profitable business will be done this year."[4]

The drought also affected business. It had begun in 1859 and caused corn prices to double by 1860.[5] Kingsbury noted that corn and wheat crops had failed in the Rio Abajo, the area south of Santa Fe, leaving farmers there with nothing to sell and no income with which to buy.[6]

Given the shortage of cash, Kingsbury had trouble collecting old bills and he became increasingly reluctant to sell more goods on credit. His disenchantment with his debtors and with New Mexico grew accordingly. "Honest men are so scarce," he told Webb, "they might . . . bear a premium but everything else is below par."[7] As usual Kingsbury reported repeatedly that business was "dull," but now he was convinced that he and Webb were getting out of the business just in time.

Once again Kingsbury's pessimism proved excessive. By March 31 he had reduced the inventory to $9,500 (it stood at $22,000 to $23,000 in late November), and in early April he sold much of that inventory to

1. Kingsbury to Webb, Santa Fe, May 6, 1860, MHS.
2. Ibid., Apr. 21, 1860, MHS.
3. Frazer, *Forts and Supplies*, 148-51.
4. Webb to Kingsbury, Hamden, CT, May 17, 1860, MHS.
5. Frazer, *Forts and Supplies*, 154.
6. Kingsbury to Webb, Santa Fe, May 6, 1860, MHS.
7. Ibid., Apr. 7, 1860, MHS.

Simon Delgado.[8] Kingsbury retained some $2,500 worth of liquor, purchased for resale to the Exchange Hotel, and the "irons" for the statehouse, whose construction halted. The statehouse remained unfinished until 1889.[9]

Kingsbury had reduced his inventory because he needed to move into smaller quarters. In February, Fauntleroy had leased Kingsbury's store to the firm of Seligman and Clever, effective June 1.[10] Kingsbury had to sell his inventory or move it before then. Luckily, he had made the sale to Delgado. At the end of April he sold some of his excess furniture and moved into two rooms across from the Exchange Hotel. One room served as his office and sleeping quarters; the other housed the liquor and the statehouse irons, the firm's white elephant. Whereas the old store had cost $75 a month, the new one cost $10. Kingsbury would be money ahead, for he planned to stay for at least another year.

Although he had disposed of most of the inventory, Kingsbury had yet to collect payment. Delgado had made his purchases on credit. He was to pay $5,000 on January 1, 1861, and the balance—the exact amount still awaiting determination—on April 1, 1861.[11] Kingsbury also needed to dog other creditors, traveling that spring below Albuquerque, as far as Los Lunas, to collect debts. Tidying up these loose ends would, he thought, take another year. He did not believe he could leave Santa Fe before May 1861,[12] but the end was now more clearly in sight.

Meanwhile, Kingsbury's business reports to Webb continued to reveal the saga of life in the Anglo-American community in Santa Fe. War with Navajos loomed on the western horizon even as Comanches and Kiowas continued raids to the east; almost three hundred New Mexico citizens lost their lives to Indian attacks in 1859 and 1860.[13] Kingsbury apparently found relief from bouts of boredom with stories of his countrymen's drunkenness, gambling, violence, an occasional homicide, and a spectacular fire that exploded a keg of gunpowder in the storeroom of a store that Kingsbury & Webb had occupied earlier. The store and its contents were completely destroyed. The episode led some of the citizenry to plan to form a fire department and to find safer ways to store gunpowder. Meanwhile, Kingsbury continued to regard Santa Fe as a disorderly frontier town, with too much whiskey and fighting, and too many murders, hot tempers, and swindlers. One Louis Dorrence was sentenced to receive thirty lashes on the main plaza for stealing a calf valued at $8. Someone broke into the courthouse and stole the indictments that a grand jury had handed down against a number of gamblers. "There being no inditments [*sic*] in court against the parties they will all go free," Kingsbury explained to Webb.[14]

∼

8. Ibid., Apr. 14, 1860, MHS.
9. Sze and Spears, *Santa Fe Historic Neighborhood Study*, 46.
10. Kingsbury to Webb, Santa Fe, Mar. 3, 1860, MHS.
11. Ibid., Apr. 7, 1860, MHS.
12. Ibid., Apr. 14, 1860, MHS.
13. Horn, *New Mexico's Troubled Years*, 80.
14 Kingsbury to Webb, Santa Fe, Mar. 10, 1860, MHS.

Letter no. 136, Kingsbury to Webb, January 1, 1860

I have again to report that I am without advices from you since my last. In that I notified you that I had sent to Doan King & Co $4,511.55 and to Mr. Messervy $5,266.25. These two sums closes all the debts of the firm that I know of. In the same letter I informed you that you would receive direct from Washington two quarters salaries of $333. and cents each, one T. H. Means and the other Philip Smith. These I hope you have already got. The other one I spoke of that is D. J. Millers you will not get. Whiting made out the papers and sent them off directing that a draft for the amt. be sent direct to Mr. [Leonard] Rose, at this place so you will not get this for the present.

Mr. Rose starts this morning for Ft. Union for the purpose to delivering his Beef Cattle.

I got out the Attachment against G. A. J. Noel and have suspended the levy for 15 days, with the understanding that they will take Corn to Albuquerque and turn it into Cash and with the money pay us. If we get the full amt. of our debt in 15 days I am to dismiss the Attachment, if not then the Sheriff will go on with the papers in his hands and make what he can out of them. I believe however the money will be paid within the time al[l]owed, & we will have no further trouble in the matter.

Rosenstein paid $1,500.+ some time ago, said he had nothing for me this trip, but that I must wait untill he comes up again when he would settle all.

My sales for the month of Dec. Amt. to $5,450.+ Collections for the same time $11,000.+ This leaves me a surplus and I have put it into checks and send the same herewith to you as follows viz—Check No. 356 dated Santa Fe N. M. No 22nd 1859. at sight on the Asst. Treas. of the U.S. at New York for One hundred dollars, drawn by J. L. Donaldson A. Q. M. payable to the order of Lt. L. W. O'Bannon A. A. Q. M. by him endorsed to us. $100.00

Also Check No. 357 of the same tenor &
Date for One hundred dollars   100.00
Also Check No. 366, of the same tenor &
date for Two hundred and fifty dollars   250.00
Also Check No. 164 dated Albuquerque N. M.
Nov. 27th 1859, at sight on the Asst.
Treas. of the U.S. at New York, for
Five Hundred dollars, drawn by James
Longstreet[15] Pay Master U.S.A. payable
to the order of Lt. R. V. Bonneau and
by him endorsed to our order.   500.00
                                                                        $950.00

Also Check No. 167 of the same effect

15. Although James Longstreet is only mentioned in passing, he merits identification because of his subsequent role in the Confederate army, where he served as a lieutenant general and became known as "Lee's Warhorse."

and date for Three hundred dollars   300.00
<u>Also</u> Check No. 26, dated Santa Fe New
Mexico Dec. 7th 1859 at sight on the
Asst. Treas. of the U.S. at New York
for Five hundred dollars, drawn by
Alex. M. Jackson Secty of Territory
of New Mexico, payable to order of
Joseph Cummings & by him endorsed
to our order   500.00
<u>Also</u> Check No. 443, dated Santa Fe
N.M. January 1st 1860, at sight on
the Asst. Treas. of the U.S. at New
York for Thirty two hundred and fifty
dollars, drawn by J. L. Donaldson
on A.Q.M. payable to our order   <u>3,250.00</u>
    Making in all $5,000.00

Which amount I have charged on our books to your Stock a/c,—
and you will please receive it as a portion of your original capital.

Soon as my collections will permit I shall send you another round
sum. I don't want to send you little driblets, and when I get enough for
a respectable remittance will send it. I think now I shall be able to get
enough to you to cover your present wants and meet your farm note,
without relying upon anything from Tom's papers. However his papers
are good that is the two quarters on El Paso route <u>$8,125.00</u> and you
certainly should get the handling of this money soon. Don't forget to
advise me soon as you get it.

I am really an[n]oyed at not getting regular replies from you, I
know you must write but from some cause the letters do not come
promptly.

By the mail that came yesterday I have a letter from Doan King &
Co. stating that mine to them of 12th Nov. covering remittances of
<u>$3,0021.99</u> to meet the first freight note had been duly received. So I
know by this that the mail got through safe which took the papers for
you conserning the purchase of Magruder's farm. I trust you may have
received them in due time. After paying our Notes in St. Louis, Doan
King & Co. will have in their hands to our credit, somewhere between
$40 or $50.+. Now if we owe any little bills there that will come within
this sum, you can instruct them to pay the same.

I think of nothing more now and will close for the present, wishing
you a happy New Year.

Letter no. 137, Kingsbury to Webb, Santa Fe, January 8, 1860

I have now the pleasure to acknowledge receipt of yours of Dec.
7th. I am much relieved to know that you are going to Batesville

[Arkansas], and shall look with much interest for your report from there, to know how you find matters. In reply to your question, I would reply that it is fully understood that in case the place is sold before we get possession he is to be credited with what his agent sold it for be it more or less. If more than $4,250.+ he is to have the balance and if less he will still owe us the deficiency but I fear there is no such good luck for us as to find it sold. I trust you will give yourself time to examine into the matter in all particulars, and be fully posted before you leave the place. Two of the town lots which are reserved, are deeded to his wife, by this I am led to believe that she can have no further lein on the balance, but you will know all long before this. Tom turned over to us 4 notes of Rose's all fully secured both by the personal Effects at the Exchange & the real Estate at Des Moine. One note is already paid, & one more will be paid before the property here is turned over. The mortgage still holds good on this property & by this sale & transfer does not lessen its validity in any particular as long as I can find the property the mortgage holds good even if it passes through a dozen hands. There is no danger of our getting further implicated with Tom. I shall go no further than your letters and instructions justify me. I have tried to explain to you fully just how it stands and think you must understand it. If he deposits money with you, you are to notify me of the amt. and I will pay the same out here under his instructions. If he does not deposit any with you then I pay nothing here. When Rose's notes are paid, and you get the $8,125+ for mail service, then we are fully covered for all Tom owes us, and this closes our risk with him.

When you get home, I wish you would take an hour and devote it to my letters. Take each one up carefully and read them through, and you will find I have guarded every point and there is no danger of our getting further in with him if you follow what I have written.

You have not replied to my letters fully. I suppose if was because you wrote in a hurry. Did you send that draft back to St. Vrain? Did you get the certificate for mail service for the last quarter Sept. 30th '59 before the draft got to you? And is it sure now?

I was forced to go on with the attachment against Noel at San Miguel. The levy was made and they gave security in twice the amt: that the property should be forthcoming at the next term of court, which is in March. So the matter stands for the present.

I think you now must feel entirely relieved in regard to funds for your private affairs. By last mail I sent you checks on New York amt.g to $5,000.+ which I trust you have received. Soon as I can get in any more money I shall send it. At all events by the end of Feby. or 1st March I will make up a remittance for you. So you may now rest easy. I have nothing favorable this week to report in the way of business, all quiet and very dull. In fact I have done nothing but sit and hold the

lines, am just where I started. I expect Mr. Rose back in a few days and
hope in next letter can report some receipts from him.

I have got that Old Note against Merrill settled by taking 50 cents
on the dollar. We have some luck yet. If I could only summon sufficient patience I believe I can bring everything out streight & to your
entire satisfaction. We shall see in time.

Letter no. 138, Kingsbury to Webb, Santa Fe, January 15, 1860

I wrote you by last mail, since then I have nothing from you. I am
looking anxiously for your next letter as I hope to hear all about how
you find the Arkansas Farm. Well the presant month is half gone and I
have nothing favorable to report in the way of business. Everything is
as dull as it can be. My sales are very small, money is very scarce, and it
is really hard times with the people. I never saw it so hard to collect
little bills. I thought I had a good excuse in urging these little matters
through, it being the first of the year, but so far for all my work with
them I have hardly got paid for shoe leather. I have frequent applications every day to <u>Loan</u>, in sums of $1 up. They come and say they
must & will have it, excuses on my part will not satisfy the hungry
wolves. I am compeled to deny them in the plainest terms and actualy
quarrel to keep what I have got. If something does not turn up to
relieve money mattters I do not know what will become of the Territory. I am really afraid to sell goods anymore on credit. They [*sic*] way
things look now we cannot be to[o] thankful that we are ready to quit,
and above all that we are having no more goods coming to put
through. No I am every day more & more convinced that we have not
commenced this winding up to[o] soon. I only wish I could see my
way out of the woods now. We have a large amt. at stake in the Territory and I assure you it will be no easy job to get it in.[16]

Mr. Rose has turned in his cattle and got the money for them. He
has paid me out of it $2,500, + $2,000 on the March note and $500 on
open account. He has finally got clear of his salt by selling it on credit
to July 1st with Moore & Rees as security.

Joe Hersch has sold all his goods in store to his two Nephews in a
lump for <u>$15,000</u> on one year credit. Rents them his store for 1 year at
$25 per month. They have now possession, and Joe has a little office.
Gives his whole time to his mill and to closing up. What his next
moove will be I cannot say. He talks of taking his train in by the way
of Pike's Peak and to load with groceries here to take to that place.
Whiting just now tells me that the Dept. have established a new rule.
That is that they will not issue Warrants for salaries, except in the
name of the person who performed the service. If this is so then I
must get Power's of Atty. for you to endorse and receipt thoes two

16. See intoduction to chapter 12.

salary warrants or you will have to send them to me to have them endorsed here.

I won't write any more now. I am in a bad humor anyhow. I have been disapointed in nearly all I have undertaken to do since the month came in.

P.S. They have introduced a set of Resolutions in the Counsil against Judge Benedict denouncing him as an habitual drunkard, being drunk in the bench and asleep while lawyers were addressing him, with sundry other charges, and carried them by 8 votes to 4. This is a bad lick at the Judge's dignity and the worst of it is that it is too true.[17]

Letter no. 139, Kingsbury to Webb, January 21, 1860

I have nothing particular or encouraging to write, every thing is as dull as it can be, and only send a few lines now to keep my promise good that I would write every week. By the mail of today I have the pleasure to acknowledge receipt of yours of Dec. 27th containing deed to Col. Fauntleroy all safe. There was no special hurry with this document, but I am glad to get it and know that you are satisfied with the sale. With regard to the Magruder matter, I have still considerable anxiety and should have felt much easier if you could have gone there at once,[18] as it is I fear that you will miss Tom and in your delay in getting to Batesville may make a great difference in that business. However I hope for the best, and trust you may find all right there. You state that you are going by the way of Washington. I trust that while there you may have the good luck to secure a certificate for that last mail draft of Tom's, and that your next letter will bring me the good news.

My collections this month have not been near as good as I would like. Still they continue to come in slow & I want to send you another remittance of $5,000. and will just as soon as I can get the amt. together. I still hope by the end of this month to be able to do it, shall strain every point to do it. Should Col. Collins get a deposit at New York I may anticipate a little and send you a check next week. One good thing we are out of debt, and what is due us is our own. I can see far enough ahead to know that I can supply all your wants and you can rest easy relying that I will send you funds just as fast as I can get it in.

I have nothing more now and will close.

P.S. You ask "has Capt. & family come to the States yet?" Who do you mean? I understand it must be Capt. Shoemaker, if so, he went sometime ago. I do not know where he is now. He left 3 of the daughters here with Houghton's family. Maj. Fry is <u>still</u> here, says nothing about going in.

17. According to Webb, who expressed sorrow that "Benedict is behaving himself so badly," news of the judge's predicament was "in all the papers." Webb to Kingsbury, New Haven, CT, Feb. 16, 1860, MHS. Benedict's biographer does not mention this episode, but does describe a successful campaign to block his reappointment for the same reasons in 1865. Hunt, *Kirby Benedict*, 183-90. See Kingsbury to Webb, Santa Fe, Apr. 7, 1860, MHS.

18. Webb had postponed his trip to Arkansas in the hopes of seeing Tom Bowler when he came east. Webb to Kingsbury, Hamden, CT, Dec. 27, 1859, MHS.

Letter no. 140, Kingsbury to Webb, Santa Fe, January 29, 1860

I am now in receipt of yours of 1st inst. written while at Washington. I am glad to know that you have obtained the certificate all right.

I sent you a few lines last week, but nothing important, and at this time I am still dry of news, business still continues exceedingly dull. I have made out to get together the sum I wanted to send to you and herewith enclose the following, viz., Check No. 89. dated Santa Fe N.M. October 1st 1859 at sight on the Asst. Treas. of the U. S. at New York for One Thousand dollars, drawn by J. L. Collins Supt. Ind. Aff. N. Mexico payable to our order, 1,000.00. Also, Check No. 482, dated Santa Fe. N.M. January 29th 1860, at sight on the Asst. Treas. of the U. S. at New York for Four Thousand dollars, drawn by J. L. Donaldson A.Q.M. payable to our order, $4,000.00.

Making in all $5,000.00, Which amt: I have charged to your stock account, and you will please receive it as another remittance or portion of your Original Capital. Send them to be collected at once and let me know when you are in receipt of the specie. I shall take off Trial Balance to Feby 1st and hope to have it all corrected to send to you by next mail. You will then see how all things stand on our books.

You will remember that Tom's note to us is drawing Interest and I shall want to know when you realize the actual money on these certificates, so that I can keep the interest account correct with him. I will do my best to keep everything secure & safe at the Exchange.

Nothing more now.

Letter no. 141, Kingsbury to Webb, Santa Fe, February 5, 1860

Dear Sir, My last from you was of Jany 1st from Washington to which I replied last week, at which time I sent you two Checks on the Asst. Treas. at N.Y.—one No. 89 drawn by J. L. Collins Supt. Ind. Aff. N.M. for $1,000.+ and one No 482 drawn by J. L. Donaldson A.Q.M. for $4,000.+ in all $5,000.+, which amount I trust you have received all safe.

Business for the month of Jany. proved very dull. My sales only amt. to ($1,225.+) One thousand two hundred and twenty five dollars. Collections for the same time amt: to $5,200.+

According to promise in my last I now enclose Trial Balance from our books showing the exact state of all accounts up to Feby 1st. Since it was taken off I have collected from Mr. Rose $1,000.+ which reduces his balance that much. I think I will be able to collect well this month, but with regard to sales it looks exceedingly gloomy just now. I wrote you some time ago that Weirick was thinking of going to the State[s]. He finally determined to go and left yesterday with [Jacob] Amberg's mule train. He takes with him a small box for you, containing the

Onion seed and wheat from Mr. [Donaciano] Vigil, also your bundles of private papers. They are all packed in a soap box. He will take it as far as St. Louis & there turn it over to Adam's Exp.

I still have Talisford [Talisforo] with me and if business is not more lively I shall try to get along without any further assistance.

[missing page] Henry Oneil, H. Mercure, Dr. Kavanaugh, &c. &c. are the sufferers. All the loose men about town and we have a large number of them are flat broke. I never saw at one time here so many desperatoes [sic]. They somehow manage to keep themselves in Whiskey and consequently fighting & quarreling all the time. Last night at a bile [baile] in Ivers [Lt. J. C. Ives?] house Joe Batesell (you may remember him. On the 4th of July he [k]nocked old [Lt. Julien] May down and pounded him right in front of the store) was cut with a knife by another American and expired immediately. A few weeks ago Rogers who was running Hirsche's [Hersch's] mill shot a Mexican in Joe's store blowing the whole top of his head off. He fell like a leaf. Rogers was allowed to give bail & has since run off leaving his securities to suffer. The young quails are to[o] numerous for me to attempt to state them.

The Hon. Legislature have got through their labors for this session. [Levi] Keithley was speaker of the House. He introduced a bill to repeal the Slave law which was past the session before, & it kicked up a big fuss. There was strong talk of Tar & feathers &c. Turned him out of his chair and finally compeled him to resign altogether and leave town.[19]

Letter no. 142, Kingsbury to Webb, Santa Fe, February 12, 1860

I sent you a few lines under date of the 5th inst., and enclosed Trial Balance of our books up to Feby. 1st. The mail arrived last night and I have again to report that I am still without advices from you, your last is of Jany. 1st.

My collections have started off well this month. I enclose a list that you may see who & what they are. You will notice that I have got from Noel on a/c $245.+ I think now I will get the balance from him before Court, at least I have his promise to that effect. My sales are limited, scarce anything charged, and the larger part of Cash Sales since the 1st is for little things sold to the Exchange. I miss Weirick much. I am lonesome and being constantly confined to the store is tedious. Dr. [J. J.] Beck has sold out their old stock clean that is all the trash and asst.d goods to Dold at Las Vegas for first cost & one cent a pound freight. The 1 cent is added to cover insurance & expenses in the states, so Dold gets the goods at States cost without freight on the plains. Beck retains all the Liq[u]ors and groceries, and I mistrust that he has a partial bargain made with Webber for these.[20] For the last six

19. For an interesting discussion of this effort in the House of Representatives of the Territory of New Mexico to repeal the so-called Otero Slave Code see Hunt, *Kirby Benedict*, 115-16, which agrees with and amplifies Kingsbury's description.

20. We have been unable to determine Webber's full name.

weeks I have been trying hard to close out our Stock to Beuthner and had considerable incouragements from him, but if he should accept my offer now I should be obliged to back out because I don't consider it safe to trust him. I have <u>private</u> information and in such a manner that I consider it reliable, that he has lost lately gambling between 10 & 12 Thousand dollars. So I cut off this string & have one less to my bow. I will keep the goods till they rot before I will place them in doubtfull hands and have a big debt to fret over.

[Manuel] Wood the gambler (who wone that money from A. Leckendorf) has got Col. Street's house (it is the Hunt house which McKutchen bought of him) is making extensive improvements there and will turn it into a Fonda on a grand scale in op[p]osition to the Exchange. At present the place cannot support two such houses, and if there is not a great change one or the other must go under.[21] Wood cannot get under way for some time yet. I have a letter from Doan King & Co. stating that they have rec.d mine of Dec. 24th with the remittances to meet our last freight note.

[Letter no. 143 is a summary of letter no. 141, Feb. 5, 1860 and letter no. 142, Feb. 12, 1860, which Kingsbury sent to Webb when the originals went astray. Webb eventually received the originals, which we have reproduced here. Since Kingsbury's summary letter contains no new information we have not reproduced it.]

Letter no. 144, Kingsbury to Webb, Santa Fe, February 19, 1860

Dear Sir, Another mail in and not a syllable from you. It is really too bad but I must take it patiently. I have very little news to send you. Business is very dull. I am doing the best I can, but everything appears to go slow. I have rec.d this week from Noel the balance on his note he also paid $20 toward the costs. I now dismiss the suit and pay all the costs.

Chas. Larange [La Rouge] has been putting me off from time to time with fair promises and got me to wait with him untill the 1st of this month at which time I had his promise in the strongest terms that we should be paid. On the last of Jany. he left town to be gone about 4 days to give him time to go to San Alfonso [Ildefonso] and back. He did not return promptly and I mistrusted he was trifling with me. I waited untill the 14th & no word from him. His wife could give me no satisfaction as to his wherabouts. Thinking I had sufficient cause I got out an attachment, and levied on everything I could find of his. The Sheriff found in the house about $300 in cash, took it & all the goods also levied on three pieces of real estate. Up to the present Charlie has not turned up, no one can account for his absence. There appears to be an impression out that he has been fouly delt with, but I am led to

21. Wood's enterprise became the El Dorado Hotel, located on lower San Francisco street on the site of today's El Dorado Hotel. Sze and Spears, *Santa Fe Historic Neighborhood Study*, 8.

believe he has run off. He owes in town between $4,000 & $5,000.+ Our attachment is first and if it sticks in court, we have sufficient secured to save every cent of our debt. Geo. Estes has sold out his stock to Vincente Garcia. He closed out at first cost, that is all the goods he had left which he brought from the States at cost there without freight. It will amt. to $3,500 or 4,000 and I think it is a pretty good bargain on both sides. Geo. I expect will go in to the States for more goods. Dold is here now recovering the stock he bought of Beck. I heard yesterday that he Dold, had agreed to take all Weinheim's goods & settle his debts and then take Weinheim in his employ at $200. per month. It is stated to me in such a way that I am led to believe it, though I see no moove there yet. My sales this month are a little better than they were last, still they are a long way short of satisfying me. The best feature in it is that the most or greater part of what I have sold has been for <u>cash in hand</u>, in truth.

I am really afraid to sell goods on credit for I don't know who to trust. On this subject of selling out I am bound to wait a while at least, in the first place the amt. is still to[o] large to make a profitable sale and then with the present appearance of things I am not willing to trust it out. When I talk of selling at <u>cost & freight</u> I am only laughed at. So at present I see nothing but to hold on to the willows and take it poco poco.

Col. Fauntleroy is making extensive preparations to march against the Navajoes. Another war with them is open and the Campaign will start as soon as practicable. This may help matters & things some.[22]

I am getting along very well without Weirick. I have cleaned out one corner of the bale room and brought my chamber furniture in, so that I am very comfortably fixed in the store.

I am trying hard to fix up another remittance to send you by next mail.

Letter no. 145, Kingsbury to Webb, Santa Fe, February 25, 1860

I wrote you last week that I had taken out an Attachment & levied on all I could find belonging to Chas. La Rouge. I think there is plenty secured to save us in full. He is still missing and if he will only stay away a few days longer there will be no trouble to make the attachment hold. Court commences the 1st Monday in next month and I am in hopes to get a judgement at this term & have the matter closed up at once.

Geo. Estes tells me that he is not going in but will send orders by Henry Mercure to fill, & will have the goods here at the regular time in the Spring. He still keeps possession of the little store. There is another little stir in Jerusalem. Weinheim's creditors have got to quareling among themselves. I am glad that we are out of the ring. I

22. War had indeed broken out, with Navajos fighting what one historian called a "war of reprisal." Before Fauntleroy could attack the Navajos, however-er, a large number of Navajos attacked Fort Defiance, on the edge of the Navajo country, in April 1860. Then, trouble with Comanches and Kiowas diverted his attention to the eastern plains. McNitt, *Navajo Wars*, 382-85, 387. The quote is on 385.

know now that I done well to get the settlement I did a year ago there. It appears that Gold did not want the goods, but wanted him on a salary to go on business to Pike's Peak. Weinheim want[ed] to go, & here the fuss commences. At the time of my compromise, the balance of the Creditors appointed two trustees to take charge over him to keep the place agoing and realize his a/c's and stock. They to receive his collection every night & watch him that he did not gamble or make improper disposition of his effects, and the funds rec.d by them to be paid pro rata to all the creditors. Now Cleaver and Spiegelberg being the two principal creditors take the responsibility of disposing of the stock for their own benefit without consulting the trustees, and actually did sell, to Louis Gold. Thereupon the Trustees, got out a writ of replevy and retook the goods & now Gold has commensed a suit against Cleaver & Spiegelberg for damages in not complying with the sale to him. Let them go it. As I said before we are out of the net, and they cannot squeeze us.

I have now rec.d yours of Jany. 27 and Feby. 2nd. I am relieved to know that the Arkansas farm is no worse.[23] I have seen Magruder about the mortgage. There is a poor show of hurrying him in the matter. He assures me that Dr. Allen has plenty in his hands and ought to be able to take it up. This is about our only show. Mack is a poor stick. He is still playing all he can, has been obliged to sell his corn & wheat to meet gambling debts, and left his store a/c's unpaid. He owes now more than all his goods in store are worth, and as for his back a/c's I imagine they are not worth much. We are lucky to get the farm. As it is I am sure I could not make 50 cents on the dollar out of him here. He acts like a crazy man, would play still stronger but his ready cash is low and his credit with the sports is none to good. If he gets in $15 or 20 during the day he is sure to go up for it before morning. It is a regular thing with him and I see no stop with him untill he goes through with the last dollar.

So far I have been able to exchange all my St. Louis checks for checks on New York. This idea had suggested itself to me before I got your letter & had put it in practice. I have no acknowledgement from Messervy yet about the money I sent him.

Mr. Rose I believe to be a good man but he likes to play too well to be entirely safe. He will play & I cannot prevent it. So far he has been successful both in his business & with cards, but in time may slip up. I am not sorry to see him give up the house. They will commense taking stock there on Monday. He has been paying along pretty well this month, in cash, & other papers well secured, so that his open a/c is now reduced to $1,000.+ This balance I am in hopes to get settled in a short time either by cash, or good notes of those who owe him. Now I am in considerable anxiety to find out more of the character & ability of the new firm. There are three of them and all straingers to me.[24]

23. Webb had been to Arkansas and described Magruder's farm as run-down but potentially valuable to anyone willing improve it. Because he thought it "dear as a speculation for us to hold," Webb had made arrangements for Dr. Allen, Magruder's agent in Batesville, to act as Kingsbury's agent to try to sell or lease the property. Webb to Kingsbury, Hamden, CT, Jan. 27, 1860, MHS.

24. Among the new proprietors was a J. G. Marsh, whom Kingsbury described in a letter to Webb. Kingsbury to Webb, Santa Fe, Apr. 21, 1860, MHS.

My collections have kept up pretty fair and I now send you all I have got in & <u>a little</u> more. You will find herewith the following check, viz. Check No. 347, dated Santa Fe N.Y. [*sic*] Nov. 9th 1859 at sight on the Asst. Treas. of the U.S. at New York for <u>Five hundred dollars</u>, drawn by J. L. Donaldson, A.Q.M. payable to the order of Lt. Horace Randal A.A.Q.M. by him in blank the name is written so close up that I must send it as it is in blank. $ 500.00.

<u>Also</u> check No. 172 dated Albuquerque Dec. 1st 1859. at sight on the Asst. Treas. of the U.S. at New York for Two hundred dollars, drawn by James Longstreet Pay Master U.S.A. payable to the order of William Fitzsimmons & by him endorsed in blank, the name is written length ways, & this to must go in blank. $ 200.00.

<u>Also</u> Check No. 1310, dated Santa Fe. N.M. February 4th 1860, at sight on the Asst. Treas of the U.S. at New York for <u>One thousand dollars</u> drawn by B. Grayson, Bvt. Col. & C.S.—payable to the order of Joseph Hersch and by him endorsed to our order $1,000.00.

<u>Also</u> Check No. 1311 of same date, tenor & effect, for <u>Four hundred dollars</u>. $ 400.00

<u>Also</u> Check 34, dated Santa Fe N.M. 30th Sept. 1859 at sight on the Asst. Treas. of the U.S. at New York for <u>One thousand dollars</u>. drawn by J. A. Mac Capt. Top.l Eng.s payable to order of 1st Lt. Lt. W. O'Bannion U.S.A. by him endorsed to our order $1,000.00.

<u>Also</u>, check No. 730 dated Santa Fe N.M. Feby. 26th 1860 at sight on the Asst. Treas. of the U.S. at New York for <u>Nineteen hundred dollars</u>, drawn by Cary H. Fry Pay Master U.S.A. payable to our order

<u>$1,900.00</u>

Making in all $5,000.00

Which amt: I have charged to your <u>stock</u> account, and you will please receive it as another remittance or portion of your original capital. After receipt of this there will still remain to your Cr. on this account $6,000.+ which I am in hope I will be able to collect next month, at all events shall start it to you soon as collected so as to close this account. The amt. of the mail certificates when collected you will take on your private a/c, which will place our private accounts more equal. After that we can begin to divide. I begin to feel now that we have a fair prospect of eventually realizing something for our past six years labor. I thank you for the suggestions about my future arraingements.[25] It is my intention if I have the good luck to get clear here, to leave free & untram[m]eled by any business operation. I look upon all future matters in this world as uncertain and consequently give myself no uneasiness about what I am to do. Of course I look ahead and can see pretty well in the dark, but have no wish to engage in anything now untill I get entirely clear of this business. And then I shall be ready & very willing to consult with you. I had not thought to trouble you with my money after it is realized. I imagined you might have

25. Tom Bowler had apprently told Webb that Kingsbury was thinking about running the Batesville farm himself. Webb was concerned that farming might not suit Kingsbury, and encouraged him to think about a more active form of business before making any final decisions. Webb to Kingsbury, Hamden, CT, Jan. 27, 1860, MHS.

enough to do in taking care of your own, but since you make the offer yourself, I may be very glad to avail myself of it untill I can come myself and see to it in person. But I haven't got anything I can call my own yet.

The prospects must indeed be very flattering before I would consent to enter the Dry goods business. I saw the whole workings of that business for 8 years in Boston and was heartily sick of the whole operation. I have no confidence in the business. It is altogether to[o] risky to suit me, too much <u>credit</u>.

My view is this when I leave here I ought to have enough if properly managed to support me. I have no ambition to get large riches, and take corisponding risks. If I again enter active business it must be in something which is cash and commands <u>cash</u>. I do not intend to invest my hard earnings in a <u>credit</u> business. I would rather put my money where it would be <u>safe</u> at 6% and go to work again on a salary if I choose, rather than take the chances in a <u>credit</u> business. That real Estate operation might suit me, but the whole thing is so far off that I will not allow my mind to speculate upon it. I have enough here to attend to at present.

You may rely that I will not do anything hasty, my main safe guard has always been <u>caution</u>, and I shall look well before I jump after getting clear here. I shall take some time to look about and deside upon my future course. By all means sell that farm when you can get a fair price for it. I haven't the first practable idea of farming and am rather old to begin to learn now. If my life & health are continued I have no doubt something will turn up for me in the future. There will be a place for me to fill and I shall be directed to it.

I am looking for Vincente St. Vrain to come up in a week or two & will then enquire of him about that Watts draft.

I don't think we will have much money to divide before about July next after Col. Fauntleroy pays the note for real Estate. By that time I hope to get enough together to make it an object to place it on interest.

Nothing more now.

Letter no. 146, Kingsbury to Webb, Santa Fe, March 3, 1860

Another mail arrived but no letter from you. I suppose it is because I received two last time.

Chas. LeRouge [La Rouge] is still missing. I understand that his wife says she does not intend to contest the attachment. I am in hopes to get judgment this court. I my last letter I sent you drafts on the Asst. Treas. at New York amt.g to $5,000.+ on your stock a/c which I hope you have rec.d all safe. I have now a letter from Messervy acknowledgeing receipt of mine with the money stating that all the drafts were paid, and containing our note canceled in full with all the interest. Among those drafts sent to him was one of the Banker Hood. So by this I know it was paid promptly. I shall take no private drafts unless I am forced to. I have looked my papers all over carefully and see nothing to indicate that the $9.00 had been paid. I discover that you rec.d $22.05 for damage on Looking Glasses, but see no charge where you had paid anything on that account.

My sales for the month of Feby. amount to $2,275.00 making the whole sales so far this year $65,000+ which according to my estimates will bear a gross profit of $13,000+. My figures show that the stock now on hand at cost & freight ought to amt. to $15,500.+ and to the best of my judgement I believe it will hold out fully & perhaps exceed those figures. Seligman & Cleaver have got from Col. Fauntleroy a lease of this store for 3 years with the privalidge of 5 more at $1,000.+ per annum, commencing on the 1st day of June next. So I must manage to give them possession at that time. I am really in hopes something will turn up so that I can dispose of our whole stock of asst.d goods before that date. I do not fancy the idea of being compeled to remain here and retail the broken remnants of unasorted goods which will be left at that time. It would be slow & hard work. I see no prospect of a customer at present, but if one should offer, I am disposed to sell very low rather than let it go by. I have been trying hard to strike a trade with Simon Delgado but he always replies that there is still too much of it that the amt. is too large for him.

My collections for Feby. amt. to $6,4000.+ of it I sent you $5,000+. I had to pay Weirick when he left, so that it leaves me but a small balance on hand. When I get your a/c current I will take off another Trial Balance and will then make up a statement of all our business in round numbers, so that you can see in a small compass just how matters stand.

I have got nothing special this week to give you in the way of news. Mr. [J. G.] Marsh[26] (Mr. Rose's successor) did not get here as soon as expected. He came with the mail today. Rose will give him possession on Monday and they will then commence taking a/c of stock.

Woods has got his house [the El Dorado] pretty well under way and is expecting to open sometime next week. He has plenty of means and I cannot tell what effect this opposition may have on the Exchange. I should feel better if it had not started. You will find herewith a note signed by Sylvester Mowry, dated Messilla [Mesilla] Arizona Oct. 9th 1859 payable 6 mos after date, at the Bank of the Metropolis Washington D.C., to the order of Chas. A. Hoppin for Five hundred dollars $500.+. I want you to send this on for Collection and do your best to get the money for it. I have no reason to suppose that it will not be paid promptly, but in case it should not, then have it protested but at the same time keep the paper and try every possible means to make the money out of him. I state this because I fear that

26. This was not the famous John Marsh (see G. D. Lyman, *John Marsh, Pioneer: The Life Story of a Trail-Blazer on Six Frontiers.* [New York: C. Scribner's Sons, 1931]), who was murdered in California; this John Marsh died of tuberculosis in Santa Fe in 1861.

the chances would be very slim in getting it here out of Hoppin &
Appell [Appel] in case anything should be wrong with Mowry. The
note was given for ¼ part of a mine which he (Mowry) bought. It was
a legitimate transaction, and should be paid promptly and probably
will be without a word. But I am getting to mistrust everybody. I have
been desieved so often that I do not know who to trust or what will
turn up next, and imagine all possible difficulties.

I see by the New Orleans papers that the Post Office bill which was
defeated last year has been taken up since the organization and passed.
I hope this bill has given you some money.[27]

Do write me regularly and long letters. I want your cooperation to
keep up my spirits and help me through.

P.S. I have a horrid & fatal affair to tell you of. It happend between
Henry Oneil and Dr. [J. J.] Beck (The executor of P[reston] Beck's
Estate) in which the Dr. was killed. The Dr. was a quick, passionate
man. Henry had been in the counting room with him had a long &
pleasant chat over a bottle of wine about 9 o'clock in the evening.
Henry went out & the Dr followed him called him on one side for
some private business. It appears the Dr. wanted him to sign some sort
of a paper which H. thought unnecessary and objected, whereupon the
Dr. flew into a pashen [*sic*] took his coat off & finally drew his Knife
and ran Henry round thoes trees which are boxed in front of the store.
Henry finally to passify him consented to sign the paper. They both
entered the counting room. The Dr. immediately turned the Key &
told him if he did not sign it he would kill him right there. Henry
wanted him to wait untill morning. The Dr. would not consent, and
drew his knife again. Henry then beg[g]ed him to let the Clerk who
was present go for his books that they might fix it right. This he would
not consent to. You shall sign it and right here now. He then through
[threw] his knife on the little office bed went to the desk and commenced to write but was so excited that he could not. He then ordered
his clerk to write as he should dictate. Henry again urged that the
matter should be put off untill morning, whereupon the Dr. commenced abusing him with words, and finally raised a chair to hit him,
but drop[p]ed it & drew his pistol, Henry cool all the time and trying
to passify him. He then laid the pistol on the table. After a few more
remarks, Henry being near the fireplace, the Dr jumped at him to
ketch him by the throat. Henry's beard being long he caught by that,
and pushed him over behind the desk by the safe door. Henry got his
beard loose and the Dr. said "damn you I will kill you any how", went
to the bed for the knife. In the meantime Henry recovered himself and
drew his pistol. The Dr. then coming to him with the knife Henry
fired, the ball taking effect in the Dr's left eye. He immediately fell and
expired in about 10 minutes, never spoke.

Henry gave himself up immediately, and after the hearing of the

27. This bill apparently freed up money to pay mail
contractors, who could then afford to pay Webb &
Kingsbury.

case was set at liberty. He is feeling very bad about the affair, regrets it exceedingly, but was absolutely obliged to do it to save himself. It is the clearest case of self defence I ever heard. Henry has the sympathy of the whole community.

The Dr. was engaged to Miss Nelly Shoemaker. They were to be married some time in April. I am told he made a will before he went to California and gave her all his property which is said to be worth at least $50,000.+ The will is now in her possession, but not opened yet. It will probably be opened & read in court on Monday.[28]

Letter no. 147, Kingsbury to Webb, Santa Fe, March 10, 1860

Dear Sir, Again and no letter from you. The old saying that no news is good news may do very well but it is certainly very unsatisfactory to me just now not to hear from you. I want a reply on the subject of those Clerks drafts. I am urging a settlement with Mr. Rose and the whole thing must be delayed on account of these drafts. Miller's papers which were started a week after those went for you have now been replied to and the draft is now here. We have Washington date here to Feby. 16th and I am at a loss to understand why it is that I have no letter from you.

I have got our judgement against Chas. La Rouge. His wife did not contest it but some of the other creditors have been trying hard to up set our lean [lien] as the <u>first</u> attachment. They are trying to compell the Sherriff to alter his return so that all may come in on the same footing. So far he has refused and by his just return we have the preference over all others. They have instatuted a suit against him in the matter. What effect it will have against us I cannot yet see, but think we are right and the result must be given in our favor. At all events it will <u>delay</u> us in realizing our cash which were it not for this we ought to make at once.

Wood's new house (The El Dorado) opened to day with a grand free blow out. It was a very nice entertainment. It is arrainged with a goodeal of taste and being new and clean shows to advantage. The whole house is richly fitted up and of course at a corisponding cost. I think myself that it is too far from the Plaza to pay, but Quin Sabi [*quien sabe*]!!![29]

Last week I sent you a note against Sylvester Mowry for $500.+ to collect. Let me know how this turns out soon as you can.

Business is pretty fair so far this month. Collections limited but sales rather incouraging. Considering all things I have no reason to complain.

Sydney & Jim Hubbell[30] last summer bought out Branfords property in Albuquerque. Had some 20 Wagon loads of goods from the

28. Dr. Beck was the J. J. Beck listed in the *Santa Fe Weekly Gazette* on May 13, 1858 as the executor of Preston Beck Jr.'s estate. Ellen Shoemaker was probably the daughter of Capt. William Shoemaker, who had been in charge of stores at Fort Union. Bloom, ed., "Historical Society Minutes," 276.

29. Kingsbury's assessment may have been correct. By November the El Dorado had closed, although the bar continued to do business. Kingsbury to Webb, Santa Fe, Nov. 4, 1860, MHS.

30. We have not identified Sydney, but "James Lawrence Hubbell, of Connecticut, settled in the Southwest after serving in the Mexican-American War and being discharged in Santa Fe. One of his sons, Lorenzo, founded the Hubbell trading post at Ganado, Arizona, which is today a National Historic Site." McNitt, *Navajo Wars*, 172 n. 4.

states and have been spending on a large scale there. They also had a
saw mill out in the mountains. Today I hear that they have made an
assignment which I suppose to mean that they have failed. We have
nothing at stake there.

We have had a terrable fire. Our old store is now nothing but a
mass of ruins.[31] The fire broke out in the back end of the long room
that we used for hard ware. The alarm was given at a little after 3
o'clock in the morning. When discovered it had made considerable
headway and must have been burning for some time. It was a long
time before the town could be arroused & people get there. I was one
of the few that went into the store but the smoke was so dense that we
were compeled to leave with empty hands, not a rag was saved not
even their books. The loss is not less than $25,000 to 30,000. The prin-
cipal part of which falles on Joe Hersch.[32] It is true he had sold the
goods to his nephews but it is on credit, and they have nothing now
since the fire. They lost everything & owe him. The wind was high &
blowing from the north. By pulling down the portal of Blumners corner and of Juaneta's we saved their houses. It was a fearful sight. At
one time the mill was in great danger the wind carrying the flames
directly to it, but by great exertions the portal was cut down and two
rooms torn down so that the connection was broken just in time to
save his grainery & mill. Down to the Grainery which is w[h]ere our
grosery wherehouse used to be, is burnt up clean, nothing left but the
walls. Joe [Hersch] will I understand commence to rebuild immediately. The cause of the fire is not known. This fire takes about half of
what Joe was worth. The young men had bought some goods at
Spiegelberg also some of Seligman & Clever—not much at S & C,
perhaps $2,500+ to 3,000+ of Spiegelberg. They fortunately owe us
nothing. I could have sold them but I demanded Joe as security & they
did not like the terms went off and bought of Spiegelberg. At the time
their reply to me was that they thought their stock was security
enough for all they wanted. I knew they owed for the whole of it and
more and did not feel satisfied to sell them & as it has turned out it is
fortunate that I did not sell them.

Louis Dorrence was indicted for stealing a calf valued at $8.00
which he butchered after 10 at night. On trial he was convicted and
sentenced to receive 30 lashes in the public plaza. On petition the Gov.
[Rencher] pardoned him the lashes, but that he should pay for the
calf, costs &c. which in all is about $100.+. It made considerable stir in
town & from all I can learn, I am led to believe that he was really
guilty & ought to have suffered the full penalty of the law. The night
before commencement of this court the Clerks Office was broken
open, and a whole bundle of inditements stolen. It contained all the
gambling inditements which were found by the Grand jury at last
March term. All the parties were under heavy bonds & by this little

31. Perhaps a structure in the rear of the compound, between the plaza and the Rio Chiquito
(today's Water St.) which Webb & Kingsbury had
just sold to Col. Fauntleroy.

32. The fire destroyed the store operated by Hersch's two nephews, who had leased it from him. See
chapter 12.

manovre [*sic*] there being no inditements in court against the parties they will all go free.

While the fire excitement is up, we are trying to form a fire company. The citizens have had a meeting and I think it will go through. A comte [committee] was appointed to draft resolutions to be offered at an adjourned meeting to be held next Tuesday. It is proposed to form a Company—provided with Buckets, axes, spades, pick & hooks, to act under proper offices so in case of necessity there may be some system and may be of much service. We will have the implements deposited at a convenient place at or near the Plaza. We also want some method of alarm, and while this thing is under consideration we intend to move the subject of Powder. See if we cannot have some regulation about it. The way it is kept here now is altogether too daingerous. Amberg has in his house about two wagon Loads & Spiegelberg about 30 kegs, nearly every house has more or less. At the fire there was about 1/2 keg exploded. The roof had burnt off before the explosion, it went up and done no harm. At the time I was not more than 40 or 50 feet from it.

I hear Dr. [J. J.] Beck's will read. He gave his <u>whole property</u> after paying his debts & funeral expenses to Miss Nelly Shoemaker his intended wife and made her the sole executrix. It was opened in the Probate court and letters granted to her. It is reported here if the will should be contested that it will not stand. Under the law here a man cannot give his property to a strainger to the prejudice of desendents or anticedents except a certain portion of his estate and the law prescribes what portion that shall be. Now Dr. Beck's parents are both living & if they contest the will it will probably fall.[33]

I think of nothing more now.

Letter no. 148, Kingsbury to Webb, Santa Fe, March 18, 1860

I have nothing particular to write since my last, just send a few lines now to let you know that I have rec.d yours of Feby. 16th with a/c current, also of the 18th with notice that you have got the $666.66 all of which is very acceptable news. I can now fix up my books and adjust a settlement with Mr. Rose. I have some fair promises of some collections to come in this week. If they hold good I shall try to send you by next mail another remittance.

Letter no. 149, Kingsbury to Webb, Santa Fe, March 24, 1860

Dear Sir, I sent you only a few lines last week. I had nothing special to write and at the time I was suffering with one of my old head aches. I have made the entries in our books to corrispond with your account current, closed the a/c and brought the balance of $134.39 down to your credit. Your account is correct as far as I know, except a little matter

33. Both Beck estates generated a significant amount of litigation in the years ahead. A daughter of Preston Beck's, Cirilia, complicated an already confusing situation. The 1860 census lists her as a six-year-old living with a twenty-two-year-old woman named Josefa Salazar. Salazar was a woman of property, owning $1,000 in real estate and $200 in personal property, an amount unusual for the neighborhood in which she lived. 1860 New Mexico Census, 60.

which you paid to Doan King <u>$2.00</u> for recording mortgage which I mistrust you have ommitted to take Cr. for. The $666.66 afterward I have charged to your agent a/c and if you get that $500. from Mowry take it up in this account. Business has been pretty lively this week. I talked around that I was to close would sell cheap & c & c. untill I got some of our friends to come and look. The result is that I have sold several bills low, just to start them about half I get cost for and the balance at a fair profit. I sold about $3,000. I want to keep it up and try to sell in small bills. I sold the show case just as it stood goods and all for $325. on this I made at least $75. and got clear of a lot of Odds & Ends. My sales has made some talk and considerable stir. I shall try to keep the mill agoing & if possible while the excitement is up wind it up. I think it is risky to wait much longer. Now is the time. Later will be too near time for new goods & then they will not look at mine. I also had a piece of good luck. I have collected from Clift $150.+ which is just like so much found. He went to a monte bank with $3 and with it wone $240. out of which I secured before he left the room $150. My collections have been pretty fair, and I can now send you the sum which I wanted to, in sending this remittance now I do not anticipate over $1,000 to 1,500. Send each of the checks for collections soon as you can, and when you have realized the <u>money</u> let me know it. I always want to know that you have got the <u>money on the drafts.</u>

You will find herewith

Draft No. 154 dated Fort Bliss Texas June 29th 1859 at sight on the Asst. Treas. of the U. S. at New York for <u>Two hundred and four 12/100 dollars</u> drawn by Thos. G. Rhett, paymaster U.S.A., payable to the order of B. S. Dowell, by him to E. Medina, by him to [name illegible] by him to us.	204.12
<u>Also</u> Check No. 664, dated Santa Fe N.M. Dec. 18th 59 at sight on the Asst. Treas. of the U.S. at N. York for <u>Two hundred Eighty nine & 41/100 dollars</u>, drawn by Cary H. Fry Pay. Mas. U.S.A., payable to the order of Elsberg & Amberg by them to our order	289.47
<u>Also</u> Check No. 449, dated Santa Fe N.M. Jany. 6th 1860 at sight on the Asst. Treas. of the U.S. at New York for One hundred dollars, drawn by J. L. Donaldson A.Q.M. payable to the order of Lt. L. W. O'Bannon A.A.Q.M. by him End. to us.	100.00
<u>Also</u> First or Original of Exchange No. 8674 dated (Canal & Banking Co.) New Orleans, Jany 26th 1860 at sight on Mssrs. M. Morgan & Sons New York for <u>Nine hundred dollars</u> drawn by A. H. [name illegible—Ken?] Cashier, payable to the order of Wm. L. Beall, by him endorsed to our order	900.00

<u>Also</u> Treas. Warrant No. 2312 pt. 1858 dated Washington
Feby. 6th 1860, at sight on the Asst. Treas. of the U.S.
at New York for <u>Three hundred and thirty three</u>
<u>33/100</u> dollars, drawn by Wm. B. Randolph Act.g Treas.
of the U. S. registered by F. Bigger, payable to order
of D. J. Miller, Clerk &c. by him End. to us.   333.33
<u>Also</u> Draft to 11.438 dated New York Feby. 17th 1860,
at three days after sight on E. Cauldwell Treas. Am.
Bap. Mis. Society No. 115 Nafsan Lt. New York
Room No. 5, drawn by Benj. M. Hill Secretary for
<u>Seventy five dollars</u> payable to the order of S. Gorman
by him End. to us   75.00
<u>Also</u>, Check No. 114, dated Santa Fe N.M. March
10th 1860, at sight on the Asst. Treas. of the U.S. at
New York, for <u>Six hundred and fifty 47/100 dollars,</u>
drawn by J. L. Collins, Supt. Ind. Aff. N. Mex.
payable to our order.   650.47
<u>Also</u> Check No. 1348 dated Santa Fe N.M. March 25th
1860, at sight on the Asst. Treas of the U.S. at New York
for <u>One Thousand dollars</u> drawn by John B. Grayson
Bvt. Lt. Col. of C.S. payable to our order   1,000.00
<u>Also</u> Check No. 568, dated Santa Fe March 13th 1860
at sight on the Asst. Treas. of the U.S. at New York for
Twenty four hundred and forty seven 61/100 dollars,
drawn by J. L. Donaldson, A.Q.M. payable to our order   2,447.61
              Making in all $6,000.00

Which amt. I send you on your stock account 1 original Capital.
This now closes that a/c in full and if you have got Bowler's drafts to
place on your private a/c we will stand equal or nearly so on our books,
so that after this all that we realize will be subject to division between
us.

I have also made arraingements by which you will again recieve
direct from Washington two salary drafts, one Philip Smith for
$333.00 and one Thos. Means $334.00, both due and payable to their
order and I herewith enclosed a Power of Atty. from Each of them
giving you authority. Endorse the same in their stead, so as to have
time & that you may get the money at once. When received take up
the amts. on your agent account and inform me. The drafts goes to the
credit of different parties on our books when I learn from you that you
have actually received the <u>money</u> on them.

I have now rec.d yours of Feby. 25th. I am glad to know that the
first $5,000 reached you safely. I hope all the drafts I send are paid
promptly. If they are not or there is any delay with them, you should
advise me as soon as possible.

With regard to my loan bill I am not quite certain whether the firm
should pay it or me. We are still working for the interest of each and I

must hesitate before I adopt you[r] suggestion. Should I get clear of these goods and commencing traveling for collecting &c &c. them of course my expenses will be charged to expense account.[34]

Rose has not completed his settlement entirely with Marsh & Co. yet, so I cannot tell you how things are there, but one thing is certain, Marsh understands that we have the first mortgage in all in the house and we are perfectly secure. It is only a question of time, and we get 10% untill our money is due & paid. Rose has paid his March Note in full. The next is due in Sept. next. Rose estimates that he made in the year $12,000.+ one half of which he has still to collect.

Letter no. 150, Kingsbury to Webb, Santa Fe, March 24, 1860

Under another envelope today I send you nine checks in all amt.g to $6,000.+ which sum when rec.d will just balance & close your stock a/c or original capitol. I hope you will get it safe. Don't forget to tell me when you have <u>actually</u> rec.d the money on these. Of course I want to know of ther safe arrival to your hands, but I also want to know that they are <u>all paid</u>. I shall try to take off Trial Balance first April. Soon as I can get more money will continue to send it to you, and if you can make it earn anything for us up to the time we may want to devide. It would be well to put it at interest where it would be secure. When I send will write more fully about it.

In haste.

P.S. That little draft for $24.50 favor of Wm. George was presented and paid March 12th 1860.

Letter no. 151, Kingsbury to Webb, Santa Fe, March 31, 1860

Dear Sir, I am now in receipt of yours of the 4th inst., noticing receipt of <u>$8.28</u> which amt. I will charge as you say to your agent a/c in order that my accounts may corrispond with yours. You say my last is of Feby. 25th since that date I have not failed to send you a letter by each & every mail.

Last week I sent you <u>nine</u> checks in all amt.g to <u>$6,000.+</u> on your stock a/c which I hope you have rec.d. Herewith you will find duplicate of No 8.674 for $900, the original of which was enclosed last week.

When you have rec.d the above $6,000. it will close your stock a/c, or in other words it will make the full sum of $36,000 which I have sent you to reimburse you for your original investment in our business. Our debts are all paid, and all that remains to make us equal in money matters is that your private a/c should show the same amt. drawn that mine does. In order to accomplish this I wish you to take from the amt. in your hands as agent a sufficient sum to make your private a/c

34. "I have been thinking since 1st Jany. that you had better charge your board bills since that time to expense account, and continue doing so until our business is closed up." Webb to Kingsbury, Hamden, CT, Feb. 25, 1860, MHS.

equal with mine. Then all the monies which you have left or will received as agent, will be joint and equal property subject to be divided whenever we get ready to do so. I will immediately take off Trial Balance to April 1st and try to have it corrected so as to send you by next mail. You will then know exactly how much to draw on you private a/c and also as to all the open balances on our books.

My sales this month sum up well. They amt. to $7,500.+ This leaves a stock on hand according to my estimate of about $9,500.+ of which at least $2,500. is in full bbls of Liquor for the Exchange. This would leave a balance of $7,000.+ in asst. goods which as the amt. is in reach of many who buy their goods here. I am really in hopes to find a purchaser for them before new goods can arrive from the states. There never was an old stock here which looked cleaner than this does. I have worked off nearly all the old trash & remnants. The heaviest portion is in Hams, (which are on hand by the stopage of the Neosho mail contract) manta, Lienzo, tickings, hickory [illegible], Brogans and good staple goods. I have not a yard of Calico in the house. I have taken out the counter table and in their place have piled all the full packages so as to have everything in sight. The shelves are filled up to the cuppord [cupboard] in the counting room from there back they are empty. My collections have also been fair. They amt. to $5,679. Also rec.d of Col. Fauntleroy on a/c of Real Estate note $1,000 making in all $6,679. In this is counted the $666.66 which you rec.d for Washington but was placed to the credit of parties here on my books.

I flatter myself that you cannot fail to be pleased with this month's transactions.

The Navajo war has been suspended by express orders from Washington,[35] and if reports be true there is to be extensive movement and chainge of the troops which are here. The report is the orders are rec.d for all of the 3rd infantry to repair at once to the Rio Grande.[36] I expect it means to the Texas & Mexican border. Whether other troops will be ordered here to protect the posts in New M. or no I cannot say. If, however, all the troops are taken from here and we are left without protection you can imagine our condition and also form some opinion of what will become of the merchants. I predict that all will break or fall like a rowe of bricks set up on end about 4 inches apart. They will all tumble at once. It will be worse than 52 under Sumner's commands.[37]

We have a small balance to our credit in the hands of Doan King & Co. at St. Louis of $49.08 as per their a/c Jany. 27th 1860, less whatever amt. you may have instructed them to pay. I wish you would draw for this amount so as to close our account with them, and when rec.d let me know the figures, how much they paid to Kirkman & Luke &c. &c.

35. If Kingsbury's statement is true that war against the Navajos was ordered suspended, Washington quickly reversed its decision after a band of Navajos attacked Fort Defiance in the early morning of April 30, 1860. The Indians' move precipitated an active campaign by Col. E. R. S. Canby during the winter of 1860-61, as well as initiating independent action on the part of the citizens of Santa Fe. Twitchell, *Leading Facts*, 316-17; Horn, *New Mexico's Troubled Years*, 80-81.

36. The Third Regiment had been ordered to Texas as part of the massive reorganization of the Department of New Mexico that Colonel Fauntleroy had recommended. See the introduction to this chapter. The Third Regiment would be relieved by the Fifth Regiment. Frazer, *Forts and Supplies*, 152.

37. Kingsbury is probably referring to Sumner's decision in 1852 to withdraw his main force from the settled portion of New Mexico in order to pursue a campaign against the Apaches. Sumner's plan caused a worried Governor Calhoun to prepare an evacuation of women and children from Santa Fe. Sumner later decided against the Apache campaign. Horn, *New Mexico's Troubled Years*, 31.

Letter no. 152, Kingsbury to Webb, Santa Fe, April 7, 1860

Dear Sir, I have now rec.d yours of March 16th—am sorry to find that my letters to you have been detained. I hope they may have come to hand before this but for fear not I now enclose copies of the two which you said by your letter was missing when you [word missing].

Chas. La Rouge is still missing and no satisfactory account of his disapearance.[38] I still trust & have good reason to believe that we are all safe here. Ashurst is now in Taos at Court, when he returns I will try to tell you the particulars more deffinately of how we stand in that matter and the prospects.

Weirick left to go home on a visit, no other reason that I know off. There was no misunderstanding between us, parted most friendly and in fact had I objected he would not have left me. It is his intention to return again in June or July. He knows our intention to close and has no expectation of our wanting his services further. He took your address and if he should go will come & see you. I can tell you very little about that fuss at Mesilla in addition to the newspaper reports. I believe myself that the whole thing grew out of a Fandango row by drunken California desperadoes. It is all quiet there now, that is I haven't heard of any more quarelling. The difficulties in Chihuahua have compeled all the Americans to leave.[39] This I believe is true but I doubt any real trouble between our people and the Mexicans on our line. I had intended to tell you before this that since that resolution (it did not pass the house) the Judge [Benedict] has been perfectly straight and appears like an other man. By this mail we have the full particulars of the disposition of the Troops which are coming. The present posts are nearly all to be broken up and the troops to be consentrated in about 4 locations only. This will open a harvest for a few, but as a general thing all who have anything at stake look with trembling at what must be the immediate result of all these places being broken up.[40]

True goods are a [illegible] here now, everything is at a discount. Honest men are so scarce that they might possibly bear a premium but everything else is way below par. Santa Fe now as far as business is conserned is about on a par with Algodanes [Algodones] or any other little stopping place that you choose to imagine. I am sure if you had been here though the last 3 months you would have had the blues ten times worse than I have had them.

Herewith you will find Trial Balance up to April 1st also a statement which I have taken from the balance sheet the better to enable you to see at a glance how our a/c's all stand. You will see by this that I want you to take from your agent a/c $6,000 & transfer it to your private a/c, so that our private a/c's may be equal or nearly so. The $1,000.+ I had to my Cr. on stock a/c I have transferred to my private

38. Webb was unhappy about their prospects of collecting any money from Charles La Rouge. "When men of his stamp get in difficulty they have not the energy or perseverance to get out. . . . I can never form any idea of what becomes of a Frenchman when they are missing. He may have committed suicide or run off, or be hid somehwere on a spree." Webb to Kingsbury, New Haven, CT, Mar. 16, 1860, MHS.

39. Civil war, known as the War of Reform, raged across Mexico as Benito Juárez and his liberal supporters tried to regain power. The city of Chihuahua had been under siege that winter. Almada, *Resúmen de historia*, 258.

40. In March Gen. Winfield Scott had issued orders to transfer two-thirds of the troops from Utah to New Mexico to eliminate four of the twelve existing posts in New Mexico, and to relocate five posts. Only Fort Garland, Fort Stanton, and Fort Bliss were to remain where they were. In fact only Cantonment Burgwin, Los Lunas, and eventually Fort Defiance were abandoned before the outbreak of the Civil War. Frazer, *Forts and Supplies*, 151-52, 163.

a/c so that both our stock a/c's are now closed on our books. My last letter gave you the transactions for the previous month in round numbers, but now with the aid of this trial Balance you can see just how all the a/c's are. I form no estimate for bad debts because I give up no a/c as long as there is any show. Of course we must loose some, how much we will find out full soon enough. One thing sure, I will collect it all if I can.

I have now something to say which gives me pleasure. I have just now closed the trade with Simon Delgado for all our goods except the Liquors. I have sold him everything at first cost, a regular bill made of every item and 20% to be added to the foot of the bill. $5,000.+ he is to pay on the 1st day of Jany. next & the balance whatever it may be on the 1st day of April. I have made the sacrifice at the start and am delighted even at this low price to place our old remnants in hand that I think is perfectly safe. Since we have been in business I have never felt the want of your presence so much in any one transaction as with this, but I have taken the responsibility and closed the bargain. For my part I am perfectly satisfied, and I trust I have done for the best. I shall commence invoicing them on Monday and hope to get through & have them delivered before or by next Saturday so that I can report the result.

By my last letter I estimated what I have today sold at $7,000.+ that is at cost & full freight so I believe this sale will bring us about ½ (half) freight, and if it will average that we are all right.

This is all word, keep quiet untill I get all figured up and can show you the exact results. Don't get in a stew. I have not lost my balance yet and have confidence enough in myself that I will be able to wind everything up right and after a little when my hands are full of this old stock I will start of[f] in good earnest for collecting.

Letter no. 153, Kingsbury to Webb, Santa Fe, April 14, 1860

Dear Sir, The mail is just in, but not a word from you. I do hope you are getting all my letters regular. I have not failed to write you every week for a long time.

In my last I sent you Trial Balance from our books up to April 1st, also a statement taken from the same to enable you at a glance to see just how all our matters stand by our Book, and also requested you to take from your agent a/cs of monies in your hands $6,000.+ & place it to your private a/c so as to make our private a/c's more equal. I also notified you of my sale to Simon Delgado. The bill amt.d to $7,627.20. The goods are delivered. Herewith you will find a copy of the bill so that you may know what the stock consisted of. He has not had time yet to examine the invoice and I have not got his notes but will try to get them before my next letter. Since I have had time to go over the sale with the amt. of the bill before me I am more than pleased with the trade under all circumstances as I see them I am delighted to get clear of them on such favorable terms. I believe Simon to be perfectly safe. You will also find a statement of what I have still on hand amt.g to $2,749.82 which together with what was sold to Simon & previous to his purchase this month, makes the round sum of $11,500.+ against my estimate which was $9,500, showing a margin of $2,000.+ profit on my transactions for this year over and above all the loss on the sale to Simon. My calculation is now to make enough on the $2,749.82 to cover all expenses of closing up the business and if I have the good luck to realize what is already bargained for, that is put these Liquors through the Exchange at my prices and get the money for them there is margin enough and they ought to bear it. Collections are very slow so far this month. You will notice that my deposit accounts are nearly all closed. I have desided not to take any more, and consequently cannot anticipate my collections in future remittances. What I send from now on will only be what is actually realized. I now enclose certificate of deposit No 258, dated Washington City March 17th 1860 signed by Sweeny Rittenhouse Faut & Co. for One thousand dollars, for monies deposited in their Banking House by T. F. Bowler to the credit of R. Frank Green, and by him endorsed payable to our order. ($1,000.+) which amt. I have charged to your agent account. You will collect it at once and take it up on that a/c. I shall continue to send you funds on this a/c as fast as my collection come in. Now with regard to investing it. If you can make this money earn anything well and good, but by all means place it where it will be safe. Look more to this point than to the amt. of interest you may have offered. Perhaps you can do better with it by letting out for a stated period rather than on call. My part of it I shall not want untill I come in, and from all matters now before me I cannot think of starting before May of next year. However in renting this money must use you own judgment. You will be equally interested with me and I will be satisfied with you management of it. I only wish to urge upon you not to take any extra risk with the view of obtaining a large interest. Use every precaution to have it secure even if it does not earn a cent for the whole time.

This is all now. Do write me every week.

P.S. I believe I told you before that Seligman & Clever had rented this store from the 1st of June. I shall now try to get them to take it from the first of May and let off for the last month also try to sell them some of our extra fixtures. I have hired two rooms for an Office & Store room opposite the Exchange for $10 per month. Shall sleep there. It is the rooms belonging to the Chavis [word illegible] adjoining where Juan Sena used to keep. I can be very comfortable there and also be handy to the Plaza. Shall keep my horse in Gilchrist's correll.

Rose to feed him and have the use of him untill I want him. I cannot rely on the saddle and if I travel it is necessary for me to have some sort of a vehicle. This Buggy is a good one has been sold two or 3 times for $300 & 350. The horse I valued at $200, and as I will not be hurried I think he can take me wherever I wish to go. It will be cheaper to feed one animal than two, forage is just now very high. Corn is worth from $6 to 8 Fanegas. I got 5 thrown in, in the trade.

Dr. Connelly has drawn out from [Henry] Winslow and closed their business. I am told it has left Winslow very poor. He had ex[h]austed everything and more too.

Letter no. 154, Kingsbury to Webb, Santa Fe, April 21, 1860

My last to you was of the 14th inst. covering Certificate of deposit No. 253 dated Washington City Mar. 17th 1860, signed by Sweeny Rittenhouse Faut & Co. for One thousand dollars ($1,000.+) for monies deposited in their Banking House by T. F. Bowler to the credit of R. Frank Green, and by him endorsed payable to our order. Also copy of bill sold to Simon Delgado and memo. of what was still in had all of which I trust you have received.

I am now in receipt of yours of March 29th—you notice receipt of all of mine of March 3rd except one of Feby 25th in that I sent you drafts amt.g to $5,000.+ I am extremely uneasy about it and shall be untill I get further advises from you. Herewith you will find a memo. of the Checks, and in case you have not got them, send at once to the Asst. Treas. and have the payment of them stopped untill I can get duplicates or certificates, or find out what has become of the originals. The worst fe[a]ture in it is that Two of the Checks were so endorsed that I was compeled to send them payable to bearer. I am at a loss to comprehend why there is so much irregularity in my letters reaching you. They are always properly mailed here, but as you have got all so far except Feby. 25th I am really in hopes it is safe and only detained on the way. If it should be lost or stolen, it will be a very hard matter to replace those checks.

I also send memo. of remittances sent you under date of March 24th $6,000.+ for fear this to[o] may be detained if they should be slow in getting to you. After waiting a reasonable time you will take proper steps to prevent them being collected by anyone else.

I hope [Sylvester] Mowry will pay their note when it is due. I have got nothing out of [Alex] Duvall yet. He had a fair prospect of getting the sutlership at Ft. Stanton, but since all the posts are to be broken up that with the rest there will be a surplus of sutlers who have no show.[41] I have written to Duvall but got no reply yet. He was only here a short time. The note was not due then. I try my best to get him to pay me.

41. Fort Stanton, however, was one of the three forts that survived the shake-up. See note 40.

Offered to allow a good discount &c. &c. but could get nothing. All the satisfaction I could get was that when he gets home would then send to me. The most he lost here was on <u>Cr.</u> I think by this that he had no money. I learned afterward that he stayed several weeks in Albuquerque on a spree most of the time, and this is the last I have heard of him. I understand Pinkney Tully is his silent partner, and at Mesilla. They are considered to be well worth at least <u>$20,000</u>. They have sold out all their goods, have a large amt. to collect, and have a mule train worth from $8 to 10,000. I hear that the train is now <u>hired</u> to Hart and freighting for him.

Frank is certainly acting very strainge.[42] He denies most positively hav[ing] any interest or connection with Woods. And yet his actions would seem to show that he was the principal of the house [the El Dorado hotel]. Through the Territory it is known more as Green's house than as Woods and from all I can see Frank is using all his influence to assist and build up that place. They have got all the <u>Play</u> there. There has not been a [monte] bank open at the Exchange for some time. It is very dull at both places. Marsh [the new owner of the Exchange] has not made more than Expenses since he got possession. He has taken advantage of the dull times and is putting the house in full repair. That is painting, papering & cleaning up. The material was all on hand, Rose had it brought out last fall, and the expense is but a trifle to put it on. Marsh is the principal man, and the only one here yet. He is a young man, and very steady, has his wife with him. I like him very well. He is not as much of a business man as Rose, but he is a man who will wear well, and I think has a good show to be popular here. One thing I am sorry to see. He does not look strong, and I believe he has got or is predisposed to consumption.

Chas. LaRouge is still missing. Ashurst stayed at Rio Ariba court and only got home this evening. I have not had a chance to talk with him yet.

I am getting perfectly disgusted. There is hardly a man here whose word in regard to money matters is worth a straw. I am loosing all confidence in everybody. True money is very scarce. The result is everybody takes advantage of it. The cry is "I have no money," "I expected so & so," "I have been disapointed" &c. &c. This comes from men who ought to have plenty to meet all demands.

If you could only hear the fair promises I have every day, & only made to be broken, You would understand why I am out of patience.

I have been urging little a/cs the whole week, & only got about $20 where I ought to have received $500. I am trying now to get Cleaver [Clever] to take the store from May 1st so as to get clear of paying rent for the last month of May. I am compeled to pay untill June 1 if he don't take it off my hands.

42. Webb was worried about Frank Green's behavior: "Tom Bowler informed me that Frank was helping Woods fix up his house. I cannot see what Frank is about. By assisting an opposition, he not only imperils the indebtedness of the Exchange to him and Tom, but by establishing another hotel the value of the Exchange property is depreciated." Webb to Kinsgbury, Hamden, Ct, Mar. 29, 1860, MHS.

Letter no. 155, Kingsbury to Webb, Santa Fe, April 23, 1860

I have already closed and mailed my letter to you to go by this mail. I want now to tell you about a big operation of stealing which has been going on at Fort Union. Van Bocklin [William K. Van Bokkelen] was Q.M. there and was to be relieved by Lt. Jones[43] (The officer which I introduced to you one day in the Store, you may remember him you liked his appearances & was pleased with him.) Lt. Jones rec.d all the corn in a lump, directly was ordered to send 1,500 Fanegas to Albuquerque. After this was taken out of the store house, it made such a big hole that he was sure that he had receipted for more than the house contained in the first place. This led to a strict examination and it was discovered that 600,000 lbs. of corn or about $22,000 worth was missing. The result was that they immediately sent information here to the Q.M., Maj. [J. L.] Donaldson, to stop paying the receipts which had been given at Union for corn. Being satisfied that the amt. short had never been rec.d there although the person receiving had given receipts for that amt. This man has gone to the States, and of the receipts stopped [John or Andrew?] Dold and Metzscan has got $15,000+. The balance I believe of all the corn which is there actually and the $7,000 has already been paid for. Now where the swindling was, remains to be proven. Now if Dold & Metzscan are honest then the whole swindling of $22,000.+ has been paid. But it comes very hard on Dold and this he gives me now for an excuse for not having the money to pay us which is due since the 1st of this month $1,700. He is good and can pay us but we will have to wait untill he gets through this affair or gets the amt. some other way. He tells me that when he started his brother to the States not long since he sent all the money he had with him, depending upon the sale of his corn to meet some debts here. Now that this swindle on Govt. has been practised & carried out there is no question, and who are the guilty it is not yet known, but the whole crowd Las Vegas, Tecolote, Moro, Sepio [Sapello] & in fact all who had anything to do at the Fort is suspissioned.[44]

The Q.M. being out of funds these receipts were given and they have been floating about as Cash untill money could come to meet them. Dold claims that some of his receipts is for corn delivered himself & by persons who were owing him, others he took in trade, others in collections, others again he bought for Cash.

If reports be true there has been swindling at that Post ever since it was established and all sorts of congectures [sic] are now thrown against all persons in that vacinity who have accumulated any money. This appears to be the bigist that has yet been discovered, though many do not hesitate to say that it is no new thing that all out there are conserned or are knowing to these matters, only that this time they happened to get caught, and Dold & Frank Metzscan happened this

43. We have been unable to identify Lt. Jones.
44. This episode was not discussed in the standard histories, such as Frazer's *Forts and Supplies* or Emmett's *Fort Union*, although such fraud was commonplace if Webb is to be believed. "That there has always been `gouging' in the contracts at Forts Union and Stanton I never had a doubt, but this is not a matter which interests us, except to watch out and protect our own interests. . . . No contractor could be expected to insure Govt. against errors in issue or stealing of corn in their warehouses for 4, 6, or 8 months from the time of delivery. And altho there may have been fraud, their own agents must have been parties to it, and at this late day, they must eventually stand it." Webb to Kingsbury, Hamden, CT, May 17, 1860, MHS.

time to be a little behind. In writing this I only tell you what I hear. Capt. Van Bocklin is personally responsible for the defficiency and if he cannot place it on someone it will <u>break him.</u>

Letter no. 156, Kingsbury to Webb, Santa Fe, April 30, 1860

Again I have to say that I have no letter from you. You can imagine my anxiety in being so long kept in suspense about the remittances of $15,000.+ Feby. 25th.

I have been pretty busy the last week fixing my new quarters & mooving. I am now writing in my new office and feel quite comfortable. I have two rooms at $10.+ per month, in the back room I have all the Liquors & State House irons nicely stored away. The front room I have arrainged for my office and sleeping appartment.

I sold to Seligman & Clever fixtures of the old store, Clock, Tables, &c., &c. amt.g to $68.+ They they [*sic*] have agreed to pay $50.+ for giving them possession of the house May 1st instead of June 1st so that we loose only $25 there in rent. Chas. LaRouge has at last turned up. He has come home all safe & sound. He has been so report says to El Paso. That is all I know of his absence. After consulting with Ashurst & the Sheriff I have their assurances that we are all safe there. The personal property will be sold now in a short time. We will then receive the proceeds and also the $300. Cash which is still in the Sheriffs hands. The real Estate has to be apprized [appraised] and can not be sold untill next term of Court which is in August. I have not seen Charlie, in fact have no business with him. It is now entirely in the hands of Officers of the court. I have some hope that he will be able to raise the cash to satisfy the judgment in full before the time expires for selling the real Estate. If not I suppose I will have to buy it in order to save us.

Sales this month foot up <u>$8,880.+</u>, Collections for the same time amt. to <u>$2,200.+</u>

I am now all ready and shall start this morning for Albuquerque to look after Simon Rosenstein's a/c and some others. I shall try to be home again by next Saturday. If not will send you a line or two from there.

This is all now, yours in haste.

Letter no. 157, Kingsbury to Webb, Santa Fe, May 6, 1860

I have now got both of yours of April 7th and am much relieved to know that you have at last got mine of Feby. 25th all Safe. I got home last night and am pretty tired, got very little encouragement for my trip. The only satisfaction I have is what information I got and that is not very encouraging, not a cent more did I collect. I found that

Simon [Rosenstein] had gone to the States to buy goods—left a clerk in charge of his affairs. He has a large stock on hand but no money. Said he hoped to collect and be able to pay us next month. One object I had in going was the hope of meeting A. Duvall. When I got there I found that he had gone to Fort Stanton[45] (this is one of the Posts that will not be abandoned) with a view of getting the Sutlership there. He has a very good show for it. It lays between him and Sumoski.[46] Sumoski is now sutler at Fort Craig[47] and there is a strong effort on the part of the Officers and others to keep up this place. If they succeed he will be retained there and Duvall will have no opposition at Stanton. I will send the note down by Ashurst against Duvall. If they cannot be collected I have instructed him to get them secured in the best way possible. If he can do no better to take a mortgage on the property for which they were given. I fear Duvall has no money and I know he is hard run. I went as far as Los Lunes [Lunas]. Saw [Nat] Macrae. Nat is broke, we may get something but the show is very slim. He has behaved badly, would have been able to pay everyone in full but has gambled off and paid about $3,500 or $4,000. The Post is broken up and everything will be removed from there this week. This leaves him entirely helpless. He has in goods about $2,500 which he has assigned to Jaramilla there a man of confidence and debts outstanding about $500 which he has assigned for the benefit of his crediters, when realized to be paid pro rata to all. As near as I could learn he must owe about $7,000. To Beck's house $2,000, Spiegelbergs $2,000, these are the principal debts. The other $2,000 is divided in small amts.

I found Albuquerque full of stores and all loaded down with goods. I think there is twice as many goods there as there is in Santa Fe. The hard times which I have been anticipating is now just beginning to take as serious shape & is being felt. The failure of the corn crop last year is a severe matter. The people are poor no corn to sell and only about ½ crop of Wheat. (Flour is now selling @ $10.+ a sack 100 lbs.) Of course they have nothing to pay the old a/c with and cannot make new ones and must do without. So that all the little stores find themselves over stocked cannot collect & of course cannot pay and now their big stocks are all due. I believe that ¾ the merchants in the Territory today are broke. That is if they were compeled to settle up, but by having time many will be able to realize and work out. I am much alarmed about our outstanding a/cs. I find it impossible to push them. They must have time, all I can do is to watch and try to prevent any undue advantages being taken against us. The most trying and vexatious part of our whole business is now before me. How thankful we ought to be that we have no goods coming out this year. You may think that I am over anxious, and draw unfair conclusions. I hope it is so but I cannot believe that I am mistaken. If you live one year & get a

45. A military reservation established for the Mescalero Apaches in 1855, in present Lincoln County.

46. We have been unable to identify Sumoski.

47. On the west side of the Rio Grande, thirty-five miles below Socorro. Established in 1851 to protect that part of the Rio Grande Valley.

just report from this country at that time, you will then see whether I am right or not. I hear while below that Winslow owed Connelly on their settlement $35,000.+ and I believe it is true. Already the Jews have shut up two stores in Albuquerque, divided the goods and got about 40% in old Trash.

Taos is at present in better condition than any other part of the Territory. Their wheat last year was good. Pikes Peak was a good market for their Flour and this has helped out the whole upper country. Flour & Taos lightening[48] brings a good lot of dust from the Peak, not much of it comes to the credit of those engaged, St. Vrain, [Joseph] Doyle, Peter Joseph, Rutherford, Posthoff & some others. Rutherford has sent some gold there and soon as it is sold we will get what he owes us.

Magruder is talking about going with his goods, but on the road somewhere between Albuquerque and this new Post to be built at Bear Springs in place of Ft. Defiance. [He] expects to get the agency to supply to Govt. with forage and keep sort of a half way house.[49]

I understand that some of the St. Louis creditors are dissatisfied with Hubbel[l]'s Assignment and are about to attach what they can find. Marsh has now got his Bar room & Billiard finished new sealings [ceilings] papered & painted. It really looks very nice and inviting. He has been doing very well the last two or three weeks. Has taken in at the Billiard Tables as high as $30 in one day.

Being away this week I have collected nothing about town. Shall commence tomorrow and try to make up a list to send you in my next so you may see what success I have.

Letter no. 158, Kingsbury to Webb, Santa Fe, May 12 1860

I am now in receipt of yours of 19th ult. and relieved to know that you have got mine of Mar. 24th with draft for $6,000.+ all safe and without delay.

I presume all the remittances which I have sent you are paid promptly or you would inform me of the failure.

I now send the list of collections which I finished. It is very slim. I am ashamed of it, but I have been running the whole week and collected all I could. Besides this I have got in about $45.+ from my small a/c book. The fact is there is no money here and it is next to impossible to collect. I hope that Faunt[leroy?] draft on Boston was duly honored. We are in good luck even to get that much secured. Duvall has not ret.d. I inclose a little note from Ashurst on the subject.

I now enclose to you draft dated Santa Fe, May 1st 1860, on David Barten Esq., Winchester Va. payable July 1st 1860 for Eight Thousand dollars ($8,000.+) drawn by Thos. F. Fauntleroy, payable to our order. I have given him a receipt for this draft and when I hear that it has been

48. Taos Lightning, a term long used by mountain men to describe a locally produced whiskey that was sold in the southern Rockies.

49. Fort Defiance was abandoned and its replacement, which Col. Fauntleroy named for himself, was built in the new location at Ojo del Oso or Bear Springs. Frazer, *Forts and Supplies*, 157. The new location, in the Wingate Valley near present-day Gallup, was 126 miles west of Albuquerque and 40 miles south of Fort Defiance, and had been a popular stopping spot for Navajos. In 1846, it was the site of the first of many Anglo-American-Navajo treaties. McNitt, *Navajo Wars*, 117, 391-92. Today Fort Wingate Military Reservation occupies the site.

paid the amt. is to be credited on his note. I secured this draft now and send it that you may have it there to present at maturity. The Col. recommends The Farmers Bank of Va. at Winchester Va. Joseph H. Sherard cast as a safe establishment for us to collect it through. Let me know when you realize the money on this so that I can adjust the interest with him here.

I am really in hopes that my collection next week will amt. to something. At all events I shall try to make up a small remittance to send in my next.

Jim Johnson has arrived from the States. Kitchen is freighting for him an early train. They look for the waggons in a few days. He will occupy the old Beck house. I hope new goods will stir up things a little and give new life to business.

We got clear of our goods just in time. I forgot to tell you that I had secured Simon Delgado's notes for the purchase according to agreement. The only deduction he has claimed so far is for Three Bacon hams and some of the cheese which he has found to be spoiled.

Joe Hersch has got his new wall all up ready for roofing. Has made three stores in the place of the old one. He has bought out the stock of the Jew House which I told you had started here last fall with a new stock which Parker freighted out for them, so it appears Joe will go to [word illegible] again. Chas. La Rouge had the misfortune to loose his wife this week. She died of grief, just the same as Drew's wife did.[50] When she found that Charlie had gone, she eat [*sic*] nothing, denied herself sleep & became perfectly ex[h]austed until nature broke up the house. When he returned she was too far gone to recover and is now at rest beyond the cares of this world. She leaves 5 little children. I am sorry for them. Charlie keeps himself very close. I have not met him since his return. His few goods are being sold by the Sheriff today.

I learn today that Lt. Cogswell has gone to the States on recruiting service. He owes us five dollars cash balance. He probably forgot it. I have written to him explaining the matter and requested him to enclose the amt. to you. When rec.d take it up on your agent a/c and notify me. A large number of officials have already left Col. Bonneville, Lt. O'Bannon, Lt. Wilkins, Capt. Sykes, Capt. Wainwright, and others will go down. O'Bannon goes on leave and will come to see you.

Letter no. 159, Kingsbury to Webb, Santa Fe, May 19, 1860

I have nothing from you this time. By last mail I sent you Draft on David Barten Esq. payable July 1st 1860 at Winchester Va. for Eight Thousand dollars ($8,000.+) dated Santa Fe May 1st 1860, drawn by Col. T. L. Fauntleroy payable to our order, which I hope you have received. I now enclose Check no. 777 dated Santa Fe, N.M. April 27,

50. The widow of William Drew. See chapter 12.

1860, at sight on the Asst. Treas. of the U.S. at New York, for Three Hundred dollars, drawn by Cary H. Fry Pay Mas. U.S.A. payable to the order of Debus & Schwarzkopf and by them endorsed to our order. <u>Also</u>, Check no. 4 dated Santa Fe N. Mex. May 19th 1860 at sight on the Asst. Treas. of the U.S. at New York for Two Thousand dollars, drawn by J. L. Collins, Supt. Ind. Affs. N. Mex. payable to our order. Making in all $2,300, which amt. I have charged to your agent account. Send them on at once for collection. I have plenty of fair promises and ought to have some more funds to send soon. Don't fail to report payment of the different checks which I send. Nothing more now.

Letter no. 160, Kingsbury to Webb, Santa Fe, May 28, 1860

I have now the pleasure to acknowledge receipt of yours of May 4th. Am glad to know that you had rec.d the two Salary warrants and would also like to know if the Power of Atty's were sufficient for you to collect the money on them.

By last mail I sent you two checks amt.g to <u>$2,300.+</u> viz Check No. 777 dated Santa Fe NM, April 27th 1860, at sight on the Asst. Treas. of the U. S. at New York for $300.+ drawn by Cary H. Fry Pay Master USA payable to the order of Debus & Schwartzkopf and by them endorsed to our order. <u>Also</u>, Check No. 4 dated Santa Fe N. Mex. May 19th 1860 at sight on the Asst. Treas. of the U. S. at New York for $2,000.+ drawn by J. L. Collins, Supt. Ind. Affs. N. Mex., payable to our order, which checks I hope you have rec.d all safe before this.

I am doing my best and using every reasonable exertion with my collections, but have very little encouragement. It is slow tedious work. Johnson's goods got here on the 14 or 15th. He finds goods a drug, he has had some little retail of things which were actually wanted, but I have see[n] only one bill at wholesale go from his house that was about $1,000.+ to old man [Alexander] Hatch. Spiegelbergs first train 26 Wagons unloaded Saturday. He will have a pretty fair run, as he has many strikers dependent upon him for goods.

One Mexican train has also got in. Gaspar Ortiz's wagons loaded with groceries for himself & Anastancio Sandoval. So you see that right early in the season the town has a fair lot of goods to start with. I hope now things will liven up a little, if not I shall fly off the handle with the blues.

Magruder did not take the place which he went to look at, was afraid of the Indians. Has since sold his little stock to Col. [?] Hopkins, who will carry on the same store. His sale amt.s to near <u>$1,500.+</u> Mack now talks of going back to the States soon as he can collect enough to pay off what he owes here.

Blumner has also sold out what he had to a young man name[d]

Schwartzkopf brother to the one who is partner with Debus the Tailor. His remnant came to near $2,000.+ and will get it in 3 & 4 months. He also gets $30. per month for the store rent.

Elias T. Clark of Rio Ar[r]iba died last week of dropsy, his remains were brought here and inter[r]ed by the Odd Fellows. Report says that his estate will not pay his debts in full.

I have not a word yet from Duvall. He went to Tecolote from Stanton to see Moore about buying the stock which Moore & Rees have at Stanton. I have written to Appel untill I am tired without so much as getting a reply. By this mail I got a letter from Hoppin which in a measure explains the reason. I will enclose his letter that you may know as much about it as I do. I am extremely anxious to know whether or not that draft which you rec.d of S. R. F. & Co. on Boston has been paid.

I am constantly stirring up all our old nest eggs, but with very little success. Rosenstein has not returned yet, his clerk sent me last week $300.+ on account. If I succeed in collecting anything this week I shall send you some checks by next mail.

This is all now. If you do not write me regular, I shall soon feel disposed to curtail my letters. Tell me all about the farm and private matters if you can find nothing else to write, but by all means let me know if the checks & other money papers which I send you are paid or not—up to the present you only acknowledge receipt of my remittances & then leave me in the dark as to whether they are paid or not. Now many of these papers, I take conditionally and do not wish to settle with the parties here untill I know for certain that you have rec.d the <u>cash</u> or <u>actual money</u>.

P.S. I have got a very severe cold, am almost sick today.

14.

"At a stand still"

Summer and Autumn 1860

Letters 161–181

Trading in Santa Fe had changed dramatically for John Kingsbury. With most of his merchandise gone, and no new stock on order, the sales part of his operations had dwindled and he devoted himself to collecting outstanding accounts. But money remained tight and Kingsbury took little satisfaction in dunning his former customers. He achieved meager results, he told Webb, and he often received "hard words."[1] Moreover, he could only spend so much time at cajoling people to pay or threatening to take them to court. Otherwise he was idle. He grew "very tired of doing nothing," as he explained to Webb.[2]

Despite his enforced leisure and the poor returns for his efforts, Kingsbury had reason to stay. Former customers, most of them in Santa Fe, still owed substantial sums that would not be paid without vigorous attention from either Kingsbury or Webb. Moreover, however scant his collections, Kingsbury continued to make progress. His monthly collections, as he reported them to Webb, totaled: May, $2,000; June, $4,300; July, $3,350; August, $1,500; September, $2,700; October, $1,450, November, $700. Nonetheless, the year ended with creditors still owing the firm $17,500.[3] Tom Bowler, and the successive owners of the Exchange Hotel—Rose and J. G. Marsh, represented the major unpaid accounts.[4] Colonel Fauntleroy came through with the final payment on the target date of June 1, for the real estate that he had purchased from Kingsbury & Webb. Kingsbury found Fauntleroy penny-pinching and intimidating, and the two had unpleasant disagreements before the deal was finished, but Kingsbury's preoccupation with the sale of the real estate finally ended. Other worries, however, took its place.[5]

For Kingsbury, and probably for other merchants as well, a pall seemed to descend over the territory. By fall it was clear that the corn crop had failed for a second year, and wheat had also done poorly. Business, Kingsbury told Webb, was "perfectly stagnant" and he feared he might have to remain in Santa Fe another year.[6] In late spring a new rush to Colorado, known to Kingsbury and others as the Pike's Peak region, had seemed to promise "a large emigration & plenty of money."[7] Santa Fe's resident population of gamblers headed north to tap the bonanza. Summer had

1. Kingsbury to Webb, Santa Fe, July 8, 1860, MHS.

2. Ibid., July 22, 1860, MHS.

3. These figures derive from Kingsbury's monthly reports in his letters; the $17,500 figure is from January 5, 1861.

4. Kingsbury to Webb, Santa Fe, Sept. 8 and Sept. 20, 1860, MHS.

5. Fauntleroy gave Kingsbury a draft dated May 12, which Kingsbury sent to Webb for collection. Kingsbury learned from Webb on August 12 that the draft had been honored. Ibid., Aug. 4 and Aug. 12, 1860.

6. Ibid., Sept. 2, 1860, MHS.

7. Ibid., June 9, 1860, MHS.

hardly begun, however, before the boom in Colorado turned to a bust and the "sports," Kingsbury reported, returned "broke" to Santa Fe. By late autumn, the gamblers were followed by the current season's wave of disillusioned "Pike's Peakers," some of whom drifted through Santa Fe, paused to reequip, and headed to new disappointments in the San Juan Mountains of present-day southeastern Colorado or to more prosperous diggings in Arizona.[8] Meanwhile, Indian raids to the east of Santa Fe continued to make mail delivery uncertain, and war with the Navajos had intensified. At one point, Kingsbury noted, Navajos had made off with a large mule train just twelve miles from Santa Fe. Despite a vigorous offensive by both regulars and volunteers (more volunteers than at any time since Spain ruled the region), early December saw the war with the Navajos end "for this season," as Kingsbury put it, and without much result.[9] Before the year ended, the freighting company of Majors and Russell flooded Santa Fe with low-priced groceries and liquors, putting still more pressure on local merchants.[10] Little wonder that when work slowed and he had little to occupy his attention, Kingsbury grew "homesick, discontented, &c."[11]

~

Letter no. 161, Kingsbury to Webb, Santa Fe, June 9, 1860

I have now received yours of May 17th. I am disapointed that you do not tell me whether those last two Clerks Warrants were paid or not. The parties are not willing to wait longer & claim that they are paid and want credit now. I also would like to know if you have got the money for Murry's note. In fact it is my wish that you report that receipt of every draft check or remittance which is actuly realized and paid. I have been urging & requesting this of you for some time and yet you don't appear to understand me, many of the papers I send I get from parties here conditionally and I always wish to know as soon as possible whether they are honored promptly or no so that I may settle advisedly with those whome I still hold responsible. I did not write last week. I had no letter from you and nothing particular to say.

Mr. [Alex] Duvall is now here. He tells me that he has got the sutlership at Ft. Stanton has bought out Mr. Rees interest there and will have Moore for a partner. In order to accomplish this he was compeled to use all his ready cash and that we must wait on him untill the 1st of August, at which time he assures me on his honor that it shall be forthcoming. His train went to San Antonio freighted with copper and has freight back, under charge of his partner. He represents that they have plenty to meet every cent they owe and a large amt. more only that it is not available now.

I still have hope that H. & A. will be able to pay the $1,300.+ by indulging them. Their property is securely bound for it and I do not

8. Ibid., July 8 and Dec. 2, 1860. For the San Juan and Arizona booms, see Smith, *Rocky Mountain West*, 13-14, and Paul, *Mining Frontiers*, 155-58.

9. McNitt, *Navajo Wars*, 393; Kingsbury to Webb, Santa Fe, Dec. 2, 1860, MHS.

10. Kingsbury to Webb, Santa Fe, Dec. 2, 1860, MHS.

11. Ibid., July 22, 1860, MHS.

wish to take it only as a last resort. I am in corispondence with both of them and think I can urge them by letter quite as well as to go in person. When I find that the money will not come then as a last resort I will go down and buy in their property, but I have still good reason to believe that this debt will yet be paid in full. Money is very scarce and it is almost impossible for good sound men to pay up. I am making very poor head way in collecting yet I am using every exertion, during the month of May the whole sum of my collections amounted to ($2,000.+) Two thousand dollars.

I am gratified and pleased to know that you are satisfied with my sale to Delgado.[12] I think it is one of the best things I ever accomplished in our business, & now only hope it will turn out right. He has been assorting up by fresh purchase, and is doing to all appearance a good business. I feel perfectly easy about that debt.

I have no excuse to make for Frank. I don't like his manouvering and have very little to do with him. That certificate I was compeled to take of him, in order to secure sundry open balances, and would regret exceedingly if it should not be paid.[13]

I heard today that Otero is doing all in his power to oppose & prevent Tom getting anything for his Niesctho [Neosho] route.[14] It is also reported here that Judge Watts has bought a house at Washington and has removed there with his family. I have not had a word from Bowler direct since he left here. You have a better chance to know his movements than I have. We have notice here that he has the appointment of Sutler at this new post to be established some where near Hatches Rancho, to be called Fort Butler, which is to take the place of Santa Fe, Albuquerque & Ft. Union, to be a 6 company post and when in full operation will probably be the headquarters also.[15] His appointment is direct from the Secty. of War and is very unsatisfactory to the Officers here, not so much against him, but they think the Secty. of War is to[o] fast and depriving them of their right to select a sutler to their own notion as has always been the custom heretofore.

Business is very dull, new goods are a perfect drag on the market, very few important sales that I can hear of. I have not heard Moore's name mentioned in connection with that affair at Union. I understand that he lost the govt. freight contract. I don't know why—but it is a heavy strike on him, as he had contracted & sublet a large portion of it and now all are on him for damages.[16] Dold has paid what he owes us, and I now send you the check which I rec.d of him in payment. Check No. 1453 dated Santa Fe N.M., June 4th 1860, at sight on the Asst. Treas. of the U.S. at New York, for Seventeen hundred dollars $1,700.+ drawn by John B. Grayson, Bvt. Lt. Col. & C. S. payable to our order.

<u>Also</u>, Check No. 386 dated Albuquerque N.M. May 24th 1860 at sight on the Asst. Treas. of the U. S. at New York for Three hundred dollars ($300.+) drawn by James Longstreet Paymaster U.S.A. payable to the order of Simon Rosenstein and by him endorsed to our order.

12. Webb had written that he considered it a "first rate sale." Webb to Kingsbury, Hamden, CT, May 17, 1860, MHS

13. Webb, too, was concerned about Frank Green's behavior and at a loss to explain it: "I cannot see why Frank Green should interest himself so much in arranging a new hotel. If he has not interest, <u>and everything is all right</u>, why does he not sustain the establishment and property in which he has an interest? I cannot account for his course." Ibid.

14. Kingsbury was referring to Tom Bowler's claim against the government regarding his mail route. See chapter 12.

15. Fauntleroy had proposed a post, to be located somewhere in the valley of the Canadian River, to function much as Kingsbury believed. Because of Fauntleroy's reservations about the location of such an important depot, construction of Fort Butler got under way slowly. In fact part of a garrison had been assigned, contracts had been let, and a sutler, apparently Tom Bowler, selected from a larger-than-usual pool of applicants, before the fort actually existed. Frazer, *Forts and Supplies*, 152, 170-72.

16. Government freighting contracts had become big business as the U.S. Army established itself across the Southwest. For example, in 1851, fifteen contractors using 626 wagons hauled 3,131,175 pounds of supplies west from Fort Leavenworth, for which the government paid $2,094,408.51. Of those 626 wagons, 452 were destined for New Mexico. Walker, *Wagonmasters*, 145, 237.

Making in all $2,000.+ which amt. I have charged to you agent account.

You say that you have loaned $4,000.+ at 6% on a note payable April 1st, 1860. Do you mean April 1st, 1861? or am I to understand that the note is already past due. I am confident it is all right & probable it is an error in writing. I hope the $8,000.+ Fauntleroy draft will be [paid] promptly at maturity and also all the other money papers which I have sent and that you can place the money in safe had at a fair interest. However, let me urge you again not to take any extra risks for a big premium.

Hovey is expected to return by every mail. Many are looking for him and expect money from him on his arrival. I hope when he does come he will bring plenty of the con que. It will help me much in many accounts which I have about town. Also in one endorsed note against him for $575. I thought after getting clear of the goods that I could do much by mooving about amongst those outside [of Santa Fe] who owe us but I find that I can accomplish much more (anyhow for the present) by staying right here. This is the time when most of the merchants visit Santa Fe and this is the headquarters for all govt. payments and I stand a fair chance to get a sight of them all when they get any money. Then by looking at our balances you will see that the principal amts. are people who live right here in town, and I don't feel safe to leave sight of any of them even for a short trip. Think it is really necessary that I should be here ready to jump any of them at the least crooked movement.

Marsh is doing very well now. His table is full and he has a very quiet orderly house. The El Dorado, is going down and must eventually close unless their games help them out. This chance is now very slim owing to the want and scarcity of ready money, we have a small claim there for which I shall sue in next court unless paid before.

Accounts from Pikes Peak are very flattering, a large emigration & plenty of money. All the sports who can get away are breaking for the diggings, but it does not appear to relieve the town much of that class. Fresh ones come from below about as fast as they leave above. Maj. Wells is about the only one left here now of the old set.

Do write me a few lines every night so as to make up a letter for me to send once a week.

Letter no. 162, Kingsbury to Webb, Santa Fe, June 17, 1860

I have no letter from you by this mail. I sent you last week by the Over Land mail, a letter with the following described checks viz. Check No. 1453 dated Santa Fe N.M. June 4th 1860 at sight on the Asst. Treas. of the U.S. at New York for Seventeen hundred dollars

($1,700.00) drawn by John B. Grayson Bvt. Lt. Col. & C. S. payable to our order.

Also, Check No. 386, dated Albuquerque, N.M. May 24th 1860, at sight on the Asst. Treas. of the U.S. at New York for Three Hundred dollars ($300.+) drawn by James Longstreet Pay Master U.S.A payable to the order of Simon Rosenstein and by him endorsed to our order. Making $2,000 which I hope you have rec.d all safe and in due time.

We have had two through mails by the Ind. rout this week & another to come in tomorrow or next day. It is reported here that Col. St. Vrain & Hovey have bought out Hall & Porter and that from this on the mail by this route will start regular and go through on time.[17] Hovey has not ret.d yet. His note will be due tomorrow. Col. Street is his agent, but I am confident that there will be no chance to get the money until Hovey gets back. I still hold Mr. Rose for the Note & look to him as the only real responsible name on it.

All the trains appear to be getting here in good season this season. Three have arrived since my last. The town is now full of fine new goods but I can discover no new life in business. They all have a good chance to open their goods without being pushed.

Weirick has returned with Amberg's Train. I have given him a bed in my Office. He is doing nothing at present but is relying on a situation from Bowler at one of the Sutler Posts. He tells me that Bowler has an interest in three Pawnee Fork, Ft. Butler and at Bear Springs in the Navajo country. I fear that Tom is starting too many fires and that he will yet burn his fingers. Don't take any of his money now in case he has any to leave with you, because it is impossible for me to collect with any certainty and if he should leave with you a large amt. I could not pay it here as soon as he might want it.

Letter no. 163, Kingsbury to Webb, Santa Fe, June 24, 1860

I am again without a note from you. I am quite uneasy to hear about those last clerks' salarys, and also about that certificate of $1,000.+ deposit with Faunt. &c. which I got of Frank Green.

Herewith you will please find the following remittances, which is all the ready funds which I have realized up to the present. Check #1439 dated Santa Fe N.M. May 20th 1860 at sight on the Asst. Treas. of the U.S. at New York for Two Hundred and fourteen dollars drawn by John B. Grayson Bvt. Lt. Col. & C. S. payable to the order of L. Meyer and by him endorsed to us. ($214.00)

Also, Check #825, dated Santa Fe N.M. June 14th 1860, at sight on the Asst. Treas. of the U.S. at New york for One Hundred and twenty five dollars drawn by J. L. Donaldson, A.Q.M. payable to the order of L. Meyer and by him endorsed to us. ($125.00)

Also, Check #851 dated Santa Fe N.M. June 24, 1860 at sight on the

17. Although the people of Santa Fe were generally dissatisfied with the quality of mail service provided by Hall and Porter and would probably have been very happy to see someone else take over the contract, this rumor was not true. Taylor, *First Mail West*, 71-75.

Asst. Treas. of the U.S. at New York, for Four Hundred dollars, drawn by J. L. Donaldson, A.Q.M. payable to our order ($400.00)

Also, Draft #55 dated Santa Fe N.M. June 18, 1860 at six days sight on Mssrs. Clark Dodge &Co. New York for One Hundred dollars, drawn by D. Hood payable to the order of J. G. Marsh & Co. and by them endorsed to our order 100.00

Making in all $839.00
which amt. I have charged to your agent account.

I have also made arraingements by which you will again receive direct from the Dept. at Washington a Warrant on the Treasury at New York for the Salary of Philip Smith $333.+ for services in the Offices of Survey Genl. for the Terr. of N.M. from April 1st 1860 to July 1st 1860 one quarter, the warrants will be issued payable to his order, and sent to you, and herewith you will find his Power of Atty. to endorse the same in his stead, when you receive this <u>money</u> let me know so that I can settle with the partners here.

P.S. Judge Houghton has not yet returned is looked for every day. I hope when he does come he will have means. He was sadly in debt when he left. There is a great excitement in the Southern part of the Territory owing to the discovery of Gold about 15 miles west of the Old Copper mines.[18] The reports come here so well authenticated that there must be some truth in it. They find rich quarts [quartz] and gulch washings. Mesilla, Franklin, El Paso & Las Cruces and all that vacinity are wild with the fever and every man that can leave has gone out. The over land stages have lost many of their men and are offering $150+ per month for drivers. I have seen some beautifull & rich samples said to be from there. It is all most to good to be true. I only hope that it is a reality and no humbug. Reports from Pikes Peak vary every week, some of the sports have already returned and say that it is all a humbug, that of all the gold hunters put together that they will not average 50 a day to the man while it costs labor[er]s from $1.50 to @4 a day to live. The great speculation there they say is in town & city lots. The whole cry there is buy, barter or sell lots, one thing certain a large emigration is pouring in even larger than last year and as a general thing they come much better provided than they did last season, both in money, stock & mashinery.[19]

Joe Hersch has sold his real Estate to Gaspar & Rafael Ortiz for $16,000.+ cash to be paid July 1, 1860. Joe to finish rebuilding the burnt part according to his plans, and they give Joe one store & the mill for 4 years free of rent. At the end of that time Joe will be entitled to his engine & all the mashinery in the mill & can remove it at his option.

For the last 3 or 4 Weeks a destructive fire has been raging in the Mountains North & East from Santa Fe. They say the timber has burnt off a streak of 150 to 200 miles. This morning the bodies of 2

18. A reference to the discovery of placer gold that May at Pinos Altos, west of the old Santa Rita copper mines and north of present-day Silver City.

19. After the winter of 1859-60 the rush to the diggings in Colorado resumed in full force. Historian Duane Smith wrote that "as was the case in California in the 1850s, the immigrants kept coming. Samuel Mallory coming over the Platte route that spring reported, 'I think we see as many as 50 wagons per day.'" Most of these gold-seekers fared no better financially than those of the year before, although daily existence had improved slightly with the advent of roads, the influx of goods, and the establishment of small settlements. Smith, *Colorado Mining*, 13.

men (Mexicans) was brought in. They were surrounded by the fire near Tesuce [Tesuque] and burnt to death, a goodeal of stock has also been burnt.

    J.M.K.

Letter no. 164, Kingsbury to Webb, Santa Fe, June 30, 1860

I am now in receipt of yours of May 31st—am really glad to get even a note from you again.

I am a little disapointed to find that the amt. still unpaid by Magruder was so large but it was well to pay it & have it out of the way. I will do my best to collect it of him here but must say I think the chances are very slim. I may be forced to sue for it and if so I have not got a particle of substancial evidence in my hands to sustain legal action against him. If you have got his original mortgage to Burr and Burr's receipt showing that the amt. of his claim was against the property at the date of my purchase or previous & then that I have paid it (or you as my Atty.) I wish you would send it to me, if I had the papers now I think I might save that sum or a portion of it by stop[p]ing the payments of Col. Hopkins to him.

Now in regard to the offer as reported by Mr. Allen. In the first place I took that farm as the only chance to save our debt & not as a speculation. You have seen it and know much better about it than I do and I am a little surprised that you should waist a reply from me about it. For my part I would be willing to take that offer for it or even less if you say so. But on the other hand of course we want to get all that we can for it. The real question is this, not whether it is worth more than the present offer, but in its present condition will it sell for more, and by holding it is the prospect of increase in value more than equal to the interest considering always contingencies & risk. The farm as it is now rented does not bring 6% on the amt. offered. From the information on your trip then you ought to be the best judge of all these points. We are not forced to sell now under a sacrifice but if you think this is a fair offer, by all means secure the trade at once, if you can get the notes to draw 10% all the better, if not take 6% only be satisfied yourself—and you will always find me content.

I prefer not to write to Mr. Allen but will leave it with you so that there may be no conflicting instructions. I would suggest this however, in case you deside to close the bargain and he who made the offer still sticks to it. That you get the papers carefully made to secure beyond a question the $1,000 forfiture, & in case of nonpayment of the first note, or any following one that all notes not due shall by the failure become all due & payable at that date. The whole to be secured by a deed of trust with power to sell by giving short notice.

By last mail I sent you checks amt.g to $839.+ also arrainged for you to receive $333.+ for salary of P. Smith, as per the enclosed memo. which I hope you have received all safe.

I now enclose draft no. 11624 dated New York May 30th 1860 at 3 days after sight on E. Cauldwell Treas. American Bap. Home Mis. Socty. No 115 Nafsan St. New York (room no. 5) for One hundred and thirty six 70/100 dollars, drawn by B. M. Hill Secty. payable to order of Saml. Gorman and by him endorsed to our order, $136.70

Also, Draft No. 11.625 of exactly the same date, tenor & effect as above, for One hundred and twenty five dollars   125.00

Also, First of Exchange no. 17 dated Tubac, Arizona June 15th 1860 at 30 days sight in C. S. Brown Secty. S.E. & M. Co. 88 Wall St. N.Y. for One thousand one hundred and seven 40/100 dollars, drawn by J. H. Lathrop, Director, payable to the order of Hoppin & Appel & by them endorsed to our order

1,107.40

1,369.10

which amt. I have charged to your agt. a/c.

I wish when you have time you would make up your agent a/c and send it to me that I may make all necessary entries from it on our books, such as exchanges &c. I don't mean to be in a hurry about it but do it when you have leasure and when I get it I will take off another Trial Balance & send you copy.

My Collections for the month sum up ($4,300.+) Four thousand three hundred dollars. Business of all sorts is & still continues very dull. Santa Fe is perfectly dead. Up to the present I have got nothing from the sheriff on C. La Rouge debt. The other creditors served on him a formal protest & he has desided to hold the money untill court and only pay it over on order of the court. I am sick of law & in my collections will only use it as a last resort. Charlie was this week married again. I enclose you a letter from Judge Hoppin which will give you the most plausible information that I have heard from the new gold mines. Weirick for the present has take a situation with Seligman & Clever at our old corner.

Hovey and Tom Bowler are expected by every stage. Tom's line is very much in debt. He must come soon & fix things.

Nothing more now

Letter no. 165, Kingsbury to Webb, Santa Fe, July 8, 1860

I am now in receipt of yours of June 8 am glad & relieved to know that all the previous & pending remittances had been paid. With regard to that Fauntleroy draft, I fear I cannot recover the exchange from him. He is a hard customer in money matters, very close & unreasonable to deal with. However, I will try it, but I must ask of you to send me a bill of the Exchange or some evidence of the actual amt.

paid. He is a man who would require this, and knowing him as well as I do I would hardly venture to ask him for it without something of this sort in my hands. As an instance to show you how close he is, at the end of 4 months he came to me and wanted our rent $300.+ endorsed on his note to stop the interest on that sum.

By last mail I sent you remittances amt.g to $1,369.10 including First of Exchange for $1,107.40 second of which you will find herewith. also memo. of the others. I hope my last reached you safely.

I am sorry to be obliged still to report the dull state of everything in the way of business. I never saw such times for money and old residents say that for 15 years there has been nothing like it. Removing the troops has in a great measure stop[p]ed the army expenses, and no new ones arrived yet to take their place. Then there are no. Govt. expenses all the appropriations for the Ter. having already been expended so that now everything is completely at a stand still. I am pushing everything in my power with collections knowing that the older they get the harder they are, but it is no use. I only get my labor for my pains and in many instances hard words besides. I must again urge upon you to be cautious with what I send you. We will have no margin to loose any of that which is actually realized.

If there is not soon a chainge here for the better we will in spite of all I can do be obliged to suffer a large loss on our outstanding accounts. One great source of satisfaction to me is the fact that we are out of debt, and that we have not now a big stock of goods to pack.

Many of the Sports who went out to Pikes Peak are returning and all so far have come back broke. The new mines below still keep up an excitement and some little gold is being got there but <u>water</u> is very scarce, and provisions very high.

I begin to be a little uneasy about the balance which Bowler still owes us. I doubt his solvency and fear that he is not business man enough to streigthen up things and cover his & Frank's extravagance. Nothing but a liberal appropriation by Congress on his claim will let him out. I am sorry now that you did not let me get those mortgages transferred and secured in our own name, rather than to hold them as they now are only as <u>colateral</u>. I look upon his <u>three</u> sutlerships as a humbug and only 3 more leavers to help break him, as long as he can keep up it is all well, but he is not the man to manage so much property. I have got in a little money this week and when I can get enough more to make a respectable remittance will send it.

Nothing more now.

P.S. When I took that draft of the Col. I was in hopes that the time difference of your getting the money there or me here, which is one month or ½ of, would be equal to all the expense of collecting. If the amt. is promptly paid you see you will have it at once, where if he had paid it here to me, the time which it would take to reach you would be equal to ½ %.

Letter no. 166, Kingsbury to Webb, Santa Fe, July 15, 1860

I have nothing from you to reply to at this time.

Since my last I have had the good luck to get a settlement with Magruder. I am well satisfied with it although it is rather a hard one. He claims that on adjusting his account with them on the 8th of Sept. 1855 he owed them according to their own statement only $268.82, with Int. at 10% to June 1st 1860 is $396.00 for which amt. he has given me an order on Col Hopkins accepted by him payable Jany. 10th 1861. This I have taken & think it far better than to risk a law suit with him and pay lawyers fees which would be nearly equal to the difference. I think this order of $396.00 is good and will certainly be paid in case the old Col. lives that long. Now about the difference of $70.42 our only show to get this amt. is to recover it again from Burr & Co.—and possibly it would be worth the effort at any rate we can loose nothing by trying. Mack does not claim any error in the credits or that any one has been omitted and can only account for the difference by the manner in which the interest is calculated. The way in which Burr's a/c is made out ex[h]orts compound interest to which Mack objects as unreasonable & unjust and not according to their original understanding. I send you a statement over Magruder's signature asserting his statements, and it may assist you to recover of Burr the $70.42. Now I know nothing of the justice in the promises and only hope that Burr will be willing to refund the difference, but in regard to this settlement with Mack, which I have just accomplished it was a Hobson's choise. Take what he was willing to give or run the risk and a big risk of getting nothing. He is still playing off every ready cent he can raise. This week he has sold or disposed of his watch to get money to play on. He is a used up man in every sense. I am sure it is lucky for us that I have secured what I have got and if you cannot get the difference from Burr we must make the best of it and congratulate ourselves that it is no worse.

I have now the pleasure to report that I have actually received $676.25 on account of our judgment against Chas. LaRouge. This is the cash which was levied upon and the net proceed of the few goods which were sold under the hammer. I feel now considerable incouragement that we will get the balance of our claim there in full. The three pieces of Real Estate are advitized by the Sheriff to be sold on the 6th of Aug. next. Now I know that he does not want this sale to go on, that he has already satisfied the other creditors which had commenced suit against him in such a manner that they have withdrawn the suits, and I have still hope that he will be able to raise enough to satisfy the balance of our execution before the day of sale. He is trying his best &

I hope he may succeed for I am sure we had much rather have the money that his property.

I now enclose you the following Checks viz.
Check No. 442, dated Albuquerque N.M. June 28th
1860 at sight on the Asst. Treas. of the U.S. at New
York for Thirty dolls. drawn by James Longstreet
Paymaster U.S.A. payable to the order of Maj.
C. H. Fry and by him endorsed to the order of Geo.
T. Beall and by him endorsed to our order $30.00
<u>Also</u>, Check No. 19 dated Santa Fe N.M.
July 7th 1860 at sight on the Asst. Treas. of the
U.S. at New York for Seventy Six & 50/100
dollars, drawn by J. L. Collins Supt. of Ind.
Aff. N. Mex. payable to our order $76.50
<u>Also</u>, Check no. 878 dated Santa Fe N.M.
July 15th 1860 at sight on the Asst. Treas. of
the U.S. at New York for Two Thousand dollars
drawn by J. L. Donaldson A.Q.M. payable
to our order   2,000.00
    Making in all $2,106.50
which amt. is charged to your agent account. This takes all that I have collected up to the present time.

I think of nothing more now. I hope those crops will soon be in a condition that you can find time to write to me regular.

P.S. Has my little colt arrived yet? What is the sex, color and name. Are the fine points beginning to show yet? In case it has no name and is a horse colt call it "<u>Brag</u>" if of the other sex call it what you please.

Tell me how is José conducting himself since he has been with you? Is he giving you satisfaction and himself justice? I would like to hear of his doing well.[20]

Hovey has returned, report says that he has plenty of means to meet all his liabilities, but not yet in proper shape to be available. I hope they may soon mature. Our Tom has not yet returned. Fort Butler & the New post in the Navajo country the Officers are unable to deside upon the locality to place them and to the present nothing has been done but submit the matter to Washington so that anyhow this year will pass without building, and next year probably there will be a new Secty of War, and Tom's sutlerships will be a fizzle.[21]

    J.M.K.

Letter no. 167, Kingsbury to Webb, Santa Fe, July 22, 1860

Yours of June 21st is now before me and contence [contents] noted. I enclose herewith a memo. of the checks which I sent you by last mail, and trust that they have reached you all safe. I have nothing for

20. Webb had sent José to Webb's father for the summer, where he was doing tolerably well, but Webb despaired of his ever becoming a responsible "straightforward man." Webb to Kingsbury, Hamden, CT, Aug. 13, 1860, MHS.
21. This is in fact what happened. See note 15.

you this week of interest. I am getting along very slow with collections, find that their is no use in fretting. I must turn over a new leaf and try to take it easy. It is impossible for me to chainge matters, and I must take them as they come along. It is hard and I am already very tired of doing nothing, particularly as I have so much on my mind and find that I accomplish so little. There is no pleasure for me in being idle. It only makes me homesick, discontented, &c. &c. and I long to get away.

I feel very much like a person in the Depot waiting for the cars, afraid to look out the back door for fear they will pass, and I be left. Here I must watch and it is all lost time. I must grant your request & excuse you, but hope you will after a while find time to send me long letters.[22]

Letter no. 168, Kingsbury to Webb, Santa Fe, July 29, 1860

I have nothing from you this week. I look for next mail to bring me a reply about the Fauntleroy draft.

I have now got our claim at the El Dorado in such a shape that I think it is secure. I have taken security for the amt. payable Oct. 1st and suspend the suit.

Money is really very tight and I have done scarce anything this week. I have a fair prospect to get the $575 from Hovey in a day or two. I have take[n] active measures with it and if the money does not come shall put it through this court. I think there is names enough on it to force the payment from some of them.

Tom has now returned. He finds matters very much complicated and himself in a tight place. His aim now is to sell out, realize what he can, and pay up. While at Washington he sent Hart in a/c $5,000.— paid Beck & Johnson off and sent Frank $9,000.+. By his books he finds the Frank has let that new house have near $6,000.+ of this money and left the mail debts unpaid. His a/cs show that Woods & Co. owe this to the mail firm, and yet he cannot find on what terms [words illegible] or reason this was done, and Frank still persists in stating that he has got nothing to do with that House or its conserns. The establishment has been running behind ever since they started. They pay nothing to anyone and I look upon the whole consern as rotten to the core and think the bubble must explode.

Frank's movements are to[o] obscure for me to fathom, and I don't pretend to understand them. But this much I do know that he has been so far implicated in the management of the affairs of that house that I think there would be no difficulty in binding him before any jury.

Poor Tom I don't know how he will get out. His intention is to get clear of all connection with Frank, and any sacrifice even if it takes the last cent he has got and then commence the world again in his own book. But the stick is he cannot cipher up how to do it without still being in debt, and he wants to get out and save his credit. I have nothing important in the way of business to report.

[P.S.] Tom left his wife and children with his mother in Mo.

Letter no. 169, Kingsbury to Webb, Santa Fe, August 4, 1860

Yours of July 6th is now before me. I believe I have rec.d all your letters and acknowledged the same in due time. I see plainly that you still do not understand my request. It appears to me a very simple one, and yet hard for you to comprehend. I have always given you credit for acknowledging receipt of the papers which I send you. Now what I request in addition is for you to tell me at as early day as possible whether they are promptly paid and honored or not or in other words whether you got the money for them or not. Now to explain the matter more fully I will take up the two letters to which you refer me, first April 19th in this you say you have rec.d for Mowry's note a draft from L. R. Faut & Co. on Boston, for $498.75. Now how am I to know whether you ever got this amt. unless you tell me. I know only what you tell me "that you have got a draft" and of course I want to hear you say that the same draft is paid or that it was not paid. Then again those two clerks salaries you say you rec.d the warrants, but how am I to know whether the warrants were paid or not except guessing at it. Your subsequent letters have explained these two matters and I know now that they were paid. But at the time you left me entirely in the dark about them.

In my collections, I am compelled to take such drafts as I can get. If I rec.d the cash and could buy remittances I could get such as would be perfectly good without a question. Then to know that you rec.d them would be sufficient and I could feel easy, but as long as I am obliged to take all sorts, I can't but feel uneasy untill I get word from you that they have actually been paid. True with Govt. checks there is but little risk, yet knowing the private transactions of some who draw I am forced to be suspicious of them, and then all private drafts. I must get word from you as to their payment before I am satisfied or can settle with the parties here for I seldom take one without still holding the parties here untill I can hear.

Here is a list which I wait to hear from 1860.

Sent you

May 12	draft drawn by Col. T. F. Fauntleroy for		$8,000.00
June 24	" " " D. Hood	"	$100.00
" "	Power of Atty. Philip Smith	"	$333.00
" "	Missionary draft #11624	"	$136.70

		ditto #11625	$125.00
		Mining Co. draft #17	$1,107.40
	herewith draft drawn by D. Hood		$578.91

In case you have already sent notice of any of the above being paid of course it is unnessary to repeat it.

I would like very much to get your account current as agent and must request you to send it as soon as you can find time to make it up. I really need it before I can take off another Trial Balance from our Books, as there are sundry items to enter from it which I can come at in no other way.

My sales during the month of July amt. to $1,200.+ collections for the same time amt. to $3,350.+. Considering the times these figures look very well & we have sufficient reason to be satisfied.

I now enclose Treasury Warrant #8586 part 317—dated Washington July 7th 1860 at sight on the Asst. Treas. of the U.S. at New York for Six hundred and twenty five dollars, signed W. C. Price Treas. of the U.S. F. Biggs register of the Treasy. payable to the order of Kirby Benedict U. S. Judge. (Quarterly Salaries) and by him endorsed to our order

$625.00.

Also, Draft No. 73 dated July 30th 1860 at sight on Mssrs. Clark Bro. Co. Bankers at St. Louis for Five hundred and seventy eight 91/100 dollars drawn by D. Hood, payable to the order of John M. Kingsbury and by him endorsed to our order.   578.91

"Note" This draft no. 73. I rec.d of O. P. Hovey for his note. It is one of those papers I was obliged to take. Send it at once for collection and let me hear the results as I still hold Mr. Rose for it and will not release him untill I hear that you have got the money.

Making in all $1,203.91

Which amt. I have charged to your agent account. I just learn from Mr. Ashurst that Duvall when here left with him sundry claims against persons here which should have been paid before this with instruction to turn the same over to us when collected, but he (Ashurst) now tells me that he has failed to get the money, that it is impossible to get them to pay up. The result is we must still wait & take the chances with Duvall. I mention to you the above the show Duvall's inclination & intention to pay up.

This is all now.

Letter no. 170, Kingsbury to Webb, Las Vegas, August 12, 1860

I have at last run away from Santa Fe for a little recreation will spend a week at the Springs.[23]

I rec.d yours of the 17th with notice of the payment of Col. Fauntleroy's drafts in my settlement with him. I will try to get him to allow the $70.+ exchange.

The day came to sell Charlie's [La Rouge's] Property. The Sheriff

23. Kingsbury apparently went to the hot springs near Las Vegas (5.5 miles from town), later known as Montezuma Hot Springs. In 1863 a visitor noted that the springs were "an unfailing specific for the worst forms of venereal disease" and that they attracted health-seekers "all the way from Denver." Strate, ed., *West by Southwest*, 120.

commenced to cry the sale when Charlie came to me and said he did not like to see his property sacrificed at a forced sale. There was no one present with money & that it would bring nothing. He had raised $400.+ if I would take that he would give me on the first day of November 200 sacks of corn with security that it should be forthcoming. I stop[p]ed the sale, took the cash, & his note for the corn with Ivers for security and then stayed the judgment untill Nov. 1st. So by this move I have got $400.+ in cash from him and the property is still bound under the execution for the balance. All the difference is that I allow him 3 months longer to pay the balance either in corn or the money. I think this is the best thing I could do. If I had not taken this proposition I should have been compelled to buy in the property, which of course we did not want, and then under the law he would have had the privilege of redeeming it in one year. The balance now is only about $300. & I think this he can raise, or at any rate we will get the corn which I can at once turn into cash. I neglect nothing by leaving at this time. All my matters are in a stand still condition and will do just as well as though I was at home. Money is so scarce that I cannot collect little bills & for the larger ones I must give them time. Six companys had arrived at Taos from Salt Lake & were expected at Santa Fe every day when I left.[24] I understand that the Col. would distribute them in the most favorable places to prevent the Navajoes from continuing their depredations. There is a strong effort also to get the Gov. [Rencher] to call for volunteers and the impression was when I left that he would call for 4 companies & that the Commander (Fauntleroy) would sanction it.

This movement if it goes on well will help matters a little, and must cause some money to be expended in the settlements. The crops this year are almost a failure particularly the corn. Wheat is pretty fair but corn will be scarce & high next winter. The poor people have suffered so much this spring & summer for something to eat that they will not sell as freely as formerly. They want to keep some and those who will have a cirplus [surplus] are asking now the same price as for old corn $7.+ to $10.+

All I have got to do is to lay quiet and when an opportunity offers get in whatever I can. I begin to think now that after all I may do better then all my fears.

This is all now.

Letter no. 171, Kingsbury to Webb, Santa Fe, August 18, 1860

I got back today all safe and well, had a pleasant trip and feel refreshed by my leave of absence.

Last week I sent you a few lines from Las Vegas, giving you a full account of my adjustment with Chas. La Rouge.

I now find your letter of July 21st before me. I cannot know any-

24. "Five companies of the Seventh Infantry, withdrawn from the Mormon campaign in Utah, arrived in Santa Fe on August 17." McNitt, *Navajo Wars*, 390. See chapter 13.

thing about the investments which you are making except what you tell me, I mean as to the risk, but this much you may be assured that I have the utmost confidence that you are not taking any extra chances with our joint funds and let it turn out as it may I shall be fully content and satisfied with what you may do in the [knowledge] that you are doing everything for the best.[25] I just learn that the overland mail contractors have refused to take any mail matter except the legitimate mail from St. Louis to Cal. & that the last three mails started from here to go that way have been sent back to go over the Independence route. I have written you regular every week, but by this move on the part of the mail arraingement you will probably get mine all in a lump. Under date of Aug. 4th I sent you two remittances memo. of which you will find herewith. This is the last which I have started to you and I trust that it has reached you safely by this time. I am anxious to hear on a/c of that "Hood" draft & sorry that there should have been any delay with it.

I have just rec.d from Ashurst $177.50 for account of A. Duvall, which Mr. A. says is all that he has been able to realize for this purpose up to the present. As I came through Tecolote I learned there that Duvall had got a contract to supply Ft. Stanton with corn. It is a large contract at a good price on which he will have a good margin for profit. So by being patient with him I think our chances is fair with what he is to pay us. I think of nothing more now of any importance.

The Gov. has not called for Volunteers. Col. Fauntleroy I understand will not aquies [acquiesce] in it & so they will not be called on for the present.[26]

Letter no. 172, Kingsbury to Webb, Santa Fe, September 2, 1860

I had nothing particular to send last week and did not write to you. Yours of Aug. 7th is now before me. The paper to establish a claim against Magruder will now be unnessary. I hope you will have the good luck to recover from Burr & Co. the $70 odd dollars difference which Mack would not pay.

If Mr. Allen succeeds in making a sale of the Farm let me know when you get the papers all fixed and in your hands.

I am glad to know that you have got the money on P. Smiths salary. I expect to get his Salary for the next quarter, will get it so as to send you at the close of this month. I expected this last letter from you to tell me also about the $100 Hood draft at 6 days time, which I sent you at the same time, perhaps however that you had not got returns from it when you wrote. Will look for advise about it in your next. I on receipt of the bill for collecting the $8000.+ tried my best to get it from the Col. [Fauntleroy].[27] He opposed it resolutely, and I in turn insisted on its payment by him, asserting every possible argument I could think of

25. Webb had written a brief note explaining that he had invested $5,000 at 7 percent in Bank of Commerce, New York. Webb to Kingsbury, Hamden, CT, July 21, 1860, MHS.

26. While Rencher had supported volunteer action against the Navajos the year before (see chapter 12), he was not interested in calling out civilians in 1860, by which time Washington had recognized the urgency of the Navajo situation and had directed Fauntleroy to address it. Moreover, the region was swarming with the newly arrived troops from Utah, unlike in 1859 when soldiers were scarce. Keleher, *Turmoil in New Mexico*, 104-5. Rencher's resistance to volunteer action proved futile, as well as unpopular. The citizens of Santa Fe raised an unauthorized militia that marched against the Navajos that fall. Horn, *New Mexico's Troubled Years*, 82.

27. Webb had incurred some expense in trying to collect the money owed them by Fauntleroy. As he explained to Kinsgsbury: "Col. Fauntleroy can have no good excuse for refusing to pay the expenses of collecting and exchange on his draft. The money was due in Santa Fe, and in cash which was as good to us as cash in New York. He choose [sic] to draw on Virginia, and, of course is bound for the expenses. I will get the bill of expenses from the cashier of the Bank and enclose to you." Webb to Kingsbury, Hamden, CT, Aug. 7, 1860, MHS.

in our favor. I never talked so hard for the like sum of money in my life and believe I would not undertake it again for twice the amt. He finally paid it but under protest that I must refer it for final settlement to arbitration. I took the money thinking that perhaps on reflection he might see the justice of our demands and that would be the end of it. But on attempting to make the entries in our book I found that I had made a gross error in the a/c which I rendered him by allowing him one month rent $75.+ more than he was entitled to. This was a gross mistake of my own & I have no one to blame for it but myself. I immediately claimed of him that I had made an error by allowing him $75 to[o] much in the a/c I had rendered. He remarked that he did not examine closely the paper, that he had left it in his room, & would look to it, since which I have not heard from him. He won't do to tye too [tie to], nothing but his money & official rank makes him a <u>man</u>. I cannot discover the first principle of justice in his composition. This is just a true report of how the matter stands now. How I will get through with it remains to be proven. I have been vexed with myself ever since I discovered this error. Don't scold. I feel bad enough about it anyhow. With most persons it could be rectified soon as it was explained but with him I think it a great chance whether I ever get it back or not. My collections for the month of Aug. amt. to $1,500.+ these are small figures, but I have done the best I could and conceive that I have neglected nothing. Business still continues very dull, throughout the whole Territory. I don't believe that there is a store in Santa Fe that has made expenses since Jany. last. It is truly unpleasant to see how perfectly stagnant business is. The crop of corn is allmost an entire failure this year. Wheat is good, they will realize more than an average crop. I now enclose you War Warrant #9486 part 9291 dated Washington 24th May 1860, at sight on the Asst. Treas. of the U.S. at New York for Five hundred dollars, signed by W. C. Price, Treas. of the U.S. registered May 24th 1860 F. Briggs regist. of the Treasury payable to order of 2nd Lt. T. W. Walker 3rd Infty. and by him endorsed to our order. $500.00

<u>Also</u>, Check #951 dated Santa Fe N.M.
Sept. 2nd 1860 at sight on the Asst. Treas. of
the U.S. at New York for One Thousand dollars,
drawn by J. L. Donaldson A.Q.M. payable to our order $1,000.00
   Making in all $1,500.00
which amt. I have charged to your agent account.

   Many thanks for the consolation at the close of your letter.[28] From every indication I will be bound to take matters as they come and that will be slow enough. I am trying my best to keep coll[ecting] but I am so impatient that it is hard work and almost next to impossible. If I had any assurance that I could leave next Spring at the time or any where near it, that I had set, I would try to be contented untill then,

28. Again, Webb had tried to encourage Kingsbury: "You must not get nervous, keep your courage up, and take things slowly, yet watch closely. We must expect to loose some, and if we loose more than we expected, and have done all in our power to protect ourselves we must not cry." Ibid.

but the way I see things now I fear that there is no hope for me before next fall, and no certainty even then.

Tom has sold out his El Paso Stage line to Elsberg & Amberg for $15,000.+ they to pay the cash or satisfy his creditors as he shall direct, as far as that sum will reach. Tom will start down this week to turn over the Stock &c. and give them possession. He tells me that he thinks with this amt. he can pay all the legitimate debts of the mail and that he will get clear and save the Exchange property.[29]

This is all now,

P.S. If you please, do send me you agt. a/c soon as you can find time to make it out. Have you ever drawn that small balance from Doan King & Co. St. Louis?

Letter no. 173, Kingsbury to Webb, Santa Fe, September 8, 1860

I have now got yours of Aug. 13th—I have done nothing this week.

I send herewith a letter from Ashurst which will show how matters stand with Duvall. I believe we will get this money after a while. The [Nat] Macrae debt I count a total loss. It will be a scratch if we ever recover a cent there. He is laying about Albuquerque & living like a lo[a]fer. I have some little doubt now about the balance due from Rosenstein. He may pay it but it will be slow. He bought goods in the states & I know that he is paying his debts there to the pr[ejudice] of those he owes here. He is a grand scamp & is capable of doing almost anything. Still I believe he can pay us if he will.

If all goes well at the Exchange, no accident by fire & we will recover there all that Tom owes us, but to keep the house up during the dull times and opposition this Spring I had to be easy with them and help them all that I could and still must be lenient with them untill they have time to realize & collect their accounts.

I have now got to pull through that mill about $8,000.+ and have still on hand for them Liquors not delivered about $1,000.+ They are doing very well now and shortly will be able to pay a good portion but it will take time to get the whole thing wound up. Will probably be one of the last to get off of our books. He Marsh has got 400 head of cattle on the road if these get here safe and can effect a sale to Col. Grayson he will be out of the woods at once. The cattle are from Arkansas and coming on Tom's <u>Neiotio</u> [Neosho] route. They look for them now to arrive every day.

Mr. Rose has determined again to go to California, is making preparations to get off some time this month.

I sent you last week two drafts amt.g to $1,500.+ which I hope you have rec.d all safe before this. You will find herewith a memo. of them.

29. Webb was happy to hear that Tom Bowler had finally sold his mail contract, and advised that "he should take his business in charge himself and get rid of Frank as soon as he can." Ibid., Sept. 24, 1860, MHS.

I am sorry the colt did not come. I had counted a good deal on it. Am disapointed.[30]

Ellison is about & just the same as ever. When they started for court at Las Vegas, the Judge [Benedict] & all hands were tight [ie., drunk], the driver Bully Welch, Houghton & Col. Street. They had not reached the rock corral when Ellison got uneasy at the speed, thought they would never get to Pigeon's & took the lines from the driver. Did not drive 500 yards before he hit a stump & upset the whole crowd. The carriage was pretty badly broke but they made out to fix up & go on. In the turn over Judge Benedict fell under the others & hurt his left arm pretty bad. It swelled up directly but they all thought it was not serious as he could move his fingers. Since he has got back & the swelling gone down he finds that the small bone at the elbow was dislocated & is now set itself in the place it was [k]nocked too, and will be a permanent injury to him. He can use the arm but it will be stiff. The others got off with slight bru[i]ses.[31] At the court old man Hatch was indited for putting his brand on cattle that were proved to be stolen, 9 head and all fresh branded. At the court here last month, Rogers, the machinist, I think you know him a short thick set man, perhaps he was with Leitensdorfer when you was here. He was afterwards employed as engineer & Blacksmith at the Gov's. mill. Was convicted of murder for shooting a mexican in a drunken spree last Christmas day and is to be hung on the 14th this month.

The Navajoes are still very bad and running at large through the whole Territory.

The El Paso stage which left here last Monday week was attacted by them at this end of the Jornada. The mules all taken & the contence [contents] of the stage, mail &c. scattered in every direction. <u>Deavers</u> was the conductor and had only one man (mexican) out rider, with him. They were both killed and were buried at Fort Craig. It is Deaver who ran so long on the Independence route, and drove your carriage when you went in with your family.[32]

Tom is now gone below with Amberg to turn over the things on the line.

Col. Fauntleroy [h]as been very busy & I let him alone this week. This is all now.

Letter no. 174, Kingsbury to Webb, Santa Fe, September 20, 1860

My last to you was under date of the 8th inst since which I have not had a word from you, but this time I was in hopes to get letters every week.

The whole of this month so far I have been sitting here like a bump on a log doing nothing in the way of collections. It is hard luck but I am doing the best I can.

30. Apparently Webb had promised Kingsbury a foal, but the mare did not "take." Ibid., Aug. 13, 1860, MHS.

31. Webb's only comment was, "I see by your letter that the battle still wages with John Barleycorn. I had hoped that Judge Benedict would give the bottle up. Tell Ellison to keep sober. I am sorry to hear that he is so bad a driver." Ibid., Oct. 11, 1860, MHS.

32. Some of the Navajo perpetrators of this attack were captured, wounded, or killed in mid-October. McNitt, *Navajo Wars*, 396-98.

Marsh is disapointed with his Cattle. He has heard from them. They got out a good piece and were obliged to stop owing to the want of water & grass. The road is completely dried up and if they had pushed on would have run a big risk of loosing the whole outfit. They may get through this fall, but he is fearful that they must lay over untill Spring. Mr. Rose is nearly ready to start for California, will get off next week. He says what Marsh owes him must pay what he owes us and makes no other alternate for us but wait for that house to realize the amt. His property in the States is still bound & in case of accident we have that to fall back on. It is drawing 10% and is probably perfectly safe. All that frets me about it is the prospect of it taking so long to realize it. Yet if those cattle get here safe there is some chance of our getting out in a reasonable time, say one year.

The new Post at Bear Spring called Ft. Fauntleroy is being established.[33] Tom has sent our goods in charge of his partner "Gilespe" for the sutler's store. They bought them off Spiegelberg.

Dr. Connelly was freighting corn out there for the troops and the Indians run off all the mules of his train (75) within 4 miles of the new Post. There is a strong demonstration being made now against the Navajoes. There are now in the field 15 or 16 companies regulars, and one Co. volunteers from each County in the Territory. These are called out & equipped by the Citizens without the consent of either the Governor or Col. Fauntleroy[34] and in addition "Piffer" [Albert H. Pfeiffer] sub Ind. Agt. starts today from Abique [Abiquiú] with 500 to 600 Utahs. Think this is the commencement only of a protracted war with those Navajoes. They must be exterminated or they will be worse than ever when this Compagne [campaign] closes.

Col. Fauntleroy is such a Bear I have not ventured to ask him yet for the $75. To tell the truth I am afraid of him.

Letter no. 175, Kingsbury to Webb, Santa Fe, September 30, 1860

I am now in receipt of yours of 1st inst. with notices of protest of drafts for $1,107.40/100. I am much annoyed at this result from the time which elapsed it must have been accepted, and from this I judge that the paper in itself is all right as far as the parties here are conserned and was protested for want of funds only. I hope the only difficulty in the matter is a question of time and that you will be able to make the money out of the parties there. I have sent the notices forward but fear that there is a poor show of getting any thing here. We still hold the property as security of H. & A. [Hoppin & Appel] but they can ill afford to loose this amt. of cash, and for all conserned and ourselves in particular I do hope you can get the money on it there. If you succeed it is like so much made.

I have rec.d this week $300.+ on account from Simon Rosenstein.

33. See chapter 13.
34. Kingsbury was nearly correct. Companies of volunteers from five counties followed the movements of fourteen companies of regular forces, the disapproval of Gov. Rencher and Col. Fauntleroy notwithstanding. McNitt, *Navajo Wars*, 390–99. See note 26.

My whole collections for this month amt. to $2,700.+

I am setting my pegs now to get the amt. due us for those State House Irons. Houghton has taken it in hand for us and he thinks that he can get us the money in a few months. I don't count much on it but at the same time think it best to get the matter stirred up & perhaps it may go through. I don't intend that they shall go out of my hands untill they are paid for.

Herewith you will find Draft dated Santa Fe July 30 1860, at sight on Hon. Joseph Holt, Post Master General Washington City—D.C. for Four Thousand and Sixty two 50/100 dollars ($4,062.50/100) being for service on mail route #12,851 from July 1st to Sept. 30th 1860 inclusive, drawn by T. F. Bowler contractor and attested by David V. Whiting, Postmaster, payable to your order. Also letter of advice to the Postmaster Genl. concerning the same subject.

This amt. when realized we get from Simon Delgado on a/c of his note to us due Jany. 1st 1860. The departments are intitled to the whole month of October to adjust their accounts, and you may not get his money untill some time in November. Do your best however to recover it and use your own discresion in case there are any small stoppages or deductions. Soon as you can get this draft settled and realized let me know and give me the net amt. rec.d with a statement of all deductions or costs which may accrue, as I am only to allow Delgado to actual amt. which we may realize on it.

I have also made arraingements for you to receive direct from the department $275.00 for service of Philip Smith in the officer here of Surveyor Genl. from July 1st to Sept. 30th inclusive and herewith send you his power of Atty. to endorse the warrant. This amt. is due at once & you should receive it at once. Let me hear the result of this as soon as you can. I get it from J. G. Marsh &Co. and only credit to them when I know that you have got the money.

When the above amts. are realized take them up on your account as agent.

I have some ready cash now on hand and when I can get some more to put with it will send you a remittance. This is all now.

P.S. Tom has returned all safe, he tells me that the mail which the Indians took on the Jornada is his loss. He had to allow Amberg $1,500.+ for it. He has raised the mortgage on the Hotel and paid up as far as his funds would go, and finds now that he owes still some $5,000.+ mail debts. His draft which I send you now he gave Simon [Rosenstein or Delgado?] to secure him some time ago for certain endorsements on loaned money which Tom raised on Simon's name of Mercure over a year ago.

Tom has now got the Hotel, garden & the concord Buggey with one pr. of good mules left all free to raise the $5,000.+ He told me yesterday that young Dr. Beck (a Nephew of Preston) offered him $7,000.+ cash for the Exchange Property.[35] He has set his price at $8,000+ and don't want to let it go for less. Both are pretty stiff & I don't think they will trade, however it is possible they may. Tom talks of leaving soon to spend another winter in Washington looking after his claims there. He has great faith in getting it through next session [of congress] & if he can, would like to hold the Exchange as it pays $100.+ a month rent. He values the gardain at $4,000+ says that it cost him with the improvements more, but I doubt if at the present time he could raise $2,000.+ for it.

Last mail brought him word that his wife has a fine little Boy all getting along well. She is still with his mother in Missouri.

J.M.K.

Letter no. 176, Kingsbury to Webb, Santa Fe, October 6, 1860

Dear Sir, I have now got yours of Sept. 11th with the protested draft returned. I am sorry you failed to get the money on this paper, as I see no show to get it here. I will hold the draft untill I hear from the notices which I have sent & then if H. & A. [Hoppin & Appel] want it will send it to them, and look to their mortgage to save us. In the mean time I hope to realize the Duvall notes so that the amt. will be that much less.

In my last I sent you Bowlers mail draft on the Dept. for $4,062.50 for services on El Paso route from July 1st to Sept. 30, 1860 inclusive also Power of Atty from P. Smith to receive $275.00. I feel uneasy to hear from this letter as I look upon the mail as very unsafe, on account of the Indians and count it a near scratch if they continue to get through safe.

I now enclose draft No. 116 dated Santa Fe N.M.
Oct. 4th 1860 at sight on Mssrs. Clark Brothers
& Co. Bankers, Saint Louis Mo. for Five Hundred
dollars ($500.+) drawn by D. Hood, payable to the
order of John W. Dune and by him endorsed to our order $500.00
"Note" This draft I got from Debus & Schwarzkopf
let me know the cost of collecting it. They are to
pay the expense.
Also, draft #353 dated Mesilla, Sept. 28th 1860 at
Ten days after sight on J. V. P. Gardner Treas.
Overland Mail Co. 84 Broadway N.Y. for Three
Hundred dollars, drawn by G. Hawley Supt.
payable to our order $300.00
Also, draft #87 dated Mesilla Sept. 17th 1860 at one
day after sight on Lovell Colls & Co. 86 Front St.
N. York for One Hundred dollars, payable to the
order of T. F. Bowler and by him endorsed to our order   100.00

35. Deed records from 1861 indicate that Bowler retained ownership of the Exchange. We assume that in selling it to Leonard Rose, then later to John Marsh, Bowler carried a mortgage. See Kingsbury to Webb, Santa Fe, Feb. 24, 1861, MHS.

drawn by Hayward & McGrorty

Also, draft Dated Oct. 5th 1860 at sight on Wm. T.
Smithson Banker at Washington City for Four
Hundred and ten dollars drawn by Robt. A. Mathews
payable to the order of T. F. Bowler & by him
endorsed to our order.   410.00
"Note" This draft I collected from Tom for our claim
on Beck. This transaction is all legitimate. Tom sold
Mathews a pair of mules for this draft. He Mathews
was just starting for the States & was tipsy when he
made the draft which is the cause of its being written
so bad and the word Washington City left out. It is
right & aught [ought] to be paid. I know that he got
the mules & money with Mr. Smithson

   Making in all $1,310.00
which amt. I have charged to your agent account. All these drafts I get
in collections some directly & some indirectly I want you to loose no
time in having them presented and shall want to hear the result of
each at the earliest period you can send me word. Don't forget the
exchange on the St. Louis draft $500.+ I will get it of Debus when I
know what it is. I have still some Cash on hand, but will keep it for
the present as just now none of the Officers are drawing on New York
Treas. & I had rather keep the money than put it in other drafts.

 The Navajoes run off all the mules of Elsberg & Amberg's train
which only arrived here from the States a few days ago. They took
them within twelve miles of town some 200 in all. A party followed
immediately & picked up some 70 or 80 which give out, but the Indians got off with the balance & all the best animals. So it goes. They
are just clearing the Rio Baja [Abajo] of every hoof that they can find.

 Mr. Marsh's partner in the Cattle (It seems that the cattle are a separate partnership business) got here today by the Southern Mail. Say
that the hird [herd] are coming on and if they escape the Indians
should get here by the 15 to 20th of this month. There is 600 Head.

 This is all now

Letter no. 177, Kingsbury to Webb, Santa Fe, October 27, 1860

 I am now in receipt of yours of Sept. 24th I am very glad to know
that the draft for $578.91 on St. Louis was paid.

 Col. Fauntleroy has been away from town for some time on a Court
Marshal [Martial]. I shall try to get our little difference settled when
he returns. I have no reply yet from Hoppin & Appel about the
protested draft. I know that they are poor & it will be a heavy blow for
them just now if they have to loose it. I have now got a letter from Dr.
Steck stating that he had made arraingements with Mr. Duvall by
which he (Dr. Steck) had agreed to place to the Cr. of Duvall $1,000.+

on our books, and that he would send us a draft for that sum to be
paid on the first of Jany next. I have again made a compromise with
Chas. La Rouge and got a settlement in full with him. I found that he
had not got the corn & it would be impossible for him to pay the balance in Corn as agreed, so I told him if he would pay me at once the
value of the corn as it [he] took it at (it is now high and worth more)
in cash that I would let him off provided he would pay the Sheriff's
fees which was $17,50. He complied and I got from him this certificate
of deposit for $532.85 which you will find herewith giving him the diff-
erence in cash. I presume that the paper is good & that there can be
no question about it. So this will wind up one of my hard cases.

   Marsh's cattle have got through safe with comparative small loss.
Out of the lot of 600 they lost 70 head. I find now that there are three
partners in this lot of cattle which leaves 200 for Marsh's part. He tells
me that 100 only are Beef cattle and the balance cows & young stock,
and he thinks that he had better keep the Beef for the Hotel. It will
last him a year and will count more to him in the end to use it that to
sell at present prices & be thrown on the market to get his beef as he
can. The cows he will put on his Gallenos ranch untill he can dispose
of them. In fact He keeps the whole lot there and sends for a few head
as he needs them. As this has turned out I see no chance of our getting
ready cash out of them, though it is a good thing that they have come.
His expense for beef is a heavy item and always cash. They have now a
year's stock and if the Comanches do not take them it will materially
lessen their cash expenses.

I now enclose to you certificate of deposit No. 297
made by Thomas F. Bowler at the Banking house
of Sweeny Rittenhouse Faut & Co. at Washington
City, dated Washington Aug. 25th 1860 payable at
sight on his endorsement for Five Hundred and
thirty four 85/100 dollars, said certificate signed by
them and endorsed to our order by him $534.85
Also Check No. 621 dated Fort Bliss Texas September 16th
1860 at sight on the Asst. Treas. of the U. S. at New
York for Seven hundred and fifty dollars signed by
Thos. G. Rhett paymaster U.S.A. payable to the order
of Joseph Magoffin & by him endorsed to our order   750.00
Also, Treasury Warrant No. 8904 part 699 dated
Washington Oct. 1st 1860 at sight on the Asst. Treas.
of the U.S. at New York for Six hundred and twenty
five dollars signed by W. C. Price Treas. of the U. S.
& registered by C. T. Torres Act.g register of the
Treasury payable to the order of Kirby Benedict
U. S. Judge and by him endorsed to our order   625.00
   Making in all $1,909.85
which amt. I have charged to your agent account.

Judge Houghton has considerable confidence that he will get the State House money for us and has directed his agent at Washington to send the amt. direct to you at New Haven, as soon as it is paid. Our bill is $912.41+ there may be some deduction for collecting. Houghton is now in Albuquerque when he returns I will ge the name & address of his agent there & send is to you that you may corrispond with him at once. See how the case stands, what the prospects are &c. &c.

P.S. Have you heard from Batesville yet?

Letter no. 178, Kingsbury to Webb, Santa Fe, November 4, 1860

I have now the pleasure to note the receipt of yours of Oct. 11th. This looks more like a letter than anything I have rec.d from you for a long time, and I return many thanks.[36] I had been sending you full letters and trying my best to be faithfull in posting you on everything in any way connected with our business, and looked for your sympathy and incouragement in return. Your silence only indicated that you had but little interest in what I was doing or at least it appeared so to me and I confess that I took it pretty hard. I hope from this on you will not fail to reply promptly and fully to all matters where money is conserned. I need confirmation from you on many of them and if you are not prompt in replying it places me in an awkward position with the different parties here.

In my last I sent you remittances amt.g to $1,909.85, memo. of which you will find herewith. I trust they have reached you safely and will be duly paid. In making up this remittance it took all the money I have realized up to the present time leaving me only about $40 on hand. My collections for the month of October sum up $1,450.+ all told. This is small figures but times are hard and this was all that I was able to accomplish. I hope to come out better this month but cannot tell now. The prospect now is bad it looks dull enough ahead. We can now set Macrae's debt down as a total loss. Beck & Johnson attached everything in the Assignees hands and succeeded in making the suit stick and have sold everything for their own benefit. They realized about $850.+ and the balance of the creditors will get nothing.

I have been working Rosenstein for sometime on the very grounds which you suggest. The amt. is now so reduced there that I have much hope to get it all in time. I am keeping sharp watch on the Exchange, but cannot hurry things there. They must have their own time. Marsh is the principal man, in fact he is the only man I depend upon and he is in very delicate health.

You will see on my last Trial Balance an a/c against E. Harris. He was sutler at Cantonment Burgwin.[37] When they broke up the post he took his goods, stock &c. to Pike's Peak in hopes to realize them there without loss. I have not rec.d a cent yet and if he is not honest this

36. Kingsbury was justifiably miffed since Webb's letters from this time amount to nothing more than a few paragraphs; Webb had turned his attention to farming.

37. Cantonment Burgwin was established in 1852 as a temporary post. Built out of green pine logs, by 1859 it had rotted to the point that some complained of the smell. Frazer, *Forts and Supplies*, 68, 94. Abandoned in the reorganization of 1860, the fort deteriorated and disappeared. The site was acquired by Southern Methodist University in the mid-1960s; the reconstructed fort presently serves as a classroom/library building.

can be counted with the bad ones. He owes in Santa Fe about $4,000, and also some small debts in Taos. He has been gone so long that the impression here is that he has run off but nothing certain known. I learned indirectly that he was established at Colorado City and I have desided to give our claim to Houghton who will start in a few days for Denver City & must pass Colorado on the way for him to do the best he can with it.

There is nothing done on the State House this year and probably will not now untill next Spring. I understand it is to be done by contract. Several estimates have been submitted in all of which I have been careful to have our irons mentioned as on hand and necessary for the work and as yet unpaid. I am confident we will be paid but when I have no Idea. As I stated to you in a previous letter I was stirring in this Affair and had got Houghton with the view of getting it paid at once direct from the Appropriation. The whole thing is now in the hands of John H. Peters, Esq. Washington City, who has instructions to send you the money in case it is paid. By writing to him direct you may learn immediately just how the matter stands and what the prospects are. They are still in my possession though they are considered delivered. I intend to hold them untill the money comes. Still if any contracts should leave them on our hands there is poor show of realizing anything out of them. This is why I have been active in getting them placed in all the estimates. Now I come again to Hoppin and Appel. I must get you to make further efforts in this matter and help me if you can. I have just got a letter from them in reply to my notice of the protested draft in which they say that Col. Andrew Talcott the present superintendent of the Mines writes them under date of Oct. 15th that "The mail of Saturday brought letters from the Cincinnati Office to 22 Sept. In which I am assured that all the drafts drawn by Mr. Lathrop with my approval will very soon be paid, Mr. Chas. D. Posten was at that time in New York making arraingements to come out with funds sufficient to settle the accounts for which no drafts have been drawn & I am led to expect his arrival within a fortnight." Now if this be true it is possible that at this time there is funds with the Secty at N.Y. to meet this draft, and it strikes me that it would be well for you to try and get this amt. there on that Second of Exchange which you have still on hand. Send it by express or private hands or by some one who will spend time to find that Mr. Brown and if he has got the money but should refuse to pay on that paper (Having accepted the First) try to have the money retained or get it by giving security untill I can again return you the original which he accepted. I consider all the parties here as doubtfull and so far out of my reach that I think it worth the effort even at some Costs to try and secure it there if possible. True the mortgage on the land is good but if we can get this draft paid it is like so much gain to both them & us.

I am sorry to hear that your lady is so sadly afflicted. Hope with you that it may prove nothing serious and that it can be easily & permanently removed.[38]

With very kind regards to All

P.S. Don't be uneasy about that Farm [Magruder's] if you cannot sell it at a fair price. Keep it untill I come home, it can't run off, and by waiting perhaps we can save ourselves on it. Don't indicate to Dr. Allen an over anxiety to push the sale.

You ask about Tom, from what I can learn he is getting along but poorly. He is now in trouble with his sutlership at Fort Fauntleroy. The officers there are opposed to the Appointment on the ground that the Secty. of War had no right to appoint a sutler that they did not choose, and the Board of Administration have put the prices of his goods at or less than they are worth in St. Louis and say that they have done so to run him off. He has now on the way 3 wagon loads which he bought of Moore and has sent Dr. Kavanaugh out there to take charge of his interest with strong letters in hopes that he Kavanaugh can satisfy the Officers and get the appointment in which case Tom will resign & be privately interested with Kavanaugh.

[Ft.] Butler is not yet established but will probably be soon, for that place he has made the same arrangemnt with Moore that is that Moore is to try to get the Appointment in case he does Tom will resign. Moore will then furnish all the goods, attend to all the business Tom not to appear or have anything to do with it and is to receive from Moore ⅓ of the net profit. Tom is now thinking of leaving soon for Washington. He wants to be there in December to follow up his claim for Mail Damages. He will probably leave and in order to go he must leave all his business in this Country at six & sevens. It appears that he has got no settlement yet with Frank and cannot until all the old debts are paid. Tom takes the rent of the Exchange and has taken everything that he can out of Frank's hands. Frank is very crooked and getting more so every day, is drinking hard. His word cannot be relied upon in any matter whatever. He with his family still occupy the house at the gardain. I hear from Col. St. Vrain that Frank wanted to go to Pike's Peak and had partially made arrangements to go in company with him. It will be a good thing for Tom if he goes & does not return. Tom tells me that his sutlership with Gordan at Pawnee Fork is doing first rate making money fast but I have learned to look upon everything with suspition and don't believe it. One thing sure Tom is trusting everything to others and is liable to be swindled on all sides. I have no confidence that he will get his claim against Govt. and if he does not, it is my private opinion that he is broke as flat as a flounder and must work for his living.[39]

This is in private of course. Don't let him have any money if he applies to you this winter. J.M.K.

38. Webb had mentioned that Lillie was in poor health: "We have discovered a tumor on her shoulder which causes her some trouble and pain in using her arm, and much anxiety of mind. We hope it will prove nothing very serious but expect it will have to be removed." Webb to Kingsbury, Hamden, CT, Oct. 11, 1860, MHS.

39. Kingsbury is again referring to Tom Bowler's claim against the government for payment on his Neosho to Albuquerque mail route.

P.S. As I had already predicted the El Dorado has closed that is all but the Bar room. That is still going on and I suppose that they are still prepaired to keep open banking tables but have had no games there for some time. They closed the eating apartment and discharged all their Bo[a]rders on the 1st of this month. Marsh's table is now full and crowded and on the whole I should think he was doing a pretty fair business in his house. The greatest trouble he has is with his collections. Money is so scarce that he cannot collect cost and I fear that the house is making many doubtfull a/cs but it cannot well be avoided. I believe he is using every diligence and is doing the best he can. What little play is now going on is here at the Exchange, but it is quite limited and in reality amt.s to almost nothing.

Many thanks for your sympathy at my loss in a sister & for your promptness in being willing to go there [Boston] at my request, but on reflection I think it will not be nessesary at present. I am disposed to extend to him every charity and am willing to give him a chance to reform if he will before I return. I am very anxious that he should turn over a new leaf and be a man. Keep charge of his little ones and set them a proper example, in this I am willing to assist him untill he is out of the mill. [I] have no wish whatever to interfere with his family only as a last resort and I fear even at the worst I should have no power there, as he will never consent to be separated from them. Now my only hope is in his reforming. If he does not I shall stop my assistance and thereby through stern necesity force some sort of a change there. Either compel him to take care of them himself turn them over to me, or trust them to the cold charity of the world.[40]

J.M.K.

[P.S.] The Navajoes are becoming very bold & have nearly got possession of the whole Territory. The fact is they go just where they please killing & robbing all the while. We have had much excitement here with them this week. They first killed a herder near rock corral, cry of Indians soon filled the town, several Americans who started out that way on their regular business were turned back by the reports of Mexicans. There was no mounted troops here. The Col. [Fauntleroy] finally sent out all he had here which was only a small detachment here in charge of Gov't. property, about 15 strong & they went out against the foe in two wagons. Of course they saw no Indians, reports continuing to come in, & the dead bodies of 3 Herders, Pino of Delgado & Sandoval, also having arrived, created much excitement. Finally Simon Delgado applied to the Governor for arms, and got up a party of mounted Mexicans about 45 strong, and started out. Found the Indians consentrated near Galisteo, a large number some say 40 others as high as 60. Any rate the Indians were strong & bold enough to stand in the open plain and did fight from Eleven A.M. until 3 P.M.

40. Kingsbury's sister, who was described as being in poor health (see chapter 7), had died in Boston. Webb to Kingsbury, Hamden, CT, July 6, 1860, MHS. One of the children to whom he refers could be the nephew with whom he lived out his later years in Boston. See Afterword.

Jesus Baca, Miguel Pino and other good fighting men were of the party. They lost three men killed on the ground & 5 wounded, two of which have died since. They all report having killed 13 Indians & wounded many more. The Mexicans also lost about half of their horses, two or 3 shot but the balance run off by the Indians. My boy Talisforo went & was in the fight. From him I learn that only about half the men went into the fight (mexicans I mean) the others were about 2 miles behind, staid there looking on and left the foremost party to fight it out alone. They were in too tight place to run & had to stand & fight it out. From him I infer that the Mexicans were whip[p]ed & that both Mex & Indians were glad to quit.

When this word got here, the 15 strong were mounted & started (horses having arrived in the meantime) on a forced charge to <u>Gallisteo</u>, and was at the seat of Battle next day at sun up, but no Indians to be seen except the dead on the field. Information since proves that while the troops were going to meet them they were coming this way and while the troops were looking for them at the place of the battle, the Indians with about 100 head of Horses, Ponies & Mules were making for the river and actually passed just below <u>Agua frio</u> [Agua Fria] between the <u>Serriga</u> [Cienega] and the <u>Mesa</u>, and crossed out at <u>San Alfonso</u> [Ildefonso], but are still small parties of two to 5 roving about. At Johnsons in the <u>Cannion</u> only yesterday two came there took his horse out killed it, took what they wanted of the meat & left. Word from below states that they are running over the whole <u>Rio Abajo</u> at large, making just such depredations as their fancy leads them to. Really the Territory is now at their mercy. I fear this mail may be in dainger of being cut off, and am quite uneasy about sending these drafts at this time!

Letter no. 179, Kingsbury to Webb, Santa Fe, November 25, 1860

I am now in receipt of yours of Oct. 27th and 31st, many of your questions I have anticipated. Fort Defiance is not broken up, Webber is still there as suttler and must be doing well. The stock and fixtures at the El Dorado have been sold at Auction, Frank Green & Woods were the principal purchasers. The affairs at that house are so mixed up that I do not pretend to understand them. I heard yesterday that what Frank bought he could have by paying the cash as other purchasers, and that they are held for him to pay for or no delivery. Frank's word is not worth a straw and I am sorry to say that I don't believe that Tom's is much better. I am sorry for them, I believe they are both used up. As for Woods I don't know anything about his means. The little claim we had against that house was paid on the security—which I got and I am done with them. Woods may be able to settle up and try to open the house again, but I hope not. There was an Appropriation passed last

winter for our State House of $60,000.+ some of the old claims have
already been paid our of this money direct, and I am in hope to get our
claim paid in the same way and have taken the proper steps, all of
which you are duly advized. The understanding is that the State
House must be complete with this $60,000.+ and is to be let on Con-
tract. Up to the present it is not awarded to anyone & whoever may
get it can do nothing untill next spring or summer.

My last to you was of Nov. 4th since then I have made a trip to
Albuquerque got $300. from Simon [Rosenstein] and his promise that
we should be paid in full before the 1st of Jany., the balance due is
about $450. & I trust he will make his word good. I could not induce
him to give a note. I also succeeded in getting a settlement in full with
Townsend at Algodones. Houghton was going to Denver with Col. St.
Vrain, but by some misunderstanding as to the time Houghton did not
meet him and the Col. left without him so Houghton will not go at
present and I do not send the a/c against Harris. Perhaps it is just as
well. I have but little confidence in Houghton. He is really poor, and if
he got anything out of Harris might have used it for his own necessity.
This Harris a/c looks bad to me, and I fear that we will loose it anyhow. I don't see how I can reach him or get hold of him. I can't think
of going myself and I don't know who to trust with it. I believe I will
let it rest awhile perhaps something may turn up.

I am not uneasy about that Arkansas Farm. I believe we will get
even there. Mack ain't worth $5.00 it is no use to ask him for that diff-
erence in interest. We must stand it and count it in the Cost of the
farm. We are lucky to get what we did.

Bowler tells me today that he has got notice from the Dept. that
they have deducted $100.+ from his P. O. Draft so I presume you have
recd the money less the $100. stopage.

I am sorry not to get you account current. I shall not take off a Trial
Balance untill First of Jany, and still hope to get your a/c before that
time. I wish you would keep a separate account of all monies received
in the way of Interest or dividends on our joint funds, not get it mixed
up in any way with your Agt. a/c for the firm. Anything that this
money may make or earn has nothing to do with our books here or
business in this country and I don't care to know anything about it
untill I get home. That is I am not particular for you to render any a/c
of it to me here, only just keep a carefull account of all the figures,
items, &c. and we can easily adjust it when we meet.

[Charles] Blumner was appointed deputy Marshal for taking the
Census in this County. The work is done and the papers go to the
Dept. by this mail. He says that he is entitled to $1053. & 54/100—one
half of which will be paid immediately on the receipt of his returns
and the balance as soon as they can be examined and errors rectified.
Now he wants to pay this money to us, has instructed the Dept. to
send his draft or Warrants to you at New Haven, payable at the Asst.

Treasury at New York. These will probably be issued payable to his order and herewith you will find Power of Atty from him for you to endorse and receive the same. The above amt. $1053.54/100 is what he claims, but it is subject to any little deductions which they choose to make. They will pay only according to their own account, but it cannot vary much from this sum. All is take whatever they send you and I am to give him credit here on his a/c for the same. Be particular to notify me of the <u>Amts. as you receive them with the dates</u>, as he (Blumner) is to pay us interest on what he owes us untill you receive this money. This is all now.

Letter no. 180, Kingsbury to Webb, Santa Fe, December 2, 1860

I have just got your two letters of Nov. 7th, I am relieved to know that the P.O. Draft is realized. This is so much to us collected from Delgado. I am also glad to know you had got the P. Smith draft. I suppose there could be no question about its payment & that you got it on presentation. I am sorry to see the result of this Mathews draft. I fear Tom will not have the ready means to refund me the amt. He is now gone out with a party to assist in selecting a place to establish the long talked of "Fort Butler."[41] When he returns (I look for him in a few days) I shall get him to arrainge it if possible. My letter which accompanied the draft to you explains just how Tom got the draft. He has no security & I fear that he will come out minus his mules. Tom owed Beck $200. for corn used on the mail line, and I took this draft giving Tom in Cash $210.+ and the other $200 when paid was to go to Beck's Cr. on our books. So if Tom can not pay it we are in $210.

My last to you was under date of Nov 25th and in it I sent you Power of Atty. to receive and endorse drafts which will be sent you direct from the Dept. for his services in taking the U.S. Census for this County. I hope that you have rec.d it all safe.

The mail so far has got through all safe, and I am in hopes there will be no trouble on the line this winter. I think you had better continue your letters by this line at any rate for the present. It is understood here that the Over land line will not take our mail either to or from. They only contract to carry the through mail for California. By sending on that line I might not get them.

My whole collections for the month of Nov. sum up ($700.+) Seven hundred dolls. Truly discouraging, but I assure you I have done all I could. To this may be added $3952.60 and $275.+ which you rec.d. Times are very hard, how thankfull I am not to have a stock of Goods on hand!! It is a great comfort to be out of debt these hard times. I don't believe that there is a merchant in the Territory today can say that he is out of debt or even easy and tell the truth.

I am very uneasy to hear the result of the balance of drafts sent Oct. 6th which you have rec.d. I hope no more will be protested.

41. One of the reasons for the delay in the establishment of Fort Butler was the army's inability to select a suitable site. See note 15.

P.S. I have very little reliable information about the Navajo war. I think it is at about a close for this season. They have killed altogether about fifty Indians, and captured considerable stock. How much I don't know and cannot rely upon reports. The Volunteers are returning the time having expired for which they enlisted. They did not do much. At present we have many Pikes Peakers passing through here. They are a hard looking set of people and mostly broke, some going to the gold mines in Arizona and some to the new diggings on St. Juan River.[42] This is up beyond Abique [Abiquiú] somewhere between the Navajo & Utah Country. There must be now at this last place on the road there some 500 or 600. Most of them come here by way of Taos for provisions. Corn & Flour is very high and is about the only thing that commands <u>Cash</u>. When I saw Winslow he was making preparations to leave with his family for the states, is probably off by this time. They go with some Officer who is going in on leave. The little he can realize from the sale of his household furniture is his only means. He talked of stop[p]ing at Kansas City with the view of going into business or get some employment there. He was used up here and got to feel it before he left.

I don't remember whether I told you in my last letter or not, that Majors & Russell have <u>100 wagon loads</u> of Groceries & fancy & staple Liquors, which will arrive here in a few days. These will be forced on the market to be sold cheap for cash. I am privately told that they are embarassed and have sent these goods here to raise the wind. All I can say is they will have a nice time with them, but it will be a hard blow on the merchants here who have regular stocks on hand which they must realize. I look upon the Territory as broke all through and you will soon see what I predicted last winter & spring coming true. Those who have been selling goods to this Country must look out or they will slip up. Don't you recomend anyone who may come your way & want to buy on <u>Cr.</u>

J.M.K.

Letter no. 181, Kingsbury to Webb, Santa Fe, December 22, 1860

My last to you was under date of Dec. 2nd since then I have rec.d nothing from you as there has been no through mail from Ind. and now the mails from here stop at Union. Do not go farther on a/c of no mail coming from the States, and as an excuse report that they are affraid of Indians and cannot go without an escort which has not been granted up to the present.

I write these few lines and start it by the overland route that you may hear from me, but have little confidence that it will go through. I have nothing of importance to communicate, every thing here is as dull as it can be. Tom has not been able yet to raise the money to

42. The San Juan River boom, described as "one of the most improbable rushes" by historian Duane Smith, ended almost immediately. Prospectors from the so-called Pike's Peak rush tried their luck in "just about the most isolated, inaccessible, and even inhospitable spot in [far southwestern] Colorado." Lack of food, cold weather, poor returns, and hostile Utes all contributed to the abandonment of the placers after one short season. Smith, *Colorado Mining*, 14.

refund us for that protested draft. He is now trying to raise the wind by mortgageing the Exchange again. He is out of funds and wants money to take him to Washington to look after his claim there. Then besides he owes several pressing debts here which must be paid, and his only show to meet them is to mortgage the house again. If he succeeds I think he will pay us for this draft.

On the 1st of next month I intend to take off a Trial Balance and as soon as corrected will send you a copy that you may see all the a/c. I will also send your agent a/c in full as it stands on our Books at present.

I have got Dr. Steck's draft on Col. Collins, which when paid is to go to the credit of Duvall's notes, but am waiting on Collins for the money. He will pay it soon as he gets some funds. he is short now and cannot meet it. I am in hopes to get it before the 1st of the month.

This is all now.

15.

"Free from this Prison"

Winter and Spring 1861

Letters 182–194

In the winter of 1860–61, Kingsbury continued preparations to leave New Mexico forever. One by one he sold the firm's horse, buggy, and safe, and he continued to try to collect outstanding accounts. But if New Mexico's economy had seemed gloomy in 1860, the new year seemed hopeless. In February he collected nothing. "Money is not to be had," he explained to Webb.[1] Moreover, Kingsbury learned that American troops might be withdrawn from New Mexico because of growing tensions between North and South. If that happened his world would collapse and he would be forced to leave precipitously: "A white man would not be safe here among the Mexicans & Indians, with the troops away."[2]

Desperate to collect something on overdue bills, Kingsbury became more aggressive and inventive. The largest sums owed Kingsbury & Webb were from several owners of the Exchange Hotel, Tom Bowler, and the men who succeeded him, Leonard Rose and J. G. Marsh. His own debts to Kingsbury aside, Marsh apparently needed to pay Rose and Bowler before they could pay Kingsbury. So Marsh, whom Kingsbury regarded as a friend, had to succeed at turning a profit at the Exchange before Kingsbury could settle his accounts and leave Santa Fe. Prospects looked glum. Marsh's hotel operated in the same difficult economy that Kingsbury lamented. Marsh, too, did business on credit. Moreover, time had confirmed Kingsbury's fears about Marsh's poor health. By January Kingsbury knew that Marsh suffered from consumption, the same disease that had killed Kingsbury's wife.[3] Kingsbury persuaded the ailing Marsh to sign over his farm in Missouri as partial payment of his debt to Webb & Kingsbury, and he brokered an intricate deal that would enable Rose and Bowler to pay much of their debt to Webb & Kingsbury as well. Kingsbury completed the arrangements just in time. By March 10, Marsh had died, survived by his wife and two-month-old child.

That deal completed, Kingsbury made further preparations to leave. He packed a trunk to ship ahead, including in it chili and wheat that Webb had requested.[4] Webb probably intended to experiment with the

1. Kingsbury to Webb, Santa Fe, Feb. 24, 1861, MHS.
2. Ibid., Feb. 24, 1861, MHS.
3. Ibid., Jan. 20, 1861, MHS.
4. Ibid., Mar. 30, 1861, MHS.

New Mexico wheat on his Hamden farm, Spring Glen, where he had become increasingly absorbed in agriculture. The distinctive New Mexico chili, however, Webb wanted for his personal consumption. Kingsbury, apparently still waiting for Webb to tell him that he could leave Santa Fe, explained to Webb that he had packed the chili inside the trunk, "but you can't get it untill I come with the key so if you want chili bad you must order me in to open it."[5]

Before Kingsbury started east, he traveled south to pursue the firm's last outstanding account of consequence—that of [Chas. A.] Hoppin & Nathan Appel. In April, he traveled south to Mesilla—near today's Las Cruces, New Mexico—to try to reach a settlement. Four weeks later, about May 5, he returned triumphant to Santa Fe. He had worked out a compromise with Hoppin & Appel, taking a loss in exchange for a cash settlement and some bank notes. Earlier a despondent Kingsbury had expressed concern to Webb that he was "getting lazy & loosing my energies." His success in Mesilla buoyed his spirits—"John is himself again," he told Webb.[6]

That same month Kingsbury left Santa Fe, apparently for the last time. Some unsettled accounts remained, as did some unsold merchandise—liquor and the iron work for the capitol building that would finally become the federal courthouse upon completion in 1889.[7] Kingsbury entrusted the collections and the inventory to his long-time employee, [Tom] Weirick, in whom he had great confidence. And he also left a will with Weirick. News of the firing on Fort Sumter on April 12 and the outbreak of the Civil War had reached Santa Fe and left Kingsbury apprehensive. His journey would take him not only through the country of hostile Indians, but also through the lands of hostile whites.

❧

Letter no. 182, Kingsbury to Webb, Santa Fe, January 5, 1861

I have now before me yours of Nov. 20th with notice of the Sale, terms &c. of Batesville Farm. I think with you that it is a good sale for us, and I am much relieved to have it so far settled and off my mind.[8] Hopkins' acceptance will soon be due and I count upon him to pay it promptly.

I have recovered the $5 Exchange on the St. Louis draft. Bowler mortgaged the Exchange property and his gardain to Joe Mercure for $5,000.+ This placed him in funds to pay off pressing accounts & gave him means to start for Washington. He left last Monday by the Ind[ependence] route, said he intended to go immediately through & would take his family along as he did last winter. You may expect a visit from them. He paid me the $410.+ for R. A. Mathews draft

5. Ibid., Apr. 7, 1830, MHS.

6. Ibid., Mar. 3 and May 5, 1861, MHS.

7 Kingsbury had continued to try to get the federal government to pay for the "irons." Ibid., Oct. 27 and Nov. 4, 1860, and Mar. 3, 1861, MHS.

8. Webb was able to sell the farm for $4,500, due in installments over four years, which he considered a good price for ridding themselves of a potential problem. The buildings were dilapidated and in need of extensive repairs and people were in the habit of stealing the wood and fences. Webb to Kingsbury, Hamden, CT, Nov. 20, 1860, MHS.

protested. I am getting very impatient to hear about the result of that Overland Mail draft $300. & Hayward and McGorty's for $100.+ sent you Oct. 6th.

Herewith you will find Trial Balance from our books up to Jany. 1st 1861. Showing a correct balance of all our a/c at that date. I also send a copy of your Agent a/c as it stands on our books—examine it carefully & notify me of what items are omitted so that I can make the necessary entries.

Did Lt. Cogswell ever send you the $5. which I loaned him. By our books we have a balance in the hands of Doan King & Co. at St. Louis of $49.08. By this mail I have requested them to forward this amt. to you less the Exchange. This amt. is correct unless you have drawn on them or instructed them to pay for us since Jany 27th 1860. You will notice that I have a little over $3,000. cash on hand, it is impossible to send you this at present as there is no good Exchange to be had, none of the Officers are drawing. Since taking off the Trial Balance I have collected the sum of $1,156.25 on papers sent us by Dr. Steck said amt. goes to the credit of notes against A. Duvall. I am in hopes now that Duvall will be able to pay the balances soon. To assist you in any calculation you may wish to make I will state that I have still on hand 1 Cask Pell. Brandy, 3 Bbl. Atwoods Spirits and one Keg Stoughton Bitters. I expect the Spirits have evaporated about half. I have also the Buggy & Harness on hand. The Horse I sold for $150.+ cash. Corn is selling for $9.50 per Fanega and I came to the conclusion that it would not pay to keep him. I shall sell the Buggy at the first fair offer. For the present I have the use of a horse belonging to Marsh which I can drive whenever I wish.

If I had things at the Exchange in a more secure shape I should feel that the weight of my work here was done. As it is I shall try every nerve to get off by April or May next, by that time I will get the other payment from Delgado, and in the mean time shall try to get all other matters in a proper shape so that I can leave them. What do you think about it? I shall not feel free to leave without your concent. So you think it will pay for me to stay longer or is it really necessary that I should. Our books show an outstanding amt. good, bad & indiferent of about $17,500 together with interest & stock on hand, say in round numbers $20,000.+ with ordinary luck by the middle of April I am confident that one half say $10,000+ of this will be realized, then will it pay for me to stay here on expenses looking after the balance? I would like to get a long letter from you with your views &c.

P.S. Is there any hope of getting anything on that old matter from Forsythe?

Letter no. 183, Kingsbury to Webb, Santa Fe, January 20, 1861

My last to you was of Jany. 5th with Trial Balance also your Agt. a/c in full as it stands on our books. I expect a long letter and full one in reply.

Since then I have collected from Marsh some $1,500.+ which goes to the Cr. of Bowler's note. Tom could not well give me the additional security which you suggest and in that part of the Exchange debt I feel pretty safe as all the property of Rose in the States is mortgaged for it and still in our hands. The stick with me is about the $3,000 which J. G. Marsh & Co. owe us and for which we have no security whatever—even this part of it would not look so bad were it not for the condition of Marsh's health. He has confirmed consumption and it is may opinion that he can not live long. I would not be surprised any day to know that he is confined to his room. He is still about and does the best he can. In a house like that you know that there is much for the proprietor to attend to in person and if he is layed up, many things must be neglected and go [w]rong. Soon as an opportunity offers I shall try to get this debt in better shape.

The Southern mail to day brought me your two letters of Dec. 11th and 25th. I expect they came by the way of San Antonio Texas. Our mail is used up. We have big reports about Inds. & heavy snow, but I believe the real cause is want of funds & proper management. Our latest dates by that line are Dec. 13th so we are far behind in political news and the great interests of the day.[9] I am relieved to hear that my last drafts were all paid, but it does appear strange that you say nothing about two sent Oct. 6th (Overland Mail $300.00 & Hayward & McGrorty $100). When you got these drafts you remark on their being a hard lot, which I knew very well but they came in collections & I was very glad to get them, and of course corispondingly anxious to hear the results. The amt. is small, and as you have not sent them back I <u>presume</u> that they were paid. I have not settled with the parties here & will not untill I hear from you about those papers. I am looking for Duvall here every week, he has been doing well at his post, and I expect that he will be able to pay us the balance when he comes. T. H. Hopkins paid $100.+ on a/c was all he could raise will pay up as fast as he can. He is honest can & will pay all be giving him a little more time. I also got a letter today from Rosenstein stating that I could draw on him at sight for the balance due us, which I shall do & send down by Maj. [J. L.] Donaldson who leaves for Albuq. in the morning.

On the strength of your letter I immediately put all my funds together & took Maj. Donaldson's draft on New York for the amt. which you will find herewith. I consider him the safist man here & know he would not draw if there was not funds there to meet it.

9. Webb's letters had contained his assessments of the political turmoil occurring in the East, opinions with a decidedly mercantile orientation. "The election of Abe Lincoln to the Presidency is creating a great excitement South, and the prospect is that several states will secede. This is creating a panic among merchants and brokers and the prospect is that there will be many failures and little business this winter." Ibid., New Haven, CT, Nov. 20, 1860, MHS. The next month he predicted the secession of the border states following the lead of the cotton states further south. "The border slave states will be ruined unless they go with the south. It deprives them of a market for their slave property to remain with the north and it will be unprofitable for them to hold their slaves, unless they can have a market for the surplus. Both sections [North and South] are mad." Ibid., Dec. 11, 1860, MHS.

Whatever you do with our funds it is all right, only let me again urge
you to be cautious & carefull, then should any of your investments
turn out bad why we will make the best of it. I shall be satisfied knowing that you are doing what you think for the best. From all I can learn
times must be very hard in the States, and ready cash should pay well
but don't let this leade you to take extra risks.[10] It is better for us to
consider the security rather than the profit that might arise. I see that
Exchange in all parts is high & in St. Louis specie is 7 to 10% premium.

Now this Check is specie & if it is at a premium with you you
should get the advantage of it.

You will find herewith Check No. 1138 dated Santa Fe N.M. Jany.
20th 1861 at sight on the Asst. Treas. of the U.S. at New York for Five
Thousand Six Hundred dollars ($5,600.00) drawn by J. L. Donaldson
A.Q.M. payable to our order, —which amt. I have charged to your
agent account. What specie I collect from this on I shall hold untill I
hear from you further as to the safety of these Official Govt. Checks,
in the mean time shall take all I can get on accounts.

What do you think about Land Warrants? Will they be good if the
Union desolves?[11] Would it be safe to buy them at a low price, say 50
cents per acre for 160? I could buy some at this price now & perhaps
they will be obliged to sell for less. I shall not touch them unless you
advise it.

I asked Ashurst about the Magruder Deed. He says that the law
here where it was executed does not require witnesses, that it was
acknowledged before the clerk of the court who is a proper and legal
officer and better than any witnesses.

Blumner has notice from the Dept. that his papers were rec.d &
that his pay would be sent to you as requested, but that it would be
necessary for you to have power to receipt & sign in his staid [stead]
for the same. I hope the Power of Atty. sent is sufficient to cover all
the grounds. It was intended to give you full power.

Letter no. 184, Kingsbury to Webb, Santa Fe, January 27, 1861

Since my last I have no word from you. Mine was under date of
20th inst., covering remittance of the following discription, viz. Check
No. 1138, dated Santa Fe N.M. Jany. 20th 1861, at sight on the Asst.
Treas. of the U.S. at New York for Five Thousand Six hundred dollars
($5,600.+) drawn by J. L. Donaldson A.Q.M. payable to our order,
which I hope you have received and got the money for it without trouble. Blumner is getting very uneasy to hear how much you have
received for him.

I have nothing important to write since my last in the way of business. We have had heavy snow and very Cold weather of late. They

10. Times were indeed difficult in the States.
Webb had written "You will see by the stock reports
that everything is a dead smash in N[ew] Y[ork]."
Ibid., Dec. 11, 1860, MHS.

11. Although behind in political news from
Washington, the southern mails had probably
brought reports of South Carolina's secession from
the Union on December 20, 1860—the first of
eleven states to secede that winter.

Webb had advised Kingsbury to hold on to the
land warrants until he heard further from Webb.
"They ought to be good in any event against the
public lands, but the passage of the Homestead bill
will of course depreciate their value." Ibid., Hamden, Feb. 16, 1861, MHS.

have just got through putting up Ice at the Fonda. It is from 10 to 12 inches thick. The extreme cold has kept Marsh in his room most of the time. I have seen him out only once or twice this week and then only for about ½ hour at a time, so that I have had no chance to talk about business with him.

Our files of papers from the States are so incomplete that we know little of what is doing or going on there. We have all sorts of reports and so wild & conflicting that I hardly know what to think or believe. I have held on to the idea that there would be some sort of a compromise and all the trouble settled but I am alone here now in this opinion. If they push matters get into a Civil war it will last for years or at any rate till all the people are ruined. I can see no benefit for either side by war.

Rosenstein has paid the balance which closes his account in full.

I have got another $100. from Hopkins. He still owes $196, which I hope to get soon. I still look for Duvall soon.

This is all now.

Letter no. 185, Kingsbury to Webb, Santa Fe, February 10, 1861

I wrote you last under date of Jany. 27th. Duvall has not come yet. T. H. Hopkins has paid the balance on his acceptance to us in full. My whole collections for the month of Jany. sum up $3,400.+ most of the items which make this some [sum] I have already noted to you so that you know who it came from.

I have now got your letter of Jany. 15th. Blumner is very anxious about his pay & I am at a loss to know why it has not been sent you or at least the first half. Other assistant Marshal's here who were imployed on the same class of work have already rec.d Treas. Warrants for the first half. Your letter is of the 15th which should be ample time for the first payment of $1,500 to reach you from the Batesville farm if it was paid prompt, as you say nothing about it, I fear that there is some trouble about it, and shall be uneasy untill I hear from you on the subject.

I do hope that you will be able to get the money for those State House irons through Mr. Peters. Let me know all that you can learn from him about it.

I am getting impatient to hear the final results with that [Hoppin & Appel] Mining draft. I fear that you will get nothing there & that I must go down to Messilla [Mesilla] and close that mortgage by buying in the property but I cannot make any move in the matter untill I get a desided reply about that Draft.

You will see in the last list of Notes one against Mr. Kozlowski for $321.32. This man keeps the house on the road that Jim Gray had near Pecos Chirch.[12] I have give my best to collect it & am tired with his

12. A native of Warsaw, Poland, Martin Kozlowski came to the United States in 1853 with his English wife. He served in the U.S. Army for five years. Mustered out in in New Mexico in 1858, he settled near the center of the abandoned pueblo of Pecos, along the route of the Santa Fe Trail, where he operated an inn (which Kingsbury tells us he acquired from one Jim Gray). Kozlowski dismantled parts of the old Pecos mission church to use as building material. For more, including his apparently spurious claim to that land, see Hall, *Four Leagues of Pecos*, 122-24.

promises. He owens [*sic*] the house & I shall put this note in next court (which is in March) and try to make the money in that way. Times are still very hard and I see no immediate relief. If anything it looks worse ahead.

The people are very poor, grain and everything in the eating line is very high.[13] There must be much suffering through the Territory. The Officers have had no money for some time, have been going ahead on credit. By my last paper (Jany. 18th) I see that the Army bill has passed. I hope this will place them in funds, and that soon things will be a little easier here. I have not collected a single cent so far this month and it is already ⅓ gone. It is impossible for Marsh to collect close or anywhere near it, and if things continue in this way as dull as it is they will Eat him out. His health is very bad and I am confident that he is failing fast. He has kept his room most of the time for the last three or four weeks. He is really unable to attend to his business & it is going behind. His partner is out on the ranch in charge of the herd of cattle. In fact he has had very little to do in and about the house and is not fit or calculated for it. He is a good safe man but the ranch is his appropriate place. If Marsh should die I am satisfied that the whole thing will go to <u>pot</u>. At all events it looks bad, and I have been in a stew about it for some time, and had determined to take anything I could get for our claim. I know that Marsh had a farm in Missouri but I did not want it only as a last resort. In view of all the facts as I see them I did not think it was safe to wait longer and yesterday I made the proposition to him and have bought his farm for $2,500.+ to be credited on his a/c. I took it at his own price. I made the trade intirely in the dark at a haphazard chance. It is a second Magruder operation & I only hope that it may turn out as well, but there is yet one trouble in the way. He has not got the deeds here or a discription of the property so as to give the proper transfer must send there for them, and I fear that he may not live for these to get here. He is exceedingly sensitive and I have to deal delicately with him. I wanted an immediate bill of sale which he seamed to think unnecessary. He is an honest good man & while he lives his word is as good as his signature. The purchase is all made in good faith & I have not the least doubt but that he will execute the papers, but in view of contingencies I am not willing to trust it & in a few days soon as I can consistently approach him I shall try to get a bond for the deed, from him & his wife and then when the other papers come, have it all fixed in proper shape. His mother now occupies the place, being alone she wishes to leave it and I have got him to write to her to leave it in charge of a neighbor, with instructions to rent it to some one or place it in charge of a responsible person who will take care of the place, insuring him that he shall not be disturbed in his crop this year. Now I will describe to you what he tells me about the place. It is situated in the South west

13. New Mexico had endured a drought for the second year in a row in 1860. See chapters 13 and 14.

of Missouri about 20 miles from Neosho. 160 acres land in 3 pieces,
1 ps. 80 & 2 pcs of 40 each, making 160 acres of which 120 is prairie &
40 timber. On the 80 Acre piece is two small houses one story high,
one a cement house the other a small cottage frame house. Nearby is a
frame barn roofed but not closed in. The houses about 6 years old and
in good repair, about 60 acres of this lot under cultivation and fenced
in. Good spring water and plenty of it. Is three miles from a good
mining district. He has owned it 3 years, bought it to live on but found
his health would not permit it. It is in a valley & a beautifull place. He
says that the houses are worth about $1,200.+ This is all I know about
it—deducting this $2,500. off his a/c there is a balance of <u>$800.</u> which I
would be very glad to get secured in some way. Will take anything that
I can get.

This is all now.

Letter no. 186, Kingsbury to Webb, Santa Fe, February 24, 1861

The mail has arrived and I am really disapointed to get no letter
from you. We have by this mail dates to Feby. 6th while my last from
you is of Jany. 15th.

I have a bond for a deed written out for that Mo. Farm & would
have had it signed before this but Mrs. Marsh is laid up with child
birth. I could not press the matter for her signature just now and so
the matter stands for the present.

I have found a purchaser for Marsh to buy him out in the
Exchange. Got the party together & they have agreed upon terms &
to give possession on the 1st of March. I am assisting Marsh in taking
a/c stock. If the bargain sticks and all goes well I will get cash for the
last Note due us from Rose, to help the trade. I have sold the balance
of our a/c against Marsh to the New purchaser for 50% Cash. I am
Rose's agent and have taken the whole responsibility of the bargain for
him. I release Marsh & take the New Man by his paying this March
note & a mortgage on all the stock as security for the balance due to
Rose. You may not exactly understand this trade, but it is all right provided the transfer goes on. We will get our $3,000—Cash which will
close Tom's Note and 50 cents on the dollar for the balance against
Marsh after deducting the $2,500. for farm & my a/c will have about
$700.+ so we loose $350.+ there and get clear.

Duvall has not come yet. The snow has detained him, it has been 2
& 3 feet deep from [Fort] Stanton to Albuquerque.

I have sold our old <u>Safe</u> for $100.+ cash. This is all the money I
have got in so far this month. Not a $ in collections. I am as cross as a
bear, but it is no use. The money is not to be had. It is really hard
times. the Military are in debt on all sides, the Navajo War has
ex[h]austed all their funds, and there has no money reached here yet

from the New appropriation. In view of the difficulties in the States, it is believed here at headquarters by all the Officers that the troops will all be ordered to the States & New Mexico left to take care of herself. If it should turn out so you can count on my leaving with the troops. A white man would not be safe here among the Mexicans & Indians, with the troops away.

Letter no. 187, Kingsbury to Webb, Santa Fe, March 3, 1861

My last to you was of the 24th ult—I am still without advices from you, and at a loss to account for it.

I have been hard at work the whole week taking a/c of stock for Marsh. He could not do it & finally left it all to me. The new proprietor is in possession but I have not got the bill corrected & papers signed. Will probably get it all fixed in a few days. Think there will be no trouble and all go streight [straight].

The Bond for a deed from Marsh & Wife for the Mo. Farm is signed & in my possession which obligates them to make a Warrantee deed of the same to me soon as the correct boundaries & numbers can be ascertained.

I have to report the gross amt. of my collections for the month of Feby., <u>Nothing</u>.

Duvall has not made his appearance yet and I do not know what to think about him. We should get our money there but when it will come I cannot say. I can do nothing with the Hoppin & Appel debt untill I hear more from you. It is not safe to go down [to Mesilla] now but I want to go soon and get it fixed up in some shape or other.

I am also very anxious to hear what luck you have with Blumner's Paper. Will they pay you the money or no, and what amt.?[14]

Do you get any encouragement from Peters about the pay for the State House Irons?[15] I count on Delgado to pay up prompt on the first of next month, hope he will not disapoint me, though I count on nothing certain these days.

How is Tom Bowler getting along with his claim at Washington?

Maj. [Cary M.] Fry has been ordered to Texas and has started with his family, if he goes east will call and see you.

All the departments here are still out of cash & paying nothing, money is scarce & hard times. No business doing. I am all impatient but cannot hurry things. My accounts are now in a shape that I must wait and let them take their own course. When shall I get free from this Prison? It looks like my time would never come. I fear that I will be kept here till fall. Do write & liven me up. I have been disapointed so much that I have no confidence in any thing. Am getting lazy & fear that I am loosing my energies.

14. Kingsbury was referring to the money the government owed Charles Blumner in payment for his work as assistant marshall and, it would appear, census taker in Santa Fe in 1860.

15. In a letter that Kingsbury apparently never received, Webb had written: "Mr. Peters informed me that owing to objection being made by Mr. Otero against the payment of the claims against the State House fund, the Secretary of the Treasury has declined to pay any more claims out of the appropriation. He thought within a month he would be able to collect it, when he would inform me. I have not heard from him yet. I can't see how we are to get it without a new appropriation, but things are so unsettled it is hard to judge what the prospects are for anything." Webb to Kingsbury, Hamden, CT, Feb. 16, 1861, MHS.

Letter no. 188, Kingsbury to Webb, March 10, 1861

I am still without a letter from you, am almost in dispair of ever getting one again. Your last is of Jany. 15th & a little short, hasty note at that. I fear that you may be in trouble. I hope you have no sickness in your family.

I was not far out of the way in my opinion about my friend Marsh. The poor man has gone to his long home, and is now free from the cares & troubles of this world. He died on the 7th. He leaves a young wife & babe but little over two months old. Poor woman she takes it very hard. I am sorry for her. Owing to his feeble health I could not get the stock finished and closed up, and now I have sent out to the Ranch for his partner to come in and close up. The papers transfer the leases &c. before any letters of Administration are taken out. I hope to get all fixed right yet.

Since my last I have got a settlement in full with old man Hatch. that is I have an order on the Quarter Master covering the balance of his a/c which will be paid when there is any funds. Everything still dull & quiet. I have put no suits in this court except one little one for $25.00. I have commenced suit on note against Kozlowski. It is in San Miguel district & will get it to trial at the end of this month. Have no doubt but that I will get a judgement on it and think the money can be made.

This is all now.

Letter no. 189, Kingsbury to Webb, Santa Fe, March 17, 1861

I have still no letter from you. I think well now next mail I must certainly get one, and live on hopes the whole week only to be doubly disapointed when the mail does come. It is real[l]y to bad—just imagine yourself here and you will know how I feel.

I sent you a few lines last week. Since then I have got matters & things fixed up at the Exchange, and in the settlement there have received $2,839.50 which goes to the credit of Tom's note to us, also $369.56 which is in full for our debt there of $738.56. This however is in a duplicate receipt on the two drafts: Quarter Master and can only be paid when the Govt. shall place him in funds.

We will loose the discount I have made—$369.28. Also whatever loss many be sustained in realizing the money on that Farm. I am now in a little stew about these farm papers or deed. Do not exactly see how I am to get them in proper shape. Any Administrator appointed here would not have jurisdiction over property and effects beyond the limits of this Territory. The bond I have got I think is sufficient to hold the place. I must take out letters or get some one to do so in Mo.

This may be accompanied with some trouble and expense. I have managed this whole affair at the Exchange with the utmost care and caution & trust that we will come out all right in the end. It has been my worst egg, and caused me more anxiety than all the balance of our collections. I am well pleased with what I have accomplished so far, and glad to see my way so far out of that dark hole.

I have made up the brandy, have about 4 Bbls—still must try to put this through that mill also the cask of bitters. I have sold the Buggy for $200.+ and taken the money prompt. It was a poor speculation but perhaps the benefits of its use was equal to all the loss. If I get this $200. I am satisfied.

I am now after Hoppin & Appel and Duvall with a sharp stick.

Times are very hard, no money, and nearly everybody throughout the Territory cramped. The poor especially are suffering. Courts have been appointed to raise funds & charity subscriptions to buy provisions to keep the destitute from starving.

I have just received from Simon Delgado One thousand dollars on account of his note due April 1st. He has turned this over to us as soon as he could raise it, and says he may be obliged to ask a little indulgence on the balance, as he may not have it prompt on the day the note will be due. I enclose this $1,000.00 to you in the following draft, viz. draft no. 1 dated Santa Fe N.M. March 16th 1861 at three days after sight on Messrs. M. Williamson & Co. Philadelphia—for One Thousand dollars drawn by Beck & Johnson payable to the order of Webb & Kingsbury, which amount I have charged to your agent account, ($1,000.+) Send this for collection at once.

Nothing more at present.

Letter no. 190, Kingsbury to Webb, Santa Fe, March 24, 1861

I wrote you last week under date of 17th enclosing Draft No. 1 dated Santa Fe N.M. March 16th 1861 at three days sight on Messrs. M. Williamson & Co. Philadelphia for One Thousand dollars, drawn by Beck & Johnson payable to our order, which letter I hope you have received all safe, for this draft I paid the specie, less 1% allowance for exchange & costs for collecting. I took it under the representation that it was unquestionable & drawn against money with them on deposit for a long and would be honored promptly. I trust you will have no trouble with it.

Since then I have rec.d yours of Feby 16th with "Protest" and of the 27th explaining the matter more fully. I feel easy in regard to it being satisfied that it has been paid as there indicated. I called upon the Maj. and have a sufficient explanation from him why the delay, but it is unnecessary to repeat it here as you probably have the money for it long ago. The Maj. is one of the most correct men in every respect that I have ever met in this country, and I place implicit reliance & confidence in what he tells me.

These two letter are the first and all that I have rec.d from you since yours of Jany 15th. By them I know that you have rec.d mine of Jany. 20 & 27th, but I have no reply from you to mine of the 5th Jany. with Trial Balance, and all previous unsettled matters. If you have written the letters have never reached me, and I am still in the dark with regard to those two checks sent Oct 6th ($300 & $100.+) also as to the result of Blumners papers, State House Claim, Hoppin & Appel mining drafts, and sundry other important items, and I am anxious in no small degree to read your reply to mine of Jany. 5th. The seeds and chili I will if possible get together and start to you by next mail stage. I am sorry to disapoint Master Jimmy but Pinones [piñons] are not to be had. There has been none for the last two or three years.

The following is a list of my letters Dec. 22, Jany. 5th, 20th, 27th, Feby. 10th, 24th, March 3rd, 10th, & 17th and the only direct reply to any of these, is to that of Jany 27th.

This week I have rec.d an other $1,000. from Delgado on a/c. Soon as the Maj. gets authority to draw again, I can start to you one of his checks for about $5,000.+ I have confidence he will not give me a check that is not good, and I feel safe to take <u>his</u> exchange and shall do so unless advised by you that our Govt. is no longer good to pay its debts.

We have advises here that the Overland Mail by El Paso is discontinued, so we must depend upon the Ind. line for all our Mail.[16] In directing your letters you had better mark them "via Independence Mo."—by this you see that I expect you to continue to write me untill such time as you hear from me positively that I am starting in. I feel so uncertain about it yet that I am not willing for you to stop writing. If I can get two or three of the principal a/cs on our books closed up, I shall be tempted to leave immediately that it is accomplished. I am anxious to be on the spot & get those Farm papers completed. However, when I do get ready to start you shall have due notice. I am greatly annoyed about the Hoppin & Appel debt. I do not want their Lands, and fear that they cannot be sold for cash. To push the sale would compel us to buy in the property. Now how to act for the <u>best</u> in this matter I am unable to deside. Then Duvall is treating us with silent contempt. I cannot get a word from him. A trip out to him would be daingerous and were I to go, have no assurance that I would get a cent. I hope to get some news soon that will assist me to deside upon these two points.

16. The political events of the spring of 1861 created complications for the Butterfield Company, which ran the overland route from St. Louis to El Paso to California. Shortly after Texas seceded from the Union in February, Texans at Fort Chadbourne confiscated the company's property. Congress officially discontinued the route on March 2. Taylor, *First Mail West*, 85-86.

Letter no. 191, Kingsbury to Webb, Santa Fe, March 30, 1861

I wrote you last week. Since then we have a through mail from Ind. and I have again to say that it brought me nothing from you. So today I have the blues and am pretty well down at the heel.

In my last I stated that I would by this stage start you a package with seed &c. I have since changed my mind and desided not to do so. The charge by mail is 50 cents per pound & I concluded that with the express charges it would be a little to[o] expensive. Then I have been unable to get any onion seed, and the Wheat this year is very poor, grain small & not filled out. I have sent out in the country to get some of the best to be had. The chile I have got & is already ground. Talis-foro wished to show his friendship and with his own money bought one string, ground it, and put it in with the rest, "Con cinco estar mucho" [with five (strings) it is much]. I am packing a trunk with keep sakes & other extra baggage to send by a train to start next week. Shall put the chile in and also the wheat if I get it in time. If I can get a few onion seed will send them by mail.

Duvall came in town last night. I met him this morning. He told me his principal business here is to settle with me, and gave me his word that tomorrow he would fix everything satisfactory. The offices have no funds and the best I can expect from him is to get receipts on some one of them to be paid when in funds. Now if he keeps his word and comes up to the mark all right, all I will have to fret over is that Hoppin & A. outfit. I sometimes think it is not worth a second thought and feel disposed to let it go to pot.

Simon Delgado has today paid me the balance and settled his note in full.

I have got a judgment against Kozlowski for the amt. of his note and interest. Ashurst writes me that he has ordered a stay of execution untill 18th of June, being assured that the money will be forthcoming at that time, and a poor show to make it now. The house & fixtures he finds were deeded to his boy at the time of purchase, so that we cannot touch it. So after all we must wait his pleasure.

This is all now,

[P.S.] I have also got an accepted order on John Dold & Bro. for $200. at 30 day for the Buggy, so I consider this safe. Payable at Santa Fe April 28th 1861.

Letter no. 192, Kingsbury to Webb, Santa Fe, April 7, 1861

I have now got yours of Feby 12th. I anticipated that you would have some trouble in getting that money from Batesville.[17] I hope you

17. The farm's purchaser had taken possession but had not paid the first installment. Webb to Kingsbury, New Haven, CT, Feb. 12, 1861, MHS.

have still the papers in such a shape that they cannot get the advantage of us. I returned the draft to Hoppin & Appel sometime ago without waiting your reply, and now enclose to you their answer that you may see what prospect there is there. I have no hope but still I have desided to go down, will start tomorrow morning. It will probably take me 3 weeks. I go with the determination to get it settled if possible in some shape, have no idea how I will come out. I feel sure that the money coming to Blumner will be sent to you and that the papers are all right. The blank receipts which they refer to have been rec.d here, and signed by him and sent back <u>with instructions again</u> to send the amt. to you. Now if they send Warrants to you made in his favor, that Power of Atty. certainly gives you authority to sign his name and you will get the money by so doing.[18] If the drafts should be made to your own order why so much the better. I trust you have got it all before this time & that you have started notice of the same so that I can make a final settlement here with Blumner.

You mention the amt. we had at the Exchange as the principal item for me to close before I can leave. My previous letters will inform you how I have managed this debt. The face of Tom's note is paid in full & I have got $1,255.+ dollars interest on it leaving still a balance of $214. interest due on it, and to secure this $214 I have got notes belonging to Rose in my hands of over $6,000.+ The Marsh part of the debt you already know how I have got it fixed. Duvall settled the balance due from him with interest by giving me a receipt on Maj. Donaldson A.Q.M. and today I have taken from the Maj. his conditional draft on New York for all the receipts I had on him. The condition is endorsed on the back of it, that we are to wait and not protest the draft untill funds are placed there to meet it. Now the supposition is that by the time you can present this draft the money will be there & it will be paid at sight. If however, there is no funds, why hold it a short time & it will be paid out of the first that comes.

viz.

Check No. 1165 dated Santa Fe N.M. April 6th 1861 at sight on the Asst. Treas. of the U.S. at New York for Six Thousand dollars, $6,000.00 drawn by J. L. Donaldson A.Q.M. payable to our order.

Also Thirteen Coupons for Interest due on the first day of May 1861. Certificates No. 81, 87, 86, 84, 85, 82, 83, 88, 91, 90, 89, 92, and 93 City Sav. Stock S. Felt Treasurer, payable at City Bank New York to bearer for Thirty five dollars Each   455.00

Making   6,453.00

which amt. I have charged to your agent account.

The Trunk I mentioned in my last I have started by Gallegos waggons to Bernard & Co. West Port and paid the freight that far. It is marked "James J. Webb New Haven, Conn. by Adams Exp." Look out for this trunk and keep it for me untill I come. The chile & wheat is

18. Washington refused to pay Webb on Blumner's behalf based on a power of attorney. Ibid.

inside but you can't get it untill I come with the key so if you want chile bad you must order me in to open it.

Many thanks for your invitation. I shall come direct to your house & stay till you get tired of me. I only wish I was with you now.[19]

P.S. I could not get onion seeds.

Letter no. 193, Kingsbury to Webb, Santa Fe, May 5, 1861

Dear Sir, I have just returned after an absence of four weeks. I am back again all safe, though I had a hard and exciting trip, and with all I have the extreem pleasure to report a full and final settlement of the H & A debt. I realized in Cash out of it $1045.00 making a sacrifice of the balance of the debt to secure this. We are now done with them & the debt is cancelled in full. I think I mentioned to you before that I feared that I was loosing my energies. In accomplishing this settlement it called into practice every talent of business that I possess and when finally closed, I could not refrain from the expression to myself John is himself again. I am well satisfied and when I can explain to you all the sircumstances I feel sure that you will be satisfied with the settlement. My expenses on the trip are $127.87.+ My last to you was of April 7 notifying you that I had that day under another envelope sent you a check for $6000. and 13 coupons for interest amt.g to $455. — which I hope you have received all safe and that you have now the money for them. I now find before me 3 letters from you of March 12th, 21st & April 5th. Yours of Feby. 16th has never reached me. The papers which Mr. Marsh sent to his mother for have not got here yet. I look for them by every mail. I think now that I can manage matters here so that I can leave in 2 or 3 weeks. If you want a letter to meet me send to the care of Bernard & Co. at West Port. I have a good many little things to fix up yet, but am in hopes that in 2 or 3 weeks I can see my way clear to leave, and this is my intention now and shall get off unless something turns up in the mean time to prevent. My intention is to go streight to you, and then if necessary return and make a special trip about those farms.[20] I am anxious now that these Marsh farm papers should come. There is no conveyance there from Ind. or West Port except private. And then when I visit those places I wish to feel free to allow all the time necessary to close up properly. There is no use to make expenses just to go there without I can stay to fix things right and I imagine that it will take time, and I am not willing to stay on the road untill I first visit home. I have given Blumner Cr. for the $263. Am in hopes you will receive the balance on his papers so that I can settle with him before I leave. Let me again urge you to be carefull & cautious with our funds. Keep it safe. If you can do no better, buy a good safe and lock it up. Our news is that War has commenced and if

19. Webb was aware of his junior partner's unhappy situation and wrote a word of encouragement in February: "I am anxious that you should come in as soon as you can get matters arranged so you can leave, but it would be better to wait untill [*sic*] you can so arrange our business that you or myself would not have to return. You have had an arduous and unpleasant task, and I am not unmindfull [*sic*] of the sacrifice of comfort you have made for the promotion of my interest and pleasure. I hope the time will soon arrive when you can leave, and when you do leave I want you to make my house your home so long as it is your pleasure." Ibid.

20. Since the farms were in Missouri and Arkansas, Webb & Kingsbury were unable to do anything about them until the Civil War ended, although Webb had advised Kinsgsbury to stop and see the them on his way in. Ibid., Hamden, CT, Mar. 12, 1861, MHS. See Afterword.

so, don't hazzard our funds in attempting to make interest. Let it rest untill I come.

I now enclose draft No. 163 dated Mesilla Feby 26th 1861 at 10 days after sight for Five Hundred dollars drawn by Wm. Buckley Supt. on Fred. Cook Esq. Treasurer Overland Mail Co. No. 84 Broadway New York, payable to order of N. J. Davis by him endorsed to order of Leonart & Maurin and by them end. to our order $500.00 and effect in every particular for 500.00,

                   Making $1000.00

which I have charged to your agent account. These two drafts I got out of the H. & A. debt, and I believe that they are as good exchange as any govt. check. Send them at once for acceptance. I hope you will get the money prompt without trouble. I am indeed grieved to hear of the affliction on your wife.[21] You both have my full sympathy in this heavy trial. I trust for your sakes that it may soon be removed & she be again restored to perfect health. True this is a world of trials, where none escape. At the very moment that our highest earthly ambition seems at hand and in our grasp, some unforeseen circumstance steps in and proves to us that all here is uncertain, and to have true treasures & safe they must be found in another world, where there is no change. I trust in this case that the worst is passed, that she has recovered entirely and may be long spaired to make your hearth glad, that happy years may be your portion here, and united have strength from the only true & sure source for every immergancy [*sic*] in this life. And above all when this life is passed and accomplished have a jenuine [*sic*] pas[s]port awaiting you & yours to that world without end, where sorrows & trials never enter. Accept my kind regards & sympathy. I look anxiously for your next letter in hopes it may bring assurance of her improvement.

Letter no. 194, Kingsbury to Webb, Santa Fe, May 12, 1861

I wrote you last week giving you the result of my trip below, and enclose to you two drafts Nos. 163 & 164, both dated Mesilla Feby 26th 1861 at 10 days after sight on Fred. Cook Esq. Treasurer Overland Mail Co. No. 84 Broadway New York. Each for the sum of Five Hundred dollars drawn by Wm Buckley Supt. payable to order of N. J. Davis by him end. to order of Leonard & Maurin and by them end. to our order, making $1,000.+ Which I trust you have received all safe and that they are promptly accepted & paid when due.

I have now rec.d yours of April 15th. Otero has gone below & I cannot see him to learn about the Irons or to know what the objections are.[22] I hope the papers are in a condition to bring the money some day. I have placed the 4 34/100 Exchange to your credit. I have desided to leave all our unsettled business with Weirick. He is better

21. Webb had mentioned in March that his wife, Lillie, had "been confined to the house for seven weeks with rheumatism—has suffered a great deal, and quite emaciated." Webb to Kingsbury, Hamden, CT, Mar. 21, 1861, MHS. By April her condition had grown worse:. "I cannot write you a very long or very full letter. My mind is filled with anxiety and trouble on account of my wife's sickness. I can see but little improvement since I wrote you last. She is gradually failing in strength, and it seems that unless she can get some relief soon she cannot last long. You would hardly recognize her. She is as helpless as a new born infant, except the use of her hands, and one of them is almost useless. I hope for the best, but fear that you will never meet her again on earth. She sends love, says she often thinks of you in your lonely condition, and with almost a sisterly affection. May God in His infinite mercy spare us all to meet again. Mrs. W. says `tell John I am very sick, and if we never meet on earth I hope to meet him in heaven.'" Ibid., New Haven, CT, Apr. 13, 1861, MHS.

acquainted with the detail than any one else and I think will due [*sic*] quite as well for us as anyone. What he may recover we will be sure to get. He has my confidence and I am willing to trust him. I think now that I cannot get ready to leave before the 27th.

I have also just rec.d your old letter of Feby 16th. I see nothing in it that requires a reply now. If it had come in proper time would have saved me much anxiety. It is with deep regret that I read the continued failing of your wife. I do hope she may yet recover. I cannot realize that she is so low as your letter indicates. May God sustain you in this dark hour, trust him and He will take you safely through. It is the only refuge. You have my sympathy and prayers. I acknowledge the kind message from Mrs. W. God grant that her wish may be realized.

In the present excited state of Affairs in the States, I confess that it is not without some fear that I start in.[23] Knowing what a long road I have to travel before I can meet you. I do not hesitate knowing in whence I trust. Should any accident befall me, you will find all our business papers in proper shape, and <u>my Will</u> I leave with Weirick. Have constituted you and him my executors, the paper will explain itself. This I have done to cover contingencies yet I hope to meet you again & that very soon.

23. "We have advices to-day that War has commenced, and there is no knowing when it will end or what will be the result. I have no doubt it will be a long and bloody contest." Ibid.

Afterword

On May 20, 1861, John Kingsbury left Santa Fe for the last time. In keeping with his cautious nature, he tied up the various loose strings of the firm's business to the best of his ability: he packed and marked the books and ledgers, which he shipped to Webb in Connecticut, he placed all of Webb & Kingsbury's unsettled New Mexico business in Tom Weirick's hands, and he drew up his Will. The outbreak of the Civil War had introduced the likelihood that his journey through the settled parts of the nation would be more perilous than the trek across the western wilderness, and he expressed trepidation for what might lie ahead.[1] What Kingsbury's last letters from Santa Fe do not convey is the pleasure and relief he must have felt at the prospect of returning to friends and family in the East. At last he was free from the obligations keeping him in Santa Fe.

If the pessimistic tone of Kingsbury's correspondence from the latter part of his tenure in Santa Fe stands in contrast to the interest and enthusiasm of his earliest letters, one can hardly be surprised. The young trader of 1853 had regarded Santa Fe as the means by which he could win prosperity and happiness. In accepting Webb's offer of a junior partnership, Kingsbury must have felt his future was assured: he would make money, establish contacts for himself in the business and political world through both Webb and Messervy, marry the woman he loved, restore her health by bringing her to New Mexico, and raise a family. He apparently considered the worldly success he had achieved by 1861 small compensation, however, for the personal losses he had sustained. Though his letters never mentioned them after the sad events of 1857, the deaths of his wife, Kate, and his young son, George, seemed to have dampened Kingsbury's enthusiasm for trading under difficult, and sometimes violent, circumstances in the West. The recurrent themes in his letters from 1857 to 1861 include his loneliness, his desire to return to the East, and Webb's seeming inattention and neglect. Attending to the firm's business in Santa Fe had deteriorated from an exciting means of providing for his family into a lonesome duty to be endured with fortitude.

But John Kingsbury had done his duty. His journey home, accompanied by José Hernández, apparently passed uneventfully.[2] Webb directed a letter to Kingsbury in Westport instructing him to stop off in Arkansas and Missouri to check on their farms. He based his advice on the grounds that "hailing from New Mexico and not being affiliated with northern interests, and knowing nothing of the condition of either

1. Kingsbury to Webb, Santa Fe, May 12, 1861, MHS; ibid., May 19, 1861, HHS.
2. Anonymous manuscript, Misc. File, Box 8, Webb Papers, MHS.

northern or southern affairs, you would be able to get along without being suspected of anything wrong, better than if you were to come on here and return."[3] Whether Kingsbury followed Webb's advice is not known, but 1861 was an inauspicious year to try to dispose of real estate in the border states. The farms remained in their possession throughout the Civil War.[4]

By late summer, John Kingsbury had begun to reestablish himself in Boston. He was thirty-two years old, owned property amounting to at least $24,000, and could consider himself relatively free of professional and personal encumbrances.[5] Although a few outstanding business matters remained to be discussed with Webb, they had entered the final stages of their partnership and their correspondence diminished. Kingsbury must have faced a world of decisions that summer—from mundane choices about his domestic arrangements to more significant questions about his future occupation and investments—but he did not describe them in frequent letters to Webb. The picture of Kingsbury's life after returning from Santa Fe becomes increasingly blurred as the years progress.

The contours of Kingsbury's life emerge most clearly during the early war years. Among the first and most painful tasks awaiting his attention in 1861 was a letter to James Webb comforting him on the loss of his wife of seven years. Lillie Webb had finally succumbed to the illness that had plagued her throughout the spring, leaving behind a disconsolate husband and a six-year-old son. His own experience in losing a wife enabled Kingsbury to write movingly to his former partner and friend:

Dear friend,

I have just got your note confirming my worst fears. I feel for you in your present sorrow. You have my sympathy and prayers.

I can realize [only too] well your deep grief [words missing] your lot now [is] to mourn but not as one without hope. I pray you may have tears to weep, and bless the hand that called her home. She has gone to her rest, far from the cares & trials of this life, there to receive the crown full & happy with those who have gone before. You have now a treasure in our fathers house, where rust and sin cannot enter. You have much to live for. Your labor is not finished. Your duty to yourself & those around you have a claim upon your energy, be faithful and true [and] reward is sure. [words missing]

He who notes the sparrows fall will not be unmindfull of you. He knows the end from the beginning and what is for our best good. "How wonderfull O God are thy ways & past finding out." We here are short sighted, but all things will be made known to us some day. God be ever present with you & may his holy spirit sustain & comfort you.[6]

3. Webb to Kingsbury, Hamden, CT, May 27, 1861, MHS.

4. Kingsbury to Webb, Boston, Nov. 7, 1865, HHS.

5. The estimate of his personal worth is based on the 1860 New Mexico Census (p. 487). His age is borne out by both the 1860 New Mexico Census and his death certificate.

6. Kingsbury to Webb, Boston, Aug. 15, 1861, MHS.

Webb recovered from his grief sufficiently to remarry within the next two years.[7] No records exist to indicate that Kingsbury remarried. He apparently remained a widower for the rest of his life, but perhaps not a lonely one. The letters he directed to Webb over the years hint at his close involvement with his own family. His sister who died in 1860 had left children. At the time Kingsbury had expressed his concern for their well-being, since their father had a history of alcoholism and seemed unable to hold a job.[8] Now that he lived in the same city, Kingsbury could perhaps take a more active part in their lives, beyond the financial assistance he had been extending them up to the time of his sister's death. He certainly pursued that course with his other sister, Anne, and her two little girls.[9] She, too, had entered into a difficult marriage, one troubled by her husband's inability to find permanent employment. As Kingsbury confided to Webb, "If he does not get work, I think they must brake [*sic*] up there, and I want to be here on the spot to see to them."[10]

In addition to his own family, Kingsbury maintained close relations with the family of his wife, visiting the Messervys and Kate's Grandfather Passarow in Salem and entertaining them on their visits to Boston.[11] Surviving letters also indicate that he stayed in contact with associates in Santa Fe, who kept him supplied with gossip about the town and its citizens. In 1863, for example, George Beall wrote with the news that Frank Green was now a salaried employee at the Exchange hotel, working as the superintendent for $300 a month; merchant Charles P. Clever had sold out to his partner Siegmund Seligman in order to practice law, and had become the attorney general for the territory; and Francisco Pino had died of heart disease in January.[12] Later that year Joab Houghton wrote that the main plaza had been enclosed with palings and planted with grass and, alarmingly, that fellow merchant "Jo. Mercure went raving crazy and was taken in three weeks ago to an Assylum [*sic*] at St. Louis, his brother Henry will wind up his business. It is feared that Jo. is incurable."[13]

In a time of war, Kingsbury found himself at loose ends professionally. He never served in the military, but the threat of having to take up arms seems to have hung over him.[14] In 1863, he wrote Webb that "I shall not go to California at present. I have escaped the first draft under the conscript law."[15] The effect of the war on investment markets, as well, left him uncertain about how to manage the money he had earned in Santa Fe. Many northern businessmen shared Kingsbury's pessimism in the war's first year, fearing it would precipitate bankruptcies throughout the business community.[16] Kingsbury's immediate instinct had been to "save most by keeping still as to transactions." But as the war progressed and government contracts stimulated the industrial economy, Kingsbury admitted that his caution had caused him to fall "a goodeal behind, counting Gold as the bases [*sic*] at its present price. I could not today convert my papers into specie less than a discount of about $6,000.+."[17] As of

7. Within a year or so of Lillie's death, Webb married a widowed cousin of his stepmother. Anonymous manuscript, Misc. File, Box 8, Webb Papers, MHS. A condolence note written at the time of Webb's death confirms that the surviving Mrs. Webb was Jimmie's stepmother. Misc. File, Box 8, Webb Papers, MHS.

8. Webb to Kingsbury, Hamden, CT, June 18, 1858, MHS; Kingsbury to Webb, Santa Fe, Nov. 4, 1860, MHS.

9. Kingsbury to Webb, Boston, Aug. 20, 1863, and Sept. 23, 1863, HHS.

10. Ibid., Aug. 23, 1861, HHS.

11. Ibid., May 21, 1863, and Sept. 23, 1863, HHS.

12. Ibid., May 21, 1863, HHS.

13. Joab Houghton to Kingsbury, Fort Union, Aug. 28, 1863, HHS. Joseph Mercure died at the crossing of the Arkansas River, and his body was returned to Santa Fe for burial. *Santa Fe Weekly Gazette*, Sept. 5, 1863, and Nov. 14, 1863.

14. Kingsbury is not listed in either the *Index to Massachusetts Soldiers, Sailors and Marines in the Civil War* or in the *Index to Army Records*.

15. Kingsbury to Webb, Boston, July 20, 1863, HHS.

16. Porter and Livesay, *Merchants and Manufacturers*, 119.

17. Ibid., 120; Kingsbury to Webb, Boston, Aug. 23, 1861, and Feb. 17, 1863, HHS.

May, 1863, he was "still doing nothing and am quite tired of it long ago."[18]

Ironically, at the same time Kingsbury experienced difficulty in settling into an occupation, José Hernández, the maker of fair promises and fresh starts, found a niche for himself, at least for a time. He joined the First Battalion, Cavalry, Connecticut Volunteers, and was posted to Wheeling, Virginia, and Georgetown. He saw action and was wounded sometime in late 1862 or early 1863, but had recovered sufficiently by the spring to resume duty. By the fall of 1863 he found himself in Harper's Ferry, Virginia.[19]

Throughout the early war years, José wrote to Webb, expressing his sadness at the death of Lillie Webb, whom he had regarded as a mother, and his sense of homesickness for the Webb family. Occasionally he sent money for Webb to deposit on his behalf.[20] Before the war's end, however, José's letters to Webb stopped. Perhaps Confederates captured him or he may have been wounded and returned to Webb's farm in Connecticut, or did something to warrant a break in his relations with Webb. The last reference to José Hernández in the Webb Papers is poignant, consisting of two postcards addressed to Jimmie Webb after James J. Webb's death. In them Samuel G. Bean of Las Cruces, New Mexico wrote to inquire "if you are the same Webb that used to merchandise in Santa Fe and Chihuahua there is a party wants to communicate with you." Apparently Jimmie answered in the affirmative because Bean's next postcard related that

> There is a Mexican here named Joe Hernandez who says he went in with your father as far as St. Louis in 1849—he was taken into the states by Kingsbury when six year old and says he recollects your mother and Aunt Hannah and knows where you was born in Santa Fe. He speaks good English. S. G. Bean.[21]

The cessation of letters from José, the death of his wife Lillie and his remarriage, and the gradual diminution of letters from John Kingsbury, all occurring within a span of two years, marked the final stages of James J. Webb's transition from Santa Fe trader to Connecticut gentleman farmer. Time and distance gradually severed his ties with New Mexico. Although he maintained contact with many of his western comrades for the remainder of his days, he clearly found his new life in Hamden absorbing. The care with which he preserved so many of his personal records demonstrates his respect for the past, yet Webb's focus seemed firmly directed toward the present and future. His farm, Spring Glen, provided him with a suitable outlet for his energies. Continuing with the interest in agriculture that he occasionally expressed in his letters to Kingsbury, Webb occupied his time by improving his property and undertaking a variety of agricultural experiments that eventually rendered his farm one of the most productive in the state.[22] He continued to indulge his

18. Kingsbury to Webb, Boston, May 21, 1863, HHS.

19. Hernández to Webb, Camp Connecticut, Wheeling, VA, Mar. 4, 1862, HHS; ibid., Camp Buckingham, near Georgetown, Sept. 28, 1862; ibid., Camp Carroll, Baltimore, March 5, 1863; and ibid., Harper's Ferry, VA, Sept. 21, 1863, HHS.

20. Ibid., Harpers Ferry, VA, Sept. 21, 1863, HHS.

21. Postcards, S. G. Bean to Jimmie Webb, Las Cruces, NM, n.d., Misc. File, Box 8, Webb Papers, MHS.

22. Anonymous manuscript, Misc. File, Box 8, Webb Papers, MHS; James J. Webb obituary, 1889, Misc. File, Box 8, Webb Papers, MHS.

interest in politics and by 1863 was serving his district in the Connecticut state legislature.[23]

By the time Webb took public office, only two pieces of business of the firm of Webb & Kingsbury remained to be settled: reimbursement for the ironwork intended for the territorial capitol, and the disposal of the farms in Missouri and Arkansas. The question of the ironwork reached a resolution of sorts that year. Joab Houghton, the contractor in charge of building the capitol, wrote to Kingsbury in August to inform him that Judge Peters, the man who collected building funds from the federal government and disbursed them to the various contractors, had died owing money to a number of people involved in the project, including Houghton and Webb & Kingsbury. Judge Watts had written to Houghton enumerating specific claims on the building funds that had been paid to Peters on behalf of individuals who never received their money. In light of Watts's letter, Houghton wrote:

> I may have been used and as it turns out was deceived in Judge Peters but I had the best reasons to have confidence in him. From the time I was in Washington in 1852 up to the time of the last transaction I had intrusted to him claims to the amt. of several thousand dollars in which he was always successful and always though drawing the money himself was prompt and correct in accounting and did his work for reasonable compensation. I fear all is lost, but I shall continue to try and if you see any chance for <u>pitching in</u>, do so.[24]

Nothing exists to indicate that Webb & Kingsbury received their due compensation. Most likely they did not. Whether the ironwork, which Kingsbury had left in Santa Fe, ever found its way into the territorial capitol, now the federal courthouse, remains open for conjecture.

The ultimate fate of the farms in Missouri and Arkansas proves equally puzzling. The last surviving letter in the correspondence of Kingsbury and Webb deals with this final bit of business between the two men but again, no evidence survived to indicate if and how they resolved the matter. In November 1865, Kingsbury volunteered to Webb to go west after the first of the year to pay the back taxes and try to dispose of both pieces of property: "I shall be at liberty to leave for six months if necessary . . . when I do go I want to be able to accomplish something, not mearly [sic] go there, turn right around & come back only to go again." What occupied Kingsbury until the first of the year and whether he did venture west in the spring may never be known, because at this point, with his last letter from Boston in 1865, he recedes from the historical record.

James J. Webb, in contrast, seemed destined for prominence, whether in New Mexico or Connecticut. His interest in farming evolved into a passion that thrust him into the forefront of agricultural activities in his

23. Anonymous manuscript, Misc. File, Box 8, Webb Papers, MHS.
24. Joab Houghton to Kingsbury, Fort Union, NM, Aug. 28, 1863, HHS.

home state. He became a member, and later the president, of the Connecticut Agricultural Society, lectured publicly on the subject, and helped to establish the Connecticut Agricultural Experiment Station in New Haven, near Hamden.[25] Hoping that his son, Jimmie, would share in his enthusiasm, he sent him to the Massachusetts Agricultural College, where he earned a bachelor of science degree in 1873. What Webb characterized as the bitterest disappointment of his life occurred, however, when Jimmie forsook the plow in order to enter Yale Law School.[26] Webb reconciled himself to the idea of an advocate in the family, and Jimmie Webb enjoyed a successful career, the capstone of which was his appointment as a Connecticut Superior Court judge.[27]

James J. Webb died at his estate in Hamden on March 22, 1889, at the age of 71, having lived a life blessed with adventure and prosperity.[28] According to probate records, he left an estate valued at $53,249.35, of which all but $10,000 was invested in his house and farm.[29] His former partner, William Messervy, whom Webb had outlived by three years, had shared in that good fortune as well, sending his son, George, to Harvard and then to St. Louis to attend Washington University School of Law.[30] Messervy's probate file includes administrative records, but no will or valuation of his estate. Nevertheless, his income was apparently sufficient for him to provide his unmarried sister, Eliza Ann, with an estate worth $20,000 at the time of her death in 1893.[31]

What of John Kingsbury? The public records yield very little information. In 1878, Kingsbury had returned to the Boston City Directory, whose pages he had not graced since 1861. Had he lived in Boston quietly during those years? Or had he been off on another adventure? In 1878 he boarded at a home at 84 Zeigler Street. By 1880, he had a place of business at 2 Change Ave. He bought his own house in 1885, at 71 Dale, in the then prosperous and comfortable suburb of Roxbury.[32] The census of 1900 reveals that he shared that home with his nephew, Charles Goodwin, and Goodwin's family. Throughout the 1890s, he worked as an accountant and treasurer, apparently retiring around 1902 at the age of 73. While we can draw few conclusions about the circumstances in which he lived his later life, we do know something of the way in which he departed it. On August 21, 1907, forty-six years after he retired from the Santa Fe trade, John Kingsbury died of apoplexy in his home in Roxbury, at the age of 78. He was buried in the Mt. Hope Cemetery.[33]

25. Anonymous manuscript and James J. Webb obituary, 1889, Misc. File, Box 8, Webb Papers, MHS.

26. Anonymous manuscript, Misc. File, Box 8, Webb Papers, MHS.

27. Webb, *Adventures*, 22.

28. Ibid., 37.

29. James J. Webb Probate Estate File, No. 28,722, New Haven District, Connecticut, Connecticut State Archives, Harford. Our thanks to Mark L. Gardner for passing this information along to us.

30. Messervy died in Salem on March 1, 1886. William S. Messervy, Docket #63106, Salem Probate Court, Salem, MA. George P. Messervy, *National Cyclopaedia of American Biography*, vol. 26 (New York: J. T. White, 1891-1984).

31. William S. Messervy, Docket #63106, and Eliza A. K. Messervy, Docket #73775, Salem Probate Court, Salem, MA.

32. Mary Price, Boston historic preservationist, interview with Jane Elder, Pink Adobe Restaurant, Old Santa Fe Trail, Santa Fe, July 6, 1994.

33. This information is based on a survey of the Boston City Directories from 1861 through 1907, as well as the 1900 U.S. Census for Boston, vol. 79, E. B. 1476, sheet 10, line 28; death certificate of John M. Kingsbury, editors' files.

Appendix

Names listed in the master accounts ledger of Webb & Kingsbury

Ashurst, M.
Akerman, Thos. S.
Abbott, John C.
Abrahams & Rosenthal
Abadie, E. H. Dr.
Abel, John N.
Allen, Thomas
Alexander, G. M.
Abréu, Francisco

Bowler, Thos. F.
Baca, Francisco
Beuthner, Solomon
Blumner, Chas.
Beck, P., Jr.
Baird, S. M.
Bartels, Louis
Beck & Johnson
Boggs, Thomas
Baca y Salazar, Jesus Ma.
Baca, Franc.o Tomas
Beuthner, Sampson
Bonneville, Col. B. L. E.
Bailey, Henry
Bowler, Thos. F., Special a/c
Baca & St. Vrain
Berthold Rozier & Co.
Branford, Edwd.
Beall Geo. F. & Co.
Beaubien & Miller
Benedict, K.
Bonneau, Lt. R. V.

Cunningham, F. A., P. M.
Cunningham, F. A.
Collins & Davis
Carter, George

Cordova, Miguel
Cunningham, S.
Connelly, Henry
Clift, J. H.
Collins, James L.
Connelly & Mitchell
Cumming, James
Capoulade, Joseph
Connelly & Co.
Corondolet Mining Co.
Clark, Elias T.
Clitz, Lt. H. B.
Connelly & Amberg
Clemens, R. E.
Collins, James L., Supt. Ind.
  Affs.
Conklin & Clift
Cary, Robert
Connelly, H. & Co.

Doan King & Co.
Deavenport, J. J.
Davis, W. W. H.
Dodge, Henry L.
Delgado, Simon
Debus & Bunker
Davis, W. W. H., Secty.
De Leon, D. C., Dr.
Drew, William
Demarais, M.
Delgado, Pablo & F.
Dold, John
de Dios, Juan
Debus, W.
Davidson, W. A.
Debus, W. & Co.
Doyle, J. B.
Debus & Schwarzkopf

Mercure, J. & H.
Meriwether, Raymond
Messervy & Webb
Moore & Rees
Messervy, Wm. S.
Morris, Maj. G.
Mitchell, Wm. C.
Messervy, Wm. S., Agent
Meyer & Ott
Mayer, A. G.
Miller, David J.
Magruder, C. B.
Mercure, Henry
Moya, Doña Dolorez
McGehee, John G.
Montezuma Lodge, Masons
Montezuma Lodge, I.O.O.F.
Mercure, Joseph
Marsh, J. G. & Co.

Notes Payable
Noel, G. A. J.
Notes Receivable
Nichols, Maj. Wm. A.
New Mexico Mining Co.

Oneil, Henry
Ortiz, Francisco y Delgado
Owens, Richard
Olives, Francisco
Ortiz, F. y Salazar
O'Bannon, Lt. L. W.

Penitentiary Fund
Pueblo Indian Fund
Pelham, William
Posthoff & Loeb
Pino, Miguel E.
Perea & Hubbel
Pfieffer, A. H.
Parker, Chas. G. & Co.
Profit & Loss

Real Estate
Robles, Cecillo

Riddlesbarger, J. & Co.
Ramirez, Serafin
Rencher, Gov. A.
Rosenstine, Simon
Rowland, Thomas
Rutherfurd, Wm.
Rose, Leonard

Scofield, C. D.
Smith, Hugh N.
Sherman, O. W.
Sanchez, Francisco
Steck, Michael
Sanches, Juan
Shaw, Rev. J. M.
Spencer, Chas. L.
Sabine, James E.
Smith, Isaiah
St. Vrain, Ceran
Shoemaker, W. R., Capt.
Spiegelberg S. J. & Bro.
Sturgis, Lt. L. D.
Spiegelberg, Elias
Sena Jesus Ma. y Baca
Sandoval, Anastacio
State House Fund
Seligman & Cleaver
Sachs, Moses
Sundry Accounts
St. Vrain, Vincente
Speigelberg Beuthner & Co.
Sloan, Dr. Wm. J.
Secretary Territory of N.M.
Spiegelberg, S. J. & L.
Spiegelberg, Solomon
Street, W. A.
Simpson, Richard
St. Vrain, V. & Co.
Staab, L.
Sena, Pablo Anto.

Tapia, Juan C.
Tolhurst, Rev. F.
Thayer, Charles
Tillman Rozier & Co.
Townsend, E. C.

United States

Vigil, Donaciano
Valle, Alexander

Webb, James J.
Webb, James J., Private a/c
Ward, John
Wheaton, T. D.
Watts, John S.
Whiting, D. V.
Wilbar, A. P.
Weirick, T. A.
Webb, James J., agent
Weinheim & Co.
Wells, J. R. Maj.
Webber, John
Weinheim, S.
Weirick, Spencer T.
Wilkins, Lt. John D.
Winslow, Henry
Wood, E. M. & Co.

Yager Hays & Co.
Yager & Kerr

Zeckendorf, A.
Zeckendorf, Louis
Zeckendorf, A & L.

Sources

UNPUBLISHED SOURCES

Beinecke Library, Yale University, New Haven, Connecticut. Papers of W. W. H. Davis.

DeGolyer Library, Southern Methodist University, Dallas, Texas. Correspondence of John M. Kingsbury to James J. Webb, 1858–1860.

Hamden Historical Society, Hamden, Connecticut. James J. Webb Collection.

Missouri Historical Society, St. Louis, Missouri. James J. Webb Papers. A description of the James J. Webb Papers, consisting of eight boxes and 21 volumes of material, is available from the Missouri Historical Society.

Museum of New Mexico Manuscript Collection, Santa Fe, New Mexico. Hiltrud von Brandt Collection.

New Mexico State Records Center and Archives, Santa Fe, New Mexico. J. J. Webb Collection, 1854–1864; Hist. File #66, Territorial Period; Santa Fe County Deed Books; Record Book of the Secretary of the Treasury, Santa Fe, 1853–1858.

NEWSPAPERS

The Salem Gazette
Santa Fe Weekly Gazette

CITY DIRECTORIES

Boston City Directories, 1848–1907
Salem City Directories, 1846, 1850, 1855, 1857, 1859

CENSUSES

Boston, Massachusetts, 1900
Essex County, Massachusetts, 1850
Santa Fe, New Mexico, 1850 and 1860

BOOKS

Almada, Francisco R. *Resúmen de historia del estado de Chihuahua.* Mexico: Libros Mexicanos, 1955.

Ault, Phil. *Wires West: The Story of the Talking Wires.* New York: Dodd, Mead & Company, 1974.

Barbour, Barton H., ed. *Reluctant Frontiersman: James Ross Larkin on the Santa Fe Trail, 1856–1857.* Albuquerque: University of New Mexico Press, published in cooperation with the Historical Society of New Mexico, 1990.

Barry, Louise. *The Beginning of the West: Annals of the Kansas Gateway to the American West, 1540–1854.* Topeka: Kansas State Historical Society, 1972.

Baxter, John O. *Las Carneradas: Sheep Trade in New Mexico, 1700–1860.* Albuquerque: University of New Mexico Press, 1987.

Bieber, Ralph Paul. *The Papers of James J. Webb, Santa Fe Merchant, 1848–1861.* Reprinted from Washington University Studies Vol. XI, Humanistic Series, No. 2, 1924.

Bode, Carl, ed. *Midcentury America: Life in the 1850s.* Carbondale: Southern Illinois University Press, 1972.

Boyd, E. *Popular Arts of Spanish New Mexico.* Santa Fe: Museum of New Mexico Press, 1974.

Boyle, Susan Calafate. *Comerciantes, Arrieros, y Peones: The Hispanos and the Santa Fe Trade.* Southwest Cultural Resources Center Professional Papers No. 54, 1994.

Brewerton, George D. *Overland with Kit Carson: A Narrative of the Old Spanish Trail in '48.* New York: Coward–McCann, Inc., 1930.

Brown, William E. *The Santa Fe Trail.* St. Louis: The Patrice Press, 1988.

Carson, Gerald. *The Social History of Bourbon: An Unhurried Account of Our Star–Spangled American Drink.* Lexington: University Press of Kentucky, 1963.

Carter, Harvey Lewis. *'Dear Old Kit': The Historical Christopher Carson.* Norman: University of Oklahoma Press, 1968.

Chalfant, William Y. *Dangerous Passage: The Santa Fe Trail and the Mexican War.* Norman: University of Oklahoma Press, 1994.

Chaput, Donald. *Francois X. Aubry: Trader, Trailmaker and Voyageur in the Southwest, 1846-1854.* Glendale, CA: The Arthur H. Clark Company, 1975.

Chávez, Angélico. *Trés Macho—He Said: Padre Gallegos of Albuquerque, New Mexico's First Congressman.* Santa Fe: William Gannon, 1985.

Chávez, Thomas E. *Manuel Alvarez, 1794–1856: A Southwestern Biography.* Niwot, Co: University Press of Colorado, 1990.

Cochran, Thomas C. *Business in American Life: A History.* New York: McGraw-Hill Book Company, 1972.

Colwell, Stephen. *The Ways and Means of Payment: A Full Analysis of the Credit System with Its Various Modes of Adjustment.* Philadelphia: J. B. Lippincott & Co., 1860.

Conkling, Roscoe P., and Margaret Conkling. *The Butterfield Overland Mail, 1857–1869.* 2 vols. Gelndale: Arthur H. Clark, 1947.

Connor, Seymour V. and Jimmy M. Skaggs. *Broadcloth and Britches: The Santa Fe Trade.* College Station: Texas A&M University Press, 1977.

Cronon, William. *Nature's Metropolis: Chicago and the Great West.* New York: W. W. Norton & Company, 1991.

Davis, W. W. H. *El Gringo: or, New Mexico and Her People.* 2nd ed. Santa Fe: The Rydal Press, 1938.

Dodge, Bertha, S. *The Road West: Saga of the 35th Parallel.* Albuquerque: University of New Mexico Press, 1980.

Douglass, Elisha P. *The Coming of Age of American Business: Three Centuries of Enterprise, 1600–1900.* Chapel Hill: University of North Carolina Press, 1971.

Drumm, Stella M., ed. *Down the Santa Fe Trail and Into Mexico: The Diary of Susan Shelby Magoffin, 1846–1847.* 1926. New Haven: Yale University Press, 1962.

Ellis, Bruce. *Bishop Lamy's Santa Fe Cathedral.* Albuquerque: University of New Mexico Press, 1985.

Emmett, Chris. *Fort Union and the Winning of the Southwest.* Norman: University of Oklahoma Press, 1965.

Faragher, John Mack. *Men and Women on the Overland Trail.* New Haven: Yale University Press, 1979.

Faragher, John Mack, et al. *Out of Many: A History of the American People.* Englewood Cliffs, NJ: Prentice Hall, 1994.

Fierman, Floyd S. *Guts and Ruts: The Jewish Pioneer on the Trail in the American Southwest.* New York: KTAV Publishing House, Inc., 1985.

Franzwa, Gregory M. *The Santa Fe Trail Revisited.* St. Louis: The Patrice Press, 1989.

Frazer, Robert W. *Forts and Supplies: The Role of the Army in the Economy of the Southwest, 1846–1861.* Albuquerque: University of New Mexico Press, 1983.

Garber, Paul. *The Gadsden Treaty.* Philadelphia: The Press of the University of Pennsylvania, 1923.

Gardner, Mark L., ed. *Brothers on the Santa Fe and Chihuahua Trails:*

Edward James Glasgow and William Henry Glasgow, 1846–1848. Niwot, CO: University Press of Colorado, 1993.

———. *The Mexican Road: Trade, Travel, and Confrontation on the Santa Fe Trail.* Manhattan, KS: Sunflower University Press, 1989.

Goetzmann, William H. *Army Exploration in the American West, 1803–1863.* Austin: Texas State Historical Association, 1991.

Gregg, Josiah. *Commerce of the Prairies.* Edited by Max L. Moorhead. Norman: University of Oklahoma Press, 1954.

Griswold, Robert L. *Family and Divorce in California, 1850–1890: Victorian Illusions and Everyday Realities.* Albany: State University of New York Press, 1982.

Hafen, LeRoy R., ed. *The Mountain Men and the Fur Trade of the Far West.* Vol. 5. Glendale, CA: The Arthur H. Clark Company, 1968.

Hafen, LeRoy R., and Ann W. Hafen, eds. *Reports from Colorado: The Wildman Letters, 1859–1865, with Other Related Latters and Newspaper Reports, 1859.* Glendale, CA: The Arthur H. Clark Company, 1961.

Hall, G. Emlen. *Four Leagues of Pecos: A Legal History of the Pecos Grant, 1800–1933.* Albuquerque: University of New Mexico Press, 1984.

Hammond, George. *Alexander Barclay, Mountain Man.* Denver: Fred A. Rosenstock, Old West Publishing Company, 1976.

Heitman, Francis B. *Historical Register and Dictionary of the United States Army.* 2 vols. Washington: Government Printing Office, 1903.

Hertzog, Peter. *La Fonda: The Inn of Santa Fe.* Santa Fe: The Press of the Territorian, 1962.

Horgan, Paul. *Lamy of Santa Fe: His Life and Times.* New York: Farrar, Straus and Giroux, 1975.

Horn, Calvin. *New Mexico's Troubled Years: The Story of the Early Territorial Governors.* Albuquerque: Horn & Wallace, Publishers, 1963.

Huning, Franz. *Trader on the Santa Fe Trail; Memoirs of Franz Huning.* Albuquerque: University of New Mexico Press, 1973.

Hunt, Aurora. *Kirby Benedict: Frontier Federal Judge.* Glendale, CA: The Arthur H. Clark Co., 1961.

Jackson, W. Turrentine. *Wagon Roads West: A Study of Federal Road Surveys and Construction in the Trans-Mississippi West, 1846–1869.* Berkeley: University of California Press, 1952.

Johnson, Emory R., et al. *History of Domestic and Foreign Commerce of the United States.* 2 vol. 1922 reprint. Washington, D.C.: Carnegie Institution of Wasington, 1915.

Jones, Billy M. *Health-Seekers in the Southwest, 1817–1900.* Norman: University of Oklahoma Press, 1967.

Josephy, Alvin M., Jr. *The Civil War in the American West.* New York: Alfred A. Knopf, 1991.

Keleher, William A. *Turmoil in New Mexico, 1846–1868.* Santa Fe: The Rydal Press, 1952.

Kenner, Charles Leroy. *A History of New Mexican-Plains Indian Relations.* Norman: Oklahoma University Press, 1969.

Lamar, Howard Roberts. *The Far Southwest, 1846–1912: A Territorial History.* New Haven: Yale University Press, 1966.

Larson, Robert W. *New Mexico's Quest for Statehood, 1846–1912.* Albuquerque: University of New Mexico Press, 1968.

The Legislative Blue Book of the Territory of New Mexico with the Rules of Order, Fundamental Law, Official Register and Record, Historical Data, Compendium of Facts, Etc., Etc. Comp. by W. G. Ritch. 1882. Albuquerque: University of New Mexico Press, 1968.

Loomis, Sylvia Glidden, ed. *Old Santa Fe Today.* Santa Fe: The School of American Research, 1966.

McNitt, Frank. *Navajo Wars: Military Campaigns, Slave Raids, and Reprisals.* Albuquerque: University of New Mexico Press, 1972.

Majors, Alexander. *Seventy Years on the Frontier: Alexander Majors' Memoirs of a Lifetime on the Border.* Ed. by Prentiss Ingraham. Chicago: Rand, McNally & Company, 1893.

Meriwether, David. *My Life in the Mountains and on the Plains: the Newly Discovered Autobiography by David Meriwether.* Ed. by Robert A. Griffen. Norman: University of Oklahoma Press, 1965.

Messervy, J. A. *Généalogie de la Famille Messervy.* Jersey: Imprimé au Bureau de la "Nouvelle Chronique," 11, Place Royale, 1899.

Montgomery, Florence M. *Textiles in America, 1650–1870.* New York: W. W. Norton & Company, [1984].

Moorhead, Max L. *New Mexico's Royal Road: Trade and Travel on the Chihuahua Trail.* Norman: University of Oklahoma Press, 1954.

Myres, Sandra L. *Westering Women and the Frontier Experience, 1800–1915.* Albuquerque: University of New Mexico Press, 1982.

Napton, William B. *Over the Santa Fe Trail 1857.* Introduction by Donald C. Cutter. Santa Fe: Stagecoach Press, 1964.

Noble, David Grant, ed. *Santa Fe: History of an Ancient City.* Santa Fe: School of American Research Press, 1989.

Oberly, James W. *Sixty Million Acres: American Veterans and the Public Lands before the Civil War.* Kent, Ohio: The Kent State University Press, 1990.

Oliva, Leo E. *Soldiers on the Santa Fe Trail.* Norman: University of Oklahoma Press, 1967.

Paul, Rodman Wilson. *Mining Frontiers of the Far West, 1848–1880.* New York: Holt, Rinehart & Winston, 1963.

Poldervaart, Arie W. *Black-Robed Justice*. Vol. 13 of *Publications in History*. Historical Society of New Mexico, 1948.

Porter, Glenn, and Harold C. Livesay. *Merchants and Manufacturers: Studies in the Changing Structure of Nineteenth-Century Marketing*. Baltimore: The Johns Hopkins Press, 1971.

Rittenhouse, Jack D. *The Santa Fe Trail: A Historical Bibliography*. Albuquerque: University of New Mexico Press, 1971.

Russell, Marian. *Land of Enchantment: Memoirs of Marian Russell Along the Santa Fe Trail*. Afterword by Marc Simmons. 1954. Albuquerque: University of New Mexico Press, 1981.

Salpointe, John Baptist. *Soldiers of the Cross. Notes on the Ecclesiastical History of New Mexico, Arizona, and Colorado*. Banning, CA: St. Boniface's Industrial School, 1898.

Sherman, John. *Santa Fe: A Pictorial History*. Norfolk/Virginia Beach, VA: Donning Company, Publishers, 1983.

Simmons, Marc. *Following the Santa Fe Trail: A Guide for Modern Travelers*. Santa Fe: Ancient City Press, 1987.

———. *Murder on the Santa Fe Trail: An International Incident*. El Paso: Texas Western Press, 1987.

Smith, Duane A. *Colorado Mining: A Photographic History*. Albuquerque: University of New Mexico Press, 1977.

———. *Rocky Mountain West: Colorado, Wyoming, and Montana, 1859–1915*. Albuquerque: University of New Mexico Press, 1992.

Steele, Thomas J., S.J. *Folk and Church in Nineteenth Century New Mexico*. Colorado Springs: The Hulbert Center Press of the Colorado College, 1993.

Strate, David K., ed. *West by Southwest: Letters of Joseph Pratt Allyn, a Traveller along the Santa Fe Trail, 1863*. Dodge City: Kansas Heritage Center, 1984.

Sze, Corinne P. and Beverley Spears. *Santa Fe Historic Neighborhood Study*. Santa Fe: City of Santa Fe, 1988.

Taylor, Morris F. *First Mail West: Stagecoach Lines on the Santa Fe Trail*. Albuquerque: University of New Mexico Press, 1971.

Taylor, Morris. *Trinidad, Colorado Territory*. Trinidad: Trinidad State Junior College, 1966.

Thrapp, Dan L. *Encyclopedia of Frontier Biography*. Glendale, CA: A. H. Clark Co., 1988.

Tobias, Henry J. *A History of the Jews in New Mexico*. Albuquerque: University of New Mexico Press, 1990.

Twitchell, Ralph Emerson. *Leading Facts of New Mexican History*. 5 vols. 1911–12. Albuquerque: Horn & Wallace, 1963.

Unruh, John D., Jr. *The Plains Across: The Overland Emigrants and the Trans-Mississippi West, 1840–1860.* Urbana: University of Illinois Press, 1979.

Wagoner, Jay J. *Early Arizona, Prehistory to Civil War.* Tucson: University of Arizona Press, 1975.

Walker, Henry Pickering. *The Wagonmasters: High Plains Freighting from the Earliest Days of the Santa Fe Trail to 1880.* Norman: University of Oklahoma Press, 1966.

Wallace, Ernest, and E. Adamson Hoebel. *The Comanches: Lords of the South Plains.* Norman: University of Oklahoma Press, 1952.

Walton, Gary M., and Hugh Rockoff. *History of the American Economy.* New York: Harcourt Brace Jovanovich, Publishers, 1990.

Watts, John S. *Indian Depredations in New Mexico.* Washington, DC: Gideon, 1858.

Webb, James Josiah. *Adventures in the Santa Fé Trade, 1844–1847.* Ed. by Ralph P. Bieber. Glendale, CA: The Arthur H. Clark Company, 1931.

Weber, David J. *The Mexican Frontier, 1821–1846: The American Southwest Under Mexico.* Albuquerque: University of New Mexico Press, 1982.

Weber, David J. Richard H. Kern: *Expeditionary Artist in the Far Southwest, 1848–1853.* Albuquerque: University of New Mexico Press, 1985.

Westphall, Victor. *Mercedes Reales: Hispanic Land Grants of the Upper Rio Grande Region.* Albuquerque: University of New Mexico Press, 1983.

White, Richard. *It's Your Misfortune and None of My Own: A New History of the American West.* Norman: University of Oklahoma Press, 1991.

Windham, Margaret Leonard, ed. *New Mexico 1850 Territorial Census.* 4 vols. Albuquerque: New Mexico Genealogical Society, 1976.

ARTICLES

Atherton, Lewis E. "The Santa Fe Trader as Mercantile Capitalist." *MHR* 77 (Oct. 1982):1–12

Bender, A. B. "Frontier Defense in the Territory of New Mexico, 1853–1861." *NMHR* 9 (Oct. 1934):345–436.

Bieber, Ralph P., ed. "Letters of William Carr Lane, 1852–1854." *NMHR* 3 (April 1928):179–203.

Bieber, Ralph P. "Some Aspects of the Santa Fe Trade, 1848–80." *MHR* 18 (Jan. 1924):158–66.

Binkley, William Campbell, ed. "Reports from a Texas Agent in New

Mexico, 1849." In *New Spain and the Anglo American West*. Ed. by George P. Hammond. Lancaster, Pa.: privately printed, 1932.

Bloom, L. B., ed. "Historical Society Minutes, 1859–1863." *NMHR* 18 (July 1943):247–311.

Bloom, L. B., ed. "Historical Society Minutes, 1859–1863. (Concl.)." *NMHR* 18 (Oct. 1943):394–428.

Carson, Wm. G. B., ed. "William Carr Lane Diary." *NMHR* 39 (July 1964):274–332.

Chávez, Angélico. "New Names in New Mexico, 1820–1850." *El Palacio* 64 (Sept.-Oct. 1957):291–318.

Cook, Mary Jean, ed. "Reminiscences of Andrew Bowdry Baird." *Compadres: Friends of the Palace of the Governors Newsletter* 2 (Oct.-Dec. 1993):3–8.

Dunham, Harold H. "Ceran St. Vrain." In *The Mountain Men and the Fur Trade of the Far West*. Ed. by LeRoy R. Hafen. Glendale, CA: The Arthur H. Clark Company, 1968.

Elder, Jane Lenz, and David J. Weber. "'Without a Murmur': The Death of Kate Kingsbury on the Santa Fe Trail." In *The Mexican Road: Trade, Travel, and Confrontation on the Santa Fe Trail*. Ed. by Mark Gardner. Manhattan, KS: Sunflower Univesity Press, 1989.

Frazer, Robert W. "Purveyors of Flour to the Army: Department of New Mexico, 1849–1861." *NMHR* 47 (1972):213–38.

Gardner, Kathryn Davis. "Conn and Hays: Council Grove's Trail Merchants." In Gardner, ed., *The Mexican Road*.

Gardner, Mark L. "Trade with New Mexico, 1860." Reprinted from the *Sacramento Daily Union*, Oct. 30, 1860. *Wagon Tracks* 9 (Nov. 1994):17–21.

Gorman, [Mrs. Samuel]. "Samuel Gorman." *Old Santa Fe* 1 (Jan. 1914):308–331.

Lecompte, Janet. "The Independent Women of Hispanic New Mexico, 1821–1846." *Western Historical Quarterly* 12 (Jan. 1981):17–35.

McMurtrie, Douglas C. "The History of Early Printing in New Mexico, with a Bibliography of the Known Issues of the New Mexican Press, 1834–1860." *NMHR* 4 (Oct. 1929):372–410.

Meyer, Marian. "100 Years of Area History Engraved on Tombstones." *Journal North, The Albuquerque Journal* (8 June 1985):6.

Möllhausen, Heinrich Baldwin. "Over the Santa Fe Trail through Kansas in 1858." Translated by John A. Burzle. Ed. by Robert Taft. *Kansas Historical Quarterly* 16 (Nov. 1948):337–80.

Parish, William J. "The German Jew and the Commercial Revolution in Territorial New Mexico, 1850–1900." *New Mexico Quarterly* 29 (Autumn 1959):307–32.

Sandoval, David A. "Gnats, Goods, and Greasers: Mexican Merchants on the Santa Fe Trail." In Gardner, ed. *The Mexican Road.*

_____. "Montezuma's Merchants: Mexican Traders on the Santa Fe Trail." In Leo E. Oliva, ed. *Adventures on the Santa Fe Trail.* Topeka: Kansas State Historical Society, 1988.

_____. "Who Is Riding the Burro Now?: A Bibliographical Critique of Scholarship on the New Mexican Trader." In *Essays and Monographs in Colorado History*, no. 6 (1987):75–92.

Simmons, Marc. "Santa Fe in the Days of the Trail." In Noble, ed., *Santa Fe*, 115–28.

Smith-Rosenberg, Carroll. "The Female World of Love and Ritual: Relations Between Women in Nineteenth-Century America." In *The American Family in Social-Historical Perspective.* Ed. by Michael Gordon. New York: St. Martin's Press, 1983.

Tittman, Edward D., "The Exploitation of Treason." *NMHR* 4 (April 1929):128–45.

Townley, John. "The New Mexico Mining Company." *NMHR* 46 (Jan. 1971):57–73.

Waldrip, William I. "New Mexico During the Civil War." *NMHR* 28 (Oct. 1953):251–90.

Weber, David J. "John Rowland." In *The Mountain Men and the Fur Trade of the Far West.* Ed. by LeRoy R. Hafen. Glendale: Arthur H. Clark, 1966.

_____, ed. "Samuel Ellison on the Election of 1857." *NMHR* 44 (July 1969):215–21.

_____. "'Scarce More Than Apes': Historical Roots of Anglo-American Stereotypes of Mexicans." In *New Spain's Far Northern Frontier: Essays on Spain in the American West, 1540–1821.* Ed. by David J. Weber. Albuquerque: University of New Mexico Press, 1979.

Westphall, Victor. "Fraud and Implications of Fraud in the Land Grants of New Mexico." *NMHR* 49 (July 1974):189–218

Whilden, Charles E. "Letters from a Santa Fe Army Clerk, 1855–56." Ed. by John Hammond Moore. *NMHR* 40 (April 1965):141–64.

Index

JANE LENZ ELDER, Associate Director of the William P. Clements Center for Southwest Studies at Southern Methodist University, is the author of many articles and exhibit catalogs, including *The Literature of Beguilement: Promoting Hispanic North America from Columbus to Today*. She is currently working on a history of Texas's Interstate Theatre Circuit.

DAVID J. WEBER is the Robert and Nancy Dedman Professor of History and Director of the William P. Clements Center for Southwest Studies at Southern Methodist University. A past president of the Western History Association, he is the author of numerous prize-winning books and articles, including *The Spanish Frontier in North America*, which was nominated for a Pulitzer Prize.